THE
GEORGIA
ALMANAC

AND BOOK OF FACTS

THE GEORGIA ALMANAC

AND BOOK OF FACTS

Edited by
James A. Crutchfield

Project Editor
Julia M. Smithson

Assistant
Mary Ann Drewry McNeese

RUTLEDGE HILL PRESS
Nashville, Tennessee

Dedicated to the citizens of Georgia,
especially those who helped in compiling this almanac

Published in Nashville, Tennessee, by Rutledge Hill Press, Inc., 513 Third Avenue South,
Nashville, Tennessee 37210

Typography by ProtoType Graphics, Inc., Nashville, Tennessee

Library of Congress Cataloging-in-Publication Data

The Georgia almanac and book of facts.

Includes index.
1. Georgia—Miscellanea.   I. Crutchfield, James
Andrew, 1938–   .
F286.G35   1986   975.8   86–25981
ISBN 0-934395-33-0
ISBN 0-934395-34-9 (pbk.)

Manufactured in the United States of America
1 2 3 4 5 6 7 8 9—92 91 90 89 88 87 86

CONTENTS

PREFACE

To my knowledge, *The Georgia Almanac and Book of Facts* represents the first effort to put between two covers a compendium of facts about Georgia. To be sure, there are volumes of statistical data. There are also scores of lists, descriptions, and information about individual subjects of interest to Georgians. But the most important feature of *The Georgia Almanac and Book of Facts* is that all of these figures, tables, charts, and other information have been synthesized into a readable whole that gives insight into Georgia and its citizens.

There long has been a need for an accurate, up-to-date, inexpensive handbook containing vital information about Georgia. You will find *The Georgia Almanac and Book of Facts* to be that handbook, and it is sure to become one of the most referenced volumes in your home or office. It is planned that this book will be updated regularly. The publishers would be happy to hear from you regarding data you would like to see included in future editions.

—James A. Crutchfield

ACKNOWLEDGMENTS

In compiling *The Georgia Almanac,* many books, institutions, state departments, and individuals were consulted. We would like to acknowledge these sources for the information provided that made this almanac possible.

Books, periodicals, and other written resources: *The American Counties,* Joseph Nathan Kane, The Scarecrow Press, Inc.; *American FORTS Yesterday and Today,* Bruce Grant; *America's Medal of Honor Recipients,* Highland Publishers; *Broadcasting/Cablecasting Yearbook, 1986,* Broadcasting Publications, Inc.; *Catalogue of National Historic Landmarks,* U.S. Department of the Interior; *CBS News Almanac,* Hammond Almanac, Inc.; *Colonial Georgia—A History,* Kenneth Coleman; *The Encyclopedia Americana International Edition,* Grolier Incorporated; *The Encyclopedia of the South,* Green Springs, Inc.; *Famous Georgians,* Kenneth Coleman and Jackie Erney; *Georgia Agricultural Facts,* Georgia Crop Reporting Service, 1985 Edition, Georgia Department of Agriculture; *Georgia Airport Directory,* Georgia Department of Transportation, Bureau of Aeronautics; *Georgia—A Short History,* E. Merton Coulter; *The Georgia County Guide,* Cooperative Extension Service, The University of Georgia; "Georgia History Calendar, 1986", Zell Miller; *Georgia Official Directory of the United States Congressmen, State and County Officers; Georgia: This Way to Fun,* Georgia Department of Industry and Trade, Tourist/Communications Division; *Great Georgians,* Zell Miller; *Historical Statistics of the South, 1790–1970,* Donald B. Dodd, Wynelle S. Dodd; *The Indians of the Southeastern United States,* John R. Swanton; *Information Please Almanac,* Houghton-Mifflin Company; *International Television Almanac,* Richard Gertner, Editor; *Know Your Georgia,* C. J. Holleran; *Legal Distilled Spirits: 1985,* Cooperative Extension Service, College of Agriculture, University of Georgia; *The License Plate Book,* Thompson C. Murray; *Merit Students Encyclopedia,* MacMillen Educational Company; *Minerals Yearbook,* U.S. Department of the Interior, Bureau of the Mines; "Musical America" Magazine by High Fidelity; *The Naming of America,* Alan Wolk; *Notable Names in American History,* James T. White & Co.; *The Official Museum Directory (1986),* The American Association of Museums; *The Original Tennessee Homecoming Cookbook,* Rutledge Hill Press; *Population Comparison—Large Cities in the Southeast,* U.S. Department of Commerce, Bureau of the Census; *Rand McNally 1986 Commercial Atlas and Marketing Guide; Reader's Digest Almanac & Yearbook,* Reader's Digest Association; *This Is Your Georgia,* Bernice McCullar; *TV and Radio Directory 3,* the 1986 Media Encyclopedia, Working Press of the Nation; *Twelfth Annual Report on the Work of the Georgia Courts,* Judicial Council of Georgia; *Travel South,* Oxmoor House, Inc.; *U.S. Postal Service 1985 Zip + 4 Code State Directory; Who Was Who In America,* Who's Who, Inc.; *The World Almanac and Book of Facts, 1986,* Newspaper Enterprise Association, Inc.; *1985–1986 Local Chamber Directory,* Business Council of Georgia; and *1986 Georgia Newspaper Directory,* Georgia Press Association.

The following state and federal agencies generously provided information related to their work. American Association of State and Local History, Nashville, Tennessee; Atlanta Symphony Orchestra; Delta Airlines; Federal Reserve Bank of Atlanta, Statistical Reports Department; Georgia Department of Archives & History; Georgia Department of Human Resources; Georgia Department of Industry and Trade, Tourist/Communications Division; Georgia Department of Labor, Employment Security Agency, Labor Information Systems; Georgia Department of Natural Resources, Parks and Historic Sites Division; Georgia Department of Revenue, Alcohol & Tobacco Tax Unit, Motor Vehicle Unit; Georgia Department of Transportation; Georgia Forestry Commission; Georgia Peanut Commission; Grand Lodge of Georgia, F. & A.M.; "Miss Georgia" Pageant; Nashville Sounds Baseball Team; Nashville Public Library Reference Desk; National Forestry Service, Department of Agriculture; Office of the Secretary of State; State of Georgia Sports Hall of Fame; The University of Georgia, College of Agriculture; U.S. Army Corps of Engineers; U.S. Department of Commerce, U.S. Weather Bureau, Bureau of the Census; U.S. Department of the Interior, Fish and Wildlife Service, National Park Service; and Vanderbilt Joint University Libraries.

Special appreciation is due the following individuals who were helpful in directing us to the most useful, up-to-date sources and in many cases provided the information we needed: George E. Briggs; Max Cleland; Alice Cormany; Dr. George E. Drewry; Steve Eng; Molly J. M. Perry; Judge J. Clayton Stephens, Jr.; Larry W. Thompson; and all the employees of Rutledge Hill Press.

INDEX

THE
GEORGIA
ALMANAC

AND BOOK OF FACTS

THE GEORGIA ALMANAC

AND BOOK OF FACTS

AGRICULTURE

Georgia leads the nation as the largest producer of peanuts and pecans. The state ranked second in poultry sales (eggs, broilers and chickens) and third in peaches and egg production.

The most important cash field crops of 1984 were peanuts, soybeans, tobacco, corn, and wheat in that order.

Sales of commercial broilers led the livestock market as the top money maker by a wide margin. Second to fifth places were taken by eggs, hogs, cattle and calves and dairy products.

Lists of County Extension Directors, Experiment Stations, and a chart showing the number of farms, the average farm size, and the average dollar value per farm for all Georgia counties, follow.

COUNTY EXTENSION DIRECTORS

Appling
County Office Complex
400 East Park
Baxley 31513
912-367-2372

Atkinson
Philip R. Torrance
County Agriculture Bldg.
Cogdell Road
Pearson 31642
912-422-3277

Bacon
Danny Stanaland
County Office Bldg.
Alma 31510
912-632-5601

Baker
Lanier Jordan
Agriculture Bldg.
Flint St.

Newton 31770
912-734-5252

Baldwin
Carol Sirmans
Federal Bldg.
East Hancock St.
Milledgeville 31061
912-453-4394

Banks
John W. Mitchell
County Office Bldg.
Homer 30547
404-677-2245

Barrow
Kate Nicholson
Federal Bldg.
Winder 30680
404-867-7581

Bartow
320 West Cherokee Ave.

Cartersville 30120
404-382-2324

Ben Hill
Duren E. Bell
515 West Magnolia St.
Fitzgerald 31750
912-423-2360

Berrien
Paul D. Wigley
102 North McKinley Ave.
Nashville 31639
912-686-5431

Bibb
Griffith Bldg.
145 First St.
Macon 31201
912-744-6338

Bleckley
John P. Parks
Post Office Bldg.

Second St.
Cochran 31014
912-934-6917

Brantley
Robert T. Boland, Jr.
County Office Bldg.
Burton St.
Nahunta 31553
912-462-5724

Brooks
Agriculture Bldg.
Moultrie Hwy. #33
Quitman 31643
912-263-4103

Bryan
J. Rastus Byrd
Courthouse Annex
Pembroke 31321
912-653-2231

Bulloch
Gary L. Lee
Federal Bldg.
North Main St.
Statesboro 30458
912-764-6101

Burke
W. H. Craven, Jr.
Agriculture Bldg.
Waynesboro 30830
404-554-2119

Butts
Carl F. Varnadoe
County Courthouse
Jackson 30233
404-775-2601

Calhoun
E. Harold Wilson
County Office Bldg.
Highway 37
Morgan 31766
912-849-2685

Camden
Dan Williams
Atkinson Bldg.
4th St.
Woodbine 31569
912-576-5601

Candler
Brad Phillips
310 West Broad St.

Metter 30439
912-685-2408

Carroll
Carl E. Brack
Agriculture Bldg.
102 City Hall Ave.
Carrollton 30117
404-834-1490

Catoosa
Steve Moraltakis
105 Maple St.
Ringgold 30736
404-935-4211

Charlton
R. Terry Thigpen
100 Third St.
Folkston 31537
912-496-2040

Chatham
Billy Myers
Old County Courthouse
2nd Floor
130 Bull St.
Savannah 31412
912-944-2291

Chattahoochee
Not Organized

Chattooga
Ted M. Clark
Post Office Bldg.
Summerville 30747
404-857-1410

Cherokee
George E. Jones
100 North St.
B-3
Canton 30114
404-479-1966

Clarke
Dan K. Gunnels
2152 West Broad St.
Athens 30606
404-546-8330

Clay
William O. Kenyon
Killingsworth Bldg.
South Washington
Fort Gaines 31751
912-768-2247

Clayton
Kathleen Wages
104 Courthouse Annex
McDonough St.
Jonesboro 30236
404-478-9911

Clinch
Audrey B. James
Courthouse Annex
Homerville 31634
912-487-2169

Cobb
Bruce E. Beck
County Bldg.
10-East Park Square
Suite 330
Marietta 30060
404-429-3330

Coffee
Rick Reed
105 Tanner St.
2nd Floor
Douglas 31533
912-384-1402

Colquitt
R. Douglas Durham
County Government Bldg.
Highway 319
Moultrie 31768
912-985-1321

Columbia
Wendell T. Stubbs
County Administration
    Bldg.
Columbia Road
Appling 30802
404-541-0557

Cook
Glenn Beard
Courthouse Annex
North Parrish Ave.
Adel 31620
912-896-4040

Coweta
Donald J. Morris
County Office Bldg.
Newnan 30264
404-253-2450

Crawford
Vernon Alligood
234 Wright Ave.

Roberta 31078
912-836-3121

Crisp
George B. Lee
County Courthouse
Cordele 31015
912-273-1217

Dade
Betty W. Gass
Extension Bldg.
Case Ave.
Trenton 30752
404-657-4116

Dawson
Courthouse
Dawsonville 30534
404-265-2442

Decatur
Ernest S. Purcell, Jr.
Agriculture Bldg.
Vada Highway
Bainbridge 31717
912-246-4528

DeKalb
W. A. Steagall
101 Court Square
East Ponce DeLeon
Decatur 30030
404-371-2821

Dodge
Garlon E. Rogers
Agriculture Bldg.
Anson Ave.
Eastman 31023
912-374-4702

Dooly
Charlie E. Ellis
County Agriculture Bldg.
Union St.
Vienna 31092
912-268-4171

Dougherty
Rhen Bishop
County Agriculture Bldg.
1016 Lowe Rd.
Albany 31706
912-436-7216

Douglas
Joan H. Douglas
6754 Broad St.

Douglasville 30134
404-949-2000

Early
C. Wayne Tankersley
Agriculture Bldg.
114 Magnolia
Blakely 31723
912-723-3072

Echols
R. Larry Corbett
Courthouse
Statenville 31648
912-559-5562

Effingham
Susan Epling
Treutlen Bldg.
Pine Street
Springfield 31329
912-754-6071

Elbert
Robert G. Perkins
Courthouse
Elberton 30635
404-283-3001

Emanuel
Jack Harrell
County Office Bldg.
Swainsboro 30401
912-237-9933

Evans
Joan Strickland
Courthouse Office Bldg.
Claxton 30417
912-739-1292

Fannin
Mary Jane Jones
Courthouse
Blue Ridge 30513
404-632-3061

Fayette
Joan F. Williams
100 McDonough Rd.
Fayetteville 30214
404-461-4580

Floyd
Louie C. Canova
County Government Bldg.
201 North 5th St.
Rome 30161
404-295-6210

Forsyth
Hugh M. McMillian
County Government Bldg.
101 Maple St.
Cumming 30130
404-887-2418

Franklin
Roy L. Deason
Cole Building
Royston Rd.
Carnesville 30521
404-384-2843

Fulton
Hal E. Tatum
506 County Administration
Bldg.
Atlanta 30303
404-572-3261

Gilmer
Ronnie H. Gheesling
9 Dalton St.
Ellijay 30540
404-635-4426

Glascock
Frank M. Watson
Courthouse
Main St.
Gibson 30810
404-598-2811

Glynn
J. Rudolph Beggs
Office Park Bldg.
Room 232
1803 Gloucester St.
Brunswick 31521
912-265-0610

Gordon
Jack N. Dyer
Northwest Branch
Experiment Station
Calhoun 30701
404-629-8685

Grady
Perry L. Pope
Agri-Center
65 11th Avenue
Northeast
Cairo 31728
912-377-1312

Greene
Mike Abernathy
County Office Bldg.

3

201 North Main
Greensboro 30642
404-453-2083

Gwinnett
John W. Baughman, Jr.
Lawrenceville Square
Suite 10
140 Clayton St. Southeast
Lawrenceville 30245
404-962-1480

Habersham
Helen Barrett
Market Bldg.
Habersham Ave.
Clarkesville 30523
404-754-2318

Hall
Robert H. Lowe
Hall County Courthouse
Gainesville 30501
404-536-6681

Hancock
Juanita Williams
Federal Bldg.
Broad St.
Sparta 31087
404-444-6596

Haralson
John C. Callaway, Jr.
County Office Bldg.
Buchanan 30113
404-646-5288

Harris
Winifred Parker
Courthouse
Hamilton 31811
404-628-4824

Hart
B. Edward Page
Courthouse Annex
Hartwell 30643
404-376-3134

Heard
Michael O. Bunn
Courthouse
Franklin 30217
404-675-3513

Henry
Millard F. Daniel
Administration Bldg.

Phillips Dr.
McDonough 30253
404-957-1533

Houston
David P. Mills
Agriculture Bldg.
733 Carroll St.
Perry 31069
912-987-2028

Irwin
Gary C. Tankersley
Courthouse
Ocilla 31774
912-468-7409

Jackson
Patricia Bell
Courthouse Annex
120 Randolph St.
Jefferson 30549
404-367-8789

Jasper
Mell. J. Tanner
Post Office Bldg.
Washington St.
Monticello 31064
404-468-6479

Jeff Davis
James R. Reid
County Agriculture Bldg.
Hazlehurst 31539
912-375-2631

Jefferson
Johnnie G. Dekle
Family & Children Services
  Bldg.
Louisville 30434
912-625-3007

Jenkins
Harold N. Brantley
209 Daniel Street
Millen 30442
912-982-4408

Johnson
Beeman C. Keen, Jr.
County Office Bldg.
College St.
Wrightsville 31096
912-864-3373

Jones
Diane W. Annis

Zackary Bldg.
Atlanta Rd. and Jackson St.
Gray 31032
912-986-3948

Lamar
212 Gordon Rd.
Barnesville 30204
404-358-0281

Lanier
J. Benjamin Tucker
Courthouse
Lakeland 31635
912-482-3895

Laurens
Paul Riddle
Telfair St.
Dublin 31021
912-272-2277

Lee
Roy D. Goodson
Government Bldg.
Railroad St.
Leesburg 31763
912-759-6426

Liberty
Leon J. Peebles
137 South Main St.
Hinesville 31313
912-876-2133

Lincoln
William W. Rahn
Courthouse
Humphrey St.
Lincolnton 30817
404-359-3233

Long
Courthouse
Highway 99
Ludowici 31316
912-545-9549

Lowndes
John A. Baker
Civic Center
Highway 84 East
Valdosta 31601
912-242-1858

Lumpkin
Kenneth G. Beasley
109 Enota St.
  Northeast

4

Dahlonega 30533
404-864-2275

Macon
N. Stewart Newberry
Courthouse Annex
100 Sumter St.
Oglethorpe 31068
912-472-7588

Madison
Larry E. Pierce
Agriculture Service Bldg.
Danielsville 30633
404-795-2281

Marion
James T. Howell
Old Elementary School
  Bldg.
Rogers St.
Buena Vista 31803
912-649-2625

McDuffie
Howell R. Roberts
161 Ansley Dr.
Thomson 30824
404-595-1815

McIntosh
John V. Bryson
Courthouse Bldg.
Highway 17
Darien 31305
912-437-6651

Meriwether
Willis A. Godowns
Extension Bldg.
Williams St.
Greenville 30222
404-672-4235

Miller
William A. Inglett
Agriculture Center
406 West Crawford St.
Colquitt 31737
912-758-3416

Mitchell
Clifford E. Lee
28 Court St.
Camilla 31730
912-336-8464

Monroe
J. Cecil Daniels

County Office Bldg.
90 Culloden Rd.
Forsyth 31029
912-994-1118

Montgomery
David Curry
County Office Bldg.
Mt. Vernon 30445
912-583-2240

Morgan
Courthouse
Corner Hancock and
  Jefferson St.
Madison 30650
404-324-2214

Murray
Louis Dykes
County Office Bldg.
Highway 76 East
Chatsworth 30705
404-695-3031

Muscogee
Richard Smith
Columbus Government
  Center
Ground Floor
Columbus 31993
404-324-7711
  ext. 215

Newton
Michael R. Welborn
1115 Usher St.
  Northeast
Covington 30209
404-786-2574

Oconee
John T. Brannen
Courthouse Annex
Water St.
Watkinsville 30677
404-769-5207

Oglethorpe
Jeanette Brooks
Multi-Purpose Bldg.
Lexington 30648
404-743-8341

Paulding
Post Office Bldg.
Dallas 30132
404-445-3885

Peach
County Agriculture Bldg.
Everett Square
Fort Valley 31030
912-825-6466

Pickens
Richard Jasperse
Edge Bldg.
108-1 Court Street
Jasper 30143
404-692-2531

Pierce
John Ed Smith
County Agriculture Bldg.
Blackshear 31516
912-449-4733

Pike
Judith Reid
Pike County Office Bldg.
Gwyn St.
Zebulon 30295
404-567-8948

Polk
Paul E. Thompson
Courthouse Annex Bldg.
Cedartown 30125
404-748-3051

Pulaski
W. Timothy Hall
County Extension Bldg.
Lumpkin St.
Hawkinsville 31036
912-783-1171

Putnam
David B. Lowe
302 West Marion St.
Eatonton 31024
404-485-4151

Quitman
Wm. Tom Jennings
Old Bank Bldg.
Georgetown 31754
912-334-4303

Rabun
Peter Marziliano
Main St.
Clayton 30525
404-782-3113

Randolph
Mike Matthews

County Office Bldg.
Church and Webster St.
Cuthbert 31740
912-732-2311

Richmond
Clyde E. Lester
Room 332 City-County
Bldg.
Greene St.
Augusta 30911-3099
404-828-6812

Rockdale
Barbara McCarthy
920-A Main St.
Conyers 30207
404-922-7750
ext. 211

Schley
M. Wilson Weathersby
Extension Bldg.
Highway 19 North
Ellaville 31806
912-937-2601

Screven
Lamar E. Zipperer
Post Office Bldg.
Sylvania 30467
912-564-2064

Seminole
Robert F. Spitaleri
Courthouse Annex
Donalsonville 31745
912-524-2326

Spalding
William L. Wages, Jr.
Courthouse Annex
119 East Soloman
Griffin 30224
404-228-9900

Stephens
James E. Peeples
Courthouse Annex
Tugalo St.
Toccoa 30577
404-886-4046

Stewart
Irene G. DuBose
Courthouse
Broad St.
Lumpkin 31815
912-838-4908

Sumter
Timothy L. Lawson
603 Spring St.
Americus 31709
912-924-4476

Talbot
Paul M. Bulloch
Courthouse
Talbotton 31827
404-665-3230

Taliaferro
Not Organized

Tattnall
Maxwell Smith
301-S City Hall
Glennville 30427
912-654-2593

Taylor
James H. Willis
Community Service Center
Highway 137 West
Butler 31006
912-862-5496

Telfair
Wm. A. McKinnon
Telfair Center for
Community Development
McRae 31055
912-868-6489

Terrell
Terrell County Agriculture
Bldg.
440 South Main St.
Dawson 31742
912-995-2165

Thomas
H. Glynn Griner
County Agriculture Bldg.
207 North Madison
Thomasville 31792
912-226-3954

Tift
Lamar G. Martin
County Administration
Bldg.
225 Tift Ave.
Tifton 31794
912-386-3600

Toombs
Aurice A. Hartley

Agriculture Bldg.
W. Broad St.
Lyons 30436
912-526-3101

Towns
C. Moye Walker
Courthouse
Hiawassee 30546
404-896-2024

Treutlen
Mickey R. Palmer
County Bldg.
First St.
Soperton 30457
912-529-3766

Troup
James W. Williams
416 Pierce St.
LaGrange 30240
404-884-6686

Turner
James C. Griffeth
Route 2
Box 23
Ashburn 31714
912-567-3448

Twiggs
Daniel Howard
Courthouse Annex
Magnolia St.
Jeffersonville 31044
912-945-3391

Union
R. Neal Moon
Haralson Memorial Civic
Center
Blairsville 30512
404-745-2524

Upson
Donnie W. Tyler
County Extension Bldg.
321 North Hightower St.
Thomaston 30286
404-647-8989

Walker
Tony L. Howell
Federal Bldg.
110 North Main St.
LaFayette 30728
404-638-2548

Walton
E. Eugene Anderson
Courthouse Annex
126 Court St.
Monroe 30655
404-267-2104

Ware
Tony A. Otts
County Office Bldg.
Waycross 31501
912-285-6161

Warren
Jerry D. Holcomb
Post Office Bldg.
104 Allen St.
Warrenton 30828
404-465-2136

Washington
Gerald D. Andrews
Courthouse
Sandersville 31082
912-552-2011

Wayne
Jim Fountain

Post Office Bldg.
Jesup 31545
912-427-6865

Webster
David J. Wagner
Courthouse Annex
Preston 31824
912-828-2325

Wheeler
David H. Williams
Neighborhood Service
  Center
Alamo 30411
912-568-7138

White
J. Michael Harris
Courthouse
South Main St.
Cleveland 30528
404-865-2832

Whitfield
Larry W. Thomas
420 North Hamilton St.
Dalton 30720

404-278-8207

Wilcox
County Agriculture Bldg.
2nd St.
Rochelle 31079
912-365-2323

Wilkes
Carl W. Tankersley
Courthouse
Rm. B-02
23 Court St.
Washington 30673
404-678-2332

Wilkinson
Courthouse Annex
Main St.
Irwinton 31042
912-946-2367

Worth
Thomas E. Cary
County Government Bldg.
Franklin St.
Sylvester 31791
912-776-4419

EXPERIMENT STATIONS

1. **College Station, Athens**
   Clive Donoho, Jr., Associate Dean and
     Director
   College of Agriculture
   Experiment Stations
   107 Conner Hall
   The University of Georgia
   Athens 30602, 404-542-2151

2. **Georgia Station, Experiment**
   Charles W. Laughlin, Associate
     Director, Northern Region, and
     Resident Director, Georgia Station
   Experiment 30212, 404-228-7263

3. **Coastal Plain Station, Tifton**
   W. C. McCormick, Associate Director,
     Southern Region, and Resident
     Director, Coastal Plain Station
   Tifton 31793, 912-386-3338

4. **Georgia Mountain Branch Station,
   Blairsville**
   James W. Dobson, Superintendent
   Blairsville 30512, 404-745-2655

5. **Northwest Georgia Branch Station,
   Calhoun**
   Edward G. Worley, Superintendent
   Calhoun 30701, 404-629-2696

6. **Central Georgia Branch Station,
   Eatonton**
   Grady V. Calvert, Superintendent
   Eatonton 31024, 404-485-6015

7. **Southeast Georgia Branch Station,
   Midville**
   Charles E. Perry, Superintendent
   Midville 30441, 912-589-7472

8. **Southwest Georgia Branch Station,
   Plains**
   Robert B. Moss, Superintendent
   Plains 31780, 912-824-4375

9. **Attapulgus Extension & Research
   Center, Attapulgus**
   Darble Granberry, Superintendent
   Extension Research Center
   Attapulgus 31715, 912-465-3421

7

★ Experiment Station
■ Branch Station
▲ Extension Research Station

FARMS

County	Number of farms	Average size (in acres)	Average dollar value of land and buildings per farm	County	Number of farms	Average size (in acres)	Average dollar value of land and buildings per farm
Georgia Total	49,630	248	225,092	Baldwin	148	300	189,480
Appling	653	205	159,668	Banks	414	113	119,046
Atkinson	267	341	240,588	Barrow	421	94	114,024
Bacon	422	216	185,621	Bartow	463	224	176,635
Baker	178	863	785,562	Ben Hill	232	282	228,910

County	Number of farms	Average size (in acres)	Average dollar value of land and buildings per farm	County	Number of farms	Average size (in acres)	Average dollar value of land and buildings per farm
Berrien	556	282	302,277	Gordon	578	147	168,369
Bibb	167	144	143,066	Grady	625	259	347,176
Bleckley	249	294	198,610	Greene	236	244	183,411
Brantley	345	116	128,794	Gwinnett	492	68	165,358
Brooks	521	379	279,841	Habersham	409	103	151,851
Bryan	93	270	169,742	Hall	874	76	136,678
Bulloch	702	336	288,856				
Burke	390	698	466,085	Hancock	151	316	174,040
Butts	171	176	162,953	Haralson	321	120	112,664
Calhoun	135	836	775,570	Harris	255	244	152,643
				Hart	548	124	113,113
Camden	59	577	228,085	Heard	190	189	141,437
Candler	261	269	182,510	Henry	426	138	194,462
Carroll	868	112	117,528	Houston	295	345	375,254
Catoosa	315	125	235,324	Irwin	419	363	299,516
Charlton	130	284	191,862	Jackson	782	111	143,566
Chatham	59	216	216,542	Jasper	232	291	166,328
Chattahoochee	18	283	133,000				
Chattooga	292	213	140,688	Jeff Davis	394	270	248,673
Cherokee	611	75	141,943	Jefferson	391	403	294,074
Clarke	102	148	245,235	Jenkins	251	427	284,486
				Johnson	304	279	126,385
Clay	94	588	405,404	Jones	184	217	186,277
Clayton	81	88	169,642	Lamar	238	176	204,929
Clinch	115	182	125,017	Lanier	172	301	181,605
Cobb	264	66	233,496	Laurens	803	265	198,971
Coffee	833	241	183,595	Lee	186	900	1,049,102
Colquitt	867	250	248,096	Liberty	61	327	217,295
Columbia	222	187	228,018				
Cook	380	238	242,134	Lincoln	182	241	166,341
Coweta	376	179	184,793	Long	104	156	149,019
Crawford	153	296	234,837	Lowndes	548	223	224,352
				Lumpkin	289	102	185,453
Crisp	226	545	584,597	Macon	267	522	441,775
Dade	183	192	152,650	Madison	582	110	134,679
Dawson	192	94	141,786	Marion	147	305	169,007
Decatur	484	402	386,368	McDuffie	216	246	196,625
DeKalb	95	54	171,553	McIntosh	29	176	99,207
Dodge	482	274	178,002	Meriwether	380	240	188,313
Dooly	304	539	578,197				
Dougherty	199	544	617,789	Miller	342	366	363,280
Douglas	151	97	116,517	Mitchell	578	409	460,590
Early	389	495	444,332	Monroe	172	341	257,320
				Montgomery	274	305	203,190
Echols	110	163	122,855	Morgan	355	310	273,563
Effingham	293	254	211,116	Murray	310	127	117,445
Elbert	368	171	118,813	Muscogee	49	242	184,085
Emanuel	519	328	206,482	Newton	286	177	140,262
Evans	211	264	200,137	Oconee	295	205	236,990
Fannin	233	91	78,528	Ogelthorpe	351	199	154,407
Fayette	253	126	297,423				
Floyd	504	186	160,796	Paulding	296	97	109,301
Forsyth	631	78	136,141	Peach	179	304	373,212
Franklin	665	122	118,728	Pickens	228	96	95,671
				Pierce	491	209	176,073
Fulton	379	112	218,794	Pike	292	191	160,524
Gilmer	272	116	149,526	Polk	327	145	87,278
Glascock	96	295	146,688	Pulaski	188	476	317,117
Glynn	55	180	142,564	Putnam	167	271	201,964

County	Number of farms	Average size (in acres)	Average dollar value of land and buildings per farm	County	Number of farms	Average size (in acres)	Average dollar value of land and buildings per farm
Quitman	34	687	501,500	Towns	176	77	128,892
Rabun	143	81	118,189				
				Treutlen	195	278	143,185
Randolph	162	763	594,469	Troup	291	190	170,076
Richmond	139	179	170,058	Turner	324	354	350,889
Rockdale	128	111	204,820	Twiggs	149	270	213,711
Schley	111	341	302,743	Union	307	92	126,870
Screven	409	450	245,068	Upson	243	205	146,193
Seminole	232	428	382,901	Walker	584	180	150,438
Spalding	262	158	159,813	Walton	462	174	192,881
Stephens	221	77	86,412	Ware	394	172	142,183
Stewart	111	610	445,162	Warren	168	356	219,964
Sumter	360	538	565,231				
				Washington	379	351	223,509
Talbot	144	289	177,292	Wayne	416	166	140,663
Taliaferro	82	271	149,975	Webster	106	557	413,396
Tattnall	631	205	182,219	Wheeler	260	302	191,258
Taylor	204	441	250,735	White	320	73	115,113
Telfair	425	235	169,654	Whitfield	422	112	135,961
Terrell	229	675	536,550	Wilcox	304	374	324,161
Thomas	540	399	334,374	Wilkes	382	317	234,594
Tift	393	279	353,921	Wilkinson	162	292	244,333
Toombs	407	242	184,765	Worth	557	353	336,426

AIRLINES

Listed below are the air carriers which operate within the State of Georgia.

Air Atlanta
Airborne Express (air freight only)
Air Express International Airlines
    (air freight only)
Air Jamaica Limited
Air Wisconsin (air freight only)
American Airlines
Bahamasair
Bankair, Inc.
British Caledonian Airways
Continental Airlines
Delta Air Lines
Delta Connection
DHL Airlines, Inc.
Eagle Airline
Eastern Air Lines, Inc.
Eastern Atlantis Express
Eastern Metro Express
Evergreen International Airlines, Inc.
    (air freight only)
Federal Express (air freight only)

Flight Line, Inc.
Flying Tiger Line (air freight only)
KLM-Royal Dutch Airlines
Lufthansa German Airlines
Midwest Express Airlines, Inc.
Northwest Orient Airlines, Inc.
Ozark Air Lines, Inc.
Pan American World Airways, Inc.
Pan Am Express
People Express Airlines, Inc.
Piedmont Aviation, Inc.
Piedmont Commuter System
Republic Airlines
Sabena Belgian World Airlines
Saber Aviation, Inc. (air freight only)
Summit Airlines, Inc. (air freight only)
Sunbird Airlines, Inc.
Trans World Airlines, Inc.
United Airlines
Zantop International Airlines, Inc.
    (air freight only)

AIRPORTS

City	Airport name	Runway length (in feet)
Adel	Cook County	4,000
Albany	Albany-Dougherty County	6,600
Alma	Alma-Bacon County	5,000
Americus	Souther Field	5,000
Ashburn	Turner County	3,250
Athens	Athens Municipal	4,992
Atlanta	DeKalb-Peachtree	5,001
Atlanta	Fulton County-Brown Field	5,796
Atlanta	Wm. B. Hartsfield Atlanta Int'l	11,889
Augusta	Bush Field	8,000
Augusta	Daniel Field	3,877
Bainbridge	Decatur County Industrial Air Park	5,100
Baxley	Baxley Municipal	3,800
Blairsville	Blairsville	3,200
Blakely	Early County	3,200
Brooklet	Davis Air Park	2,700
Brunswick	Glynco Jetport	8,000
Brunswick	Jekyll Island	3,700
Brunswick	Malcolm McKinnon	5,466
Buena Vista	Marion County	3,200
Butler	Butler Municipal	2,700
Cairo	Cairo-Grady County	3,000
Calhoun	Tom B. David	4,600
Camilla	Camilla-Mitchell County	3,200
Canon	Franklin County	3,500
Canton	Cherokee County	3,400
Carrollton	West Georgia Regional	5,000
Cartersville	Cartersville	4,000
Cedartown	Cornelius Moore	4,000
Claxton	Claxton-Evans County	4,000
Cochran	Cochran	3,200
Columbus	Columbus Metropolitan	7,000
Cordele	Crisp County-Cordele	5,000
Cornelia	Habersham County	3,750
Covington	Covington Municipal	3,000
Cumming	Mathis	1,550
Cuthbert	Cuthbert-Randolph	3,000
Dahlonega	Lumpkin County-Wimpy's	3,000
Dalton	Dalton Municipal	5,000
Darien	Eden Field	3,000
Dawson	Dawson Municipal	2,790
Donalsonville	Donalsonville Municipal	5,000
Douglas	Douglas Municipal	5,000
Dublin	W. H. "Bud" Barron	5,000
Eastman	Eastman-Dodge County	4,500
Eatonton	Putnam County	3,000
Elberton	Elbert County-Patz Field	3,400

11

City	Airport name	Runway length (in feet)
Ellijay	Gilmer County	3,500
Fairburn	South Fulton Sky Port	2,690
Fitzgerald	Fitzgerald Municipal	5,000
Folkston	Davis Field	2,500
Fort Gaines	Fort Gaines-Clay County	2,837
Fort Valley	Duke	3,370
Gainesville	Lee Gilmer Memorial	5,000
Greensboro	Green County Airpark	3,300
Griffin	Griffin-Spalding County	3,300
Hampton	Henry County-Bear Creek	3,375
Hawkinsville	Hawkinsville-Pulaski County	3,000
Hazlehurst	Hazlehurst	4,500
Hinesville	Liberty County	3,700
Homerville	Homerville	4,000
Irwinville	Crystal Lake Air Park	3,000
Jasper	Pickens County	3,600
Jefferson	Jackson County	4,100
Jesup	Jesup-Wayne County	3,800
Jonesboro	South Expressway	2,980
LaFayette	Barwick-LaFayette	4,780
LaGrange	Callaway	5,000
Lawrenceville	Gwinnett County-Briscoe Field	4,000
Louisville	Louisville Municipal	3,500
Macon	Herbert Smart-Downtown	4,696
Macon	Lewis B. Wilson	6,500
Madison	Madison Municipal	3,800
Marietta	McCollum	4,580
McRae	Telfair-Wheeler County	4,000
Metter	Metter Municipal	3,100
Milledgeville	Baldwin County	5,000
Millen	Millen	3,000
Monroe	Monroe-Walton County Airport	3,300
Montezuma	Dr. C. P. Savage Sr.	3,200
Moultrie	Moultrie Municipal	3,000
Moultrie	Spence Field	3,000
Nahunta	Brantley County	3,000
Nashville	Berrien County	3,000
Newnan	Newnan-Coweta County	4,000
Peachtree City	Falcon Field	4,600
Perry	Perry-Fort Valley	5,000
Pine Mountain	Callaway Gardens-Harris County	5,000
Quitman	Quitman-Brooks County	3,600
Reidsville	Reidsville	3,800
Resaca	Zack	2,900
Rome	Richard B. Russell	4,999
St. Marys	St. Marys	5,000
Sandersville	Kaolin Field	3,800
Savannah	Savannah International	9,000
Soperton	Treutlen County	2,725

City	Airport name	Runway length (in feet)
Statesboro	Statesboro Municipal	5,000
Stockbridge	Berry Hill	3,000
Stone Mountain	Stone Mountain	3,000
Swainsboro	Emanuel County	4,180
Sylvania	Plantation Air Park	5,000
Sylvester	Sylvester-Worth County	3,400
Thomaston	Reginald Grant Memorial	3,000
Thomasville	Thomasville Municipal	5,000
Thomson	Thomson-McDuffie County	5,000
Tifton	Henry Tift Myers	4,650
Toccoa	Toccoa-R. G. Letourneau Field	4,000
Valdosta	Valdosta Municipal	6,302
Vidalia	Vidalia Municipal	5,000
Warm Springs	Roosevelt Memorial	3,000
Warner Robins	Warner Robins Air Park	2,845
Washington	Washington-Wilkes County	3,400
Waycross	Waycross-Ware County	5,045
Waynesboro	Burke County	3,200
Williamson	Peach State Glider Port	3,300
Winder	Winder	4,600
Woolsey	Rust Air Strip	2,000
Wrens	Wrens Memorial	3,000
Zebulon	Ridgeview Farm	2,100

ALCOHOL

The following list shows the counties in which liquor sales are legal only in certain cities, and the "wet" cities.

County	Town	County	Town
Barrow	Winder	Haralson	Buchanan
Calhoun	Edison, Leary	Henry	Locust Grove
Chattahoochee	Cusseta	Jackson	Arcade
Clay	Fort Gaines	Jasper	Monticello
Colquitt	Moultrie	Jefferson	Louisville
Columbia	Grovetown	Johnson	Wadley, Wrightsville
Coweta	Grantville	Marion	Buena Vista
Dooly	Unadilla, Vienna	Meriwether	Greenville, Luthersville, Woodbury
Douglas	Douglasville (Package Liquor)	Monroe	Forsyth (Package Liquor)
Elbert	Elberton	Montgomery	Uvalda
Fayette	Peachtree City	Morgan	Madison, Rutledge
Floyd	Rome	Newton	Covington
Franklin	Canon, Lavonia	Paulding	Hiram, Braswell, Dallas
Gordon	Calhoun	Peach	Byron
Greene	Siloam, White Plains	Pickens	Nelson
Gwinnett	Lilburn, Suwanee	Pike	Zebulon
Habersham	Mt. Airy	Randolph	Coleman
Hall	Gainesville	Screven	Hiltonia, Newington
Hancock	Sparta	Schley	Ellaville

County	Town	County	Town
Stephens	Martin	Twiggs	Jeffersonville
Stewart	Lumpkin, Richland	Walker	Lookout Mountain
Rabun	Sky Valley	Walton	Walnut Grove
Talbot	Talbotton, Geneva, Woodland	Washington	Tennelle, Sandersville
		Wheeler	Glenwood
Taylor	Reynolds	White	Helen
Telfair	Scotland, Lumber City	Whitefield	Dalton
Thomas	Thomasville	Wilcox	Abbeville
Treutlen	Soperton	Wilkes	Washington
Troup	LaGrange, West Point		

Clinch, Jasper: Private club referendum to issue licenses to private clubs only in a normally all dry area. County commissioner can issue letter of approval for license.

Below is a map showing which counties prohibit the sale of liquor and which allow it only in certain cities, as well as those which allow it county-wide.

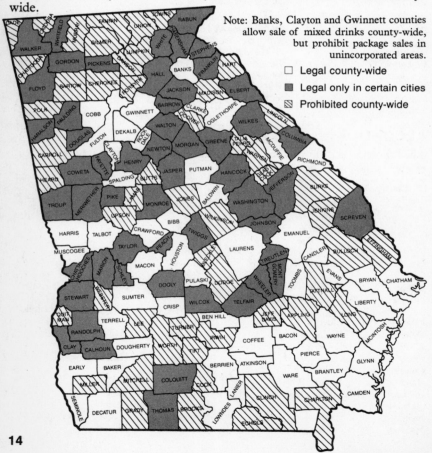

Note: Banks, Clayton and Gwinnett counties allow sale of mixed drinks county-wide, but prohibit package sales in unincorporated areas.

☐ Legal county-wide

■ Legal only in certain cities

▨ Prohibited county-wide

BANKING

The chart below shows, as of June 30, 1985, the number of banking institutions, as well as total deposits, in thousands of dollars in each Georgia county.

County	Banks	Total Deposits	County	Banks	Total Deposits
Appling	2	55,575	Dooly	3	56,974
Atkinson	2	16,840	Dougherty	4	539,069
Bacon	2	45,476	Douglas	3	155,015
Baker	1	7,840	Early	2	46,999
Baldwin	3	174,588	Echols	0	0
Banks	1	17,237	Effingham	0	0
Barrow	2	102,477	Elbert	2	139,191
Bartow	3	69,190	Emanuel	4	109,964
Ben Hill	2	71,123	Evans	2	45,555
Berrien	3	57,418	Fannin	1	40,863
Bibb	3	482,115	Fayette	2	74,938
Bleckley	2	42,369	Floyd	5	385,354
Brantley	0	0	Forsyth	2	86,080
Brooks	3	39,659	Franklin	3	111,576
Bryan	1	25,666	Fulton	12	101,740,025
Bulloch	3	189,894	Gilmer	2	69,651
Burke	4	70,373	Glascock	1	3,234
Butts	1	27,813	Glynn	3	379,107
Calhoun	3	33,262	Gordon	1	101,795
Camden	4	43,741	Grady	3	64,809
Candler	2	48,837	Greene	3	97,977
Carroll	6	253,365	Gwinnett	7	443,261
Catoosa	2	80,823	Habersham	3	199,462
Charlton	2	59,847	Hall	2	353,974
Chatham	7	5,642,767	Hancock	2	29,474
Chattahoochee	0	0	Haralson	5	99,899
Chattooga	2	77,792	Harris	1	31,208
Cherokee	3	202,734	Hart	1	24,467
Clarke	2	243,187	Heard	1	12,565
Clay	0	0	Henry	3	126,916
Clayton	2	97,265	Houston	3	89,302
Clinch	1	21,324	Irwin	2	44,027
Cobb	6	812,046	Jackson	4	92,037
Coffee	5	160,185	Jasper	2	39,198
Colquitt	2	105,944	Jeff Davis	2	36,041
Columbia	2	65,063	Jefferson	4	76,374
Cook	3	44,336	Jenkins	2	33,533
Coweta	4	190,514	Johnson	1	20,315
Crawford	1	16,377	Jones	2	21,592
Crisp	2	77,729	Lamar	2	62,682
Dade	1	21,400	Lanier	1	23,655
Dawson	1	20,696	Laurens	6	253,078
Decatur	1	34,598	Lee	1	9,338
DeKalb	4	250,529	Liberty	2	86,832
Dodge	4	84,409	Lincoln	1	23,474

County	Banks	Total Deposits	County	Banks	Total Deposits
Long	0	0	Spalding	2	230,064
Lowndes	5	217,188	Stephens	2	101,293
Lumpkin	2	72,069	Stewart	2	16,854
Macon	0	0	Sumter	2	91,232
Madison	2	24,863	Talbot	2	20,890
Marion	0	0	Taliaferro	1	15,314
McDuffie	1	64,191	Tattnall	4	78,894
McIntosh	1	22,870	Taylor	2	34,817
Meriwether	5	80,492	Telfair	4	46,043
Miller	1	19,282	Terrell	2	67,724
Mitchell	3	85,932	Thomas	4	118,906
Monroe	3	64,662	Tift	3	121,654
Montgomery	3	58,849	Toombs	4	107,500
Morgan	2	33,942	Towns	1	38,011
Murray	2	88,778	Treutlen	1	20,079
Muscogee	3	925,367	Troup	6	276,876
Newton	3	132,157	Turner	2	58,286
Oconee	1	36,062	Twiggs	1	5,977
Oglethorpe	2	28,119	Union	2	65,624
Paulding	2	98,112	Upson	3	125,470
Peach	3	101,303	Walker	3	118,320
Pickens	2	63,986	Walton	4	150,613
Pierce	3	44,562	Ware	2	112,741
Pike	2	34,653	Warren	1	16,297
Polk	1	46,717	Washington	3	85,329
Pulaski	2	57,765	Wayne	0	0
Putnam	2	56,500	Webster	1	4,362
Quitman	0	0	Wheeler	1	9,866
Rabun	2	80,933	White	2	137,920
Randolph	2	38,069	Whitfield	3	384,190
Richmond	2	695,518	Wilcox	5	26,972
Rockdale	2	138,989	Wilkes	2	83,457
Schley	1	12,902	Wilkinson	3	37,363
Screven	3	76,615	Worth	2	57,173
Seminole	2	41,504			

BASEBALL

Atlanta is the only city in Georgia with a major league baseball team, the *Atlanta Braves*. The Braves play their home games in Atlanta Stadium, which has a capacity of 52,934 people. The fence distances at Atlanta Stadium are: left, 330 feet; center, 402 feet; and right, 330 feet. For ticket or game information pertaining to the Atlanta Braves, call 404-577-9100.

The Atlanta Braves finished the 1986 season in last place in the Eastern Division of the National League, with 72 wins and 89 losses for an average of .447.

Dale Murphy, a Brave, led the National League in runs, with 118, and in home runs, with 37, in 1985.

On April 8, 1974, Hank Aaron, of the Braves, broke Babe Ruth's career home run record by hitting his 715th homer over the left-center field fence at Atlanta.

Two other cities in Georgia have AA baseball clubs, associated with the Southern Association: *Savannah Braves*, affiliated with the Atlanta Braves; and *Columbus Astros*, affiliated with *Houston Astros*.

BASKETBALL

There is one professional basketball team in Georgia, the *Atlanta Hawks*. The Hawks are in the Central Division of the Eastern Conference of the National Basketball Association.

The Hawks finished the 1985–1986 season in 2nd place in their division with 50 wins, 32 losses, and a .610 winning percentage.

For ticket or game information on the Atlanta Hawks, call 404-681-3600.

BICENTENNIAL CELEBRATION OF THE U.S. CONSTITUTION

In 1788, Georgia became the fourth state of the "New United States of America" by unanimously ratifying the Federal Constitution. The Commission in charge of the celebration plans for 1988 is listed below.

Commission Chair	Commission Vice-Chair	Contact Person
Honorable Thomas O. Marshall	Honorable Max Cleland	Ms. Helen P. Dougherty
Chief Justice	Secretary of State	Special Assistant to the
Supreme Court of Georgia	Room 214 State Capitol	Secretary of State
Room 528 Judicial Building	Atlanta, Georgia 30334	Room 214 State Capitol
Atlanta, Georgia 30334		Atlanta, Georgia 30334
		404-656-2881

BOUNDARIES

Georgia is touched by portions of five states. These five states and a brief history of each follow.

Alabama. Derived from a Creek Indian phrase meaning "Here We Rest." In the early 1700s several Spanish expeditions visited the state. In 1702 the French founded Mobile and settled near Tallapoosa. Alabama became a territory in 1817, a state in 1819. Montgomery was the first capital of the Confederacy.

Florida. According to Herrera, historian to the King of Spain, Ponce de Leon "Believing that land to be an island, they named it *Florida*, because it appeared very delightful, having many pleasant groves . . . the Spaniards call *Pasqua de Flores*, or Florida."

17

South Carolina. Named alternatively after French King Charles IX and English kings Charles I and II. In 1690 North and South Carolina became separate entities, and in 1712 they became separately known as North and South Carolina.

North Carolina. *See* South Carolina.

Tennessee. Originally part of North Carolina, Tennessee became a territory of the United States in 1790 and later, in 1796, achieved statehood as the 16th state in the Union.

CHAMBERS OF COMMERCE

A Chamber of Commerce is a voluntary organization of the business community. It unites business and professional individuals and firms, thus creating a central agency which lends itself to improving business and building a better community.

The major responsibility of the Chamber of Commerce is the community's economic well-being. It works to increase wealth and prosperity by facilitating the growth of existing businesses and fostering new ones. This new wealth can be directed toward establishing and improving educational and cultural facilities in order to create the proper business climate for attracting more business and industry.

The Chamber of Commerce meets this responsibility in three steps:

1. It examines community needs to determine what must be done to make it a better place to live and do business.

2. It channels community resources to the fulfillment of these needs.

3. It organizes and develops the necessary leadership to guarantee that the organization will become an effective force for expansion and improvement.

The following list includes all Chambers of Commerce in Georgia, along with their principal contact person.

Adel
See Cook County Chamber of Commerce

Albany
Albany Chamber of Commerce
P.O. Box 308
Albany 31702, 912-883-6900
C. Lamar Clifton, Executive Vice President

Alma
Alma-Bacon County Chamber of Commerce
P.O. Box 450
Alma 31510, 912-632-5859
Bobby A. Wheeler, Sr., Executive Director

Americus
Americus-Sumter County Chamber of Commerce
P.O. Box 724, 400 West Lamar Street
Americus 31709, 912-924-2646
John Rivers, President

Ashburn
See Turner County Chamber of Commerce

Athens
Athens Area Chamber of Commerce
P.O. Box 948, 300 North Thomas St.
Athens 30603, 404-549-6800
Allen D. Stephenson, Executive Vice President

Atlanta
Atlanta Chamber of Commerce
1300 North Omni International
Atlanta 30303, 404-521-0845

Gerald L. Bartels, Executive Vice President
Business Council of Georgia
1280 South Omni International
Atlanta 30335, 404-223-2264
Gene Dyson, CAE President

Chamber of Commerce of the United States
223 Perimeter Center Parkway, Suite 115
Atlanta 30346, 404-393-0140
Harry Cowan, Manager/Southeastern
  Region

Women's Chamber of Commerce of Atlanta
1776 Peachtree St., 634 South Tower
Atlanta 30309, 404-892-0538
Marilyn J. Somers, Executive Director

Augusta
Greater Augusta Chamber of Commerce
P.O. Box 657, 600 Broad St. Plaza
Augusta 30903, 404-722-0421
Charles H. Bellmann, Executive Vice
  President

Bainbridge
Bainbridge-Decatur County Chamber of
  Commerce
P.O. Box 736
Bainbridge 31717, 912-246-4774
David W. Booker, Executive Director

Banks County
Banks County Chamber of Commerce
P.O. Box 57
Homer 30547, 404-677-2108
Lucille B. Mabry, Executive Director

Barnesville
Barnesville-Lamar County Chamber of
  Commerce
109 Forsyth Street
Barnesville 30204, 404-358-2732
Sue Bankston, Executive Secretary

Barrow County
Barrow County Chamber of Commerce
P.O. Box 456—Old Railroad Station
Winder 30680, 404-867-9444
Cora Lou Nix, Executive Director

Baxley
Baxley-Appling County Chamber of
  Commerce
P.O. Box 413, 301 West Parker Street
Baxley 31513, 912-367-7731
E. Lanier Browning, Jr., Executive Vice
  President

Berrien County
Berrien County Chamber of Commerce

P.O. Box 217, 108 S. Jefferson Street
Nashville 31639, 912-686-5123
Sue G. Browning, Manager/Secretary

Blackshear
See Pierce County Chamber of Commerce

Blairsville
Blairsville-Union County Chamber of
  Commerce
P.O. Box 727
Blairsville 30512, 404-745-5789
Louise M. Sprayberry, Executive Secretary

Blakely
Blakely-Early County Chamber of
  Commerce
P.O. Box 189, 52 Court Square
Blakely 31723, 912-723-3741
Nancy J. Kinsey, Executive Director

Blue Ridge
See Copper Basin-Fannin Chamber of
  Commerce

Brantley County
Brantley County Chamber of Commerce
P.O. Drawer B, Highway 301
Nahunta 31553, 912-462-6282
Barbara Chancey, Executive Secretary

Brunswick
Brunswick-Golden Isles Chamber of
  Commerce
P.O. Box 250, 4 Glynn Avenue
Brunswick 31520, 912-265-0620
Lee F. Davenport, Jr. Executive Director

Burke County
Burke County Chamber of Commerce
536 Liberty Street
Waynesboro 30830, 404-554-5451
Jayne F. Brinson, Executive Vice President

Business Council of Georgia
1280 South Omni International
Atlanta 30335, 404-223-2264
Gene Dyson, CAE, President

Butts County
Butts County Chamber of Commerce
P.O. Box 147
Jackson 30233, 404-775-4839
Don Earnhart, President

Cairo
Cairo-Grady County Chamber of
  Commerce, Inc.
P.O. Box 387, 961 North Broad Street
Cairo 31728, 912-377-3663
Peggy Chapman, Executive Vice President

19

Calhoun
See Gordon County Chamber of Commerce

Camden
Camden/Kings Bay Area Chamber of
Commerce
P.O. Box 1797, Highway 40
Kingsland 31548, 912-729-5840

Camilla
Camilla Chamber of Commerce
P.O. Box 226
Camilla 31730, 912-336-5255
Phyllis S. Weathersby, Executive Director

Canton
See Cherokee County Chamber of
Commerce

Carnesville
See Franklin County Chamber of
Commerce

Carroll County
Carroll County Chamber of Commerce
435 North Park Street
Carrollton 30117, 404-832-2446
William T. Nunis, Executive Director

Carrollton
See Carroll County Chamber of Commerce

Cartersville
Cartersville-Bartow County Chamber of
Commerce
P.O. Box 307
Cartersville 30120, 404-382-1466
Tim L. Chason, Executive Vice President

Cedartown
Cedartown Chamber of Commerce, Inc.
201 East Avenue
Cedartown 30125, 404-748-3220, Ext. 23
Jean B. Brumby, Executive Secretary

Chatsworth
Chatsworth-Murray County Chamber of
Commerce
P.O. Box 327, Fort Street
Chatsworth 30705, 404-695-6060
Calvin R. Means, Executive Vice President

Chattooga County
Chattooga County Chamber of Commerce
P.O. Box 217, 108 Washington Ave.
Summerville 30747, 404-857-4033
Suzan B. Spivey, Executive Director

Cherokee County
Cherokee County Chamber of Commerce
P.O. Box 757, 101 West Main Street

Canton 30114, 404-479-1994 or 1995
Jack E. Whitmire, Executive Vice
President

Claxton
Claxton-Evans County Chamber of
Commerce & Industrial Development
Authority
P.O. Box 655
Claxton 30417, 912-739-1391
Ms. Elissa H. Hall, Executive Director

Clayton
See Rabun County Chamber of Commerce

Clayton County
Clayton County Chamber of Commerce
P.O. Box 774, 8712 Tara Blvd.
Jonesboro 30237, 404-478-6549
Phil Mellor, Executive Vice President

Clinch County
Clinch County Chamber of Commerce
604 East Dame Avenue
Homerville 31634, 912-487-2360
Harry James, Executive Director

Cobb County
Cobb Chamber of Commerce
P.O. Box Cobb
Marietta 30065-2429, 404-980-2000
Phil Sanders, Executive Vice President

Cochran
Cochran-Bleckley Chamber of Commerce
P.O. Box 462, 401 Second Street
Cochran 31014, 912-934-2965
Mary Y. Brown, Executive Secretary

College Park
See South Fulton Chamber of Commerce

Columbus
Columbus Chamber of Commerce
P.O. Box 1200, 1344 13th Avenue
Columbus 31902, 404-327-1566
Joe F. Ragland, Executive Vice President

Commerce
See Jackson County Chamber of Commerce

Conyers
Conyers-Rockdale Chamber of Commerce
P.O. Box 483, 1186 Scott Street
Conyers 30207, 404-483-7049
Randolph B. Cardoza, Executive Vice
President

Cook County
Cook County Chamber of Commerce
P.O. Box 481, 120 North Burwell Avenue

Adel 31620, 912-896-7200
Ms. Willie Paulk, Executive Vice President

Copper Basin-Fannin
Copper Basin-Fannin Chamber of
Commerce
P.O. Box 875
Blue Ridge 30513, 404-632-5680
Dale Huddleson, Executive Director

Cordele
Cordele-Crisp Chamber of Commerce
P.O. Box 158, 302 East 16th Avenue
Cordele 31015, 912-273-1668
Don Sims, Executive Vice President

Cornelia
See Habersham County Chamber of
Commerce

Covington
See Newton County Chamber of Commerce

Cumming
Cumming-Forsyth County Chamber of
Commerce
P.O. Box 711, 115 W. Main St.
Cumming 30130, 404-887-6461
M. "Mac" Berston, Executive Director

Cuthbert
Cuthbert-Randolph Chamber of
Commerce, Inc.
P.O. Box 31, Plum Street on the Square
Cuthbert 31740, 912-732-2683
Cherrie Y. King, Secretary

Dahlonega
Dahlonega-Lumpkin County Chamber of
Commerce
Box 2037
Dahlonega 30533, 404-864-3513
Betty Wilson-Wojcik, Executive Director

Dallas
See Paulding County Chamber of
Commerce

Dalton
Dalton-Whitfield Chamber of Commerce
P.O. Box 99, 524 Holiday Avenue
Dalton 30720-0099, 404-278-7373
Charles H. Van Rysselberge, Executive
Vice President

Darien
See McIntosh County Chamber of
Commerce

Dawson
See Terrell County Chamber of Commerce

Dawson County
Dawson County Chamber of Commerce
P.O. Box 299
Dawsonville 30534, 404-265-6278 or 2667
Johnnie E. Sweatte, President

Dawsonville
See Dawson County Chamber of Commerce

Decatur
See DeKalb Chamber of Commerce

DeKalb County
DeKalb Chamber of Commerce
750 Commerce Dr., Suite 201
Decatur 30030, 404-378-8000
James W. Dunn, Executive Vice President

Donalsonville
Donalsonville-Seminole County Chamber of
Commerce
P.O. Box 713, Highway 84 East
Donalsonville 31745, 912-524-2588
Debbie N. Moulton, Executive Secretary

Douglas
Douglas-Coffee County Chamber of
Commerce
Lock Drawer 1607
Douglas 31533, 912-384-1873
Max Lockwood, Executive Vice President

Douglas County
Douglas County Chamber of Commerce
P.O. Box 395, 2145 Slater Mill Road
Douglasville 30133, 404-942-5022
Bob Arnold, Executive Director

Douglasville
See Douglas County Chamber of Commerce

Dublin
Dublin-Laurens County Chamber of
Commerce
P.O. Box 818, 1009 Bellevue Avenue
Dublin 31021, 912-272-5546
Harold O. Duncan, Executive Director

Eastman
Eastman-Dodge County Chamber of
Commerce
P.O. Drawer 550, 201 2nd Avenue
Eastman 31023, 912-374-4723
John M. Crichton, Executive Director

East Point
See South Fulton County Chamber of
Commerce

Eatonton
Eatonton-Putnam Chamber of Commerce

P.O. Box 656, 105 Sumter Street
Eatonton 31024, 404-485-7701
Roddie Anne Blackwell, Executive Vice
President

Elbert County
Elbert County Chamber of Commerce, Inc.
P.O. Box 537, 148 College Avenue
Elberton 30635, 404-283-5651
Dorothy L. McDonald, Executive Vice
President

Elberton
See Elbert County Chamber of Commerce

Ellijay
Ellijay-Gilmer County Chamber of
Commerce
P.O. Box 818, Broad Street
Ellijay 30540, 404-635-7400
W. E. "Gene" Wright, Executive Director

Fannin County
See Copper Basin-Fannin Chamber of
Commerce

Fayette County
Fayette County Chamber of Commerce
P.O. Box 276, 695 Jeff Davis Drive
Fayetteville 30214, 404-461-9983
Robert E. Simmons, Executive Vice
President

Fayetteville
See Fayette County Chamber of Commerce

Fitzgerald
Fitzgerald Chamber of Commerce
P.O. Box 218, 805 South Grant Street
Fitzgerald 31750, 912-423-9357
Mrs. Joni L. Pigg, Executive Director

Folkston
Folkston-Charlton County Chamber of
Commerce
P.O. Box 756, 202 W. Main St.
Folkston 31537, 912-496-2536
Virginia S. Wade, Executive Director

Forsyth
See Monroe County Chamber of Commerce

Fort Gaines
Fort Gaines Chamber of Commerce
P.O. Box 298, 203 Washington St.
Fort Gaines 31751, 912-768-2934
James E. Coleman, President

Fort Oglethorpe
Fort Oglethorpe Area Chamber of
Commerce

P.O. Box 2263, Battlefield Parkway
Fort Oglethorpe 30742, 404-866-0036
Judy G. Hodges, Executive Secretary

Fort Valley
See Peach County Chamber of Commerce

Fulton County
See North Fulton County or South Fulton
County or Sandy Springs Chamber of
Commerce

Franklin
Franklin Chamber of Commerce
P.O. Box 265
Franklin 30217, 404-675-3301
Bryan Owensby, President

Franklin County
Franklin County Chamber of Commerce
P.O. Box 151, Athens Street
Carnesville 30521, 404-384-4659
Peggy Vaughan, Secretary

Gainesville-Hall County
Gainesville-Hall County Chamber of
Commerce
P.O. Box 374, 230 Sycamore Street
Gainesville 30503, 404-532-6206
Clifton McDuffie, Executive Vice President

Glennville
Glennville Area Chamber of Commerce
134 South Main Street
Glennville 30427, 912-654-2000
Irene G. Smith, Executive Secretary

Gordon County
Gordon County Chamber of Commerce
102 Court Street
Calhoun 30701, 404-629-6912
Phillip E. Overton, Executive Vice
President

Greater Valley
Greater Valley Area Chamber of Commerce
P.O. Box 584, 42 Broad Street
West Point 31833, 205-642-1411
C. Thom Robinson, Executive Director

Greene County
Greene County Chamber of Commerce
P.O. Box 403, Greene County Office Bldg.
Greensboro 30642, 404-453-7592
Ana S. Anest, Executive Director

Greensboro
See Greene County Chamber of Commerce

Greenville
See Meriwether County Chamber of
Commerce

Griffin
Griffin Area Chamber of Commerce
P.O. Box 73, 111 West Taylor Street
Griffin 30224, 404-227-3264
Mildred C. Sawyer, Executive Vice
President

Gwinnett County
Gwinnett County Chamber of Commerce
P.O. Box 1245, 1230 Atkinson Road
Lawrenceville 30246, 404-963-5128
John Sawyer, Executive Vice President

Habersham County
Habersham County Chamber of Commerce
P.O. Box 366, Railroad Depot
Cornelia 30531, 404-778-4654
Barbara P. Kerby, Executive Secretary

Hapeville
Hapeville Chamber of Commerce
P.O. Box 82489
Hapeville 30354, 404-767-4244
James E. Clay, Executive Secretary

Hart County
Hart County Chamber of Commerce, Inc.
P.O. Box 793, Carolina Street
Hartwell 30643, 404-376-8590
Mrs. Teresa B. Shirley, Executive Secretary

Hartwell
See Hart County Chamber of Commerce

Hawkinsville
Hawkinsville-Pulaski County Chamber of
Commerce
P.O. Box 447, Lumpkin & Broad Streets
Hawkinsville 31036, 912-783-1717
Betty Smyth, Executive Secretary

Hazlehurst
Hazlehurst-Jeff Davis County Chamber of
Commerce
P.O. Box 536, Hinson Street
Hazlehurst 31539, 912-375-4543
Verle L. Thigpen, Executive Vice President

Helen
Greater Helen Area Chamber of Commerce
P.O. Box 192
Helen 30545, 404-878-2181
Helen D. Fincher, Executive Director

Henry County
Henry County Chamber of Commerce
1310 Highway 20, West
McDonough 30253, 404-957-5786
Nettye V. Clifton, Executive Vice President

Hinesville
Hinesville-Liberty County Chamber of
Commerce
P.O. Box 405, 100 Commerce Street
Hinesville 31313, 912-368-4445
Betty M. Slater, Executive Director

Hogansville
Hogansville Chamber of Commerce
P.O. Box 572, 100 Maple Drive
Hogansville 30230, 404-637-4529
R. T. Hammond, President

Homer
See Banks County Chamber of Commerce

Homerville
See Clinch County Chamber of Commerce

Irwin County
Irwin County Chamber of Commerce
P.O. Box 104, Irwin Avenue
Ocilla 31774, 912-468-9114
Mary Nelms, Executive Director

Jackson
See Butts County Chamber of Commerce

Jackson County
Jackson County Area Chamber of
Commerce
P.O. Box 399, 117 Athens Street
Jefferson 30549, 404-367-9090
Claude Fullerton, Jr., Executive Director

Jasper
See Pickens County Chamber of Commerce

Jefferson
See Jackson County Chamber of Commerce

Jefferson County
Jefferson County Chamber of Commerce
P.O. Box 24, 211 E. 7th Street
Louisville 30434, 912-625-8134
Bill Sawyer, Executive Director

Jeffersonville
See Twiggs County Chamber of Commerce

Jenkins County
Jenkins County Chamber of Commerce and
Development Auth.
200 Southside Cotton Avenue
Millen 30442, 912-982-5595
Caren Oglesby, Executive Vice President

Jesup
See Wayne County Chamber of Commerce

Jonesboro
See Clayton County Chamber of Commerce

LaFayette
LaFayette Area Chamber of Commerce
P.O. Box 985, 304 North Main Street
LaFayette 30728, 404-638-1930
Mrs. Katherine C. Derrick, Executive
Secretary

LaGrange
LaGrange Area Chamber of Commerce
P.O. Box 636, 221 Bull Street
LaGrange 30241, 404-884-8671
Jane L. Fryer, Executive Director

Lavonia
Lavonia Chamber of Commerce
Old Railroad Depot, General Delivery
Lavonia 30553, 404-356-8202
Jeanette Weldon, Executive Secretary

Lawrenceville
See Gwinnett County Chamber of
Commerce

Louisville
See Jefferson County Chamber of
Commerce

Lumpkin
See Stewart County Chamber of Commerce

Lyons
Lyons-Toombs County Chamber of
Commerce
P.O. Box 49, 417 North State Street
Lyons 30436, 912-526-6216
Betty Bazemore, Secretary

Macon
Greater Macon Chamber of Commerce
P.O. Box 169, 305 Coliseum Drive
Macon 31298, 912-741-8000
Glenn E. West, CCE, Executive Vice
President

Macon County
Macon County Chamber of Commerce
P.O. Box 308, 316 South Dooley Street
Montezuma 31063, 912-472-2391
Mrs. Helen G. Garr, Executive Vice
President

Madison
Madison-Morgan County Chamber of
Commerce
P.O. Box 826, 120 Main Street
Madison 30650, 404-342-4454
Yvonne D. DeVane, Executive Director

Manchester
See Meriwether County Chamber of
Commerce

Marietta
See Cobb Chamber of Commerce

McDonough
See Henry County Chamber of Commerce

McIntosh County
McIntosh Chamber of Commerce
P.O. Box 1497, Fort King George & US 17
Darien 31305, 912-437-4192 or 6684
Robert Walczak, President

McRae
See Telfair County Chamber of Commerce

Meriwether County
Meriwether County Chamber of Commerce
P.O. Box 9
Warm Springs, 31830-0009, 404-655-2558
Allen G. Nicas, Executive Director

Metter
Metter-Candler County Chamber of
Commerce
P.O. Box 497, 410 S.W. Broad Street
Metter 30439, 912-685-2159
Cal Dean, Executive Director

Millen
See Jenkins County Chamber of Commerce

Milledgeville
Milledgeville-Baldwin County Chamber of
Commerce
P.O. Box 751, 130 S. Jefferson Street
Milledgeville 31061, 912-453-9311
Linda Southerland, Executive Vice
President

Monroe
See Walton County Chamber of Commerce

Monroe County
Monroe County Chamber of Commerce
P.O. Box 811, 102 E. Johnston Street
Forsyth 31029, 912-994-9239
Rita B. Duke, Executive Director

Montezuma
See Macon County Chamber of Commerce

Monticello
Monticello-Jasper County Chamber of
Commerce
P.O. Box 133
Monticello 31064, 404-468-2116
Mell Tanner, President

Moultrie
Moultrie-Colquitt County Chamber of
Commerce
P.O. Box 487, 329 North Main Street
Moultrie 31768, 912-985-2131
Sam Lofton, Executive Vice President

Nahunta
See Brantley County Chamber of
Commerce

Nashville
See Berrien County Chamber of Commerce

Newnan
Newnan-Coweta Chamber of
Commerce, Inc.
P.O. Box 1103, 1 Savannah Street
Newnan 30264, 404-253-2270
Inez W. Slaton, Executive Director

Newton County
Newton County Chamber of Commerce
P.O. Box 168, 1121 Floyd Street
Covington 30209, 404-786-7510
Art Cassella, Executive Director

North Fulton
North Fulton Chamber of Commerce
P.O. Box 846, 1025 Old Roswell Road
Roswell 30077, 404-993-8808
Delouis J. West, Executive Director

Ocilla
See Irwin County Chamber of Commerce

Oconee County
Oconee County Chamber of Commerce
P.O. Box 338, Hwy. 441, Main Street
Watkinsville 30677, 404-769-5197
John W. McNally, Executive Director

Oglethorpe
Oglethorpe Chamber of Commerce
P.O. Box 178, 214 Sumter Street
Oglethorpe 31068, 912-472-7733
John Coogle, President

Paulding County
Paulding County Chamber of Commerce
150 East Memorial Drive
Dallas 30132, 404-445-6016
Mary Dean Gravett, Secretary

Peach County
Peach County Chamber of Commerce
P.O. Box 1238, 114 Vineville Street
Fort Valley 31030, 912-825-3733
Herman L. Stine, Executive Vice President

Pearson
Pearson Chamber of Commerce
P.O. Box 601
Pearson 31642
Phil Torrance, Secretary

Pelham
Pelham Chamber of Commerce
P.O. Box 151, Park Plaza #2
Pelham 31779, 912-294-4924
Don Gray, Executive Secretary

Perry
Perry Area Chamber of Commerce
P.O. Box 592, 1207 Washington Street
Perry 31069, 912-987-1234
Ann H. Conner, Executive Vice President

Pickens County
Pickens County Chamber of Commerce
P.O. Box 327
Jasper 30143, 404-692-5600
Stanley Dean, President

Pierce County
Pierce County Chamber of Commerce
P.O. Box 47, South Central Avenue
Blackshear, 31516, 912-449-4741
Robert M. Williams, Jr., Executive
Director

Pike County
Pike County Chamber of Commerce, Inc.
P.O. Box 317, Pike County Courthouse
Zebulon 30295, 404-567-8734
Grover Anderson, Secretary/Treasurer

Pine Mountain
Pine Mountain Chamber of
Commerce, Inc.
P.O. Box 483
Pine Mountain 31822, 404-628-4171
Martha F. M. Chewning,
Secretary/Treasurer

Quitman
Quitman-Brooks County Chamber of
Commerce
900 East Screven Street
Quitman 31643, 912-263-4841
Bythel Warrell, Executive Director

Rabun County
Rabun County Chamber of Commerce
P.O. Box 761, Highway 441 North
Clayton 30525, 404-782-4812
Marge Striggow, Executive Director

Reidsville
See Tattnall County Chamber of Commerce

Ringgold-Catoosa County
Ringgold-Catoosa County Chamber of
Commerce
P.O. Box 52, 305 E. Nashville Street
Ringgold 30736, 404-935-5200
Diann Smith, Executive Director

Rockmart
Rockmart Chamber of Commerce
P.O. Box 636, 200 South Marble Street
Rockmart 30153, 404-684-5454, Ext. 18
Ann E. Beck, Executive Director

Rome
Rome Area Chamber of Commerce
P.O. Box 406, 424 Broad Street
Rome 30161, 404-291-7663
Bruce S. Schlosberg, Executive Vice
President

Roswell
See North Fulton Chamber of Commerce

Royston
Royston-Franklin Springs Chamber of
Commerce
P.O. Box 304, Depot Street
Royston 30662, 404-245-9293
C. Donald Johnson, Jr., President

Saint Simons Island
Saint Simons Island Chamber of Commerce
Neptune Park
St. Simons Island 31522, 912-638-9014
Mrs. Jean S. Alexander, Executive
Secretary

Sandersville
See Washington County Chamber of
Commerce

Sandy Springs
Sandy Springs Chamber of Commerce, Inc.
6065 Roswell Road, NE, Suite 726
Sandy Springs 30328, 404-252-4800
Raymond L. Higgins, Executive Director

Savannah
Savannah Area Chamber of Commerce
301 West Broad Street
Savannah 31499, 912-233-3067
David A. Young, President

Screven County
Screven County Chamber of Commerce
101 South Main Street
Sylvania 30467, 912-564-7878
Norma K. Howard, Executive Director

Soperton
Soperton-Treutlen Chamber of Commerce

P.O. Box 296
Soperton 30457, 912-529-6868
John N. Smith, President

South Fulton
South Fulton Chamber of Commerce
6400 Shannon Parkway
Union City 30291, 404-964-1984 or 1985
Otis D. Viall, Executive Director

South Georgia
See Thomasville

Sparta
Sparta-Hancock County Chamber of
Commerce
P.O. Box 452
Sparta 31087, 404-444-5715
Marian A. Davis, Executive Director

Statesboro
Statesboro-Bulloch County Chamber of
Commerce
323 South Main Street
Statesboro 30458, 912-764-6111
George A. Hanson, Executive Director

Stewart County
Stewart County Chamber of Commerce
P.O. Box 1021
Lumpkin 31815, 912-838-4326
Ms. Gina Mathis, Secretary-Treasurer

Summerville
See Chattooga County Chamber of
Commerce

Swainsboro
Swainsboro-Emanuel County Chamber of
Commerce
124 North Main Street
Swainsboro 30401, 912-237-6426
Richard L. James, CCE, Executive Vice
President

Sylvania
See Screven County Chamber of Commerce

Sylvester
See Worth County Chamber of Commerce

Tattnall County
Tattnall County Chamber of Commerce
P.O. Box 769, Brazell Street
Reidsville 30453, 404-577-4713
Rubye T. Smith, Executive Secretary

Telfair County
Telfair County Chamber of Commerce
120 East Oak Street
McRae 31055, 912-868-6365

Kathleen Johnson Clark, Executive
Director

Terrell County
Terrell County Chamber of Commerce
P.O. Box 405, 158 E. Lee Street
Dawson 31742, 912-995-2011
Ima A. Rude, Executive Secretary

Thomaston
Thomaston-Upson County Chamber of
Commerce
P.O. Box 827, 310 North Church Street,
Ste. C
Thomaston 30286, 404-647-9686
O. Kirk Straughan, Executive Vice
President

Thomasville
Thomasville-Thomas County Chamber of
Commerce
P.O. Box 560, 401 South Broad Street
Thomasville 31799, 912-226-9600
Lloyd E. Eckberg, CCE, Executive Vice
President

South Georgia Chamber of Commerce
P.O. Box 2036
Thomasville 31799, 912-226-9600
Lloyd E. Eckberg, CCE, President

Thomson
Thomson-McDuffie Chamber of Commerce
136 Railroad Street
Thomson 30824, 404-595-5963
William E. Drew, Executive Vice President

Tift County
Tift County Chamber of Commerce
P.O. Box 165, 100 Central Avenue
Tifton 31793, 912-382-6200
Kenneth J. O'Neill, Executive Vice
President

Tifton
See Tift County Chamber of Commerce

Toccoa
Toccoa-Stephens County Chamber of
Commerce
P.O. Box 577, 901 E. Currahee St.
Toccoa 30577, 404-886-2132
Robert H. Evans, Executive Vice President

Turner County
Turner County Chamber of Commerce
P.O. Drawer 608, 121 College St.
Ashburn 31714, 912-567-2541
Marvin Raines, Executive Director

Twiggs County
Twiggs County Chamber of Commerce
P.O. Box 231
Jeffersonville 31044, 912-945-3915
Ms. J. E. Beck, Sr., President

Tybee Island
Tybee Island Chamber of Commerce
P.O. Box 491, 209 Butler Avenue
Tybee Island 31328, 912-786-5444
Earl R. Anderson, President

Unadilla
Unadilla Chamber of Commerce
P.O. Box 176
Unadilla 31091, 912-627-3207
Charles Goodroe, President

Union City
See South Fulton Chamber of Commerce

United States Chamber of Commerce
See Atlanta

Valdosta
Valdosta-Lowndes County Chamber of
Commerce
P.O. Box 790, 416 N. Ashley St.
Valdosta 31601, 912-247-8100
John B. Lastinger, Executive Vice
President

Vidalia
Vidalia Chamber of Commerce
P.O. Box 306, 104 East First Street
Vidalia 30474, 912-537-4466
Victor Cross, Executive Vice President

Vienna
Vienna-Dooly County Chamber of
Commerce
P.O. Box 394
Vienna 31092, 912-268-4554
Stanley Gambrell, Executive Director

Walton County
Walton County Chamber of Commerce
P.O. Box 89, 323 W. Spring Street
Monroe 30655, 404-267-6594
Frances E. Enslen-Jones, Executive
Director

Warm Springs
See Meriwether County Chamber of
Commerce

Warner Robins
Warner Robins Chamber of Commerce
1420 Watson Boulevard
Warner Robins 31093, 912-922-8585
Dick Walden, Executive Vice President

Warrenton
Warren County Chamber of Commerce
P.O. Box 27
Warrenton 30828, 404-465-2680
Diane Raley, President

Washington
See Wilkes County Chamber of Commerce

Washington County
Washington County Chamber of Commerce
P.O. Box 582
Sandersville 31082, 912-552-3288
Adilene H. Prescott, Secretary

Watkinsville
See Oconee County Chamber of Commerce

Waycross
Waycross-Ware County Chamber of
Commerce
424 Hicks Street
Waycross 31502, 912-283-3742
Tom Boland, Executive Vice President

Wayne County
Wayne County Chamber of Commerce
P.O. Box 70, 124 NW Broad Street
Jesup 31545, 912-427-2028
William E. Durrett, Executive Director

Waynesboro
See Burke County Chamber of Commerce

West Point
See Greater Valley Chamber of Commerce
Mrs. Marian A. Sumner, President

Wilkes County
Wilkes County Chamber of Commerce
P.O. Box 661, 25 E. Square
Washington 30673, 404-678-2013
Russ Everett, Executive Director

Winder
See Barrow County Chamber of Commerce

Women's Chamber
See Atlanta

Worth County
Worth County-Sylvester Chamber of
Commerce
P.O. Box 768, 301 E. Franklin Street
Sylvester 31791, 912-776-7718
David H. Duggan, Executive Director

Wrightsville
Wrightsville-Johnson County Chamber of
Commerce
P.O. Box 189
Wrightsville 31096, 912-964-9693
Danny O. Evans, President

Zebulon
See Pike County Chamber of Commerce

GEORGIA AREA PLANNING AND DEVELOPMENT COMMISSIONS

Altamaha Georgia Southern APDC
P.O. Box 328, 505 W. Parker Street
Baxley 31513, 912-367-3648
Ted Fortino, Executive Director

Atlanta Regional Commission
Suite 1801, 100 Edgewood Avenue, NE
Atlanta 30335, 404-656-7700
Harry West, Executive Director

Central Savannah River APDC
P.O. Box 2800, 2123 Wrightsboro Road
Augusta 30904, 404-737-1823
Tim F. Maund, Executive Director

Chattahoochee-Flint APDC
P.O. Box 2308, 6 Shenandoah Blvd.
Newnan 30264, 404-253-8521
David T. Barrow, Executive Director

Coastal APDC
P.O. Box 1917

Brunswick 31521, 912-264-7363
Vernon D. Martin, Executive Director

Coosa Valley APDC
P.O. Drawer H, Jackson Hill Drive
Rome 30163, 404-295-6485
C. D. Rampley, Executive Director

Georgia Mountains APDC
P.O. Box 1720
Gainesville 30503, 404-536-3431
Dr. Sam Dayton, Executive Director

Heart of Georgia APDC
501 Oak Street
Eastman 31023, 912-374-4771
Nicky Cabero, Executive Director

Lower Chattahoochee APDC
P.O. Box 1908, 930 2nd Avenue
Columbus 31994, 404-324-4221
Ron Starnes, Executive Director

McIntosh Trail APDC
P.O. Drawer A
Barnesville 30204, 404-358-3647
Lanier E. Boatwright, Executive Director

Middle Flint APDC
P.O. Box 6, 203 East College Street
Ellaville 31806, 912-937-2561 or GIST
345-1204
Bobby L. Lowe, Executive Director

Middle Georgia APDC
600 Grand Building
Macon 31201, 912-744-6160 or GIST
321-6160
James Tonn, Executive Director

North Georgia APDC
503 West Waugh Street
Dalton 30720, 404-272-2300 or GIST
234-2300
George Sutherland, Executive Director

Northeast Georgia APDC
305 Research Drive

Athens 30610, 404-548-3141
Clinton Lane, Executive Director

Oconee APDC
P.O. Box 707, 3014 Heritage Road
Milledgeville 31061, 912-453-5327 or GIST
404-324-5372
J. E. Gentry, Executive Director

South Georgia APDC
P.O. Box 1233, 327 West Savannah Ave.
Valdosta 31601, 912-333-5277 or GIST
349-5277
Hal Davis, Executive Director

Southeast Georgia APDC
P.O. Box 2049, 3243 Harris Road
Waycross 31501, 912-285-6097
Nash Williams, Executive Director

Southwest Georgia APDC
P.O. Box 346, Broad Street
Camilla 31730, 912-336-5616 or GIST
341-4315
Carroll C. Underwood, Executive Director

CLIMATE

Georgia's climate is mild, with 65 °F. (18 °C) being the average annual temperature. For the most part the winters are short and mild and the summers warm and humid.

The map and charts on pages 30 and 31 reveal the high and low temperatures (Fahrenheit on left; Celsius on right) that can normally be expected for each of the twelve months in the northern, middle, and southern parts of Georgia.

COASTLINE & SHORELINE

General coastline figures represent lengths of the seacoast outline. The coastlines of sounds and of bays are included to a point where they narrow to the width of 30 minutes of latitude, and the distance across at such point is included. Total shorelines include the outer coast, offshore islands, sounds, bays, and rivers to the head of tidewater or to a point where tidal waters narrow to a width of 100 feet.

Coastline
100 miles

Shoreline
2,344 miles

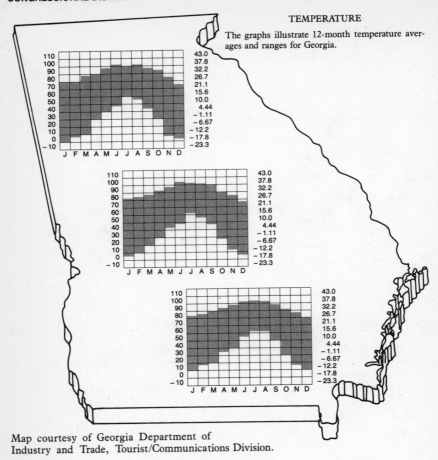

TEMPERATURE

The graphs illustrate 12-month temperature averages and ranges for Georgia.

Map courtesy of Georgia Department of Industry and Trade, Tourist/Communications Division.

CONGRESSIONAL DISTRICTS

Georgia is divided into ten Congressional districts, as shown on the accompanying map on page 32. The representatives are listed with their Washington, D.C. addresses and telephone numbers.'

District 1
Lindsay Thomas
Washington, D.C. 20515
202-225-5831

District 2
Charles Hatcher
Washington, D.C. 20515
202-225-3631

District 3
Richard Ray
Washington, D.C. 20515
202-225-5901

District 4
Pat Swindall
Washington, D.C. 20515
202-225-4272

Annual Precipitation

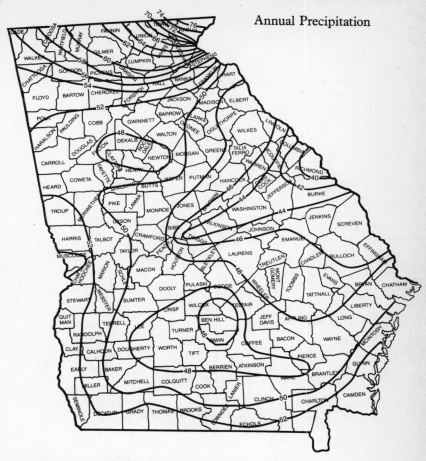

Mean annual precipitation in inches. Amounts shown in 2-inch intervals.

District 5
Wyche Fowler, Jr.
Washington, D.C. 20515
202-225-3801

District 6
Newt Gingrich
Washington, D.C. 20515
202-225-4501

District 7
George (Buddy) Darden
Washington, D.C. 20515
202-225-2931

District 8
J. Roy Rowland
Washington, D.C. 20515
202-225-6531

District 9
Ed Jenkins
Washington, D.C. 20515
202-225-5211

District 10
Doug Barnard, Jr.
Washington, D.C. 20515
202-225-4101

United States
Congressional Districts

CONGRESSIONAL MEDAL OF HONOR

The Congressional Medal of Honor is the highest United States military decoration and is awarded in the name of Congress to members of the Armed Forces for gallantry and bravery beyond the call of duty in action against the enemy. Georgia recipients of the Congressional Medal of Honor, their rank, units, and hometowns follow.

ARMY-AIR FORCE

Brown, Bobbie E., Capt., 1st Inf. Div. (Atlanta).
Carter, Mason, 1st Lt., 5th U.S. Inf. (Augusta).
*Durham, Harold Bascom, Jr., 2d Lt., 1st Inf. Div. (Atlanta) (b. N.C.).
Garlington, Ernest A., 1st Lt. 7th U.S. Cav. (Athens) (b. S.C.).

Jackson, Joe M., Lt. Col., USAF (Newnan).

*Johnston, Donald R., Spec. 4, 1st Cav. Div. (Columbus).

Lee, Daniel L., 1st Lt., 117th Cav. Rec. Sq. (Alma).

McLerry, Finnis D., Plat. Sgt., 198th Inf. Brig. Ameri. Div. (Fort Benning) (b. Tex.).

*McKibben, Ray, Sgt., 17th Cav. (Felton).

McKinney, John R., Sgt., 33d Inf. Div. (Woodcliff).

Ray, Ronald Eric, Capt., 25th Inf. Div. (Cordele).

*Story, Luther H., Pfc., 2d Inf. Div. (Buena Vista).

*Wilbanks, Hilliard A., Capt., 21st Tact. Air Support Squadron (Cornelia).

NAVY-MARINE CORPS

Davis, Raymond G., Lt. Col., USMC, 1st Marine Div. (Atlanta).

*Davis, Rodney Maxwell, Sgt., USMC, 1st Marine Div. (Macon).

*Dyess, Aquilla James, Lt. Col., USMCR (Augusta).

*Elrod, Henry Talmage, Capt., USMC (Ashburn).

Leland, George W., GM, USN (Savannah).

Livingston, James E., Capt., USMC (McRae).

*Phillips, Lee H., Cpl., USMC, 1st Marine Div. (Ben Hill).

Pless, Stephen W., Maj., USMC, 1st Mar. Aircraft Wing (Newnan).

*Thomason, Clyde, Sgt., USMCR (Atlanta).

* Posthumous award

It is noteworthy that the first Medals of Honor ever bestowed were awarded to the nineteen Union Army volunteers who in 1862 captured the locomotive, *General*, at Big Shanty, Georgia and sabotaged vital Confederate facilities between Atlanta and Chattanooga. All nineteen men were captured, and eight were tried and executed. Eventually, all in the party were awarded medals, some posthumously.

CONSTITUTION

Since 1777, Georgia has had eight constitutions. The last, adopted in 1945, is one of the few in the United States that requires a state to operate on a "pay-as-you-go" basis. Amendments to the constitution can be proposed by the legislature, or by a special convention called by the legislature, but become effective only after being approved by a majority of Georgia's voters in a statewide election.

PREAMBLE

To perpetuate the principles of free government, insure justice to all, preserve peace, promote the interest and happiness of the citizen and of the family, and transmit to posterity the enjoyment of liberty, we the people of Georgia, relying upon the protection and guidance of Almighty God, do ordain and establish this Constitution.

ARTICLE I.
BILL OF RIGHTS
Section I.
Rights of Persons

Paragraph I. **Life, liberty, and property.** No person shall be deprived of life, liberty, or property except by due process of law.

Paragraph II. **Protection to person and property; equal protection.** Protection to person and property is the paramount duty of government and shall be impartial and complete. No person shall be denied the equal protection of the laws.

Paragraph III. **Freedom of conscience.** Each person has the natural and inalienable right to worship God, each according to the dictates of that person's own conscience; and no human authority should, in any case, control or interfere with such right of conscience.

Paragraph IV. **Religious opinions; freedom of religion.** No inhabitant of this state shall be molested in person or property or be prohibited from holding any public office or trust on account of religious opinions; but the right of freedom of religion shall not be so construed as to excuse acts of licentiousness or justify practices inconsistent with the peace and safety of the state.

Paragraph V. **Freedom of speech and of the press guaranteed.** No law shall be passed to curtail or restrain the freedom of speech or of the press. Every person may speak, write, and publish sentiments on all subjects but shall be responsible for the abuse of that liberty.

Paragraph VI. **Libel.** In all civil or criminal actions for libel, the truth may be given in evidence; and, if it shall appear to the trier of fact that the matter charged as libelous is true, the party shall be discharged.

Paragraph VII. **Citizens, protection of.** All citizens of the United States, resident in this state, are hereby declared citizens of this state; and it shall be the duty of the General Assembly to enact such laws as will protect them in the full enjoyment of the rights, privileges, and immunities due to such citizenship.

Paragraph VIII. **Arms, right to keep and bear.** The right of the people to keep and bear arms shall not be infringed, but the General Assembly shall have power to prescribe the manner in which arms may be borne.

Paragraph IX. **Right to assemble and petition.** The people have the right to assemble peaceably for their common good and to apply by petition or remonstrance to those vested with the powers of government for redress of grievances.

Paragraph X. **Bill of attainder; ex post facto laws; and retroactive laws.** No bill of attainder, ex post facto law, retroactive law, or laws impairing the obligation of contract or making irrevocable grant of special privileges or immunities shall be passed.

Paragraph XI. **Right to trial by jury; number of jurors; selection and compensation of jurors.**

(a) The right to trial by jury shall remain inviolate, except that the court shall render judgment without the verdict of a jury in all civil cases where no issuable defense is filed and where a jury is not demanded in writing by either party. In criminal cases, the defendant shall have a public and speedy trial by an impartial jury; and the jury shall be the judges of the law and the facts.

(b) A trial jury shall consist of 12 persons; but the General Assembly may prescribe any number, not less than six, to constitute a trial jury in courts of limited jurisdiction and in superior courts in misdemeanor cases.

(c) The General Assembly shall provide by law for the selection and compensation of persons to serve as grand jurors and trial jurors.

Paragraph XII. **Right to the courts.** No person shall be deprived of the right to prosecute or defend, either in person or by an attorney, that person's own cause in any of the courts of this state.

Paragraph XIII. **Searches, seizures, and warrants.** The right of the people to be secure in their persons, houses, papers, and effects against unreasonable searches and seizures shall not be violated; and no warrant shall issue except upon probable cause supported by oath or affirmation particularly describing the place or places to be searched and the persons or things to be seized.

Paragraph XIV. **Benefit of counsel; accusation; list of witnesses; compulsory process.** Every person charged with an offense against the laws of this state shall have the privilege and benefit of counsel; shall be furnished with a copy of the accusation or indictment and, on demand, with a list of the witnesses on whose testimony such charge is founded; shall have compulsory process to obtain the testimony of that person's own witnesses; and shall be confronted with the witnesses testifying against such person.

Paragraph XV. **Habeas corpus.** The writ of habeas corpus shall not be suspended unless, in case of rebellion or invasion, the public safety may require it.

Paragraph XVI. **Self-incrimination.** No person shall be compelled to give testimony tending in any manner to be self-incriminating.

Paragraph XVII. **Bail; fines; punishment; arrest, abuse of prisoners.** Excessive bail shall not be required, nor excessive fines imposed, nor cruel and unusual punishments inflicted; nor shall any person be abused in being arrested, while under arrest, or in prison.

Paragraph XVIII. **Jeopardy of life or liberty more than once forbidden.** No person shall be put in jeopardy of life or liberty more than once for the same offense except when a new trial has been granted after conviction or in case of mistrial.

Paragraph XIX. **Treason.** Treason against the State of Georgia shall consist of insurrection against the state, adhering to the state's enemies, or giving them aid and comfort. No person shall be convicted of treason except on the testimony of two witnesses to the same overt act or confession in open court.

Paragraph XX. **Conviction, effect of.** No conviction shall work corruption of blood or forfeiture of estate.

Paragraph XXI. **Banishment and whipping as punishment for crime.** Neither banishment beyond the limits of the state nor whipping shall be allowed as a punishment for crime.

Paragraph XXII. **Involuntary servitude.** There shall be no involuntary servitude within the State of Georgia except as a punishment for crime after legal conviction thereof or for contempt of court.

Paragraph XXIII. **Imprisonment for debt.** There shall be no imprisonment for debt.

Paragraph XXIV. **Costs.** No person shall be compelled to pay costs in any criminal case except after conviction on final trial.

Paragraph XXV. **Status of the citizen.** The social status of a citizen shall never be the subject of legislation.

Paragraph XXVI. **Exemptions from levy and sale.** The General Assembly shall protect by law from levy and sale by virtue of any process under the laws of this state a portion of the property of each person in an amount of not less than $1,600.00 and shall have authority to define to whom any such additional exemptions shall be allowed; to specify the amount of such exemptions; to provide for the manner of exempting such property and for the sale, alienation, and encumbrance thereof; and to provide for the waiver of said exemptions by the debtor.

Paragraph XXVII. **Spouse's separate property.** The separate property of each spouse shall remain the separate property of that spouse except as otherwise provided by law.

Paragraph XXVIII. **Enumeration of rights not denial of others.** The enumeration of rights herein contained as a part of this Constitution shall not be construed to deny to the people any inherent rights which they may have hitherto enjoyed.

Section II.
Origin and Structure of Government

Paragraph I. **Origin and foundation of government.** All government, of right, originates with the people, is founded upon their will only, and is instituted solely for the good of the whole. Public officers are the trustees and servants of the people and are at all times amenable to them.

Paragraph II. **Object of government.** The people of this state have the inherent right of regulating their internal government. Government is instituted for the protection, security, and benefit of the people; and at all times they have the right to alter or reform the same whenever the public good may require it.

Paragraph III. **Separation of legislative, judicial, and executive powers.** The legislative, judicial, and executive powers shall forever remain separate and distinct; and no person discharging the duties of one shall at the same time exercise the functions of either of the others except as herein provided.

Paragraph IV. **Contempts.** The power of the courts to punish for contempt shall be limited by legislative acts.

Paragraph V. **What acts void.** Legislative acts in violation of this Constitution or the Constitution of the United States are void, and the judiciary shall so declare them.

Paragraph VI. **Superiority of civil authority.** The civil authority shall be superior to the military.

Paragraph VII. **Separation of church and state.** No money shall ever be taken from the public treasury, directly or indirectly, in aid of any church, sect, cult, or religious denomination or of any sectarian institution.

Paragraph VIII. **Lotteries.** All lotteries, and the sale of lottery tickets, are hereby prohibited; and this prohibition shall be enforced by penal laws, except that the General Assembly may by law provide that the operation of a nonprofit bingo game shall not be a lottery and shall be legal in this state. The General Assembly may by law define a nonprofit bingo game and provide for the regulation of nonprofit bingo games.

Paragraph IX. **Sovereign immunity of the state from suit.**

(a) Sovereign immunity extends to the state and all of its departments and agencies. However, the defense of sovereign immunity is waived as to any action ex contractu for the breach of any written contract now existing or hereafter entered into by the state or its departments and agencies. Also the defense of sovereign immunity is waived as to those actions for the recovery of damages for any claim against the state or any of its departments and agencies for which liability insurance protection for such claims has been provided but only to the extent of any liability insurance provided. Moreover, the sovereign immunity of the state or any of its departments and agencies may hereafter be waived further by Act of the General Assembly which specifically provides that sovereign immunity is hereby waived and the extent of the waiver. No waiver of sovereign immunity shall be construed as a waiver of any immunity provided to the state or its departments and agencies by the United States Constitution. The provisions of this paragraph shall not have the effect of permitting the state or any of its departments or agencies to interpose the defense of sovereign immunity as to any action against the state or any of its departments or agencies filed prior to January 1, 1983, if such defense could not have been interposed on December 31, 1982.

(b) The General Assembly may provide by law for the processing and disposition of claims against the state which do not exceed such maximum amount as provided therein.

Section III.
General Provisions

Paragraph I. **Eminent domain.**

(a) Except as otherwise provided in this Paragraph, private property shall not be taken or damaged for public purposes without just and adequate compensation being first paid.

(b) When private property is taken or damaged by the state or the counties or municipalities of the state for public road or street purposes, or for public transportation purposes, or for any other public purposes as determined by the General Assembly, just and adequate compensation therefor need not be paid until the same has been finally fixed and determined as provided by law; but such just and adequate compensation shall then be paid in preference to all other obligations except bonded indebtedness.

(c) The General Assembly may by law require the condemnor to make prepayment against adequate compensation as a condition precedent to the exercise of the right of eminent domain and provide for the disbursement of the same to the end that the rights and equities of the property owner, lien holders, and the state and its subdivisions may be protected.

(d) The General Assembly may provide by law for the payment by the condemnor of reasonable expenses, including attorney's fees, incurred by the condemnee in determining just and adequate compensation.

(e) Notwithstanding any other provision of the Constitution, the General Assembly may provide by law for relocation assistance and payments to persons displaced through the exercise of the power of eminent domain or because of public projects or programs; and the powers of taxation may be exercised and public funds expended in furtherance thereof.

Paragraph II. **Private ways.** In case of necessity, private ways may be granted upon just and adequate compensation being first paid by the applicant.

Paragraph III. **Tidewater titles confirmed.** The Act of the General Assembly approved December 16, 1902, which extends the title of ownership of lands abutting on tidal water to low water mark, is hereby ratified and confirmed.

ARTICLE II.
VOTING AND ELECTIONS
Section I.
Method of Voting; Right to Register and Vote

Paragraph I. **Method of voting.** Elections by the people shall be by secret ballot and shall be conducted in accordance with procedures provided by law.

Paragraph II. **Right to register and vote.** Every person who is a citizen of the United States and a resident of Georgia as defined by law, who is at least 18 years of age and not disenfranchised by this article, and who meets minimum residency requirements as provided by law shall be entitled to vote at any election by the people. The General Assembly shall provide by law for the registration of electors.

Paragraph III. **Exceptions to right to register and vote.**

(a) No person who has been convicted of a felony involving moral turpitude may register, remain registered, or vote except upon completion of the sentence.

(b) No person who has been judicially determined to be mentally incompetent may register, remain registered, or vote unless the disability has been removed.

Section II.
General Provisions

Paragraph I. **Procedures to be provided by law.** The General Assembly shall provide by law for a method of appeal from the decision to allow or refuse to allow any person to register or vote and shall provide by law for a procedure whereby returns of all elections by the people shall be made to the Secretary of State.

Paragraph II. **Run-off election.** A run-off election shall be a continuation of the general election and only persons who were entitled to vote in the general election shall be entitled to vote therein; and only those votes cast for the persons designated for the runoff shall be counted in the tabulation and canvass of the votes cast.

Paragraph III. **Persons not eligible to hold office.** No person who is not a registered voter or who has been convicted of a felony involving moral turpitude, unless that person's civil rights have been restored, or who is the holder of public funds illegally shall be eligible to hold any office or appointment of honor or trust in this state. Additional conditions of eligibility to hold office for persons elected on a write-in vote and for persons holding offices or appointments of honor or trust other than elected offices created by this Constitution may be provided by law.

Paragraph IV. **Recall of public officials holding elective office.** The General Assembly is hereby authorized to provide by general law for the recall of public officials who hold elective office. The procedures, grounds, and all other matters relative to such recall shall be provided for in such law.

Paragraph V. **Vacancies created by elected officials qualifying for other office.** The office of any state, county, or municipal elected official shall be declared vacant upon such elected official qualifying, in a general primary or general election, or special primary or special election, for another state, county, or municipal elective office or qualifying for the House of Representatives or the Senate of the United States if the term of the office for which such official is qualifying for begins more than 30 days prior to the expiration of such official's present term of office. The vacancy created in any such office shall be filled as provided by this Constitution or any general or local law. This provision shall not apply to any elected official seeking or holding more than one elective office when the holding of such offices simultaneously is specifically authorized by law.

Section III.
Suspension and Removal
of Public Officials

Paragraph I. **Procedures for and effect of suspending or removing public officials upon felony indictment.**

(a) As used in this Paragraph, the term "public official" means the Governor, the Lieutenant Governor, the Secretary of State, the Attorney General, the State School Superintendent, the Commissioner of Insurance, the Commissioner of Agriculture, the Commissioner of Labor, and any member of the General Assembly.

(b) Upon indictment for a felony by a grand jury of this state, which felony indictment relates to the performance or activities of the office of any public official, the Attorney General or district attorney shall transmit a certified copy of the indictment to the Governor or, if the indicted public official is the Governor, to the Lieutenant Governor who shall, subject to subparagraph (d) of this Paragraph, appoint a review commission. If the indicted public official is the Governor, the commission shall be composed of the Attorney General, the Secretary of State, the State School Superintendent, the Commissioner of Insurance, the Commissioner of Agriculture, and the Commissioner of Labor. If the indicted public official is the Attorney General, the commission shall be composed of three other public officials who are not members of the General Assembly. If the indicted public official is not the Governor, the Attorney General, or a member of the General Assembly, the commission shall be composed of the Attorney General and two other public officials who are not members of the General Assembly. If the indicted public official is a member of the General Assembly, the commission shall be composed of the Attorney General and one member of the Senate and one member of the House of Representatives. If the Attorney General brings the indictment against the public official, the Attorney General shall not serve on the commission. In place of the Attorney General, the Governor shall appoint a retired Supreme Court Justice or a retired Court of Appeals Judge. The commission shall provide for a speedy hearing, including notice of the nature and cause of the hearing, process for obtaining witnesses, and the assistance of counsel. Unless a longer period of time is granted by the appointing authority, the commission shall make a written report within 14 days. If the commission determines that the indictment relates to and adversely affects the administration of the office of the indicted public official and that the rights and interests of the public are adversely affected thereby, the Governor or, if the Governor is the indicted public official, the Lieutenant Governor shall suspend the public official immediately and without further action pending the final disposition of the case or until the expiration of the officer's term of office, whichever occurs first. During the term of office to which such officer was elected and in which the indictment occurred, if a nolle prosequi is entered, if the public official is acquitted, or if after conviction the conviction is later overturned as a result of any direct appeal or application for a writ of certiorari, the officer shall be immediately reinstated to the office from which he was suspended. While a public official is suspended under this Paragraph and until final conviction, the officer shall continue to receive the compensation from his office.

(c) Unless the Governor is the public officer under suspension, for the duration of any suspension under this Paragraph, the Governor shall appoint a replacement officer except in the case of a member of the General Assembly. If the Governor is the public officer under suspension, the provisions of Article V, Section I, Paragraph V of this Constitution shall apply as if the Governor were temporarily disabled. Upon a final conviction with no appeal or review pending, the office shall be declared vacant and a successor to that office shall be chosen as provided in this Constitution or the laws enacted in pursuance thereof.

(d) No commission shall be appointed for a period of 14 days from the day the indictment is received. This period of time may be extended by the Governor. During this period of time, the indicted public official may, in writing, authorize the Governor or, if the Governor is the indicted public official, the Lieutenant Governor to suspend him from office. Any such voluntary suspension shall be subject to the same conditions for review, reinstatement, or declaration of vacancy as are provided in this Paragraph for a nonvoluntary suspension.

(e) After any suspension is imposed under this Paragraph, the suspended public official may petition the appointing authority for a review. The Governor or, if the indicted public official is the Governor, the Lieutenant Governor may reappoint the commission to review the suspension. The commission shall make a written report within 14 days. If the commission recommends that the public official be reinstated, he shall immediately be reinstated to office.

(f) The report and records of the commission and the fact that the public official has or has not been suspended shall not be admissible in evidence in any court for any purpose. The report and record of the commission shall not be open to the public.

(g) The provisions of this Paragraph shall not apply to any indictment handed down prior to January 1, 1985.

(h) If a public official who is suspended from office under the provisions of this Paragraph is not first tried at the next regular or special term following the indictment, the suspension shall be terminated and the public official shall be reinstated to office. The public official shall not be reinstated under this subparagraph if he is not so tried based on a continuance granted upon a motion made only by the defendant.

ARTICLE III.
LEGISLATIVE BRANCH
Section I.
Legislative Power

Paragraph I. **Power vested in General Assembly.** The legislative power of the state shall be vested in a General Assembly which shall consist of a Senate and a House of Representatives.

Section II.
Composition of General Assembly

Paragraph I. **Senate and House of Representatives.**

(a) The Senate shall consist of not more than 56 Senators, each of whom shall be elected from single-member districts.

(b) The House of Representatives shall consist of not fewer than 180 Representatives apportioned among representative districts of the state.

Paragraph II. **Apportionment of General Assembly.** The General Assembly shall apportion the Senate and House districts. Such districts shall be composed of contiguous territory. The apportionment of the Senate and of the House of Representatives shall be changed by the General Assembly as necessary after each United States decennial census.

Paragraph III. **Qualifications of members of General Assembly.**

(a) At the time of their election, the members of the Senate shall be citizens of the United States, shall be at least 25 years of age, shall have been citizens of this state for at least two years, and shall have been legal residents of the territory embraced within the district from which elected for at least one year.

(b) At the time of their election, the members of the House of Representatives shall be citizens of the United States, shall be at least 21 years of age, shall have been citizens of this state for at least two years, and shall have been legal residents of the territory embraced within the district from which elected for at least one year.

Paragraph IV. **Disqualifications.**

(a) No person on active duty with any branch of the armed forces of the United States shall have a seat in either house unless otherwise provided by law.

(b) No person holding any civil appointment or office having any emolument annexed thereto under the United States, this state, or any other state shall have a seat in either house.

(c) No Senator or Representative shall be elected by the General Assembly or appointed by the Governor to any office or appointment having any emolument annexed thereto during the time for which such person shall have been elected unless the Senator or Representative shall first resign the seat to which elected; provided, however, that, during the term for which elected, no Senator or Representative shall be appointed to any civil office which has been created during such term.

Paragraph V. **Election and term of members.**

(a) The members of the General Assembly shall be elected by the qualified electors of their respective districts for a term of two years and shall serve until the time fixed for the convening of the next General Assembly.

(b) The members of the General Assembly in office on June 30, 1983, shall serve out the remainder of the terms to which elected.

(c) The first election for members of the General Assembly under this Constitution shall take place on Tuesday after the first Monday in November, 1984, and subsequent elections biennially on that day until the day of election is changed by law.

Section III.
Officers of the General Assembly

Paragraph I. **President and President Pro Tempore of the Senate.**

(a) The presiding officer of the Senate shall be styled the President of the Senate.

(b) A President Pro Tempore shall be elected by the Senate from among its members. The President Pro Tempore shall act as President in case of the temporary disability of the President. In case of the death, resignation, or permanent disability of the President or in the event of the succession of the President to the executive power, the President Pro Tempore shall become President and shall receive the same compensation and allowances as the Speaker of the House of Representatives. The General Assembly shall provide by law for the method of determining disability as provided in this Paragraph.

Paragraph II. **Speaker and Speaker Pro Tempore of the House of Representatives.**

(a) The presiding officer of the House of Representatives shall be styled the Speaker of the House of Representatives and shall be elected by the House of Representatives from among its members.

(b) A Speaker Pro Tempore shall be elected by the House of Representatives from among its members. The Speaker Pro Tempore shall become Speaker in case of the death, resignation, or permanent disability of the Speaker and shall serve until a Speaker is elected. Such election shall be held as provided in the rules of the House. The General Assembly shall provide by law for the method of determining disability as provided in this Paragraph.

Paragraph III. **Other officers of the two houses.** The other officers of the two houses shall be a Secretary of the Senate and a Clerk of the House of Representatives.

Section IV.
Organization and Procedure of the General Assembly

Paragraph I. **Meeting, time limit, and adjournment.**

(a) The Senate and House of Representatives shall organize each odd-numbered year and shall be a different General Assembly for each two-year period. The General Assembly shall meet in regular session on the second Monday in January of each year, or otherwise as provided by law, and may continue in session for a period of no longer than 40 days in the aggregate each year. By concurrent resolution, the General Assembly may adjourn any regular session to such later date as it may fix for reconvening. Separate periods of adjournment may be fixed by one or more such concurrent resolutions.

(b) Neither house shall adjourn during a regular session for more than three days or meet in any place other than the state capitol without the consent of the other. Following the fifth day of a special session, either house may adjourn not more than twice for a period not to exceed seven days for each such adjournment. In the event either house, after the thirtieth day of any session, adopts a resolution to adjourn for a specified period of time and such resolution and any amendments thereto are not adopted by both houses by the end of the legislative day on which adjournment was called for in such resolution, the Governor may adjourn both houses for a period of time not to exceed ten days.

(c) If an impeachment trial is pending at the end of any session, the House shall adjourn and the Senate shall remain in session until such trial is completed.

Paragraph II. **Oath of members.** Each Senator and Representative, before taking the seat to which elected, shall take the oath or affirmation prescribed by law.

Paragraph III. **Quorum.** A majority of the members to which each house is entitled shall constitute a quorum to transact business. A smaller number may adjourn from day to day and compel the presence of its absent members.

Paragraph IV. **Rules of procedure; employees; interim committees.** Each house shall determine its rules of procedure and may provide for its employees. Interim committees may be created by or pursuant to the authority of the General Assembly or of either house.

Paragraph V. **Vacancies.** When a vacancy occurs in the General Assembly, it shall be filled as provided by this Constitution and by law. The seat of a member of either house shall be vacant upon the removal of such member's legal residence from the district from which elected.

Paragraph VI. **Salaries.** The members of the General Assembly shall receive such salary as shall be provided for by law, provided that no increase in salary shall become effective prior to the end of the term during which such change is made.

Paragraph VII. **Election and returns; disorderly conduct.** Each house shall be the judge of the election, returns, and qualifications of its members and shall have power to punish them for disorderly behavior or misconduct by censure, fine, imprisonment, or expulsion; but no member shall be expelled except by a vote of two-thirds of the members of the house to which such member belongs.

Paragraph VIII. **Contempts, how punished.** Each house may punish by imprisonment, not extending beyond the session, any person not a member who shall be guilty of a contempt by any disorderly behavior in its presence or who shall rescue or attempt to rescue any person arrested by order of either house.

Paragraph IX. **Privilege of members.** The members of both houses shall be free from arrest during sessions of the General Assembly, or committee meetings thereof, and in going thereto or returning therefrom, except for treason, felony, or breach of the peace. No member shall be liable to answer in any other place for anything spoken in either house or in any committee meeting of either house.

Paragraph X. **Elections by either house.** All elections by either house of the General Assembly shall be by recorded vote, and the vote shall appear on the respective journal of each house.

Paragraph XI. **Open meetings.** The sessions of the General Assembly and all standing committee meetings thereof shall be open to the public. Either house may by rule provide for exceptions to this requirement.

Section V.
Enactment of Laws

Paragraph I. **Journals and laws.** Each house shall keep and publish after its adjournment a journal of its proceedings. The original journals shall be the sole, official records of the proceedings of each house and shall be preserved as provided by law. The General Assembly shall provide for the publication of the laws passed at each session.

Paragraph II. **Bills for revenue.** All bills for raising revenue, or appropriating money, shall originate in the House of Representatives.

Paragraph III. **One subject matter expressed.** No bill shall pass which refers to more than one subject matter or contains matter different from what is expressed in the title thereof.

Paragraph IV. **Statutes and sections of Code, how amended.** No law or section of the Code shall be amended or repealed by mere reference to its title or to the number of the section of the Code; but the amending or repealing Act shall distinctly describe the law or Code section to be amended or repealed as well as the alteration to be made.

Paragraph V. **Majority of members to pass bill.** No bill shall become law unless it shall receive a majority of the votes of all the members to which each house is entitled, and such vote shall so appear on the journal of each house.

Paragraph VI. **When roll-call vote taken.** In either house, when ordered by the presiding officer or at the desire of one-fifth of the members present or a lesser number if so provided by the rules of either house, a roll-call vote on any question shall be taken and shall be entered on the journal. The yeas and nays in each house shall be recorded and entered on the journal upon the passage or rejection of any bill or resolution appropriating money and whenever the Constitution requires a vote of two-thirds of either or both houses for the passage of a bill or resolution.

Paragraph VII. **Reading of general bills.** The title of every general bill and of every resolution intended to have the effect of general law or to amend this Constitution or to propose a new Constitution shall be read three times and on three separate days in each house before such bill or resolution shall be voted upon; and the third reading of such bill and resolution shall be in their entirety when ordered by the presiding officer or by a majority of the members voting on such question in either house.

Paragraph VIII. **Procedure for considering local legislation.** The General Assembly may provide by law for the procedure for considering local legislation. The title of every local bill and every resolution intended to have the effect of local law shall be read at least once before such bill or resolution shall be voted upon; and no such bill or resolution shall be voted upon prior to the second day following the day of introduction.

Paragraph IX. **Advertisement of notice to introduce local legislation.** The General Assembly shall provide by law for the advertisement of notice of intention to introduce local bills.

Paragraph X. **Acts signed.** All Acts shall be signed by the President of the Senate and the Speaker of the House of Representatives.

Paragraph XI. **Signature of Governor.** No provision in this Constitution for a two-thirds' vote of both houses of the General Assembly shall be construed to waive the necessity for the signature of the Governor as in any other case, except in the case of the two-thirds' vote required to override the veto or to submit proposed constitutional amendments or a proposal for a new Constitution.

Paragraph XII. **Rejected bills.** No bill or resolution intended to have the effect of law which shall have been rejected by either house shall again be proposed during the same regular or special session under the same or any other title without the consent of two-thirds of the house by which the same was rejected.

Paragraph XIII. **Approval, veto, and override of veto of bills and resolutions.**

(a) All bills and all resolutions which have been passed by the General Assembly intended to have the effect of law shall become law if the Governor approves or fails to veto the same within six days from the date any such bill or resolution is transmitted to the Governor unless the General Assembly adjourns sine die or adjourns for more than 40 days prior to the expiration of said six days. In the case of such adjournment sine die or of such adjournment for more than 40 days, the same shall become law if approved or not vetoed by the Governor within 40 days from the date of any such adjournment.

(b) During sessions of the General Assembly or during any period of adjournment of a session of the General Assembly, no bill or resolution shall be transmitted to the Governor after passage except upon request of the Governor or upon order of two-thirds of the membership of each house. A local bill which is required by the Constitution to have a referendum election conducted before it shall become effective shall be transmitted immediately to the Governor when ordered by the presiding officer of the house wherein the bill shall have originated or upon order of two-thirds of the membership of such house.

(c) The Governor shall have the duty to transmit any vetoed bill or resolution, together with the reasons for such veto, to the presiding officer of the house wherein it originated within three days from the date of veto if the General Assembly is in session on the date of transmission. If the General Assembly adjourns sine die or adjourns for more than 40 days, the Governor shall transmit any vetoed bill or resolution, together with the reasons for such veto, to the presiding officer of the house wherein it originated within 60 days of the date of such adjournment.

(d) During sessions of the General Assembly, any vetoed bill or resolution may upon receipt be immediately considered by the house wherein it originated for the purpose of overriding the veto. If two-thirds of the members to which such house is entitled vote to override the veto of the Governor, the same shall be immediately transmitted to the other house where it shall be immediately considered. Upon the vote to override the veto by two-thirds of the members to which such other house is entitled, such bill or resolution shall become law. All bills and resolutions vetoed during the last three days of the session and not considered for the purpose of overriding the veto and all bills and resolutions vetoed after the General Assembly has adjourned sine die may be considered at the next session of the General Assembly for the purpose of overriding the veto in the manner herein provided. If either house shall fail to override the Governor's veto, neither house shall again consider such bill or resolution for the purpose of overriding such veto.

(e) The Governor may approve any appropriation and veto any other appropriation in the same bill, and any appropriation vetoed shall not become law unless such veto is overridden in the manner herein provided.

Paragraph XIV. **Jointly sponsored bills and resolutions.** The General Assembly may provide by law for the joint sponsorship of bills and resolutions.

Section VI.
Exercise of Powers

Paragraph I. **General powers.** The General Assembly shall have the power to make all laws not inconsistent with this Constitution, and not repugnant to the Constitution of the United States, which it shall deem necessary and proper for the welfare of the state.

Paragraph II. **Specific powers.**

(a) Without limitation of the powers granted under Paragraph I, the General Assembly shall have the power to provide by law for:

(1) Restrictions upon land use in order to protect and preserve the natural resources, environment, and vital areas of this state.

(2) A militia and for the trial by courts-martial and nonjudicial punishment of its members, the discipline of whom, when not in federal service, shall be in accordance with law and the directives of the Governor acting as commander in chief.

(3) The participation by the state and political subdivisions and instrumentalities of the state in federal programs and the compliance with laws relating thereto, including but not limited to the powers, which may be exercised to the extent and in the manner necessary to effect such participation and compliance, to tax, to expend public money, to condemn property, and to zone property.

(4) The continuity of state and local governments in periods of emergency re-

sulting from disasters caused by enemy attack including but not limited to the suspension of all constitutional legislative rules during such emergency.

(5) The participation by the state with any county, municipality, nonprofit organization, or any combination thereof in the operation of any of the facilities operated by such agencies for the purpose of encouraging and promoting tourism in this state.

(6) The control and regulation of outdoor advertising devices adjacent to federal aid interstate and primary highways and for the acquisition of property or interest therein for such purposes and may exercise the powers of taxation and provide for the expenditure of public funds in connection therewith.

(b) The General Assembly shall have the power to implement the provisions of Article I, Section III, Paragraph I(b.); Article IV, Section VIII, Paragraph II; Article IV, Section VIII, Paragraph III; and Article X, Section II, Paragraph XII of the Constitution of 1976 in force and effect on June 30, 1983; and all laws heretofore adopted thereunder and valid at the time of their enactment shall continue in force and effect until modified or repealed.

Paragraph III. **Powers not to be abridged.** The General Assembly shall not abridge its powers under this Constitution. No law enacted by the General Assembly shall be construed to limit its powers.

Paragraph IV. **Limitations on special legislation.**

(a) Laws of a general nature shall have uniform operation throughout this state and no local or special law shall be enacted in any case for which provision has been made by an existing general law, except that the General Assembly may by general law authorize local governments by local ordinance or resolution to exercise police powers which do not conflict with general laws.

(b) No population bill, as the General Assembly shall define by general law, shall be passed. No bill using classification by population as a means of determining the applicability of any bill or law to any political subdivision or group of political subdivisions may expressly or impliedly amend, modify, supersede, or repeal the general law defining a population bill.

(c) No special law relating to the rights or status of private persons shall be enacted.

Paragraph V. **Special limitations.**

(a) The General Assembly shall not have the power to grant incorporation to private persons but shall provide by general law the manner in which private corporate powers and privileges may be granted.

(b) The General Assembly shall not forgive the forfeiture of the charter of any corporation existing on August 13, 1945, nor shall it grant any benefit to or permit any amendment to the charter of any corporation except upon the condition that the acceptance thereof shall operate as a novation of the charter and that such corporation shall thereafter hold its charter subject to the provisions of this Constitution.

(c) The General Assembly shall not have the power to authorize any contract or agreement which may have the effect of or which is intended to have the effect of defeating or lessening competition, or encouraging a monopoly, which are hereby declared to be unlawful and void.

(d) The General Assembly shall not have the power to regulate or fix charges of public utilities owned or operated by any county or municipality of this state, except as authorized by this Constitution.

Paragraph VI. **Gratuities.**

(a) Except as otherwise provided in the Constitution, (1) the General Assembly shall not have the power to grant any donation or gratuity or to forgive any debt or obligation owing to the public, and (2) the General Assembly shall not grant or authorize extra compensation to any public officer, agent, or contractor after the service has been rendered or the contract entered into.

(b) All laws heretofore adopted under Article III, Section VIII, Paragraph XII of the Constitution of 1976 in force and effect on June 30, 1983, shall continue in force and effect and may be amended if such amendments are consistent with the authority granted to the General Assembly by such provisions of said Constitution.

Section VII.
Impeachments

Paragraph I. **Power to impeach.** The House of Representatives shall have the sole power to vote impeachment charges against any executive or judicial officer of this state or any member of the General Assembly.

Paragraph II. **Trial of impeachments.** The Senate shall have the sole power to try impeachments. When sitting for that purpose, the Senators shall be on oath, or affirmation, and shall be presided over by the Chief Justice of the Supreme Court. Should the Chief Justice be disqualified, then the Presiding Justice shall preside. Should the Presiding Justice be disqualified, then the Senate shall select a Justice of the Supreme Court to preside. No person shall be convicted without concurrence of two-thirds of the members to which the Senate is entitled.

Paragraph III. **Judgments in impeachment.** In cases of impeachment, judgments shall not extend further than removal from office and disqualification to hold and enjoy any office of honor, trust, or profit within this state or to receive a pension therefrom, but no such judgment shall relieve any party from any criminal or civil liability.

Section VIII.
Insurance Regulation

Paragraph I. **Regulation of insurance.** Provision shall be made by law for the regulation of insurance.

Paragraph II. **Issuance of licenses.** Insurance licenses shall be issued by the Commissioner of Insurance as required by law.

Section IX.
Appropriations

Paragraph I. **Public money, how drawn.** No money shall be drawn from the treasury except by appropriation made by law.

Paragraph II. **Preparation, submission, and enactments of general appropriations bill.**

(a) The Governor shall submit to the General Assembly within five days after its convening in regular session each year a budget message and a budget report, accompanied by a draft of a general appropriations bill, in such form and manner as may be prescribed by statute, which shall provide for the appropriation of the funds necessary to operate all the various departments and agencies and to meet the current expenses of the state for the next fiscal year.

(b) The General Assembly shall annually appropriate those state and federal funds necessary to operate all the various departments and agencies. To the extent that federal funds received by the state for any program, project, activity, purpose, or expenditure are changed by federal authority or exceed the amount or amounts appropriated in the general appropriations Act or supplementary appropriation Act or Acts, or are not anticipated, such excess, changed or unanticipated federal funds are hereby continually appropriated for the purposes authorized and directed by the federal government in making the grant. In those instances where the conditions under which the federal funds have been made available do not provide otherwise, federal funds shall first be used to replace state funds that were appropriated to supplant federal funds in the same state fiscal year. The fiscal year of the state shall commence on the first day of July of each year and terminate on the thirtieth of June following.

(c) The General Assembly shall by general law provide for the regulation and management of the finance and fiscal administration of the state.

Paragraph III. **General appropriations bill.** The general appropriations bill shall embrace nothing except appropriations fixed by previous laws; the ordinary expenses of the executive, legislative, and judicial departments of the government; payment of the public debt and interest thereon; and for support of the public institutions and educational interests of the state. All other appropriations shall be made by separate bills, each embracing but one subject.

Paragraph IV. **General appropriations Act.**

(a) Each general appropriations Act, now of force or hereafter adopted with such amendments as are adopted from time to time, shall continue in force and effect for the next fiscal year after adoption and it shall then expire, except for the mandatory appropriations required by this Constitution and those required to meet contractual obligations authorized by this Constitution and the continued appropriation of federal grants.

(b) The General Assembly shall not appropriate funds for any given fiscal year which, in aggregate, exceed a sum equal to the amount of unappropriated surplus expected to have accrued in the state treasury at the beginning of the fiscal year together with an amount not greater than the total treasury receipts from existing revenue sources anticipated to be collected in the fiscal year, less refunds, as estimated in the budget report and amendments thereto. Supplementary appropriations, if any, shall be made in the manner provided in Paragraph V of this section of the Constitution; but in no event shall a supplementary appropriations Act continue in force and effect beyond the expiration of the general appropriations Act in effect when such supplementary appropriations Act was adopted and approved.

(c) All appropriated state funds, except for the mandatory appropriations required by this Constitution, remaining unexpended and not contractually obligated at the expiration of such general appropriations Act shall lapse.

Paragraph V. **Other or supplementary appropriations.** In addition to the appropriations made by the general appropriations Act and amendments thereto, the General Assembly may make additional appropriations by Acts, which shall be known as supplementary appropriation Acts, provided no such supplementary appropriation shall be available unless there is an unappropriated surplus in the state treasury or the revenue necessary to pay such appropriation shall have been provided by a tax laid for such purpose and collected into the general fund of the state treasury. Neither house shall pass a supplementary appropriation bill until the general appropriations Act shall have been finally adopted by both houses and approved by the Governor.

Paragraph VI. **Appropriations to be for specific sums.**

(a) Except as hereinafter provided, the appropriation for each department, officer, bureau, board, commission, agency, or institution for which appropriation is made shall be for a specific sum of money; and no appropriation shall allocate to any object the proceeds of any particular tax or fund or a part or percentage thereof.

(b) An amount equal to all money derived from motor fuel taxes received by the state in each of the immediately preceding fiscal years, less the amount of refunds, rebates, and collection costs authorized by law, is hereby appropriated for the fiscal year beginning July 1, of each year following, for all activities incident to providing and maintaining an adequate system of public roads and bridges in this state, as authorized by laws enacted by the General Assembly of Georgia, and for grants to counties by law authorizing road construction and maintenance, as provided by law authorizing such grants. Said sum is hereby appropriated for, and shall be available for, the aforesaid purposes regardless of whether the General Assembly enacts a general appropriations Act; and said sum need not be specifically stated in any general appropriations Act passed by the General Assembly in order to be available for such purposes. However, this shall not preclude the General Assembly from appropriating for such purposes an amount greater than the sum specified above for such purposes. The expenditure of such funds shall be subject to all the rules, regulations, and restrictions imposed on the expenditure of appropriations by provisions of the Constitution and laws of this state, unless such provisions are in conflict with the provisions of this paragraph. And provided, however, that the proceeds of the tax hereby appropriated shall not be subject to budgetary reduction. In the event of invasion of this state by land, sea, or air or in case of a major catastrophe so proclaimed by the Governor, said funds may be utilized for defense or relief purposes on the executive order of the Governor.

(c) A trust fund for use in the reimbursement of a portion of an employer's workers' compensation expenses resulting to an employee from the combination of a previous disability with subsequent injury incurred in employment may be provided for by law. As authorized by law, revenues raised for purposes of the fund may be paid into and disbursed from the trust without being subject to the limitations of subparagraph (a) of this Paragraph or of Article VII, Section III, Paragraph II.

(d) As provided by law, additional penalties may be assessed in any case in which any court in this state imposes a fine or orders the forfeiture of any bond in the nature of the penalty for all offenses against the criminal and traffic laws of this state or of the political subdivisions of this state. The proceeds derived from such additional penalty assessments may be allocated for the specific purpose of meeting any and all costs, or any portion of the cost, of providing training to law enforcement officers and to prosecuting officials.

(e) The General Assembly may by general law approved by a three-fifths' vote of both houses designate any part or all of the proceeds of any state tax now or hereafter levied and collected on alcoholic beverages to be used for prevention, education, and treatment relating to alcohol and drug abuse.

Paragraph VII. **Appropriations void, when.** Any appropriation made in conflict with any of the foregoing provisions shall be void.

Section X.
Retirement Systems

Paragraph I. **Expenditure of public funds authorized.** Public funds may be expended for the purpose of paying benefits and other costs of retirement and pension systems for public officers and employees and their beneficiaries.

Paragraph II. **Increasing benefits authorized.** Public funds may be expended for the purpose of increasing benefits being paid pursuant to any retirement or pension system wholly or partially supported from public funds.

Paragraph III. **Retirement systems covering employees of county boards of education.** Notwithstanding Article IX, Section II, Paragraph III(a)(14), the authority to establish or modify heretofore existing local retirement systems covering employees of county boards of education shall continue to be vested in the General Assembly.

Paragraph IV. **Firemen's Pension System.** The powers of taxation may be exercised by the state through the General Assembly and the counties and municipalities for the purpose of paying pensions and other benefits and costs under a firemen's pension system or systems. The taxes so levied may be collected by such firemen's pension system or systems and disbursed therefrom by authority of the General Assembly for the purposes therein authorized.

Paragraph V. **Funding standards.** It shall be the duty of the General Assembly to enact legislation to define funding standards which will assure the actuarial soundness of any retirement or pension system supported wholly or partially from public funds and to control legislative procedures so that no bill or resolution creating or amending any such retirement or pension system shall be passed by the General Assembly without concurrent provisions for funding in accordance with the defined funding standards.

Paragraph V-A. **Limitation on involuntary separation benefits for Governor of the State of Georgia.** Any other provisions of this Constitution to the contrary notwithstanding, no past, present, or future Governor of the State of Georgia who ceases or ceased to hold office as Governor for any reason, except for medical disability, shall receive a retirement benefit based on involuntary separation from employment as a result of ceasing to hold office as Governor. The provisions of any law in conflict with this Paragraph are null and void effective January 1, 1985.

Paragraph VI. **Involuntary separation; part-time service.**

(a) Any public retirement or pension system provided for by law in existence prior to

47

January 1, 1985, may be changed by the General Assembly for any one or more of the following purposes:

(1) To redefine involuntary separation from employment; or

(2) To provide additional or revise existing limitations or restrictions on the right to qualify for a retirement benefit based on involuntary separation from employment.

(b) The General Assembly by law may define or redefine part-time service, including but not limited to service as a member of the General Assembly, for the purposes of any public retirement or pension system presently existing or created in the future and may limit or restrict the use of such part-time service as creditable service under any such retirement or pension system.

(c) Any law enacted by the General Assembly pursuant to subparagraph (a) or (b) of this Paragraph may affect persons who are members of public retirement or pension systems on January 1, 1985, and who became members at any time prior to that date.

(d) Any law enacted by the General Assembly pursuant to subparagraph (a) or (b) of this Paragraph shall not be subject to any law controlling legislative procedures for the consideration of retirement or pension bills, including, but not limited to, any limitations on the sessions of the General Assembly at which retirement or pension bills may be introduced.

(e) No public retirement or pension system created on or after January 1, 1985, shall grant any person whose retirement is based on involuntary separation from employment a retirement or pension benefit more favorable than the retirement or pension benefit granted to a person whose separation from employment is voluntary.

ARTICLE IV.
CONSTITUTIONAL BOARDS AND COMMISSIONS
Section I.
Public Service Commission

Paragraph I. **Public Service Commission.**

(a) There shall be a Public Service Commission for the regulation of utilities which shall consist of five members who shall be elected by the people. The Commissioners in office on June 30, 1983, shall serve until December 31 after the general election at which the successor of each member is elected. Thereafter, all succeeding terms of members shall be for six years. Members shall serve until their successors are elected and qualified. A chairman shall be selected by the members of the commission from its membership.

(b) The commission shall be vested with such jurisdiction, powers, and duties as provided by law.

(c) The filling of vacancies and manner and time of election of members of the commission shall be as provided by law.

Section II.
State Board of Pardons and Paroles

Paragraph I. **State Board of Pardons and Paroles.** There shall be a State Board of Pardons and Paroles which shall consist of five members appointed by the Governor, subject to confirmation by the Senate. The members of the board in office on June 30, 1983, shall serve out the remainder of their respective terms, provided that the expiration date of the term of any such member shall be December 31 of the year in which the member's term expires. As each term of office expires, the Governor shall appoint a successor as herein provided. All such terms of members shall be for seven years. A chairman shall be selected by the members of the board from its membership.

Paragraph II. **Powers and authority.**

(a) Except as otherwise provided in this Paragraph, the State Board of Pardons and Paroles shall be vested with the power of executive clemency, including the powers to grant reprieves, pardons, and paroles; to commute penalties; to remove disabilities imposed by law; and to remit any part of a sentence for any offense against the state after conviction.

(b) When a sentence of death is commuted to life imprisonment, the board shall not have the authority to grant a pardon to the convicted person until such person has served at least 25 years in the penitentiary; and such person shall not become eligible for parole at any time prior to serving at least 25 years in the penitentiary. When a person is convicted of armed robbery, the board shall not have the authority to consider such person for pardon or parole until such person has served at least five years in the penitentiary.

(c) Notwithstanding the provisions of subparagraph (b) of this Paragraph, the General Assembly, by law, may prohibit the board from granting and may prescribe the terms and conditions for the board's granting a pardon or parole to:

(1) Any person incarcerated for a second or subsequent time for any offense for which such person could have been sentenced to life imprisonment; and

(2) Any person who has received consecutive life sentences as the result of offenses occurring during the same series of acts.

(d) The chairman of the board, or any other member designated by the board, may suspend the execution of a sentence of death until the full board shall have an opportunity to hear the application of the convicted person for any relief within the power of the board.

(e) Notwithstanding any other provisions of this Paragraph, the State Board of Pardons and Paroles shall have the authority to pardon any person convicted of a crime who is subsequently determined to be innocent of said crime.

Section III.
State Personnel Board

Paragraph I. **State Personnel Board.**

(a) There shall be a State Personnel Board which shall consist of five members appointed by the Governor, subject to confirmation by the Senate. The members of the board in office on June 30, 1983, shall serve out the remainder of their respective terms. As each term of office expires, the Governor shall appoint a successor as herein provided. All such terms of members shall be for five years. Members shall serve until their successors are appointed and qualified. A member of the State Personnel Board may not be employed in any other capacity in state government. A chairman shall be selected by the members of the board from its membership.

(b) The board shall provide policy direction for a State Merit System of Personnel Administration and may be vested with such additional powers and duties as provided by law. State personnel shall be selected on the basis of merit as provided by law.

Paragraph II. **Veterans preference.** Any veteran who has served as a member of the armed forces of the United States during the period of a war or armed conflict in which any branch of the armed forces of the United States engaged, whether under United States command or otherwise, and was honorably discharged therefrom, shall be given such veterans preference in any civil service program established in state government as may be provided by law. Any such law must provide at least ten points to a veteran having at least a 10 percent service connected disability as rated and certified by the Veterans Administration, and all other such veterans shall be entitled to at least five points.

Section IV.
State Transportation Board

Paragraph I. **State Transportation Board; commissioner.**

(a) There shall be a State Transportation Board composed of as many members as there are congressional districts in the state. The member of the board from each congressional district shall be elected by a majority vote of the members of the House of Representatives and Senate whose respective districts are embraced or partly embraced within such congressional district meeting in caucus. The members of the board in office on June 30, 1983, shall serve out the remainder of their respective terms. The General Assembly shall provide by law the procedure for the election of members and for filling vacancies on the board. Members shall serve for terms of five years and until their successors are elected and qualified.

(b) The State Transportation Board shall select a commissioner of transportation, who shall be the chief executive officer of the Department of Transportation and who shall have such powers and duties as provided by law.

Section V.
Veterans Service Board

Paragraph I. **Veterans Service Board; commissioner.**

(a) There shall be a State Department of Veterans Service and Veterans Service Board which shall consist of seven members appointed by the Governor, subject to confirmation by the Senate. The members in office on June 30, 1983, shall serve out the remainder of their respective terms. As each term of office expires, the Governor shall appoint a successor as herein provided. All such terms of members shall be for seven years. Members shall serve until their successors are appointed and qualified.

(b) The board shall appoint a commissioner who shall be the executive officer of the department. All members of the board and the commissioner shall be veterans of some war or armed conflict in which the United States has engaged. The board shall have such control, duties, powers, and jurisdiction of the State Department of Veterans Service as shall be provided by law.

Section VI.
Board of Natural Resources

Paragraph I. **Board of Natural Resources.**

(a) There shall be a Board of Natural Resources which shall consist of one member from each congressional district in the state and five members from the state at large, one of whom must be from one of the following named counties: Chatham, Bryan, Liberty, McIntosh, Glynn, or Camden. All members shall be appointed by the Governor, subject to confirmation by the Senate. The members of the board in office on June 30, 1983, shall serve out the remainder of their respective terms. As each term of office expires, the Governor shall appoint a successor as herein provided. All such terms of members shall be for seven years. Members shall serve until their successors are appointed and qualified. Insofar as it is practicable, the members of the board shall be representative of all areas and functions encompassed within the Department of Natural Resources.

(b) The board shall have such powers and duties as provided by law.

Section VII.
Qualifications, Compensation, Removal from Office,
and Powers and Duties of Members of
Constitutional Boards and Commissions

Paragraph I. **Qualifications, compensation, and removal from office.** The qualifications, compensation, and removal from office of members of constitutional boards and commissions provided for in this article shall be as provided by law.

Paragraph II. **Powers and duties.** The powers and duties of members of constitutional boards and commissions provided for in this article, except the Board of Pardons and Paroles, shall be as provided by law.

ARTICLE V.
EXECUTIVE BRANCH
Section I.
Election of Governor and Lieutenant Governor

Paragraph I. **Governor: term of office; compensation and allowances.** There shall be a Governor who shall hold office for a term of four years and until a successor shall be chosen and qualified. Persons holding the office of Governor may succeed themselves for one four-year term of office. Persons who have held the office of Governor and have succeeded themselves as hereinbefore provided shall not again be eligible to be elected to that office until after the expiration of four years from the conclusion of their term as Governor. The compensation and allowances of the Governor shall be as provided by law.

Paragraph II. **Election for Governor.** An election for Governor shall be held on Tuesday after the first Monday in November of 1986, and the Governor-elect shall be installed in office at the next session of the General Assembly. An election for Governor shall take place quadrennially thereafter on said date unless another date be fixed by the General Assembly. Said election shall be held at the places of holding general elections in the several counties of this state, in the manner prescribed for the election of members of the General Assembly, and the electors shall be the same.

Paragraph III. **Lieutenant Governor.** There shall be a Lieutenant Governor, who shall be elected at the same time, for the same term, and in the same manner as the Governor. The Lieutenant Governor shall be the President of the Senate and shall have such executive duties as prescribed by the Governor and as may be prescribed by law not inconsistent with the powers of the Governor or other provisions of this Constitution. The compensation and allowances of the Lieutenant Governor shall be as provided by law.

Paragraph IV. **Qualifications of Governor and Lieutenant Governor.** No person shall be eligible for election to the office of Governor or Lieutenant Governor unless such person shall have been a citizen of the United States 15 years and a legal resident of the state six years immediately preceding the election and shall have attained the age of 30 years by the date of assuming office.

Paragraph V. **Succession to executive power.**

(a) In case of the temporary disability of the Governor as determined in the manner provided in Section IV of this article, the Lieutenant Governor shall exercise the powers and duties of the Governor and receive the same compensation as the Governor until such time as the temporary disability of the Governor ends.

(b) In case of the death, resignation, or permanent disability of the Governor or the governor-elect, the Lieutenant Governor or the Lieutenant Governor-elect, upon becoming the Lieutenant Governor, shall become the Governor until a successor shall be elected and qualified as hereinafter provided. A successor to serve for the unexpired term shall be elected at the next general election; but, if such death, resignation, or permanent disability shall occur within 30 days of the next general election or if the term will expire within 90 days after the next general election, the Lieutenant Governor shall become Governor for the unexpired term. No person shall be elected or appointed to the office of Lieutenant Governor for the unexpired term in the event the Lieutenant Governor shall become Governor as herein provided.

(c) In case of the death, resignation, or permanent disability of both the Governor or the Governor-elect and the Lieutenant Governor or the Lieutenant Governor-elect or in case of the death, resignation, or permanent disability of the Governor and there shall be no Lieutenant Governor, the Speaker of the House of Representatives shall exercise the powers and duties of the Governor until the election and qualification of a Governor at a special election, which shall be held within 90 days from the date on which the Speaker of the House of Representatives shall have assumed the powers and duties of the Governor, and the person elected shall serve out the unexpired term.

Paragraph VI. **Oath of office.** The Governor and Lieutenant Governor shall, before entering on the duties of office, take such oath or affirmation as prescribed by law.

Section II.
Duties and Powers of Governor

Paragraph I. **Executive powers.** The chief executive powers shall be vested in the Governor. The other executive officers shall have such powers as may be prescribed by this Constitution and by law.

Paragraph II. **Law enforcement.** The Governor shall take care that the laws are faithfully executed and shall be the conservator of the peace throughout the state.

Paragraph III. **Commander in chief.** The Governor shall be the commander in chief of the military forces of this state.

Paragraph IV. **Veto power.** Except as otherwise provided in this Constitution, before any bill or resolution shall become law, the Governor shall have the right to review such bill or resolution intended to have the effect of law which has been passed by the General Assembly. The Governor may veto, approve, or take no action on any such bill or resolution. In the event the Governor vetoes any such bill or resolution, the General Assembly may, by a two-thirds' vote, override such veto as provided in Article III of this Constitution.

Paragraph V. **Writs of election.** The Governor shall issue writs of election to fill all vacancies that may occur in the Senate and in the House of Representatives.

Paragraph VI. **Information and recommendations to the General Assembly.** At the beginning of each regular session and from time to time, the Governor may give the General Assembly information on the state of the state and recommend to its consideration such measures as the Governor may deem necessary or expedient.

Paragraph VII. **Special sessions of the General Assembly.**

(a) The Governor may convene the General Assembly in special session by proclamation which may be amended by the Governor prior to the convening of the special session or amended by the Governor with the approval of three-fifths of the members of each house after the special session has convened; but no laws shall be enacted at any such special session except those which relate to the purposes stated in the proclamation or in any amendment thereto.

(b) The Governor shall convene the General Assembly in special session for all purposes whenever three-fifths of the members to which each house is entitled certify to the Governor in writing, with a copy to the Secretary of State, that in their opinion an emergency exists in the affairs of the state. The General Assembly may convene itself if, after receiving such certification, the Governor fails to do so within three days, excluding Sundays.

(c) Special sessions of the General Assembly shall be limited to a period of 40 days unless extended by three-fifths' vote of each house and approved by the Governor or unless at the expiration of such period an impeachment trial of some officer of state government is pending, in which event the House shall adjourn and the Senate shall remain in session until such trial is completed.

Paragraph VIII. **Filling vacancies.**

(a) When any public office shall become vacant by death, resignation, or otherwise, the Governor shall promptly fill such vacancy unless otherwise provided by this Constitution or by law; and persons so appointed shall serve for the unexpired term unless otherwise provided by this Constitution or by law.

(b) In case of the death or withdrawal of a person who received a majority of votes cast in an election for the office of Secretary of State, Attorney General, State School Superintendent, Commissioner of Insurance, Commissioner of Agriculture, or Commissioner of Labor, the Governor elected at the same election, upon becoming Governor, shall have the power to fill such office by appointing, subject to the confirmation of the Senate, an individual to serve until the next general election and until a successor for the balance of the unexpired term shall have been elected and qualified.

Paragraph IX. **Appointments by Governor.** The Governor shall make such appointments as are authorized by this Constitution or by law. If a person whose confirmation is required by the Senate is once rejected by the Senate, that person shall not be renominated by the Governor for appointment to the same office until the expiration of a period of one year from the date of such rejection.

Paragraph X. **Information from officers and employees.** The Governor may require information in writing from constitutional officers and all other officers and employees of the executive branch on any subject relating to the duties of their respective offices or employment.

Section III.
Other Elected Executive Officers

Paragraph I. **Other executive officers, how elected.** The Secretary of State, Attorney General, State School Superintendent, Commissioner of Insurance, Commissioner of Agriculture, and Commissioner of Labor shall be elected in the manner prescribed for the election of members of the General Assembly and the electors shall be the same. Such executive officers shall be elected at the same time and hold their offices for the same term as the Governor.

Paragraph II. **Qualifications.**

(a) No person shall be eligible to the office of the Secretary of State, Attorney General, State School Superintendent, Commissioner of Insurance, Commissioner of Agriculture, or Commissioner of Labor unless such person shall have been a citizen of the United States for ten years and a legal resident of the state for four years immediately preceding election or appointment and shall have attained the age of 25 years by the date of assuming office. All of said officers shall take such oath and give bond and security, as prescribed by law, for the faithful discharge of their duties.

(b) No person shall be Attorney General unless such person shall have been an active-status member of the State Bar of Georgia for seven years.

Paragraph III. **Powers, duties, compensation, and allowances of other executive officers.** Except as otherwise provided in this Constitution, the General Assembly shall prescribe the powers, duties, compensation, and allowances of the above executive officers and provide assistance and expenses necessary for the operation of the department of each.

Paragraph IV. **Attorney General; duties.** The Attorney General shall act as the legal advisor of the executive department, shall represent the state in the Supreme Court in all capital felonies and in all civil and criminal cases in any court when required by the Governor, and shall perform such other duties as shall be required by law.

Section IV.
Disability of Executive Officers

Paragraph I. **"Elected constitutional executive officer," how defined.** As used in this section, the term "elected constitutional executive officer" means the Governor, the Lieutenant Governor, the Secretary of State, the Attorney General, the State School Superintendent, the Commissioner of Insurance, the Commissioner of Agriculture, and the Commissioner of Labor.

Paragraph II. **Procedure for determining disability.** Upon a petition of any four of the elected constitutional executive officers to the Supreme Court of Georgia that another elected constitutional executive officer is unable to perform the duties of office because of a physical or mental disability, the Supreme Court shall by appropriate rule provide for a speedy and public hearing on such matter, including notice of the nature and cause of the accusation, process for obtaining witnesses, and the assistance of counsel. Evidence at such hearing shall include testimony from not fewer than three qualified physicians in private practice, one of whom must be a psychiatrist.

Paragraph III. **Effect of determination of disability.** If, after hearing the evidence on disability, the Supreme Court determines that there is a disability and that such disability is permanent, the office shall be declared vacant and the successor to that office shall be chosen as provided in this Constitution or the laws enacted in pursuance thereof. If it is determined that the disability is not permanent, the Supreme Court shall determine when the disability has ended and when the officer shall resume the exercise of the powers of office. During the period of temporary disability, the powers of such office shall be exercised as provided by law.

ARTICLE VI.
JUDICIAL BRANCH
Section I.
Judicial Power

Paragraph I. **Judicial power of the state.** The judicial power of the state shall be vested exclusively in the following classes of courts: magistrate courts, probate courts, juvenile courts, state courts, superior courts, Court of Appeals, and Supreme Court. Magistrate courts, probate courts, juvenile courts, and state courts shall be courts of limited jurisdiction. In addition, the General Assembly may establish or authorize the establishment of municipal courts and may authorize administrative agencies to exercise quasi-judicial powers. Municipal courts shall have jurisdiction over ordinance violations and such other jurisdiction as provided by law. Except as provided in this paragraph and in Section X, municipal courts, county recorder's courts and civil courts in existence on June 30, 1983, and administrative agencies shall not be subject to the provisions of this article.

Paragraph II. **Unified judicial system.** All courts of the state shall comprise a unified judicial system.

Paragraph III. **Judges; exercise of power outside own court; scope of term "judge."** Provided the judge is otherwise qualified, a judge may exercise judicial power in any court upon the request and with the consent of the judges of that court and of the judge's own court under rules prescribed by law. The term "judge," as used in this article, shall include Justices, judges, senior judges, magistrates, and every other such judicial office of whatever name existing or created.

Paragraph IV. **Exercise of judicial power.** Each court may exercise such powers as necessary in aid of its jurisdiction or to protect or effectuate its judgments; but only the superior and appellate courts shall have the power to issue process in the nature of mandamus, prohibition, specific performance, quo warranto, and injunction. Each superior court, state court, and other courts of record may grant new trials on legal grounds.

Paragraph V. **Uniformity of jurisdiction, powers, etc.** Except as otherwise provided in this Constitution, the courts of each class shall have uniform jurisdiction, powers, rules of practice and procedure, and selection, qualifications, terms, and discipline of judges. The provisions of this Paragraph shall be effected by law within 24 months of the effective date of this Constitution.

Paragraph VI. **Judicial circuits; courts in each county; court sessions.** The state shall be divided into judicial circuits, each of which shall consist of not less than one county. Each county shall have at least one superior court, magistrate court, a probate court, and, where needed, a state court and a juvenile court. The General Assembly may provide by law that the judge of the probate court may also serve as the judge of the magistrate court. In the absence of a state court or a juvenile court, the superior court shall exercise that jurisdiction. Superior courts shall hold court at least twice each year in each county.

Paragraph VII. **Judicial circuits, courts, and judgeships, law changed.** The General Assembly may abolish, create, consolidate, or modify judicial circuits and courts and judgeships; but no circuit shall consist of less than one county.

Paragraph VIII. **Transfer of cases.** Any court shall transfer to the appropriate court in the state any civil case in which it determines that jurisdiction or venue lies elsewhere.

Paragraph IX. **Rules of evidence; law prescribed.** All rules of evidence shall be as prescribed by law.

Section II.
Venue

Paragraph I. **Divorce cases.** Divorce cases shall be tried in the county where the defendant resides, if a resident of this state; if the defendant is not a resident of this state, then in the county in which the plaintiff resides, provided that any person who has been a resident of any United States army post or military reservation within the State of Georgia for one year next preceding the filing of the petition may bring an action for divorce in any county adjacent to said United States army post or military reservation.

Paragraph II. **Land titles.** Cases respecting titles to land shall be tried in the county where the land lies, except where a single tract is divided by a county line, in which case the superior court of either county shall have jurisdiction.

Paragraph III. **Equity cases.** Equity cases shall be tried in the county where a defendant resides against whom substantial relief is prayed.

Paragraph IV. **Suits against joint obligors, copartners, etc.** Suits against joint obligors, joint tort-feasors, joint promisors, copartners, or joint trespassers residing in different counties may be tried in either county.

Paragraph V. **Suits against maker, endorser, etc.** Suits against the maker and endorser of promissory notes, or drawer, acceptor, and endorser of foreign or inland bills of exchange, or like instruments, residing in different counties, shall be tried in the county where the maker or acceptor resides.

Paragraph VI. **All other cases.** All other civil cases, except juvenile court cases as may otherwise be provided by the Juvenile Court Code of Georgia, shall be tried in the county where the defendant resides; venue as to corporations, foreign and domestic, shall be as provided by law; and all criminal cases shall be tried in the county where the crime was committed, except cases in the superior courts where the judge is satisfied that an impartial jury cannot be obtained in such county.

Paragraph VII. **Venue in third-party practice.** The General Assembly may provide by law that venue is proper in a county other than the county of residence of a person or entity impleaded into a pending civil case by a defending party who contends that such person or entity is or may be liable to said defending party for all or part of the claim against said defending party.

Paragraph VIII. **Power to change venue.** The power to change the venue in civil and criminal cases shall be vested in the superior courts to be exercised in such manner as has been, or shall be, provided by law.

Section III.
Classes of Courts of Limited Jurisdiction

Paragraph I. **Jurisdiction of classes of courts of limited jurisdiction.** The magistrate, juvenile, and state courts shall have uniform jurisdiction as provided by law. Probate courts shall have such jurisdiction as now or hereafter provided by law, without regard to uniformity.

Section IV.
Superior Courts

Paragraph I. **Jurisdiction of superior courts.** The superior courts shall have jurisdiction in all cases, except as otherwise provided in this Constitution. They shall have exclusive jurisdiction over trials in felony cases, except in the case of juvenile offenders as provided by law; in cases respecting title to land; in divorce cases; and in equity cases. The superior courts shall have such appellate jurisdiction, either alone or by circuit or district, as may be provided by law.

Section V
Court of Appeals

Paragraph I. **Composition of Court of Appeals; Chief Judge.** The Court of Appeals shall consist of not less than nine judges who shall elect from among themselves a Chief Judge.

Paragraph II. **Panels as prescribed.** The Court of Appeals may sit in panels of not less than three Judges as prescribed by law or, if none, by its rules.

Paragraph III. **Jurisdiction of Court of Appeals; decisions binding.** The Court of Appeals shall be a court of review and shall exercise appellate and certiorari jurisdiction in all cases not reserved to the Supreme Court or conferred on other courts by law. The decisions of the Court of Appeals insofar as not in conflict with those of the Supreme Court shall bind all courts except the Supreme Court as precedents.

Paragraph IV. **Certification of question to Supreme Court.** The Court of Appeals may certify a question to the Supreme Court for instruction, to which it shall then be bound.

Paragraph V. **Equal division of court.** In the event of an equal division of the Judges when sitting as a body, the case shall be immediately transmitted to the Supreme Court.

Section VI.
Supreme Court

Paragraph I. **Composition of Supreme Court; Chief Justice; Presiding Justice; quorum; substitute judges.** The Supreme Court shall consist of not more than nine Justices who shall elect from among themselves a Chief Justice as the chief presiding and administrative officer of the court and a Presiding Justice to serve if the Chief Justice is absent or is disqualified. A majority shall be necessary to hear and determine cases. If a Justice is disqualified in any case, a substitute judge may be designated by the remaining Justices to serve.

Paragraph II. **Exclusive appellate jurisdiction of Supreme Court.** The Supreme Court shall be a court of review and shall exercise exclusive appellate jurisdiction in the following cases:

(1) All cases involving the construction of a treaty or of the Constitution of the State of Georgia or of the United States and all cases in which the constitutionality of a law, ordinance, or constitutional provision has been drawn in question; and

(2) All cases of election contest.

Paragraph III. **General appellate jurisdiction of Supreme Court.** Unless otherwise provided by law, the Supreme Court shall have appellate jurisdiction of the following classes of cases:

(1) Cases involving title to land;
(2) All equity cases;
(3) All cases involving wills;
(4) All habeas corpus cases;
(5) All cases involving extraordinary remedies;
(6) All divorce and alimony cases;
(7) All cases certified to it by the Court of Appeals; and
(8) All cases in which a sentence of death was imposed or could be imposed.
Review of all cases shall be as provided by law.

Paragraph IV. **Jurisdiction over questions of law from state or federal appellate courts.** The Supreme Court shall have jurisdiction to answer any question of law from any state or federal appellate court.

Paragraph V. **Review of cases in Court of Appeals.** The Supreme Court may review by certiorari cases in the Court of Appeals which are of gravity or great public importance.

Paragraph VI. **Decisions of Supreme Court binding.** The decisions of the Supreme Court shall bind all other courts as precedents.

Section VII.
Selection, Term, Compensation, and Discipline of Judges

Paragraph I. **Election; term of office.** All superior court and state court judges shall be elected on a nonpartisan basis for a term of four years. All Justices of the Supreme Court and the Judges of the Court of Appeals shall be elected on a nonpartisan basis for a term of six years. The terms of all judges thus elected shall begin the next January 1 after their election. All other judges shall continue to be selected in the manner and for the term they were selected on June 30, 1983, until otherwise provided by local law.

Paragraph II. **Qualifications.**

(a) Appellate and superior court judges shall have been admitted to practice law for seven years.

(b) State and juvenile court judges shall have been admitted to practice law for five years.

(c) Probate and magistrate judges shall have such qualifications as provided by law.

(d) All judges shall reside in the geographical area in which they are selected to serve.

(e) The General Assembly may provide by law for additional qualifications, including, but not limited to, minimum residency requirements.

Paragraph III. **Vacancies.** Vacancies shall be filled by appointment of the Governor except as otherwise provided by law in the magistrate, probate, and juvenile courts.

Paragraph IV. **Period of service of appointees.** An appointee to an elective office shall serve until a successor is duly selected and qualified and until January 1 of the year following the next general election which is more than six months after such person's appointment.

Paragraph V. **Compensation and allowances of judges.** All judges shall receive compensation and allowances as provided by law; county supplements are hereby continued and may be granted or changed by the General Assembly. County governing authorities which had the authority on June 30, 1983, to make county supplements shall continue to have such authority under this Constitution. An incumbent's salary, allowance, or supplement shall not be decreased during the incumbent's term of office.

Paragraph VI. **Judicial Qualifications Commission; power; composition.** The power to discipline, remove, and cause involuntary retirement of judges shall be vested in the Judicial Qualifications Commission. It shall consist of seven members, as follows:

(1) Two judges of any court of record, selected by the Supreme Court;

(2) Three members of the State Bar of Georgia who shall have been active status members of the state bar for at least ten years and who shall be elected by the board of governors of the state bar; and

(3) Two citizens, neither of whom shall be a member of the state bar, who shall be appointed by the Governor.

Paragraph VII. **Discipline, removal, and involuntary retirement of judges.**

(a) Any judge may be removed, suspended, or otherwise disciplined for willful misconduct in office, or for willful and persistent failure to perform the duties of office, or for habitual intemperance, or for conviction of a crime involving moral turpitude, or for conduct prejudicial to the administration of justice which brings the judicial office into disrepute. Any judge may be retired for disability which constitutes a serious and likely permanent interference with the performance of the duties of office. The Supreme Court shall adopt rules of implementation.

(b) (1) Upon indictment for a felony by a grand jury of this state or by a grand jury of the United States of any judge, the Attorney General or district attorney shall transmit a certified copy of the indictment to the Judicial Qualifications Commission. The commission shall, subject to subparagraph (b)(2) of this Paragraph, review the indictment, and, if it determines that the indictment relates to and adversely affects the administration of the office of the indicted judge and that the rights and interests of the public are adversely affected thereby, the commission shall suspend the judge immediately and without further action pending the final disposition of the case or until the expiration of the judge's term of office, whichever occurs first. During the term of office to which such judge was elected and in which the indictment occurred, if a nolle prosequi is entered, if the public official is acquitted, or if after conviction the conviction is later overturned as a result of any direct appeal or application for a writ of certiorari, the judge shall be immediately reinstated to the office from which he was suspended. While a judge is suspended under this subparagraph and until final conviction, the judge shall continue to receive the compensation from his office. For the duration of any suspension under this subparagraph, the Governor shall appoint a replacement judge. Upon a final conviction with no appeal or review pending, the office shall be declared vacant and a successor to that office shall be chosen as provided in this Constitution or the laws enacted in pursuance thereof.

(2) The commission shall not review the indictment for a period of 14 days from the day the indictment is received. This period of time may be extended by the commission. During this period of time, the indicted judge may, in writing, authorize the commission to suspend him from office. Any such voluntary suspension shall be subject to the same conditions for review, reinstatement, or declaration of vacancy as are provided in this subparagraph for a nonvoluntary suspension.

(3) After any suspension is imposed under this subparagraph, the suspended judge may petition the commission for a review. If the commission determines that the judge should no longer be suspended, he shall immediately be reinstated to office.

(4) The findings and records of the commission and the fact that the public official has or has not been suspended shall not be admissible in evidence in any court for any purpose. The findings and records of the commission shall not be open to the public.

(5) The provisions of this subparagraph shall not apply to any indictment handed down prior to January 1, 1985.

(6) If a judge who is suspended from office under the provisions of this subparagraph is not first tried at the next regular or special term following the indictment, the suspension shall be terminated and the judge shall be reinstated to office. The judge shall not be reinstated under this provision if he is not so tried based on a continuance granted upon a motion made only by the defendant.

Paragraph VIII. **Due process; review by Supreme Court.** No action shall be taken against a judge except after hearing and in accordance with due process of law. No removal or involuntary retirement shall occur except upon order of the Supreme Court after review.

Section VIII.
District Attorneys

Paragraph I. **District attorneys; vacancies; qualifications; compensation; duties; immunity.**

(a) There shall be a district attorney for each judicial circuit, who shall be elected circuit-wide for a term of four years. The successors of present and subsequent incumbents shall be elected by the electors of their respective circuits at the general election held immediately preceding the expiration of their respective terms. District attorneys shall serve until their successors are duly elected and qualified. Vacancies shall be filled by appointment of the Governor.

(b) No person shall be a district attorney unless such person shall have been an active-status member of the State Bar of Georgia for three years immediately preceding such person's election.

(c) The district attorneys shall receive such compensation and allowances as provided by law and shall be entitled to receive such local supplements to their compensation and allowances as may be provided by law.

(d) It shall be the duty of the district attorney to represent the state in all criminal cases in the superior court of such district attorney's circuit and in all cases appealed from the superior court and the juvenile courts of that circuit to the Supreme Court and the Court of Appeals and to perform such other duties as shall be required by law.

(e) District attorneys shall enjoy immunity from private suit for actions arising from the performance of their duties.

Paragraph II. **Discipline, removal, and involuntary retirement of district attorneys.** Any district attorney may be disciplined, removed or involuntarily retired as provided by general law.

Section IX.
General Provisions

Paragraph I. **Administration of the judicial system; uniform court rules; advice and consent of councils.** The judicial system shall be administered as provided in this Paragraph. Not more than 24 months after the effective date hereof, and from time to time thereafter by amendment, the Supreme Court shall, with the advice and consent of the council of the affected class or classes of trial courts, by order adopt and publish uniform court rules and record-keeping rules which shall provide for the speedy, efficient, and inexpensive resolution of disputes and prosecutions. Each council shall be comprised of all of the judges of the courts of that class.

Paragraph II. **Disposition of cases.** The Supreme Court and the Court of Appeals shall dispose of every case at the term for which it is entered on the court's docket for hearing or at the next term.

Section X.
Transition

Paragraph I. **Effect of ratification.** On the effective date of this article:

(1) Superior courts shall continue as superior courts.

(2) State courts shall continue as state courts.

(3) Probate courts shall continue as probate courts.

(4) Juvenile courts shall continue as juvenile courts.

(5) Municipal courts not otherwise named herein, of whatever name, shall continue as and be denominated municipal courts, except that the City Court of Atlanta shall retain its name. Such municipal courts, county recorder's courts, and Civil Courts of Richmond and Bibb counties, and administrative agencies having quasi-judicial powers shall continue with the same jurisdiction as such courts and agencies have on the effective date of this article until otherwise provided by law.

(6) Justice of the peace courts, small claims courts, and magistrate courts operating on the effective date of this Constitution and the County Court of Echols County shall become and be classified as magistrate courts. The County Court of Baldwin County and the County Court of Putnam County shall become and be classified as state courts, with the same jurisdiction and powers as other state courts.

Paragraph II. **Continuation of judges.** Each judge holding office on the effective date of this article shall continue in office until the expiration of the term of office, as a judge of the court having the same or similar jurisdiction. Each court not named herein shall cease to exist on such date or at the expiration of the term of the incumbent judge, whichever is later; and its jurisdiction shall automatically pass to the new court of the same or similar jurisdiction, in the absence of which court it shall pass to the superior court.

ARTICLE VII.
TAXATION AND FINANCE
Section I.
Power of Taxation

Paragraph I. **Taxation; limitations on grants of tax powers.** The state may not suspend or irrevocably give, grant, limit, or restrain the right of taxation and all laws, grants, contracts, and other acts to effect any of these purposes are null and void. Except as otherwise provided in this Constitution, the right of taxation shall always be under the complete control of the state.

Paragraph II. **Taxing power limited.**

(a) The annual levy of state ad valorem taxes on tangible property for all purposes, except for defending the state in an emergency, shall not exceed one-fourth mill on each dollar of the assessed value of the property.

(b) So long as the method of taxation in effect on December 31, 1980, for the taxation of shares of stock of banking corporations and other monied capital coming into competition with such banking corporations continues in effect, such shares and other monied capital may be taxed at an annual rate not exceeding five mills on each dollar of the assessed value of the property.

Paragraph III. **Uniformity; classification of property; assessment of agricultural land; utilities.**

(a) All taxes shall be levied and collected under general laws and for public purposes only. Except as otherwise provided in subparagraph (c), all taxation shall be uniform upon the same class of subjects within the territorial limits of the authority levying the tax.

(b) (1) Except as otherwise provided in this subparagraph (b), classes of subjects for taxation of property shall consist of tangible property and one or more classes of intangible personal property including money.

(2) Subject to the conditions and limitations specified by law, each of the following types of property may be classified as a separate class of property for ad valorem property tax purposes and different rates, methods, and assessment dates may be provided for such properties:

(A) Motor vehicles, including trailers.

(B) Mobile homes other than those mobile homes which qualify the owner of the home for a homestead exemption from ad valorem taxation.

(c) Tangible real property, but no more than 2,000 acres of any single property owner, which is devoted to bona fide agricultural purposes shall be assessed for ad valorem taxation purposes at 75 percent of the value which other tangible real property is assessed. No property shall be entitled to receive the preferential assessment provided for in this subparagraph if the property which would otherwise receive such assessment would result in any person who has a beneficial interest in such property, including any interest in the nature of stock ownership, receiving the benefit of such preferential assessment as to more than 2,000 acres. No property shall be entitled to receive the preferential assessment provided for in this subparagraph unless the conditions set out below are met:

(1) The property must be owned by:

(A) (i) One or more natural or naturalized citizens;

(ii) An estate of which the devisee or heirs are one or more natural or naturalized citizens; or

(iii) A trust of which the beneficiaries are one or more natural or naturalized citizens; or

(B) A family-owned farm corporation, the controlling interest of which is owned by individuals related to each other within the fourth degree of civil reckoning, or which is owned by an estate of which the devisee or heirs are one or more natural or naturalized citizens, or which is owned by a trust of which the beneficiaries are one or more natural or naturalized citizens, and such corporation derived 80 percent or more of its gross income from bona fide agricultural pursuits within this state within the year immediately preceding the year in which eligibility is sought.

(2) The General Assembly shall provide by law:

(A) For a definition of the term "bona fide agricultural purposes," but such term shall include timber production;

(B) For additional minimum conditions of eligibility which such properties must meet in order to qualify for the preferential assessment provided for herein, including, but not limited to, the requirement that the owner be required to enter into a covenant with the appropriate taxing authorities to maintain the use of the properties in bona fide agricultural purposes for a period of not less than ten years and for appropriate penalties for the breach of any such covenant.

(3) In addition to the specific conditions set forth in this subparagraph (c), the General Assembly may place further restrictions upon, but may not relax, the conditions of eligibility for the preferential assessment provided for herein.

(d) The General Assembly may provide for a different method and time of returns, assessments, payment, and collection of ad valorem taxes of public utilities, but not on a greater assessed percentage of value or at a higher rate of taxation than other properties, except that property provided for in subparagraph (c).

Section II.
Exemptions from Ad Valorem Taxation

Paragraph I. **Unauthorized tax exemptions void.** Except as authorized in or pursuant to this Constitution, all laws exempting property from ad valorem taxation are void.

Paragraph II. **Exemptions from taxation of property.**

(a) (1) Except as otherwise provided in this Constitution, no property shall be exempted from ad valorem taxation unless the exemption is approved by two-thirds of the members elected to each branch of the General Assembly in a roll-call vote and by a majority of the qualified electors of the state voting in a referendum thereon.

(2) Homestead exemptions from ad valorem taxation levied by local taxing jurisdictions may be granted by local law conditioned upon approval by a majority of the qualified electors residing within the limits of the local taxing jurisdiction voting in a referendum thereon.

(3) Laws subject to the requirement of a referendum as provided in this subparagraph (a) may originate in either the Senate or the House of Representatives.

(4) The requirements of this subparagraph (a) shall not apply with respect to a law which codifies or recodifies an exemption previously authorized in the Constitution of 1976 or an exemption authorized pursuant to this Constitution.

(b) The grant of any exemption from ad valorem taxation shall be subject to the conditions, limitations, and administrative procedures specified by law.

Paragraph III. **Exemptions which may be authorized locally.**

(a) (1) The governing authority of any county or municipality, subject to the approval of a majority of the qualified electors of such political subdivision voting in a referendum thereon, may exempt from ad valorem taxation, including all such taxation levied for educational purposes and for state purposes, inventories of goods in the process of manufacture or production, and inventories of finished goods.

(2) Exemptions granted pursuant to this subparagraph (a) may only be revoked by a referendum election called and conducted as provided by law. The call for such referendum shall not be issued within five years from the date such exemptions were first granted and, if the results of the election are in favor of the revocation of such exemptions, then such revocation shall be effective only at the end of a five-year period from the date of such referendum.

(3) The implementation, administration, and revocation of the exemptions authorized in this subparagraph (a) shall be provided for by law. Until otherwise provided by law, the grant of the exemption shall be subject to the same conditions, limitations, definitions, and procedures provided for the grant of such exemption in the Constitution of 1976 on June 30, 1983.

(b) That portion of Article VII, Section I, Paragraph IV of the Constitution of 1976 which authorized local exemptions for certain property used in solar energy heating or cooling systems and in the manufacture of such systems is adopted by this reference as a part of this Constitution as completely as though incorporated in this Paragraph verbatim. This subparagraph (b) is repealed effective July 1, 1986.

Paragraph IV. **Current property tax exemptions preserved.** Those types of exemptions from ad valorem taxation provided for by law on June 30, 1983, are hereby continued in effect as statutory law until otherwise provided for by law. Any law which reduces or repeals any homestead exemption in existence on June 30, 1983, or created thereafter must be approved by two-thirds of the members elected to each branch of the General Assembly in a roll-call vote and by a majority of the qualified electors of the state or the affected local taxing jurisdiction voting in a referendum thereon. Any law which reduces or repeals exemptions granted to religious or burial grounds or institutions of purely public charity must be approved by two-thirds of the members elected to each branch of the General Assembly.

Paragraph V. **Disabled veteran's homestead exemption.** Except as otherwise provided in this paragraph, the amount of the homestead exemption granted to disabled veterans shall be the greater of $32,500.00 or the maximum amount which may be granted to a disabled veteran under Section 802 of Title 38 of the United States Code as hereafter amended. Such exemption shall be granted to: those persons eligible for such exemption on June 30, 1983; to disabled American veterans of any war or armed conflict who are disabled due to loss or loss of use of one lower extremity together with the loss or loss of use of one upper extremity which so affects the functions of balance or propulsion as to preclude locomotion without the aid of braces, crutches, canes, or a wheelchair; and to disabled veterans hereafter becoming eligible for assistance in acquiring housing under Section 801 of the United States Code as hereafter amended. The General Assembly may by general law provide for a different amount or a different method of determining the amount of or eligibility for the homestead exemption granted to disabled veterans. Any such law shall be enacted by a simple majority of the votes of all the members to which each house is entitled and may become effective without referendum. Such law may provide that the amount of or eligibility for the exemption shall be determined by reference to laws enacted by the United States Congress.

Section III.
Purposes and Method of State Taxation

Paragraph I. **Taxation; purposes for which powers may be exercised.**

(a) Except as otherwise provided in this Constitution, the power of taxation over the whole state may be exercised for any purpose authorized by law. Any purpose for which the powers of taxation over the whole state could have been exercised on June 30, 1983, shall continue to be a purpose for which such powers may be exercised.

(b) Subject to conditions and limitations as may be provided by law, the power of taxation may be exercised to make grants for tax relief purposes to persons for sales tax paid and not otherwise reimbursed on prescription drugs. Credits or relief provided hereunder may be limited only to such reasonable classifications of taxpayers as may be specified by law.

Paragraph II. **Revenue to be paid into general fund.**

(a) Except as otherwise provided in this Constitution, all revenue collected from taxes, fees, and assessments for state purposes, as authorized by revenue measures enacted by the General Assembly, shall be paid into the general fund of the state treasury.

(b) (1) As authorized by law providing for the promotion of any one or more types of agricultural products, fees, assessments, and other charges collected on the sale or processing of agricultural products need not be paid into the general fund of the state treasury. The uniformity requirement of this article shall be satisfied by the application of the agricultural promotion program upon the affected products.

(2) As used in this subparagraph, "agricultural products" includes, but is not limited to, registered livestock and livestock products, poultry and poultry products, timber and timber products, fish and seafood, and the products of the farms and forests of this state.

Paragraph III. **Grants to counties and municipalities.** State funds may be granted to counties and municipalities within the state. The grants authorized by this Paragraph shall be made in such manner and form and subject to the procedures and conditions specified by law. The law providing for any such grant may limit the purposes for which the grant funds may be expended.

Section IV.
State Debt

Paragraph I. **Purposes for which debt may be incurred.** The state may incur:

(a) Public debt without limit to repel invasion, suppress insurrection, and defend the state in time of war.

(b) Public debt to supply a temporary deficit in the state treasury in any fiscal year created by a delay in collecting the taxes of that year. Such debt shall not exceed, in the aggregate, 5 percent of the total revenue receipts, less refunds, of the state treasury in the fiscal year immediately preceding the year in which such debt is incurred. The debt incurred shall be repaid on or before the last day of the fiscal year in which it is incurred out of taxes levied for that fiscal year. No such debt may be incurred in any fiscal year under the provisions of this subparagraph (b) if there is then outstanding unpaid debt from any previous fiscal year which was incurred to supply a temporary deficit in the state treasury.

(c) General obligation debt to acquire, construct, develop, extend, enlarge, or improve land, waters, property, highways, buildings, structures, equipment, or facilities of the state, its agencies, departments, institutions, and of those state authorities which were created and activated prior to November 8, 1960.

(d) General obligation debt to provide educational facilities for county and independent school systems and to provide public library facilities for county and independent school systems, counties, municipalities, and boards of trustees of public libraries or boards of trustees of public library systems, and, when the construction of such educational or library facilities has been completed, the title to such facilities shall be vested in the respective local boards of education, counties, municipalities, or public library boards of trustees for which such facilities were constructed.

(e) Guaranteed revenue debt by guaranteeing the payment of revenue obligations issued by an instrumentality of the state if such revenue obligations are issued to finance:

(1) Toll bridges or toll roads.

(2) Land public transportation facilities or systems.

(3) Water facilities or systems.

(4) Sewage facilities or systems.

(5) Loans to, and loan programs for, citizens of the state for educational purposes.

Paragraph II. **State general obligation debt and guaranteed revenue debt; limitations.**

(a) As used in this Paragraph and Paragraph III of this section, "annual debt service requirements" means the total principal and interest coming due in any state fiscal year. With regard to any issue of debt incurred wholly or in part on a term basis, "annual debt service requirements" means an amount equal to the total principal and interest payments required to retire such issue in full divided by the number of years from its issue date to its maturity date.

(b) No debt may be incurred under subparagraphs (c), (d), and (e) of Paragraph I of this section or Paragraph V of this section at any time when the highest aggregate annual debt service requirements for the then current year or any subsequent year for outstanding general obligation debt and guaranteed revenue debt, including the proposed debt, and the highest aggregate annual payments for the then current year or any subsequent fiscal year of the state under all contracts then in force to which the provisions of the second paragraph of Article IX, Section VI, Paragraph I(a) of the Constitution of 1976 are applicable, exceed 10 percent of the total revenue receipts, less refunds of the state treasury in the fiscal year immediately preceding the year in which any such debt is to be incurred.

(c) No debt may be incurred under subparagraphs (c) and (d) of Paragraph I of this section at any time when the term of the debt is in excess of 25 years.

(d) No guaranteed revenue debt may be incurred to finance water or sewage treatment facilities or systems when the highest aggregate annual debt service requirements for the then current year or any subsequent fiscal year of the state for outstanding or proposed guaranteed revenue debt for water facilities or systems or sewage facilities or systems exceed 1 percent of the total revenue receipts less refunds, of the state treasury in the fiscal year immediately preceding the year in which any such debt is to be incurred.

(e) The aggregate amount of guaranteed revenue debt incurred to make loans for educational purposes that may be outstanding at any time shall not exceed $18 million, and the aggregate amount of guaranteed revenue debt incurred to purchase, or to lend or deposit against the security of, loans for educational purposes that may be outstanding at any time shall not exceed $72 million.

Paragraph III. **State general obligation debt and guaranteed revenue debt; conditions upon issuance; sinking funds and reserve funds.**

(a) (1) General obligation debt may not be incurred until legislation is enacted stating the purposes, in general or specific terms, for which such issue of debt is to be incurred, specifying the maximum principal amount of such issue and appropriating an amount at least sufficient to pay the highest annual debt service requirements for such issue. All such appropriations for debt service purposes shall not lapse for any reason and shall continue in effect until the debt for which such appropriation was authorized shall have been incurred, but the General Assembly may repeal any such appropriation at any time prior to the incurring of such debt. The General Assembly shall raise by taxation and appropriate each fiscal year, in addition to the sum necessary to make all payments required under contracts entitled to the protection of the second paragraph of Paragraph I(a), Section VI, Article IX of the Constitution of 1976, such amounts as are necessary to pay debt service requirements in such fiscal year on all general obligation debt.

(2) (A) The General Assembly shall appropriate to a special trust fund to be designated "State of Georgia General Obligation Debt Sinking Fund" such amounts as are necessary to pay annual debt service requirements on all general obligation debt. The sinking fund shall be used solely for the retirement of general obligation debt payable from the fund. If for any reason the monies in the sinking fund are insufficient to make, when due, all payments required with respect to such general obligation debt, the first revenues thereafter received in the general fund of the state shall be set aside by the appropriate state fiscal officer to the extent necessary to cure the deficiency and shall be deposited by the fiscal officer into the sinking fund. The appropriate state fiscal officer may be required to set aside and apply such revenues at the suit of any holder of any general obligation debt incurred under this section.

(B) The obligation to make sinking fund deposits as provided in subparagraph (2)(A) shall be subordinate to the obligation imposed upon the fiscal officers of the state pursuant to the provisions of the second paragraph of Paragraph I(a) of Section VI of Article IX of the Constitution of 1976.

(b) (1) Guaranteed revenue debt may not be incurred until legislation has been enacted authorizing the guarantee of the specific issue of revenue obligations then proposed, reciting that the General Assembly has determined such obligations will be self-liquidating over the life of the issue (which determination shall be conclusive), specifying the maximum principal amount of such issue and appropriating an amount at least equal to the highest annual debt service requirements for such issue.

(2) (A) Each appropriation made for the purposes of subparagraph (b)(1) shall be paid upon the issuance of said obligations into a special trust fund to be designated "State of Georgia Guaranteed Revenue Debt Common Reserve Fund" to be held together with all other sums similarly appropriated as a common reserve for any payments which may be required by virtue of any guarantee entered into in connection with any issue of guaranteed revenue obligations. No appropriations for the benefit of guaranteed revenue debt shall lapse unless repealed prior to the payment of the appropriation into the common reserve fund.

(B) If any payments are required to be made from the common reserve fund to meet debt service requirements on guaranteed revenue obligations by virtue of an insufficiency of revenues, the amount necessary to cure the deficiency shall be paid from the common reserve fund by the appropriate state fiscal officer. Upon any such payment, the common reserve fund shall be reimbursed from the general funds of the state within ten days following the commencement of any fiscal year of the state for any amounts so paid; provided, however, the obligation to make any such reimbursements shall be subordinate to the obligation imposed upon the fiscal officers of the state pursuant to the second paragraph of Paragraph I(a) of Section VI, Article IX of the Constitution of 1976 and shall also be subordinate to the obligation to make sinking fund deposits for the benefit of general obligation debt. The appropriate state fiscal officer may be required to apply such funds as provided in this subparagraph (b)(2)(B) at the suit of any holder of any such guaranteed revenue obligations.

(C) The amount to the credit of the common reserve fund shall at all times be at least equal to the aggregate highest annual debt service requirements on all outstanding guaranteed revenue obligations entitled to the benefit of the fund. If at the end of any fiscal year of the state the fund is in excess of the required amount, the appropriate state fiscal officer, as designated by law, shall transfer the excess amount to the general funds of the state free of said trust.

(c) The funds in the general obligation debt sinking fund and the guaranteed revenue debt common reserve fund shall be as fully invested as is practicable, consistent with the requirements to make current principal and interest payments. Any such investments shall be restricted to obligations constituting direct and general obligations of the United States government or obligations unconditionally guaranteed as to the payment of principal and interest by the United States government, maturing no longer than 12 months from date of purchase.

Paragraph IV. **Certain contracts prohibited.** The state, and all state institutions, departments and agencies of the state are prohibited from entering into any contract, except contracts pertaining to guaranteed revenue debt, with any public agency, public corporation, authority, or similar entity if such contract is intended to constitute security for bonds or other obligations issued by any such public agency, public corporation, or authority and, in the event any contract between the state, or any state institution, department or agency of the state and any public agency, public corporation, authority or similar entity, or any revenues from any such contract, is pledged or assigned as security for the repayment of bonds or other obligations, then and in either such event, the appropriation or expenditure of any funds of the state for the payment of obligations under any such contract shall likewise be prohibited.

Paragraph V. **Refunding of debt.** The state may incur general obligation debt or guaranteed revenue debt to fund or refund any such debt or to fund or refund any obligations issued upon the security of contracts to which the provisions of the second paragraph of Paragraph

I(a), Section VI, Article IX of the Constitution of 1976 are applicable. The issuance of any such debt for the purposes of said funding or refunding shall be subject to the 10 percent limitation in Paragraph II(b) of this section to the same extent as debt incurred under Paragraph I of this section; provided, however, in making such computation the annual debt service requirements and annual contract payments remaining on the debt or obligations being funded or refunded shall not be taken into account. The issuance of such debt may be accomplished by resolution of the Georgia State Financing and Investment Commission without any action on the part of the General Assembly and any appropriation made or required to be made with respect to the debt or obligation being funded or refunded shall immediately attach and inure to the benefit of the obligations to be issued in connection with such funding or refunding. Debt incurred in connection with any such funding or refunding shall be the same as that originally authorized by the General Assembly, except that general obligation debt may be incurred to fund or refund obligations issued upon the security of contracts to which the provisions of the second paragraph of Paragraph I(a), Section VI, Article IX of the Constitution of 1976 are applicable and the continuing appropriations required to be made under this Constitution shall immediately attach and inure to the benefit of the obligation to be issued in connection with such funding or refunding with the same force and effect as though said obligations so funded or refunded had originally been issued as a general obligation debt authorized hereunder. The term of a funding or refunding issue pursuant to this Paragraph shall not extend beyond the term of the original debt or obligation and the total interest on the funding or refunding issue shall not exceed the total interest to be paid on such original debt or obligation. The principal amount of any debt issued in connection with such funding or refunding may exceed the principal amount being funded or refunded to the extent necessary to provide for the payment of any premium thereby incurred.

Paragraph VI. **Faith and credit of state pledged debt may be validated.** The full faith, credit, and taxing power of the state are hereby pledged to the payment of all public debt incurred under this article and all such debt and the interest on the debt shall be exempt from taxation. Such debt may be validated by judicial proceedings in the manner provided by law. Such validation shall be incontestable and conclusive.

Paragraph VII. **Georgia State Financing and Investment Commission; duties.** There shall be a Georgia State Financing and Investment Commission. The commission shall consist of the Governor, the President of the Senate, the Speaker of the House of Representatives, the State Auditor, the Attorney General, the director, Fiscal Division, Department of Administrative Services, or such other officer as may be designated by law, and the Commissioner of Agriculture. The commission shall be responsible for the issuance of all public debt and for the proper application, as provided by law, of the proceeds of such debt to the purposes for which it is incurred; provided, however, the proceeds from guaranteed revenue obligations shall be paid to the issuer thereof and such proceeds and the application thereof shall be the responsibility of such issuer. Debt to be incurred at the same time for more than one purpose may be combined in one issue without stating the purpose separately but the proceeds thereof must be allocated, disbursed and used solely in accordance with the original purpose and without exceeding the principal amount authorized for each purpose set forth in the authorization of the General Assembly and to the extent not so used shall be used to purchase and retire public debt. The commission shall be responsible for the investment of all proceeds to be administered by it and, as provided by law, the income earned on any such investments may be used to pay operating expenses of the commission or placed in a common debt retirement fund and used to purchase and retire any public debt, or any bonds or obligations issued by any public agency, public corporation or authority which are secured by a contract to which the provisions of the second paragraph of Paragraph I(a) of Section VI, Article IX of the Constitution of 1976 are applicable. The commission shall have such additional responsibilities, powers, and duties as are provided by law.

Paragraph VIII. **State aid forbidden.** Except as provided in this Constitution, the credit of the state shall not be pledged or loaned to any individual, company, corporation, or association. The state shall not become a joint owner or stockholder in or with any individual, company, association, or corporation.

Paragraph IX. **Construction.** Paragraphs I through VIII of this section are for the purpose of providing an effective method of financing the state's needs and their provisions and any law now or hereafter enacted by the General Assembly in furtherance of their provisions shall be liberally construed to effect such purpose. Insofar as any such provisions or any such law may be inconsistent with any other provisions of this Constitution or of any other law, the provisions of such Paragraphs and laws enacted in furtherance of such Paragraphs shall be controlling; provided, however, the provisions of such Paragraphs shall not be so broadly construed as to cause the same to be unconstitutional and in connection with any such construction such Paragraphs shall be deemed to contain such implied limitations as shall be required to accomplish the foregoing.

Paragraph X. **Assumption of debts forbidden; exceptions.** The state shall not assume the debt, or any part thereof, of any county, municipality, or other political subdivision of the state, unless such debt be contracted to enable the state to repel invasion, suppress civil disorders or insurrection, or defend itself in time of war.

Paragraph XI. **Section not to unlawfully impair contracts or revive obligations previously voided.** The provisions of this section shall not be construed so as to:

(a) Unlawfully impair the obligation of any contract in effect on June 30, 1983.

(b) Revive or permit the revival of the obligation of any bond or security declared to be void by the Constitution of 1976 or any previous Constitution of this state.

ARTICLE VIII.
EDUCATION
Section I.
Public Education

Paragraph I. **Public education; free public education prior to college or postsecondary level; support by taxation.** The provision of an adequate public education for the citizens shall be a primary obligation of the State of Georgia. Public education for the citizens prior to the college or postsecondary level shall be free and shall be provided for by taxation. The expense of other public education shall be provided for in such manner and in such amount as may be provided by law.

Section II.
State Board of Education

Paragraph I. **State Board of Education.**

(a) There shall be a State Board of Education which shall consist of one member from each congressional district in the state appointed by the Governor and confirmed by the Senate. The Governor shall not be a member of said board. The ten members in office on June 30, 1983, shall serve out the remainder of their respective terms. As each term of office expires, the Governor shall appoint a successor as herein provided. The terms of office of all members appointed after the effective date of this Constitution shall be for seven years. Members shall serve until their successors are appointed and qualified. In the event of a vacancy on the board by death, resignation, removal, or any reason other than expiration of a member's term, the Governor shall fill such vacancy; and the person so appointed shall serve until confirmed by the Senate and, upon confirmation, shall serve for the unexpired term of office.

(b) The State Board of Education shall have such powers and duties as provided by law.

(c) The State Board of Education may accept bequests, donations, grants, and transfers of land, buildings, and other property for the use of the state educational system.

(d) The qualifications, compensation, and removal from office of the members of the board of education shall be as provided by law.

Section III.
State School Superintendent

Paragraph I. **State School Superintendent.** There shall be a State School Superintendent, who shall be the executive officer of the State Board of Education, elected at the same time and in the same manner and for the same term as that of the Governor. The State School Superintendent shall have such qualifications and shall be paid such compensation as may be fixed by law. No member of the State Board of Education shall be eligible for election as State School Superintendent during the time for which such member shall have been appointed.

Section IV.
Board of Regents

Paragraph I. **University System of Georgia; board of regents.**

(a) There shall be a Board of Regents of the University System of Georgia which shall consist of one member from each congressional district in the state and five additional members from the state at large, appointed by the Governor and confirmed by the Senate. The Governor shall not be a member of said board. The members in office on June 30, 1983, shall serve out the remainder of their respective terms. As each term of office expires, the Governor shall appoint a successor as herein provided. All such terms of members shall be for seven years. Members shall serve until their successors are appointed and qualified. In the event of a vacancy on the board by death, resignation, removal, or any reason other than the expiration of a member's term, the Governor shall fill such vacancy; and the person so appointed shall serve until confirmed by the Senate and, upon confirmation, shall serve for the unexpired term of office.

(b) The board of regents shall have the exclusive authority to create new public colleges, junior colleges, and universities in the State of Georgia, subject to approval by majority vote in the House of Representatives and the Senate. Such vote shall not be required to change the status of a college, institution or university existing on the effective date of this Constitution. The government, control, and management of the University System of Georgia and all of the institutions in said system shall be vested in the Board of Regents of the University System of Georgia.

(c) All appropriations made for the use of any or all institutions in the university system shall be paid to the board of regents in a lump sum, with the power and authority in said board to allocate and distribute the same among the institutions under its control in such way and manner and in such amounts as will further an efficient and economical administration of the university system.

(d) The board of regents may hold, purchase, lease, sell, convey, or otherwise dispose of public property, execute conveyances thereon, and utilize the proceeds arising therefrom; may exercise the power of eminent domain in the manner provided by law; and shall have such other powers and duties as provided by law.

(e) The board of regents may accept bequests, donations, grants, and transfers of land, buildings, and other property for the use of the University System of Georgia.

(f) The qualifications, compensation, and removal from office of the members of the board of regents shall be as provided by law.

Section V.
Local School Systems

Paragraph I. **School systems continued; consolidation of school systems authorized; new independent school systems prohibited.** Authority is granted to county and area boards of education to establish and maintain public schools within their limits. Existing county and independent school systems shall be continued, except that the General Assembly may provide by law for the consolidation of two or more county school systems, independent school systems, portions thereof, or any combination thereof into a single county or area school system under the control and management of a county or area board of education, under such terms and conditions as the General Assembly may prescribe; but no such consolidation shall become effective until approved by a majority of the qualified voters voting thereon in each separate school system proposed to be consolidated. No independent school system shall hereafter be established.

Paragraph II. **Boards of education.** Each school system shall be under the management and control of a board of education, the members of which shall be elected or appointed as provided by law. School board members shall reside within the territory embraced by the school system and shall have such compensation and additional qualifications as may be provided by law.

Paragraph III. **School superintendents.** There shall be a school superintendent of each system who shall be the executive officer of the board of education and shall have such qualifications, powers, and duties as provided by general law.

Paragraph IV. **Changes in school boards and superintendent.**

(a) The composition of school boards, the term of office, and the methods of selecting board members and school superintendents, including whether elections shall be partisan or nonpartisan, shall be as provided by law applicable thereto on June 30, 1983, but may be changed thereafter only by local law, conditioned upon approval by a majority of the qualified voters voting thereon in the system affected. It shall not be necessary for a local law which reapportions election districts from which members of a local board of education are elected to be conditioned on the approval of the voters as herein required.

(b) School systems which are authorized on June 30, 1983, to make the changes listed in subparagraph (a) of this Paragraph by local law without a referendum may continue to do so.

Paragraph V. **Power of boards to contract with each other.**

(a) Any two or more boards of education may contract with each other for the care, education, and transportation of pupils and for such other activities as they may be authorized by law to perform.

(b) The General Assembly may provide by law for the sharing of facilities or services by and between local boards of education under such joint administrative authority as may be authorized.

Paragraph VI. **Power of boards to accept bequests, donations, grants, and transfers.** The board of education of each school system may accept bequests, donations, grants, and transfers of land, buildings, and other property for the use of such system.

Paragraph VII. **Special schools.**

(a) The General Assembly may provide by law for the creation of special schools in such areas as may require them and may provide for the participation of local boards of education in the establishment of such schools under such terms and conditions as it may provide; but no bonded indebtedness may be incurred nor a school tax levied for the support of special schools without the approval of a majority of the qualified voters voting thereon in each of the systems affected. Any special schools shall be operated in conformity with regulations of the State Board of Education pursuant to provisions of law. The state is authorized to expend funds for the support and maintenance of special schools in such amount and manner as may be provided by law.

(b) Nothing contained herein shall be construed to affect the authority of local boards of education or of the state to support and maintain special schools created prior to June 30, 1983.

Section VI.
Local Taxation for Education

Paragraph I. **Local taxation for education.**

(a) The board of education of each school system shall annually certify to its fiscal authority or authorities a school tax not greater than 20 mills per dollar for the support and maintenance of education. Said fiscal authority or authorities shall annually levy said tax upon the assessed value of all taxable property within the territory served by said school system, provided that the levy made by an area board of education, which levy shall not be greater than 20 mills per dollar, shall be in such amount and within such limits as may be prescribed by local law applicable thereto.

(b) School tax funds shall be expended only for the support and maintenance of public schools, public vocational-technical schools, public education, and activities necessary or incidental thereto, including school lunch purposes.

(c) The 20 mill limitation provided for in subparagraph (a) of this Paragraph shall not apply to those school systems which are authorized on June 30, 1983, to levy a school tax in excess thereof.

(d) The method of certification and levy of the school tax provided for in subparagraph (a) of this Paragraph shall not apply to those systems that are authorized on June 30, 1983, to utilize a different method of certification and levy of such tax; but the General Assembly may by law require that such systems be brought into conformity with the method of certification and levy herein provided.

Paragraph II. **Increasing or removing tax rate.** The mill limitation in effect on June 30, 1983, for any school system may be increased or removed by action of the respective boards of education, but only after such action has been approved by a majority of the qualified voters voting thereon in the particular school system to be affected in the manner provided by law.

Paragraph III. **School tax collection reimbursement.** The General Assembly may by general law require local boards of education to reimburse the appropriate governing authority for the collection of school taxes, provided that any rate established may be reduced by local act.

Section VII.
Educational Assistance

Paragraph I. **Educational assistance programs authorized.**

(a) Pursuant to laws now or hereafter enacted by the General Assembly, public funds may be expended for any of the following purposes:

(1) To provide grants, scholarships, loans, or other assistance to students and to parents of students for educational purposes.

(2) To provide for a program of guaranteed loans to students and to parents of students for educational purposes and to pay interest, interest subsidies, and fees to lenders on such loans. The General Assembly is authorized to provide such tax exemptions to lenders as shall be deemed advisable in connection with such program.

(3) To match funds now or hereafter available for student assistance pursuant to any federal law.

(4) To provide grants, scholarships, loans, or other assistance to public employees for educational purposes.

(5) To provide for the purchase of loans made to students for educational purposes who have completed a program of study in a field in which critical shortages exist and for cancellation of repayment of such loans, interest, and charges thereon.

(b) Contributions made in support of any educational assistance program now or hereafter established under provisions of this section may be deductible for state income tax purposes as now or hereafter provided by law.

Paragraph II. **Guaranteed revenue debt.** Guaranteed revenue debt may be incurred to provide funds to make loans to students and to parents of students for educational purposes, to purchase loans made to students and to parents of students for educational purposes, or to lend or make deposits of such funds with lenders which shall be secured by loans made to students and to parents of students for educational purposes. Any such debt shall be incurred in accordance with the procedures and requirements of Article VII, Section IV of this Constitution.

Paragraph III. **Public authorities.** Public authorities or public corporations heretofore or hereafter created for such purposes shall be authorized to administer educational assistance programs and, in connection therewith, may exercise such powers as may now or hereafter be provided by law.

Paragraph IV. **Waiver of tuition.** The Board of Regents of the University System of Georgia shall be authorized to establish programs allowing attendance at units of the University System of Georgia without payment of tuition or other fees, but the General Assembly may provide by law for the establishment of any such program for the benefit of elderly citizens of the state.

ARTICLE IX.
COUNTIES AND MUNICIPAL CORPORATIONS
Section I.
Counties

Paragraph I. **Counties a body corporate and politic.** Each county shall be a body corporate and politic with such governing authority and with such powers and limitations as are provided in this Constitution and as provided by law. The governing authorities of the several counties shall remain as prescribed by law on June 30, 1983, until otherwise provided by law.

Paragraph II. **Number of counties limited; county boundaries and county sites; county consolidation.**

(a) There shall not be more than 159 counties in this state.

(b) The metes and bounds of the several counties and the county sites shall remain as prescribed by law on June 30, 1983, unless changed under the operation of a general law.

(c) The General Assembly may provide by law for the consolidation of two or more counties into one or the division of a county and the merger of portions thereof into other counties under such terms and conditions as it may prescribe; but no such consolidation, division, or merger shall become effective unless approved by a majority of the qualified voters voting thereon in each of the counties proposed to be consolidated, divided, or merged.

Paragraph III. **County officers; election; term; compensation.**

(a) The clerk of the superior court, judge of the probate court, sheriff, tax receiver, tax collector, and tax commissioner, where such office has replaced the tax receiver and tax collector, shall be elected by the qualified voters of their respective counties for terms of four years and shall have such qualifications, powers, and duties as provided by general law.

(b) County officers listed in subparagraph (a) of this Paragraph may be on a fee basis, salary basis, or fee basis supplemented by salary, in such manner as may be directed by law. Minimum compensation for said county officers may be established by the General Assembly by general law. Such minimum compensation may be supplemented by local law or, if such authority is delegated by local law, by action of the county governing authority.

(c) The General Assembly may consolidate the offices of tax receiver and tax collector into the office of tax commissioner.

Paragraph IV. **Civil service systems.** The General Assembly may by general law authorize the establishment by county governing authorities of civil service systems covering county employees or covering county employees and employees of the elected county officers.

Section II.
Home Rule for Counties and Municipalities

Paragraph I. **Home rule for counties.**

(a) The governing authority of each county shall have legislative power to adopt clearly reasonable ordinances, resolutions, or regulations relating to its property, affairs, and local government for which no provision has been made by general law and which is not inconsistent with this Constitution or any local law applicable thereto. Any such local law shall remain in force and effect until amended or repealed as provided in subparagraph (b). This, however, shall not restrict the authority of the General Assembly by general law to further define this power or to broaden, limit, or otherwise regulate the exercise thereof. The General Assembly shall not pass any local law to repeal, modify, or supersede any action taken by a county governing authority under this section except as authorized under subparagraph (c) hereof.

(b) Except as provided in subparagraph (c), a county may, as an incident of its home rule power, amend or repeal the local acts applicable to its governing authority by following either of the procedures hereinafter set forth:

(1) Such local acts may be amended or repealed by a resolution or ordinance duly adopted at two regular consecutive meetings of the county governing authority not less than seven nor more than 60 days apart. A notice containing a synopsis of the proposed amendment or repeal shall be published in the official county organ once a week for three weeks within a period of 60 days immediately preceding its final adoption. Such notice shall state that a copy of the proposed amendment or repeal is on file in the office of the clerk of the superior court of the county for the purpose of examination and inspection by the public. The clerk of the superior court shall furnish anyone, upon written request, a copy of the proposed amendment or repeal. No amendment or repeal hereunder shall be valid to change or repeal an amendment adopted pursuant to a referendum as provided in (2) of this subparagraph or to change or repeal a local act of the General Assembly ratified in a referendum by the electors of such county unless at least 12 months have elapsed after such referendum. No amendment hereunder shall be valid if inconsistent with any provision of this Constitution or if provision has been made therefor by general law.

(2) Amendments to or repeals of such local acts or ordinances, resolutions, or regulations adopted pursuant to subparagraph (a) hereof may be initiated by a petition filed with the judge of the probate court of the county containing, in cases of counties with a population of 5,000 or less, the signatures of at least 25 percent of the electors registered to vote in the last general election; in cases of counties with a population of more than 5,000 but not more than 50,000, at least 20 percent of the electors registered to vote in the last general election; and, in cases of a county with a population of more than 50,000, at least 10 percent of the electors registered to vote in the last general election, which petition shall specifically set forth the exact language of the proposed amendment or repeal. The judge of the probate court shall determine the validity of such petition within 60 days of its being filed with the judge of the probate court. In the event the judge of the probate court determines that such petition is valid, it shall be his duty to issue the call for an election for the purpose of submitting such amendment or repeal to the registered electors of the county for their approval or rejection. Such call shall be issued not less than ten nor more than 60 days after the date of the filing of the petition. He shall set the date of such election for a day not less than 60 nor more than 90 days after the date of such filing. The judge of the probate court shall cause a notice of the date of said election to be published in the official organ of the county once a week for three weeks immediately preceding such date. Said notice shall also contain a synopsis of the proposed amendment or repeal and shall state that a copy thereof is on file in the office of the judge of the probate court of the county for the purpose of examination and inspection by the public. The judge of the probate court shall furnish anyone, upon written request, a copy of the proposed amendment or repeal. If more than one-half of the votes cast on such question are for approval of the amendment or repeal, it shall become of full force and effect; otherwise, it shall be void and of no force and effect. The expense of such election shall be borne by the county, and it shall be the duty of the judge of the probate court to hold and conduct such election. Such election shall be held under

the same laws and rules and regulations as govern special elections, except as otherwise provided herein. It shall be the duty of the judge of the probate court to canvass the returns and declare and certify the result of the election. It shall be his further duty to certify the result thereof to the Secretary of State in accordance with the provisions of subparagraph (g) of this Paragraph. A referendum on any such amendment or repeal shall not be held more often than once each year. No amendment hereunder shall be valid if inconsistent with any provision of this Constitution or if provision has been made therefor by general law.

In the event that the judge of the probate court determines that such petition was not valid, he shall cause to be published in explicit detail the reasons why such petition is not valid; provided, however, that, in any proceeding in which the validity of the petition is at issue, the tribunal considering such issue shall not be limited by the reasons assigned. Such publication shall be in the official organ of the county in the week immediately following the date on which such petition is declared to be not valid.

(c) The power granted to counties in subparagraphs (a) and (b) above shall not be construed to extend to the following matters or any other matters which the General Assembly by general law has preempted or may hereafter preempt, but such matters shall be the subject of general law or the subject of local acts of the General Assembly to the extent that the enactment of such local acts if otherwise permitted under this Constitution:

(1) Action affecting any elective county office, the salaries thereof, or the personnel thereof, except the personnel subject to the jurisdiction of the county governing authority.

(2) Action affecting the composition, form, procedure for election or appointment, compensation, and expenses and allowances in the nature of compensation of the county governing authority.

(3) Action defining any criminal offense or providing for criminal punishment.

(4) Action adopting any form of taxation beyond that authorized by law or by this Constitution.

(5) Action extending the power of regulation over any business activity regulated by the Georgia Public Service Commission beyond that authorized by local or general law or by this Constitution.

(6) Action affecting the exercise of the power of eminent domain.

(7) Action affecting any court or the personnel thereof.

(8) Action affecting any public school system.

(d) The power granted in subparagraphs (a) and (b) of this Paragraph shall not include the power to take any action affecting the private or civil law governing private or civil relationships, except as is incident to the exercise of an independent governmental power.

(e) Nothing in subparagraphs (a), (b), (c), or (d) shall affect the provisions of subparagraph (f) of this Paragraph.

(f) The governing authority of each county is authorized to fix the salary, compensation, and expenses of those employed by such governing authority and to establish and maintain retirement or pension systems, insurance, workers' compensation, and hospitalization benefits for said employees.

(g) No amendment or revision of any local act made pursuant to subparagraph (b) of this section shall become effective until a copy of such amendment or revision, a copy of the required notice of publication, and an affidavit of a duly authorized representative of the newspaper in which such notice was published to the effect that said notice has been published as provided in said subparagraph has been filed with the Secretary of State. The Secretary of State shall provide for the publication and distribution of all such amendments and revisions at least annually.

Paragraph II. **Home rule for municipalities.** The General Assembly may provide by law for the self-government of municipalities and to that end is expressly given the authority to delegate its power so that matters pertaining to municipalities may be dealt with without the necessity of action by the General Assembly.

Paragraph III. **Supplementary powers.**

(a) In addition to and supplementary of all powers possessed by or conferred upon any county, municipality, or any combination thereof, any county, municipality, or any combination thereof may exercise the following powers and provide the following services:

(1) Police and fire protection.

(2) Garbage and solid waste collection and disposal.

(3) Public health facilities and services, including hospitals, ambulance and emergency rescue services, and animal control.

(4) Street and road construction and maintenance, including curbs, sidewalks, street lights, and devices to control the flow of traffic on streets and roads constructed by counties and municipalities or any combination thereof.

(5) Parks, recreational areas, programs, and facilities.

(6) Storm water and sewage collection and disposal systems.

(7) Development, storage, treatment, purification, and distribution of water.

(8) Public housing.

(9) Public transportation.

(10) Libraries, archives, and arts and sciences programs and facilities.

(11) Terminal and dock facilities and parking facilities.

(12) Codes, including building, housing, plumbing, and electrical codes.

(13) Air quality control.

(14) The power to maintain and modify heretofore existing retirement or pension systems, including such systems heretofore created by general laws of local application by population classification, and to continue in effect or modify other benefits heretofore provided as a part of or in addition to such retirement or pension systems and the power to create and maintain retirement or pension systems for any elected or appointed public officers and employees whose compensation is paid in whole or in part from county or municipal funds and for the beneficiaries of such officers and employees.

(b) Unless otherwise provided by law,

(1) No county may exercise any of the powers listed in subparagraph (a) of this Paragraph or provide any service listed therein inside the boundaries of any municipality or any other county except by contract with the municipality or county affected; and

(2) No municipality may exercise any of the powers listed in subparagraph (a) of this Paragraph or provide any service listed therein outside its own boundaries except by contract with the county or municipality affected.

(c) Nothing contained within this Paragraph shall operate to prohibit the General Assembly from enacting general laws relative to the subject matters listed in subparagraph (a) of this Paragraph or to prohibit the General Assembly by general law from regulating, restricting, or limiting the exercise of the powers listed therein; but it may not withdraw any such powers.

(d) Except as otherwise provided in subparagraph (b) of this Paragraph, the General Assembly shall act upon the subject matters listed in subparagraph (a) of this Paragraph only by general law.

Paragraph IV. **Planning and zoning.** The governing authority of each county and of each municipality may adopt plans and may exercise the power of zoning. This authorization shall not prohibit the General Assembly from enacting general laws establishing procedures for the exercise of such power.

Paragraph V. **Eminent domain.** The governing authority of each county and of each municipality may exercise the power of eminent domain for any public purpose.

Paragraph VI. **Special districts.** As hereinafter provided in this Paragraph, special districts may be created for the provision of local government services within such districts; and fees, assessments, and taxes may be levied and collected within such districts to pay, wholly or partially, the cost of providing such services therein and to construct and maintain facilities therefor. Such special districts may be created and fees, assessments, or taxes may be levied and collected therein by any one or more of the following methods:

(a) By general law which directly creates the districts.

(b) By general law which requires the creation of districts under conditions specified by such general law.

(c) By municipal or county ordinance or resolution, except that no such ordinance or resolution may supersede a law enacted by the General Assembly pursuant to subparagraphs (a) or (b) of this Paragraph.

Paragraph VII. **Community redevelopment.**

(a) The General Assembly may authorize any county, municipality, or housing authority to undertake and carry out community redevelopment, which may include the sale or other disposition of property acquired by eminent domain to private enterprise for private uses.

(b) In addition to the authority granted by subparagraph (a) of this Paragraph, the General Assembly is authorized to grant to counties or municipalities for redevelopment purposes and in connection with redevelopment programs, as such purposes and programs are defined by general law, the power to issue tax allocation bonds, as defined by such law, and the power to incur other obligations, without either such bonds or obligations constituting debt within the meaning of Section V of this article, and the power to enter into contracts for any period not exceeding 30 years with private persons, firms, corporations, and business entities. Notwithstanding the grant of these powers pursuant to general law, no county or municipality may exercise these powers unless so authorized by local law and unless such powers are exercised in conformity with those terms and conditions for such exercise as established by that local law. The provisions of any such local law shall conform to those requirements established by general law regarding such powers. No such local law, or any amendment thereto, shall become effective unless approved in a referendum by a majority of the qualified voters voting thereon in the county or municipality directly affected by that local law.

Paragraph VIII. **Limitation on the taxing power and contributions of counties, municipalities, and political subdivisions.** The General Assembly shall not authorize any county, municipality, or other political subdivision of this state, through taxation, contribution, or otherwise, to appropriate money for or to lend its credit to any person or to any nonpublic corporation or association except for purely charitable purposes.

Paragraph IX. **Immunity of counties, municipalities, and school districts.** The General Assembly may waive the immunity of counties, municipalities, and school districts by law.

Section III.
Intergovernmental Relations

Paragraph I. **Intergovernmental contracts.**

(a) The state, or any institution, department, or other agency thereof, and any county, municipality, school district, or other political subdivision of the state may contract for any period not exceeding 50 years with each other or with any other public agency, public corporation, or public authority for joint services, for the provision of services, or for the joint or separate use of facilities or equipment; but such contracts must deal with activities, services, or facilities which the contracting parties are authorized by law to undertake or provide.

(b) Subject to such limitations as may be provided by general law, any county, municipality, or political subdivision thereof may, in connection with any contracts authorized in this Paragraph, convey any existing facilities or equipment to the state or to any public agency, public corporation, or public authority.

(c) Any county, municipality, or any combination thereof, may contract with any public agency, public corporation, or public authority for the care, maintenance, and hospitalization of its indigent sick and may as a part of such contract agree to pay for the cost of acquisition, construction, modernization, or repairs of necessary land, buildings, and facilities by such public agency, public corporation, or public authority and provide for the payment of such services and the cost to such public agency, public corporation, or public authority of acquisition, construction, modernization, or repair of land, buildings, and facilities from revenues realized by such county, municipality, or any combination thereof from any taxes authorized by this Constitution or revenues derived from any other source.

Paragraph II. **Local government reorganization.**

(a) The General Assembly may provide by law for any matters necessary or convenient to authorize the consolidation of the governmental and corporate powers and functions vested in municipalities with the governmental and corporate powers and functions vested in a county or counties in which such municipalities are located; provided, however, that no such consolidation shall become effective unless separately approved by a majority of the qualified voters of the county or each of the counties and of the municipality or each of the municipalities located within such county or counties containing at least 10 percent of the population of the county in which located voting thereon in such manner as may be prescribed in such law. Such law may provide procedures and requirements for the establishment of charter commissions to draft proposed charters for the consolidated government, and the General Assembly is expressly authorized to delegate its powers to such charter commissions for such purposes so that the governmental consolidation proposed by a charter commission may become effective without the necessity of further action by the General Assembly; or such law may require that the recommendation of any such charter commission be implemented by a subsequent local law.

(b) The General Assembly may provide by general law for alternatives other than governmental consolidation as authorized in subparagraph (a) above for the reorganization of county and municipal governments, including, but not limited to, procedures to establish a single governing body as the governing authority of a county and a municipality or municipalities located within such county or for the redistribution of powers between a county and a municipality or municipalities located within the county. Such law may require the form of governmental reorganization authorized by such law to be approved by the qualified voters directly affected thereby voting in such manner as may be required in such law.

(c) Nothing in this Paragraph shall be construed to limit the authority of the General Assembly to repeal municipal charters without a referendum.

Section IV.
Taxation Power of County and Municipal Governments

Paragraph I. **Power of taxation.**

(a) Except as otherwise provided in this Paragraph, the governing authority of any county, municipality, or combination thereof may exercise the power of taxation as authorized by this Constitution or by general law.

(b) In the absence of a general law:

(1) County governing authorities may be authorized by local law to levy and collect business and occupational license taxes and license fees only in the unincorporated areas of the counties. The General Assembly may provide that the revenues raised by such tax or fee be spent for the provision of services only in the unincorporated areas of the county.

(2) Municipal governing authorities may be authorized by local law to levy and collect taxes and fees in the corporate limits of the municipalities.

(c) The General Assembly may provide by law for the taxation of insurance companies on the basis of gross direct premiums received from insurance policies within the unincorporated areas of counties. The tax authorized herein may be imposed by the state or by counties or by the state for county purposes as may be provided by law. The General Assembly may further provide by law for the reduction, only upon taxable property within the unincorporated areas of counties, of the ad valorem tax millage rate for county or county school district purposes or for the reduction of such ad valorem tax millage rate for both such purposes in connection with imposing or authorizing the imposition of the tax authorized herein or in connection with providing for the distribution of the proceeds derived from the tax authorized herein.

Paragraph II. **Power of expenditure.** The governing authority of any county, municipality, or combination thereof may expend public funds to perform any public service or public function as authorized by this Constitution or by law or to perform any other service or function as authorized by this Constitution or by general law.

Paragraph III. **Purposes of taxation; allocation of taxes.** No levy need state the particular purposes for which the same was made nor shall any taxes collected be allocated for any particular purpose, unless otherwise provided by this Constitution or by law.

Section V.
Limitation on Local Debt

Paragraph I. **Debt limitations of counties, municipalities, and other political subdivisions.**

(a) The debt incurred by any county, municipality, or other political subdivision of this state, including debt incurred on behalf of any special district, shall never exceed 10 percent of the assessed value of all taxable property within such county, municipality, or political subdivision; and no such county, municipality, or other political subdivision shall incur any new debt without the assent of a majority of the qualified voters of such county, municipality, or political subdivision voting in an election held for that purpose as provided by law.

(b) Notwithstanding subparagraph (a) of this Paragraph, all local school systems which are authorized by law on June 30, 1983, to incur debt in excess of 10 percent of the assessed value of all taxable property therein shall continue to be authorized to incur such debt.

Paragraph II. **Special district debt.** Any county, municipality, or political subdivision of this state may incur debt on behalf of any special district created pursuant to Paragraph VI of Section II of this article. Such debt may be incurred on behalf of such special district where the county, municipality, or other political subdivision shall have, at or before the time of incurring such debt, provided for the assessment and collection of an annual tax within the special district sufficient in amount to pay the principal of and interest on such debt within 30 years from the incurrence thereof; and no such county, municipality, or other political subdivision shall incur any debt on behalf of such special district without the assent of a majority of the qualified voters of such special district voting in an election held for that purpose as provided by law. No such county, municipality, or other political subdivision shall incur any debt on behalf of such special district in an amount which, when taken together with all other debt outstanding incurred by such county, municipality, or political subdivision and on behalf of any such special district, exceeds 10 percent of the assessed value of all taxable property within such county, municipality, or political subdivision. The proceeds of the tax collected as provided herein shall be placed in a sinking fund to be held on behalf of such special district and used exclusively to pay off the principal of and interest on such debt thereafter maturing. Such moneys shall be held and kept separate and apart from all other revenues collected and may be invested and reinvested as provided by law.

Paragraph III. **Refunding of outstanding indebtedness.** The governing authority of any county, municipality, or other political subdivision of this state may provide for the refunding of outstanding bonded indebtedness without the necessity of a referendum being held therefor, provided that neither the term of the original debt is extended nor the interest rate of the original debt is increased. The principal amount of any debt issued in connection with such refunding may exceed the principal amount being refunded in order to reduce the total principal and interest payment requirements over the remaining term of the original issue. The proceeds of the refunding issue shall be used solely to retire the original debt. The original debt refunded shall not constitute debt within the meaning of Paragraph I of this section; but the refunding issue shall constitute a debt such as will count against the limitation on debt measured by 10 percent of assessed value of taxable property as expressed in Paragraph I of this section.

Paragraph IV. **Exceptions to debt limitations.** Notwithstanding the debt limitations provided in Paragraph I of this section and without the necessity for a referendum being held therefor, the governing authority of any county, municipality, or other political subdivision of this state may, subject to the conditions and limitations as may be provided by general law:

    (1) Accept and use funds granted by and obtain loans from the federal government or any agency thereof pursuant to conditions imposed by federal law.

    (2) Incur debt, by way of borrowing from any person, corporation, or association as well as from the state, to pay in whole or in part the cost of property valuation and equalization programs for ad valorem tax purposes.

Paragraph V. **Temporary loans authorized.** The governing authority of any county, municipality, or other political subdivision of this state may incur debt by obtaining temporary loans in each year to pay expenses. The aggregate amount of all such loans shall not exceed 75 percent of the total gross income from taxes collected in the last preceding year. Such loans shall be payable on or before December 31 of the calendar year in which such loan is made. No such loan may be obtained when there is a loan then unpaid obtained in any prior year. No such county, municipality, or other political subdivision of this state shall incur in any one calendar year an aggregate of such temporary loans or other contracts, notes, warrants, or obligations for current expenses in excess of the total anticipated revenue for such calendar year.

Paragraph VI. **Levy of taxes to pay bonds; sinking fund required.** Any county, municipality, or other political subdivision of this state shall at or before the time of incurring bonded indebtedness provide for the assessment and collection of an annual tax sufficient in amount to pay the principal and interest of said debt within 30 years from the incurring of such bonded indebtedness. The proceeds of this tax, together with any other moneys collected for this purpose, shall be placed in a sinking fund to be used exclusively for paying the principal of and interest on such bonded debt. Such moneys shall be held and kept separate and apart from all other revenues collected and may be invested and reinvested as provided by law.

Paragraph VII. **Validity of prior bond issues.** Any and all bond issues validated and issued prior to June 30, 1983, shall continue to be valid.

Section VI.
Revenue Bonds

Paragraph I. **Revenue bonds; general limitations.** Any county, municipality, or other political subdivision of this state may issue revenue bonds as provided by general law. The obligation represented by revenue bonds shall be repayable only out of the revenue derived from the project and shall not be deemed to be a debt of the issuing political subdivision. No such issuing political subdivision shall exercise the power of taxation for the purpose of paying any part of the principal or interest of any such revenue bonds.

Paragraph II. **Revenue bonds; special limitations.** Where revenue bonds are issued by any county, municipality, or other political subdivision of this state in order to buy, construct, extend, operate, or maintain gas or electric generating or distribution systems and necessary appurtenances thereof and the gas or electric generating or distribution system extends beyond the limits of the county in which the municipality or other political subdivision is located, then its services rendered and property located outside said county shall be subject to taxation and regulation in the same manner as are privately owned and operated utilities.

Paragraph III. **Development authorities.** The development of trade, commerce, industry, and employment opportunities being a public purpose vital to the welfare of the people of this state, the General Assembly may create development authorities to promote and further such purposes or may authorize the creation of such an authority by any county or municipality or combination thereof under such uniform terms and conditions as it may deem necessary. The General Assembly may exempt from taxation development authority obligations, properties, activities, or income and may authorize the issuance of revenue bonds by such authorities which shall not constitute an indebtedness of the state within the meaning of Section V of this article.

Paragraph IV. **Validation.** The General Assembly shall provide for the validation of any revenue bonds authorized and shall provide that such validation shall thereafter be incontestable and conclusive.

Paragraph V. **Validity of prior revenue bond issues.** All revenue bonds issued and validated prior to June 30, 1983, shall continue to be valid.

Section VII.
Community Improvement Districts

Paragraph I. **Creation.** The General Assembly may by local law create one or more community improvement districts for any county or municipality or provide for the creation of one or more community improvement districts by any county or municipality.

Paragraph II. **Purposes.** The purpose of a community improvement district shall be the provision of any one or more of the following governmental services and facilities:

(1) Street and road construction and maintenance, including curbs, sidewalks, street lights, and devices to control the flow of traffic on streets and roads.

(2) Parks and recreational areas and facilities.

(3) Storm water and sewage collection and disposal systems.

(4) Development, storage, treatment, purification, and distribution of water.

(5) Public transportation.

(6) Terminal and dock facilities and parking facilities.

(7) Such other services and facilities as may be provided for by general law.

Paragraph III. **Administration.**

(a) Any law creating or providing for the creation of a community improvement district shall designate the governing authority of the municipality or county for which the community improvement district is created as the administrative body or otherwise shall provide for the establishment and membership of an administrative body for the community improvement district. Any such law creating or providing for the creation of an administrative body for the community improvement district other than the municipal or county governing authority shall provide for representation of the governing authority of each county and municipality within which the community improvement district is wholly or partially located on the administrative body of the community improvement district.

(b) Any law creating or providing for the creation of a community improvement district shall provide that the creation of the community improvement district shall be conditioned upon:

(1) The adoption of a resolution consenting to the creation of the community improvement district by:

(A) The governing authority of the county if the community improvement district is located wholly within the unincorporated area of a county;

(B) The governing authority of the municipality if the community improvement district is located wholly within the incorporated area of a municipality; or

(C) The governing authorities of the county and the municipality if the community improvement district is located partially within the unincorporated area of a county and partially within the incorporated area of a municipality; and

(2) Written consent to the creation of the community improvement district by:

(A) A majority of the owners of real property within the community improvement district which will be subject to taxes, fees, and assessments levied by the administrative body of the community improvement district; and

(B) The owners of real property within the community improvement district which constitutes at least 75 percent by value of all real property within the community improvement district which will be subject to taxes, fees, and assessments levied by the administrative body of the community improvement district; and for this purpose value shall be determined by the most recent approved county ad valorem tax digest.

(c) The administrative body of each community improvement district may be authorized to levy taxes, fees, and assessments within the community improvement district only on real property used nonresidentially, specifically excluding all property used for residential, agricultural, or forestry purposes and specifically excluding tangible personal property and intangible property. Any tax, fee, or assessment so levied shall not exceed 2½ percent of the assessed value of the real property or such lower limit as may be established by law. The law creating or providing for the creation of a community improvement district shall provide that taxes, fees, and assessments levied by the administrative body of the community improvement district shall be equitably apportioned among the properties subject to such taxes, fees, and assessments according to the need for governmental services and facilities created by the degree of density of development of each such property. The law creating or providing for the creation of a community improvement district shall provide that taxes, fees, and assessments levied by the administrative body of the community improvement district shall be equitably apportioned among the properties subject to such taxes, fees, and assessments according to the need for governmental services and facilities created by the degree of density of development of each such property. The law creating or providing for the creation of a community improvement district shall provide that the proceeds of taxes, fees, and assessments levied by the administrative body of the community improvement district shall be used only for the purpose of providing governmental services and facilities which are specially required by the degree of density of development within the community improvement district and not for the purpose of providing those governmental services and facilities provided to the county or municipality as a whole. Any tax, fee, or assessment so levied shall be collected by the county or municipality for which the community improvement district is created in the same manner as taxes, fees, and assessments levied by such county or municipality. The proceeds of taxes, fees, and assessments so levied, less such fee to cover the costs of collection as may be specified by law, shall be transmitted by the collecting county or municipality to the administrative body of the community improvement district and shall be expended by the administrative body of the community improvement district only for the purposes authorized by this Section.

Paragraph IV. **Debt.** The administrative body of a community improvement district may incur debt, as authorized by law, without regard to the requirements of Section V of this Article, which debt shall be backed by the full faith, credit, and taxing power of the community improvement district but shall not be an obligation of the State of Georgia or any other unit of government of the State of Georgia other than the community improvement district.

Paragraph V. **Cooperation with local governments.** The services and facilities provided pursuant to this Section shall be provided for in a cooperation agreement executed jointly by the administrative body and the governing authority of the county or municipality for which the community improvement district is created. The provisions of this section shall in no way limit the authority of any county or municipality to provide services or facilities within any community improvement district; and any county or municipality shall retain full and complete authority and control over any of its facilities located within a community improvement district. Said control shall include but not be limited to the modification of, access to, and degree and type of services provided through or by facilities of the municipality or county. Nothing contained in this Section shall be construed to limit or preempt the application of any governmental laws, ordinances, resolutions, or regulations to any community improvement district or the services or facilities provided therein.

Paragraph VI. **Regulation by general law.** The General Assembly by general law may regulate, restrict, and limit the creation of community improvement districts and the exercise of the powers of administrative bodies of community improvement districts.

ARTICLE X.
AMENDMENTS TO THE CONSTITUTION
Section I.
Constitution, How Amended

Paragraph I. **Proposals to amend the Constitution; new Constitution.** Amendments to this Constitution or a new Constitution may be proposed by the General Assembly or by a constitutional convention, as provided in this article. Only amendments which are of general and uniform applicability throughout the state shall be proposed, passed, or submitted to the people.

Paragraph II. **Proposals by the General Assembly; submission to the people.** A proposal by the General Assembly to amend this Constitution or to provide for a new Constitution shall originate as a resolution in either the Senate or the House of Representatives and, if approved by two-thirds of the members to which each house is entitled in a roll-call vote entered on their respective journals, shall be submitted to the electors of the entire state at the next general election which is held in the even-numbered years. A summary of such proposal shall be prepared by the Attorney General, the Legislative Counsel, and the Secretary of State and shall be published in the official organ of each county and, if deemed advisable by the "Constitutional Amendments Publication Board," in not more than 20 other newspapers in the state designated by such board which meet the qualifications for being selected as the official organ of a county. Said board shall be composed of the Governor, the Lieutenant Governor, and the Speaker of the House of Representatives. Such summary shall be published once each week for three consecutive weeks immediately preceding the day of the general election at which such proposal is to be submitted. The language to be used in submitting a proposed amendment or a new Constitution shall be in such words as the General Assembly may provide in the resolution or, in the absence thereof, in such language as the Governor may prescribe. A copy of the entire proposed amendment or of a new Constitution shall be filed in the office of the judge of the probate court of each county and shall be available for public inspection; and the summary of the proposal shall so indicate. The General Assembly is hereby authorized to provide by law for additional matters relative to the publication and distribution of proposed amendments and summaries not in conflict with the provisions of this Paragraph.

If such proposal is ratified by a majority of the electors qualified to vote for members of the General Assembly voting thereon in such general election, such proposal shall become a part of this Constitution or shall become a new Constitution, as the case may be. Any proposal so approved shall take effect as provided in Paragraph VI of this article. When more than one amendment is submitted at the same time, they shall be so submitted as to enable the electors to vote on each amendment separately, provided that one or more new articles or related changes in one or more articles may be submitted as a single amendment.

Paragraph III. **Repeal or amendment of proposal.** Any proposal by the General Assembly to amend this Constitution or for a new Constitution may be amended or repealed by the same General Assembly which adopted such proposal by the affirmative vote of two-thirds of the members to which each house is entitled in a roll-call vote entered on their respective journals, if such action is taken at least two months prior to the date of the election at which such proposal is to be submitted to the people.

Paragraph IV. **Constitutional convention; how called.** No convention of the people shall be called by the General Assembly to amend this Constitution or to propose a new Constitution, unless by the concurrence of two-thirds of the members to which each house of the General Assembly is entitled. The representation in said convention shall be based on population as near as practicable. A proposal by the convention to amend this Constitution or for a new Constitution shall be advertised, submitted to, and ratified by the people in the same manner provided for advertisement, submission, and ratification of proposals to amend the Constitution by the General Assembly. The General Assembly is hereby authorized to provide the procedure by which a convention is to be called and under which such convention shall operate and for other matters relative to such constitutional convention.

Paragraph V. **Veto not permitted.** The Governor shall not have the right to veto any proposal by the General Assembly or by a convention to amend this Constitution or to provide a new Constitution.

Paragraph VI. **Effective date of amendments or of a new Constitution.** Unless the amendment or the new Constitution itself or the resolution proposing the amendment or the new Constitution shall provide otherwise, an amendment to this Constitution or a new Constitution shall become effective on the first day of January following its ratification.

ARTICLE XI.
MISCELLANEOUS PROVISIONS
Section I.
Miscellaneous Provisions

Paragraph I. **Continuation of officers, boards, commissions, and authorities.**

(a) Except as otherwise provided in this Constitution, the officers of the state and all political subdivisions thereof in office on June 30, 1983, shall continue in the exercise of their functions and duties, subject to the provisions of laws applicable thereto and subject to the provisions of this Constitution.

(b) All boards, commissions, and authorities specifically named in the Constitution of 1976 which are not specifically named in this Constitution shall remain as statutory boards, commissions, and authorities; and all constitutional and statutory provisions relating thereto in force and effect on June 30, 1983, shall remain in force and effect as statutory law unless and until changed by the General Assembly.

Paragraph II. **Preservation of existing laws; judicial review.** All laws in force and effect on June 30, 1983, not inconsistent with this Constitution shall remain in force and effect; but such laws may be amended or repealed and shall be subject to judicial decision as to their validity when passed and to any limitations imposed by their own terms.

Paragraph III. **Proceedings of courts and administrative tribunals confirmed.** All judgments, decrees, orders, and other proceedings of the several courts and administrative tribunals of this state, heretofore made within the limits of their several jurisdictions, are hereby ratified and affirmed, subject only to reversal or modification in the manner provided by law.

Paragraph IV. **Continuation of certain constitutional amendments for a period of four years.**

(a) The following amendments to the Constitution of 1877, 1945, and 1976 shall continue in force and effect as part of this Constitution until July 1, 1987, at which time said amendments shall be repealed and shall be deleted as a part of this Constitution unless any such amendment shall be specifically continued in force and effect without amendment either by a local law enacted prior to July 1, 1987, with or without a referendum as provided by law, or by an ordinance or resolution duly adopted prior to July 1, 1987, by the local governing authority in the manner provided for the adoption of home rule amendments to its charter or local act: (1) amendments to the Constitution of 1877 and the Constitution of 1945 which were continued in force and effect as a part of the Constitution of 1976 pursuant to the provisions of Article XIII, Section I, Paragraph II of the Constitution of 1976 which are in force and effect on the effective date of this Constitution; (2) amendments to the Constitution of 1976 which were ratified as general amendments but which by their terms applied principally to a particular political subdivision or subdivisions which are in force and effect on the effective date of this Constitution; (3) amendments to the Constitution of 1976 which were ratified not as general amendments which are in force and effect on the effective date of this Constitution; and (4) amendments to the Constitution of 1976 of the type provided for in the immediately preceding two subparagraphs (2) and (3) of this Paragraph which were ratified at the same time this Constitution was ratified.

(b) Any amendment which is continued in force and effect after July 1, 1987, pursuant to the provisions of subparagraph (a) of this Paragraph shall be continued in force and effect as a part of this Constitution, except that such amendment may thereafter be repealed but may not be amended.

(c) All laws enacted pursuant to those amendments to the Constitution which are not continued in force and effect pursuant to subparagraph (a) of this Paragraph shall be repealed on July 1, 1987. All laws validly enacted on, before, or after July 1, 1987, and pursuant to the specific authorization of an amendment continued in force and effect pursuant to the provisions of subparagraph (a) of this Paragraph shall be legal, valid, and constitutional under this Constitution. Nothing in this subparagraph (c) shall be construed to revive any law not in force and effect on June 30, 1987.

(d) Notwithstanding the provisions of subparagraphs (a) and (b), the following amendments to the Constitutions of 1877 and 1945 shall be continued in force as a part of this Constitution: amendments to the Constitution of 1877 and the Constitution of 1945 which created or authorized the creation of metropolitan rapid transit authorities, port authorities, and industrial areas and which were continued in force as a part of the Constitution of 1976 pursuant to the provisions of Article XIII, Section I, Paragraph II of the Constitution of 1976 and which are in force on the effective date of this Constitution.

Paragraph V. **Special commission created.** Amendments to the Constitution of 1976 which were determined to be general and which were submitted to and ratified by the people of the entire state at the same time this Constitution was ratified shall be incorporated and made a part of this Constitution as provided in this Paragraph. There is hereby created a commission to be composed of the Governor, the President of the Senate, the Speaker of the House of Representatives, the Attorney General, and the Legislative Counsel, which is hereby authorized and directed to incorporate such amendments into this Constitution at the places deemed most appropriate to the commission. The commission shall make only such changes in the language of this Constitution and of such amendments as are necessary to incorporate properly such amendments into this Constitution and shall complete its duties prior to July 1, 1983. The commission shall deliver to the Secretary of State this Constitution with those amendments incorporated therein, and such document shall be the Constitution of the State of Georgia. In order that the commission may perform its duties, this Paragraph shall become effective as soon as it has been officially determined that this Constitution has been ratified. The commission shall stand abolished upon the completion of its duties.

Paragraph VI. **Effective date.** Except as provided in Paragraph V of this section, this Constitution shall become effective on July 1, 1983; and, except as otherwise provided in this Constitution, all previous Constitutions and all amendments thereto shall thereupon stand repealed.

CORPS OF ENGINEERS LAKES

Since the late 1940s, the Corps of Engineers has constructed nine large multi-purpose reservoirs on the major rivers of Georgia. These dams and lakes, built to provide flood control, hydroelectric power, and navigation to the people of the Southeast, have also found their place through the years among the major recreation attractions in the state. The latest figures show visitations at these lakes exceeded 51 million annually. And four of the State's lakes are among the eight most popular Corps-built lakes in the nation. Lake Lanier, northeast of Atlanta, currently holds the Corps' national record for annual visitations with 13 million.

Although Georgia is blessed with many lakes, six of the Corps-operated lakes—Hartwell, Clark Hill, Lanier, Seminole, Walter George, and West Point—are the largest in the state. Total area of all nine publicly-owned lakes is 289,000 acres, with a combined shoreline length of 4,300 miles.

Because of the popularity of these lakes, the Corps of Engineers is deeply involved in the field of outdoor recreation. Development includes a wide variety of recreational facilities, including marinas, boat launching ramps, picnic and camping facilities, hiking trails, swimming beaches, fish attractors, and much more. Some of the lakes, such as newly developed West Point Lake on the Chattahoochee River near LaGrange, have special fishing piers and other features designed for the elderly and the handicapped. In addition, West Point, as a recreation demonstration project, is designed to have such extra features as basketball and tennis courts, a children's fishing pond, and a rifle and pistol range.

For more information on facilities at individual lakes, contact the Resource Manager.

Allatoona Lake. Resource Manager, U.S. Army, Corps of Engineers, P.O. Box 487, Cartersville 30120. On the Etowah River northwest of Atlanta, the 12,000-acre lake has over 270 miles of shoreline. The Etowah Indian Mounds and Kennesaw Mountain Battlefield are within a few miles of the lake.

Carters Lake. Resource Manager, U.S. Army, Corps of Engineers, P.O. Box 42, Oakman 30732. In North Georgia's Blue Ridge, 2 hours north of Atlanta. This 400-foot-deep lake is one of Georgia's newest lakes.

Clark Hill Lake. Resource Manager, U.S. Army, Corps of Engineers, Clark Hill Lake, Clark Hill, S.C. 29821. This 70,000-acre lake, on the Georgia–South Carolina border near Augusta is the largest Corps-managed lake in the state. It is especially known for its fine fishing and has some of the state's best publicly-owned hunting lands.

Hartwell Lake. Resource Manager, U.S. Army, Corps of Engineers, P.O. Box 278, Hartwell 30643. Located on the Savannah River in the rolling country of the upper Piedmont Plateau, Hartwell Lake is easily accessible from Interstate 85. There are 4 marinas and 3 state parks on the lake, as well as 68 other developed public areas.

Lake George W. Andrews. Resource Manager, U.S. Army, Corps of Engineers, P.O. Box 281, Fort Gaines 31751. This lake is the smallest Corps-built lake in Georgia. In spite of its small size, it has a wide range of facilities, including boat ramps and provisions for tent camping.

Lake Seminole. Resource Manager, U.S. Army, Corps of Engineers, P.O. Box 96, Chattahoochee, FL 32324. A renowned fishing hole (specialty, large mouth bass), 5,000-acre Lake Seminole is located in the warm subtropical lowlands of South Georgia where Alabama, Georgia, and Florida join. Its 37,000 acres offer year-round fishing, boating, and camping opportunities.

Lake Sidney Lanier. Resource Manager, U.S. Army, Corps of Engineers, P.O. Box 567, Buford 30518. A 38,000-acre lake with 550 miles of shoreline, including Lanier Islands, a developed outdoor recreation facility.

Walter F. George Lake. Resource Manager, U.S. Army, Corps of Engineers, P.O. Box 281, Fort Gaines 31751. South of Columbus, this lake has long been recognized as one of Georgia's finest fishing lakes. The Eufala National Wildlife Refuge for migratory birds is also located on project lands.

West Point Lake. Resource Manager, U.S. Army, Corps of Engineers, P.O. Box 574, West Point 31833. Located on the Chattahoochee River, about 3 miles north of West Point. The lake is 25,900 acres, with 37 recreational areas and 11 parks, and a public overlook.

COUNTY NAME ORIGINS

Georgia contains 159 counties. Each county name, the year of its establishment, and a brief biographical sketch (when available) of the person for whom it was named, follow.

Appling County. Established 1818; named in honor of DANIEL APPLING. Served as Lieutenant Colonel in War of 1812. He was awarded the sword by the legislature of Georgia; but he died in 1818, before it was presented to him.

Atkinson County. Established 1917; named in honor of WILLIAM YATES ATKINSON. Served as fifty-third governor of Georgia. Also served in Georgia assembly.

Bacon County. Established 1914; named in honor of AUGUSTUS OCTAVIUS BACON. Confederate Army officer. Served in State House of Representatives, 1871-86; serving 2 years as Speaker pro tempore and 8 years as Speaker. U.S. Senator, 1895-1914.

Baker County. Established 1825; named in honor of COLONEL JOHN BAKER.

Baldwin County. Established 1803; named in honor of ABRAHAM BALDWIN. Educator, president of University of Georgia. Served in State House of Representatives, 1785; Continental Congress, 1785-88; federal constitutional convention, 1787; U.S. representative, 1789-99 and senator, 1799-1807.

Banks County. Established 1858; named in honor of RICHARD BANKS. A noted physician.

Barrow County. Established 1914; named in honor of DAVID CRENSHAW BARROW. A University of Georgia professor who later served as Chancellor of the university, 1907-25.

Bartow County. Established 1832; named in honor of FRANCIS S. BARTOW. An army general who was killed July 21, 1861 at Manassas Plains. (Bartow County was formerly Cass County. The name was changed December 6, 1861.)

Ben Hill County. Established 1906; named in honor of BENJAMIN HARVEY HILL. Served in State House of Representatives, 1851; State Senate, 1859-60; delegate to Confederate Provisional Congress, 1861; senator, Confederate Congress, 1861-65; U.S. representative, 1875-77; and senator, 1877-82.

Berrien County. Established 1856; named in honor of JOHN MACPHERSON BERRIEN. After serving as a lawyer, judge and officer of the cavalry, he served in the State Senate, 1822-23; U.S. Senate, 1825-29. He was U.S. Attorney General in President Andrew Jackson's cabinet, 1829-31, before serving 3 more terms in the U.S. Senate, 1841-52.

Bibb County. Established 1822; named in honor of WILLIAM WYATT BIBB. A physician who served as a state representative, 1803-05; U.S. representative, 1807-13; senator, 1813-16, before becoming territorial governor of Alabama, 1817-19, and later first governor of the State of Alabama, 1819-20.

Bleckley County. Established 1912; named in honor of LOGAN EDWIN BLECKLEY. After serving as solicitor general of Atlanta, 1852–56, he fought in the War Between the States. Later he became Supreme Court reporter, 1864–67; associate justice of the South Carolina Supreme Court, 1875–80; chief justice, 1887–94; secretary to the governor.

Brantley County. Established 1920; named in honor of BENJAMIN D. BRANTLEY.

Brooks County. Established 1858; named in honor of PRESTON SMITH BROOKS.

Bryan County. Established 1793; named in honor of JONATHAN BRYAN.

Bulloch County. Established 1796; named in honor of ARCHIBALD BULLOCH. The first governor of Georgia under American rule, 1776–77, was also a lieutenant in the South Carolina regiment, 1757; Speaker of the Georgia Royal Assembly, 1775–76; and Continental Congress.

Burke County. Established 1777; named in honor of EDMUND BURKE. A member of British Parliament in 1765 who urged the repeal of the Stamp Act and advised conciliation with the American colonies.

Butts County. Established 1825; named in honor of SAM BUTTS. An army officer killed January 27, 1814 at the Battle of Chillabee.

Calhoun County. Established 1854; named in honor of JOHN CALDWELL CALHOUN. A South Carolina legislator who served in their House of Representatives, 1808–09, and represented his state in the U.S. House of Representatives, 1811–17 and Senate, 1832–43, 1845–50. He served in President Monroe's cabinet, 1817–25, as secretary of war, and President Tyler's cabinet, 1844–45, as secretary of state. He served as vice president under presidents John Quincy Adams and Andrew Jackson, 1825–32.

Camden County. Established 1777; named in honor of CHARLES PRATT, EARL OF CAMDEN. A member of British Parliament who opposed as unconstitutional the Stamp Act and tax of American colonies as unconstitutional. He was Lord Chancellor, 1766–70, and Lord President of Council, 1782, 1784–94.

Candler County. Established 1914; named in honor of ALLEN DANIEL CANDLER. A Civil War soldier who was injured at Kennesaw Mountain and lost an eye at Jonesboro. After serving as an educator he became mayor of Gainesville, 1872; was in State House of Representatives, 1873–77; Senate, 1878–79; U.S. representative, 1883–91; secretary of state for Georgia, 1894–98; governor, 1899–1902.

Carroll County. Established 1826; named in honor of CHARLES CARROLL. Signer of the Declaration of Independence who served as senator from Maryland, 1777–1800.

Catoosa County. Established 1853; named in honor of CHIEF CATOOSA. Indian chief.

Charlton County. Established 1854; named in honor of ROBERT MILLEDGE CHARLTON. State legislator, 1829; U.S. District Attorney, 1830; Superior Court judge, eastern district, 1832; U.S. senator, 1852–53; mayor of Savannah.

Chatham County. Established 1777; named in honor of WILLIAM PITT, EARL OF CHATHAM. English nobleman, entered Parliament, 1735. Secretary of state and leader of House of Commons, 1756.

Chattahoochee County. Established 1854; named for the Indian word which translates "painted stone."

Chattooga County. Established 1838; named for the CHATTOOGA RIVER.

Cherokee County. Established 1831; named in honor of the CHEROKEE INDIAN TRIBE.

Clarke County. Established 1801; named in honor of ELIJAH CLARKE. Twice wounded Georgia militia officer who fought at Alligator Creek, 1778; Wofford's Iron Works, 1780; Musgrove's Mill, 1780; Augusta, 1780; and Long Cane, S.C., 1780.

Clay County. Established 1854; named in honor of HENRY CLAY. Kentucky congressman, 1803; U.S. senator, 1806-07, 1810-11; representative from Kentucky, 1811-14, 1815-21, and 1823-25; secretary of state to President Adams. Ran unsuccessfully three times for the presidency, 1824, 1832 and 1844.

Clayton County. Established 1858; named in honor of AUGUSTIN SMITH CLAYTON. Member and clerk of House of Representatives, 1810-15; Superior Court judge, 1819-25; and U.S. representative, 1832-35.

Clinch County. Established 1850; named in honor of DUNCAN LAMONT CLINCH. Third Infantry Army officer who fought in first and second Seminole Wars. U.S. representative, 1844-45.

Cobb County. Established 1832; named in honor of THOMAS WILLIS COBB. U.S. representative, 1817-21, 1823-24; U.S. senator, 1824-28; Superior Court judge, 1828.

Coffee County. Established 1854; named in honor of JOHN COFFEE. Georgia militia officer wounded in Creek Indian Battle, 1814; state senator, 1819-27; U.S. Representative, 1833-36.

Colquitt County. Established 1856; named in honor of WALTER TERRY COLQUITT. Chattahoochee circuit court judge, 1826; Methodist clergyman, 1827; Senate, 1834 and 1837; U.S. representative, 1839-40, 1842-43; U.S. Senator, 1843-48.

Columbia County. Established 1790; named in honor of CHRISTOPHER COLUMBUS. Italian navigator who sailed from Spain and discovered San Salvador in 1492.

Cook County. Established 1918; named in honor of PHILIP COOK. Senator, 1859, 1860, 1863 and 1864; Confederate Army officer; U.S. representative, 1873-83; secretary of state, 1890-94.

Coweta County. Established 1826; named in honor of an Indian chief.

Crawford County. Established 1822; named in honor of WILLIAM HARRIS CRAWFORD. Representative, 1803-07; U.S. senator, 1807-13; Senate president pro tempore, 1812; U.S. minister to France, 1813-15; U.S. secretary of war in President Madison's cabinet, 1815-16; secretary of the Treasury in President Madison's cabinet, 1816-25; circuit judge, 1827-34.

Crisp County. Established 1905; named in honor of CHARLES FREDERICK CRISP. Confederate soldier held as prisoner of war, 1864-65; circuit court solicitor general, 1872-77; Superior Court judge, 1877-82; U.S. representative, 1883-96.

Dade County. Established 1837; named in honor of FRANCIS LANGHORNE DADE. Officer in U.S. Infantry, killed in ambush by Seminole chiefs Micanope and Jumper, December 28, 1835.

Dawson County. Established 1857; named in honor of WILLIAM CROSBY DAWSON. Representative, compiler, laws of Georgia, 1820-30; fought in Creek War, 1836; U.S. representative, 1836-41; Superior Court judge, Ocmulgee Circuit, 1845; U.S. senator, 1849-55.

Decatur County. Established 1823; named in honor of STEPHEN DECATUR. Commander of schooner Enterprise in Tripolitan War and United States in War of 1812; forced Barbary Pirates to submit to terms. Killed in a duel with Commodore James Barrow, 1820.

DeKalb County. Established 1822; named in honor of JOHANN DEKALB. French army officer who aided American colonists; was commissioned major general in Continental Army, 1777; died of injury at battle of Camden, N.J., 1780.

Dodge County. Established 1870; named in honor of WILLIAM EARLE DODGE. Delegate to peace convention to prevent Civil War in 1861; U.S. representative from New York, 1866-67.

87

Dooly County. Established 1821; named in honor of JOHN DOOLY. Georgia militia officer who was killed with his family by Tories in 1780.

Dougherty County. Established 1853; named in honor of CHARLES DOUGHERTY. Judge of the western circuit.

Douglas County. Established 1870; named in honor of STEPHEN ARNOLD DOUGLAS. Illinois House of Representatives, 1836–37; land office registrar; Illinois Secretary of State, 1840–41; representative and senator from Illinois. Defeated by Abraham Lincoln for the presidency, 1860.

Early County. Established 1818; named in honor of PETER EARLY. Twenty-fifth governor of Georgia, 1813–15; U.S. representative, 1803–07; Superior Court judge; state senator, 1815–17.

Echols County. Established 1858; named in honor of ROBERT M. ECHOLS. Georgia assembly; infantry officer U.S. Regiment, 1847; killed at Natural Bridge, Mexico, Dec. 3, 1847.

Effingham County. Established 1777, named in honor of THOMAS HOWARD, ninth baron Howard, third earl of Effingham, 1763; officer of British army, favored colonists in struggle for independence.

Elbert County. Established 1790; named in honor of SAMUEL ELBERT. Governor of Georgia, 1785; grenadier company officer; expedition against English in east Florida; defended Savannah; wounded and taken prisoner Briar Creek, 1779.

Emanuel County. Established 1812; named in honor of DAVID EMANUEL. Twentieth governor of Georgia, 1801; Revolutionary War; Georgia legislature; president Georgia Senate.

Evans County. Established 1914; named in honor of CLEMENT ANSELM EVANS. Judge; state senator, 1859; Army officer wounded at Gettysburg; Methodist minister, 1866.

Fannin County. Established 1854; named in honor of JAMES WALKER FANNIN. War hero killed, March 27, 1836.

Fayette County. Established 1821; named in honor of MARQUIS DE LAFAYETTE. Resigned from French military service to aid American cause of independence; commissioned Major General in Continental Army, 1777; returned to Paris, 1781; became commander-in-chief of the National Guard, 1789; captured by Austrians, 1792; revisited U.S. in 1784 and 1824–25.

Floyd County. Established 1832; named in honor of JOHN FLOYD. Officer of the Georgia militia; fought Creek and Choctaw Indians; State House of Representatives, 1820–27; U.S. representative, 1827–29.

Forsyth County. Established 1832; named in honor of JOHN FORSYTH. Attorney general of Georgia, 1808; U.S. representative; U.S. senator; U.S. minister to Spain, 1819–23; thirty-first governor of Georgia, 1827–29; U.S. secretary of state under presidents Jackson and Van Buren, 1834–41.

Franklin County. Established 1784; named in honor of BENJAMIN FRANKLIN. Printer; founded Pennsylvania "Gazette," 1728; clerk of Pennsylvania General Assembly; postmaster of Philadelphia; provincial assembly; deputy postmaster general of the British North American Colonies; Continental Congress; signed the Declaration of Independence, 1776; Pennsylvania constitutional convention, 1776; commissioner and minister to France, 1776–85; governor of Pennsylvania, 1785–88; federal constitutional convention, 1787.

Fulton County. Established 1853; named in honor of ROBERT FULTON. Inventor, experimented with a submarine boat in France, 1801; built the Clermont, a steamboat, which sailed up the Hudson River, 1807.

Gilmer County. Established 1832; named in honor of GEORGE ROCKINGHAM GILMER. Officer in campaign against Creek Indians; House of Representatives, 1818, 1819 and 1824; U.S. representative, 1827–29, 1833–35; governor, 1829–31, 1837–39.

Glascock County. Established 1857; named in honor of THOMAS GLASCOCK. Georgia constitutional convention; officer in War of 1812; Seminole War, 1817; House of Representatives, 1821, 1823, 1831, 1834 and 1839; U.S. representative, 1835–39.

Glynn County. Established 1777; named in honor of JOHN GLYNN.

Gordon County. Established 1850; named in honor of WILLIAM WASHINGTON GORDON. Graduated West Point, 1814; Third Lieutenant, 1815; aide to General Gaines, resigned 1815; first president of Georgia Central Railroad.

Grady County. Established 1905; named in honor of HENRY WOODFIN GRADY. Newspaperman; Georgia representative of *New York Herald,* 1871; editor and part owner of *Atlanta Constitution,* 1880.

Greene County. Established 1786; named in honor of NATHANAEL GREENE. Officer Continental Army, 1775; commanded Army of the South, 1780; president of the court of inquiry for Major Andre.

Gwinnett County. Established 1818; named in honor of BUTTON GWINNETT. Second president of Georgia Provisional Council; signer of the Declaration of Independence, 1776; Georgia constitutional convention, 1777; acting president and commander-in-chief of Georgia, 1777; killed in a duel with General Lachlan McIntosh.

Habersham County. Established 1818; named in honor of JOSEPH HABERSHAM. Served as officer of the First Georgia Regiment, 1776; Continental Congress, 1785–86; postmaster general, 1795–1801.

Hall County. Established 1818; named in honor of LYMAN HALL. Ninth governor of Georgia Provisional Council, 1774–75; signer of Declaration of Independence, 1776; physician; governor of Georgia, 1783.

Hancock County. Established 1793; named in honor of JOHN HANCOCK. First governor of Massachusetts (Commonwealth). Massachusetts provincial legislature, 1766–72; served three terms in Continental Congress, was president one term; first signer of the Declaration of Independence, 1776; major general of Massachusetts Militia; Massachusetts constitutional convention, 1780; governor of Massachusetts; 1780–85 and 1787–93.

Haralson County. Established 1856; named in honor of HUGH ANDERSON HARALSON. Representative, 1831–32; Senator, 1837–38; major general Georgia militia, 1838–50; U.S. Representative, 1843–51.

Harris County. Established 1827; named in honor of CHARLES HARRIS. Lawyer, alderman or mayor of Savannah, Georgia for about 30 years; offered many judicial posts but declined them.

Hart County. Established 1853; named in honor of NANCY MORGAN HART. Married Benjamin Hart of Kentucky, moved to Elbert County, Georgia, mother of six sons and two daughters; a sharpshooter and patriot reported to have routed and captured many Tories.

Heard County. Established 1830; named in honor of STEPHEN HEARD. Sixth governor; Battle of Kettle Creek, 1781; president of Georgia council, 1782; chief justice inferior court.

Henry County. Established 1821; named in honor of PATRICK HENRY. Virginia House of Burgesses, 1765; Continental Congress, 1774–76; governor of Georgia, 1776–79 and 1784–86; Virginia constitutional convention, 1788.

Houston County. Established 1821; named in honor of JOHN HOUSTOUN. Chairman of Georgia Sons of Liberty, 1774; Continental Congress, 1775–76; executive council, 1777; governor, 1778 and 1784.

89

Irwin County. Established 1818; named in honor of JARED IRWIN. Officer of Georgia militia; constitutional convention, 1789; representative, 1790; governor, 1796–98 and 1806–09; permanent constitutional convention, 1798.

Jackson County. Established 1796; named in honor of JAMES JACKSON. Served as lieutenant in Revolutionary War, wounded at Midway, Georgia; brigadier general, 1778; U.S. representative, 1789–91; U.S. senator, 1793–95; governor, 1798–1801; U.S. senator, 1801–06.

Jasper County. Established 1801; named in honor of WILLIAM JASPER. Officer in Colonel William Moultrie's Second South Carolina Infantry, 1775; distinguished himself during attack on Fort Moultrie, June 28, 1776; killed while planting South Carolina flag at battle of Savannah, October 9, 1779.

Jeff Davis County. Established 1905; named in honor of JEFFERSON DAVIS. Graduated U.S. Military Academy, 1828; Black Hawk War, 1830–31; representative from Mississippi, 1845–46; commanded Mississippi Riflemen, 1846; with General Taylor in Mexico, 1846; declined appointment as brigadier general, 1847; senator from Mississippi, 1847–51; U.S. secretary of war in cabinet of President Pierce, 1853–57; senator from Mississippi, 1857–61; major general of Mississippi militia, 1861; president of provisional Confederate congress, 1861; president of the Confederacy, 1862; captured, 1865; indicted for treason, 1866; paroled, 1867.

Jefferson County. Established 1796; named in honor of THOMAS JEFFERSON. Virginia House of Burgesses, 1769–74; signer of Declaration of Independence, 1776; governor of Virgina, 1779–81; Virginia house of delegates, 1782; Continental Congress, 1783–85; U.S. Minister to France, 1784–87; U.S. Secretary of State in cabinet of President Washington, 1790–93; vice president of the U.S., 1797–1801; President of the United States, 1801–09.

Jenkins County. Established 1905; named in honor of CHARLES JONES JENKINS. State legislature, 1830; Georgia attorney, 1831; solicitor general middle circuit, 1831; elected ten times to legislature, 1836–49; speaker of the house, 1840, 1843 and 1845; senator, 1856; supreme court, 1860; governor, 1865–68; president constitutional convention, 1877.

Johnson County. Established 1858; named in honor of HERSCHEL VASPASIAN JOHNSON. U.S Senator, 1848–49; Superior court judge of Ocmulgee circuit, 1849–53; governor, 1853–57; senator in Second Confederate Congress, 1862–65; president of constitutional convention, 1865; elected senator but not permitted to qualify, 1866; judge of the middle circuit, 1873–80.

Jones County. Established 1807; named in honor of JAMES JONES. First lieutenant Georgia militia, 1790; House of Representatives, 1796–98; constitutional convention, 1798; U.S. representative, 1799–1801.

Lamar County. Established 1920; named in honor of LUCIUS QUINTUS CINCINNATUS LAMAR. Georgia House of Representatives, 1853; representative from Mississippi, 1857–60 and 1873–77; lieutenant colonel and colonel 18th Mississippi regiment; diplomatic mission to Russia, France and England for the Confederate States, 1863; professor, University of Mississippi, 1866–67; senator from Mississippi, 1877–85; secretary of the Interior in President Cleveland's cabinet, 1885–88; U.S. Supreme Court justice, 1888–93.

Lanier County. Established 1919; named in honor of SIDNEY LANIER. Tutor, Oglethorpe College, 1860–61; private in Macon volunteers, 1861; wrote "Tiger Lilies" and many other poems; practiced law at Macon, 1868–72; lecturer in English literature of Johns Hopkins University.

Laurens County. Established 1807; named in honor of JOHN LAURENS. Served in Revolutionary War under General George Washington; wounded at battle of Germantown, October 4, 1777; captured one of the redoubts at Yorktown, Virginia; received Cornwallis' sword. Killed in skirmish, Combahee River, South Carolina, 1782.

Lee County. Established 1826; named in honor of RICHARD HENRY LEE. Justice of the peace Westmoreland County, Virginia, 1757; Virginia House of Burgesses, 1758–75; Continental

Congress, 1774–80; signer of the Declaration of Independence, 1776; Virginia House of Delegates, 1777, 1780 and 1785; Continental Congress, 1784–87; senator from Virginia, 1789–92.

Liberty County. Established 1777; Descriptive.

Lincoln County. Established 1796; named in honor of BENJAMIN LINCOLN. Major general in Continental Army, 1776; at siege of Yorktown, received sword of Cornwallis, 1781; secretary of war, 1781–83; stopped Shay's Rebellion, 1787; lieutenant governor of Massachusetts, 1788; Collector of the Port, Boston, Massachusetts, 1789–1808.

Long County. Established 1920; named in honor of CRAWFORD WILLIAMSON LONG. Physician; used sul-ether in surgical operation at Jefferson, 1841.

Lowndes County. Established 1825; named in honor of WILLIAM JONES LOWNDES. South Carolina House of Representatives, 1806–10; captain of militia, 1807; representative from South Carolina, 1811–22; died at sea, 1822.

Lumpkin County. Established 1832; named in honor of WILSON LUMPKIN. House of Representatives, 1808–12; Senate, 1812–15; U.S. representative, 1815–17 and 1827–31; governor, 1831–35; U.S. senator, 1837–41.

Macon County. Established 1837; named in honor of NATHANIEL MACON. Revolutionary War; North Carolina senate, 1780–82, 1784 and 1785; representative from North Carolina, 1791–1815; Speaker House of Representatives, 1801–07; senator from North Carolina, 1815–28; president North Carolina constitutional convention, 1835.

Madison County. Established 1811; named in honor of JAMES MADISON. First general assembly of Virginia, 1776; Continental Congress, 1780–83 and 1786–88; federal constitutional convention, 1787; representative from Virginia, 1789–97; U.S. secretary of state in cabinet of President Jefferson, 1801–09; President of the U.S., 1809–17.

Marion County. Established 1827; named in honor of FRANCIS MARION. Brigadier general, commander of Marion's brigade, known as "the Swamp Fox"; harassed English troops in the Revolutionary War; won battle of Eutaw Springs; served in South Carolina state Senate, 1782–90.

McDuffie County. Established 1870; named in honor of GEORGE McDUFFIE. South Carolina House of Representatives, 1818–20; Representative from South Carolina, 1821–34; governor of South Carolina, 1834–36; senator from South Carolina, 1842–46.

McIntosh County. Established 1793; named in honor of WILLIAM McINTOSH. Creek Indian chief, leader of Lower Creeks served in Seminole War, 1817–18; brigadier general U.S. Army, killed by his tribesmen who considered him a traitor.

Meriwether County. Established 1827; named in honor of DAVID MERIWETHER. Elected thirteen times to Kentucky legislature, 1832–83; Kentucky constitutional convention, 1849; Kentucky secretary of state, 1851; senator from Kentucky, 1852; governor of New Mexico territory, 1853–55; Kentucky House of Representatives, 1858–85; Speaker, Kentucky House of Representatives, 1859.

Miller County. Established 1856; named in honor of ANDREW JACKSON MILLER. House of Representatives, 1836; Senate, 1838–56; Superior Court judge.

Mitchell County. Established 1857; named in honor of HENRY MITCHELL. General.

Monroe County. Established 1821; named in honor of JAMES MONROE. Revolutionary War; Virginia legislature; Continental Congress, 1783–86; Virginia senator, 1790–94; served two terms as governor of Virginia (Commonwealth); U.S. secretary of state under President James Madison; President of the U.S., 1817–25.

Montgomery County. Established 1793; named in honor of RICHARD MONTGOMERY. Pro-

91

vincial Congress, 1775; brigadier general Continental Army; killed leading assault against Quebec, 1775.

Morgan County. Established 1807; named in honor of DANIEL MORGAN. Teamster under General Braddock, 1755; lieutenant in Pontiac's War, 1764; captain in Dunmore's War, 1774; captain Virginia riflemen, 1775; captured at Quebec, December 31, 1775; colonel of Virginia regiment, 1776; brigadier general at battle of Saratoga, 1780; defeated General Tarleton at battle of Cowpens, 1781; commanding Virginia militia suppressed Whiskey Insurrection in Pennsylvania, 1794; Representative from Virginia, 1797-99.

Murray County. Established 1832; named in honor of THOMAS W. MURRAY. Legislature, 1818, speaker of the house; nominated for U.S. Congress but died before election.

Muscogee County. Established 1826; named in honor of MUSCOGEE INDIAN TRIBE.

Newton County. Established 1821; named in honor of JOHN NEWTON. Sergeant who, with William Jasper, captured ten British soldiers who were taking colonial prisoners to Savannah to be hanged.

Oconee County. Established 1875. Indian word for "the place of springs" or "the water eyes of the hills."

Oglethorpe County. Established 1793; named in honor of JAMES EDWARD OGLETHORPE. First governor under the trustees. Colonizer; landed at Charleston, 1733; returned to England, 1734; second trip, 1736; advocated religious freedom; returned to England, 1743; surrendered charter of Georgia, 1752; general commander of English forces, 1765.

Paulding County. Established 1832; named in honor of JOHN PAULDING. One of the captors of Major John Andre, 1780; received silver medal from Congress and pension of $200.

Peach County. Established 1924. Descriptive, Georgia peach.

Pickens County. Established 1853; named in honor of ANDREW PICKENS. Fought Cherokee Indians, 1760; captain to brigadier general Revolutionary War, 1779-81; awarded sword by Congress for victory at Cowpens, 1781; fought Cherokee Indians, 1782; South Carolina House of Representatives, 1781-94; South Carolina constitutional convention, 1790; representative from South Carolina, 1793-95; major general of militia, 1795; South Carolina House of Representatives, 1800-12.

Pierce County. Established 1857; named in honor of FRANKLIN PIERCE. New Hampshire House of Representatives, 1829-33; representative from New Hampshire, 1833-37; senator from New Hampshire, 1837-42; colonel in Mexican war; brigadier general, 1847; New Hampshire constitutional convention, 1850; president of the U.S., 1853-57.

Pike County. Established 1822; named in honor of ZEBULON MONTGOMERY PIKE. Soldier and explorer; Pike's peak (first sighted by him) bears his name; colonel in War of 1812, was killed in Toronto, Canada.

Polk County. Established 1851; named in honor of JAMES KNOX POLK. Chief clerk Tennessee senate, 1821-23; Tennessee House of Representatives, 1823-25; representative from Tennessee, 1825-39; governor of Tennessee, 1839-41; President of the U.S., 1845-49.

Pulaski County. Established 1808; named in honor of CASIMIR PULASKI. Polish nobleman who came to America in 1777 to aid American independence; fought at Brandywine and Germantown; mortally wounded at siege of Savannah, 1779.

Putnam County. Established 1807; named in honor of ISRAEL PUTNAM. Served in French and Indian War, 1754-63; Pontiac's War, 1764; major general Continental Army, 1775-79; commanded at New York and Philadelphia.

Quitman County. Established 1858; named in honor of JOHN ANTHONY QUITMAN. Mississippi House of Representatives, 1826-27; chancellor of Mississippi, 1828-35; president Mississippi senate, 1835-36; acting governor of Mississippi, 1835-36; judge high court of errors and appeals, 1838; brigadier general volunteers, 1846; major general regular army, 1847; governor of Mississippi, 1850-51; representative from Mississippi, 1855-58.

Rabun County. Established 1819; named in honor of WILLIAM RAYBUN. State assembly; president of Senate; governor, 1817-19, died in office, 1819.

Randolph County. Established 1828; named in honor of JOHN RANDOLPH. Representative from Virginia, 1799-1813, 1815-17, 1819-25, 1827-29 and 1833; senator from Virginia, 1825-27; Virginia constitutional convention, 1829; U.S. minister to Russia, 1830-31; fought duel with Henry Clay, 1826.

Richmond County. Established 1777; named in honor of CHARLES LENNOX, THIRD DUKE OF RICHMOND. Third son of second Duke of Richmond; British Minister Extraordinary in Paris, 1765; secretary of state for Southern Department, 1766; resigned, 1767; favored American colonies and wanted troops withdrawn, 1778.

Rockdale County. Established 1870. Descriptive.

Schley County. Established 1857; named in honor of WILLIAM SCHLEY. Superior Court judge, 1825-28; House of Representatives, 1830; U.S. representative, 1833-35; governor, 1835-37.

Screven County. Established 1793; named in honor of JAMES SCREVEN. Served as officer of 3rd Georgia Rangers, 1776; resigned, 1778; brigadier general Georgia militia; killed at Midway Church, Liberty County, Georgia.

Seminole County. Established 1920; named in honor of the SEMINOLE INDIAN TRIBE.

Spalding County. Established 1851; named in honor of THOMAS SPALDING. House of Representatives, 1794; constitutional convention, 1798; Senate, 1805-06; commissioner to determine Georgia-Florida boundary line.

Stephens County. Established 1905; named in honor of ALEXANDER HAMILTON STEPHENS. House of Representatives, 1836-41; Senate, 1842; U.S. representative, 1843-59; vice president of Confederate provisional government, 1861; imprisoned for five months, 1865; elected senator by Georgia, but did not present his credentials as Georgia was not readmitted to representation, 1866; U.S. representative, 1873-82; governor, 1882-83.

Stewart County. Established 1830; named in honor of DANIEL STEWART. Brigadier general, Continental Army.

Sumter County. Established 1831; named in honor of THOMAS SUMTER. Lieutenant colonel Sixth Continental Regiment; brigadier general of militia, 1780; voted the thanks of Congress, 1781; South Carolina state senate, 1781-82; Representative from South Carolina, 1789-93 and 1797-1801; Senator from South Carolina, 1801-10.

Talbot County. Established 1827; named in honor of MATTHEW TALBOT. Member state constitutional convention, 1798; Senator, 1808; president of Senate, 1818-23; ex officio governor, 1819.

Taliaferro County. Established 1825; named in honor of BENJAMIN TALIAFERRO. Officer in Revolutionary War; president state senate; delegate state constitutional convention, 1798; U.S. representative, 1799-1802; Superior Court judge.

Tattnall County. Established 1801; named in honor of JOSIAH TATTNALL. In Revolutionary War under General Anthony Wayne, 1782; colonel of Georgia regiment promoted to brigadier general, 1801; House of Representatives, 1795 and 1796; U.S. senator, 1796-99; governor, 1801-02.

Taylor County. Established 1852; named in honor of ZACHARY TAYLOR. Twelfth president of the U.S., 1849-50.

Telfair County. Established 1807; named in honor of EDWARD TELFAIR. Member of state council of safety in 1775 and 1776; delegate to the Provincial Congress at Savannah in 1776; member of the Continental Congress, 1777-79 and 1780-83; one of the signers of the Articles of Confederation and delegate to constitutional convention; governor, 1786 and 1790-93.

Terrell County. Established 1856; named in honor of WILLIAM TERRELL. Physician; House of Representatives, 1810-13; U.S. representative, 1817-21.

Thomas County. Established 1825; named in honor of JETT THOMAS. Captain of artillery under General John Floyd; major general, state militia; built state capitol at Milledgeville, 1807.

Tift County. Established 1905; named in honor of NELSON TIFT. Founded Augusta guards, 1835; Baker County inferior court, 1840-41 and 1849; colonel militia Baker County, 1840; House of Representatives, 1841, 1847, 1851-52; editor Albany "Patriot," 1845-58; captain in Confederate Navy, 1861; U.S. representative, 1868-69.

Toombs County. Established 1905; named in honor of ROBERT TOOMBS. Commanded a company in Creek War serving under General Scott, 1836; House of Representatives, 1837-40 and 1841-44; U.S. representative, 1845-53; U.S. senator, 1853-61; Confederate provisional congress; secretary of state of the Confederate States; brigadier general Confederate Army.

Towns County. Established 1856; named in honor of GEORGE WASHINGTON BONAPARTE TOWNS. House of Representatives, 1829-30; Senate, 1832-34; U.S. representative, 1835-36, 1837-39 and 1846-47; governor, 1847-51.

Treutlen County. Established 1917; named in honor of JOHN ADAM TREUTLEN. Provincial Congress, 1775; first governor under the constitution, 1777-78.

Troup County. Established 1826; named in honor of GEORGE MICHAEL TROUP. House of Representatives, 1803-05; U.S. Representative, 1807-15; U.S. Senator, 1816-18; governor, 1823-27; U.S. Senator, 1829-33.

Turner County. Established 1905; named in honor of HENRY GRAY TURNER. Private Confederate Army, 1861; advanced to captain; wounded at battle of Gettysburg; House of Representatives, 1874-76, 1878 and 1879; U.S. representative, 1881-97; associate justice Supreme Court, 1903.

Twiggs County. Established 1809; named in honor of JOHN TWIGGS. Major general, 1781; aide of General Greene; commissioner to negotiate treaty with the Creek Indians, 1783.

Union County. Established 1832. Descriptive.

Upson County. Established 1824; named in honor of STEPHEN UPSON. Graduated from Yale.

Walker County. Established 1833; named in honor of FREEMAN WALKER. House of Representatives, 1807-11; mayor of Augusta, 1818-19; U.S. senator, 1819-21; mayor of Augusta, 1823.

Walton County. Established 1818; named in honor of GEORGE WALTON. Secretary Provisional Congress, 1774; delegate Continental Congress, 1776-81; signer Declaration of Independence, 1776; colonel of militia captured at battle of Savannah; held prisoner until 1779; governor, 1779-80; chief justice, 1783-86; governor, 1789; judge of Superior Courts of eastern judicial circuit, 1790; chief justice, 1793; U.S. senator, 1795-96; judge of the middle circuit 1799-1804.

Ware County. Established 1824; named in honor of NICHOLAS WARE.

Warren County. Established 1793; named in honor of JOSEPH WARREN. Physician; president of Provincial Congress, 1775; major general Continental Army, 1775; killed at battle of Breed's Hill (Bunker Hill), June 17, 1775.

Washington County. Established 1784; named in honor of GEORGE WASHINGTON. Successfully led Continental Armies to victory in Revolutionary War, 1781; presided over federal constitutional convention, 1787; first President of the U.S., 1789–97.

Wayne County. Established 1803; named in honor of ANTHONY WAYNE. Nicknamed "Mad Anthony"; army officer wounded at Three Rivers Battle, 1776; captured at Stony Point; awarded thanks and gold medal from Congress, 1779; after serving in Pennsylvania was U.S. Representative, 1791–92; returned to lead Army to victory over Indians at Fallen Timbers, 1793.

Webster County. Established 1853; named in honor of DANIEL WEBSTER. Served as a New Hampshire Representative, 1813–17; Massachusetts Representative, 1823–27; Senator, 1827–41, 1845–50; was Secretary of State in the cabinets of Presidents Tyler, 1841–43, and Fillmore, 1850–52.

Wheeler County. Established 1912; named in honor of JOSEPH WHEELER. Army officer; U.S. Representative from Alabama, 1881–82, 1883 and 1885–1900; returned to Army; helped negotiate surrender of Spanish Army in Cuba, 1898; authored many books.

White County. Established 1857; named in honor of DAVID T. WHITE.

Whitfield County. Established 1851; named in honor of GEORGE WHITEFIELD. A clergyman of the Church of England who arrived in Savannah, 1738; built an orphanage there in 1740; was compiler of hymnbook, 1753.

Wilcox County. Established 1857; named in honor of JOHN WILCOX. Army officer.

Wilkes County. Established 1777; named in honor of JOHN WILKES. A member of England's House of Commons who, during the American Revolution, favored the colonies.

Wilkinson County. Established 1803; named in honor of JAMES WILKINSON. Army officer in Revolutionary War; fought against Indians; was representative of U.S. in Louisiana Territory take-over; served there as first governor, 1805–07; led attacks by troops against Canadian border, War of 1812.

Worth County. Established 1853; named in honor of WILLIAM JENKINS WORTH. Much honored military officer who served as commandant at U.S. Military Academy, 1820–28; and following numerous other awards was presented sword by Congress, 1847.

COUNTY SEATS

County	County Seat	Zip Code	County	County Seat	Zip Code
Appling	Baxley	31513	Bulloch	Statesboro	30458
Atkinson	Pearson	31642	Burke	Waynesboro	30830
Bacon	Alma	31510	Butts	Jackson	30233
Baker	Newton	31770	Calhoun	Morgan	31766
Baldwin	Milledgeville	31061	Camden	Woodbine	31569
Banks	Homer	30547			
Barrow	Winder	30680	Candler	Metter	30439
Bartow	Cartersville	30120	Carroll	Carrollton	30117
Ben Hill	Fitzgerald	31750	Catoosa	Ringgold	30736
Berrien	Nashville	31639	Charlton	Folkston	31537
			Chatham	Savannah	31402
Bibb	Macon	31202	Chattahoochee	Cusseta	31805
Bleckley	Cochran	31014	Chattooga	Summerville	30747
Brantley	Nahunta	31553	Cherokee	Canton	30114
Brooks	Quitman	31643	Clarke	Athens	30601
Bryan	Pembroke	31321	Clay	Ft. Gaines	31751

COUNTY SEATS

County	County Seat	Zip Code	County	County Seat	Zip Code
Clayton	Jonesboro	30236	Lanier	Lakeland	31615
Clinch	Homerville	31634	Laurens	Dublin	31021
Cobb	Marietta	30060	Lee	Leesburg	31763
Coffee	Douglas	31533	Liberty	Hinesville	31313
Colquitt	Moultrie	31768	Lincoln	Lincolnton	30817
Columbia	Appling	30802	Long	Ludowici	31316
Cook	Adel	31620	Lowndes	Valdosta	31601
Coweta	Newnan	30263	Lumpkin	Dahlonega	30533
Crawford	Knoxville	31050	Macon	Oglethorpe	31068
Crisp	Cordele	31015	Madison	Danielsville	30633
Dade	Trenton	30752	Marion	Buena Vista	31803
Dawson	Dawsonville	30534	McDuffie	Thomson	30824
Decatur	Bainbridge	31717	McIntosh	Darien	31305
DeKalb	Decatur	30030	Meriwether	Greenville	30222
Dodge	Eastman	31023	Miller	Colquitt	31737
Dooly	Vienna	31092	Mitchell	Camilla	31730
Dougherty	Albany	31701	Monroe	Forsyth	31029
Douglas	Douglasville	30134	Montgomery	Mt. Vernon	30445
Early	Blakely	31723	Morgan	Madison	30650
Echols	Statenville	31648	Murray	Chatsworth	30705
Effingham	Springfield	31329	Muscogee	Columbus	31902
Elbert	Elberton	30635	Newton	Covington	30209
Emanuel	Swainsboro	30401	Oconee	Watkinsville	30677
Evans	Claxton	30417	Oglethorpe	Lexington	30648
Fannin	Blue Ridge	30513	Paulding	Dallas	30132
Fayette	Fayetteville	30214	Peach	Ft. Valley	31030
Floyd	Rome	30161	Pickens	Jasper	30143
Forsyth	Cumming	30130	Pierce	Blackshear	31516
Franklin	Carnesville	30521	Pike	Zebulon	30295
Fulton	Atlanta	30303	Polk	Cedartown	30125
Gilmer	Ellijay	30540	Pulaski	Hawkinsville	31036
Glascock	Gibson	30810	Putnam	Eatonton	31024
Glynn	Brunswick	31520	Quitman	Georgetown	31754
Gordon	Calhoun	30701	Rabun	Clayton	30525
Grady	Cairo	31728	Randolph	Cuthbert	31740
Greene	Greensboro	30642	Richmond	Augusta	30903
Gwinnett	Lawrenceville	30245	Rockdale	Conyers	30207
Habersham	Clarkesville	30523	Schley	Ellaville	31806
Hall	Gainesville	30501	Screven	Sylvania	30467
Hancock	Sparta	31087	Seminole	Donalsonville	31745
Haralson	Buchanan	30113	Spalding	Griffin	30223
Harris	Hamilton	31811	Stephens	Toccoa	30577
Hart	Hartwell	30643	Stewart	Lumpkin	31815
Heard	Franklin	30217	Sumter	Americus	31709
Henry	McDonough	30253	Talbot	Talbotton	31827
Houston	Perry	31069	Taliaferro	Crawfordville	30631
Irwin	Ocilla	31774	Tattnall	Reidsville	30453
Jackson	Jefferson	30549	Taylor	Butler	31006
Jasper	Monticello	31064	Telfair	McRae	31055
Jeff Davis	Hazlehurst	31539	Terrell	Dawson	31742
Jefferson	Louisville	30434	Thomas	Thomasville	31792
Jenkins	Milen	30442	Tift	Tifton	31794
Johnson	Wrightsville	31096	Toombs	Lyon	30436
Jones	Gray	31032	Towns	Hiawassee	30546
Lamar	Barnesville	30204	Treutlen	Soperton	30457

County	County Seat	Zip Code	County	County Seat	Zip Code
Troup	LaGrange	30240	Wayne	Jesup	31545
Turner	Ashburn	31714	Webster	Preston	31824
Twiggs	Jeffersonville	31044	Wheeler	Alamo	30411
Union	Blairsville	30512	White	Cleveland	30528
Upson	Thomaston	30286	Whitfield	Dalton	30720
Walker	Lafayette	30728	Wilcox	Abbeville	31001
Walton	Monroe	30655	Wilkes	Washington	30673
Ware	Waycross	31501	Wilkinson	Irwinton	31042
Warren	Warrenton	30828	Worth	Sylvester	31791
Washington	Sandersville	31082			

COURTS

SUPREME COURT

The court holds three terms of court each year, beginning in September, January and April, and hears no oral arguments in August or December. Court is virtually always held in Atlanta, although the court is authorized to sit and may schedule sessions in other locations such as at an accredited law school in order to demonstrate its procedure to students.

To qualify for office as a justice, a person must be at least 30 years of age, a citizen of the state for three years and a practicing attorney for seven years. Justices are elected to six-years terms in statewide nonpartisan elections. Any vacancies on the court are filled by appointment of the governor.

Supreme Court
244 Washington St., S.W.
Atlanta 30334
404-656-3470

Harold N. Hill, Jr.
Chief Justice
Thomas O. Marshall
Presiding Justice

Harold G. Clarke
George T. Smith
Hardy Gregory, Jr.
Charles L. Weltner
Richard Bell

COURT OF APPEALS

The Court of Appeals is authorized to exercise appellate jurisdiction in all cases where exclusive jurisdiction is not reserved to the Supreme Court or conferred on other courts.

The Court of Appeals consists of nine judges divided into three panels of three judges each. Under the court's rules, the judges elect a chief judge for a term of two years, with an automatic rotation of the office of chief judge based on seniority of service. The chief judge is responsible for the administration of the court and appoints three divisional presiding judges who, along with the chief judge, form the executive council. Any decision rendered by a division is final unless a single judge dissents, whereupon the case is considered by all nine judges. In the instance of an equal division of judges hearing a case in full, the case is transferred to the Supreme Court.

Judges of the Court of Appeals are elected to terms of six years in state-

COURTS

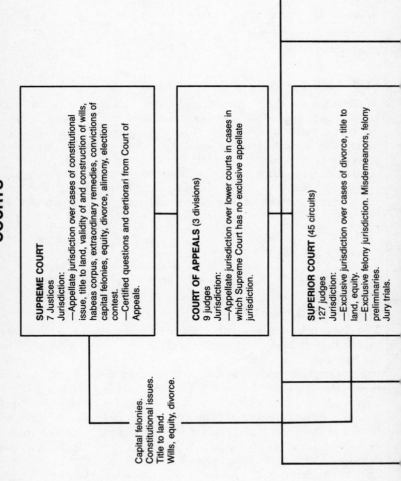

SUPREME COURT
7 Justices
Jurisdiction:
—Appellate jurisdiction over cases of constitutional issue, title to land, validity of and construction of wills, habeas corpus, extraordinary remedies, convictions of capital felonies, equity, divorce, alimony, election contest.
—Certified questions and certiorari from Court of Appeals.

COURT OF APPEALS (3 divisions)
9 judges
Jurisdiction:
—Appellate jurisdiction over lower courts in cases in which Supreme Court has no exclusive appellate jurisdiction.

SUPERIOR COURT (45 circuits)
127 judges
Jurisdiction:
—Exclusive jurisdiction over cases of divorce, title to land, equity.
—Exclusive felony jurisdiction. Misdemeanors, felony preliminaries.
Jury trials.

Capital felonies.
Constitutional issues.
Title to land.
Wills, equity, divorce.

STATE COURT
(63 courts)
79 judges; 31 full-time, 48 part-time.
Jurisdiction:
—Civil law actions except cases within the exclusive jurisdiction of superior court.
—Misdemeanors, felony preliminaries.
Jury trials.

JUVENILE COURT
(159 courts)
51 judges; 10 full-time, 41 part-time (3 state court judges serve as part-time juvenile court judges). Superior court judges serve in counties without independent juvenile courts.
Jurisdiction:
—Deprived, unruly, delinquent juveniles.
No jury trials.

CIVIL COURT
(2 courts)
3 judges
Jurisdiction:
—Issue warrants. Misdemeanor and felony preliminaries.
—Civil tort and contract cases under $7,500 for Bibb County, under $25,000 for Richmond County.
Jury trials.

MUNICIPAL COURT
(1 court)
1 judge
Jurisdiction:
—Civil law and landlord tenant cases (civil) under $7,500.
—Misdemeanor guilty pleas and preliminary hearings. Warrants.
Jury trials in civil cases.

PROBATE COURT
(159 courts)
159 judges
Jurisdiction:
—Exclusive jurisdiction in probate of wills, administration of estates, appointment of guardians, mentally ill, involuntary hospitalizations, marriage licenses.
—Traffic in some counties.
—Truancy in some counties.
—Hold courts of inquiry.
—Issue search warrants and arrest warrants in certain cases.
Jury trials in Clayton County only.

MAGISTRATE COURT
(159 courts)
159 chief magistrates and 265 magistrates; 39 also serve probate, juvenile, civil or municipal courts.
Jurisdiction:
—Issue search and arrest warrants, felony and misdemeanor preliminaries.
—Civil claims of $2,500 or less, dispossessories, distress warrants, county ordinances.
No jury trials.

COUNTY RECORDER'S COURT
(4 courts)
7 judges
Jurisdiction:
—County ordinances, criminal warrants and preliminaries.

MUNICIPAL COURTS
(Approximately 390 courts active)
Jurisdiction:
—Ordinance violations, traffic, criminal preliminaries.
No jury trials.

wide nonpartisan elections. A vacancy in any judgeship is filled by gubernatorial appointment.

The court sits in Atlanta and holds three terms of court per year.

Court of Appeals	Harold T. Banke	Judges:
Judicial Building, 4th floor	Chief Judge	George H. Carley
Atlanta 30334	Presiding Judges:	John W. Sognier
404-656-3450	Braswell D. Deen, Jr.	Marion T. Pope, Jr.
	William LeRoy McMurray, Jr.	Robert Benham
	A.W. Birdsong, Jr.	Dorothy Toth Beasley

SUPERIOR COURTS

Located in each of the state's 159 counties, superior courts are organized by judicial circuits, or groups of counties. There are 45 circuits, which vary in size and population, as well as in the number of judges serving them. From one to eight counties comprise the circuits, with the single-county circuits generally located in or near the several large metropolitan areas of the state. In the 45 circuits, the number of superior court judges per circuit ranges from one judge in each of three circuits (Appalachian, Piedmont, Rockdale) to twelve judges in the Atlanta Judicial Circuit.

For the purpose of administration, the judicial circuits are organized into 10 administrative districts whose boundaries correspond roughly to those of Georgia's U.S. congressional districts. The superior court judges of each district elect one among their number to serve as district administrative judge. The administrative judges are authorized by statute to utilize caseload and other information for management purposes and to assign superior court judges, with their approval, to other counties or circuits as needed.

All superior court judges are elected in nonpartisan elections by voters of each circuit to terms of four years. Certain vacancies and new judgeships may be filled by appointment of the governor.

Below is a list of each county name, superior court circuit, and the telephone number of each superior court judge.

County	Superior Court Circuit	Judge Superior Court Telephone	County	Superior Court Circuit	Judge Superior Court Telephone
Appling	Brunswick	912-367-2155	Bulloch	Ogeechee	912-764-9607
Atkinson	Alapaha	912-686-2180	Burke	Augusta	404-554-2279
Bacon	Waycross	912-384-0587	Butts	Flint	404-358-2300
Baker	South Georgia	912-246-1111	Calhoun	South Georgia	912-246-1111
Baldwin	Ocmulgee	912-453-4270	Camden	Brunswick	912-576-5308
Banks	Piedmont	404-677-4413	Candler	Middle	912-237-4566
Barrow	Piedmont	404-367-8672	Carroll	Coweta	404-832-0525
Bartow	Cherokee	404-386-3714	Catoosa	Lookout Mtn.	404-935-4047
Ben Hill	Cordele	912-423-5120	Charlton	Waycross	912-283-2880
Berrien	Alapaha	912-686-2180	Chatham	Eastern	912-944-4767
Bibb	Macon	912-744-6233	Chattahoochee	Chattahoochee	404-324-7711
Bleckley	Oconee	912-783-1696	Chattooga	Lookout Mtn.	404-857-2017
Brantley	Waycross	912-384-0587	Cherokee	Blue Ridge	404-479-1966
Brooks	Southern	912-985-1598	Clarke	Western	404-354-2767
Bryan	Atlantic	912-653-2027	Clay	Pataula	912-723-3126

County	Superior Court Circuit	Judge Superior Court Telephone	County	Superior Court Circuit	Judge Superior Court Telephone
Clayton	Clayton	404-478-9911	Lanier	Alapaha	912-686-2180
Clinch	Alapaha	912-487-2280	Laurens	Dublin	912-272-4131
Cobb	Cobb	404-429-3164	Lee	Southwestern	912-924-2269
Coffee	Waycross	912-384-0587	Liberty	Atlantic	912-653-2017
Colquitt	Southern	912-985-1598	Lincoln	Toombs	404-595-4437
Columbia	Augusta	404-828-6733			
Cook	Alapaha	912-896-7397	Long	Atlantic	912-653-2027
Coweta	Coweta	404-253-8175	Lowndes	Southern	912-333-5130
Crawford	Macon	912-746-8260	Lumpkin	Northeastern	404-536-6681
Crisp	Cordele	912-273-7950	Macon	Southwestern	912-924-2269
			Madison	Northern	912-283-8363
Dade	Lookout Mtn.	404-657-4778	Marion	Chattahoochee	404-571-4700
Dawson	Northeastern	404-536-6681	McDuffie	Toombs	404-595-3982
Decatur	South Georgia	912-246-1111	McIntosh	Atlantic	912-653-2027
DeKalb	Stone Mtn.	404-371-2226	Meriwether	Coweta	404-672-4416
Dodge	Oconee	912-783-1696	Miller	Pataula	912-758-2177
Dooly	Cordele	912-273-3632			
Dougherty	Dougherty	912-432-6295	Mitchell	South Georgia	912-246-1111
Douglas	Douglas	404-949-2000	Monroe	Flint	912-994-6614
Early	Pataula	912-723-3126	Montgomery	Oconee	912-783-1696
Echols	Southern	912-242-3663	Morgan	Ocmulgee	404-342-0672
			Murray	Conasauga	404-695-4811
Effingham	Ogeechee	912-754-6071	Muscogee	Chattahoochee	404-571-4811
Elbert	Northern	404-283-8363	Newton	Alcovy	404-786-2584
Emanuel	Middle	912-237-4566	Oconee	Western	404-354-2767
Evans	Atlantic	912-653-2029	Oglethorpe	Northern	404-283-8363
Fannin	Appalachian	404-632-2225	Paulding	Tallapoosa	404-445-8871
Fayette	Griffin	404-277-7539			
Floyd	Rome	404-291-5121	Peach	Macon	912-825-8454
Forsyth	Blue Ridge	404-887-8564	Pickens	Appalachian	404-632-2225
Franklin	Northern	404-283-8363	Pierce	Waycross	912-384-0587
Fulton	Atlanta	404-572-2571	Pike	Griffin	404-228-9900
			Polk	Tallapoosa	404-748-2515
Gilmer	Appalachian	404-291-9251	Pulaski	Oconee	912-783-1696
Glascock	Toombs	404-595-4437	Putnam	Ocmulgee	404-485-7530
Glynn	Brunswick	912-265-7335	Quitman	Pataula	912-334-2578
Gordon	Cherokee	404-629-8509	Rabun	Mountain	404-754-6274
Grady	South Georgia	912-377-7349	Randolph	Pataula	912-732-2010
Greene	Ocmulgee	912-453-4270			
Gwinnett	Gwinnett	404-962-1416	Richmond	Augusta	404-821-2357
Habersham	Mountain	404-754-6274	Rockdale	Rockdale	404-922-7750
Hall	Northeastern	404-536-6681	Schley	Southwestern	912-924-2269
Hancock	Ocmulgee	404-444-5746	Screven	Ogeechee	912-564-2091
			Seminole	Pataula	912-723-3126
Haralson	Tallapoosa	404-646-3803	Spalding	Griffin	404-228-9900
Harris	Chattahoochee	404-327-5710	Stephens	Mountain	404-886-7525
Hart	Northern	404-376-7151	Stewart	Southwestern	912-924-2269
Heard	Coweta	404-675-3700	Sumter	Southwestern	912-924-2269
Henry	Flint	404-957-1876	Talbot	Chattahoochee	404-324-7711
Houston	Houston	912-987-2110			
Irwin	Tifton	912-382-1556	Taliaferro	Toombs	404-595-3982
Jackson	Piedmont	404-367-8672	Tattnall	Atlantic	912-557-6393
Jasper	Ocmulgee	912-453-4270	Taylor	Chattahoochee	912-862-5420
Jeff Davis	Brunswick	912-375-3359	Telfair	Oconee	912-783-1696
			Terrell	Pataula	912-723-8232
Jefferson	Middle	912-552-3227	Thomas	Southern	912-226-5112
Jenkins	Ogeechee	912-764-6704	Tift	Tifton	912-382-1556
Johnson	Dublin	912-272-4131	Toombs	Middle	912-552-3227
Jones	Ocmulgee	912-986-6671	Towns	Mountain	404-754-6274
Lamar	Flint	404-358-2300	Treutlen	Dublin	912-272-4131

County	Superior Court Circuit	Judge Superior Court Telephone	County	Superior Court Circuit	Judge Superior Court Telephone
Troup	Coweta	404-884-5226	Wayne	Brunswick	912-427-3761
Turner	Tifton	912-567-2011	Webster	Southwestern	912-924-2269
Twiggs	Dublin	912-272-4131	Wheeler	Oconee	912-783-1696
Union	Mountain	404-754-6274	White	Northeastern	404-865-2613
Upson	Griffin	404-647-3020	Whitfield	Conasauga	404-278-0047
Walker	Lookout Mtn.	404-638-1650	Wilcox	Cordele	912-273-7950
Walton	Alcovy	404-267-4571	Wilkes	Toombs	404-678-1455
Ware	Waycross	912-287-4309	Wilkinson	Ocmulgee	912-453-4270
Warren	Toombs	404-465-3946	Worth	Tifton	912-382-1556
Washington	Middle	912-552-3227			

STATE COURTS

State courts retain jurisdiction over trials of nonfelony (misdemeanor, traffic) criminal cases and exercise civil jurisdiction over all general civil actions regardless of the amount claimed, unless exclusive jurisdiction is vested in the superior court. Uniform state court jurisdiction also includes hearing applications for and issuing search and arrest warrants, holding courts of inquiry and punishing contempts by fine ($500 or less) and/or imprisonment (20 days or less). State courts have also been granted constitutional jurisdiction to review decisions of lower courts as may later be provided by statute.

Like superior court judges, state court judges are selected in nonpartisan elections by voters of the respective counties and serve terms of four years. Vacancies and new judgeships may be filled by appointment of the governor in certain instances.

JUVENILE COURTS

The express purpose of Georgia's juvenile courts, as construed by the state's codified proceedings, is to protect the well-being of children, to provide guidance and control conducive to a child's welfare and the best interests of the state and to secure as nearly as possible care equivalent to parental care for a child removed from the home.

The juvenile court's exclusive original jurisdiction extends to cases involving delinquent children alleged to have committed noncapital offenses and unruly children under the age of 17, deprived children under the age of 18 and juvenile traffic offenders under 16 years of age. In addition, the juvenile court has jurisdiction over custody and child support proceedings referred from the superior court and in cases involving termination of parental rights and enlistment in the military services and consent to marriage for minors. Appeals from the juvenile court in all cases of final judgement are to the Court of Appeals or the Supreme Court.

Juvenile court judges are required by statute to participate in annual training programs sponsored by the Institute of Continuing Judicial Education.

Judges serving separate juvenile courts serve terms of four years. Upon judicial appointment, a person must be over 30 years of age and a citizen of the state for three years, as well as having practiced law for at least three years.

The Council of Juvenile Court Judges is composed of all judges of the courts exercising jurisdiction over juveniles. The membership includes 51 full or part-time juvenile court judges and 58 superior court judges exercising juvenile court jurisdiction. The primary concern of the council is contributing to more effective administration and operation of the state's juvenile courts.

Council of Juvenile Court Judges
244 Washington St., S.W.
Atlanta 30334
404-656-6411

J. Chris Perrin
Executive Director
Mike Sanford
Juvenile Court Specialist

Additional information about Georgia courts can be obtained from:

Judicial Council of Georgia
Administrative Office of the Courts
244 Washington Street, S.W.
Suite 550
Atlanta 30334

Max Cleland
Secretary of State
Elections Division
110 State Capitol
Atlanta 30334

PROBATE COURTS

The probate court exercises exclusive jurisdiction in the probate of wills, the administration of estates, the appointment of guardians and the involuntary hospitalization of incapacitated adults and other dependent individuals. Probate judges are also authorized to perform certain administrative functions such as issuing marriage licenses, pistol permits and delayed birth certificates.

Depending on the particular county, probate judges may be responsible for holding habeas corpus hearings, supervising local elections or presiding over criminal preliminaries. Probate courts may also hear traffic cases and try violations of state game and fish laws, unless there is a demand for a jury trial, in which instance a case would be transferred to the superior court.

One probate judge serves in each of Georgia's 159 counties. Probate judges are elected in partisan elections by the voters of each county to a term of four years. In most counties, a vacancy in office is filled through special election ordered by an official serving as interim judge. In other counties, designated or appointed persons fill the particular vacancy until the next succeeding general election.

Candidates for the office of probate judge must be a county resident for at least two years, have attained the age of 25 and have obtained a high school diploma or its equivalent. In counties with a population of more than 100,000, candidates must be 30 years of age and either a practicing attorney for three years or have served as probate court clerk for at least five years prior to election as judge.

State law requires probate judges to fulfill initial and annual training requirements by attending seminars conducted by the Institute of Continuing Judicial Education and planned together with the Executive Probate Judges Council. The council is a nonfunded state agency charged with the responsibility of advising and coordinating with the Institute concerning matters of continuing education for probate judges.

MAGISTRATE COURTS

The statewide system of magistrate courts replaced justice of the peace, small claims and other existing, similar courts as courts with uniform jurisdiction in 1983.

A chief magistrate and one or more magistrates serve each county. The chief magistrate makes appointments to fill vacancies in the office of magistrate (with concurrence of superior court judges), assigns cases among and decides disputes between other magistrates and sets court sessions as necessary.

Chief magistrates are elected in partisan elections. The term of an appointed magistrate runs concurrently with the four year term of the chief magistrate.

Magistrates are required by law to be residents of the county for one year preceding the beginning of their term of office, to be at least 25 years of age and to have a high school education. Judges of courts replaced by magistrate courts who became magistrates by virtue of a statutory grandfather clause are exempt from these qualifications, but additional qualifications may be imposed for any county through local law. All non-lawyer magistrates are required to successfully complete initial certification courses and annual recertification programs approved by the Georgia Magistrate Courts Training Council and conducted by the Institute of Continuing Judicial Education. Attorney magistrates are exempt from the initial training requirements.

As provided by law, judges of other limited jurisdiction courts may also serve as judge of a magistrate court.

OTHER COURTS

Along with the two appellate and five trial courts, approximately 400 local courts form the Georgia court system. Several special courts and numerous courts serving incorporated municipalities operate under a variety of names with varying jurisdictions.

Originally created by statute or constitutional provision, certain special courts have limited civil and criminal jurisdiction throughout the county. Such courts are the civil courts located in Bibb and Richmond counties and the Municipal Court of Columbus. Special courts authorized to exercise criminal jurisdiction only are the county recorder's courts of Chatham, De-Kalb and Gwinnett counties and the consolidated government of Columbus-Muscogee County.

The 1983 constitution classified existing and future local city, mayor's, municipal, recorder's and police courts under the umbrella term "munici-pal courts" to designate them as a group of courts having jurisdiction over ordinance violations and other matters as may be statutorily provided. (One exception is the City Court of Atlanta which retains its original name.) Numbering approximately 390, active municipal courts try local traffic of-fenses, exercise criminal jurisdiction of magistrate courts and may have concurrent jurisdiction over cases involving one ounce or less of marijuana.

CRIME

Number of crimes reported, 1983.

County	Total	Violent Crimes				Property Crimes			
		Murder	Rape	Robbery	Aggravated Assault	Burglary	Larceny	Motor Vehicle Theft	Arson
Appling	294	0	1	0	22	89	169	13	0
Atkinson	53	0	1	0	4	18	27	3	0
Bacon	149	1	4	5	18	40	76	5	0
Baker	—	—	—	—	—	—	—	—	—
Baldwin	1,658	3	22	26	144	585	803	69	6
Banks	164	0	1	1	8	46	97	9	2
*Barrow	649	3	5	4	36	212	344	39	6
Bartow	1,242	2	12	17	54	316	718	117	6
Ben Hill	663	2	3	10	40	228	352	24	4
Berrien	268	0	4	5	35	72	135	17	0
*Bibb	8,922	20	69	260	498	2,059	5,418	569	29
Bleckley	61	0	0	2	4	26	28	1	0
Brantley	19	0	0	0	7	7	4	1	0
Brooks	236	0	3	0	30	99	97	6	1
Bryan	243	0	2	3	22	60	143	13	0
Bulloch	1,358	0	6	22	72	276	937	41	4
Burke	658	4	5	10	89	221	298	25	6
*Butts	147	0	2	2	2	87	52	2	0
Calhoun	50	0	1	0	17	18	14	0	0
Camden	426	1	3	7	41	137	211	25	1
Candler	28	0	0	0	1	6	19	2	0
Carrroll	2,472	3	17	27	107	714	1,473	119	12
*Catoosa	703	0	2	7	14	237	358	78	7
Charlton	181	0	1	7	19	61	84	8	1
*Chatham	16,207	27	144	556	775	3,868	9,981	753	103
*Chattahoochee	—	—	—	—	—	—	—	—	—
Chattooga	359	0	1	5	13	119	193	25	3
*Cherokee	1,191	0	7	8	42	455	563	108	8

CRIME

County	Total	Violent Crimes				Property Crimes			
		Murder	Rape	Robbery	Aggravated Assault	Burglary	Larceny	Motor Vehicle Theft	Arson
*Clarke	4,953	8	40	76	278	1,263	3,069	202	17
Clay	9	0	0	0	1	2	6	0	0
*Clayton	7,755	3	34	188	187	2,310	4,478	526	29
Clinch	76	0	0	1	1	34	38	2	0
*Cobb	15,279	10	70	241	585	4,119	8,823	1,352	79
Coffee	668	2	2	8	53	192	373	32	6
Colquitt	1,011	1	3	33	37	292	594	39	12
*Columbia	966	1	7	9	42	336	505	56	10
Cook	269	0	1	13	35	83	125	12	0
*Coweta	829	0	1	12	54	283	427	48	4
Crawford	87	0	0	1	6	31	38	9	2
Crisp	1,015	3	7	18	123	319	516	28	1
*Dade	162	1	1	3	7	67	51	32	0
Dawson	96	1	0	1	2	33	53	5	1
Decatur	706	6	3	20	77	198	363	39	1
*DeKalb	25,141	13	161	736	666	6,801	14,625	1,993	146
Dodge	53	0	0	1	0	20	32	0	0
Dooly	—	—	—	—	—	—	—	—	—
*Dougherty	6,122	16	68	173	415	1,850	3,402	183	15
*Douglas	1,859	4	8	22	116	524	998	175	12
Early	259	4	4	3	41	83	116	7	1
Echols	1	0	0	0	0	1	0	0	0
*Effingham	250	0	1	0	12	96	120	17	4
Elbert	308	0	1	6	31	106	151	9	4
Emanuel	240	1	0	4	23	76	127	8	1
Evans	21	0	0	0	2	8	10	1	0
Fannin	177	1	0	2	6	75	72	15	6
*Fayette	736	0	1	7	18	219	451	34	6
Floyd	2,845	4	9	43	130	835	1,615	189	20
*Forsyth	836	0	1	3	25	217	520	65	5
Franklin	220	1	7	7	11	74	99	18	3
*Fulton	66,572	167	811	4,311	5,811	17,464	33,141	4,815	52
Gilmer	119	1	0	0	2	46	58	8	4
Glascock	—	—	—	—	—	—	—	—	—
Glynn	4,582	8	58	118	427	1,266	2,514	179	12
Gordon	1,078	3	5	11	29	285	668	74	3
Grady	181	0	1	9	6	79	76	10	0
Greene	326	0	3	10	41	142	121	8	1
*Gwinnett	7,437	4	35	85	372	2,179	4,127	602	33
Habersham	64	0	2	0	1	19	37	4	1
Hall	3,038	4	16	35	166	808	1,772	215	22
Hancock	—	—	—	—	—	—	—	—	—
Haralson	469	0	1	6	29	154	248	30	1
Harris	303	0	2	4	26	141	110	17	3
Hart	138	0	0	0	3	50	74	11	0
Heard	44	0	0	0	0	26	15	2	1
*Henry	1,044	1	12	23	54	309	560	79	6
*Houston	2,408	2	17	33	92	741	1,413	100	10
Irwin	138	0	2	3	9	57	62	5	0
*Jackson	554	0	7	7	23	202	270	34	11
Jasper	72	1	0	1	1	40	28	1	0
Jeff Davis	163	0	0	4	14	41	95	7	2
Jefferson	280	1	5	1	38	94	126	10	5

106

County	Total	Violent Crimes				Property Crimes			
		Murder	Rape	Robbery	Aggravated Assault	Burglary	Larceny	Motor Vehicle Theft	Arson
Jenkins	147	1	1	2	13	53	71	3	3
Johnson	1	0	0	0	1	0	0	0	0
*Jones	244	1	2	1	6	122	101	9	2
Lamar	269	0	5	7	26	58	159	10	4
Lanier	165	1	1	2	18	52	83	7	1
Laurens	1,237	2	10	16	101	378	696	33	1
*Lee	140	0	0	0	3	52	78	7	0
Liberty	1,357	2	19	34	93	441	689	74	5
Lincoln	90	0	0	0	3	49	36	2	0
Long	—	—	—	—	—	—	—	—	—
Lowndes	3,861	7	26	33	39	1,277	2,306	154	19
Lumpkin	208	1	0	1	16	57	123	6	4
Macon	275	1	0	2	19	101	148	4	0
*Madison	194	0	1	0	14	88	78	12	1
Marion	3	0	0	0	2	1	0	0	0
*McDuffie	101	0	0	2	9	42	42	6	0
McIntosh	207	0	0	4	10	84	99	10	0
Meriwether	333	2	5	5	34	134	132	19	2
Miller	40	0	0	1	4	11	21	1	2
Mitchell	598	0	3	9	61	145	355	23	2
Monroe	504	0	12	10	72	135	244	28	3
Montgomery	—	—	—	—	—	—	—	—	—
Morgan	124	0	1	2	5	64	49	3	0
Murray	300	0	3	2	14	95	144	41	1
*Muscogee	6,940	10	59	248	332	1,969	3,834	440	48
*Newton	1,201	4	7	18	79	339	707	44	3
*Oconee	8	0	0	0	1	3	4	0	0
Oglethorpe	73	0	0	1	4	33	33	2	0
*Paulding	505	1	2	3	15	192	254	34	4
*Peach	282	0	1	5	18	75	164	19	0
Pickens	92	0	0	1	5	26	46	12	2
Pierce	49	0	3	0	7	9	27	3	0
Pike	60	0	0	0	2	20	34	4	0
Polk	589	1	3	8	67	177	283	44	6
Pulaski	260	3	1	4	21	85	138	8	0
Putnam	199	0	0	0	12	94	85	6	2
Quitman	3	1	0	0	0	1	1	0	0
Rabun	116	0	0	0	2	56	52	6	0
Randolph	103	0	0	1	15	31	54	2	0
*Richmond	8,939	18	95	332	340	2,886	4,753	484	31
*Rockdale	1,341	2	9	10	83	318	825	90	4
Schley	8	0	0	0	0	7	1	0	0
Screven	140	1	1	1	8	51	74	4	0
Seminole	217	2	2	3	26	64	108	12	0
*Spalding	2,628	5	32	71	220	628	1,531	125	16
Stephens	613	3	4	9	24	231	316	24	2
Stewart	19	0	0	1	1	8	9	0	0
Sumter	1,126	2	11	18	123	278	658	26	10
Talbot	—	—	—	—	—	—	—	—	—
Taliaferro	—	—	—	—	—	—	—	—	—
Tattnall	89	0	0	2	1	38	43	5	0
Taylor	77	0	1	2	12	24	34	4	0
Telfair	65	0	0	0	1	41	21	2	0

County	Total	Violent Crimes				Property Crimes			
		Murder	Rape	Robbery	Aggravated Assault	Burglary	Larceny	Motor Vehicle Theft	Arson
Terrell	244	0	3	4	18	83	121	11	4
Thomas	1,131	3	6	32	84	268	688	42	8
Tift	1,650	4	17	45	179	402	923	75	5
Toombs	293	3	3	9	27	90	135	19	7
Towns	—	—	—	—	—	—	—	—	—
Treutlen	1	0	0	0	0	1	0	0	0
Troup	2,186	7	10	23	252	337	1,487	62	8
Turner	162	0	0	0	21	54	82	5	0
Twiggs	—	—	—	—	—	—	—	—	—
Union	16	2	0	0	1	2	9	2	0
Upson	405	1	2	3	40	149	193	17	0
*Walker	1,297	3	5	18	34	467	698	66	6
*Walton	824	0	2	10	37	290	462	20	3
Ware	1,398	1	7	27	68	393	830	58	14
Warren	—	—	—	—	—	—	—	—	—
Washington	561	1	6	20	59	179	252	38	6
Wayne	315	1	3	4	22	99	177	7	2
Webster	1	0	0	1	0	0	0	0	0
Wheeler	9	1	0	0	2	4	2	0	0
White	142	0	0	0	1	49	82	10	0
Whitfield	2,152	4	13	42	82	532	1,289	182	8
Wilcox	—	—	—	—	—	—	—	—	—
Wilkes	215	0	0	3	21	82	94	13	2
Wilkinson	—	—	—	—	—	—	—	—	—
Worth	372	0	3	4	12	139	196	14	4
State Agency	1,290	21	65	98	120	591	273	82	40
Georgia	251,164	460	2,188	8,489	15,305	70,080	137,642	15,954	1,046

*Metropolitan County
—Indicates counties not submitting to the Georgia Crime Information Center during the reporting period
NOTE: These figures solely reflect reports of incidence of crime by law enforcement agencies in each county to the Georgia Crime Information Center.

STATE PRISON INMATES' HOME COUNTY

	Males By Age, 1984					Female Total	1984 Male and Female Total
	Under 21	22–39	40–54	55–99	Total		
Appling	2	15	1	0	18	1	19
Atkinson	2	13	2	0	17	1	18
Bacon	0	16	1	0	17	0	17
Baker	1	6	0	0	7	0	7
Baldwin	11	53	10	1	75	3	78
Banks	3	10	1	0	14	0	14
*Barrow	9	30	9	0	48	6	54
Bartow	24	64	7	1	96	3	99
Ben Hill	12	39	5	1	57	4	61
Berrien	6	15	4	0	25	0	25
*Bibb	77	357	41	17	492	25	517
Bleckley	2	15	5	0	22	0	22
Brantley	0	7	0	0	7	0	7

	Males By Age, 1984					Female	1984 Male and Female
	Under 21	22–39	40–54	55–99	Total	Total	Total
Brooks	11	28	2	4	45	1	46
Bryan	7	5	2	2	16	1	17
Bulloch	4	45	5	2	56	2	58
Burke	9	33	7	0	49	3	52
*Butts	7	18	3	0	28	1	29
Calhoun	3	11	3	1	18	0	18
Camden	5	11	0	0	16	0	16
Candler	4	17	0	1	22	1	23
Carroll	19	66	12	5	102	5	107
*Catoosa	4	22	3	0	29	0	29
Charlton	2	6	2	0	10	1	11
*Chatham	74	370	45	4	493	13	506
*Chattahoochee	0	1	0	0	1	0	1
Chattooga	7	31	2	1	41	1	42
*Cherokee	10	47	10	0	67	2	69
*Clarke	35	172	19	2	228	10	238
Clay	1	4	0	0	5	0	5
*Clayton	35	203	28	8	274	12	286
Clinch	3	13	2	0	18	0	18
*Cobb	55	245	55	8	363	25	388
Coffee	4	31	4	0	39	1	40
Colquitt	21	60	8	4	93	1	94
*Columbia	4	19	1	0	24	2	26
Cook	9	17	3	3	32	1	33
*Coweta	12	76	4	3	95	4	99
Crawford	0	9	0	1	10	0	10
Crisp	6	40	3	1	50	2	52
*Dade	4	6	1	3	14	0	14
Dawson	1	10	0	0	11	1	12
Decatur	10	54	7	5	76	4	80
*DeKalb	102	472	76	9	659	37	696
Dodge	5	16	5	2	28	2	30
Dooly	4	18	0	1	23	1	24
*Dougherty	60	239	21	4	324	21	345
*Douglas	15	59	17	0	91	3	94
Early	5	24	4	1	34	2	36
Echols	0	2	3	0	5	0	5
*Effingham	4	15	0	0	19	2	21
Elbert	6	32	7	0	45	2	47
Emanuel	2	28	1	0	31	2	33
Evans	2	9	0	1	12	0	12
Fannin	1	11	4	1	17	1	18
*Fayette	4	10	2	0	16	1	17
Floyd	33	130	25	4	192	11	203
*Forsyth	4	43	12	2	61	3	64
Franklin	5	21	7	1	34	1	35
*Fulton	316	2,019	332	77	2,744	197	2,941
Gilmer	1	9	1	0	11	1	12
Glascock	1	0	0	0	1	0	1
Glynn	28	113	14	6	161	3	164
Gordon	7	39	12	3	61	1	62
Grady	13	36	6	3	58	5	63
Greene	4	26	2	0	32	2	34
*Gwinnett	32	163	27	6	228	6	234

	Males By Age, 1984					Female Total	1984 Male and Female Total
	Under 21	22–39	40–54	55–99	Total		
Habersham	8	28	2	1	39	2	41
Hall	23	140	28	2	193	13	206
Hancock	1	11	0	0	12	0	12
Haralson	3	15	10	1	29	0	29
Harris	2	9	3	2	16	1	17
Hart	1	18	4	3	26	0	26
Heard	2	4	1	1	8	0	8
*Henry	10	39	8	4	61	4	65
*Houston	20	71	11	1	103	4	107
Irwin	7	15	1	0	23	1	24
*Jackson	7	43	7	3	60	4	64
Jasper	1	12	3	0	16	0	16
Jeff Davis	3	5	0	1	9	0	9
Jefferson	5	14	5	2	26	3	29
Jenkins	2	14	5	0	21	0	21
Johnson	2	8	2	0	12	1	13
*Jones	1	12	2	0	15	1	16
Lamar	4	6	2	0	12	1	13
Lanier	4	9	1	1	15	1	16
Laurens	8	33	7	3	51	5	56
*Lee	3	11	1	0	15	1	16
Liberty	8	32	3	1	44	6	50
Lincoln	0	11	0	0	11	1	12
Long	0	11	3	0	14	1	15
Lowndes	22	104	14	3	143	9	152
Lumpkin	1	7	1	2	11	0	11
Macon	3	17	0	0	20	1	21
*Madison	7	31	3	2	43	1	44
Marion	1	8	0	0	9	0	9
*McDuffie	6	29	6	3	44	1	45
McIntosh	1	9	1	0	11	0	11
Meriwether	7	30	9	0	46	3	49
Miller	1	9	1	0	11	2	13
Mitchell	10	54	8	1	73	4	77
Monroe	7	20	1	0	28	2	30
Montgomery	1	10	0	0	11	1	12
Morgan	5	12	3	0	20	1	21
Murray	2	16	7	0	25	3	28
*Muscogee	70	420	40	12	542	25	567
*Newton	16	81	8	1	106	2	108
*Oconee	1	13	1	0	15	0	15
Oglethorpe	1	6	1	0	8	1	9
*Paulding	3	20	7	2	32	2	34
*Peach	5	35	6	1	47	0	47
Pickens	1	13	3	1	18	3	21
Pierce	3	22	0	0	25	1	26
Pike	0	1	3	1	5	1	6
Polk	6	33	6	2	47	1	48
Pulaski	0	17	1	1	19	0	19
Putnam	6	27	2	4	39	2	41
Quitman	1	2	0	0	3	0	3
Rabun	2	7	2	1	12	1	13
Randolph	5	13	2	2	22	3	25

	Males By Age, 1984					Female Total	1984 Male and Female Total
	Under 21	22–39	40–54	55–99	Total		
*Richmond	50	347	46	11	454	31	485
*Rockdale	9	40	5	1	55	1	56
Schley	0	4	0	0	4	1	5
Screven	1	15	3	2	21	0	21
Seminole	3	6	3	0	12	0	12
Spalding	24	91	12	3	130	10	140
Stephens	8	25	5	0	38	3	41
Stewart	1	8	0	0	9	0	9
Sumter	12	54	3	2	71	5	76
Talbot	1	6	3	0	10	0	10
Taliaferro	0	1	0	0	1	0	1
Tattnall	3	31	2	1	37	1	38
Taylor	2	16	0	1	19	0	19
Telfair	4	15	3	1	23	0	23
Terrell	4	18	1	1	24	0	24
Thomas	20	76	10	6	112	7	119
Tift	14	69	10	6	99	5	104
Toombs	15	30	9	1	55	1	56
Towns	0	3	1	0	4	0	4
Treutlen	0	9	1	2	12	0	12
Troup	19	77	28	5	129	10	139
Turner	1	11	0	0	12	0	12
Twiggs	0	10	0	0	10	0	10
Union	1	10	2	0	13	0	13
Upson	11	52	11	3	77	2	79
*Walker	13	43	6	1	63	2	65
*Walton	16	63	15	1	95	6	101
Ware	17	69	5	3	94	0	94
Warren	4	15	2	1	22	1	23
Washington	10	35	5	2	52	1	53
Wayne	7	29	4	1	41	2	43
Webster	0	0	0	0	0	0	0
Wheeler	2	5	2	0	9	0	9
White	1	3	0	0	4	0	4
Whitfield	20	125	26	3	174	9	183
Wilcox	8	11	4	1	24	2	26
Wilkes	2	22	4	0	28	1	29
Wilkinson	0	15	2	0	17	0	17
Worth	5	16	2	0	23	1	24
Out of State	77	718	149	30	974	42	1,016
Home County Not Reported	328	988	177	51	1,544	58	1,602
Georgia	2,201	10,662	1,701	404	14,968	763	15,731

*Metropolitan County

NOTE: Data excludes those incarcerated in a county jail awaiting transfer to a state prison

CYCLORAMA

The most moving and impressive memorial of the battle which sealed the fate of the Confederacy is the Cyclorama of the Battle of Atlanta which occurred on July 22, 1864. It is more than a painting; it is a three-dimensional panorama with narration, music and sound effects.

Measuring 50 feet in height, 400 feet in circumference, and weighing over 18,000 pounds, it was painted in 1885-6 by a group of German and Polish artists brought to America for this purpose by Mr. William Wehner, owner of the Milwaukee studio where it was set up and completed. First exhibited in Detroit in 1887, the painting traveled all over the United States before coming to its final resting place in the city whose destruction it commemorates. After several changes in ownership and many locations, the painting was brought to Atlanta in 1891 and exhibited in a building on the north side of Edgewood Avenue, near Piedmont Avenue. It was bought at auction in 1893 by Mr. George V. Gress, an Atlanta citizen, who presented it to the City of Atlanta in 1898. In 1921 the painting was transferred from an old, wooden structure at a location in Grant Park to its present location in the imposing marble building on a hillsite in the central part of the park. In 1936, by means of a WPA grant, the painting was made three-dimensional by the addition of blasted tree stumps, bushes and shrubbery that are shell-torn in effect, broken rails and cross-ties, life-like plaster figures of Confederate and Federal soldiers, and other fragments of war which form the battlefield surrounding the canvas. In viewing the painting it is difficult to determine the ending of the real and the beginning of the illusion. The special light and sound effects give the painting a realism which is startling.

The facility was re-opened in 1982 after 2 years extensive conservation of the painting/diorama and renovation of the building, which now includes a revolving seating platform.

> Grant Park, in southeast Atlanta
> 800 Cherokee Ave. S.E.
> Atlanta, Georgia 30315
> 404-624-1071

ECONOMICS

The component of greatest importance in today's economy in Georgia is manufacturing, being the leading source of jobs.

The state's labor force is broken down approximately in the following order from the greatest to the least: manufacturing industries; wholesale and retail trade; government, at federal, state, and local levels; agriculture; lumbering; mining; fishing.

An important sector of the state economy is finance, as evidenced by the mass of corporate headquarters in Atlanta. The Southeast's center for communications and transportation is Atlanta, which is also the chief distributor of goods for the area.

More than $2 billion per year is amassed from tourism in Georgia, with its urban convention centers and coastal resorts as the primary sources.

Charts reflecting business activity, economic rank, and personal income follow.

BUSINESS ACTIVITY: 1981-1982

	No. of Establishments[1]		Percent Change 1981-1982	No. of Employees[2]		Percent Change 1981-1982
	1981	1982		1981	1982	
Appling	260	261	0.4	3,516	3,652	3.9
Atkinson	77	74	—3.9	685	815	19.0
Bacon	174	175	0.6	1,917	2,364	23.3
Baker	20	24	20.0	304	343	12.8
Baldwin	544	530	—2.6	8,522	8,611	1.0
Banks	44	67	52.3	891	1,121	25.8
Barrow	335	338	0.9	6,412	6,072	—5.3
Bartow	674	676	0.3	13,501	12,948	—4.1
Ben Hill	317	307	—3.2	4,303	4,222	—1.9
Berrien	196	196	0.0	3,161	3,196	1.1
Bibb	3,391	3,395	0.1	52,161	54,024	3.6
Bleckley	174	159	—8.6	1,972	1,839	—6.7
Brantley	80	78	—2.5	500	499	—0.2
Brooks	182	178	—2.2	1,554	1,627	4.7
Bryan	112	100	—10.7	960	857	—10.7
Bulloch	685	674	—1.6	8,402	8,489	1.0
Burke	246	243	—1.2	4,368	4,132	—5.4
Butts	207	208	0.5	2,137	2,041	—4.5
Calhoun	97	91	—6.2	599	744	24.2
Camden	222	230	3.6	3,675	3,843	4.6
Candler	154	150	—2.6	1,393	1,370	—1.7
Carroll	930	948	1.9	16,261	16,713	2.8
Catoosa	333	339	1.8	5,168	5,244	1.5
Charlton	113	107	—5.3	1,082	1,059	—2.1
Chatham	4,488	4,500	0.3	68,475	69,636	1.7
Chattahoochee	64	34	—46.9	528	388	—26.5
Chattooga	256	227	—11.3	6,478	5,946	—8.2
Cherokee	551	636	15.4	6,254	6,093	—2.6
Clarke	1,783	1,787	0.2	29,638	28,965	—2.3
Clay	45	47	4.4	415	421	1.4
Clayton	2,464	2,495	1.3	46,147	36,881	—20.1
Clinch	119	114	—4.2	1,729	1,402	—18.9
Cobb	6,078	6,524	7.3	91,017	95,363	4.8
Coffee	485	498	2.7	6,107	6,029	—1.3
Colquitt	647	672	3.9	8,102	7,477	—7.7
Columbia	433	486	12.2	4,762	5,556	16.7
Cook	221	228	3.2	2,606	2,612	0.2
Coweta	581	602	3.6	10,724	10,720	—0.0
Crawford	52	57	9.6	433	352	—18.7
Crisp	436	435	—0.2	5,739	5,766	0.5
Dade	96	91	—5.2	1,460	1,337	—8.4
Dawson	57	54	—5.3	599	415	—30.7
Decatur	467	464	—0.6	7,181	7,339	2.2

113

	No. of Establishments[1]		Percent Change	No. of Employees[2]		Percent Change
	1981	1982	1981–1982	1981	1982	1981–1982
DeKalb	11,577	12,027	3.9	209,722	210,320	0.3
Dodge	372	311	—16.4	4,144	3,386	—18.3
Dooly	159	152	—4.4	1,838	1,647	—10.4
Dougherty	2,129	2,149	0.9	34,455	34,774	0.9
Douglas	700	741	5.9	7,160	7,488	4.6
Early	202	201	—0.5	3,608	3,278	—9.1
Echols	9	5	—44.4	84	58	—31.0
Effingham	158	152	—3.8	1,070	1,029	—3.8
Elbert	415	402	—3.1	5,984	5,823	—2.7
Emanuel	342	347	1.5	4,880	4,832	—1.0
Evans	183	182	—0.5	2,307	2,228	—3.4
Fannin	180	198	10.0	1,615	1,728	7.0
Fayette	398	498	25.1	4,755	4,559	—4.1
Floyd	1,445	1,444	—0.1	27,670	26,243	—5.2
Forsyth	368	420	14.1	3,791	4,400	16.1
Franklin	250	243	—2.8	3,081	3,063	—0.6
Fulton	18,310	18,104	—1.1	394,565	393,334	—0.3
Gilmer	168	172	2.4	2,724	2,358	—13.4
Glascock	23	22	—4.3	358	306	—14.5
Glynn	1,381	1,419	2.8	20,268	19,441	—4.1
Gordon	521	523	0.4	10,114	9,541	—5.7
Grady	280	294	5.0	3,605	3,783	4.9
Greene	177	162	—8.5	2,715	2,695	—0.7
Gwinnett	3,008	3,732	24.1	43,052	58,351	35.5
Habersham	461	432	—6.3	7,720	7,029	—9.0
Hall	1,568	1,596	1.8	26,741	27,129	1.5
Hancock	106	90	—15.1	931	902	—3.1
Haralson	259	273	5.4	7,015	7,126	1.6
Harris	170	147	—13.5	2,144	1,713	—20.1
Hart	218	228	4.6	4,340	4,553	4.9
Heard	38	44	15.8	808	720	—10.9
Henry	444	441	—0.7	5,012	4,522	—9.8
Houston	1,071	1,080	0.8	12,526	12,985	3.7
Irwin	124	122	—1.6	1,003	1,024	2.1
Jackson	350	339	—3.1	5,319	4,986	—6.3
Jasper	96	100	4.2	1,310	1,395	6.5
Jeff Davis	230	238	3.5	4,537	4,037	—11.0
Jefferson	245	245	0.0	3,299	3,905	18.4
Jenkins	129	135	4.7	1,615	1,466	—9.2
Johnson	112	106	—5.4	1,801	1,655	—8.1
Jones	159	127	—20.1	1,236	1,029	—16.7
Lamar	142	149	4.9	2,714	2,438	—10.2
Lanier	81	79	—2.5	540	555	2.8
Laurens	718	733	2.1	10,571	10,912	3.2
Lee	64	46	—28.1	660	557	—15.6
Liberty	329	350	6.4	3,246	3,603	11.0
Lincoln	97	80	—17.5	1,159	848	—26.8
Long	29	31	6.9	195	230	17.9

	No. of Establishments[1]		Percent Change	No. of Employees[2]		Percent Change
	1981	1982	1981–1982	1981	1982	1981–1982
Lowndes	1,535	1,536	0.1	20,157	18,675	—7.4
Lumpkin	114	129	13.2	1,426	1,367	—4.1
Macon	177	185	4.5	3,677	3,385	—7.9
Madison	159	149	—6.3	1,393	1,444	3.7
Marion	58	59	1.7	739	697	—5.7
McDuffie	328	357	8.8	5,201	4,536	—12.8
McIntoch	85	82	—3.5	1,092	959	—12.2
Meriwether	247	244	—1.2	5,971	4,838	—19.0
Miller	104	103	—1.0	752	700	—6.9
Mitchell	348	334	—4.0	4,067	4,102	0.9
Monroe	204	205	0.5	4,865	4,200	—13.7
Montgomery	131	118	—9.9	1,641	1,583	—3.5
Morgan	194	180	—7.2	2,736	2,734	—0.1
Murray	292	279	—4.5	5,547	5,033	—9.3
Muscogee	3,314	3,312	—0.1	55,982	55,828	—0.3
Newton	466	456	—2.1	6,682	6,468	—3.2
Oconee	128	139	8.6	973	1,072	10.2
Oglethorpe	70	77	10.0	426	515	20.9
Paulding	228	230	0.9	1,989	1,936	—2.7
Peach	299	272	—9.0	4,135	3,992	—3.5
Pickens	170	176	3.5	2,625	2,779	5.9
Pierce	202	202	0.0	1,708	1,780	4.2
Pike	66	62	—6.1	643	598	—7.0
Polk	465	451	—3.0	8,240	7,946	—3.6
Pulaski	180	167	—7.2	1,734	1,721	—0.7
Putnam	146	139	—4.8	2,236	2,172	—2.9
Quitman	26	25	—3.8	117	106	—9.4
Rabun	194	225	16.0	2,841	2,922	2.9
Randolph	168	158	—6.0	1,533	1,412	—7.9
Richmond	3,486	3,455	—0.9	53,254	52,003	—2.3
Rockdale	592	683	15.4	8,893	9,909	11.4
Schley	57	54	—5.3	659	635	—3.6
Screven	201	200	—0.5	3,217	2,988	—7.1
Seminole	189	180	—4.8	1,466	1,391	—5.1
Spalding	853	836	—2.0	14,142	13,610	—3.8
Stephens	411	425	3.4	7,953	7,262	—8.7
Stewart	94	95	1.1	776	742	—4.4
Sumter	582	569	—2.2	8,516	8,015	—5.9
Talbot	59	58	—1.7	441	455	3.2
Taliaferro	25	24	—4.0	164	186	13.4
Tattnall	253	254	0.4	2,688	2,752	2.4
Taylor	126	124	—1.6	1,175	1,207	2.7
Telfair	201	200	—0.5	2,516	3,073	22.1
Terrell	172	174	1.2	1,982	2,277	14.9
Thomas	798	770	—3.5	11,573	11,133	—3.8
Tift	706	700	—0.8	9,616	9,399	—2.3
Toombs	457	444	—2.8	6,270	6,076	—3.1
Towns	86	86	0.0	631	549	—13.0
Treutlen	71	73	2.8	733	737	0.5

	No. of Establishments[1]		Percent Change	No. of Employees[2]		Percent Change
	1981	1982	1981–1982	1981	1982	1981–1982
Troup	970	973	0.3	18,023	18,799	4.3
Turner	170	164	—3.5	2,135	1,876	—12.1
Twiggs	59	60	1.7	987	1,305	32.2
Union	122	112	—8.2	1,326	1,153	—13.0
Upson	398	409	2.8	8,841	8,159	—7.7
Walker	625	657	5.1	9,743	9,536	—2.1
Walton	434	422	—2.8	6,631	6,180	—6.8
Ware	828	798	—3.6	9,196	8,956	—2.6
Warren	68	69	1.5	978	1,242	27.0
Washington	315	303	—3.8	4,694	4,470	—4.8
Wayne	379	393	3.7	5,488	5,567	1.4
Webster	29	28	—3.4	246	236	—4.1
Wheeler	55	52	—5.5	436	530	21.6
White	186	202	8.6	2,111	2,126	0.7
Whitfield	1,609	1,584	—1.6	32,100	29,459	—8.2
Wilcox	93	90	—3.2	635	768	20.9
Wilkes	240	229	—4.6	3,539	3,031	—14.4
Wilkinson	131	131	0.0	2,725	2,599	—4.6
Worth	211	224	6.2	2,484	2,467	—0.7
Statewide	103	35	—66.0	1,069	1,230	15.1
Georgia	105,427	107,000	1.2	1,743,025	1,738,095	1.4

[1] An establishment is a single physical location where business is conducted or where services or industrial operations are performed.

[2] Employment is the count of employees during the pay period that includes March 12, as reported on Internal Revenue Service Form 941, or as corrected by estimates in those cases where it was incompletely or improperly reported.

ECONOMIC RANK: 1982, 1983

County	Master[1] Economic Rank	1983[2] Taxable Sales × $1,000	1982[3] Adjusted Gross Income × $1,000	1983 Net Property & Utility Digest × $1,000	1983 Mileage Rates
Appling	64	73,501	69,014	432,071	15.51
Atkinson	145	19,547	21,953	48,605	23.03
Bacon	109	66,676	36,240	80,355	16.31
Baker	148	8,220	12,033	74,348	12.86
Baldwin	39	194,353	198,857	201,639	24.15
Banks	118	24,240	30,749	84,258	12.79
Barrow	51	116,297	127,214	170,979	21.60
Bartow	23	254,844	250,340	523,810	24.29
Ben Hill	77	84,437	76,014	122,953	18.07
Berrien	91	54,925	58,727	112,201	17.05
Bibb	8	1,379,552	1,017,083	1,112,682	32.49
Bleckley	114	38,813	53,868	65,051	24.47
Brantley	123	21,221	34,544	85,421	20.08
Brooks	94	44,704	44,822	160,636	15.45

County	Master[1] Economic Rank	1983[2] Taxable Sales × $1,000	1982[3] Adjusted Gross Income × $1,000	1983 Net Property & Utility Digest × $1,000	1983 Mileage Rates
Bryan	105	55,874	52,985	76,512	19.32
Bulloch	35	197,745	170,993	303,508	12.99
Burke	55	72,060	86,452	642,603	9.58
Butts	86	81,436	65,587	84,035	28.26
Calhoun	138	16,686	24,188	83,823	15.40
Camden	72	60,053	78,139	201,178	21.25
Candler	126	46,690	29,463	65,963	14.73
Carroll	21	342,462	337,907	309,633	24.00
Catoosa	38	152,750	171,724	238,468	16.53
Charlton	130	26,447	26,411	91,676	23.26
Chatham	4	1,849,243	1,302,389	1,758,067	26.20
Chattahoochee	154	11,606	10,319	13,437	11.28
Chattooga	57	85,555	100,543	146,501	25.24
Cherokee	19	192,577	370,504	454,110	24.56
Clarke	15	690,195	438,480	656,657	31.82
Clay	152	13,918	10,744	31,374	15.19
Clayton	7	958,111	1,168,686	1,752,584	32.96
Clinch	135	26,422	25,227	74,876	25.44
Cobb	3	2,769,830	3,021,865	3,734,803	25.00
Coffee	46	147,223	112,276	212,599	19.93
Colquitt	36	206,378	164,352	301,326	13.69
Columbia	34	92,299	277,231	343,753	22.62
Cook	96	57,059	52,681	108,286	18.61
Coweta	25	230,415	267,933	437,641	19.15
Crawford	137	13,008	30,242	56,329	24.05
Crisp	56	174,018	88,102	179,461	16.62
Dade	112	41,024	43,079	73,631	21.22
Dawson	121	17,928	30,796	76,879	20.52
Decatur	48	116,685	98,982	263,990	11.64
DeKalb	2	5,139,863	4,018,820	5,080,876	31.00
Dodge	92	64,296	74,763	81,774	27.31
Dooly	103	51,073	42,039	129,726	13.58
Dougherty	10	839,098	618,462	814,122	19.31
Douglas	18	281,655	402,666	433,262	33.72
Early	85	52,833	51,454	219,535	10.63
Echols	158	1,023	6,124	42,796	17.26
Effingham	73	41,088	103,747	170,694	22.67
Elbert	60	107,803	90,188	140,272	25.29
Emanuel	66	86,962	84,086	165,209	24.41
Evans	113	58,750	39,914	66,081	16.03
Fannin	84	68,273	59,165	94,929	20.68
Fayette	30	100,235	318,789	373,687	23.91
Floyd	12	571,880	491,180	706,335	26.80
Forsyth	33	150,640	192,529	324,469	28.89
Franklin	76	82,196	73,969	101,699	21.28
Fulton	1	8,179,127	5,246,214	7,783,203	30.62

County	Master[1] Economic Rank	1983[2] Taxable Sales × $1,000	1982[3] Adjusted Gross Income × $1,000	1983 Net Property & Utility Digest × $1,000	1983 Mileage Rates
Gilmer	99	66,796	50,606	85,376	21.85
Glascock	157	2,482	10,727	23,523	17.68
Glynn	16	577,263	377,173	758,569	21.64
Gordon	41	135,475	171,127	248,653	25.47
Grady	67	85,543	76,593	173,063	18.05
Greene	101	53,637	49,401	98,768	19.78
Gwinnett	5	1,253,512	1,765,926	2,345,458	25.25
Habersham	47	149,767	133,923	178,262	21.74
Hall	11	619,511	519,865	790,346	19.02
Hancock	131	18,143	29,224	95,019	28.18
Haralson	63	70,678	102,107	152,008	36.45
Harris	75	55,602	81,172	158,824	16.80
Hart	68	80,528	80,861	143,508	22.34
Heard	119	12,346	27,341	186,627	13.62
Henry	28	153,728	274,976	333,753	34.34
Houston	14	395,104	534,841	549,298	25.06
Irwin	122	27,622	33,112	89,035	15.38
Jackson	45	147,469	128,511	189,438	23.32
Jasper	124	19,075	36,688	77,510	23.66
Jeff Davis	95	54,875	54,854	125,491	11.93
Jefferson	74	84,216	76,566	134,171	16.52
Jenkins	125	31,204	32,104	71,864	21.25
Johnson	133	25,720	33,643	49,257	20.60
Jones	78	44,928	87,605	129,872	15.60
Lamar	98	49,286	57,218	98,836	21.71
Lanier	149	17,327	18,544	35,491	18.15
Laurens	29	239,798	194,388	318,656	19.20
Lee	100	20,589	66,311	134,938	18.22
Liberty	54	121,710	91,196	173,519	16.85
Lincoln	140	15,464	28,187	50,460	19.24
Long	151	5,440	15,525	53,969	21.26
Lowndes	17	532,230	339,612	539,461	21.67
Lumpkin	102	39,817	48,454	104,253	19.38
Macon	83	54,682	53,015	202,364	14.20
Madison	81	25,642	91,512	130,870	19.94
Marion	147	14,278	19,435	51,474	16.82
McDuffie	69	82,754	91,503	121,669	15.24
McIntosh	134	31,083	28,774	61,633	30.22
Meriwether	59	93,156	95,171	144,206	22.29
Miller	132	24,002	25,490	93,559	13.61
Mitchell	62	90,689	83,815	182,856	13.10
Monroe	61	74,639	74,915	400,238	10.01
Montgomery	143	13,195	24,884	61,322	12.40
Morgan	87	68,928	58,580	118,853	16.71
Murray	71	54,646	105,967	140,095	20.56
Muscogee	9	1,322,739	910,616	1,083,996	29.16

County	Master[1] Economic Rank	1983[2] Taxable Sales × $1,000	1982[3] Adjusted Gross Income × $1,000	1983 Net Property & Utility Digest × $1,000	1983 Mileage Rates
Newton	32	163,892	216,154	264,219	24.48
Oconee	89	28,534	81,014	116,997	19.75
Oglethorpe	120	19,887	38,192	82,971	16.90
Paulding	50	75,807	157,563	173,886	30.67
Peach	65	87,269	108,992	134,585	18.50
Pickens	79	94,731	60,633	114,103	28.80
Pierce	104	37,556	51,320	104,995	20.63
Pike	129	12,390	43,950	67,271	23.00
Polk	43	137,467	170,001	199,110	24.56
Pulaski	115	43,812	44,035	73,126	18.61
Putnam	90	44,280	58,848	173,363	22.71
Quitman	159	3,966	6,005	16,978	23.25
Rabun	93	48,472	49,469	157,439	16.23
Randolph	128	41,495	30,125	69,131	14.78
Richmond	6	1,410,127	1,019,010	1,264,499	23.61
Rockdale	24	225,302	299,083	405,917	32.25
Schley	153	9,600	13,406	31,682	15.33
Screven	80	66,245	59,024	168,447	16.96
Seminole	111	51,688	35,487	90,816	17.81
Spalding	22	292,267	284,110	346,493	23.62
Stephens	53	128,833	118,495	167,014	21.61
Stewart	141	20,855	19,949	64,789	12.98
Sumter	40	171,948	143,867	275,684	10.80
Talbot	144	14,406	23,555	50,168	18.52
Taliaferro	156	3,133	6,689	31,740	11.25
Tattnall	82	65,755	68,387	131,837	11.45
Taylor	116	75,971	33,271	64,065	17.25
Telfair	106	47,445	48,468	91,674	16.72
Terrell	107	42,598	48,275	95,619	13.81
Thomas	27	245,082	202,442	310,949	21.60
Tift	37	212,193	167,286	303,120	11.77
Toombs	52	166,782	111,634	154,489	20.93
Towns	136	29,399	21,391	55,781	8.15
Treutlen	146	14,538	22,171	36,075	19.90
Troup	20	346,842	293,773	388,647	19.22
Turner	117	32,852	36,748	91,224	17.79
Twiggs	127	11,089	36,199	89,314	21.15
Union	110	38,853	35,932	93,102	13.75
Upson	44	116,878	130,219	205,904	24.00
Walker	26	159,942	284,453	348,600	18.35
Walton	42	142,441	173,674	223,582	19.60
Ware	31	275,974	190,653	299,192	20.33
Warren	139	17,974	23,244	68,560	16.78
Washington	58	96,211	90,213	184,632	20.57
Wayne	49	117,111	104,325	258,379	18.25
Webster	155	3,750	9,336	37,884	19.13

County	Master[1] Economic Rank	1983[2] Taxable Sales × $1,000	1982[3] Adjusted Gross Income × $1,000	1983 Net Property & Utility Digest × $1,000	1983 Mileage Rates
Wheeler	150	11,339	16,740	49,173	17.66
White	97	50,259	49,866	115,410	16.82
Whitfield	13	609,837	441,397	726,550	20.14
Wilcox	142	14,450	27,541	48,611	21.52
Wilkes	88	72,268	53,354	125,845	16.64
Wilkinson	108	34,136	55,778	94,758	21.21
Worth	70	54,090	81,233	185,658	16.47
Other		350	837,504		
Georgia		40,501,509	36,730,568	53,764,924	

[1] Master Economic Rank is determined by using the information of personal income, sales tax receipts, motor vehicle tags, and assessed property value.

[2] Based on sales tax

[3] Reported on Georgia returns

PERSONAL INCOME: 1982, 1983

	Total Personal Income			Per Capita Personal Income		
	(in millions of dollars)		Percent Change	(in dollars)		Rank in State
County	1982	1983	1982–1983	1982	1983	
Appling	128	134	4.4	8,102	8,307	72
Atkinson	43	46	6.6	6,981	7,458	116
Bacon	63	66	4.6	6,585	6,835	140
Baker	26	27	2.6	6,578	6,830	141
Baldwin	291	321	10.2	7,925	8,649	58
Banks	65	75	15.0	7,076	8,010	90
Barrow	191	211	10.1	8,581	9,158	37
Bartow	347	382	10.0	8,212	8,827	46
Ben Hill	122	133	9.2	7,389	8,020	88
Berrien	104	111	6.1	7,589	8,015	89
Bibb	1,464	1,583	8.1	9,547	10,202	17
Bleckley	86	92	6.8	7,998	8,540	61
Brantley	57	61	6.0	6,385	6,744	143
Brooks	96	98	2.2	6,277	6,389	154
Bryan	80	88	9.7	7,413	7,739	105
Bulloch	282	295	4.9	7,711	8,073	85
Burke	147	159	8.0	7,396	7,761	102
Butts	110	121	10.4	7,368	7,928	96
Calhoun	45	46	.6	7,915	7,985	92
Camden	143	158	10.7	9,062	9,547	27
Candler	51	53	3.6	6,786	7,033	131
Carroll	502	557	11.0	8,495	9,216	34
Catoosa	295	315	6.6	7,738	8,227	77
Charlton	49	54	9.5	6,585	7,130	130

| County | Total Personal Income | | Percent Change | Per Capita Personal Income | | Rank in State |
| | (in millions of dollars) | | | (in dollars) | | |
	1982	1983	1982–1983	1982	1983	
Chatham	2,106	2,250	6.8	10,029	10,653	10
Chattahoochee	136	141	3.7	6,550	7,177	129
Chattooga	148	161	8.9	6,869	7,492	115
Cherokee	514	577	12.2	9,010	9,637	26
Clarke	707	775	9.7	9,313	10,183	18
Clay	18	19	3.9	5,198	5,467	159
Clayton	1,581	1,732	9.5	10,151	10,987	7
Clinch	47	52	9.8	7,017	7,633	109
Cobb	4,147	4,655	12.3	12,921	13,913	1
Coffee	195	211	8.1	7,086	7,534	114
Colquitt	277	291	5.0	7,648	8,002	91
Columbia	443	495	11.8	10,088	10,698	9
Cook	85	91	7.5	6,154	6,628	145
Coweta	383	420	9.7	9,298	9,991	21
Crawford	57	60	6.0	7,923	8,446	65
Crisp	148	156	5.4	7,392	7,779	101
Dade	78	82	5.4	6,573	7,015	132
Dawson	44	49	12.8	8,447	8,885	44
Decatur	202	219	8.5	7,649	8,317	70
DeKalb	6,256	6,878	9.9	12,698	13,750	2
Dodge	121	130	7.0	7,100	7,614	110
Dooly	93	93	.1	8,710	8,795	50
Dougherty	897	961	7.2	8,721	9,355	29
Douglas	541	603	11.4	9,233	9,943	22
Early	99	103	4.2	7,410	7,756	104
Echols	14	15	7.1	6,071	6,521	148
Effingham	159	172	8.1	8,191	8,524	62
Elbert	159	172	7.9	8,367	9,031	40
Emanuel	142	150	5.3	6,680	7,002	134
Evans	66	68	3.9	7,599	7,867	99
Fannin	101	111	10.0	6,730	7,331	122
Fayette	425	491	15.5	12,587	13,455	3
Floyd	754	812	7.6	9,477	10,258	16
Forsyth	300	333	10.9	9,942	10,645	11
Franklin	126	139	10.4	8,127	8,860	45
Fulton	7,230	7,899	9.2	12,013	13,012	4
Gilmer	90	97	7.6	7,837	8,396	68
Glascock	21	22	4.5	8,750	9,325	30
Glynn	568	610	7.4	10,125	10,719	8
Gordon	259	289	11.6	8,434	9,302	31
Grady	151	159	5.7	7,509	7,873	98
Greene	78	86	10.4	6,755	7,321	123
Gwinnett	2,301	2,669	16.0	11,964	12,799	5
Habersham	198	209	5.7	7,588	7,946	94
Hall	773	843	9.1	9,882	10,613	12
Hancock	56	61	8.4	5,959	6,487	150

County	Total Personal Income			Per Capita Personal Income		
	(in millions of dollars)		Percent Change	(in dollars)		Rank in State
	1982	1983	1982–1983	1982	1983	
Haralson	163	177	8.3	8,614	9,290	33
Harris	117	128	9.5	7,546	8,112	83
Hart	147	160	9.3	7,735	8,419	66
Heard	52	58	10.3	7,927	8,576	60
Henry	377	422	11.9	9,863	10,569	14
Houston	806	871	8.1	9,957	10,607	13
Irwin	69	71	2.5	7,665	7,760	103
Jackson	208	228	9.6	7,892	8,503	63
Jasper	65	70	8.6	8,676	9,292	32
Jeff Davis	96	102	6.6	8,127	8,674	56
Jefferson	133	141	6.3	7,175	7,606	111
Jenkins	54	56	5.0	6,119	6,433	152
Johnson	58	63	7.6	6,741	7,252	126
Jones	146	159	8.9	8,382	8,899	43
Lamar	92	100	8.4	7,636	8,209	78
Lanier	37	39	6.1	6,457	6,876	138
Laurens	311	335	7.6	8,228	8,806	47
Lee	101	109	8.7	7,958	8,246	74
Liberty	308	323	4.9	7,494	7,932	95
Lincoln	49	52	6.7	7,220	7,706	107
Long	33	35	6.7	6,671	6,986	135
Lowndes	562	613	9.0	8,149	8,728	53
Lumpkin	80	87	9.5	7,085	7,717	106
Macon	88	93	6.3	6,137	6,499	149
Madison	141	155	9.7	7,659	8,267	73
Marion	36	38	6.6	6,923	7,339	121
McDuffie	149	160	7.4	7,887	8,315	71
McIntosh	49	51	4.2	5,990	6,200	157
Meriwether	143	154	8.0	6,734	7,233	127
Miller	50	52	2.7	7,207	7,389	120
Mitchell	151	160	6.4	7,028	7,419	118
Monroe	121	129	6.8	8,234	8,803	48
Montgomery	49	53	6.1	7,104	7,428	117
Morgan	99	106	7.0	8,214	8,711	54
Murray	150	168	12.1	7,214	7,982	93
Muscogee	1,613	1,748	8.4	9,197	10,002	20
Newton	315	345	9.7	8,434	9,088	38
Oconee	120	135	11.8	9,148	9,896	23
Oglethorpe	69	75	9.5	7,489	8,062	86
Paulding	220	244	10.8	8,058	8,667	57
Peach	166	179	7.9	8,963	9,645	25
Pickens	102	111	8.7	8,387	8,995	41
Pierce	85	89	4.9	6,850	7,261	124
Pike	70	76	8.1	8,255	8,922	42
Polk	266	285	7.4	8,090	8,691	55
Pulaski	76	79	4.3	8,423	8,792	51

County	Total Personal Income			Per Capita Personal Income		
	(in millions of dollars)		Percent Change	(in dollars)		Rank in State
	1982	1983	1982–1983	1982	1983	
Putnam	87	90	3.5	8,180	8,240	75
Quitman	14	15	5.7	5,967	6,329	155
Rabun	71	78	8.6	6,730	7,258	125
Randolph	59	60	2.5	6,066	6,297	156
Richmond	1,718	1,862	8.4	9,372	10,042	19
Rockdale	411	455	10.5	10,420	11,253	6
Schley	25	27	6.5	7,418	7,886	97
Screven	101	107	5.5	7,078	7,398	119
Seminole	68	71	4.3	7,632	8,088	84
Spalding	429	466	8.6	8,550	9,207	35
Stephens	171	189	10.6	7,788	8,479	64
Stewart	37	40	8.1	6,210	6,614	146
Sumter	243	266	9.3	8,072	8,800	49
Talbot	41	43	6.6	5,982	6,416	153
Taliaferro	16	17	5.3	7,686	8,145	81
Tattnall	120	125	4.2	6,823	7,012	133
Taylor	58	62	6.3	7,301	7,824	100
Telfair	88	93	6.2	7,720	8,209	78
Terrell	81	81	.3	6,728	6,752	142
Thomas	334	359	7.5	8,609	9,199	36
Tift	283	305	7.6	8,414	9,069	39
Toombs	164	175	6.5	7,148	7,563	112
Towns	37	41	9.9	6,055	6,452	151
Treutlen	38	41	7.2	6,176	6,606	147
Troup	458	500	9.1	9,025	9,822	24
Turner	78	80	2.0	8,113	8,177	80
Twiggs	61	65	6.5	6,427	6,875	139
Union	54	59	8.8	5,519	5,945	158
Upson	206	223	8.3	7,644	8,236	76
Walker	452	479	6.0	7,925	8,416	67
Walton	252	275	8.9	8,104	8,764	52
Ware	322	348	8.2	8,578	9,398	28
Warren	45	47	4.9	6,622	6,977	136
Washington	145	156	7.6	7,600	8,143	82
Wayne	174	174	.5	8,040	8,044	87
Webster	17	18	3.5	7,229	7,549	113
Wheeler	32	34	4.5	6,301	6,711	144
White	70	77	9.0	6,585	6,950	137
Whitfield	622	685	10.3	9,432	10,390	15
Wilcox	53	55	3.3	6,949	7,220	128
Wilkes	90	96	7.1	8,003	8,595	59
Wilkinson	83	90	8.3	7,913	8,391	69
Worth	136	142	4.3	7,369	7,662	108
Georgia	54,521	59,551	9.2	9,654	10,389	

EDUCATION
County Boards of Education

Atkinson
Pearson 31642
912-422-7373

Appling
Baxley 31513
912-367-3646

Bacon
601 N. Pierce St., Alma
31510
912-632-7363

Baker
P.O. Box 40, Newton 31770
912-734-5346

Baldwin
P.O. Box 1188,
Milledgeville 31061
912-452-3516

Banks
Box 1657 Homer 30547
404-677-2224

Barrow
109 Church St., Winder
30680
404-867-4527

Bartow
P.O. Box 569, Cartersville
30120
404-382-3813

Ben Hill
Courthouse, Fitzgerald
31750
912-423-3320

Berrien
P.O. Box 625, Nashville
31639
912-686-2081

Bibb
Board of Public Education
and Orphanage for Bibb
County
Box 6157, Macon 31213
912-742-8711

Bleckley
Cochran 31014
912-934-2821

Brantley
Courthouse Square,
Nahunta 31553
912-462-6176

Brooks
P.O. Box 511, Quitman
31643
912-263-7531

Bryan
P.O. Box 768, Pembroke
31321
912-653-4381

Bulloch
P.O. Box 877, Statesboro
30458
912-764-6201

Burke
P.O. Box 596, Waynesboro
30830
404-554-5101

Butts
181 N. Mulberry, Jackson
30233
404-775-7532

Calhoun
Courthouse Square,
Morgan 31766
912-849-2765

Camden
520 N. Lee St., Kingsland
31548
912-729-5687

Candler
P.O. Box 536, Metter 30439
912-685-5713

Carroll
402 Newnan St., Carrollton
30117
404-832-3568

Catoosa
Box 130, Ringgold 30736
404-935-2297

Charlton
500 S. Third St., Folkston
31537
912-496-2596

Chatham
Board of Public Education
for the City of Savannah
and County of Chatham
208 Bull St., Savannah
31401
912-234-2541

Chattahoochee
P.O. Box 188, Cusseta
31805
404-989-3678

Chattooga
P.O. Box 30, Summerville
30747
404-857-3447

Cherokee
P.O. Box 769, Canton
30114
404-479-1871

Clarke
P.O. Box 1708, Athens
30610
404-546-7721

Clay
Fort Gaines 31751
912-768-2232

Clayton
120 Smith, St., Jonesboro
30236
404-478-9991

Clinch
101 College St., Homerville
31634
912-487-5370

Cobb
P.O. Box 1088, Marietta
30061
404-422-9171

Coffee
Box 959, Douglas 31533
912-384-2086

Colquitt
1220 S. Main St., Moultrie
31768
912-985-1550

Columbia
P.O. Box 10, Appling
30802
404-541-0650

Cook
1109 N. Parrish, Adel
31620
912-896-2294

Coweta
55 Savannah St., Newnan
30263
404-253-3530

Crawford
322 Manor St., Roberta
31078
912-836-3131

Crisp
Cordele 31015
912-273-1611

Dade
P.O. Box 188, Trenton
30752
404-657-4361

Dawson
Courthouse, Dawsonville
30534
404-265-3246

Decatur
100 West St., Bainbridge
31717
912-246-5898

DeKalb
3770 N. Decatur Road,
Decatur 30032
404-296-2000

Dodge
P.O. Box 647, Eastman
31023
912-374-3783

Dooly
Courthouse, Vienna 31092
912-268-4761

Dougherty
P.O. Box 1470, Albany
31703
912-888-5800

Douglas
P.O. Box 1077,
Douglasville 30133

404-942-5411

Early
Courthouse, Blakely 31723
912-723-4337

Echols
P.O. Box 207, Statenville
31648
912-559-5734

Effingham
Ash St., Springfield 31329
912-754-6491

Elbert
50 Laurel Dr., Elberton
30635
404-283-1904

Emanuel
P.O. Box 130, Swainsboro
30401
912-237-6674

Evans
P.O. Box 826, Claxton
30417
912-739-3544

Fannin
P.O. Box 606, Blue Ridge
30513
404-632-3771

Fayette
210 Stonewall Ave.,
Fayetteville 30214
404-461-8171

Floyd
171 Chatillon Road, N.E.,
Rome 30161
404-234-1031

Forsyth
101 School St., Cumming
30130
404-887-2461

Franklin
P.O. Box 98, Carnesville
30521
404-384-4556

Fulton
786 Cleveland Ave., Atlanta
30315
404-768-3600

Gilmer
5 West Side Square, Ellijay
30540
404-635-7991

Glascock
Railroad Avenue, Gibson
30810
404-598-2291

Glynn
P.O. Box 1677, Brunswick
31521
912-265-6590

Gordon
P.O. Box 127, Calhoun
30701
404-629-7366

Grady
P.O. Box 300, Cairo 31728
912-377-3701

Greene
203 Main St., Greensboro
30642
404-453-7688

Gwinnett
52 Gwinnett Dr.,
Lawrenceville 30245
404-963-8651

Habersham
P.O. Box 467, Clarkesville
30523
404-754-2118

Hall
300 Green St., Gainesville
30501
404-536-6681

Hancock
P.O. Box 488, Sparta 31087
404-444-6621

Haralson
P.O. Box 508, Buchanan
30113
404-646-3882

Harris
P.O. Box 388, Hamilton
31811
404-628-4206

Hart
P.O. Box 696, Hartwell
30643
404-376-5141

125

Heard
Courthouse, Franklin 30217
404-675-3320

Henry
396 Tomlinson St.,
McDonough 30253
404-957-6601

Houston
1211 Washington St., Perry
30169
912-987-1929

Irwin
210 Apple St., Ocilla 31774
912-468-5524

Jackson
Washington St., Jefferson
30549
404-367-5151

Jasper
126 Courthouse, Monticello
31064
404-468-6350

Jeff Davis
Pine Forest Ave.,
Hazlehurst 31539
912-375-4286

Jefferson
P.O. Box 449, Louisville
30434
912-625-7626

Jenkins
P.O. Box 660, Millen 30442
912-982-4305

Johnson
P.O. Box 110, Wrightsville
31096
912-864-3302

Jones
Courthouse, Gray 31032
912-986-6580

Lamar
204 Gordon Rd.,
Barnesville 30204
404-358-1159

Lanier
P.O. Box 158, Lakeland
31635
912-482-3966

Laurens
2128 Court Square Sta.,
Dublin 31021
912-272-4767

Lee
Governmental Bldg.,
Leesburg 31763
912-759-6414

Liberty
P.O. Box 70, Hinesville
31313
912-876-2161

Lincoln
P.O. Box 39, Lincolnton
30817
404-359-3742

Long
Ludowici 31316
912-545-2367

Lowndes
P.O. Box 1227, Valdosta
31601
912-242-8760

Lumpkin
Courthouse Hill, Dahlonega
30533
404-864-3611

Macon
Oglethorpe 31068
912-472-8188

Madison
Royston Rd., Highway 29,
Danielsville 30633
404-795-2191

Marion
Buena Vista 31803
912-649-2234

McDuffie
P.O. Box 957, Thomson
30824
404-595-1918

McIntosh
P.O. Box 495, Darien 31305
912-437-6645

Meriwether
N. Court Square,
Greenville 30222
404-672-4297

Miller
Courthouse Square,
Colquitt 31737
912-758-5592

Mitchell
P.O. Box 588, Camilla
31730
912-336-5641

Monroe
310 Montpelier Ave.,
Forsyth 31029
912-994-2031

Montgomery
Broad/Washington St.,
Mt. Vernon 30445
912-583-2301

Morgan
1065 East Ave., Madison
30650
404-342-0752

Murray
P.O. Box 40, Chatsworth
30705
404-695-4531

Muscogee
1200 Bradley Drive,
Columbus 31994
404-324-5661

Newton
3187 Newton Dr., N.E.,
Covington 30209
404-787-1330

Oconee
School Street, Watkinsville
30677
404-769-5130

Oglethorpe
P.O. Box 190, Lexington
30648
404-743-8128

Paulding
522 Hardee St., Dallas
30132
404-445-2051

Peach
Knoxville St., Ft. Valley
31030
912-825-5933

Pickens
211 N. Main, Jasper 30143
404-692-2532

Pierce
Courthouse Annex,
Blackshear 31516
912-449-5564

Pike
Jackson St., Zebulon,
30295
404-567-8489

Polk
P.O. Box 128, Cedartown
30125
404-748-3821

Pulaski
McCormick Ave.,
Hawkinsville 31036
912-892-9191

Putnam
P.O. Box 31, Eatonton
31024
404-485-5381

Quitman
Georgetown 31754
912-334-4189

Rabun
Mt. City School Bldg.,
Clayton 30525
404-746-5376

Randolph
309 N. Webster St.,
Cuthbert 31740
912-732-2641

Richmond
2083 Heckle St., Augusta
30910-2999
404-736-8451

Rockdale
P.O. Drawer 1199, Conyers
30207
404-483-4713

Schley
Ellaville 31806
912-937-2405

Screven
P.O. Box 1668, Sylvania
30467
912-564-7114

Seminole
P.O. Box 188,
Donalsonville 31745
912-524-2433

Spalding
P.O. Drawer N, Griffin
30223
404-227-9478

Stephens
Courthouse Annex, Toccoa
30577
404-886-3783

Stewart
P.O. Box 547, Lumpkin
31815
912-838-4329

Sumter
P.O. Box 967, Americus
31709
912-924-6949

Talbot
P.O. Box 515, Talbotton
31827
404-665-8528

Taliaferro
Route 2, Park Street,
Crawfordville 30631
404-456-2575

Tattnall
Reidsville 30453
912-557-4726

Taylor
P.O. Box 1937, Butler
31006
912-862-5224

Telfair
210B E. Parsonage St.,
McRae 31055
912-868-5661

Terrell
Courthouse, Dawson 31742
912-995-4425

Thomas
P.O. Box 2300, Thomasville
31792
912-226-7102

Tift
P.O. Box 389, Tifton 31793
912-382-4000

Toombs
P.O. Box 440, Lyons 30436
912-526-3141

Towns
Courthouse, Hiawassee
30546
404-896-2279

Treutlen
202 Third Street, Soperton
30457
912-529-4228

Troup
Courthouse Annex,
LaGrange 30240
404-884-8634

Turner
213 N. Cleveland St.,
Ashburn 31714
912-567-3338

Twiggs
Intersection 16 & 96,
Jeffersonville 31044
912-945-3127

Union
School St., Blairsville 30512
404-745-2322

Upson
Courthouse, Thomaston
30286
404-647-9621

Walker
P.O. Box 29, LaFayette
30728
404-638-1240

Walton
115 Oak St., Monroe 30655
404-267-6544

Ware
P.O. Box 1789, Waycross
31501
912-283-8656

Warren
P.O. Box 228, Warrenton
30828
404-465-3383

Washington
P.O. Box 716, Sandersville
31082
912-552-3981

Wayne
555 S. Sunset Blvd., Jesup
 31545
912-427-4244

Webster
Preston 31824
912-828-3315

Wheeler
P.O. Box 427, Alamo 30411
912-568-7198

White
Courthouse, Cleveland
 30528
404-865-2315

Whitfield
P.O. Box 2167, Dalton
 30720
404-278-8070

Wilcox
Courthouse, Abbeville
 31001
912-467-2141

Wilkes
P.O. Box 279, Washington
 30673
404-678-2718

Wilkinson
P.O. Box 206, Irwinton
 31042
912-946-5521

Worth
P.O. Box 359, Sylvester
 31791
912-776-6943

The following chart is a breakdown of the population 25 years old and over by years of school completed.

County	Elementary 0–8 Years % of Total	High School 1–3 Years % of Total	4 Years % of Total	1–3 Years % of Total	4 or More Years % of Total	Median Years of School Completed
Appling	32.2	26.2	27.5	7.6	6.5	11.1
Atkinson	41.9	23.0	24.5	5.7	5.0	9.9
Bacon	33.4	24.9	29.6	5.2	6.9	10.9
Baker	43.7	27.3	18.8	5.2	4.9	9.9
Baldwin	27.0	20.1	26.1	11.3	15.4	12.1
Banks	35.5	25.0	28.5	6.1	5.0	10.9
Barrow	34.5	27.8	21.8	8.4	7.5	10.8
Bartow	35.2	24.9	25.5	8.0	6.3	10.9
Ben Hill	32.4	24.5	25.2	9.9	8.1	11.3
Berrien	32.8	26.1	27.9	7.3	5.9	11.1
Bibb	24.2	20.0	30.4	12.3	13.0	12.2
Bleckley	29.8	23.3	27.2	10.9	9.0	11.6
Brantley	28.5	23.6	36.8	6.4	4.8	11.7
Brooks	36.8	23.7	24.5	7.4	7.5	10.9
Bryan	30.6	27.6	30.3	7.2	4.4	11.2
Bulloch	27.0	21.1	24.3	12.0	15.7	12.1
Burke	38.9	22.5	21.9	8.9	7.9	10.4
Butts	31.5	24.9	29.3	7.9	6.4	11.3
Calhoun	40.6	24.7	18.6	9.0	7.2	10.4
Camden	25.8	22.7	31.9	11.5	8.2	12.0
Candler	36.3	23.0	22.0	9.7	9.1	11.0
Carroll	29.5	23.6	26.3	9.4	11.2	11.6
Catoosa	23.8	20.5	36.5	12.0	7.3	12.2
Charlton	36.8	19.7	30.7	7.4	5.5	10.8
Chatham	20.2	19.2	31.5	15.0	14.1	12.3
Chattahoochee	7.3	10.9	42.8	18.6	20.4	12.7
Chattooga	40.3	25.4	21.7	6.8	5.9	10.1
Cherokee	27.0	20.9	30.1	12.3	9.7	12.1
Clarke	17.3	15.3	20.0	12.4	35.0	12.9
Clay	38.5	24.3	19.8	7.7	9.8	10.7
Clayton	13.4	20.1	40.3	15.9	10.3	12.4
Clinch	42.1	23.5	21.8	6.0	6.5	9.8
Cobb	12.2	15.6	30.7	18.6	23.0	12.7
Coffee	33.9	22.8	23.5	11.6	8.2	11.2
Colquitt	31.5	23.4	26.8	9.9	8.4	11.5

County	Elementary 0–8 Years % of Total	High School 1–3 Years % of Total	High School 4 Years % of Total	1–3 Years % of Total	4 or More Years % of Total	Median Years of School Completed
Columbia	16.0	16.8	35.4	16.5	15.4	12.5
Cook	34.9	26.4	25.7	7.4	5.7	10.8
Coweta	29.2	24.7	26.6	9.8	9.8	11.6
Crawford	32.5	27.0	28.5	5.6	6.5	11.0
Crisp	28.4	26.5	25.9	10.3	9.0	11.6
Dade	33.2	23.0	27.1	8.9	7.8	11.1
Dawson	39.2	24.1	25.6	6.6	4.4	10.5
Decatur	32.5	22.1	27.6	9.5	8.4	11.5
DeKalb	9.9	13.2	28.2	20.8	27.9	13.0
Dodge	36.8	23.1	24.3	9.4	6.6	11.1
Dooly	39.3	26.8	16.5	9.5	8.0	10.6
Dougherty	20.8	20.7	30.0	14.3	14.2	12.3
Douglas	20.7	21.9	36.6	11.7	9.1	12.2
Early	37.3	23.9	23.0	7.2	8.6	10.9
Echols	33.8	25.2	31.4	5.8	3.9	10.9
Effingham	25.7	27.7	33.8	7.7	5.2	11.7
Elbert	30.6	28.0	26.4	7.2	7.9	11.3
Emanuel	37.7	23.9	23.4	7.8	7.2	10.7
Evans	35.4	21.6	26.9	9.0	7.2	11.2
Fannin	40.6	18.5	28.0	7.7	5.2	10.4
Fayette	11.8	14.9	37.2	19.6	16.5	12.6
Floyd	29.0	22.3	27.4	9.6	11.8	11.9
Forsyth	27.4	21.8	30.8	11.3	8.7	12.0
Franklin	33.4	28.6	21.1	9.0	7.9	10.8
Fulton	17.4	16.6	26.5	16.6	23.0	12.6
Gilmer	45.1	17.4	23.7	7.2	6.6	9.7
Glascock	43.5	24.6	21.6	5.5	4.8	9.8
Glynn	19.8	18.3	31.9	15.1	14.9	12.4
Gordon	34.5	23.4	27.1	8.2	6.8	11.1
Grady	35.0	24.4	25.3	8.4	7.0	10.9
Greene	38.6	26.5	21.8	6.8	6.3	10.5
Gwinnett	12.9	15.4	32.9	19.9	18.9	12.7
Habersham	34.1	22.4	24.6	9.6	9.3	11.2
Hall	28.4	23.5	24.5	11.5	12.2	11.8
Hancock	45.9	20.6	21.0	6.2	6.4	9.7
Haralson	32.3	25.7	26.3	8.9	6.9	11.1
Harris	30.0	20.3	24.7	13.2	11.8	12.0
Hart	29.8	32.1	22.2	8.3	7.7	11.1
Heard	37.4	27.1	22.6	8.6	4.4	10.3
Henry	21.4	24.2	33.1	11.9	9.5	12.1
Houston	14.7	16.4	40.0	15.6	13.2	12.5
Irwin	34.3	26.2	25.1	8.7	5.7	11.0
Jackson	33.9	25.4	25.3	7.5	8.0	11.1
Jasper	30.2	28.4	24.3	8.0	9.2	11.2
Jeff Davis	37.6	21.9	26.2	6.9	7.4	10.9
Jefferson	41.4	22.2	21.6	8.0	6.8	10.3
Jenkins	41.4	23.4	19.4	8.8	7.0	10.2
Johnson	39.5	25.5	23.3	5.5	6.2	10.5
Jones	24.5	21.3	33.3	10.4	10.6	12.1
Lamar	30.4	23.9	27.1	10.5	8.0	11.5
Lanier	35.0	25.7	24.1	10.0	5.3	10.8
Laurens	30.5	23.8	26.2	9.7	9.8	11.6
Lee	22.5	23.4	30.6	14.3	9.3	12.1
Liberty	15.2	15.4	42.1	15.0	12.3	12.5
Lincoln	30.3	28.6	26.7	7.1	7.3	11.3

129

EDUCATION

County	Elementary 0–8 Years % of Total	High School 1–3 Years % of Total	High School 4 Years % of Total	1–3 Years % of Total	4 or More Years % of Total	Median Years of School Completed
Long	29.5	24.3	33.0	6.8	6.4	11.6
Lowndes	22.3	20.6	30.8	13.1	13.2	12.2
Lumpkin	39.3	17.6	24.9	8.5	9.8	10.7
Macon	40.9	23.9	18.7	8.5	8.0	10.3
Madison	31.8	25.6	26.5	8.6	7.5	11.2
Marion	38.3	25.7	22.8	7.1	6.1	10.3
McDuffie	31.9	26.2	26.3	7.4	8.2	11.3
McIntosh	33.8	24.8	27.6	7.8	6.1	11.1
Meriwether	34.9	25.7	25.0	7.4	7.1	10.9
Miller	38.0	20.5	23.8	10.7	7.1	11.0
Mitchell	35.3	25.2	22.9	9.1	7.5	10.8
Monroe	32.8	21.7	28.3	7.9	9.4	11.6
Montgomery	33.0	25.1	28.2	6.6	7.1	11.1
Morgan	35.1	23.9	21.9	9.6	9.6	11.2
Murray	42.0	21.8	24.6	6.5	5.1	10.1
Muscogee	21.4	17.8	32.6	15.4	12.9	12.3
Newton	30.1	24.8	27.5	9.0	8.7	11.5
Oconee	20.7	19.2	26.3	12.6	21.2	12.4
Oglethorpe	32.8	24.6	26.1	7.0	9.5	11.3
Paulding	29.7	28.7	30.0	7.4	4.3	11.2
Peach	27.5	21.5	25.0	11.7	14.4	12.0
Pickens	40.8	21.3	22.6	8.4	6.9	10.4
Pierce	32.1	21.3	30.6	9.1	6.9	11.6
Pike	29.0	24.1	28.8	9.4	8.7	11.7
Polk	37.8	22.5	26.3	7.8	5.7	10.6
Pulaski	31.3	22.9	24.5	12.7	8.6	11.6
Putnam	31.8	21.9	28.0	9.1	9.2	11.6
Quitman	39.7	24.4	21.9	7.4	6.6	10.3
Rabun	28.9	24.8	24.4	10.5	11.4	11.6
Randolph	38.8	25.6	20.0	9.0	6.7	10.5
Richmond	21.0	17.7	32.1	14.5	14.8	12.4
Rockdale	17.0	19.5	35.7	15.1	12.6	12.4
Schley	32.3	23.3	27.0	9.0	8.4	11.2
Screven	37.4	21.1	25.2	8.9	7.4	11.0
Seminole	33.6	23.5	26.4	9.3	7.3	11.2
Spalding	31.2	24.4	25.8	9.6	9.0	11.4
Stephens	32.3	24.5	23.4	10.0	9.9	11.4
Stewart	38.5	25.7	20.2	8.0	7.7	10.6
Sumter	30.1	23.0	21.5	11.4	14.0	11.7
Talbot	37.6	22.1	25.9	6.4	8.0	10.9
Taliaferro	42.5	32.4	14.4	5.3	5.4	10.0
Tattnall	31.6	24.1	29.2	10.1	5.2	11.4
Taylor	41.6	22.4	21.6	7.1	7.4	10.0
Telfair	35.4	25.0	22.7	8.8	8.1	11.1
Terrell	36.5	26.2	19.3	8.9	9.0	10.9
Thomas	30.7	20.7	27.3	10.2	11.2	11.8
Tift	31.5	23.0	22.9	11.1	11.5	11.4
Toombs	31.0	25.0	24.8	9.9	9.3	11.4
Towns	34.3	20.6	25.6	9.6	9.9	11.3
Treutlen	45.1	21.9	20.5	6.3	6.2	9.6
Troup	35.4	22.8	22.9	8.0	10.9	10.8
Turner	35.1	25.0	23.5	8.5	7.8	11.0
Twiggs	40.5	26.0	23.3	5.2	5.1	10.1
Union	43.1	18.2	20.9	9.8	8.0	10.2

County	Elementary 0–8 Years % of Total	High School 1–3 Years % of Total	4 Years % of Total	1–3 Years % of Total	4 or More Years % of Total	Median Years of School Completed
Upson	36.4	22.2	25.7	8.7	7.1	10.9
*Walker	33.0	22.4	29.9	8.7	6.0	11.2
*Walton	34.8	27.2	23.6	7.1	7.3	10.7
Ware	28.3	24.5	26.7	10.5	10.0	11.7
Warren	45.9	22.9	19.8	3.9	7.6	9.7
Washington	36.5	25.6	23.6	5.5	8.7	10.8
Wayne	29.9	21.5	30.8	10.7	7.2	11.8
Webster	38.1	25.4	22.4	7.4	6.7	10.8
Wheeler	41.1	22.1	21.2	8.1	7.5	10.3
White	33.9	18.1	27.5	11.1	9.6	11.7
Whitfield	33.9	21.3	24.3	10.7	9.7	11.3
Wilcox	38.2	25.4	22.8	7.6	6.1	10.5
Wilkes	31.7	28.0	20.2	10.1	10.1	11.2
Wilkinson	32.0	27.5	25.1	8.2	7.3	11.1
Worth	32.4	24.2	26.1	9.5	7.8	11.1
Georgia	23.7	19.9	28.5	13.3	14.6	12.2

The chart below shows the total number of teachers in each county, the number with advanced degrees, the cost per pupil, and the beginning salary for teachers in each county.

County	Number of Teachers	Teachers[1] with Advanced Degrees	Cost Per Pupil (Dollars)	1983–1984[2] Beginning Teacher Salary
Appling	216	105	2,147	—
Atkinson	83	34	1,878	—
Bacon	117	36	1,783	—
Baker	30	8	3,017	—
Baldwin	352	195	2,047	15,169
Banks	82	26	1,792	14,429
Barrow	251	114	1,829	14,529
Bartow	414	157	2,011	15,029
Ben Hill	56	27	1,515	—
Berrien	172	78	2,007	—
Bibb	1,386	762	2,184	15,529
Bleckley	121	60	1,871	—
Brantley	123	48	1,586	—
Brooks	182	65	2,080	—
Bryan	131	53	1,615	—
Bulloch	392	226	1,831	14,579
Burke	237	69	2,044	14,929
Butts	138	68	1,891	15,129
Calhoun	92	52	2,248	—
Camden	177	66	1,870	—
Candler	86	38	1,784	14,329
Carroll	463	269	1,716	—

County	Number of Teachers	Teachers[1] with Advanced Degrees	Cost Per Pupil (Dollars)	1983–1984[2] Beginning Teacher Salary
Catoosa	381	139	1,630	15,081
Charlton	109	29	2,144	—
Chatham	1,740	823	2,329	—
Chattahoochee	22	12	2,209	14,649
Chattooga	184	84	1,836	—
Cherokee	609	276	1,771	15,834
Clarke	602	376	2,517	15,432
Clay	25	15	2,299	
Clayton	1,811	995	2,107	—
Clinch	102	41	2,102	14,729
Cobb	2,926	1,479	2,070	—
Coffee	334	138	1,806	—
Colquitt	425	192	1,885	—
Columbia	501	179	1,784	—
Cook	165	69	2,008	—
Coweta	485	265	2,041	15,582
Crawford	95	40	2,079	—
Crisp	253	132	2,018	—
Dade	121	35	1,881	14,719
Dawson	75	36	2,202	15,045
Decatur	326	129	1,735	—
DeKalb	4,204	2,994	2,646	16,500
Dodge	210	105	1,889	—
Dooly	122	69	2,002	—
Dougherty	1,008	515	2,006	—
Douglas	652	370	1,838	15,421
Early	166	93	1,955	—
Echols	34	15	2,117	—
Effingham	237	85	1,612	—
Elbert	221	86	1,791	14,529
Emanuel	242	102	1,754	14,529
Evans	102	44	1,644	—
Fannin	161	89	1,886	14,679
Fayette	479	245	1,912	16,048
Floyd	523	281	2,246	15,329
Forsyth	362	175	2,072	—
Franklin	167	67	1,662	—
Fulton	2,371	1,182	2,641	15,708
Gilmer	117	65	1,844	14,629
Glascock	37	16	1,597	—
Glynn	589	295	2,523	—
Gordon	222	127	1,781	14,929
Grady	248	100	1,798	—
Greene	135	56	2,099	—
Gwinnett	2,054	1,114	1,940	16,007
Habersham	257	136	1,917	14,329
Hall	620	359	1,936	15,511
Hancock	121	40	1,918	—

County	Number of Teachers	Teachers[1] with Advanced Degrees	Cost Per Pupil (Dollars)	1983–1984[2] Beginning Teacher Salary
Haralson	156	80	1,843	15,129
Harris	142	84	2,064	14,529
Hart	202	93	1,825	—
Heard	97	42	2,477	—
Henry	384	144	1,865	—
Houston	797	478	1,884	—
Irwin	102	46	1,983	—
Jackson	145	60	2,018	—
Jasper	84	33	2,042	—
Jeff Davis	126	55	1,527	—
Jefferson	206	59	1,681	—
Jenkins	120	51	2,121	—
Johnson	88	32	1,736	—
Jones	189	92	1,580	—
Lamar	131	46	2,124	—
Lanier	72	32	1,761	14,579
Laurens	252	123	2,333	14,829
Lee	165	89	1,772	—
Liberty	296	93	1,616	—
Lincoln	81	36	1,910	—
Long	53	16	1,864	—
Lowndes	379	196	1,858	—
Lumpkin	108	72	2,007	—
Macon	162	72	2,111	—
Madison	198	101	1,788	—
Marion	95	50	2,862	14,429
McDuffie	221	76	1,700	—
McIntosh	111	36	1,893	—
Meriwether	258	112	1,769	14,829
Miller	84	32	2,046	—
Mitchell	182	70	2,336	—
Monroe	144	46	1,955	15,140
Montgomery	66	33	1,724	14,329
Morgan	141	60	1,921	14,979
Murray	230	114	1,722	—
Muscogee	1,887	1,246	2,305	15,818
Newton	434	190	1,841	15,772
Oconee	152	93	1,865	—
Oglethorpe	106	47	1,845	—
Paulding	299	139	1,691	15,242
Peach	209	106	1,599	—
Pickens	122	55	1,971	—
Pierce	141	74	1,612	—
Pike	103	41	1,848	14,829
Polk	361	219	1,851	—
Pulaski	102	46	1,880	—
Putman	119	62	2,173	—
Quitman	17	8	2,827	—

County	Number of Teachers	Teachers[1] with Advanced Degrees	Cost Per Pupil (Dollars)	1983–1984[2] Beginning Teacher Salary
Rabun	113	48	2,105	—
Randolph	110	52	1,898	—
Richmond	1,614	570	1,940	—
Rockdale	451	259	1,991	15,719
Schley	24	14	2,186	14,329
Screven	175	77	2,150	—
Seminole	108	51	1,951	—
Spalding	539	237	1,927	15,409
Stephens	226	119	1,744	—
Stewart	82	40	2,102	—
Sumter	107	59	2,097	—
Talbot	69	32	2,033	14,629
Taliaferro	15	2	2,756	—
Tattnall	165	71	1,765	14,379
Taylor	99	50	1,925	—
Telfair	148	73	1,906	14,329
Terrell	128	60	1,790	—
Thomas	246	117	1,956	14,629
Tift	365	175	1,565	14,929
Toombs	127	49	1,679	—
Towns	41	16	1,976	14,329
Treutlen	74	33	1,617	—
Troup	205	108	1,655	—
Turner	130	62	1,818	—
Twiggs	95	41	1,913	—
Union	107	49	1,973	—
Upson	171	69	1,670	14,529
Walker	514	203	1,763	15,029
Walton	317	130	1,618	—
Ware	211	88	1,741	—
Warren	65	16	1,944	—
Washington	212	75	2,034	—
Wayne	228	100	1,754	—
Webster	20	14	2,704	—
Wheeler	73	31	1,833	14,329
White	116	69	2,369	14,329
Whitfield	500	286	1,849	15,179
Wilcox	85	55	2,086	—
Wilkes	130	44	1,970	14,629
Wilkinson	121	55	2,022	—
Worth	219	114	1,837	15,079
Total	51,102	25,845		
City Systems	8,099	4,294		
Georgia	59,201	30,139	2,103	

—Data not available

[1]Masters Degree or higher

[2]For the 1983–1984 school year, the base salary for beginning teachers was $14,329. Some school systems supplement the base salary.

Independent city systems

Independent City Systems	1983–1984				1983–1984			1983–1984[2] Beginning Teacher Salary
	Number of Schools	Enrollment	Graduates	Dropouts	Number of Teachers	Teachers[1] With Advanced Degrees	Cost Per Pupil (Dollars)	
Americus	5	3,900	242	73	205	135	1,525	—
Atlanta	118	68,732	4,487	1,322	3,818	2,135	3,003	15,876
Bremen	2	1,188	71	13	65	43	1,811	14,929
Buford	3	1,472	99	21	81	35	2,013	—
Calhoun	3	2,433	239	135	132	72	2,173	15,329
Carrollton	6	3,033	227	39	159	104	1,988	14,829
Cartersville	3	2,071	127	47	118	62	2,091	—
Chickamauga	2	1,107	88	8	52	21	1,262	—
Commerce	3	1,204	69	16	66	28	1,594	—
Dalton	9	4,152	242	101	253	173	2,813	—
Decatur	9	2,559	127	34	169	134	2,854	15,829
Dublin	6	3,535	171	106	177	92	1,647	—
Fitzgerald	3	2,370	187	83	127	55	1,616	—
Gainesville	4	3,006	205	84	179	117	2,263	15,735
Hogansville	3	982	48	23	56	17	1,648	—
Jefferson	3	1,510	85	95	86	43	1,465	14,629
LaGrange	11	4,975	261	144	299	171	1,994	14,929
Marietta	10	4,689	207	54	266	146	2,745	14,329
Pelham	3	1,859	91	46	96	35	1,526	—
Rome	13	4,811	207	155	284	148	1,959	—
Social Circle	3	989	58	22	59	23	1,812	14,829
Thomaston	4	1,702	110	42	100	38	1,861	—
Thomasville	8	3,641	260	50	220	95	2,157	—
Trion	2	1,083	68	11	48	21	1,336	—
Valdosta	9	7,357	382	218	393	162	1,675	—
Vidalia	5	2,682	119	60	138	58	1,587	—
Waycross	7	3,638	163	92	214	95	1,980	15,329
West Point	3	760	37	19	59	38	2,387	—
Totals	260	141,440	8,677	3,113	7,918	4,294		

—Data not available

[1]Masters Degree or higher

[2]For the 1983–1984 school year, the base salary for beginning teachers was $14,329. Some school systems supplement the base salary.

ELECTORAL VOTE

The state of Georgia has 12 electoral votes.

ELEVATIONS, LATITUDES, AND LONGITUDES

The average elevation in Georgia is 600 feet. Brasstown Bald is the highest point in the state with an altitude of 4,784 feet. The Atlantic Ocean is the lowest point at one foot. Georgia lies between 30° and 35° north latitude and from 81° to 85° 30' west longitude. Similar values for selected locales in the state follow.

City	Altitude	Latitude	Longitude
Albany	180	31°32'N	84°08'W
Atlanta	1,010	33°39'N	84°26'W
Augusta	148	33°22'N	81°58'W
Columbus	385	32°31'N	84°56'W
Macon	354	32°42'N	83°39'W
Savannah	46	32°06'N	81°12'W

EMPLOYMENT

ANNUAL AVERAGES, 1985

County	Labor Force	Employment	Unemployment	Unemployment Rate
Appling	8,268	7,548	720	8.7
Atkinson	3,702	3,349	353	9.5
Bacon	3,959	3,607	352	8.9
Baker	1,817	1,680	137	7.5
Baldwin	15,658	14,782	876	5.6
Banks	5,496	5,227	269	4.9
Barrow	13,665	12,606	1,059	7.7
Bartow	19,862	17,908	1,954	9.8
Ben Hill	7,369	6,794	575	7.8
Berrien	6,733	6,319	414	6.1
Bibb	70,221	65,065	5,156	7.3
Bleckley	4,478	4,133	345	7.7
Brantley	3,926	3,506	420	10.7
Brooks	6,511	6,110	401	6.2
Bryan	4,892	4,510	382	7.8
Bulloch	17,160	16,181	979	5.7
Burke	14,326	13,347	979	6.8
Butts	7,738	7,024	714	9.2
Calhoun	2,228	1,960	268	12.0
Camden	8,046	7,603	443	5.5
Candler	3,201	2,983	218	6.8
Carroll	30,033	28,017	2,016	6.7
Catoosa	17,518	16,403	1,115	6.4
Charlton	2,918	2,669	249	8.5
Chatham	93,118	86,265	6,853	7.4
Chattahoochee	3,506	3,277	229	6.5
Chattooga	8,800	7,645	1,155	13.1
Cherokee	34,057	32,849	1,208	3.5
Clarke	37,776	35,748	2,028	5.4
Clay	1,448	1,344	104	7.2
Clayton	89,658	85,023	4,635	5.2

County	Labor Force	Employment	Unemployment	Unemployment Rate
Clinch	2,993	2,794	199	6.6
Cobb	192,880	185,284	7,596	3.9
Coffee	12,411	11,275	1,136	9.2
Colquitt	16,338	15,067	1,271	7.8
Columbia	22,099	21,200	899	4.1
Cook	6,139	5,700	439	7.2
Coweta	23,736	22,486	1,250	5.3
Crawford	3,222	2,954	268	8.3
Crisp	8,775	7,836	939	10.7
Dade	5,348	4,946	402	7.5
Dawson	2,733	2,568	165	6.0
Decatur	11,064	10,253	811	7.3
DeKalb	274,798	261,606	13,192	4.8
Dodge	5,839	4,926	913	15.6
Dooly	4,454	4,039	415	9.3
Dougherty	48,734	44,361	4,373	9.0
Douglas	34,678	33,191	1,487	4.3
Early	5,542	4,949	593	10.7
Echols	1,088	1,025	63	5.8
Effingham	9,013	8,469	544	6.0
Elbert	8,686	7,746	940	10.8
Emanuel	8,358	7,579	779	9.3
Evans	3,817	3,489	328	8.6
Fannin	5,803	5,305	498	8.6
Fayette	21,377	20,662	715	3.3
Floyd	37,276	34,108	3,168	8.5
Forsyth	18,028	17,343	685	3.8
Franklin	7,882	7,308	574	7.3
Fulton	341,929	320,752	21,177	6.2
Gilmer	4,841	4,414	427	8.8
Glascock	1,159	1,079	80	6.9
Glynn	27,515	25,741	1,774	6.4
Gordon	18,112	16,528	1,584	8.7
Grady	10,048	9,297	751	7.5
Greene	5,127	4,574	553	10.8
Gwinnett	124,999	120,495	4,504	3.6
Habersham	11,583	10,871	712	6.1
Hall	43,354	40,771	2,583	6.0
Hancock	3,673	3,333	340	9.3
Haralson	8,869	8,047	822	9.3
Harris	9,243	8,706	537	5.8
Hart	9,413	8,754	659	7.0
Heard	3,002	2,701	301	10.0
Henry	23,186	22,086	1,100	4.7
Houston	36,158	33,816	2,342	6.5

County	Labor Force	Employment	Unemployment	Unemployment Rate
Irwin	5,487	5,218	269	4.9
Jackson	13,451	12,583	868	6.5
Jasper	3,198	2,895	303	9.5
Jeff Davis	6,003	5,591	412	6.9
Jefferson	7,871	7,195	676	8.6
Jenkins	3,705	3,366	339	9.1
Johnson	3,888	3,528	360	9.3
Jones	8,192	7,576	616	7.5
Lamar	4,743	4,285	458	9.7
Lanier	2,250	2,100	150	6.7
Laurens	16,573	15,029	1,544	9.3
Lee	6,209	5,729	480	7.7
Liberty	10,670	9,820	850	8.0
Lincoln	2,975	2,493	482	16.2
Long	1,570	1,409	161	10.3
Lowndes	32,351	30,202	2,149	6.6
Lumpkin	5,592	5,301	291	5.2
McDuffie	9,024	8,324	700	7.8
McIntosh	3,747	3,354	393	10.5
Macon	4,771	4,065	706	14.8
Madison	9,740	8,996	744	7.6
Marion	2,909	2,662	247	8.5
Meriwether	8,365	7,433	932	11.1
Miller	3,162	2,956	206	6.5
Mitchell	9,362	8,550	812	8.7
Monroe	7,438	6,853	585	7.9
Montgomery	3,149	2,925	224	7.1
Morgan	5,860	5,254	606	10.3
Murray	10,869	9,883	986	9.1
Muscogee	71,761	66,454	5,307	7.4
Newton	21,123	19,923	1,200	5.7
Oconee	6,981	6,671	310	4.4
Oglethorpe	4,464	4,081	383	8.6
Paulding	15,966	15,278	688	4.3
Peach	8,706	7,996	710	8.2
Pickens	5,222	4,860	362	6.9
Pierce	5,406	4,779	627	11.6
Pike	4,832	4,464	368	7.6
Polk	12,961	11,673	1,288	9.9
Pulaski	3,856	3,318	538	14.0
Putnam	5,062	4,659	403	8.0
Quitman	713	638	75	10.5
Rabun	5,585	5,177	408	7.3
Randolph	3,707	3,362	345	9.3

County	Labor Force	Employment	Unemployment	Unemployment Rate
Richmond	79,886	74,537	5,349	6.7
Rockdale	23,319	22,478	841	3.6
Schley	1,609	1,476	133	8.3
Screven	5,551	5,064	487	8.8
Seminole	3,841	3,555	286	7.4
Spalding	28,673	26,556	2,117	7.4
Stephens	10,339	9,355	984	9.5
Stewart	2,433	2,080	353	14.5
Sumter	14,592	13,344	1,248	8.6
Talbot	2,611	2,324	287	11.0
Taliaferro	670	568	102	15.2
Tattnall	6,993	6,533	460	6.6
Taylor	2,994	2,687	307	10.3
Telfair	5,054	4,576	478	9.5
Terrell	4,720	4,198	522	11.1
Thomas	18,492	16,741	1,751	9.5
Tift	16,984	15,832	1,152	6.8
Toombs	10,558	9,706	852	8.1
Towns	2,938	2,740	198	6.7
Treutlen	2,389	2,197	192	8.0
Troup	26,944	24,798	2,146	8.0
Turner	3,637	3,270	367	10.1
Twiggs	3,537	3,218	319	9.0
Union	4,101	3,713	388	9.5
Upson	12,046	10,907	1,139	9.5
Walker	25,614	23,523	2,091	8.2
Walton	18,097	16,831	1,266	7.0
Ware	16,438	14,901	1,537	9.4
Warren	2,722	2,513	209	7.7
Washington	8,068	7,426	642	8.0
Wayne	8,661	7,740	921	10.6
Webster	669	553	116	17.3
Wheeler	2,650	2,465	185	7.0
White	5,848	5,415	433	7.4
Whitfield	38,953	35,979	2,974	7.6
Wilcox	2,955	2,710	245	8.3
Wilkes	5,129	4,373	756	14.7
Wilkinson	4,390	4,088	302	6.9
Worth	7,027	6,212	815	11.6
Georgia	2,865,000	2,678,000	187,000	6.5

ENDANGERED SPECIES

The following are the federally listed endangered and threatened species.
The status code is: E–Endangered; T–Threatened.

Common Name	Scientific Name	Status
Birds		
Curlew, Eskimo	Numenius borealis	E
Eagle, bald	Haliaeetus leucocephalus	E
Falcon, American peregrine	Falco peregrinus anatum	E
Falcon, Arctic peregrine	Falco peregrinus tundrius	T
Plover, piping	Charadrius melodus	T
Stork, wood	Mycteria americana	E
Warbler (wood), Bachman's	Vermivora bachmanii	E
Woodpecker, ivory-billed	Campephilus principalis	E
Woodpecker, red-cockaded	Picoides borealis	E
Fishes		
Chub, spotfin	Hybopsis monacha	T
Darter, amber	Percina antesella	E
Darter, snail	Percina tanasi	T
Logperch, Conassauga	Percina jenkinsi	E
Madtom, yellowfin	Noturus flavipinnis	T
Mammals		
Bat, gray	Myotis grisescens	E
Bat, Indiana	Myotis sodalis	E
Manatee, West Indian (Florida)	Trichechus manatus	E
Panther, Florida	Felis concolor coryi	E
Wolf, red	Canis rufus	E
Plants		
Rattleweed, hairy	Baptisia arachnifera	E
Dropwort, canby's	Oxypolis canbyi	E
Pitcher plant, green	Sarracenia oreophila	E
Torreya, Florida	Torreya taxifolia	E
Trillium, persistent	Trillium, persistens	E
Reptiles		
Alligator, American	Alligator mississippiensis	E
Alligator, American	Alligator mississippiensis	T
Snake, eastern indigo	Drymarchon corais couperi	T
Turtle, green sea	Chelonia mydas	T
Turtle, Kemp's (Atlantic) Ridley sea	Lepidochelys kempii	E
Turtle, leatherback sea	Dermochelys coriacea	E
Turtle, loggerhead sea	Caretta caretta	T

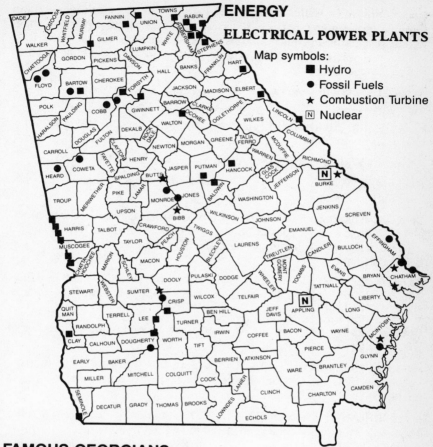

ENERGY

ELECTRICAL POWER PLANTS

Map symbols:
- ■ Hydro
- ● Fossil Fuels
- ★ Combustion Turbine
- Ⓝ Nuclear

FAMOUS GEORGIANS

The following list is merely representative of the many hundreds of Georgians—native born or "transplanted"—who have made their mark on the development of Georgia and the United States.

Aaron, Henry Louis "Hank" (1934—   ). Born in Mobile, Alabama. Baseball player, holder of 21 Major League records, including Most Home Runs. Member of the Baseball Hall of Fame. Corporate vice president of the *Atlanta Braves*.

Aiken, Conrad Potter (1889—1973). Born in Savannah. Poet, novelist, short story writer and critic. Educated at Harvard University. Works include *Selected Poems*, for which he won the Pulitzer Prize in 1930, *Blue Voyage*, *The Short Stories of Conrad Aiken*, and his autobiography, *Ushant*.

141

Anderson, James William "Bill" (1937—   ). Born in Columbia, South Carolina, grew up in Griffin and Decatur. Country music performer, songwriter, restaurant and music publishing entrepreneur. He holds 50 BMI awards and was elected to the Country Music Songwriters Hall of Fame before the age of forty.

Arnall, Ellis Gibbs. See section on Governors (1943—1947).

Arp, Bill (1826—1903). Born in Lawrenceville. Pseudonym for Charles Henry Smith. Attorney and humorist. Author of several books including *Bill Arp's Peace Papers*.

Atkinson, William Yates. See section on Governors (1894—1898).

Bainbridge, William (1774—1833). Naval officer, commanded the *U.S. Constitution*. Decatur County town named in his honor.

Baldwin, Abraham (1754—1807). Born in North Guilford, Connecticut; one of Georgia's signers of the United States Constitution in 1787. Played a key role in the establishment of the University of Georgia. U.S. representative and senator.

Bartram, William (1739—1823). Born in Philadelphia, died in Kingsessing, Pennsylvania. Early naturalist who roamed much of the state of Georgia.

Bell, Griffin B. (1918—   ). U.S. attorney general, cabinet member of Jimmy Carter.

Benning, Henry Lewis (1814—1875). Born in Virginia. Educated at the University of Georgia. Confederate general. Fort Benning named in his honor.

Berrien, John McPherson (1781—1856). Graduate of Princeton, 4 times U.S. senator, attorney general in Andrew Jackson's cabinet.

Berry, Martha (1866—1942). Born near Rome, Georgia; died in Atlanta. Educator. Became Georgia's first female member of the Board of Regents. Founder of the Berry Schools.

Bethune, Thomas Green (1849—1908). A slave on the Bethune plantation near Columbus, "Blind Tom'" became an internationally famous blind pianist and composer.

Birney, Alice McClellan (1858—1907). Born in Marietta. Founder of the National Congress of Mothers, which later became the National Parent-Teacher Association.

Blackburn, Joyce (—   ). Author of prize-winning fiction and historical biographies, including fiction for children such as *Suki and the Invisi-*

ble Peacock, Suki and the Old Umbrella, and biographies of Martha Berry, John Adams, James Edward Oglethorpe and others.

Boudinot, Elias (circa 1803—1839). Born in Georgia, murdered in Georgia. Editor of the *Cherokee Phoenix,* an Indian newspaper. Was killed for his role in the 1835 treaty with the United States.

Boynton, James S. See section on Governors (1883).

Brown, Joseph Emerson. See section on Governors (1857—1865).

Brown, Jospeh Mackey. See section on Governors (1909—1911; 1912—1913).

Brownson, Nathan. See section on Governors (1781—1782).

Brumby, Thomas M. (—   ). Spanish-American War hero from Marietta who served as Admiral Dewey's flag officer at the Battle of Manila.

Bulloch, Archibald. See section on Governors (1776—1777).

Bullock, Rufus B. See section on Governors (1868—1871).

Busbee, George Dekle. See section on Governors (1975—1983).

Butler, Selena Sloan (1872—1964). Born in Thomasville; died in Los Angeles, Ca. Educator. Founder of the Georgia Colored Parent-Teacher Association and the National Congress of Colored Parents. She fought against racial discrimination.

Caldwell, Erskine Preston (1903—   ). Born in White Oak. Noted novelist. Best known for his stories about hard times in the American South. Author of *Tobacco Road* and *God's Little Acre.*

Callaway, Cason J. (1894—1961). Textile magnate who created Callaway Gardens, the resort with botanical and vegetable gardens.

Candler, Allen Daniel. See section on Governors (1898—1902).

Carter, James Earl, Jr., "Jimmy" (1924—   ). Born in Plains. Nuclear physicist, naval officer, peanut farmer, school board member, state senator, governor, 39th president of the United States. Also see section on Governors (1971—1975).

Carter, Rosalynn Smith (1927—   ). Born in Georgia. Wife of President Jimmy Carter.

Charles, Ezzard (1922—   ). Born in Georgia. Professional boxer. Held the World Heavyweight Boxing Championship from 1949, following Joe Louis's retirement, to 1951.

Charles, Ray (1932—   ). Born in Albany. Noted blind pianist and singer. His recordings have been on the charts in country, rhythm and blues, and popular categories.

Chivers, Thomas Holley (1809—1858). Born in Washington; died in Decatur. Was a noted poet and good friend of Edgar Allan Poe. Works include *The Path of Sorrow* (1832), *The Lost Pleiad* (1845), and *Conrad and Eudora* (1834).

Clarke, Elijah (1733—1799). Born in Edgecombe County, North Carolina; died in Richmond County, Georgia. Active in the Revolution. Land speculator, involved in the Yazoo Land Frauds. Clarke County is named in his honor.

Clarke, John. See section on Governors (1819—1823).

Clay, Lucius DuBignon (1879—1978). Born in Marietta. U.S. Army general, author of *Decision in Germany* (1950). Retired in 1949, then served as ambassador in West Berlin during President Kennedy's administration.

Cobb, Howell. See section on Governors (1851—1853).

Cobb, Thomas Reade Rootes (1823—1862). Graduate of University of Georgia, author of the Confederate State Constitution, and brigadier general in the Confederacy. Co-founder of the first law school in Georgia.

Cobb, Tyrus Raymond "Ty" (1886—1961). Born in Banks County. Baseball player from 1905 to 1928. Until Pete Rose recently broke his record, Cobb had more hits (4,191) than any player in history. Member of the Baseball Hall of Fame.

Coburn, Charles (1877—1961). Born in Macon. Popular character in movies of the 1930s and 1940s.

Colquitt, Alfred Holt. See section on Governors (1877—1882).

Conley, Benjamin F. See section on Governors (1871—1872).

Cooper, Mark Anthony (1800—1885). Member of U.S. House of Representatives, pioneer iron industrialist.

Coulter, Ellis Merton (1890—1981). Born in Hickory, North Carolina; died in Atlanta. Educator and author. Taught history at the University of Georgia. His works include *The Civil War and Readjustment in Kentucky* (1926), *Georgia, A Short History* (1933), and in *The History of the South* series: *The South During Reconstruction, 1865—1877* and *The Confederate States of America, 1861—1865* (1950).

Crawford, George Walker. See section on Governors (1843—1847).

Crawford, William Harris (1772—1834). Born in Amherst County, Va.; died in Georgia. One of Georgia's most successful national politicians. U.S.

senator, president pro tempore of the Senate, U.S. minister to France, secretary of War, secretary of the Treasury, and presidential hopeful.

Davies, Myrick. See section on Governors (1781).

Dawson, William Crosby (1798—1856). Born in Greene County. Lawyer, legislator, captain of volunteers in the Indian War of 1836 in Florida, judge of the Ocmulgee judicial circuit, congressman, senator. Two cities and one county in Georgia are named for him.

Dodd, Lamar (1909—   ). Born in Fairburn. Artist and art educator, lecturer, official artist for the National Aeronautics and Space Administration.

Dorsey, Hugh Manson. See section on Governors (1917—1921).

Douglas, Melvyn (1901—1981). Born in Macon. died in New York City. Noted movie actor. Won two Academy Awards for his performances in *Hud* in 1963 and *Being There* in 1979.

Early, Peter. See section on Governors (1813—1815).

Edwards, Harry Stillwell (1855—1938). Born in Appling County. Author and columnist for the *Macon Telegraph*. Among his works are his most famous short story, "AEneas Africanus," and a tribute to his friend Sidney Lanier.

Elbert, Samuel. See section on Governors (1785—1786).

Ellis, Henry. See section on Governors (1757—1760).

Emanuel, David. See section on Governors (1801).

Felton, Rebecca Latimer (1835—1930). Born near Decatur; died in Atlanta. Was a writer and a leader for political and social reform. At the age of 87, she became the nation's first female U.S. senator.

Few, William (1748—1828). Born in Maryland; died in New York. One of Georgia's two signers of the U.S. Constitution. U.S. senator and judge. Moved to New York in 1799 where he became president of the City Bank.

Forsyth, John. See section on Governors (1827—1829).

Fremont, John Charles (1813—1890). Born in Savannah; died in New York City. Was an Army officer, explorer, senator and civil governor of California. Was the Republican Party's first presidential nominee.

George, Walter Franklin (1878—1957). Born in Webster County, Georgia. Served in the U.S. Senate for 34 years. Ambassador to NATO and special advisor to President Eisenhower. Law school at Mercer University named in his honor.

Gilmer, George Rockingham. See section on Governors (1829—1831; 1837—1839).

Gordon, John Brown. See section on Governors (1886—1890).

Gordon, William Washington (1796—1842). Educated at West Point. First President of the Central of Georgia Railroad. Third lieutenant, aide to General Gaines. Gordon County named for him.

Goulding, Dr. Frances Robert (1810—1881). Inventor of the sewing machine, wrote juvenile books *Young Marooners*, 1852, and *Marooners' Island*, 1862.

Grady, Henry Woodfin (1850—1889). Born in Athens; died in Boston, Ma. Newspaperman, editor and part owner of the *Atlanta Constitution* in the 1880s.

Graham, Patrick. See section on Governors (1752—1754).

Greene, Nathanael (1742—1786). Born in Potowomut, Rhode Island. While in command of the southern Revolutionary army, Greene conducted a notably successful campaign against the British in Georgia, forcing the enemy to retreat. Georgia honored him with the gift of Mulberry Grove, an estate on the Savannah River, where he retired after the war was won.

Griffin, Samuel Marvin. See section on Governors (1955—1959).

Gwinnett, Button. See section on Governors (1777).

Habersham, James (1713—1775). Born in England, died in Brunswick, New Jersey. Secretary and acting governor of the colony of Georgia from 1771 to 1773. Established the first orphanage in the new world. Raised and exported the first cotton ever shipped from America. Father of Joseph Habersham.

Habersham, Joseph (1751—1815). Died in Savannah. Leader of the Liberty Boys; colonel in the Continental Army. Served in the Continental Congress, speaker of the Georgia House of Representatives, mayor of Savannah, first postmaster general of the United States.

Hadas, Moses (1900—1966). Born in Atlanta; died in Aspen, Co. Classical scholar, educated at Emory University. Edited and translated many Latin, Greek, Hebrew and German works into English. His works include *A History of Greek Literature* (1950) and *Humanism: The Greek Ideal and Its Survival* (1960).

Hall, Lyman. See section on Governors (1783—1784).

Handley, George. See section on Governors (1788—1789).

Hardee, William Joseph (1815—1873). Born in Savannah; died in

Wytheville, Va. Educated at West Point. Taught at West Point, then took command of Confederate forces when Georgia seceded the Union in 1861. Attained the rank of general, and in 1864 he commanded the forces that defended Savannah against General Sherman's troops.

Hardman, Lamartine Griffin. See section on Governors (1927—1931).

Hardwick, Thomas William. See section on Governors (1921—1923).

Hardy, Oliver Norvell (1892—1957). Born in Harlem. Great comedian of Laurel and Hardy fame.

Harris, Joe Frank. See section on Governors (1983—   ).

Harris, Joel Chandler (1848—1908). Born in Eatonton. Assisted Henry W. Grady in running the *Atlanta Constitution*. Creator and author of the famous "Uncle Remus" stories. Founded the *Uncle Remus Magazine* in 1907, achieving a circulation of 200,000.

Harris, Nathaniel E. See section on Governors (1915—1917).

Hayes, Roland (1887—1976). Born in Curyville; died in Boston, Ma. International tenor. Son of a former slave, Hayes was the first black singer to get worldwide recognition in classical music.

Heard, Stephen. See section on Governors (1780—1781).

Herty, Charles (1867—1938). Born in Milledgeville. Taught Chemistry at the University of Georgia and the University of North Carolina. Concentrated on finding new industrial uses for Southern natural resources. Developed process for using pine in making wood pulp.

Hill, Benjamin Harvey (1823—1882). Born in Jasper County. Graduate of University of Georgia. Senator in the Confederate States of America. After the War Between the States, became a U.S. senator.

Hill, Joshua (1812—1891). Opponent of secession, Unionist during the war, U.S. senator (1871—1873).

Hill, Walter Barnard (1851—1905). Born in Talbot County. Lawyer and educator. Founded Georgia Bar Association. Chancellor of the University of Georgia, 1899—1905.

Hodges, Courtney (1887—1966). Born in Perry. American army officer, educated at the U.S. Military Academy at West Point. Participated in campaigns in France during World War I, served with the army of occupation in Germany in 1918. During World War II he was commanding general of the Tenth Army Corps from 1942 to 1943, and later commanded the Third Army and the First Army through many European campaigns.

Holliday, John Henry "Doc" (1852—1887). Born in Georgia; died in Colorado. Training as a dentist, Holliday migrated to Texas as a young man for health reasons. Was a friend of lawman Wyatt Earp. Participated in the gunfight at the O. K. Corral.

Holloway, Sterling (1905—   ). Born in Cedartown. Actor, comedian and recording artist, appeared in numerous commercials and is best known for being the voice of Walt Disney's Winnie the Pooh and the narrator of *Jungle Book.*

Hope, John (1868—1936). Born in Augusta; died in Atlanta. Educator and black leader. Educated at Brown University. Became the first black president of Morehouse College (1906—1929). Helped found and presided over Atlanta University. Helped organize the Commission of Interracial Cooperation.

Houstoun, John. See section on Governors (1778—1779; 1784—1785).

Howley, Richard. See section on Governors (1780).

Irwin, Jared. See section on Governors (1796—1798; 1806—1809).

Jackson, Henry Rootes (1820—1898). Born in Athens; died in Savannah. Minister to Austria, brigadier general in the Confederacy, and minister to Mexico.

Jackson, James. See section on Governors (1798—1801).

James, Harry (1916—1983). Born in Albany; died in Las Vegas, Nevada. Famed band leader of the 1940s. Was married to Hollywood "pin-up" queen, Betty Grable.

Jenkins, Charles Jones. See section on Governors (1865—1868).

Johnson, Hershel Vespasian. See section on Governors (1853—1857).

Johnson, James. See section on Governors (1865).

Johnson, Nunnally (1897—1977). Born in Georgia; died in Los Angeles, Ca. Was a noted screenwriter, director, and producer. Was responsible for such films as *The Grapes of Wrath, The Man in the Gray Flannel Suit,* and *The Three Faces of Eve.*

Johnston, Joseph Eggleston (1807—1891). Born in Prince Edward County, Va.; died in Washington, D.C. Commander of the Confederate Army opposing Sherman on his March to Atlanta in 1864.

Jones, Charles Colcock (1831—1893). Born in Savannah; died in Augusta. Was an historian and prolific writer, among his books being *The Dead Towns of Georgia* (1878).

Jones, Joseph (1833—1896). Born in Liberty County; died in New Orleans. Was a physician, surgeon in the Confederate Army, and later, responsible for archaeological digs in Tennessee. Brother of Charles C. Jones.

Jones, Noble Wimberly (circa 1724—1805). Born near London, England; died in Savannah. A physician in Savannah, member of the Continental Congress, and president of the Georgia Medical Society.

Jones, Robert Tyre, Jr., "Bobby" (1902—1971). Born in Atlanta. Noted golfer. Won the U.S. Amateur Championship in 1924, 1925, 1927, 1928, 1930; won the U.S. Open in 1923, 1926, and 1930.

Keach, Stacy (1941—   ). Born in Savannah. Movie actor, currently enjoying great success in the television series, "Mike Hammer."

Kemeys, Edward (1843—1907). Born in Georgia. Sculptor known for his animal sculptures, especially the bronze lions at the Art Institute of Chicago.

Kilpatrick, William Heard (1871—1965). Born in White Plains; died in New York City. Taught at Teachers College in Columbia University from 1909 to 1938. Among his works are *Fountains of Method*, 1925, and *Philosophy of Education*, 1951.

King, Coretta Scott (1927—   ). Born in Heiberger, Alabama. Educated at Antioch College in Ohio, and New England Conservatory of Music in Boston, Massachusetts. Met and married Martin Luther King, Jr. there. After his death, she continued to work with the Southern Christian Leadership Conference. President of the Martin Luther King, Jr. Center for Social Change.

King, Martin Luther, Jr. (1929—1968). Born in Atlanta; died in Memphis, Tennessee. Civil rights leader and organizer of the march on Washington in 1963. Assassinated in Memphis.

Knight, Gladys (1944—   ). Born in Atlanta. Popular singer and recording artist. Her group is known as "Gladys Knight and the Pips."

Lamar, Joseph Rucker (1857—1916). Born in Elbert County. Jurist. Was associate justice of the U.S. Supreme Court. Compiled *The Code of the State of Georgia* (2 vols. 1896).

Lamar, Lucius Q. C. (1825—1893). Born in Putnam County. U.S. congressman, Confederate envoy to Russia, U.S. senator, U.S. secretary of the Interior, and associate justice of the U.S. Supreme Court.

Lamar, Mirabeau Buonaparte (1798—1859). Born in Louisville. Served with Sam Houston at the Battle of San Jacinto in 1836. Was vice president of Texas in 1836 and president from 1838—1841.

Lanier, Sidney (1842—1881). Born in Macon; died in North Carolina. One of America's outstanding 19th century poets. Was a P.O.W. during the War

Between the States. Was also a novelist, musician, lawyer, and university professor. Author of *The Marshes of Glynn.*

LeConte, Joseph (1823—1901). Born in Liberty County. Noted geologist. Was professor at the University of California at Berkeley from 1869—1896. Author of *Elements of Geology.*

Lee, Brenda (1944—   ). Born in Atlanta. Popular country singer and recording artist. Resides in Nashville, Tennessee.

Lincoln, Benjamin (1733—1810). Commander of the Department of the South in 1778. Leader of unsuccessful assault on the British in Savannah.

Long, Crawford Williamson (1815—1878). Born in Danielsville; died in Athens. Introduced the use of ether as a surgical anesthetic, an event that has been described as one of the "greatest events in the history of medicine."

Longstreet, Augustus Baldwin (1790—1870). Born in Augusta; died in Mississippi. Georgia's best known antebellum author. *Georgia Scenes* is recognized as a foremost example of American humor. President of the University of Mississippi. Was the uncle of General James Longstreet and the father-in-law of L. Q. C. Lamar.

Low, Juliette Gordon (1860—1927). Born in Savannah. Organized the first group of Girl Guides, later the Girl Scouts of America, in Savannah in 1912.

Lumpkin, Joseph Henry (1799—1867). Born in Oglethorpe County; died in Athens. Graduate of Princeton, first chief justice of the Supreme Court (1845—1867). Assisted in writing the state penal code, founder of Georgia's first law school, law teacher.

Lumpkin, Wilson. See section on Governors (1831—1835).

Maddox, Lester Garfield. See section on Governors (1967—1971).

Martin, John. See section on Governors (1782—1783).

Matthews, George. See section on Governors (1787—1788; 1793—1796).

McAdoo, William Gibbs (1863—1941). Born near Marietta. Attorney and railroad company executive. U.S. secretary of the treasury. Married Woodrow Wilson's daughter, Eleanor. Was U.S. senator from California.

McCullers, Carson Smith (1917—1967). Born in Columbus. Noted author and playwright. Wrote *Member of the Wedding* in 1946.

McDaniel, Henry D. See section on Governors (1883—1886).

McDonald, Charles James. See section on Governors (1839—1843).

McGill, Ralph Emerson (1898—1969). Publisher of the *Atlanta Constitution;* author of *The South and the Southerner* (1963).

McIntosh, Lachlan (1725—1806). Born in Scotland; died in Savannah. Brigadier in the revolution, and duelist who killed Button Gwinnett. Appointed by the Continental Congress as commander of the military forces in Georgia.

Melton, James (1904—1961). Born in Moultrie. Was lead tenor for the Metropolitan Opera Company. Starred on radio's "Texaco Star Theater" and the "Telephone Hour."

Mercer, Johnny (1909—1976). Born in Savannah. Popular music composer. Best known for such hit tunes as "Jeepers Creepers," "Old Black Magic," and "Moon River" (with Henry Mancini).

Milledge, John. See section on Governors (1802—1806).

Miller, Caroline (1903—   ). Noted writer. Won the Pulitzer Prize for fiction in 1934 for *Lamb in His Bosom.*

Miller, Zell (1932—   ). Educator, author, lieutenant governor of Georgia, he has been in office longer than any other person in the state's history. Author of *Great Georgians* and *They Heard Georgia Singing.*

Mitchell, David Brydie. See section on Governors (1809—1818; 1815—1817).

Mitchell, Margaret (1900—1949). Born in Atlanta; died in Atlanta. Author of *Gone With the Wind* in 1936. Over 1,000,000 copies were sold within the first six months of publication. Named Georgia's "most famous person" by legislative action in 1985. Also see section entitled *Gone With the Wind.*

Northern, William J. See section on Governors (1890—1894).

O'Conner, Mary Flannery (1925—1964). Born in Savannah. Noted novelist and short story writer. Wrote *Wise Blood* (1952), *A Good Man Is Hard to Find and Other Short Stories* (1955), and the acclaimed *The Violent Bear It Away* (1959).

Odum, Howard Washington (1884—1954). Born in Bethlehem, Georgia. Educator and writer. Was a pioneer in Southern sociological education. Author of *The Negro and His Songs.*

Oglethorpe, James. See section on Governors (1733—1743).

Parker, Henry. See section on Governors (1751—1752).

Parks, Bert (1914—   ). Born in Atlanta. Entertainer, master of ceremonies for the Miss America Pageant from 1956 to 1979.

Price, Eugenia (—   ). Resides in Georgia. Internationally known author, whose works include the St. Simons Trilogy, *Lighthouse, New Moon*

Rising, and *Beloved Invader*, and such best-sellers as *Savannah*, and *To See Your Face Again*. Her papers are collected by the Mugar Library at Boston University.

Pulaski, Count Casimir (1748—1779). Born in Podolia, Poland. Joined forces with General Benjamin Lincoln to drive the British out of Savannah, and was mortally wounded during an attack on October 9, 1779. Fort Pulaski was named in his honor.

Rabun, William. See section on Govenors (1817—1819).

Redding, Otis (1941—1971). Born in Dawson. Writer and singer of soul ballads, including "I've Been Loving You Too Long," "Respect," and "Sitting on the Dock of the Bay."

Reece, Byron Herbert (1917—1958). Born near Choestoe. Poet, winner of national awards, including the Georgia Distinguished Writers Award. Works include *Bow Down in Jericho*, a book of poetry, and a novel, *Better a Dinner of Herbs*.

Reed, Jerry (1937—   ). Born in Atlanta. Country music singer and guitarist. One of his more popular recordings was "When You're Hot You're Hot." Co-starred with Burt Reynolds in several movies.

Reynolds, Burt (1936—   ). Born in Waycross. Popular movie actor. One of his most popular appearances was in the movie *Smoky and the Bandit*.

Reynolds, John. See section on Governors (1754—1757).

Rivers, Eurith Dickinson. See section on Governors (1937—1941).

Robinson, Jackie (1919—1972). Born in Cairo, Georgia. First black to play major league baseball in the U.S. Most valuable player in the National League in 1949. Career spanned from 1947 to 1956. Member of the Baseball Hall of Fame.

Ross, John (1790—1866). Born near Lookout Mountain, Tennessee. Served with Andrew Jackson against the Creeks in 1812. Was president of the National Council of Cherokees and later, chief of the Cherokee nation.

Ruger, Thomas Howard. See section on Governors (1868).

Rusk, Dean (1909—   ). Born in Canton. Former president of the Rockefeller Foundation. U.S. secretary of state in the Kennedy and Johnson administrations.

Russell, Richard B. See section on Governors (1931—1933).

Ryan, Father Abram Joseph (1838—1886). Catholic priest and poet. Longtime Augusta resident whose works include such Southern Confederacy tributes as *The Conquered Banner* and *Sword of Lee*.

Sanders, Carl E. See section on Governors (1963—1967).

Schley, William. See section on Governors (1835—1837).

Slaton, John Marshall. See section on Governors (1913—1917).

Smith, Charles Henry (1826—1903). Humorist who wrote under the pseudonym Bill Arp.

Smith, Hoke. See section on Governors (1907—1909; 1911).

Smith, James Milton. See section on Governors (1872—1877).

Smith, Lillian (1897—1966). Born in Jasper, Florida; died in Atlanta. Author, civil rights activist. She co-founded *The North Georgia Review* in 1936. Novels include *Strange Fruit* (1944) and *Killers of the Dream* (1949) which condemned racism. Friend of Dr. Martin Luther King, Jr., she was also on the board of Congress of Racial Equality.

Spaulding, Thomas (1774—1851). Planter and banker. Born on St. Simons Island. State legislator, U.S. congressman. Agricultural experimenter, reformer and writer. Helped develop production of Sea Island cotton and sugar along Georgian coast.

Stallings, Laurence (1894—1968). Playwright, motion picture scenarist, critic, and novelist.

Stanton, Frank Lebby (1857—1927). Journalist who wrote for the *Atlanta Constitution*. Most popular poet of the 1890s, works include *Songs from Dixie Land* (1900), and a poem which was set to music, "Mighty Lak a Rose."

Stephens, Alexander Hamilton. See section on Governors (1882—1883).

Stephens, William. See section on Governors (1743—1751).

Stevens, Ray (1939—   ). Born in Clarksdale. Lives in Nashville, Tennessee. Popular country music recording star. His hit, "The Streak," sold over 5 million copies.

Talmadge, Eugene. See section on Governors (1933—1937; 1941—1943).

Talmadge, Herman Eugene. See section on Governors (1947; 1948—1955).

Tarkenton, Fran (1940—   ). Born in Richmond, Virginia. Moved to Athens, Georgia in 1951. Starred in football at Athens High School. Was All-American quarterback at the University of Georgia. Played professional football for the Minnesota Vikings and the New York Giants.

Tattnall, Josiah. See section on Governors (1801—1802).

Telfair, Edward. See section on Governors (1786—1787; 1789—1793).

Terrell, Joseph M. See section on Governors (1902—1907).

Thompson, Melvin Ernest. See section on Governors (1947—1948).

Tomochichi (—   ). An old Creek chief who met General Oglethorpe when he landed in Georgia in 1733, and accompanied him to England in 1734. Travelled with Oglethorpe down the coast of Georgia in 1736.

Toombs, Robert Augustus (1810—1885). Born near Washington, Georgia; died in Georgia. U.S. congressman, U.S. senator. Secretary of state in the Confederate States of America. Participated in the Battles of Malvern Hill and Antietam. After the War Between the States, he never regained his U.S. citizenship.

Towns, George Washington Bonaparte. See section on Governors (1847—1851).

Treutlen, John Adam. See section on Governors (1777—1778).

Troup, George M. See section on Governors (1823—1827).

Vandiver, Samuel Ernest. See section on Governors (1959—1963).

Vinson, Carl (—1981). Lawyer and congressman. Born near Milledgeville. Member, state House of Representatives, 1902—1912. Judge of county court of Baldwin County, 1912—1914. Congressman, 1914—1965.

Walker, Clifford Mitchell. See section on Governors (1923—1927).

Walton, George. See section on Governors (1779—1780; 1789—1790).

Watson, Thomas Edward (1856—1922). Born near Thomson. U.S. congressman, writer, and leader of Georgia's agrarian revolt in the late 19th century. Author of *The Story of France*. Also served in the U.S. Senate.

Wayne, Anthony (1745—1796). Commander of the American forces in Georgia when the British evacuated Savannah in 1782. Waynesboro and Wayne County were named for him.

Wayne, James Moore (1790—1867). Born in Savannah. Graduate of Princeton. Was a U.S. congressman and an associate justice of the U.S. Supreme Court.

Wereat, John. See section on Governors (1779).

Wesley, John (1703—1791). Born in England. Founder of Methodism, and minister of the Church of England in Georgia, 1735—1736.

Wheeler, Joseph (1836—1906). Born near Augusta. Confederate lieutenant-general of Calvary. U.S. congressman after the War Between the States. Also served in the Spanish-American War.

Whitefield, George (1714—1770). Born in Gloucester, England. Came to Georgia as a missionary in 1737. Founded Bethesda Orphans Home.

White, Walter Francis (1893—1955). Negro leader and author. A leader of the National Association for the Advancement of Colored People (NAACP).

Wilson, Ellen Louise Axson (1860—1914). Born in Georgia. First wife of President Woodrow Wilson.

Wilson, Woodrow (1856—1924). Born in Virginia; grew up in Georgia during the War Between the States. Educator, scholar, writer, governor and president. Passed several bills including the Child Labor Legislation, and the Nineteenth Amendment giving women the right to vote.

Woods, William B. (1824—1887). Born in Newark, Ohio; died in Washington, D.C. Educated at Yale University. Brigadier general in the Union Army. Accompanied General Sherman on his march to the sea. Moved to Alabama to aid in reconstruction. U.S. Circuit Court judge for Georgia and neighboring states, 1869—1880, associate justice of U.S. Supreme Court, 1880.

Woodward, Joanne (1930—   ). Born in Thomasville. Noted film and television actress. Won the Academy Award in 1957 for her role in *The Three Faces of Eve*.

Wright, Sir James. See section on Governors (1760—1782).

Yerby, Frank (1916—   ). Born in Augusta. Noted novelist. Author of *The Foxes of Harrow, Goat Song, Judas, The Dahomean*, and many others.

Young, Andrew Jackson, Jr. (1932—   ). U.S. ambassador to the United Nations, civil rights leader and politician. Cabinet member of President Jimmy Carter.

FESTIVALS AND EVENTS

The following is a partial list of festivals and events with the general dates on which they usually take place. For more detailed list of events giving actual dates write: Calendar, P.O. Box 1776, Atlanta, Georgia 30301. If you desire more detailed information on a specific festival or event and no contact person is listed, consult the chamber of commerce in that area (see Chambers of Commerce chapter).

JANUARY
Fireside Arts/Crafts Show—Helen—White County, mid-January—mid-February. (Unicoi State Park, 404-878-2201)
Fasching Masquerade Karnival—Helen—White County, mid-January—mid-February. (Chamber of Commerce, 404-878-2181)

Rattlesnake Roundup—Whigham—Grady County, mid-January, Whigham High School. (Myron R. Prevatte, 912-762-4243)

FEBRUARY

Georgia Week—Savannah—Chatham County, early February, Savannah Historic District. (Marti Bowden, 912-233-7787)

Antiques at the Crossroads—Perry—Houston County, early February, National Guard Armory. (912-987-3119)

MARCH

Rattlesnake Roundup—Claxton—Evans County, mid-March. (Jimmy Waters, 912-739-3733)

St. Patrick's Festival—Dublin—Laurens County, mid-March. (Hal Ward, 912-275-0353)

St. Patrick's Day Festival—Savannah—Chathan County, March 17.

Peach Orchards in Bloom—Ft. Valley/Perry—Houston County, mid-March.

Hawkinsville Harness Festival—Hawkinsville—Pulaski County, mid- to late March.

Cherry Blossom Festival—Macon—Bibb County, mid- to late March. (Carolyn Crayton, 912-744-7429)

Historic Tour of Homes—Cuthbert—Randolph County, late March.

Great Golden Easter Egg Hunt—Jekyll Island—Glynn County, Easter.

Easter Sunrise Service—Pine Mountain—Harris County, Easter.

Tour of Homes and Gardens—St. Simons Island—Glynn County, late March.

Tour of Homes and Gardens—Savannah—Chatham County, late March.

APRIL

Master's Golf Tournament—Augusta—Richmond County, early April.

Livestock Festival—Sylvania—Screvens County, early April. (Norma K. Howard, 912-564-7878)

Westville's Spring Festival—Lumpkin, Westville—Stewart County, early April. (Jerald N. Baxter, 912-838-6310)

Atlanta Dogwood Festival—Atlanta—Fulton County, early April. (Clara L. Wells, 404-892-0539)

Georgia Steam and Gas Show—Tifton—Tift County, early April.

Berry Patch—Rome—Floyd County, mid-April.

Trout Festival—Dahlonega—Lumpkin County, mid-April.

Rose Festival—Thomasville—Thomas County, mid-April. (Ruth Willett, 912-226-9600)

Atlanta Steeplechase—Atlanta—Fulton County, early April.

Pine Tree Festival—Swainsboro—Emanuel County, late April—early May. (Ed Schwabe, 912-237-8846)

Crackerland Country Fair—Howard—Taylor County, late April. (Fred Brown, 912-862-5253)

Affair on the Square—LaGrange—Troup County, late April.

"Night in Old Savannah"—Savannah—Chatham County, Visitors' Center, late April. (Thomas E. Newsome, 912-355-2422)

Georgia Mountain Jubilee—Gainsville—Hall County, late April—early May.

MAY

Westville's May Day—Lumpkin, Westville—Stewart County, May 1. (Jerald Baxter, 912-838-6310)

Prater's Mill Country Fair—Dalton—Whitfield County, Prater's Mill, early May. (J. Alderman/J. Harrell, 404-259-3420)

156

Enterprise 80/81—Athens—Clarke County, early May.

Gum Swamp Festival—Cochran—Bleckley County, early May.

Salisbury Fair—Columbus—Muscogee County, Ironworks, early May. (Celia Page, 404-322-0756)

Cotton Pickin' Antique Arts/Crafts (Country) Fair—Gay—Meriwether County, Old Cotton Gin Complex, early May. (Joann Gay, 404-538-6814)

Mayfest—Dahlonega—Lumpkin County, Pavilion, mid-May. (Chamber of Commerce, 404-878-2181)

Blessing of the Fleet—Darien—McIntosh County, May.

Brunswick Gold Isles Spring Fiesta/Blessing of the Fleet—Brunswick—Glynn County, mid-May.

Arts Festival of Atlanta—Atlanta—Fulton County, mid-May.

Ogeechee River Raft Race—Statesboro—Bulloch County, May.

Vidalia Onion Festival—Vidalia—Toombs County, mid-May. (Priscilla Oxley, 912-537-9838)

Memorial Day Festival—Jekyll Island—Glynn County, Memorial Day. (Morgan Rodgers, 912-635-2232)

Arts & Crafts Festival—Thomasville—Thomas County, Exchange Club Fairgrounds, late May. (Al Stone, 912-226-3108)

JUNE

Helen to the Atlantic Ocean Balloon Race—Helen—White County, early June. (Chamber of Commerce, 404-878-2181)

Savannah River Days Raft Race—Augusta—Richmond County, early June.

Marigold Festival—Winterville—Clarke County, early June.

Putnam County Dairy Festival—Eatonton—Putnam County, early June.

Currahee Arts/Crafts Festival—Toccoa—Stephens County, mid-June.

Spring Lake Bluegrass Festival/Old Time Fiddler's Reunion—Rhine—Dodge County, mid-June.

Blueberry Festival—Alma—Bacon County, Recreation Park, late June. (Jerri L. Taylor, 912-632-5859)

Bluegrass Festival—Dahlonega—Lumpkin County, Music Park, late June. (Norman Adams, 404-864-7203)

JULY

Appalachian Wagon Train—Chatsworth—Murray County, Saddle Club Grounds, eary July. (C. W. Bradley, 404-695-2361)

4th of July Celebration—Colbert—Madison County, July 4.

Peachtree Road Race—Atlanta—Fulton County, 4th of July.

Watermelon Festival—Cordele—Crisp County, early July.

Masters Water Ski Tournament—Pine Mountain—Harris County, mid-July.

Blessing of the Fleet—Thunderbolt—Chatham County, July.

AUGUST

Lake Trahlyta Arts & Crafts Fair—Blairsville—Union County, Vogel State Park, early August. (David Foote, 404-745-2628)

Clown Festival—Macon—Bibb County, Museum of Arts and Sciences, early August. (Ray Hooten, 912-788-0808)

Georgia Mountain Fair—Hiawassee—Towns County, early August.

Sea Island Festival—Sea Island—Glynn County, early August.

Artifacts Fair—Macon—Bibb County, Ocmulgee National Monument, mid-August. (912-742-0447)

Gold Leaf Festival—Pelham—Mitchell County, mid-August.

Old Time Fiddlin' Convention—Dalton—Whitfield County, mid-August.

Mountain Do Arts/Crafts Festival—Buford, Lake Lanier Islands—Gwinnett County, mid- to late August. (Kurt Sutton, 404-945-6701)

Chattahoochee Mountain Fair—Clarkesville—Habersham County, Fairgrounds, late August. (Les Smith, 404-778-8207)

Tybee Regatta—Tybee Island—Chatham County, August.

SEPTEMBER

County Fair of 1896—Tifton—Tift County, Georgia Agrirama, early September. (Geraldine Walters, 912-386-3344)

Yellow Daisy Festival—Stone Mountain—DeKalb County, Park, early September. (Kathi Hayes, 404-469-9831)

Powers Crossroads Country Fair/Arts Festival—Newnan—Coweta County, Labor Day Weekend. (Harriet Alexander, 404-253-2011)

Oktoberfest—Helen—White County, early September to mid-October. (Chamber of Commerce, 404-878-2181)

Hamburg Harvest Festival—Mitchell-Glascock County, Hamburg State Park, early September. (Julian Price, 912-552-2393)

Barnesville Buggy Days—Barnesville—Lamar County, mid-September. (Sue Bankston, 404-358-2732)

Festival of the Painted Rock—Roswell—Fulton County, Chattahoochee Nature Center, mid-September. (Dotty Ertis, 404-992-2055)

Chattahoochee Folk Festival—Columbus—Muscogee County, mid-September.

Ft. Mountain Village Crafts Fair—Chatsworth—Murray County, September.

Apple Festival—Tallulah Falls—Rabun County, Terrora Visitor Center, mid- to late September. (Wanda Phillips, 404-754-3276)

Pecan Festival—Albany—Dougherty County, late September to mid-October. (Sara Pearson, 912-883-6900)

Crackerland County Fair—Howard—Taylor County, late September. (Fred Brown, 912-862-5253)

OCTOBER

Praters' Mill County Fair—Dalton—Whitfield County, early October.

Sunbelt Expo—Moultrie—Colquitt County, early October.

Andersonville Historic Fair—Andersonville—Sumter County, early October.

Cotton Pickin' Antique Arts/Crafts Fair—Gay—Meriwether County, early October. (Bill Gay, 404-538-6814)

Autumn Leaf Festival—Maysville—Banks County, early October. (Elbert Maybry, 404-652-2536)

Great Pumpkin Festival—Cochran—Bleckley County, early October. (Mary Brown, 912-934-2965)

Crowe Springs Craftsmen's Fair—Cartersville—Bartow County, mid-October.

Fabric Creations from the Mountains—Helen—White County, Unicoi State Park, mid-October. (Bob Slack, 404-878-2201 ext. 282 or 283)

Heritage Holidays—Rome—Floyd County, mid-October.

Georgia Marble Festival—Jasper—Pickens County, early to mid-October. (Lawton Baggs, 404-692-6598)

Apple Festival—Ellijay—Gilmer County, mid-October. (Gene Wright, 404-635-7400)

Sorghum Festival—Blairsville—Union County, mid-October.

Gold Rush Days—Dahlonega—Lumpkin County, Gold Museum, mid-October. (Sharon Johnson, 404-864-2257)

Fall Country Music/Bluegrass Festival—Hiawassee—Towns County, mid-October.

Scottish Festival & Highland Games—Stone Mountain Park—DeKalb County, mid-October. (Kathi Hayes, 404-469-9831)

Golden Isles Art Festival—St. Simons Island—Glynn County, Neptune Park, mid-October. (Gordi Wood, 912-638-2425)

Brown's Crossing Craftsmen's Fair—Milledgeville—Baldwin County, mid-October.

Southern Open Golf Tournament—Columbus—Muscogee County, Green Island Country Club, early to mid-October. (John Patterson, 404-324-0411)

Cherokee Fall Festival—Calhoun—Gordon County, New Echota Historic Site, late October. (Ed Reed, 404-629-8151)

War of 1812 Fair—Midway—Liberty County, Sunbury Historic Site, late October. (Don McGhee, 912-884-5999)

Six County Fair—Swainsboro—Emanuel County, late October.

Long County Wild Life Festival—Ludowici—Long County, October.

Steam & Gas Fair—Tifton—Tift County, Georgia Agrirama, late October. (Geraldine Walters, 912-386-3344)

Corn Festival—Camilla—Mitchell County, late October.

Fair of 1850—Lumpkin—Stewart County, late October to early November. (Jerald Baxter, 912-838-6310)

NOVEMBER
Mule Day—Calvary—Grady County, early November. (Charles Butler, 912-872-3211)

Pioneer Skills Day Fair—Royston—Franklin County, Victoria Bryant State Park, early November. (Robert Emery, 404-245-6270)

Red Clay Hill Arts & Crafts Festival—Calhoun—Gordon County, Cherokee Capital Fairgrounds, early November. (Sharon Harrell, 404-629-7561)

Million Pines Arts & Crafts Festival—Soperton—Treutlen County, Iva Park, early November. (Jeanne McLendon, 912-529-6611)

Fair of 1850—Westville—Stewart County, early November.

Jasper County Deer Festival—Monticello—Jasper County, early November. (Gene Bailey, 404-468-8194)

Cane Grinding Fair—Tifton—Tift County, Georgia Agrirama, mid-November. (Geraldine Walters, 912-386-3344)

Holiday Marketplace—Gainesville—Hall County, Georgia Mountain Center, mid-November. (Holly Duggan, 404-534-6080)

Piddlers & Peddlers Fair—Perry—Houston County, National Guard Armory, late November. (Norma Wilson, 912-987-2079)

DECEMBER
Old Fashion Christmas—Dahlonega—Lumpkin County, early December.

Tour of Homes—Madison—Morgan County, early December.

Sugarplum Festival—Stone Mountain—DeKalb County, Village, early to mid-December. (Betty Fogel, 404-939-7351)

Yuletide Season—Lumpkin—Stewart County, mid- to late December.
Christmas Activities and Living Nativity Pageant—Stone Mountain—DeKalb County, mid-to late December.

FINE ARTS

ATLANTA

Atlanta Symphony Orchestra
J. Thomas Bacchetti, Executive Vice
President and General Manager
Robert Shaw, Music Director and
Conductor
Robert W. Woodruff Arts Center
1280 Peachtree Street, NE (30309)
404-898-1182

AUGUSTA

Augusta Opera Company
Edward Bradberry, General Director
Imperial Theater
P.O. Box 3865
Hill Station (30904)
404-738-0451

Augusta Symphony Orchestra
Tona R. Bays, Manager
Harry M. Jacobs, Musical Director
and Conductor
Maxwell Grover Performing Arts
Theatre
Box 3684
Hill Station (30904)
404-733-9739

COLUMBUS

Columbus Symphony Orchestra
Francis Anderson, Manager
Harry Kruger, Conductor
Three Arts Theatre
P.O. Box 5631 (31906)
404-323-5059

MACON

Macon Symphony Orchestra
Hartley W. Haines, Manager
Adrian Gnam, Musical Director and
Conductor
Porter Memorial Auditorium
P.O. Box 5700 (31208)
912-474-5700/9463

Mercer University Artist Series
Dr. Robert Parris, Director
Grand Opera House/Newton House
Musical Department, Mercer Univ.
(31207)
912-744-2748

SAVANNAH

Savannah Concert Association
Martin H. Greenberg, M.D.,
President
Savannah Civic Center
701 East 44 Street (31405)
912-356-8193/236-2358

Savannah Symphony Orchestra
Marge Mazo, Acting General Manager
Philip Greenberg, Musical Director
and Conductor
Savannah Civic Center
P.O. Box 9505 (31412)
912-236-9536

STATESBORO

**Georgia Southern College Life
Enrichment Series**
Dr. John F. DeNitto, Executive
Director
McCroan Auditorium
LB 8133, Georgia Southern College
(30460)
912-681-5247

THOMASVILLE

**Thomasville Entertainment
Foundation, Inc.**
Mrs. William M. Searcy, Jr.,
Executive Director
Municipal Auditorium
323 Glenwood Drive (31792)
912-226-0432

FLORA AND FAUNA

In colonial times, Georgia was covered almost entirely with forests and the land is still heavily wooded. Much of the Appalachian and Blue Ridge mountain areas are covered with a mixture of deciduous and coniferous trees. Some of the species represented are ash *(Fraxinus)*, black walnut *(Juglans nigra)*, birch *(Betula)*, yellow poplar *(Liriodendron)*, beech *(Fagus)*, hemlock *(Tsuga)*, sweet gum *(Liquidambar styraciflua)*, red and white oak *(Quercus)*, hickory *(Carya)*, sycamore *(Platanus occidentalis)*, and loblolly pine *(Pinus taeda)*. On the Piedmont and the coastal plains, pines predominate, especially loblolly and long-leaf *(Pinus palustris)* pines. In the southern portion of the coastal plains the state tree, live oak *(Quercus virginiana)*, thrives. In sandy soil palmettos *(Sabal)* are common. Swampy and poorly drained areas are the natural habitat for tupelo gums *(Nyssa aquatica)*, bald cypresses *(Taxodium distichum* and *T. ascendens)*, and pond cypress *(T. ascendens)*. Black cherry *(Prunus serotina)*, dogwood *(Cornus)*, chestnut *(Castanea dentata)*, butternut *(Juglans cinerea)*, sweet bay *(Magnolia virginiana)*, evergreen magnolia *(Magnolia grandiflora)*, sassafras *(Sassafras albidum)*, red maple *(Acer rubrum)*, and cottonwood *(Populus deltoides)* are also indigenous to the state.

Known to the Indians as the Land of the Trembling Earth, Okefenokee Swamp is a very unusual wilderness of wild orchids , floating green lily pads *(Nymphaea odorata)* and bald cypresses with pendant tufts of Spanish moss *(Tillandsia usneoides)*.

Georgia is blessed with a great profusion of flowering plants, including the state flower, Cherokee rose *(Rosa laevigata)*. Other kinds include bellwort *(Uvularia)*, bloodroot *(Sanguinaria canadensis)*, columbine *(Aquilegia canadensis)*, galax *(Galax aphylla)*, hepatica *(Hepatica)*, trillium *(Trillium)*, mayapple *(Podophyllum peltatum)* and violet *(Viola)*. Species of flame azalea *(Azalea calendulacea)*, rhododendron, redbud *(Cercis canadensis)*, mimosa, and laurel are some of the shrubs and small flowering trees which abound in Georgia.

Of the larger animals still found in the state, white-tailed deer are the most plentiful. In the Okefenokee Swamp and the northern mountains black bears *(Ursus americanus)* roam, and wildcats *(Lynx)* prowl in some rural areas. The wooded areas are profuse with muskrat *(Ondatra zibethica)*, opossums *(Didelphis virginiana)*, gray squirrels *(Sciurus carolinensis)*, red squirrels *(Tamiasciurus hudsonius)*, gray foxes *(Urocyon cinereoargenteus)*, red foxes *(Vulpes vulpes)*, and raccoon *(Procyon lotor)*. Many swamps and rivers are inhabited by beaver *(Castor canadensis)* and otter *(Lutra canadensis)*.

There are more than 300 species of birds east of the Mississippi, most of which can be viewed in Georgia. Of that number, approximately 160 are indigenous to the state; 120 of them breed below the Fall Line, which is an imaginary line between the Piedmont and the coastal plain marked by waterfalls and rapids, where rivers descend abruptly from an upland to a lowland. This line not only divides the species of birds but of trees and plants as well. Many of the birds that winter in Georgia migrate from Canada and the northern United States. Anhinga or snakebird, *(Anhinga anhinga)*, clapper rail *(Rallus longirostris)*, egrets *(Egretta)*, wood duck *(Aix sponsa)*, wood ibis *(Mycteria americana)*, and many species of herons (Ardeidae) are common along the coast, in marshes, and inland swamps. In cultivated areas mourning doves *(Zenaidura macroura)* and bobwhites *(Colinus virginianus)* are plentiful and black vultures *(Coragyps atratus)*, turkey buzzards *(Cathartes aura)* and hawks (Accipitridae) are visible throughout the state. From brushy thickets the distinctive calls of the brown thrasher, the state bird *(Toxostoma rufum)*, mockingbird *(Mimus polyglottos)*, and the catbird *(Dumetella carolinensis)* ring out. Ruby-throated hummingbird *(Archilochus colubris)*, crow *(Corvus brachyrhynchos)*, robin *(Turdus migratorius)*, cardinal *(Richmondena cardinalis)*, meadowlark *(Sturnella magna)*, blue jay *(Cyanocitta cristata)* and the towhee *(Pipilo)* are familiar sights in the state. There are numerous species of sparrows (Fringillidae), wrens *(Troglodytes)*, vireos *(Vireo)* and warblers (Parulidae) also. In 1967 an ivory-billed woodpecker *(Campephilus principalis)*, which was thought to be extinct, was sighted in Georgia.

In the great Okefenokee and coastal swamps the state's largest reptile, the alligator, is found. The poisonous snakes found in the state are copperhead *(Ancistrodon contortrix,)* cottonmouth *(Ancistrodom piscivorous)*, water moccasin *(Natrix)*, coral snake *(Micrurus fulvius)*, and pygmy diamondback rattlesnake in addition to many types of nonpoisonous snakes.

Channel bass *(Sciaenops ocellatus)*, spotted weakfish *(Cynoscion regalis)*, sailfish *(Istiophorus)*, and tarpon *(Tarpon atlanticus)* are the saltwater fish most commonly found. Along the coastal areas oysters *(Ostreidae)*, crabs *(Brachyura)*, and shrimps *(Crangon)* are available. Mountain trout, bream *(Lepomis)*, pike *(Esox)*, catfish *(Nematognathi)*, and black basses *(Micropterus)* are in the lakes and streams of northern and central Georgia. The rivers of the Coastal Plain have an abundant supply of bass, drum *(Sciaenidae)*, mackerel *(Scomber scombrus)*, mullet *(Mugilidae)* and redfish *(Sebastes marinus)*.

FOOTBALL

Atlanta is the only city in Georgia with a professional football team. The *Atlanta Falcons* Club is a member of the National Football League (NFL). In Southeastern Conference (SEC) competition among college teams, the University of Georgia traditionally ranks high. Georgia Tech, once a member of the SEC, is now a member of the Atlantic Coast Conference (ACC).

For ticket or game information about the Falcons, call 404-588-1111.

Georgia Football's Major Bowl Games

Rose Bowl—Pasadena, California
1929 Georgia Tech 8, California 7
1943 Georgia 9, UCLA 0

Orange Bowl—Miami, Florida
1940 Georgia Tech 21, Missouri 7
1942 Georgia 40, Texas Christian 26
1945 Tulsa 26, Georgia Tech 12
1948 Georgia Tech 20, Kansas 14
1949 Texas 41, Georgia 28
1952 Georgia Tech 17, Baylor 14
1960 Georgia 14, Missouri 0
1967 Florida 27, Georgia Tech 12

Sugar Bowl—New Orleans, Louisiana
1944 Georgia Tech 20, Tulsa 18
1947 Georgia 20, North Carolina 10
1953 Georgia Tech 24, Mississippi 7
1954 Georgia Tech 42, West Virginia 19
1956 Georgia Tech 7, Pittsburgh 0
1969 Arkansas 16, Georgia Tech 2
1977 Pittsburgh 27, Georgia 3
1981 Georgia 17, Notre Dame 10
1982 Pittsburgh 24, Georgia 20
1983 Penn State 27, Georgia 23

Cotton Bowl—Dallas, Texas
1943 Texas 14, Georgia Tech 7
1955 Georgia Tech 14, Arkansas 6
1967 Georgia 24, Southern Methodist 9
1976 Arkansas 31, Georgia 10
1984 Georgia 10, Texas 9

Sun Bowl—Tempe, Arizona
1965 Georgia 7, Texas Tech 0
1970 Nebraska 45, Georgia 6
1971 Georgia Tech 17, Texas Tech 9

Gator Bowl—Jacksonville, Florida
1947 Maryland 20, Georgia 20
1956 Georgia Tech 21, Pittsburgh 14
1959 Arkansas 14, Georgia Tech 7
1961 Penn State 30, Georgia Tech 15
1965 Georgia Tech 31, Texas Tech 21
1971 Georgia 7, North Carolina 3

Astro-Bluebonnet Bowl—Houston, Texas
   1962 Missouri 14, Georgia Tech 10
   1978 Stanford 25, Georgia 22

Liberty Bowl—Memphis, Tennessee
   1967 N.C. State 14, Georgia 7
   1972 Georgia Tech 31, Iowa State 30

Peach Bowl—Atlanta, Georgia
   1971 Mississippi 41, Georgia Tech 18
   1973 Georgia 17, Maryland 16
   1978 Purdue 41, Georgia Tech 21

INTERESTING FOOTBALL FACTS

The University of Georgia football team was the National Champion in 1980.

Georgia was SEC champion in 1942, tied with Tennessee in 1946, 1948, 1959, tied with Alabama in 1966, 1968, 1976, 1980, 1981, and 1982.

Georgia Tech was SEC champion in 1939 (tied with Tennessee), 1943–1944, tied with Tennessee in 1951, and 1952.

The University of Georgia team was undefeated in 1980 and 1982.

The University of Georgia has furnished two Heisman Trophy winners: Frank Sinkwich in 1942 and Herschel Walker in 1982.

The University of Georgia holds the all-time scoring record for a single game against Cumberland College in 1916: 222–0.

The University of Georgia's stadium is named Sanford Stadium. It holds 82,122 people and is located in Athens.

Georgia Tech plays its home games at Grant Field in Atlanta; capacity 58,121.

1987 Schedules for Georgia and Georgia Tech follow. Games played at home are in bold.

GEORGIA		GEORGIA TECH	
Sept. 12	**Oregon State**	**Sept. 12**	**The Citadel**
Sept. 19	at Clemson	**Sept. 19**	**North Carolina**
Sept. 26	**South Carolina**	Sept. 26	at Clemson
Oct. 3	at Ole Miss	Oct. 3	at N.C. State
Oct. 10	**LSU**	**Oct. 10**	**Indiana State**
Oct. 17	at Vanderbilt	**Oct. 17**	**Auburn**
Oct. 24	**Kentucky**	Oct. 24	at Tennessee
Oct. 31	**Virginia**	Oct. 31	at Duke

Nov. 7	at Florida		Nov. 7	Virginia
Nov. 14	**Auburn**		Nov. 21	**Wake Forest**
Nov. 28	Georgia Tech		Nov. 28	**Georgia**

FORTS

Fort Allatoona. A Union-held fort saved from Confederate attack by General Sherman, with the first effective use of signals perfected by General Albert J. Myer.

Fort Augusta. Built around 1735 by Governor James E. Oglethorpe, after he designed the town of Augusta. He named the fort and the town for the mother of King George III. Both town and fort were taken by the Tories and the fort renamed Fort Cornwallis. In June, 1781, Colonel "Light Horse Harry" Lee took the fort and forced the British to surrender.

Fort Benning. Established during World War I, nine miles from Columbus. Named for Confederate General Henry L. Benning of Columbus.

Fort Cornwallis. Built around 1735 by Governor James E. Oglethorpe and originally called Fort Augusta, the fort was taken by Tory Lieutenant Colonels Brown and Grierson and the name changed to Fort Cornwallis. The Colonials captured the fort, but the British retook it. In June, 1781, Colonel "Light Horse Harry" Lee forced the British to surrender.

Fort Edwards. Built in 1789 in Watkinsville. Established as a defense against Cherokee Indians.

Fort Fidius. Built in 1793 at Milledgeville, nine years before the town became the capital of Georgia. This fort had the largest garrison of Federal troops south of the Ohio River.

Fort Frederica. Built in 1736 by Governor James E. Oglethorpe. The fort and the town surrounding it were named in honor of Frederick, the only son of King George II of England. The fort, which commanded the channel between St. Simon Island and the mainland, was erected as a defense for the English colonists in Georgia against the Spanish in Florida. In 1742 a Spanish force dispatched from Cuba threatened the English settlers, but the expedition was turned back a few miles south of the fort by General James E. Oglethorpe in the Battle of Bloody Marsh.

Fort Gaines. In Clay County, overlooking the Chattahoochee River. The fort was named for General Gaines. Today the town of Fort Gaines occupies the site.

Fort George. Built in 1761, the first fort on Cockspur Island. American patriots destroyed it in 1801.

Fort Greene. Built in 1794, a hurricane destroyed it in 1804. It was the second fort built on Cockspur Island.

Fort Grierson. Built near Fort Augusta by Tory Lieutenant Colonel Grierson. The fort was captured by the colonials and retaken by the British, but in June, 1781, Colonel "Light Horse Harry" Lee took the fort and the British surrendered.

Fort Hawkins. Built in 1806 on the Ocmulgee River, 35 miles from Milledgeville. The fort was named for Benjamin Hawkins, a Government Indian agent. Its main purpose was to protect the state against Indian insurrection, and served as a meeting place for Federal agents and Creek Indians. During the War of 1812 this fort was the assembling place for troops who were equipped and sent to the aid of General Andrew Jackson before the Battle of New Orleans.

Fort Hughes. Near the town of Bainbridge, not far from Fort Scott. Mainly an earthwork used by General Jackson's troops during the Seminole War.

Fort Jackson. Built during the War of 1812 on the Savannah River, 2 miles south of Savannah. Confederates seized it in March, 1861 and held it until Savannah was taken by the Union forces.

Fort King George. Built in 1721, near Darien at the mouth of the Altahama River. Named for King George of England, it was the first English settlement on Georgia land. The fort was built to protect the colonists from encroachments of the French and Spanish. In 1727, the fort was almost destroyed by fire. It was rebuilt but the garrision was moved to South Carolina.

Fort McAllister. Built by Confederate forces at the start of the War Between the States, on the Great Ogeechee River, 12 miles south of Savannah and opposite Genesis Point. One of the principal defenses of the city, the fort withstood attacks in 1862 and 1863. On December 13, 1864, the fort was captured, the final event of Sherman's march to the sea.

Fort McPherson. The fort was named for Union General James Birdseye McPherson, who was killed in the Battle of Atlanta. In 1883 Spelman College acquired the grounds and buildings of the fort, and the fort was moved to a location four miles south of Atlanta.

Fort Morris. Built in 1776 at Sunbury, south of Savannah. Defended by Continental troops in several attacks until 1779, when the fort was taken and destroyed by the British. The destruction of the fort brought about the end of Republican power in eastern Georgia.

Fort Mountain. Believed to have been built by De Soto in 1540 on a peak in the Cohutta Mountains, in the western portion of the state. Now a state park, the United States Forest Service has a lookout tower on the site.

Fort Oglethorpe. Near Dodge, a United States Military Post established in 1903. Named for James E. Oglethorpe, founder of Georgia.

Fort Pulaski. Built in 1829–47, the third fort on Cockspur Island. The fort was designed by Simon Bernard, Napoleon's Chief engineer, and named in honor of the Polish count Casimir Pulaski, hero of the Battle of Savannah during the American Revolution. Seized and garrisoned by the Confederates at the outbreak of the War Between the States, it was bombarded by the Federals for thirty hours on April 10–11, 1862, and was forced to surrender, due to the ineffectiveness of forts of brick and masonry against the artillery of the day. With the fall of Fort Pulaski, the Savannah River was closed to blockade runners, British merchant steam vessels who traded guns and ammunition for cotton and tobacco. The shells fired by the Federals during the siege are still embedded in its walls.

Fort St. Andrew. Built on Cumberland Island to protect the entrance to the St. Marys River.

Fort St. Simon. Built about 1736 on the eastern tip of St. Simon Island. On July 5, 1742, Spanish vessels sailed into the harbor at St. Simons, and forced General James E. Oglethorpe to retreat. The Spanish swarmed over the island, and on July 7, Oglethorpe defeated the Spanish at Grenadier Marsh, which became known as Bloody Marsh.

Fort Scott. Built in 1816 on the bank of the Flint River, near the Georgia-Florida line. The fort was the headquarters for the first Seminole War.

Fort Tyler. Built on a hill at West Point to protect the city from the fire of Federal guns in the War Between the States. The fort was named for Confederate General Robert C. Tyler, who was killed in the battle at the fort on Easter, April 16, 1865.

Fort Walker. A War Between the States fort in Atlanta, used by a Confederate battery during the Battle of Atlanta in 1864. The fort was named in honor of William T. Walker, a Confederate General killed in the Battle of Atlanta.

Fort Wayne. Built in 1762. The fort was named for General "Mad Anthony" Wayne. The fort was captured and strengthened by the British in 1779, and Americans rebuilt it during the War of 1812.

Fort Wilkinson. Built in 1796, a few miles north of Fort Fidius. The fort was named for General James Wilkinson. In 1802 representatives of 32 Creek towns signed the Indian treaty of 1802 that ceded the lands of that area to the state of Georgia.

Fort William. Built in 1736, by Governor James E. Oglethorpe on Cumberland Island. The purpose of the fort was to command the entrance to the St. Marys River.

Fort Wimberly. Built in the early 1700s by Governor James E. Oglethorpe on the Isle of Hope, south of Savannah. The fort was built to guard the narrows of the Skiaway River. The original wooden structure was replaced in 1741 by a concrete one. During the War Between the States a Confederate Battalion stationed there prevented Federal ships from passing along the inland water route.

GEOGRAPHIC CENTER

The geographic center of the state of Georgia lies 18 miles southeast of Macon.

GOLD

Gold was discovered in the mountains of northern Georgia in 1829. Almost immediately over 10,000 miners descended upon the region to try their hand at getting rich. A U.S. mint was established in nearby Dahlonega and before it became inactive, it processed millions of dollars worth of gold coins. A sad aspect of this, America's first major gold rush, was that the yellow metal's discovery sealed the fate of the Cherokee Indians who lived in the surrounding countryside. White settlers were already envious of the Cherokee's holdings; the finding of gold in the Indian lands merely brought about the inevitable sooner. The "Trail of Tears" happened shortly thereafter.

GONE WITH THE WIND

Gone With the Wind, the fiery novel set in Georgia, spanning the years before, during, and immediately after the War Between the States, was one of the best selling books ever to be published in the United States. Likewise, the movie rendition of the same has become one of Hollywood's all-time money makers. The book, written by Atlanta's Margaret Mitchell, was an immediate success upon its publication in 1936, selling over 700,000 copies in its first four months. *Gone With the Wind* won the 1937 Pulitzer Prize, and it was translated into 30 foreign languages.

Hollywood was quick to see its potential and film magnate David O. Selznick paid $50,000 Depression dollars for the film rights. The movie was no less spectacular than the book. Winner of 10 Academy Awards, it starred Clark Gable and Vivien Leigh.

Georgians in general and Atlanteans in particular are proud that one of their natives, Margaret Mitchell, contributed this outstanding piece of Southern literature to future generations of Americans.

GOVERNORS

UNDER THE TRUSTEES

Oglethorpe, James Edward, 1733—1743. Born in England on December 22, 1696. Served in House of Commons, 1722 to 1743. The death of a friend in one of England's debtor prisons caused Oglethorpe to want to do something about the prison situation. Early settlers left England November, 1732 and arrived in Savannah February, 1733. He was in charge of the government, 1733 to 1743; accepted Treaty of Frederica, 1736; defended Georgia in England, and secured regiment, 1737; fought Spanish, 1742; court-martialed, 1744. Died June 30, 1785.

THE THREE PRESIDENTS OF GEORGIA

There were three presidents that served as heads of the government in Georgia between the time Oglethorpe left and the coming of the three royal governors.

Stephens, William, 1743—1751 (President of Colony). Born in England, *c.* 1671. Served in Parliament, was a colleague of Oglethorpe. He went from England to Ireland and then to America. He was 66 years old when he came to Georgia in 1737. Oglethorpe had been too busy to keep the trustees in England informed, so Stephens was appointed secretary, and sent to help him. In 1741 the Trustees divided Georgia into two separate parishes; Stephens was made president of the one in Savannah. When Oglethorpe left Georgia, 1743, he recommended the trustees make Stephens president of all Georgia. Stephens presided over the first representative assembly, January 15, 1751. He retired April, 1751 and became the first Georgian to be pensioned. He died August, 1753.

Parker, Henry, 1751—1752. He served as an assistant to President Stephens. Was a constable, 1733; third bailiff, 1734; first bailiff, 1738 and first assistant under the new government. Became vice-president, March, 1750, and president April 8, 1751 when Stephens retired. He organized Georgia's first militia, June, 1751. He died while in office, 1752.

Graham, Patrick, 1752—1754. Was owner of a small plantation and a seller of medicines. In May, 1751, he was sent into Creek country to secure a grant of the reserved lands from the Indians to the colony of Georgia. He became president when President Parker died in 1752. Georgia became more prosperous while Graham was president. People who had moved away because of the trustees' harsh laws came back, and new settlers moved in, among them the Puritans in 1752. He was president until the first royal governor arrived in 1754.

THE THREE ROYAL GOVERNORS

By 1754, King George II and his ministers had come up with a plan to govern Georgia, since the Trustees had given up their charter. The plan was to have a royal governor, with a twelve-man advisory council named by the King, which would serve as the upper house of the Assembly. The lower house would be made up of delegates elected by the people.

Reynolds, John, 1754—1757. Born in England in 1700. Was a navy captain. Arrived in Savannah October 29, 1754 and the government was turned over to him. He did implement the royal plan of government, but was not a popular governor, and the people wanted him removed. He was summoned to England to answer charges. He was dismissed from office, and returned to the Navy, where he became an admiral. He died in 1776.

Ellis, Henry, 1757—1760. Born in England in 1721. He was a scientist and explorer. His father was wealthy but stern, and he ran away to sea when he was young. He was welcomed by the settlers, who were glad to be rid of Reynolds. He was a popular governor. There were eight parishes created during his administration, when the Church of England was the tax-supported church in Georgia. He had a good relationship with the Indians. His failing health caused him to leave Georgia in November, 1760. He died in Naples, Italy, January 21, 1800.

Wright, Sir James, 1760—1782. Believed to have been born in England, Wright grew up in South Carolina, where his father was chief justice. He held various jobs in the courts, becoming acting attorney general in 1742; attorney general, 1747—1757. He went to London for three years as provincial agent for South Carolina. He was appointed royal governor May 13, 1760. He strengthened defenses and worked at keeping the Indians friendly. He was a well respected governor until the Stamp Act, when some of the Liberty Boys suggested he be hanged. It was another ten years before he was actually arrested. He left the colony in 1776, when the patriots took control, but returned in 1779 as governor of the part of Georgia then in British hands. He left office when Savannah was surrendered to the Americans, 1782.

GOVERNORS OF THE STATE

Bulloch, Archibald, 1776—1777. Born in Charleston, South Carolina in 1730. He moved to Georgia to set up his law practice, and lived in Savannah. Was president of Provincial Congress, and in charge of the Council of Safety. When Governor Wright was arrested, Georgians took over their government and elected Bulloch. He called the first constitutional convention, October, 1775. The first legislature under the new constitution was to meet in May, 1777, to elect the first constitutional governor. But Bulloch died in March, 1777.

Gwinnett, Button, 1777. Born in Gloucestershire, England in 1732. Came from England shortly before the Revolutionary War. He was a merchant, and settled in Savannah. Elected to the Assembly in 1769. Was a delegate from Georgia to the Second Continental Congress in Philadelphia and was one of the signers of the Declaration of Independence. When Bulloch died, Gwinnett was named acting president. He served two months until an election was held and he was defeated. He died of injuries sustained in a duel, May 19, 1777.

Treutlen, John Adam, 1777—1778. Born in Austria, brought to Georgia when he was six. Was a member of the Council of Safety and Georgia's Provincial Congress. Was elected governor May, 1777 and served until the following January. When his term was up, he took his family to visit relatives in South Carolina and he vanished without a trace.

Houstoun, John, 1778—1779; 1784—1785. Was the son of a British nobleman. After serving as Mayor of Savannah, was elected to Provincial Congress, 1775, Second Provincial Congress, 1775. He was one of four men to sign an advertisement that appeared in the Savannah *Gazette* which roused Georgians to be supportive of the Revolution. He was just ending his first term as governor, 1778—1779, when the British captured Savannah. According to the constitution, he could not remain in office, so for a while Georgia had no governor. He was elected to the office again 1784 to 1785, making him the first governor to serve a second term. During his second term, forty thousand acres of land was set aside to be sold to raise funds to charter the University of Georgia.

Wereat, John, 1779. Two factions of Georgia's Patriot or Whig government developed in Augusta. One elected John Wereat head of the government, and the other elected George Walton. But January 4, 1780 they settled their differences and elected Richard Howley.

Walton, George, 1779—1780; 1789—1790. Born in Prince Edward County, Virginia, near Farmville, 1741. Was a Continental Congress delegate, signed the Declaration of Independence, and served in the Revolutionary War. Was appointed governor the first time by a separate faction that was caused by the confusion of the Revolutionary War. He only served a few months. He was elected again by a joint ballot of the State Legislature. Peace was established with the Creek Indians, a new State Constitution was ratified, and Augusta was established as the capital during his administration. Walton County, Georgia was named in his honor. He died in Georgia, near Augusta, February 2, 1804.

171

Howley, Richard, 1780. After the two factions of the Patriot or Whig government settled their differences, they elected Howley. He was also elected to Continental Congress, and a few days after taking office, he left for Washington.

Heard, Stephen, 1780—1781 (Acting Governor). Born in Ireland. As Council president, he was made acting governor while Howley served as a delegate in Washington. Later he went to North Carolina.

Davies, Myrick, 1781 (Acting Governor). When Heard went to North Carolina, Davis was made acting head of the government. He was later murdered.

Brownson, Nathan, 1781—1782. Born in Connecticut. Graduated from Yale. A doctor who was head of the hospitals in the South during the war. A member of the Continental Congress, 1776 to 1778; one of the signers of the United States Constitution. He was sent to Augusta to take over as governor, 1781. He helped design the charter for the University of Georgia.

Martin, John, 1782—1783. Born in Rhode Island. Was a member of the first Provincial Congress, 1775. Served as lieutenant during the Revolutionary War. He was elected governor near the end of the war and carried the government back to Savannah.

Hall, Lyman, 1783—1784. Born in Connecticut April 12, 1734. A doctor who graduated from Yale. Went from New England to the Carolina Colony, and then came to Georgia with the Puritans to be their doctor. Was delegate to the Continental Congress; delegate to Second Provincial Congress, 1775; a signer of the Declaration of Independence, 1776. Became governor 1783. He urged the people to set up seminaries of learning during his term, and he helped plan the University of Georgia. He died October 19, 1791.

Houstoun, John, 1784—1785 (Second Term).

Elbert, Samuel, 1785—1786. Born in South Carolina. Served on committee to arm state in readiness for war, 1776. Was general in Revolutionary War. After serving term as governor, 1785 to 1786, he served as sheriff in Chatham County.

Telfair, Edward, 1786—1787; 1789—1793. Born in Scotland, c. 1735, on the Telfair estate, "Town Head," emigrated c. 1758 to Virginia and later, in 1766, settled in Savannah, Georgia. Was a member of the Continental Congress and a signer of the Articles of Confederation. During his second term, from 1789—1793, there was conflict with the federal government regarding the Indian question defined in the Treaty of New York, which resulted in the passage of the Eleventh Amendment. Telfair County, Georgia, was named in his honor. He died September 17, 1807, in Savannah.

Mathews, George, 1787—1788; 1793—1796. Born in Augusta County,

Georgia, September 10, 1739. Commanded a company of volunteers against the Indians, 1757; fought in the Battle of Point Pleasant, 1774; also the battles of Brandywine and Germantown, where he was wounded and captured. Was a delegate to the First Congress, 1789 to 1791. Was appointed governor, 1787 to 1788. Became governor for a second term, 1793 to 1796, defeating Edward Telfair by a joint ballot of the State Legislature. The major issue of his administration was the Yazoo Land Sale. The Virginia Yazoo Company, the South Carolina Land Company and the Tennessee Land Company purchased 2,500,000 acres of land for 200,000 dollars. The purchasers failed to comply with the terms and the agreement lapsed. Five other companies combined to purchase 35,000,000 acres for 500,000 dollars and the transaction was approved by the state legislature in spite of Governor Mathews' veto. Died in Augusta, August 30, 1812.

Handley, George, 1788—1789. Less is known about him than any other governor. He was a former soldier with a valiant record and a dependable civil officer.

GOVERNORS (Following the ratification of the State Constitution)

Telfair, Edward, 1789—1793 (Second Term).

Mathews, George, 1793—1796 (Second Term).

Irwin, Jared, 1796—1798, 1806—1809, Democratic-Republican. Born in Mecklenburg County, North Carolina in 1750. After moving to Georgia, he was active in the American Revolution; commanded a Georgia militia detachment against the Indians on the Georgia frontier. Was inaugurated as governor on January 15, 1796 after being elected by a joint ballot of the State Legislature. He signed a bill during his administration, rescinding the Yazoo Land Sale, which had caused so much controversy that the State Legislature ordered that the record of the sale be removed from official records. His first term ended January 12, 1798. He assumed the office again on September 23, 1806 when Governor John Milledge resigned and remained in that capacity until his own inauguration on November 6, 1807, since he had again been elected by a joint ballot of the State Legislature. He died in Union Hill, Washington County, Georgia on March 1, 1815. Irwin County was named in his honor.

Jackson, James, 1798—1801, Democratic-Republican. Born in Moreton-Hampstead, Devonshire, England on September 21, 1757. Emigrated in 1772 to Georgia, served in the Constitutional Army during the Revolutionary War, served from 1789 to 1791 in the First Congress, served in the U.S. Senate, 1793 to 1795. He was elected governor by a joint ballot of the State Legislature, inaugurated January 12, 1796. He resigned March 3, 1801. The next day, March 4, 1801, he began a term as U.S. Senator where he served until his death March 19, 1806, in Washington. Jackson County was named in his honor.

Emanuel, David, 1801, Democratic-Republican. Born in Georgia, *c.* 1744, served in the Georgia Militia during the Revolutionary War as a captain and then as colonel. He served as president of the Georgia Senate and as such, assumed the office of governor on March 3, 1801 when Governor James Jackson resigned and served until Josiah Tattnall was inaugurated November 7, 1801. Then he returned to the Senate to serve as president until he died February 19, 1808 at his Burke County plantation. Emanuel County was named in his honor.

Tattnall, Josiah, 1801—1802, Democratic-Republican. Born near Savannah in 1764; accompanied his father to England at the outbreak of the Revolutionary War; returned to Savannah and enlisted in 1782 under General Anthony Wayne. Was U.S. Senator, 1796—1799. Elected governor by joint ballot of State Legislature and was inaugurated November 7, 1801, resigned November 4, 1802 for health reasons, traveled to Nassau, New Providence and British West Indies, where he died June 6, 1803. Tattnall County was named in his honor.

Milledge, John, 1802—1806, Democratic-Republican. Born in 1757 in Savannah; served in the Revolutionary War army and unofficially as a "Liberty Boy." He and James Jackson (another future governor) were captured by the British; they escaped, only to be held by American soldiers as spies, and at the last minute were saved from the gallows. Served in the U.S. House, 1793 to 1799; 1801 to 1802; became governor 1802. During his term he dealt with matters concerning land cessions and the Creek Indians and a road was built from Tennessee to Augusta. Greatly interested in education, and served as a trustee of the University of Georgia. He resigned during his second term to accept the U.S. Senate seat vacated by the death of James Jackson. He was a loyal supporter of Thomas Jefferson and was made president pro tempore of the Senate, 1809. He died in Augusta in 1818.

Irwin, Jared, 1806—1809 (Second Term).

Mitchell, David Brydie, 1809—1813, 1815—1817, Democratic-Republican. Born in Scotland October 22, 1766. At seventeen he moved to Savannah. Served in state General Assembly, 1794—1796; Savannah's mayor, 1801 to 1802; U.S. Attorney General, 1803 to 1805. He served three two-year terms, with emphasis on internal improvements, improving highways and building new roads, establishing better banking facilities and strengthening the militia. An act prohibiting dueling was passed during his administration. He resigned in 1817 to become Federal Indian Agent to the Creek Indians. Died April 22, 1837.

Early, Peter, 1813—1815, Democratic-Republican. Born June 30, 1773 in Madison County, Virginia. Upon completion of law school in Philadelphia, he set up practice in Washington, Georgia. Served three terms in U.S.

House of Representatives, 1801 to 1807. Was judge of the newly-created Superior Court of the Ocmulgee Circuit until he was elected governor in 1813. Unlike most of the previous governors, he cooperated fully with the federal government. He vetoed the reenactment of the so-called "Alleviating Law" (extending debtor's repayment time under certain conditions), but his veto was overridden, and he was defeated in the next election. He was promptly elected to the state Senate in 1816 by his home county, Greene. He died August 15, 1817. Early County was named in his honor.

Mitchell, David Brydie, 1815—1817 (Third Term).

Rabun, William, 1817—1819, Democratic-Republican. Born in Halifax, North Carolina on April 8, 1771. In 1775 he moved to Wilkes County, Georgia. Served six one-year terms in the state Senate starting in 1810; President of the Senate, 1812 to 1816. Was made *ex-officio* Governor March 1817 upon Governor David B. Mitchell's retirement and continued to serve one term. He served during a time of general prosperity, and due to his influence the legislature appropriated money for waterways, canals, roads and other internal improvements, and revised the penal code. The state Penitentiary was finished, and a steamboat company was chartered. He died October 25, 1819, while still in office. Rabun County was named in his honor.

Clark, John, 1819—1823, Democratic-Republican. Born in Edgecombe County, North Carolina, February 28, 1766, moved to Wilkes County, Georgia 1774. He had little formal education; joined the army at age fifteen as lieutenant. After running unsuccessfully in 1813 and 1817, he was elected governor in 1819. He served two terms, during which time a treaty was signed (1821) with the Creeks, giving the state the area between the Flint and Ocmulgee Rivers, which was divided into five new counties. On October 2, 1832 in St. Andrew's Bay, Florida, Clark died of yellow fever.

Troup, George Micheal, 1823—1827, Democratic-Republican. Born on the Tombigbee River, Alabama, September 8, 1780. His family moved to Savannah when he was two. In 1797 he graduated from Princeton. Was U.S. representative three terms, 1807 to 1815; chairman of Military Affairs Committee during the War of 1812; U.S. Senator, 1816 to 1818. He was elected governor by the legislature by a slim margin of four votes. In 1825 he was reelected in the first gubernatorial race decided by popular vote. He was an ardent supporter of States' Rights and internal improvements. The removal of the Creek Indians from the state and the making of their land accessible to white settlers took place during his terms in office. Returned to the U.S. Senate 1829, but retired in 1833 because of poor health. He died in Montgomery County on April 26, 1856. Troup County was named in his honor.

Forsyth, John, 1827—1829, Democratic-Republican. Born in Fredericksburg, Virginia on October 22, 1780. Princeton graduate, 1799; served three terms in U.S. House of Representatives, 1813 to 1818; resigned to fill short term in the U.S. Senate, 1818 to 1819. Resigned to become minister to Spain until 1823; then three more terms as U.S. representative, 1823 to 1827. Inaugurated governor November 7, 1827 following election by popular vote. He was opposed to the 1828 "Tariff of Abominations" and was in favor of neutralizing it by state action. Returned to U.S. Senate, 1829 to 1834. Joined President Andrew Jackson's cabinet as secretary of state, was reappointed by President Martin Van Buren, 1834 to 1841. Died in Washington, D.C., October 21, 1841. Forsyth County was named in his honor.

Gilmer, George Rockingham, 1829—1831, 1837—1839, Democratic-Republican. Born near Lexington, Wilkes (now Oglethorpe) County on April 11, 1790. First Lieutenant, Forty-third Regiment, U.S. Infantry, 1813 to 1815 in the campaign against the Creek Indians. Served in U.S. House of Representatives, 1819 to 1823, 1827 to 1829 as a Democrat. Served as governor 1829 to 1831 as a Democratic-Republican. His second term, 1837 to 1839 he ran as States' Rights candidate. Gold was discovered in the Nacoochee Valley, in an area belonging to the Cherokee Indians. Gold seekers presence, in spite of a proclamation demanding their departure, created troubles with the Cherokees during his first term. His second term was marked by the Panic of 1837. Author of *Sketches of Some of the First Settlers of Upper Georgia*. Gilmer died in Lexington, Georgia on November 16, 1859. Gilmer County was named in his honor.

Lumpkin, Wilson, 1831—1835, Union Party. Born in Pittsylvania County, Virginia on January 14, 1783. Served in U.S. House of Representatives, 1815 to 1817. He was appointed as a commissioner to determine the boundaries of treaties made with the Creek Indians by President James Monroe in 1818 to 1819. U.S. House of Representatives as a Jacksonian Democrat, 1826 to 1831. He took the office of governor as a Union Party candidate. His primary interest as governor was the removal of the Cherokees from north Georgia. In his second term he worked for a revision of the state's tax laws, called for a system of teacher training and mass education, a railroad to join the Ohio Valley with Georgia's coast, and State Penitentiary improvements. He died December 1, 1870 and was buried in Athens. Lumpkin County was named in his honor.

Schley, William, 1835—1837, Union Party. Born in Frederick, Maryland, December 10, 1786. Served Ninth Regiment, Georgia militia as a private; studied law; admitted to Georgia Bar 1812. Served state legislature, 1830 to 1832; U.S. House of Representatives, 1832 to 1835 as a Democrat. Elected governor as a Union Party candidate. He died November 20, 1858 and was buried near Augusta. Schley County was named in his honor.

Gilmer, George Rockingham, 1837—1839 (Second Term).

McDonald, Charles James, 1839—1843, Union Party. Born in Charleston, South Carolina, July 9, 1793. In 1794, his family moved to Hancock County, Georgia. Served in the Georgia militia as brigadier general, 1823 to 1825. Served as Democratic representative in the Georgia Legislature, 1830; state senate 1834 to 1839. Elected governor as the Union Party candidate, 1839. His term had to deal with the problems created by the Panic of 1837, and a legislature dominated by Whigs. He sought to establish a state Supreme Court, and an adequate educational system. He concentrated on the state's economy during his second term, as well as supporting the programs he began in his first administration. He died December 16, 1860 in Marietta, Georgia.

Crawford, George Walker, 1843—1847, Whig. Born in Columbia County, Georgia, December 22, 1798. Served Georgia House of Representatives, 1837 to 1843. He served one month (February to March 1843) as U.S. Representative to finish term following the death of Richard Habersham. He was inaugurated governor November 7, 1843 and was the only Whig to ever hold that office. He served two terms and was a successful and popular administrator. Sound currency, liquidation of the state bank, payment of the state debt, railroad construction, establishment of a State Supreme Court, and penal reform were some of his objectives. He served as Secretary of War in President Zachary Taylor's cabinet, 1848 to 1850. He died July 27, 1872.

Towns, George Washington Bonaparte, 1847—1851, Democrat. Born in Wilkes County, Georgia, May 4, 1801. Served as U.S. Representative 1835 to 1836, 1837 to 1839, 1846 to 1847. Served two terms as governor, 1847 to 1851 and favored the use of poll taxes, the revenue from the state railroad, and other sources of revenue to fund public education. He supported the Mexican War. He died in Macon on July 15, 1854. Towns County was named in his honor.

Cobb, Howell, 1851—1853, Constitutional Union. Born in Jefferson County, Georgia, September 7, 1815. Served as U.S. Representative, 1842 to 1851 and was Speaker of the House 1849 to 1851. Served one term as governor, 1851 to 1853. Annual legislative sessions, election of a state attorney general, Supreme Court sessions in the state capital, leasing of the state-owned Western and Atlantic Railroad, and financial aid for the State Library and education were some of his objectives. Returned to the U.S. House of Representatives in 1854. He joined President James Buchanan's cabinet as secretary of the treasury in 1857, resigned in 1860. He was President of the Provisional Congress of the Confederacy, as well as a delegate. He died while on a business trip to New York, October 9, 1868.

Johnson, Hershel Vespasian, 1853—1857, States' Rights Democratic. Born in Burke County, Georgia, September 18, 1812. Appointed to fill a vacancy in the U.S. Senate 1848 to 1849. Became governor in 1853 and served two terms. Favored public education and States' Rights. He ran unsuccessfully for vice president of the United States on the Douglas Democratic ticket in 1860. He served as judge of the Middle Circuit of Georgia from 1873 until his death, August 16, 1880.

Brown, Joseph Emerson, 1857—1865, Democrat. Born April 15, 1821 in Pickens District, South Carolina. Graduated in 1846 from Yale Law School, and began his practice in Canton, Georgia. Served in Georgia Senate, 1849—1855. Was the only Georgian to serve four successive terms as governor, 1857 to 1865. He was a strong pro-slavery states' rights leader who favored secession and made great efforts to prepare the state for war. He quarreled with President Jefferson Davis over various issues. His passion for state sovereignty weakened the Confederate war effort. At the end of the war he was jailed briefly and he resigned as governor June, 1865. He advocated Reconstruction. Served as U.S. senator, 1880 to 1891. Died November 30, 1894.

Johnson, James, 1865, Democrat (Provisional). Born February 12, 1811 in Robinson County, North Carolina. Graduated from University of Georgia in 1832 and was an attorney in Columbus. Served one term in Congress, 1851 to 1853. He opposed secession and was loyal to the Union throughout the war, unlike most Georgians. He was appointed Provisional Governor by President Andrew Johnson to help the state form a new government. During his brief tenure (June 17 to December 14, 1865) he called a state convention which ratified the 13th Amendment, disclaimed the Confederate debt, repealed the Ordinance of Secession, and wrote a new state constitution which called for the election of a governor and other state officials and Johnson gave up his position. He later served as judge of the Superior Court. He died November 20, 1891.

Jenkins, Charles Jones, 1865—1868, Constitutional Union Party. Born in Beaufort, South Carolina, January 6, 1805; moved to Jefferson County, Georgia in 1816. A lawyer who served many terms in the state House of Representatives; four sessions as Speaker. In 1852 he was National Constitutional Union Party vice presidential candidate, and in 1853 the Constitutional Union Party candidate for governor but was twice defeated. He did assume the office as governor in 1865, however, and had the difficult problems of rebuilding the state treasury and state property that had been destroyed in the War Between the States. By the end of his term there was money in the treasury and the state railroad had been repaired. He died June 14, 1883. Jenkins County was named in his honor.

Ruger, Thomas Howard, 1868 (Military Governor). Born in Livingston County, New York. Graduated from West Point in 1854, served in U.S. Army Corps of Engineers; lieutenant colonel of the Third Wisconsin Regiment (June, 1861); colonel (August, 1861); brigadier general (November, 1862); brevetted to major general for gallantry at the Battle of Franklin, Tennessee, November 30, 1864. When Governor Jenkins was removed from office for refusing to pay for the State Convention out of state funds, General Ruger was named governor of Georgia (January 17, 1868) by Major General George W. Meade, commander of the Third Military District. He served until June 28, 1868. He then served as superintendent of the U.S. Military Academy at West Point, 1871 to 1876. He died June 3, 1907.

Bullock, Rufus Brown, 1868—1871, Republican. Born in Bethlehem, New York March 28, 1834. Was a telegraphic expert and became an official of a telegraph company in Augusta, Georgia. He served the Confederacy at the outbreak of the War Between the States, even though he was opposed to secession, establishing railroad and telegraph lines. Elected governor by popular vote and took office when Governor Ruger was removed. Numerous allegations were brought against him: bribing the press, selling pardons, allowing the state penitentiary to be plundered, and encouraging corruption in state government. He resigned office October 23, 1871 and left the state when a Democratic majority returned to the state legislature and he faced the possibility of criminal indictment. He was arrested and returned to Georgia in 1876, but was acquitted on charges of embezzlement of public funds due to lack of evidence. He remained in Atlanta to be president of the Chamber of Commerce, and officer of several businesses, including director of the Union Pacific Railroad. He died April 27, 1907.

Conley, Benjamin F., 1871—1872, Republican. Born March 1, 1815 in Newark, New Jersey. He moved to Augusta, Georgia at age fifteen, where he became a successful merchant. From 1857 to 1859, he was mayor of Augusta. He retired to a plantation in Alabama rather than take part in the War Between the States. After the war, he became active in politics and became president of the state Senate. He advanced to the office of governor when Governor Bullock abruptly resigned October 30, 1871. He held that office two months and twelve days and partisan battles raged. His honesty was praised by his opponents, in spite of the fact that his vetoes were usually overridden. His brief term marked the end of Republican control in the Reconstruction era. President Grant appointed him Postmaster of the city of Atlanta, 1875 to 1883 and he died there in 1885.

Smith, James Milton, 1872—1877, Democrat. Born October 24, 1823 in Twiggs County, Georgia. Attained rank of colonel in the Confederate Army and served a year in the Confederate Congress, 1864 to 1865. He was Speaker of the Georgia House of Representatives. His inauguration as governor (January 12, 1872) marked the end of five years of Republican rule. As governor, he faced serious economic problems in the aftermath of Reconstruction. The Georgia State College of Agriculture and Mechanical Arts (in Athens), the office of State Geologist and the Department of Agriculture

179

were all created during his term in office. For six years he served the State Railroad Commission, before being appointed Judge of the Superior Court of the Chattahoochee Circuit in 1887. He died November 25, 1890.

Colquitt, Alfred Holt, 1877—1882, Democrat. Born April 20, 1824 in Walton County, Georgia. He began a long and successful career in politics after serving in the Mexican War. He served in Congress, the state legislature, and the Georgia Secession Convention before serving the Confederate Army first as a captain and later as major general. He was elected to a four-year term as governor in 1876, then reelected to a two-year term. He brought reductions in the floating and bonded debts and taxes, thus strengthening the state's financial structure. A new state Constitution was approved which served the state until 1945. Was elected to the U.S. Senate in 1883 and again in 1888. He died while serving in the Senate, March 26, 1894.

Stephens, Alexander Hamilton, 1882—1883, Democrat. Born February 11, 1812 in Wilkes County, Georgia. Served State House of Representatives, 1836 to 1841; state Senate, 1842 to 1843; and U.S. House of Representatives, 1843 to 1859. He was vice president of the Confederacy, a reluctant secessionist who believed in states' rights and constitutional law, and was involved in numerous conflicts with President Jefferson Davis over the conduct of the war. After being defeated for the Senate in 1872, he was elected U.S. Representative and served ten years. Became governor November 4, 1882 but the demands were too much in his weakened condition and he died four months later, March 4, 1883. Stephens County was named in his honor.

Boynton, James S., 1883, Democrat. Born May 7, 1833 in Henry County, Georgia. Served as colonel in Confederate Army; Mayor of Griffin, 1869 to 1872; Georgia Senate, 1880 to 1884 and was president of the Senate both terms. Became acting governor when Governor Stephens died and until May 10, 1883 when a replacement could be elected. He died December 22, 1902.

McDaniel, Henry D., 1883—1886, Democrat. Born September 4, 1836 in Monroe, Georgia. A lawyer who served in the Confederate Army, State House of Representatives and Senate before being elected governor. Strengthening the state's finances, taxing the railroads, supervising the building of a new state Capitol, and improving services for the blind, deaf and insane were some of his accomplishments. He died July 25, 1926.

Gordon, John B., 1886—1890, Democrat. Born in Upson County, Georgia February 6, 1832. Was regarded as one of the finest untrained soldiers of the Confederacy, being one of only three Georgians to attain rank of Lieutenant General. He was believed to be the head of the Ku Klux Klan in Georgia and was an adamant opponent of Radical Reconstruction. Elected to the

U.S. Senate, 1871 to 1880; became successful businessman; then elected governor 1886 and again in 1888. The state's bonded indebtedness was reduced, and there was an increase in capital, factories, railroads and population, though few reforms were enacted in his term. He toured the country lecturing on the Confederacy in his last years, and published *Reminiscences of the Civil War* in 1903. He died January 9, 1904.

Northern, William J., 1890—1894, Democrat. Born July 9, 1835 in Jones County, Georgia. An educator and president of the State Agricultural Society who served two terms in the state House of Representatives and one term in the state Senate before being elected to two terms as governor. Progress was made in the field of education and he conducted the office in an efficient and frugal manner. He was involved in religious and scholarly pursuits after his terms in office, editing *Men of Mark in Georgia,* a seven-volume collection of biographical sketches published 1907 to 1912. He served briefly as state Historian. He died March 25, 1913.

Atkinson, William Yates, 1894—1898, Democrat. Born in Meriwether County, Georgia, November 11, 1854. Served four terms in Georgia Legislature; the last one as Speaker of the House. Was chairman of the Georgia Democratic Convention in 1890. Served two terms as governor. He sought educational, electoral, and penal reforms but failed in his efforts to establish the office of Lieutenant Governor and to eliminate lynching. He publicized the Atlanta Exposition of 1895 and stressed industrial expansion. He died August 8, 1899. Atkinson County was named in his honor.

Candler, Allen Daniel, 1898—1902, Democrat. Born November 4, 1834 in Lumpkin County, Georgia. An educator and businessman who served four terms in the U.S. Congress and four years as Georgia's secretary of state before being elected to two terms as governor. He was not known for any changes or reforms but rather for being honest and frugal. His greatest service to the state came from his serving as state Historian. Twenty-eight large volumes on Georgia's colonial, revolutionary and confederate history were published. He published with Clement Evans a three-volume encyclopedia of Georgia in 1906. He died October 26, 1910. Candler County was named in his honor.

Terrell, Joseph M., 1902—1907, Democrat. Born in Meriwether County, Georgia, June 6, 1861. A lawyer who served two terms in the state House of Representatives, 1884 to 1888; Georgia Senate, 1890; state Attorney General, 1892 to 1902; and two terms as governor, 1902 to 1907. In spite of opposition from his conservative legislature, many of his progressive reforms were enacted. His most important accomplishments were in the field of education, with the establishment of the College of Agriculture, and an agricultural and mechanical school for each Congressional district was authorized. He was appointed to the U.S. Senate in 1910, following the death of Senator Alexander Clay. He resigned July 14, 1911 to resume his law practice and died November 17, 1912 in Atlanta.

Smith, Hoke, 1907—1909, 1911, Democrat. Born in Newton, North Carolina, September 2, 1855. He was active in the state Democratic Party and an avid supporter of Grover Cleveland. Was Democratic State Convention Chairman, 1888 and Democratic National Convention delegate in 1892. Was secretary of interior, 1893 to 1896 and then was out of office ten years before being elected governor in 1906. The Railroad Commission was strengthened; the convict lease system abolished; juvenile courts and a parole system were established during his term. He was defeated in his bid for reelection in 1908 but won again in 1910. In 1911 the legislature named him U.S. Senator and he resigned his position as governor. He died on November 27, 1931.

Brown, Joseph Mackey, 1909—1911, 1912—1913, Democrat. Born in Canton, Georgia, December 28, 1851. Was employed with the Western and Atlantic Railroad, 1877; appointed to the Railroad Commission, 1904; became governor 1909. He sought economy in government, lower taxes, enforcement of Prohibition, and a reduction in the power of the Railroad Commission. He was defeated in his bid for reelection by Hoke Smith but when Smith was appointed to the Senate, Brown easily won reelection. He wrote two books entitled *Mountain Campaigns in Georgia* and *Astanax* as well as numerous articles. He died March 3, 1932 at his home in Marietta.

Smith, Hoke, 1911 (Second Term).

Slaton, John Marshall, 1911—1912, 1913—1915, Democrat. Born December 25, 1866 in Meriwether County, Georgia. Graduated from the University of Georgia in 1866 and set up a law practice in Atlanta which lasted sixty-eight years. Served thirteen years in the Georgia House of Representatives, starting in 1896, and was Speaker of the House twice. He advanced to the Senate and was President of the Senate. He served two months as acting governor when Governor Smith gave up the office to become U.S. Senator (November 16, 1911 to January 10, 1912) and was later elected Governor 1913 to 1915. He was a conservative who stressed governmental frugality, tax equalization, and regulation of public utilities. Child labor legislation, the establishment of the Georgia Training School for Girls, and the creation of four new counties also took place during his term. He was unanimously elected president of the Georgia Bar Association in 1928. He died January 11, 1955.

Brown, Joseph Mackey, 1912—1913 (Second Term).

Slaton, John Marshall, 1913—1915 (Second Term).

Harris, Nathaniel E., 1915—1917, Democrat. Born in Jonesboro, Tennessee on January 21, 1846. Served in Confederate Army, graduated in 1870 from the University of Georgia and practiced law in Macon. Served four years in Georgia House of Representatives 1882 to 1886, and helped to establish the Georgia Institute of Technology. Elected to state Senate, 1894. As governor, 1915 to 1917, he struggled with dislocations caused by World War I, the renewed activity of the Ku Klux Klan, and the much divided issue of Prohibition. He was successful in securing pension increases for Confederate veterans, a compulsory education law and a fifty-year lease of the state-owned railroad. His main interest in his last years was service to Georgia Tech. He was the last Confederate veteran to serve as governor of Georgia. He died September 21, 1929.

Dorsey, Hugh Manson, 1917—1921, Democrat. Born in Fayetteville, Georgia, July 10, 1871. A member of the Georgia Bar Association; was solicitor general of the Atlanta Judicial Circuit, 1910 to 1916. During his terms as governor, he strongly objected to lynching and peonage, a system in which debtors or legal prisoners were forced to work for their creditors or those persons who leased their services from the state. He brought to public attention the unjust treatment of blacks in the state with his book *The Negro in Georgia*. He favored compulsory education for both races and conferences to discuss racial affairs. He returned to practicing law, was appointed Judge of the City Court of Atlanta, and finally Judge of the Atlanta Judicial Circuit until his death, June 11, 1948.

Hardwick, Thomas William, 1921—1923, Democrat. Born in Thomas County, Georgia, December 9, 1872. Served in state House of Representatives, 1890 to 1899, 1903 to 1914; U.S. Senate, 1914 to 1919. During his term as governor (1921 to 1923) there was a revival of the Ku Klux Klan, due to the "Red Scare" which developed after World War I. Hardwick demanded that its members unmask and end their violent activities and they retaliated by securing his defeat for reelection. He died in Sandersville, Georgia January 31, 1944.

Walker, Clifford Mitchell, 1923—1927, Democrat. Born in Monroe, Georgia, July 4, 1877. Mayor of Monroe, 1905 to 1907; served as Solicitor General of the Western Judicial Circuit of Georgia, 1909 to 1913; Attorney General of Georgia, 1914 to 1919. He served two terms as governor. Georgia received national criticism because of the state's cruel treatment of prisoners during his administration. When the use of the lash was abolished in prison camps, the Ku Klux Klan turned their wrath on him. He was in favor of the League of Nations. He died November 9, 1954.

Hardman, Lamartine Griffin, 1927—1931, Democrat. Born in Commerce, Georgia, April 14, 1856. After studying medicine and becoming a successful businessman he became a member of the Georgia House of Representatives, 1902 to 1907, and the state Senate, 1908 to 1910. He served two terms as governor, 1927 to 1931. He was an opponent to the repeal of

Prohibition; cotton production declined greatly and manufacturing took on an increasing percentage of the labor force during his administration. He died in Atlanta, February 18, 1937.

Russell, Richard B., 1931—1933, Democrat. Born November 2, 1897 in Winder, Georgia. Served state House of Representatives, 1920 to 1930; Speaker of the House, 1926 to 1930. Became governor during the Great Depression, bringing about such austerity measures as the Reorganization Act of 1931 which reduced the number of state agencies from 102 to 18. Placing all state-supported colleges under one Board of Regents was his most resolute change. Elected to U.S. Senate in 1932 and continued to serve for the next thirty-eight years. He was one of only three men ever to be elected for seven consecutive terms in the Senate and the only man to have served more than half his life there. He advocated military preparedness and states' rights. He served as a respected advisor to six presidents; chairman of the Senate Appropriations Committee; was third-in-line for presidency; and at the time of his death, January 21, 1971, was president pro tempore of the Senate.

Talmadge, Eugene, 1933—1937, 1941—1943, Democrat. Born in Forsyth, Georgia on September 23, 1884. He farmed, practiced law and operated a saw mill before being elected Commissioner of Agriculture in 1926. He served three terms before being elected governor. He was against public welfare and government debt, sought frugal government and low taxes. He often ruled by martial law and was a spokesman of the farmer. He lowered the cost of license tags, property taxes and utility rates, and used federal funds to build highways and other state services. Reelected in 1934 to a second term by an overwhelming margin. Won a third term in 1940 and a fourth in 1946, but died on December 21, 1946 before taking office.

Rivers, Eurith Dickinson, 1937—1941, Democrat. Born in Center Point, Arkansas on December 1, 1895. Was editor of a newspaper. Elected to Georgia legislature in 1924; Georgia Senate, 1926. Ran unsuccessfully for office of governor in 1928 and again in 1930. Elected to Georgia House of Representatives, 1932 and 1934; served as speaker both terms. After being elected governor in 1936, he gave complete support to Roosevelt's New Deal. State services were increased, especially welfare benefits, public health and housing, electricity expanded in rural areas, increased highway expansion, and more funds to public schools because of increased federal assistance. He was elected to a second term, but his administration was spoiled by charges of corruption and mismanagement. He died on June 11, 1967 in Atlanta.

Talmadge, Eugene, 1941—1943 (Third Term).

Arnall, Ellis Gibbs, 1943—1947, Democrat. Born in Newnan, Georgia on March 20, 1907. Elected to General Assembly, 1932; speaker pro tempore,

1933 and 1935 and attorney general of Georgia, 1939—1943. In 1943, he became governor. He sponsored numerous progressive changes that the legislature adopted; accreditation was restored to the state's colleges; elimination of the chain gang and other prison reforms; Georgia became the first state to lower the voting age to eighteen; the poll tax was abolished; without increasing taxes the state debt was paid and a new constitution was adopted. He lost a reelection bid in 1966 to Lester Maddox.

Thompson, Melvin Ernest, 1947—1948, Democrat. Born in Millen, Georgia on May 1, 1903. Was elected Georgia's first lieutenant governor in 1946. He became acting governor two days after his inauguration on January 18, 1947. Thompson succeeded to the office after Governor Ellis Arnall left office, since Governor-Elect Eugene Talmadge had died on December 21, 1946. (However, the office was controlled by Herman Talmadge, appointed by the legislature, until the state Supreme Court ruled that Thompson was the chief executive.) Thompson was more of a liberal, with emphasis on education, the passage of a sales tax, and the purchase of Jekyll Island. He died October 3, 1980.

Talmadge, Herman Eugene, 1947, 1948—1955, Democrat. Born in Telfair County, Georgia on August 9, 1913. His father, Eugene Talmadge, died before taking office to a fourth term as governor in 1947 and Talmadge was elected governor in 1947 by the Georgia Legislature. He served sixty-seven days before the state Supreme Court put him out of office. In 1948 and in 1950, he was elected a total of six years by popular vote. By introducing a three percent sales tax he was able to expand state services, especially education. Money for public schools nearly tripled and new schools were built, funded by the new State Building Authority. The State Forestry Commission was established, a network of hospitals and health facilities was constructed and the Highway Department was reorganized. He was first elected to the U.S. Senate in 1956 and served as chairman of Agriculture and Forestry. He was considered to be one of the most powerful members of the Senate.

Griffin, Samuel Marvin, 1955—1959, Democrat. Born in Bainbridge, Georgia on September 4, 1907. Elected to the General Assembly, 1934; executive secretary to Governor Rivers, 1940; U.S. Army, 1941 to 1944; adjutant general, 1944 to 1947; lieutenant governor, 1948 to 1952. Elected governor in 1954, he favored segregation and the county unit system, as did his predecessor, Governor Talmadge. Rural roads were paved through the sale of bonds; an atomic reactor was built at Georgia Tech; an eight-million-dollar science center was begun at the University of Georgia and funds were increased to public schools and the university system. When he left office he returned to Bainbridge to run the *Post-Searchlight*, the newspaper his father had edited before him and which he turned over to his son in 1963.

Vandiver, Samuel Ernest, 1959—1963, Democrat. Born July 31, 1918 in Franklin County, Georgia. He began to practice law in Winder, after serving in World War II as a pilot. Was mayor of Lavonia; aide to Governor Eugene Talmadge; Governor Herman Talmadge's campaign manager, 1948; state adjutant general 1948 to 1954; director of selective service, 1948 to 1954; and lieutenant governor, 1955 to 1959. Elected Governor in 1958 by an overwhelming majority. The problems he faced during his administration were of reapportionment and school integration. He was strongly in favor of segregation and states' rights and was hesistant to implement the rulings of the federal courts and allow the public schools to be integrated. The legislature eliminated the state's segregation laws and the county unit system which was used to nominate candidates for the Democratic primary during his term. He favored governmental efficiency, expanded tourism, the development of foreign trade, and increased funding for education. He suffered a heart attack in 1966, causing him to withdraw from his bid for reelection for governor. He served as adjutant general in 1971.

Sanders, Carl E., 1963—1967, Democrat. Born in Augusta, Georgia on May 15, 1925. Elected to state Senate, 1954; served as Senate Floor Leader, then as president pro tempore of the Senate. Elected governor 1962. Education, highway construction, hospitals and mental health facilities, recreational areas, and community airports received additional funding through his efforts. His greatest concern was education. The construction of 6,000 classrooms, the hiring of 10,000 additional teachers, and the Minimum Foundation Program (which established uniform standards for education) were his major accomplishments. When his term expired, he returned to his law practice. He ran again for governor in 1970, but was defeated by Jimmy Carter.

Maddox, Lester Garfield, 1967—1971, Democrat. Born in Atlanta, Georgia, September 30, 1915. Believing in segregation, he gained widespread attention in 1964 by closing the restaurant he had operated since 1947 rather than serve blacks. He became nationally known for his one-man campaign against the Supreme Court, President Johnson, Martin Luther King, Jr., the Atlanta newspapers, Communists and Socialists. He ran for governor in 1966 and since neither candidate had a majority (Bo Callaway—453,665; Maddox—450,626) the election was decided by the legislature which elected Maddox, 182 votes to 66. He carried out few reforms during his term, because of his political inexperience and the strange circumstances of his election. He expanded the Department of Industry and Trade, secured pay increases for teachers and state employees, released hundreds of prisoners before the expiration of their terms, and in fact appointed more blacks to office than any previous governor.

Carter, James Earl, 1971—1975, Democrat. Born in Plains, Georgia, October 1, 1924. He graduated in 1946 from United States Naval Academy at Annapolis; served on the nuclear submarine program with Admiral Hyman G. Rickover, under the auspices of the Atomic Energy Commission in 1951. He resigned from the Navy in 1953 and returned to Georgia to manage family business interests after death of his father. He served in the state Senate, 1963 to 1967; the Educational Matters Committee; and the Highways, Agriculture, and Appropriations Committees. Became governor in 1971; reorganized the state government; reinstated capital punishment for certain crimes; disclosure laws for political candidates; a "no fault" auto insurance plan; and the right by counties to vote to exempt themselves from the state's "blue laws." He was inaugurated President of the United States January 20, 1977.

Busbee, George Dekle, 1975—1983, Democrat. Born in Vienna, Georgia on August 7, 1927. During World War II, he served with the United States Naval Reserve. Served state House of Representatives, 1957 to 1974; assistant Administration Floor Leader, 1963 to 1965; Administration Floor Leader, 1966; and House Majority Leader, 1967 to 1974. The federal Equal Rights Amendment was defeated by the state legislature; new revenue sources were approved for local governments, including local sales taxes and hotel-motel taxes; and an investigation of some of Georgia's doctors for alleged overcharging was initiated by the governor.

Harris, Joe Frank, 1983— , Democrat. Born in Cartersville, Georgia on February 16, 1936. After receiving a B.A. degree from the University of Georgia, and serving in the Army, he became a businessman. Served 18 years in the state House of Representatives, the last eight of which he was chairman of the House Appropriations Committee. Education reform has been his priority in office, with $1.5 billion being appropriated without the aid of any new state taxes and he is also working to enhance economic development in the state. He has been involved in campaigns against drunk driving, child abuse, and drug trafficking.

HIGHER EDUCATION

UNIVERSITIES, COLLEGES, VOCATIONAL-TECHNICAL SCHOOLS

Abraham Baldwin Agricultural College, Tift County, Junior College (2 Yr.). A unit of the University System of Georgia, enrollment 2182, M-1154, F-1028. Tifton, GA 31793, Telephone 912-386-3230. Founded 1908.

Agnes Scott College, DeKalb County, Senior College (4 Yr.). Private, enrollment 549, M-O, F-549, Decatur, GA 30030, Telephone 404-373-2571. Founded 1889.

Albany Area Technical School, Dougherty County, Area Technical. Area school developed under State Department of Education policies, enrollment 2551, M-1156, F-1395. Albany, GA 31708, Telephone 912-888-1320.

Albany Junior College, Dougherty County, Junior College (2 Yr.). A unit of the University System of Georgia, enrollment 1964, M-744, F-1220. Albany, GA 31707, Telephone 912-888-8888. Founded 1963.

Albany State College, Dougherty County, Senior College (4 Yr.). A unit of the University System of Georgia, enrollment 1893, M-753, F-1140. Albany, GA 31705, Telephone 912-439-4234. Founded 1903.

American College for Applied Arts, Fulton County, Senior College (4 Yr.). Atlanta, GA 30342. Founded 1975.

Andrew College, Randolph County, Junior College (2 Yr.). Private, United Methodist, enrollment 320, M-168, F152. Cuthbert, GA 31740, Telephone 912-732-2171. Founded 1854.

Armstrong State College, Chatham County, Senior College (4 Yr.). A unit of the University System of Georgia, enrollment 2922, M-1098, F-1824. Savannah, GA 31406, Telephone 912-927-5243. Founded 1935.

Athens Area Technical School, Clarke County, Area Technical. Area school developed under State Department of Education policies, enrollment 4413, M-1894, F-2519. Athens, GA 30601, Telephone 404-549-2360.

Atlanta Area Technical School, Fulton County, Area Technical. Area school developed under State Department of Education policies, enrollment 7247, M-2549, F-4698. Atlanta, GA 30310, Telephone 404-758-9451. Founded 1967.

Atlanta Christian College, Fulton County, Bible College (4 Yrs.). Private, Christian, enrollment 180, M-113, F-67 (1982). East Point, GA 30344, Telephone 404-761-8861. Founded 1937.

Atlanta College of Art, Fulton County, Art College (4 Yr.). Private, enrollment 270, M-126, F-144 (1982). Atlanta, GA 30309, Telephone 404-898-1164. Founded 1928.

Atlanta Junior College, Fulton County, Junior College (2 Yr.). A unit of the University System of Georgia, enrollment 1661, M-689, F-972. Atlanta, GA 30310, Telephone 404-656-6441. Founded 1974.

Atlanta University, Fulton County, Doctoral. Private, enrollment 1065, M-507, F-558. Atlanta, GA 30314, Telephone 404-681-0251. Founded 1867.

Augusta Area Technical School, Richmond County, Area Technical. Area school developed under State Department of Education policies, enrollment, 4693, M-1980, F-2713. Augusta, GA 30906, Telephone 404-796-6900. Founded 1961.

Augusta College, Richmond County, Senior College (4 Yr.). A unit of the University System of Georgia, enrollment 4252, M-1729, F-2523. Augusta, GA 30910, Telephone 404-828-2987. Founded 1925.

Bainbridge Junior College, Decatur County, Junior College (2 Yr.). A unit of the University System of Georgia, enrollment 621, M-241, F-380. Bainbridge, GA 31717, Telephone 912-246-7941. Founded 1973.

Ben Hill-Irwin Area Technical School. Ben Hill County, Area Technical. Area school developed under State Department of Education policies, enrollment 849, M-406, F-443, Fitzgerald, GA 31750, Telephone 912-468-7487.

Berry College, Floyd County, Senior College (4 Yr.). Private, enrollment 1403, M-560, F-836. Mount Berry, GA 30149, Telephone 404-232-5374. Founded 1902.

Brenau College, Hall County, Senior College (4 Yr.). Private, enrollment 1602, M-593, F-1009. Gainesville, GA 30501, Telephone 404-534-6109. Founded 1878.

Brewton-Parker College, Montgomery County, Junior College (2 Yr.). Private, Baptist, enrollment 1277, M-667, F-610, Mount Vernon, GA 30445, Telephone 912-583-2241. Founded 1904.

Brunswick Junior College, Glynn County, Junior College (2 Yr.). A unit of the University System of Georgia, enrollment 1305, M-538, F-767. Brusnwick, GA 31520, Telephone 912-264-7235. Founded 1961.

Carroll County Area Technical School, Carroll County, Area Technical. Area school developed under State Department of Education policies, enrollment 1542, M-666, F-876. Carrollton, GA 30117, Telephone 404-834-3391.

Carver Bible Institute and College, Fulton County, Senior College (4 Yr.). Atlanta, GA 30313. Founded 1943.

Clark College, Fulton County, Senior College (4 Yr.). Private, United Methodist, enrollment 1936, M-692, F-1244. Atlanta, GA 30314, Telephone 404-681-3080. Founded 1869.

Clayton Junior College, Clayton County, Junior College (2 Yr.). A unit of the University System of Georgia, enrollment 3603, M-1487, F-2116. Morrow, GA 30260, Telephone 404-961-3400. Founded 1969.

Columbia Theological Seminary, DeKalb County, Doctoral. Private, Presbyterian, enrollment 502, M-408, F-94. Decatur, GA 30031, Telephone 404-378-8821. Founded 1828.

Columbus Area Technical School, Muscogee County, Area Technical. Area school developed under State Department of Education policies,

enrollment 3069, M-1568, F-1501. Columbus, GA 31904, Telephone 404-322-1425.

Columbus College, Muscogee County, Senior College (4 Yr.). A unit of the University System of Georgia, enrollment 4283, M-1838, F-2445. Columbus, GA 31993, Telephone 404-568-2001. Founded 1958.

Coosa Valley Area Technical School, Floyd County, Area Technical. Area school developed under State Department of Education policies, enrollment 2401, M-985, F-1416. Rome, GA 30161, Telephone 404-235-1142.

Covenant College, Dade County, Senior College (4 Yr.). Private, enrollment 515, M-267, F-248. Lookout Mountain, TN 37350, Telephone 404-820-1560.

Dalton Junior College, Whitfield County, Junior College (2 Yr.). A unit of the University System of Georgia, enrollment 1654, M-726, F-928. Dalton, GA 30720, Telephone 404-278-3113. Founded 1963.

DeKalb Area Technical School, DeKalb County, Area Technical. Area school developed under State Department of Education policies, enrollment 8084, M-3869, F-4215. Clarkston, GA 30021, Telephone 404-299-4306.

DeKalb Community College, DeKalb County, Junior College (2 Yr.). A community junior college of the public education system of DeKalb County, enrollment 14,877, M-6908, F-7969. Clarkston, GA 30021, Telephone 404-299-4331. Founded 1964.

DeVry Institute of Technology, Fulton County, Senior College (4 Yr.). Atlanta, GA 30341. Founded 1969.

Draughon's Junior College, Chatham County, Junior College (2 Yr.). Savannah, GA 31406. Founded 1899.

Emanuel County Junior College, Emanuel County, Junior College (2 Yr.). A unit of the University System of Georgia, enrollment 415, M-176, F-239. Swainsboro, GA 30401, Telephone 404-237-7831. Founded 1973.

Emmanuel College, Franklin County, Junior College (2 Yr.). Private, Pentecostal Holiness, enrollment 352, M-150, F-202, Franklin Springs, GA 30639, Telephone 404-245-7226. Founded 1919.

Emory University, DeKalb County, Doctoral. Private, Methodist, enrollment 8533, M-4511, F-4022. Atlanta, GA 30322, Telephone 404-329-6123. Founded 1836.

Floyd Junior College, Floyd County, Junior College (2 Yr.). A unit of the University System of Georgia, enrollment 1673, M-661, F-1012. Rome, GA 30161, Telephone 404-295-6323. Founded 1970.

Fort Valley State College, Peach County, Senior College (4 Yr.). A unit of the University System of Georgia, enrollment 1870, M-870, F-1000. Fort Valley, GA 31030, Telephone 912-825-6315. Founded 1895.

Gainesville Junior College, Hall County, Junior College (2 Yr.). A unit of the University System of Georgia, enrollment 1762, M-851, F-911. Gainesville, GA 30501, Telephone 404-536-5226. Founded 1964.

Georgia College, Baldwin County, Senior College (4 Yr.). A unit of the University System of Georgia, enrollment 3554, M-1487, F-2067. Milledgeville, GA 30161, Telephone 912-453-4444. Founded 1889.

Georgia Institute of Technology, Fulton County, Doctoral. A unit of the University System of Georgia, enrollment 10,912, M-8637, F-2275. Atlanta GA 30332, Telephone 404-894-2000. Founded 1885.

Georgia Military College, Baldwin County, Junior College (2 Yr.). Private, enrollment 1403, M-980, F-423. Milledgeville, GA 31061, Telephone 912-453-3481. Founded 1879.

Georgia Southern College, Bulloch County, Senior College (4 Yr.). A unit of the University System of Georgia, enrollment 7018, M-3183, F-3835. Statesboro, GA 30460, Telephone 912-681-5600. Founded 1906.

Georgia Southwestern College, Sumter County, Senior College (4 Yr.). A unit of the University System of Georgia, enrollment 2344, M-989, F-1355. Americus, GA 31709, Telephone 912-928-1279. Founded 1906.

Georgia State University, Fulton County, Doctoral. A unit of the University System of Georgia, enrollment 21,512, M-9486, F-12,026. Telephone 404-658-2000. Founded 1913.

Gordon Junior College, Lamar County, Junior College (2 Yr.). A unit of the University System of Georgia, enrollment 1506, M-546, F-960. Barnesville, GA 30204, Telephone 404-358-1700. Founded 1852.

Griffin-Spalding Area Technical School, Spalding County, Area Technical. Area school developed State Department of Education policies, enrollment 1819, M-780, F-1039. Griffin, GA 30223, Telephone 404-277-1322.

Gwinnett Area Vocational-Technical School, Gwinnett County. Area School (FY 85 first year of operation; therefore, no FY 84 enrollment data). Lawrenceville, GA 30246, Telephone 404-962-7584.

Heart of Georgia Vocational-Technical School, Laurens County. Area School, enrollment not available, Dublin, GA 31040, Telephone 912-275-0672.

Houston Area Vocational Center, Houston County, Vocational Center. Area school developed under State Department of Education policies, enrollment 1577, M-608, F-969. Warner Robins, GA 31056, Telephone 912-283-2002.

Immanuel Baptist Schools, Fulton County, Senior College (4 Yr.). Atlanta, GA 30316. Founded 1952.

Interdenominational Theological Center, Fulton County, Doctoral. Private, enrollment 310, M-253, F-57. Atlanta, GA 30314, Telephone 404-525-5926. Founded 1958.

John Marshall Law School, Fulton County, Doctoral. Atlanta, GA 30316. Founded 1952.

Kennesaw College, Cobb County, Senior College (4 Yr.). A unit of the University System of Georgia, enrollment 5383, M-2182, F-3201. Marietta, GA 30061, Telephone 404-422-8770. Founded 1963.

LaGrange College, Troup County, Senior College (4 Yr.). Private, Methodist, enrollment 947, M-397, F-550. LaGrange, GA 30240, Telephone 404-882-2911. Founded 1831.

Lanier Area Technical School, Hall County, Area Technical. Area school developed under State Department of Education policies, enrollment 2288, M-1093, F-1195. Oakwood, GA 30566, Telephone 404-536-8884.

Life Chiropractic College, Cobb County, Doctoral. Private, enrollment 1876, M-1446, F-430. Marietta, GA 30060, Telephone 404-424-0554. Founded 1974.

Macon Area Technical School, Bibb County, Area Technical. Area school developed under State Department of Education policies, enrollment 6151, M-3725, F-2426. Macon, GA 31201, Telephone 912-781-0551.

Macon Junior College, Bibb County, Junior College (2 Yr.). A unit of the University System of Georgia, enrollment 2982, M-1145, F-1837. Macon, GA 31297, Telephone 912-474-2700. Founded 1968.

Marietta-Cobb Area Vocational Technical School, Cobb County, Vocational-Technical. Area school developed under State Department of Education policies, enrollment 3766, M-1752, F-2014. Marietta, GA 30060, Telephone 404-422-1660.

Medical College of Georgia, Richmond County, Doctoral. A unit of the University System of Georgia, enrollment 2387, M-1254, F-1133. Augusta, GA 30912, Telephone 404-828-2301. Founded 1828.

Mercer University, Bibb County, Doctoral. Private, Baptist, enrollment 2880, M-1465, F-1415. Macon, GA 31207, Telephone 912-744-2700. Founded 1833.

Mercer University in Atlanta, DeKalb County, Senior College (4 Yr.). Private, Baptist, enrollment 1868, M-1001, F-867. Atlanta, GA 30341, Telephone 404-451-0331. Founded 1964.

Mercer University Southern School of Pharmacy, Fulton County, Doctoral. Private, Baptist, enrollment 316, M-191, F-125. Atlanta, GA 30312, Telephone 404-688-6291. Founded 1903.

Middle Georgia College, Bleckley County, Junior College (2 Yr.). A unit of the University System of Georgia, enrollment 1430, M-705, F-725. Cochran, GA 31014, Telephone 912-934-6221. Founded 1884.

Morehouse College, Fulton County, Senior College (4 Yr.). Private, enrollment 2056, M-2056, F-0. Atlanta, GA 30314, Telephone 404-681-2800. Founded 1867.

Morehouse School of Medicine, Fulton County, Doctoral. Private, enrollment 127, M-69, F-58. Atlanta, GA 30310, Telephone 404-752-1000.

Morris Brown College, Fulton County, Senior College (4 Yr.). Private, African Methodist Episcopal, enrollment 1268, M-549, F-719. Atlanta, GA 30314, Telephone 404-525-7831. Founded 1881.

Moultrie Area Technical School, Colquitt County, Area Technical. Area school developed under State Department of Education policies, enrollment 1164, M-561, F-603. Moultrie, GA 31768, Telephone 912-985-2297.

North Georgia College, Lumpkin County, Senior College (4 Yr.). A unit of the University System of Georgia, enrollment 1990, M-858, F-1132. Dahlonega, GA 30533, Telephone 404-864-3391. Founded 1873.

North Georgia Technical-Vocational School, Habersham County, Technical-Vocational. Area school developed under State Department of Education policies, enrollment 1921, M-995, F-926. Clarkesville, GA 30523, Telephone 404-754-2131. Founded 1943.

Oglethorpe University, DeKalb County, Senior College (4 Yr.). Private, enrollment 1029, M-422, F-607. Atlanta, GA 30319, Telephone 404-261-1441. Founded 1835.

Oxford College of Emory University, Newton County, Senior College (2 Yr.). Private, Methodist, enrollment 463, M-244, F-219 (1982). Oxford, GA 30267, Telephone 404-786-7051. Founded 1836.

Paine College, Richmond County, Senior College (4 Yr.). Private, Methodist, enrollment 752, M-240, F-512. Augusta, GA 30910, Telephone 404-722-4471. Founded 1882.

Pickens Area Technical School, Pickens County, Area Technical. Area school developed under State Department of Education policies, enrollment 1665, M-510, F-1155. Jasper, GA 30143, Telephone 404-692-3411.

Piedmont College, Habersham County, Senior College (4 Yr.). Private, Congregational, enrollment 388, M-203, F-185. Demorest, GA 30535, Telephone 404-778-8033. Founded 1897.

Phillips College, Richmond County, Junior College (2 Yr.). Augusta, GA 30902. Founded 1948.

Phillips College, Muscogee County, Junior College (2 Yr.). Columbus, GA 31901. Founded 1951.

Reinhardt College, Cherokee County, Junior College (2 Yr.). Private, Methodist, enrollment 514, M-215, F-299. Waleska, GA 30183, Telephone 404-479-1454. Founded 1883.

Savannah Area Technical School, Chatham County, Area Technical. Area school developed under State Department of Education policies, enrollment 1143, M-458, F-685. Savannah, GA 31405, Telephone 912-352-1464.

Savannah College of Art and Design, Chatham County, Senior College (4 Yr.). Private, enrollment N/A. Savannah, GA 31401, Telephone 912-236-7458.

Savannah State College, Chatham County, Senior College (4 Yr.). A unit of the University System of Georgia, enrollment 2211, M-1028, F-1183. Savannah, GA 31404, Telephone 912-356-2240. Founded 1890.

Shorter College, Floyd County, Senior College (4 Yr.). Private, Baptist, enrollment 726, M-319, F-407. Rome, GA 30161, Telephone 404-291-2121.

Southern Technical Institute, Cobb County, Senior College (4 Yr.). A unit of the University System of Georgia, enrollment 3499, M-2968, F-531. Marietta, GA 30060, Telephone 404-424-7200. Founded 1948.

South Georgia College, Coffee County, Junior College (2 Yr.). A unit of the University System of Georgia, enrollment 1172, M-522, F-650. Douglas, GA 31533, Telephone 912-384-1100. Founded 1906.

South Georgia Technical and Vocational School, Sumter County, Technical-Vocational. Area school developed under State Department of Education policies, enrollment 1638, M-169, F-737. Americus, GA 31709, Telephone 912-928-0283.

Spelman College. Fulton County, Senior College (4 Yr.). Private, enrollment 1642, M-0, F-1642. Atlanta, GA 30314, Telephone 404-681-3643. Founded 1881.

Swainsboro Area Technical School, Emanuel County, Area Technical. Area school developed under State Department of Education policies, enrollment 1507, M-634, F-873. Swainsboro, GA 30401, Telephone 912-237-6465.

Thomas Area Technical School, Thomas County, Area Technical. Area school developed under State Department of Education policies, enrollment 1179, M-503, F-676. Thomasville, GA 31792, Telephone 912-228-2387.

Thomas County Community College, Thomas County, Junior College (2 Yr.). Private, enrollment 391, M-136, F-255. Thomasville, GA 31792, Telephone 912-226-1621. Founded 1950.

Tift College, Monroe County, Senior College (4 Yr.). Private, Baptist, enrollment 494, M-59, F-435. Forsyth, GA 31029, Telephone 912-994-2515. Founded 1847.

Toccoa Falls College, Stephens County, Senior College (4 Yr.). Private, enrollment 642, M-335, F-307. Toccoa Falls, GA 30598, Telephone 404-886-6831. Founded 1907.

Troup County Area Technical School, Troup County, Area Technical. Area school developed under State Department of Education policies, enrollment 1222, M-555, F-687 LaGrange, GA 30240, Telephone 404-882-0080.

Truett-McConnell College, White County, Junior College (2 Yr.). Private, Baptist, enrollment 902, M-412, F-490. Cleveland, GA 30528, Telephone 404-865-2135. Founded 1946.

University of Georgia, The. Clarke County, Doctoral. A unit of the University System of Georgia, enrollment 25,042, M-12,577, F-12,465. Athens, GA 30602, Telephone 404-542-3030. Founded 1785.

Upson County Area Techical School, Upson County, Area Technical. Area school developed under State Department of Education policies, enrollment 797, M-410, F-387. Thomaston, GA 30286, Telephone 404-647-9616.

Valdosta Area Technical School, Lowndes County, Area Technical. Area school developed under State Department of Education policies, enrollment 1592, M-620, F-972. Valdosta, GA 31601, Telephone 912-333-5995.

Valdosta State College, Lowndes County, Senior College (4 Yr.). A unit of the University System of Georgia, enrollment 5835, M-2546, F-3289. Valdosta, GA 31698, Telephone 912-247-3226. Founded 1906.

Walker County Area Technical School, Walker County, Area Technical. Area school developed under State Department of Education policies, enrollment 2278, M-816, F-1462. Rock Springs, GA 30739, Telephone 404-764-1016.

Waycross-Ware Technical School, Ware County, Area Technical. Area school developed under State Department of Education policies, enrollment 1514, M-523, F-991. Waycross, GA 31501, Telephone 912-283-2002.

Waycross Junior College, Ware County, Junior College (2 Yr.). A unit of the University System of Georgia, enrollment 555, M-178, F-377. Waycross, GA 31501, Telephone 912-285-6135. Founded 1976.

Wesleyan College, Bibb County, Senior College (4 Yr.). Private, Methodist, enrollment 387, M-4, F-383. Macon, GA 31207, Telephone 912-477-1110. Founded 1836.

West Georgia College, Carroll County, Senior College (4 Yr.). A unit of the University System of Georgia, enrollment 6351, M-2673, F-3678. Carrollton, GA 30118, Telephone 404-834-1211. Founded 1933.

Woodrow Wilson College of Law, Fulton County, Doctoral. Atlanta, GA 30308. Founded 1932.

Young Harris College, Union County, Junior College (2 Yr.). Private, United Methodist, enrollment 382, M-169, F-213. Young Harris, GA 30582, Telephone 404-379-3112. Founded 1886.

HIGHWAYS

Georgia can boast an excellent network of Interstate, Federal, State, and County highways. According to the Department of Transportation records as of July 1, 1985, the Georgia highway mileage is as follows:

		Miles
Interstate:	Rural	902.23
	Urban	316.98
	Total	1,219.21

	Miles	Paved
State Highways	18,012.11	17,976.93
County Roads	76,038.09	37,433.14
City Streets	11,642.66	10,249.87
Other Public	326.98	190.26
Total	106,019.84	
	Miles in all Systems	

State Reservation Roads   133.07 Miles

Federal Reservation Roads 1,597.38 Miles

All interstate mileage is included in the state highway total. State and federal reservation mileage can also be included in state, county or city mileages. Other public roads include roads open to the public, but not included in the Official System Mileages for State, County and City.

HISTORICAL SOCIETIES

ALBANY
Thronateeska Heritage Foundation
100 Roosevelt Ave. (31701)
912-432-6955

ALMA
Historical Society of Alma-Bacon County
P.O. Box 2026 (31510)
912-632-8450

ALPHARETTA
Old Milton County Historical and Genealogical Society, Inc.
367 Karen Dr. (30201)

ATHENS
Athens-Clarke Heritage Foundation
Fire Hall 2, 489 Prince Ave. (30601)
404-353-1801

Southern Historical Association
Dept. of History, University of Georgia (30602)
404-542-8848

ATLANTA
Atlanta Historical Society, Inc.
3101 Andrews Dr., N.W. (30305)
404-261-1837

Georgia Trust for Historic Preservation, Inc.
1516 Peachtree St., N.W. (30309)
404-881-9980

Hart County, Georgia Historical Society
2073 McLendon Ave, N.W. (30307)
404-377-5612

Historic Preservation Section, Department of Natural Resources
270 Washington St., Room 704 (30334)
404-656-2840

AUGUSTA
Richmond County Historical Society
Reese Library, Augusta College, 2500 Walton Way (30910)
404-737-1745

BARNESVILLE
Barnesville-Lamar County Historical Society
888 Thomaston St. (30204)
404-358-1289

BAXLEY
Appling County Historical Society, Inc.
P.O. Box 1063 (31513)
912-367-2431

BLAKELEY
Early County Historical Society, Inc.
255 N. Main (31723)

BRUNSWICK
Coastal APDC Advisory Council on Historic Preservation
P.O. Box 1917 (31521)
912-264-7363

BUCHANAN
Haralson County Historical Society, Inc.
Courthouse Square (30113)

CALHOUN
Gordon County Historical Society, Inc.
P.O. Box 342 (30701)

CARROLLTON
Carroll County Historical Society, Inc.
c/o West Georgia Regional Library
P.O. Box 160 (30117)

CARTERSVILLE
Etowah Valley Historical Society
Rt. 2, Kingston (30145)

CEDARTOWN
Polk County Historical Society
P.O. Box 7 (30125)

CLEVELAND
White County Historical Society
Box 281 (30528)

CLINTON
Old Clinton Historical Society, Inc.
  (31032)
912-986-3384

COCHRAN
Bleckley County Historical Society
Middle Georgia College (31014)
912-934-6221

COLLEGE PARK
College Park Historical Society, Inc.
P.O. Box F (30337)

COLUMBUS
Historic Columbus Foundation, Inc.
P.O. Box 5312 (31906)
404-322-0756

Historic District Preservation
  Society, Inc.
P.O. Box 263 (31902)
404-571-2245

CONYERS
Rockdale County Historical Society
P.O. Box 351 (30207)

CRAWFORDVILLE
Taliaferro County Historical
  Society, Inc.
P.O. Box 32 (30631)
404-456-2140

CUTHBERT
Randolph Historical Society, Inc.
P.O. Box 456 (31740)

DALTON
Whitfield-Murray Historical
  Society, Inc.
715 Chattanooga Ave. (30720)

404-278-0217

DECATUR
DeKalb History Society
Old Courthouse on the Square (30030)
404-373-1088

DUBLIN
Laurens County Historical
  Society, Inc.
P.O. Box 1461 (31021)
912-272-9242

EAST POINT
East Point Historical Society, Inc.
City Hall Annex, 2847 Main St.
  (30344)
404-767-4656

EATONTON
Eatonton-Putnam County Historical
  Society, Inc.
P.O. Box 331 (31024)
404-485-7701

ELBERTON
Elbert County Historical
  Society, Inc.
P.O. Box 1033 (30635)

FAIRBURN
Old Campbell County Historical
  Society, Inc.
P.O. Box 153 (30213)

FAYETTEVILLE
Fayette County Historical
  Society, Inc.
P.O. Box 421 (30214)
404-461-7152

FOLKSTON
Charlton County Historical Society
Rt. 3, Box 142-C (31537)
912-496-7401

FORT GAINES
Ft. Gaines Historical Society, Inc.
P.O. Box 6 (31751)

GRIFFIN
Griffin Historical and Preservation
  Society
P.O. Box 196 (30224)

GUYTON
Guyton Historical Society
P.O. Box 15 (31312)
912-772-3344

HAWKINSVILLE
Pulaski Historical Commission, Inc.
P.O. Box 447 (31036)
912-738-1717

HINESVILLE
Liberty County Historical Society
P.O. Box 797 (31313)

JEFFERSON
Jackson County Historical Society
c/o President, Rt. 2, Box 222
Commerce (30529)

JONESBORO
Historical Jonesboro, Inc.
P.O. Box 922 (30236)

LAFAYETTE
Walker County Historical Society
P.O. Box 707 (30728)

LAGRANGE
Ockuskee Historical Society, Inc.
P.O. Box 1051 (30241)

Troup County Historical Society,
  Inc.—Archives
P.O. Box 1051 (30241)
404-884-1828

LAWRENCEVILLE
Gwinnett County Historical
  Society, Inc.
P.O. Box 261 (30246)
404-963-9584

LUMPKIN
Stewart County Historical
  Commission

P.O. Box 817 (31815)
912-838-4201

MACON
Georgia Baptist Historical Society
Mercer University Library,
  Colman Ave. (31207)
912-745-6811

Macon Heritage Foundation, Inc.
P.O. Box 6092 (31208)
912-742-5084

Middle Georgia Historical
  Society, Inc.
935 High Street (31201)
912-743-3851

METTER
Candler County Historical Society
P.O. Box 235 (30439)
912-685-2771

MILLEDGEVILLE
Old Capital Historical Society
P.O. Box 4 (31061)

MONROE
Historical Society of Walton
  County, Inc.
238 N. Broad St. 30655

MONTICELLO
Jasper County Historical
  Foundation, Inc.
128 Robert Dr. (31064)
404-468-6637

MORROW
Clayton County Heritage Association
P.O. Box 305 (30260)
404-961-3460

MOULTRIE
Colquitt County Historical Society
Norman Park, Rt. 1 (31771)

NEWNAN
Newnan-Coweta Historical Society
P.O. Box 1001 (30264)
404-251-0207

199

OXFORD
Oxford Historical Shrine Society
P.O. Box 243 (30267)

PORTAL
Portal Heritage Society
c/o Denver Hollingsworth
301 College Blvd., Statesboro (30458)
912-764-3047

REIDSVILLE
Tattnall County Historic
  Preservation, Inc.
P.O. Box 392 (30453)
912-557-4802

ROME
Northwest Georgia Historical and
  Genealogical Society
P.O. Box 2484 (30161)

ROOPVILLE
Roopville Historical Society
  and Archives
124 Old Franklin St. (30171)
404-854-4170

ROSWELL
Roswell Historical Society
P.O. Box 274 (30075)
404-992-1665

ST. MARYS
Guale Historical Society, Inc.
P.O. Box 398 (31558)

St. Marys Historic Preservation
  Commission
414 Osborne St. (31558)
912-882-4667

ST. SIMONS ISLAND
Coastal Georgia Historical
  Society—Museum of
  Coastal History
P.O. Box 1136 (31522)
912-638-4666

Historical Society of the South
  Georgia Conference, United

Methodist Church
P.O. Box 407 (31522)
912-638-4050

SAVANNAH
Coastal Heritage Society
1 Ft. Jackson Rd. (31402)
912-232-3945

Georgia Historical Society
501 Whitaker St. (31499)
912-944-2128

Historic Savannah Foundation, Inc.
P.O. Box 1733 (31402)

SOCIAL CIRCLE
Historic Preservation Society of
  Social Circle, Inc.
P.O. Box 832 (30279)
404-464-2345

SOPERTON
Treutlen County Historical Society
Truetlen County Courthouse (30457)
912-529-6711

SWAINSBORO
Emanuel Historic Preservation
  Society
P.O. Box 1101 (30401)

THOMASVILLE
Thomas County Historical
  Society, Inc.
P.O. Box 1922 (31799)
912-226-7664

VALDOSTA
Lowndes County Historical Society
P.O. Box 434 (31601)
912-247-4780

Southern Jewish Historical Society
P.O. Box 179 (31698)
912-333-5947

WASHINGTON
Washington-Wilkes Historical
  Foundation, Inc.
308 E. Robert Toombs Ave. (30673)

404-678-2105

WATKINSVILLE
Watkinsville Historical Society
Main Street (30177)

WAYNESBORO
Burke County Historical Association
c/o Mrs. Alden Dye
Quaker Rd. (30830)

WINDER
Barrow County Historical Society
409 Candler St. (30680)
404-867-9003

WRIGHTSVILLE
Johnson County Historical
  Society, Inc.
P.O. Box 86 (31096)

HISTORIC SITES

Historic Sites are features of extreme historical significance. These sites are maintained by the Georgia Department of Natural Resources. Listed below are the Historic Sites throughout the state and a brief description of each. Normal operating hours for all are: Tuesday through Saturday 9 to 5; Sunday 2 to 5:30; Closed Mondays, Thanksgiving and Christmas.

Alexander H. Stephens House and Confederate Museum. In Crawfordsville on Ga. 22. Was the antebellum home of the Vice President of the Confederacy.

Dahlonega Gold Museum. Town Square. Commemorates the country's first major gold rush near here in 1828. A branch of the U.S. Mint operated in the vicinity for 23 years.

Etowah Indian Mounds. 3 miles S.W. of Cartersville. Area was occupied between A.D. 1,000 and A.D. 1,500. Was the largest Indian town in the Etowah Valley.

Fort King George. Near Darien. Fort was the southernmost outpost of the British colonies in 1721. Formerly was an Indian village site and Spanish mission site.

Fort McAllister. Near Richmond, 10 miles E. on Ga. 144. Was the key to Savannah's fortifications during the War Between the States. Fell to Sherman in 1864.

Hofwyl-Broadfield Plantation. 7 mile S. of Darien. An antebellum rice plantation.

Jarrell Plantation. 8 miles S.E. of Juliette. A 7.5 acre working farm spanning the years from the 1840s to the 1940s, complete with animals, crops, mill, blacksmith shop, and syrup evaporators.

Kolomoki Indian Mounds. 9 miles N. of Blakely. Historic settlement dating to A.D. 800 includes seven burial and temple mounds.

Lapham-Patterson House. In Thomasville at 626 N. Dawson St. Victorian mansion built in 1884.

Midway Museum. On U.S. 17 next to Church. Raised cottage style. Furniture, documents, and artifacts date from the early 18th to the mid-19th centuries.

New Echota. Exit 131, I-75. Capital of the Cherokee Indian Nation from 1825 to 1838. Sequoyah, the inventor of the Cherokee alphabet, lived here for a time.

Sunbury. Near Midway, 8 miles E. of I-95. Marks the spot of Georgia's second largest colonial seaport. An important Revolutionary War and War of 1812 site.

Toombs House. In Washington on Augusta Road. Built in 1797, the present structure is the core of the home of Confederate General Robert Toombs.

Traveler's Rest. 6 miles W. of Toccoa on U.S. 123. Built between 1815 and 1830. Served as a plantation house, tavern, trading post, and post office. Authentic furnishings.

Vann House. U.S. 76, 3 miles W. of Chatsworth. House was built in 1804 and is a fine example of Cherokee Indian wealth and culture.

HISTORY

The following chronology only scratches the surface of Georgia's history. For brevity's sake, some important events in the state's past have been omitted. Also, see the sections "War Between the States," "Women's Rights," "Forts," and "Famous Georgians" for information about these related topics.

1540—De Soto explores region today called Georgia.

1562—French explorer, Jean Ribaut, explores the St. Marys River.

1565—The Spanish King sent Pedro Menendez de Aviles to get rid of the French. But with the French and Indians against them, the Spanish soldiers were forced back to the islands along the coast.

1679—Spanish friars, led by Father Juan Ocon, visit the Cherokee town of Coweta.

1681—Franciscans pass through Coweta.

1696—James Oglethorpe is born in England on December 22.

1715—A South Carolinian, Thomas Nairne, was the first to suggest that England colonize the area which is now Georgia. The Indians, not liking his idea, burned him at the stake.

1732—King George II of England grants a royal charter for the establishment of Georgia.

—November 17, the *Queen Anne* with 114 settlers on board and led by General James Oglethorpe, sailed from England.

1733—On February 12 the *Queen Anne* landed at the site of Savannah with the settlers who were to establish Georgia.

1734—By March Oglethorpe's followers have built 91 log houses facing the Savannah River.

1736—Oglethorpe brings many more individuals to Georgia from England, among them John and Charles Wesley.

—John Wesley, founder of Methodism, came to Georgia as missionary for the Church of England. He began what is reported to be the world's first Protestant Sunday school.

1736—Fort Frederica is built on St. Simons Island.

—The first golf course in Georgia, and possibly in the United States, was constructed by once wealthy landowners from the Scottish Highlands who settled at the present site of Darien.

1737—John Wesley was so disliked that he was forced to return to England and was replaced by George Whitefield, who established Bethesda Orphanage. He also established the first English-speaking school in the state.

1739—Tomochichi, the Indian leader who helped get the Georgia colony on its feet, dies at the age of 97.

1742—The British defeat the Spanish in the Battle of Bloody Marsh. Spanish influence wanes.

1743—The first advocate of communism, Christian Priber, died in prison on St. Simons Island. He came to Georgia from Germany and taught of the advantages of communistic government. Then he encouraged the French traders to compete with the English, was accused of being a French spy, and was arrested and imprisoned.

1751—Henry Parker organizes Georgia's first militia.

1752—Forty-three families of Puritans, with their 536 slaves, arrive in Georgia.

1754—The first of three royal governors from England arrives in Georgia after the colony's original trustees relinquish their charter.

1765—John and William Bartram travel through Georgia.

1766—The Georgia penal institutions were so filled with debtors that a law was passed by the State Legislature requiring creditors to pay for food for the people that had been thrown into jail.

1773—Slave population swells to over 15,000.

1774—The first Continental Congress meets in Philadelphia, without representation from Georgia.

1775—Georgia holds its first Provincial Congress.

1776—British warships arrive in Savannah Harbor.

—Button Gwinnett, George Walton, and Lyman Hall sign Declaration of Independence at Philadelphia.

1777—The Georgia Legislature adopts the state's first constitution.

1778—Savannah falls to British forces.

1779—Americans defeat British at Kettle Creek near Washington, Georgia. British defeat Americans at Brier Creek.

1781—Americans, under the command of General "Light Horse Harry" Lee, recapture Augusta, which has been occupied by the British since 1779.

1782—British forces surrender at Savannah.

1785—The University of Georgia is chartered.

1786—General Nathanael Greene, who had taken command of the Southern theater late in the war, dies at Mulberry Grove after retiring there in 1785.

1788—Georgia becomes the fourth state of the new United States of America by unanimously ratifying the Federal Constitution.

1790—Georgia's population is 82,548.

—The first Georgia game law was passed by the State Assembly to conserve wildlife.

1793—Eli Whitney invents the cotton gin near Savannah.

1796—The slave market in Louisville is believed to have been built when the town was the state capital, but there are no documents to prove it.

1799—The Great Seal is authorized by the Legislature.

1801—Georgia's first divorce was granted. It was required by the State Constitution that the Superior Court authorize and both Houses of Legislature agree by two-thirds majority to grant a divorce.

1802—Jekyll Island was purchased by Poulain DuBignon and became a haven for French Royalists who were fleeing the Revolution in their homeland.

1819—The steamship, *Savannah*, becomes the first such ship to cross the Atlantic Ocean.

1820—Population of the state is 340,985.

1821—Creek Indians relinquish to Georgia the land between the Flint and the Ocmulgee Rivers.

1824—A hurricane destroyed Sunbury, the second largest city of Georgia. It was the home town of Dr. Lyman Hall and Button Gwinnett, who signed the Declaration of Independence; Richard Hawley and Nathan Brownson; two governors; and other famous Georgians. After surviving an attack from the British, a hurricane, and a malaria epidemic, another hurricane destroyed it completely.

1825—Creek Chief William McIntosh is murdered.

—General LaFayette visits Georgia.

1828—The nation's first gold rush took place at Dahlonega in Lumpkin County, north Georgia.

1829—Gold is discovered at Duke's Creek in today's White County.

—Augustine S. Clayton set up the first cotton mill near Athens, operated with waterpower from the Oconee River.

1830—State's population is 516,823.

1831—United States Supreme Court rejects Cherokee plea against federal removal law.

1832—Georgia charters its first railroad.

1834—Georgian Mirabeau Lamar migrates to Texas; he will become Texas's second president.

1835—Oglethorpe University founded in Atlanta.

1836—Emory University founded in Atlanta and Wesleyan College (the first woman's college with authority to confer degrees) chartered in Macon.

1838—Cherokees "Trail of Tears" begins.

1839—The lot for the first residence in Atlanta is purchased.

1840—Georgia's population climbs to 691,392.

1842—Dr. Crawford Long, a Jefferson physician, becomes the first doctor to administer ether to kill pain during surgery.

—Sidney Lanier is born in Macon on February 3.

1846—Georgia Supreme Court meets for the first time.

1851—The Georgia Military Institute was founded at Marietta.

1860—Juliette Gordon Low, founder of the Girl Scouts, is born in Savannah.

1861—Georgia secedes from the Union on January 19.

—Governor Joseph Brown orders the State Militia to occupy Fort Pulaski.

1863—Nathan Bedford Forrest captures 1500 Union soldiers near Rome.

—Battle of Chickamauga is fought.

1864—The Battle of Atlanta begins. In November Sherman and his troops set fire to Atlanta.

1865—Georgia adopts the 13th Amendment, outlawing slavery.

1867—The first Rich's Department Store opens in Atlanta.

1868—Georgia is readmitted to the Union.

1874—On February 28 Georgia became the first state in the Union to establish a Department of Agriculture.

1875—Postwar population of Georgia is 1,184,068.

1877—Atlanta becomes permanent capital.

1878—Walter George is born near Preston on January 19.

1886—Ty Cobb is born in Banks County on December 18.

1888—The Atlanta Bar Association is organized.

—Georgia Tech begins classes.

1889—Capitol building is completed.

1892—The Coca-Cola company is granted its first charter by the Fulton Superior Court.

1895—A "moving picture show" at the Cotton States Exposition in Atlanta, believed to be the first before a paid audience.

1897—Richard Russell is born in Winder on November 2.

—February 17 the National Congress of Mothers was organized in Washington, D.C., an idea conceived by Mrs. Theodore Birney, a native of Marietta and Cobb County teacher. Later the name was changed to National Parent-Teacher Association.

1900—Margaret Mitchell is born in Atlanta on November 8.

1902—Bobby Jones is born in Atlanta on March 17.

1909—Dean Rusk is born in Cherokee County on February 9.

1912—Juliette Gordon Low organizes the first Girl Scout Troop in the United States in Savannah.

1914—Carl Vinson is sworn in as the nation's youngest member of Congress.

1915—"Nat" Harris becomes Georgia's last "Confederate Veteran" governor.

1922—Rebecca Felton becomes the nation's first female United States Senator.

1924—James Earl Carter is born in Plains.

1925—The holly bush was developed by Thomas W. Burford, botanist of Atlanta.

1928—The Cloisters opens.

1929—Martin Luther King, Jr. is born in Atlanta on January 15.

1930—Rebecca Latimer Felton dies in Atlanta on January 24.

   —Population climbs to 2,908,521.

1935—The Brown Thrasher becomes Georgia's state bird.

1936—*Gone With the Wind* is published.

1937—Okefenokee Swamp becomes a National Wildlife Refuge.

1939—The movie, *Gone With the Wind*, premiers in Atlanta.

1943—Georgia becomes first state to allow 18-year-olds to vote.

1945—Franklin Roosevelt dies at Warm Springs.

1947—The state of Georgia purchases Jekyll Island for $650,000.

1961—Baseball great Ty Cobb dies on July 17.

1962—Members of the Atlanta Symphony are killed in a Paris plane crash.

1964—Georgia voters go Republican in the presidential election.

1973—Maynard Jackson, Jr. becomes Atlanta's first black mayor.

1974—Hank Aaron hits his 715th home run in Atlanta.

1976—James Earl Carter is elected President of the United States.

1977—Toccoa Dam bursts, causing much property damage.

1979—"Georgia on My Mind" is adopted as the state song.

1980—Population of the state is 5,463,105.

1981—University of Georgia wins the national football championship.

1982—Georgia experiences the second highest population growth rate (3.2 percent since 1980) in the South Atlantic region.

1984—Georgians give Ronald Reagan 60.1 percent of the vote in the presidential election.

1985—Robert Woodruff, empire-building president of Coca-Cola Company, dies at age 95 on March 7.

HOLIDAYS AND DAYS OF SPECIAL OBSERVANCE

The following legal holidays are observed in Georgia.

New Year's Day .... January 1
Martin Luther King, Jr.'s Birthday .... January 15
  (will be observed the third Monday of January)
Robert E. Lee's Birthday .... January 19
  (will be observed the Friday following Thanksgiving)
Washington's Birthday .... February 22
  (will be observed December 24)
Confederate Memorial Day .... April 15
National Memorial Day .... May 25
Independence Day .... July 4
Labor Day .... First Monday in September
Columbus Day .... October 12
Veterans' Day .... November 11
Thanksgiving Day .... Fourth Thursday in November
Christmas Day .... December 25

HOUSING

There are approximately 2,012,640 occupied housing units in Georgia. About 60% of this amount are owner occupied units and 33% are occupied by renters.

County	Year-Round Housing Units	Owner-Occupied Housing Units	Renter-Occupied Housing Units	Mobile Homes	Housing Units Built Before 1939
Appling	5,768	3,818	1,299	1,105	953
Atkinson	2,313	1,413	596	399	437
Bacon	3,379	2,314	802	402	445
Baker	1,264	826	382	189	162
Baldwin	11,723	6,713	3,438	1,708	1,670
Banks	3,277	2,400	634	630	817
Barrow	7,768	5,228	2,086	1,153	1,452
Bartow	14,536	10,210	3,594	2,035	2,548
Ben Hill	6,184	3,828	1,842	734	1,762
Berrien	5,113	3,318	1,335	839	855

County	Year-Round Housing Units	Owner-Occupied Housing Units	Renter-Occupied Housing Units	Mobile Homes	Housing Units Built Before 1939
Bibb	55,561	31,131	21,449	1,295	10,053
Bleckley	3,920	2,587	965	396	821
Brantley	3,043	2,357	427	836	395
Brooks	5,362	3,378	1,612	750	1,698
Bryan	3,498	2,531	683	823	476
Bulloch	12,600	7,059	4,280	1,659	2,220
Burke	6,787	3,968	2,244	802	1,582
Butts	4,663	2,798	1,189	573	1,174
Calhoun	1,942	1,198	635	156	570
Camden	5,142	3,411	977	1,078	408
Candler	2,824	1,664	863	349	580
Carroll	20,276	13,297	5,705	2,626	3,835
Catoosa	13,389	10,069	2,579	1,733	1,268
Charlton	2,496	1,726	500	501	376
Chatham	76,718	42,368	28,955	3,827	13,542
Chattahoochee	3,200	473	2,539	286	486
Chattooga	8,245	5,876	1,857	781	2,133
Cherokee	17,666	13,842	3,006	2,462	2,217
Clarke	27,576	12,423	14,164	1,789	3,396
Clay	1,325	792	401	113	419
Clayton	52,989	32,458	17,991	1,568	1,057
Clinch	2,342	1,348	772	340	465
Cobb	113,271	70,759	35,836	3,252	4,526
Coffee	9,701	6,249	2,656	1,579	1,545
Colquitt	12,936	8,187	3,965	1,492	2,621
Columbia	14,010	10,326	2,508	2,056	749
Cook	4,849	3,278	1,198	587	779
Coweta	14,082	9,736	3,571	1,149	3,207
Crawford	2,546	1,816	541	527	392
Crisp	7,074	4,093	2,466	832	1,458
Dade	4,275	3,185	813	800	503
Dawson	1,818	1,405	258	341	299
Decatur	9,046	5,926	2,389	1,059	1,774
DeKalb	181,803	102,842	70,080	711	12,164
Dodge	6,394	4,379	1,488	655	1,346
Dooly	3,765	2,388	1,141	383	1,191
Dougherty	34,705	17,677	15,366	1,940	2,523
Douglas	17,746	14,067	2,844	2,254	1,223
Early	4,667	2,886	1,417	519	1,279
Echols	808	582	153	194	174
Effingham	6,265	4,754	1,033	1,421	1,013
Elbert	7,038	4,794	1,760	770	1,938
Emanuel	7,723	4,911	2,080	740	2,089
Evans	3,175	1,879	980	506	687
Fannin	6,061	4,547	975	832	1,071
Fayette	9,608	8,041	1,167	794	895
Floyd	30,173	19,182	9,295	1,989	6,618
Forsyth	10,321	7,807	1,588	2,179	1,013
Franklin	5,833	4,117	1,246	711	1,359
Fulton	246,352	104,679	120,629	964	39,273
Gilmer	4,391	3,044	893	821	657
Glascock	910	610	226	142	292
Glynn	21,894	12,800	7,026	1,855	2,732

County	Year-Round Housing Units	Owner-Occupied Housing Units	Renter-Occupied Housing Units	Mobile Homes	Housing Units Built Before 1939
Gordon	10,904	7,630	2,650	1,097	1,798
Grady	7,089	4,865	1,755	862	1,489
Greene	4,117	2,860	897	362	1,118
Gwinnett	58,015	43,115	12,112	3,581	2,994
Habersham	8,912	6,569	1,827	1,332	1,562
Hall	27,342	18,631	7,440	3,583	3,711
Hancock	3,095	1,988	803	319	971
Haralson	6,966	5,007	1,497	781	1,321
Harris	5,927	4,137	1,099	634	1,307
Hart	7,494	4,982	1,304	972	1,234
Heard	2,434	1,705	499	458	618
Henry	12,244	9,553	2,077	1,403	1,764
Houston	27,390	17,324	8,185	2,361	742
Irwin	3,326	2,121	892	354	1,104
Jackson	9,088	6,372	2,247	1,746	2,056
Jasper	2,802	1,843	710	292	869
Jeff Davis	4,042	2,784	987	602	597
Jefferson	6,503	3,966	1,980	656	1,572
Jenkins	3,282	1,945	961	380	953
Johnson	3,284	2,148	807	322	1,091
Jones	5,820	4,321	949	1,165	752
Lamar	4,297	2,840	1,170	407	1,109
Lanier	2,029	1,263	559	369	285
Laurens	13,442	8,580	3,867	1,614	2,370
Lee	3,870	2,678	964	864	265
Liberty	10,674	4,696	4,933	2,315	643
Lincoln	3,030	1,706	479	532	767
Long	1,733	1,050	486	488	272
Lowndes	24,279	13,785	8,824	2,514	3,149
Lumpkin	3,727	2,505	883	718	590
Macon	4,675	3,023	1,348	536	1,165
Madison	6,468	4,923	1,202	1,371	1,233
Marion	1,841	1,217	470	314	445
McDuffie	6,739	4,428	1,842	954	990
McIntosh	3,094	2,190	440	716	495
Meriwether	7,594	5,105	1,772	1,078	2,196
Miller	2,561	1,698	707	249	571
Mitchell	7,026	4,406	2,080	720	1,476
Monroe	4,908	3,350	1,317	621	1,212
Montgomery	2,533	1,617	597	376	789
Morgan	3,901	2,661	1,002	427	1,182
Murray	6,887	5,033	1,506	1,493	845
Muscogee	63,802	33,739	25,373	1,814	8,834
Newton	11,812	8,199	2,777	1,185	2,421
Oconee	4,488	3,194	1,043	517	811
Oglethorpe	3,131	2,347	600	550	839
Paulding	9,150	7,185	1,560	1,151	1,376
Peach	6,631	4,130	2,050	715	1,171
Pickens	4,443	3,231	930	683	963
Pierce	4,279	2,962	966	592	913
Pike	3,086	2,269	573	413	992
Polk	12,040	8,458	2,955	822	3,208
Pulaski	3,345	2,163	904	324	821

209

County	Year-Round Housing Units	Owner-Occupied Housing Units	Renter-Occupied Housing Units	Mobile Homes	Housing Units Built Before 1939
Putnam	3,659	2,541	857	491	615
Quitman	882	520	252	89	215
Rabun	4,673	3,022	869	649	754
Randolph	3,535	2,109	1,017	241	1,145
Richmond	64,763	35,211	24,290	3,243	8,944
Rockdale	12,144	9,564	2,028	1,029	938
Schley	1,235	832	293	166	418
Screven	5,501	3,278	1,491	922	1,193
Seminole	3,806	2,361	690	620	450
Spalding	17,023	10,337	5,840	1,225	3,380
Stephens	8,308	5,704	2,083	1,093	1,165
Stewart	2,086	1,258	633	221	758
Sumter	10,090	6,022	3,443	925	2,237
Talbot	2,362	1,571	515	283	693
Taliaferro	866	558	200	81	403
Tattnall	6,254	3,655	1,935	694	1,226
Taylor	2,862	1,951	702	358	723
Telfair	4,363	2,930	977	605	999
Terrell	4,138	2,329	1,510	281	1,522
Thomas	13,774	8,669	4,120	1,473	3,216
Tift	11,000	7,119	3,618	1,627	1,603
Toombs	8,345	4,884	2,788	876	1,169
Towns	3,184	1,733	291	814	326
Treutlen	2,331	1,395	678	158	492
Troup	18,316	11,266	6,189	1,054	5,141
Turner	3,208	2,006	1,072	335	761
Twiggs	3,137	2,203	609	430	498
Union	4,150	2,809	560	601	551
Upson	9,732	6,496	2,674	759	3,155
Walker	20,878	15,384	4,250	1,997	3,395
Walton	10,425	7,132	2,874	1,550	2,515
Ware	13,771	8,761	4,027	1,282	2,733
Warren	2,312	1,620	490	224	687
Washington	6,587	4,188	1,888	690	1,910
Wayne	7,586	4,932	1,947	951	1,095
Webster	828	532	224	123	246
Wheeler	1,906	1,311	422	282	471
White	4,042	2,861	638	571	613
Whitfield	23,780	15,452	7,014	2,821	2,603
Wilcox	2,773	1,972	624	284	766
Wilkes	4,165	2,899	981	392	1,139
Wilkinson	3,787	2,607	743	688	907
Worth	6,353	4,210	1,601	1,055	1,209
Georgia	2,012,640	1,216,459	655,193	152,948	296,662

INDIANS

It is difficult at this late date to attempt to determine the Indian population of North America at the beginning of European discovery and exploration. Even more difficult is to try to come up with figures for a small segment of the continent—a segment that one day would become a state of the United States. Various estimates, however, have placed the aboriginal population of the contiguous states at around one million individuals, divided among 2,000 tribes. Of these, probably less than 10,000 Indians lived in the region which became Georgia.

The accompanying map depicts the various tribes that made Georgia their home during the 17th century, a time which closely corresponds with the opening of the historic period in this part of the country. Most of the tribes shown, with the exception of the *Cherokees* in the northeast, were part of the powerful *Creek* Confederacy. Speaking languages belonging to the *Muskhogean* stock, all of these tribes maintained a similar life style, that indigenous to the southeastern part of North America. Mostly village dwell-

ers, these Indians practiced agriculture, but still depended on hunting, fishing, and gathering for a sizable portion of their livelihood.

The Cherokees, who spoke an *Iroquoian* language, lived in the northeast and comprised the largest Indian tribe in the south. Consisting at one time of an estimated 22,000 individuals, the majority lived in Tennessee and North and South Carolina. In later years, Georgia attained a sizable number of Cherokees, before they were driven west by the U.S. Government in the 1830s.

Those Muskhogean, or Creek, tribes shown on the map are:

Apalachicola	Oconee
Chiaha	Osochi
Creek	Okmulgee
Guale	Tacatacuru
Hitchiti	Tamathli
Icafui	Yamasee
Kasihta	Yui

LABOR

COMMUTERS, TRAVEL TIME, AND MODE OF TRANSPORTATION: 1980.

				Car, Truck or Van		
County	Number Worked in County of Residence	Number Worked Outside County of Residence	Mean Travel Time (Minutes)	Percent Drive Alone	Percent Carpool	Percent Public Means
Appling	3,234	1,270	19	63.9	26.0	0.4
Atkinson	1,133	759	24	61.4	30.6	0.0
Bacon	2,490	451	14	66.8	20.5	0.8
Baker	593	564	25	55.9	34.7	0.3
Baldwin	11,353	1,427	17	73.2	21.4	1.2
Banks	1,105	2,423	23	58.3	28.9	1.9
Barrow	5,535	2,887	23	64.6	30.0	0.4
Bartow	12,609	3,862	21	66.2	28.4	0.7
Ben Hill	5,067	546	14	74.0	20.1	0.4
Berrien	3,760	1,246	16	69.0	23.1	0.3
Bibb	47,752	8,203	20	69.9	22.7	3.1
Bleckley	2,557	1,370	22	57.2	32.3	1.7
Brantley	1,038	1,969	29	57.9	32.6	1.0
Brooks	2,932	1,711	20	61.6	27.7	0.6
Bryan	1,279	2,325	29	62.0	31.4	0.5
Bulloch	11,794	1,688	17	65.4	24.3	0.3
Burke	4,828	1,323	20	55.2	35.2	0.8
Butts	2,786	1,944	26	61.3	32.8	1.2
Calhoun	1,072	577	20	57.7	34.6	0.2
Camden	3,927	780	20	62.1	29.0	1.6
Candler	1,916	643	16	66.6	22.2	0.4
Carroll	16,919	4,888	21	67.5	26.8	0.9

County	Number Worked in County of Residence	Number Worked Outside County of Residence	Mean Travel Time (Minutes)	Car, Truck or Van		Percent Public Means
				Percent Drive Alone	Percent Carpool	
Catoosa	4,115	11,128	21	75.8	20.2	0.5
Charlton	1,343	912	25	52.7	38.6	1.1
Chatham	70,330	4,804	21	67.7	18.6	5.6
Chattahoochee	11,321	1,398	10	25.2	15.8	1.5
Chattooga	6,267	1,931	21	62.5	30.2	0.3
Cherokee	8,254	13,336	31	65.2	29.1	0.6
Clarke	27,649	2,899	16	66.7	20.0	3.2
Clay	627	216	17	53.5	34.7	0.5
Clayton	29,432	37,295	24	75.0	20.8	1.4
Clinch	2,208	245	17	64.5	28.1	0.5
Cobb	68,032	72,425	25	76.0	19.4	1.2
Coffee	8,304	846	16	67.4	22.6	0.8
Colquitt	9,408	1,969	19	68.3	23.3	0.6
Columbia	3,539	12,606	23	74.3	21.5	0.3
Cook	3,327	1,222	18	69.2	21.8	0.2
Coweta	10,504	4,369	23	68.4	27.0	0.3
Crawford	857	1,806	29	59.1	34.8	0.6
Crisp	4,824	805	16	67.7	23.2	0.8
Dade	1,758	2,646	26	59.4	29.5	0.5
Dawson	943	997	27	62.1	29.2	0.0
Decatur	6,355	1,107	19	66.7	25.6	0.7
DeKalb	112,887	112,110	25	69.3	17.5	9.4
Dodge	3,808	1,672	21	71.0	23.6	1.0
Dooly	2,444	771	18	61.3	27.5	0.4
Dougherty	33,615	2,088	17	73.2	19.3	1.7
Douglas	6,273	15,719	29	69.0	27.4	0.7
Early	3,540	620	16	65.0	26.8	0.5
Echols	246	472	26	64.8	29.2	0.1
Effingham	1,859	4,102	29	64.6	29.6	0.1
Elbert	6,030	1,335	18	69.7	24.5	0.2
Emanuel	6,092	917	18	64.3	28.3	0.0
Evans	2,291	596	17	61.1	25.6	0.4
Fannin	2,850	1,863	24	70.5	23.4	1.6
Fayette	4,337	7,991	27	74.0	21.8	0.9
Floyd	29,278	3,060	20	74.2	19.3	1.5
Forsyth	4,715	7,231	30	64.3	30.4	0.5
Franklin	3,443	2,322	22	63.3	28.9	0.0
Fulton	176,276	49,665	26	61.3	15.8	17.4
Gilmer	2,997	1,033	25	64.6	26.4	1.2
Glascock	363	405	22	60.1	30.8	0.0
Glynn	21,752	877	17	72.2	20.8	1.0
Gordon	9,980	2,637	18	71.3	23.2	0.3
Grady	5,107	1,655	18	62.7	27.3	0.9
Greene	3,188	740	21	55.0	36.2	1.3
Gwinnett	28,873	48,428	26	72.9	22.6	1.3
Habersham	8,281	1,541	18	68.0	24.1	1.1

County	Number Worked in County of Residence	Number Worked Outside County of Residence	Mean Travel Time (Minutes)	Car, Truck or Van		Percent Public Means
				Percent Drive Alone	Percent Carpool	
Hall	28,041	4,506	20	72.0	21.5	0.8
Hancock	1,216	1,453	27	44.2	48.0	1.2
Haralson	5,050	2,202	21	66.8	27.3	0.5
Harris	2,253	3,662	25	66.8	27.2	0.8
Hart	4,525	2,294	18	66.2	27.4	0.3
Heard	1,040	1,276	27	61.7	32.3	1.0
Henry	4,615	10,103	29	72.0	23.6	1.0
Houston	27,035	5,210	17	69.0	24.8	0.7
Irwin	1,794	1,186	19	65.6	24.7	0.2
Jackson	5,548	4,456	21	65.7	27.9	0.5
Jasper	1,635	945	27	60.4	32.9	1.5
Jeff Davis	3,614	597	15	72.1	19.7	0.0
Jefferson	4,697	1,106	18	56.4	33.9	0.5
Jenkins	2,333	659	19	62.8	27.1	0.3
Johnson	1,683	1,097	23	55.0	38.3	0.4
Jones	1,334	4,618	25	71.1	24.9	0.8
Lamar	2,497	1,870	22	62.7	30.0	0.6
Lanier	868	873	20	66.9	27.4	0.3
Laurens	11,943	1,428	18	69.0	23.8	1.3
Lee	1,120	3,631	23	71.1	23.3	0.5
Liberty	10.320	1,755	14	43.8	24.9	1.0
Lincoln	1,416	973	26	58.9	34.4	1.4
Long	392	1,175	23	58.5	35.1	0.1
Lowndes	24,675	1,919	16	71.7	19.0	0.8
Lumpkin	2,172	1,761	23	63.1	24.9	0.6
Macon	3,186	931	18	57.3	30.6	1.3
Madison	2,089	4,448	23	64.3	28.7	0.2
Marion	929	661	25	59.0	33.4	0.7
McDuffie	4,561	1,970	19	67.4	26.6	0.3
McIntosh	1,465	912	26	61.5	28.1	2.7
Meriwether	5,108	2,253	22	62.3	31.3	1.1
Miller	1,693	941	20	67.0	21.0	1.1
Mitchell	5,131	1,634	19	61.9	29.9	0.6
Monroe	3,586	1,781	23	59.9	33.5	0.5
Montgomery	1,251	1,064	19	58.9	32.2	1.0
Morgan	3,084	1,068	21	62.4	28.9	1.4
Murray	5,251	2,983	19	72.4	23.5	0.2
Muscogee	49,092	17,365	18	70.4	17.0	2.5
Newton	7,111	6,202	24	66.2	28.5	0.4
Oconee	1,425	3,948	20	71.7	22.6	0.2
Oglethorpe	1,258	2,227	26	59.4	34.9	0.8
Paulding	2,962	6,586	33	62.9	32.8	0.6
Peach	4,099	2,624	19	62.4	28.6	0.7
Pickens	3,020	1,262	26	63.8	31.6	0.2
Pierce	2,626	1,553	22	67.3	27.1	0.2
Pike	1,083	2,443	26	61.2	30.4	0.4

County	Number Worked in County of Residence	Number Worked Outside County of Residence	Mean Travel Time (Minutes)	Car, Truck or Van		Percent Public Means
				Percent Drive Alone	Percent Carpool	
Polk	8,459	3,262	21	68.1	27.4	0.7
Pulaski	2,347	892	19	59.0	29.5	2.3
Putnam	2,810	824	18	61.5	29.8	0.0
Quitman	144	413	25	57.6	37.2	0.8
Rabun	3,635	426	18	64.9	28.7	0.2
Randolph	2,297	468	16	61.7	28.5	0.2
Richmond	64,289	7,404	18	62.4	19.8	3.1
Rockdale	5,888	9,199	28	70.3	24.5	1.0
Schley	717	501	17	65.6	27.0	0.8
Screven	3,966	925	18	65.5	28.8	0.3
Seminole	2,209	896	20	64.6	26.9	0.1
Spalding	14,157	4,708	21	66.0	26.7	2.2
Stephens	7,662	1,012	16	71.0	22.6	0.2
Stewart	993	368	22	52.6	32.4	1.7
Sumter	9,308	1,149	16	65.1	26.8	1.1
Talbot	738	1,574	29	51.0	43.6	0.7
Taliaferro	262	378	25	56.2	32.6	1.0
Tattnall	3,953	1,599	19	65.6	26.0	0.2
Taylor	1,777	766	22	52.0	38.8	1.4
Telfair	2,724	1,272	19	63.8	26.9	1.0
Terrell	2,643	668	15	61.3	26.8	2.3
Thomas	12,209	975	16	68.8	22.1	0.8
Tift	10,174	863	14	71.4	19.1	0.8
Toombs	6,126	1,668	19	68.1	23.1	1.6
Towns	1,233	611	19	62.5	27.2	0.3
Treutlen	1,160	755	22	64.3	28.8	0.0
Troup	16,661	2,253	17	68.6	22.8	3.2
Turner	2,656	469	15	70.3	23.6	0.2
Twiggs	1,103	1,832	28	62.4	33.2	0.4
Union	2,414	655	22	62.7	24.3	1.0
Upson	9,328	1,161	16	63.3	29.6	0.9
Walker	9,081	11,786	23	73.1	22.7	0.3
Walton	7,086	4,780	25	61.7	32.7	0.4
Ware	11,208	1,164	16	76.8	16.6	0.9
Warren	1,135	660	21	59.7	33.5	1.1
Washington	5,846	803	18	63.0	29.7	0.4
Wayne	6,062	721	17	71.9	20.4	0.4
Webster	171	370	24	57.2	31.6	2.9
Wheeler	809	836	21	60.8	31.1	0.4
White	2,247	1,727	23	68.2	24.7	0.0
Whitfield	27,729	2,271	17	72.7	22.0	0.5
Wilcox	1,389	783	22	62.5	26.8	2.4
Wilkes	3,513	546	17	65.3	26.0	0.3
Wilkinson	2,195	1,467	21	58.2	36.6	1.1
Worth	3,449	2,379	22	61.8	29.8	0.8
Georgia	1,453,389	693,518	22	67.5	22.1	3.9

LAND AREA

Georgia, from a land area standpoint, is the largest state east of the Mississippi River. It contains 58,909.6 square miles and ranks 21st in size in the country. The state's extreme North-South length is 315 miles; extreme East-West breadth is 250 miles. The chart below gives the individual counties in Georgia, along with their areas in square miles.

County	Area in Square Miles: 1980 Total	Land	Water	County	Area in Square Miles: 1980 Total	Land	Water
Appling	512.3	510.0	2.3	Dooly	397.3	396.8	0.5
Atkinson	344.3	343.8	0.5	Dougherty	334.1	329.5	4.6
Bacon	285.8	285.7	0.2	Douglas	202.7	202.7	0.0
Baker	347.9	347.1	0.8	Early	517.7	516.1	1.6
Baldwin	267.8	257.4	10.4	Echols	420.6	420.6	0.0
Banks	233.9	233.8	0.1	Effingham	482.1	481.9	0.2
Barrow	163.1	162.6	0.5	Elbert	374.2	366.7	7.5
Bartow	470.7	456.1	14.6	Emanuel	689.6	688.3	1.3
Ben Hill	253.9	253.8	0.1	Evans	187.0	186.5	0.5
Berrien	457.8	455.7	2.1	Fannin	390.3	384.2	6.1
Bibb	255.7	253.0	2.7	Fayette	199.5	199.0	0.5
Bleckley	219.0	219.0	0.0	Floyd	520.2	518.7	1.5
Brantley	444.5	444.5	0.0	Forsyth	246.9	226.2	20.6
Brooks	497.6	491.1	6.5	Franklin	266.7	263.8	2.9
Bryan	453.1	441.3	11.8	Fulton	534.9	533.9	1.0
Bulloch	688.7	677.9	10.8	Gilmer	431.7	427.4	4.3
Burke	834.1	832.8	1.3	Glascock	144.3	144.3	0.0
Butts	189.7	186.9	2.8	Glynn	457.5	412.4	45.1
Calhoun	284.0	283.8	0.2	Gordon	355.2	355.0	0.2
Camden	689.0	649.5	39.6	Grady	459.9	459.0	0.9
Candler	248.8	248.2	0.7	Greene	406.2	389.5	16.7
Carroll	503.2	501.3	1.9	Gwinnett	436.5	435.1	1.4
Catoosa	162.4	162.4	0.0	Habersham	279.0	278.3	0.7
Charlton	782.4	779.5	2.9	Hall	427.7	379.2	48.5
Chatham	498.4	443.4	55.0	Hancock	478.8	469.7	9.1
Chattahoochee	251.2	250.1	1.1	Haralson	283.1	282.6	0.5
Chattooga	313.4	313.4	0.0	Harris	472.8	464.4	8.3
Cherokee	434.4	424.0	10.5	Hart	257.2	230.0	27.2
Clarke	121.9	121.9	0.0	Heard	301.2	291.8	9.4
Clay	216.8	196.4	20.4	Henry	321.1	320.6	0.5
Clayton	148.8	147.9	0.9	Houston	380.4	379.8	0.6
Clinch	824.0	821.4	2.6	Irwin	362.6	362.2	0.4
Cobb	344.9	343.3	1.6	Jackson	342.1	342.1	0.0
Coffee	602.9	601.9	1.0	Jasper	373.7	371.3	2.4
Colquitt	556.8	556.5	0.3	Jeff Davis	335.6	335.1	0.5
Columbia	307.8	290.2	17.6	Jefferson	531.2	529.2	2.0
Cook	232.8	232.6	0.2	Jenkins	352.7	352.6	0.1
Coweta	445.2	444.5	0.7	Johnson	306.8	306.4	0.4
Crawford	327.8	327.8	0.0	Jones	394.4	394.3	0.1
Crisp	280.7	275.0	5.7	Lamar	186.0	185.6	0.4
Dade	175.7	175.7	0.0	Lanier	199.5	193.7	5.8
Dawson	214.1	210.0	4.1	Laurens	817.0	815.7	1.3
Decatur	623.5	585.8	37.7	Lee	361.9	358.4	3.5
DeKalb	270.5	270.0	0.6	Liberty	541.9	516.7	25.2
Dodge	505.5	503.9	1.6	Lincoln	258.2	195.7	62.5

County	Area in Square Miles: 1980			County	Area in Square Miles: 1980		
	Total	Land	Water		Total	Land	Water
Long	403.2	402.1	1.1	Stephens	183.8	177.1	6.7
Lowndes	511.3	506.8	4.5	Stewart	463.3	452.3	11.0
Lumpkin	287.6	287.1	0.5	Sumter	492.1	488.5	3.6
Macon	404.3	403.8	0.5	Talbot	395.0	394.5	0.5
Madison	285.6	285.2	0.5				
Marion	366.2	366.2	0.0	Taliaferro	195.9	195.9	0.0
McDuffie	266.2	256.0	10.2	Tattnall	487.1	483.9	3.2
McIntosh	478.3	425.0	53.3	Taylor	381.9	381.7	0.3
Meriwether	506.2	505.7	0.5	Telfair	444.2	443.9	0.3
Miller	283.6	283.6	0.0	Terrell	337.5	337.0	0.5
				Thomas	552.7	550.6	2.1
Mitchell	513.9	512.4	1.5	Tift	268.8	268.4	0.3
Monroe	397.4	396.8	0.6	Toombs	372.3	371.0	1.3
Montgomery	244.7	244.2	0.5	Towns	171.2	164.9	6.3
Morgan	354.5	348.9	5.6	Treutlen	202.5	202.1	0.5
Murray	347.0	344.7	2.3				
Muscogee	220.9	217.8	3.1	Troup	445.6	414.5	31.1
Newton	279.0	277.3	1.7	Turner	289.5	289.1	0.4
Oconee	186.5	186.4	0.1	Twiggs	362.5	361.7	0.8
Oglethorpe	441.7	441.6	0.1	Union	330.0	319.9	10.1
Paulding	312.7	312.3	0.4	Upson	325.9	325.7	0.2
				Walker	446.4	446.0	0.4
Peach	151.5	151.5	0.0	Walton	330.2	330.2	0.0
Pickens	232.4	232.1	0.3	Ware	907.3	907.1	0.2
Pierce	343.9	343.9	0.0	Warren	286.0	285.5	0.5
Pike	219.3	219.3	0.0	Washington	684.4	683.5	0.8
Polk	311.5	311.4	0.1				
Pulaski	249.9	249.2	0.7	Wayne	648.3	646.9	1.4
Putnam	361.0	343.5	17.5	Webster	210.0	209.9	0.1
Quitman	161.1	146.0	15.1	Wheeler	299.3	299.1	0.2
Rabun	377.1	370.4	6.7	White	242.2	242.0	0.2
Randolph	431.0	430.5	0.5	Whitfield	290.9	290.8	0.1
				Wilcox	383.4	381.9	1.5
Richmond	328.6	325.9	2.7	Wilkes	473.8	470.1	3.7
Rockdale	132.0	132.0	0.1	Wilkinson	452.2	451.5	0.8
Schley	169.0	169.0	0.0	Worth	576.1	575.0	1.1
Screven	655.1	654.8	0.4				
Seminole	256.7	225.3	31.4	Georgia	58,909.6	58,055.8	853.8
Spalding	199.7	199.2	0.5				

LEGISLATURE

MEMBERS OF SENATE BY DISTRICTS

District 1
Portion of Chatham
J. Tom Coleman, Jr. (D)
P.O. Box 22398
Savannah 31403
912-964-7308

District 2
Portion of Chatham
Al Scott (D)
738 East Victory Drive

Savannah 31406
912-234-6420

District 3
Liberty, McIntosh; Portion of Bryan, Chatham, Glynn
Glenn E. Bryant (D)
P.O. Box 585
Hinesville 31313
912-368-3300

District 4
Bulloch, Candler, Effingham, Evans, Long, Tattnall; Portion of Bryan
Joseph E. Kennedy (D)
P.O. Box 246
Claxton 30417
912-739-1163

District 5
Portion of DeKalb

SENATORIAL DISTRICTS

Joe Burton (R)
2598 Woodwardin Road,
NE
Atlanta 30345
404-938-2730

District 6
*Bacon, Brantley, Camden,
Charlton, Pierce, Wayne;
Portion of Appling, Glynn*
Riley Reddish (D)
Cherokee Lake
Jesup 31545
912-586-6973

District 7
*Atkinson, Berrien, Clinch,
Lanier, Tift, Ware*
Ed Perry (D)
P.O. Box 496
Nashville 31639
912-686-7454

District 8
*Brooks, Cook, Echols,
Lowndes*
Loyce W. Turner (D)
608 Howellbrook Drive
Valdosta 31602

912-242-5725

District 9
Portion of Gwinnett
Tom Phillips (R)
1703 Pounds Road
Stone Mountain 30087
404-469-4735

District 10
*Decatur, Grady, Thomas;
Portion of Colquitt*
Paul H. Trulock (D)
P.O. Box 70

REPRESENTATIVE DISTRICTS

Climax 31734
912-762-4141

District 11
*Baker, Calhoun, Clay,
Early, Miller, Mitchell,
Quitman, Randolph,
Seminole, Stewart,
Webster; Portion of
Chattahoochee*
Jimmy Hodge
Timmons (D)
132 Woodlawn Street
Blakely 31723

912-849-3415

District 12
Dougherty
Al Holloway (D)
P.O. Box 588
Albany 31702
912-435-5601

District 13
*Ben Hill, Crisp, Dooly,
Irwin, Turner, Worth;
Portion of Colquitt*
Rooney L. Bowen (D)

P.O. Box 417
Vienna 31092
912-268-2400

District 14
*Lee, Macon, Peach, Schley,
Sumter, Taylor, Terrell*
Bud McKenzie (D)
P.O. Box 565
Montezuma 31063
912-472-8111

District 15
Portion of Chattahoochee,

219

Muscogee
Floyd Hudgins (D)
P.O. Box 12127
Columbus 31907
404-327-5135

District 16
*Marion, Talbot; Portion of
Muscogee*
Ted J. Land (R)
1069 Standing Boy Court
Columbus 31904
404-322-1683

District 17
*Butts, Henry; Portion of
Clayton*
Janice Horton (D)
430 Burke Circle
McDonough 30253
404-656-5079

District 18
*Houston, Twiggs; Portion of
Bibb*
Ed Barker (D)
P.O. Box 5036
Warner Robins 31099
912-922-8238

District 19
*Bleckley, Coffee, Dodge, Jeff
Davis, Pulaski, Telfair,
Wilcox*
Walter S. Ray (D)
Box 295
Douglas 31533
912-384-0200

District 20
*Johnson, Laurens,
Montgomery, Toombs,
Treutlen, Wheeler; Portion
of Appling, Washington*
Hugh Gillis, Sr. (D)
P.O. Box 148
Soperton 30457
912-529-3212

District 21
*Burke, Emanuel, Glascock,
Jefferson, Jenkins,
Screven; Portion of
Washington*
Bill English (D)
214 Golf Drive
Swainsboro 30401
912-237-6954

District 22
Portion of Richmond
Thomas F. Allgood (D)
P.O. Box 1523
Augusta 30903
404-724-6526

District 23
*Portion of Columbia,
Richmond*
Frank A. Albert (R)
3102 Walton Way Ext.
Augusta 30909
404-736-2876

District 24
*Greene, Lincoln, McDuffie,
Oglethorpe, Taliaferro,
Warren, Wilkes; Portion of
Columbia*
Sam McGill (D)
P.O. Box 520
Washington 30673
404-678-2161

District 25
*Baldwin, Hancock, Jasper,
Jones, Morgan, Putnam,
Wilkinson*
Culver Kidd (D)
P.O. Box 370
Milledgeville 31061
912-452-1420

District 26
Portion of Bibb
Richard L. Greene (D)
Suite 517
Trust Company Bank
Building
Macon 31201
912-745-7931

District 27
*Crawford, Lamar, Monroe,
Upson; Portion of Bibb*
W. F. (Billy) Harris (D)
1261 Willingham Springs
Road
Thomaston 30286
404-648-2851

District 28
Coweta, Pike, Spalding
Kyle T. Cobb (D)
P.O. Box 1010
Griffin 30224
404-228-7001

District 29
*Harris, Heard, Meriwether,
Troup; Portion of Carroll*
Quillian Baldwin (D)
P.O. Box 1364
LaGrange 30241
404-882-8122

District 30
Portion of Carroll, Douglas
Wayne Garner (D)
25 Azalea Trail
Carrollton 30117
404-834-7038

District 31
*Haralson, Paulding, Polk;
Portion of Bartow*
Nathan Dean (D)
340 Wingfoot Street
Rockmart 30153
404-684-7851

District 32
Portion of Cobb
Jim Tolleson (R)
2195 Beech Valley Drive
Smyrna 30080
404-434-3885

District 33
Portion of Cobb
Roy E. Barnes (D)
4841 Brookwood Drive
Mableton 30059
404-424-1500

District 34
*Fayette; Portion of Douglas,
Fulton*
Bev Engram (D)
749 Pinehurst Drive
Fairburn 30213
404-964-3391

District 35
Portion of Fulton
Arthur Langford, Jr. (D)
1544 Niskey Lake Trail
Atlanta 30331
404-344-6848

District 36
Portion of Fulton
David Scott (D)
190 Wendell Drive, SE
Atlanta 30315
404-622-5653

District 37
Portion of Cherokee, Cobb
Carl Harrison (R)
P.O. Box 1374
Marietta 30061
404-427-7371

District 38
Portion of Fulton
Horace Edward Tate (D)
621 Lilla Drive, SW
Atlanta 30310
404-522-7512

District 39
Portion of Fulton
Julian Bond (D)
361 West View Drive, SW
Atlanta 30310
404-758-9101

District 40
Portion of Fulton
Paul D. Coverdell (R)
2015 Peachtree Road, NE
Atlanta 30309
404-355-8880

District 41
Portion of DeKalb
James W. (Jim)
Tysinger (R)
3781 Watkins Place, NE
Atlanta 30319
404-885-5318

District 42
Portion of DeKalb
Pierre Howard (D)
500 Fidelity National Bank
Building
Decatur 30030
404-378-2566

District 43
Portion of DeKalb
Eugene Walker (D)
2231 Chevy Chase Lane
Decatur 30032
404-299-4212

District 44

Portion of Clayton
Terrell Starr (D)
4766 Tanglewood Lane
Forest Park 30050
404-366-5311

District 45
Newton, Rockdale, Walton
Harrill L. Dawkins (D)
1445-A Old McDonough
Road
Conyers 30207
404-483-0882

District 46
Clarke, Oconee; Portion of Jackson
Paul Broun (D)
165 Pulaski Street
Athens 30610
404-546-6700

District 47
Banks, Elbert, Franklin, Hart, Madison; Portion of Jackson
M. Parks Brown (D)
P.O. Box 37
Hartwell 30643
404-376-2700

District 48
Barrow; Portion of Gwinnett
Donn M. Peevy (D)
P.O. Box 862
Lawrenceville 30245
404-963-0858

District 49
Hall; Portion of Forsyth
Nathan Deal (D)
P.O. Box 2522
Gainesville 30503
404-532-9978

District 50
Dawson, Habersham, Lumpkin, Rabun, Stephens, Towns, Union, White
John C. Foster (D)
P.O. Box 100

Cornelia 30531
404-778-2919

District 51
Fannin, Gilmer, Gordon, Pickens; Portion of Cherokee, Whitfield
Max Brannon (D)
P.O. Box 1027
Calhoun 30701
404-629-4508

District 52
Floyd; Portion of Bartow
Ed Hine (D)
P.O. Box 5511
Rome 30161
404-291-2531

District 53
Chattooga, Dade, Walker; Portion of Catoosa
Waymond (Sonny)
Huggins (D)
P.O. Box 284
LaFayette 30728
404-638-1409

District 54
Murray; Portion of Catoosa, Whitfield
W. W. (Bill) Fincher, Jr. (D)
P.O. Drawer 400
Chatsworth 30705
404-695-2334

District 55
Portion of DeKalb
Lawrence (Bud)
Stumbaugh (D)
1071 Yemassee Trail
Stone Mountain 30083
404-939-2254

District 56
Portion of Cobb, Forsyth, Fulton
Haskew Brantley (R)
P.O. Box 605
Alpharetta 30201
404-475-5005

MEMBERS OF SENATE ALPHABETICALLY LISTED

Albert, Frank A. (R)
District 23

Allgood, Thomas F. (D)
District 22

Baldwin, Quillian (D)
District 29

Barker, Ed (D)
District 18

Barnes, Roy E. (D)
District 33

Bond, Julian (D)
District 39

Bowen, Rooney L. (D)
District 13

Brannon, Max (D)
District 51

Brantley, Haskew (R)
District 56

Broun, Paul (D)
District 46

Brown, M. Parks (D)
District 47

Bryant, Glenn E. (D)
District 3

Burton, Joe (R)
District 5

Cobb, Kyle T. (D)
District 28

Coleman, J. Tom (D)
District 1

Coverdell, Paul D. (R)
District 40

Dawkins, Harrill L. (D)
District 45

Deal, Nathan (D)
District 49

Dean, Nathan (D)
District 31

English, Bill (D)
District 21

Engram, Bev (D)
District 34

Fincher, W. W. (Bill) (D)
District 54

Foster, John C. (D)
District 50

Garner, Wayne (D)
District 30

Gillis, Hugh, Sr. (D)
District 20

Greene, Richard L. (D)
District 26

Harris, W. F. (Billy) (D)
District 27

Harrison, Carl (R)
District 37

Hine, Ed (D)
District 52

Holloway, Al (D)
District 12

Horton, Janice (D)
District 17

Howard, Pierre (D)
District 42

Hudgins, Floyd (D)
District 15

Huggins, Waymond
(Sonny) (D)
District 53

Kennedy, Joseph E. (D)
District 4

Kidd, Culver (D)
District 25

Land, Ted J. (R)
District 16

Langford, Arthur, Jr. (D)
District 35

McGill, Sam (D)
District 24

McKenzie, Bud (D)
District 14

Peevy, Donn M. (D)
District 48

Perry, Ed (D)
District 7

Phillips, Tom (R)
District 9

Ray, Walter S. (D)
District 19

Reddish, Riley (D)
District 6

Scott, Al (D)
District 2

Scott, David (D)
District 36

Starr, Terrell (D)
District 44

Stumbaugh, Lawrence
(Bud) (D)
District 55

Tate, Horace Edward (D)
District 38

Timmons, Jimmy
Hodge (D)
District 11

Tolleson, Jim (R)
District 32

Trulock, Paul H. (D)
District 10

Turner, Loyce W. (D)
District 8

Tysinger, James W.
(Jim) (R)
District 41

Walker, Eugene (D)
District 43

MEMBERS OF THE HOUSE OF REPRESENTATIVES BY DISTRICTS

District 1—Post 1
Portion of Dade, Walker
Donald F. Oliver (D)
P.O. Box 386

Chickamauga 30707
404-931-2829
District 1—Post 2
Portion of Dade, Walker

Forest Hays, Jr. (D)
Route 2
Flintstone 30725
404-931-2326

District 2
Portion of Catoosa
Robert G. Peters (D)
P.O. Box 550
Ringgold 30736
615-267-4471

District 3
Murray; Portion of Catoosa,
Whitfield
Tom Ramsey (D)
P.O. Box 1130
Chatsworth 30705
404-695-6642

District 4—Post 1
Fannin, Gilmer, Lumpkin,
Rabun, Towns, Union
Carlton H. Colwell (D)
P.O. Box 850
Blairsville 30512
404-745-6239

District 4—Post 2
Fannin, Gilmer, Lumpkin,
Rabun, Towns, Union
Ralph Twiggs (D)
P.O. Box 432
Hiawassee 30546
404-896-2574

District 5
Chattooga; Portion of Dade,
Walker
John G. Crawford (D)
Route 1, Box 518
Lyerly 30730
404-895-4410

District 6—Post 1
Portion of Whitfield
Roger Willams (D)
132 Huntington Road
Dalton 30720
404-278-1788

District 6—Post 2
Portion of Whitfield
Phil Foster (D)
411 College Drive,
Apt. E16
Dalton 30720
404-226-3616

District 7
Gordon
J. C. Maddox (D)
P.O. Box 577

Calhoun 30701
404-629-4407

District 8—Post 1
Pickens; Portion of Cherokee
Wendell T. Anderson,
Sr. (D)
RFD 4
Canton 30114
404-479-5559

District 8—Post 2
Pickens; Portion of Cherokee
W. G. (Bill) Hasty, Sr. (D)
Route 9, Hilton Way
Canton 30114
404-479-8528

District 9—Post 1
Dawson, Hall; Portion of
Gwinnett
Joe T. Wood (D)
P.O. Drawer 1417
Gainesville 30503
404-536-0161

District 9—Post 2
Dawson, Hall; Portion of
Gwinnett
Bobby Lawon (D)
P.O. Box 53
Gainesville 30503
404-536-2304

District 9—Post 3
Dawson, Hall; Portion of
Gwinnett
Jerry D. Jackson (D)
P.O. Box 7275
Chestnut Mountain 30502
404-967-3466

District 10
Forsyth; Portion of Cherokee
Bill H. Barnett (D)
P.O. Box 755
Cumming 30130
404-887-6582

District 11—Post 1
Habersham, Stephens,
White; Portion of Banks
Bill Dover (D)
Route 2, "Timbrook"
Clarkesville 30523
404-754-6396

District 11—Post 2
Habersham, Stephens,
White; Portion of Banks
Jeanette Jamieson (D)
P.O. Box 852
Toccoa 30577
404-886-1168

District 12
Jackson; Portion of Banks
Lauren (Bubba) McDonald,
Jr. (D)
Route 5, Dogwood Trail
Commerce 30529
404-656-5052

District 13—Post 1
Franklin, Hart; Portion of
Clarke, Madison
Louie Clark (D)
RFD 2
Danielsville 30633
404-789-2236

District 13—Post 2
Franklin, Hart; Portion of
Clarke, Madison
Billy Milford (D)
Route 3
Hartwell 30643
404-376-4427

District 14
Elbert, Oglethorpe; Portion
of Madison
Charles W. Yeargin (D)
P.O. Box 584
Elberton 30635
404-283-4376

District 15—Post 1
Portion of Bartow, Floyd
E. M. (Buddy)
Childers (D)
15 Kirkwood Street
Rome 30161
404-291-8203

District 15—Post 2
Portion of Bartow, Floyd
Forrest L. McKelvey (D)
104 Hooper Street, RFD 1
Lindale 30147
404-234-2067

District 16
Portion of Floyd
Paul E. Smith (D)
P.O. Box 486

223

Rome 30162
404-232-1997

District 17
Portion of Polk
Bill Cummings (D)
508 Morgan Valley Road
Rockmart 30153
404-684-3747

District 18
Haralson; Portion of
Paulding, Polk
Thomas B. Murphy (D)
P.O. Drawer 1076
Bremen 30110
404-537-5201

District 19
Portion of Bartow
Boyd Pettit (D)
P.O. Box 1256
Cartersville 30120
404-382-9592

District 20—Post 1
Portion of Cobb
Joe Mack Wilson (D)
77 Church Street
Marietta 30060
404-428-6581

District 20—Post 2
Portion of Cobb
A. L. (Al) Burruss (D)
P.O. Box 6338
Marietta 30062
404-973-8070

District 20—Post 3
Portion of Cobb
Bill Cooper (D)
2432 Powder Springs Road
Marietta 30064
404-943-5663

District 20—Post 4
Portion of Cobb
Steve Thompson (D)
4265 Bradley Drive
Austell 30001
404-955-0027

District 20—Post 5
Portion of Cobb
Terry Lawler (D)
P.O. Box 189
Clarkdale 30020
404-941-8613

District 21—Post 1
Portion of Cobb
Fred Aiken (R)
4020 Pineview Drive, SE
Smyrna 30080
404-432-1883

District 21—Post 2
Portion of Cobb
Johnny Isakson (R)
5074 Hampton Farms
Drive
Marietta 30067
404-973-0303

District 21—Post 3
Portion of Cobb
Bill Atkins (R)
4719 Windsor Drive
Smyrna 30080
404-435-0490

District 21—Post 4
Portion of Cobb
Frank Johnson (R)
436 Concord Road
Smyrna 30080
404-436-0780

District 21—Post 5
Portion of Cobb
Tom Wilder (R)
2920 Rockbridge Road
Marietta 30066
404-428-3762

District 22
Portion of Fulton
Mrs. Dorothy Felton (R)
465 Tanacrest Drive, NW
Atlanta 30328
404-252-4172

District 23
Portion of Fulton
Luther S. Colbert (R)
495 Houze Way
Roswell 30076
404-993-4786

District 24
Portion of Fulton
Kil Townsend (R)
56 West Paces Drive, NW
Atlanta 30327
404-261-2682

District 25
Portion of Fulton

John M. Lupton (R)
594 Westover Drive
Atlanta 30305
404-266-6346

District 26
Portion of Fulton
Jim Martin (D)
161 Spring Street, Suite 615
Atlanta 30303
404-523-0568

District 27
Portion of Fulton
Dick Lane (R)
2704 Humphries Street
East Point 30344
404-767-4451

District 28
Portion of Fulton
Bob Holmes (D)
1850 King Geo. Lane, SW
Atlanta 30331
404-755-9528

District 29
Portion of Fulton
Douglas C. Dean (D)
346 Arthur Street, SW
Atlanta 30310
404-524-3413

District 30
Portion of Fulton
Paul Bolster (D)
660 Woodland Avenue, SE
Atlanta 30316
404-627-1697

District 31
Portion of Fulton
Mable Thomas (D)
P.O. Box 573
Atlanta 30301
404-525-7251

District 32
Portion of Fulton
Mrs. Helen Selman (D)
Jones Ferry Road, Box 315
Palmetto 30268
404-463-3374

District 33
Portion of Fulton
J. C. (Julius C.) Daugherty,
Sr. (D)
202 Dougherty Building,

15 Chestnut Street, SW
Atlanta 30314
404-525-2031

District 34
Portion of Fulton
Tyrone Brooks (D)
Station A—P.O. Box 11185
Atlanta 30310–0185
404-524-5531

District 35
Portion of Fulton
J. E. (Billy) McKinney (D)
765 Shorter Terrace, NW
Atlanta 30318
404-691-8810

District 36
Portion of Fulton
G. D. Adams (D)
3417 Northside Drive
Hapeville 30354
404-761-3397

District 37
Portion of Fulton
Georganna Sinkfield (D)
179 Tonawanda Drive, SE
Atlanta 30315
404-622-1515

District 38
Portion of Fulton
Lorenzo Benn (D)
579 Fielding Lane, SW
Atlanta 30311
404-349-4325

District 39
Portion of Fulton
John W. Greer (D)
925 Healey Building
Atlanta 30303
404-524-4223

District 40
Portion of Fulton
Barbara H. Couch (D)
2864 West Roxboro Road,
NE
Atlanta 30324
404-261-1406

District 41
Portion of Douglas, Paulding
Charlie Watts (D)
505 Hardee Street
Dallas 30132

404-445-2708

District 42
Portion of Douglas
Thomas (Mac) Kilgore (D)
1992 Tara Circle
Douglasville 30135
404-352-1140

District 43
Fayette
Paul W. Heard, Jr. (R)
102 Camp Creek Court
Peachtree City 30269
404-762-9573

District 44
Portion of DeKalb
John Linder (R)
5039 Winding Branch
Drive
Dunwoody 30338
404-394-6790

District 45
Portion of DeKalb
Max Davis (R)
1177 W. Nancy Creek
Drive, NE
Atlanta 30319
404-373-3316

District 46
Portion of DeKalb
Cathey W. Steinberg (D)
1732 Dunwoody Place, NE
Atlanta 30324
404-262-2244

District 47
Portion of DeKalb
Chesley Morton (R)
3580 Coldwater Canyon
Court
Tucker 30084
404-496-0416

District 48
Portion of DeKalb
Betty Jo Williams (R)
2024 Castleway Drive, NE
Atlanta 30345
404-325-9051

District 49
Portion of DeKalb
Tom Lawrence (R)
2283 Stratmor Drive
Stone Mountain 30087

404-894-7885

District 50
Portion of DeKalb
Frank Redding (D)
P.O. Box 117
Decatur 30030
404-377-1458

District 51
Portion of DeKalb
Ken Workman (D)
3383 Hyland Drive
Decatur 30032
404-399-0711

District 52
Portion of DeKalb
Eleanor L. Richardson (D)
755 Park Lane
Decatur 30033
404-636-5892

District 53
Portion of DeKalb
Mrs. Mobley (Peggy)
Childs (D)
520 Westchester Drive
Decatur 30030
404-378-0593

District 54
Portion of DeKalb
Juanita T. Williams (D)
8 East Lake Drive, NE
Atlanta 30317
404-373-5751

District 55
Portion of DeKalb
Betty J. Clark (D)
P.O. Box 17852
Atlanta 30316
404-241-4033

District 56
Portion of DeKalb
Betty Aaron (D)
3920 John Hopkins Court
Decatur 30034
404-981-9724

District 57—Post 1
Rockdale; Portion of DeKalb
Troy Athon (D)
1161 Valley Drive, NE
Conyers 30207
404-922-1922

225

District 57—Post 2
Rockdale; Portion of DeKalb
Wm. C. (Bill) Mangum,
Jr. (D)
4320 Pleasant Forest Drive
Decatur 30034
404-681-1230

District 57—Post 3
Rockdale; Portion of DeKalb
Dean Alford (D)
20 Willowick Drive
Lithonia 30058
404-939-1047

District 58
Portion of DeKalb
Cas Robinson (D)
4720 Fellswood Drive
Stone Mountain 30083
404-296-5392

District 59
Portion of Gwinnett
Mike Barnett (R)
1472 Ridgewood Drive
Lilburn 30247
404-923-8153

District 60
Portion of Gwinnett
Charles Martin (D)
470 Hill Street
Buford 30518
404-945-5179

District 61
Portion of Gwinnett
Vinson Wall (D)
164 E. Oak Street
Lawrenceville 30245
404-963-9558

District 62
Portion of Gwinnett
Charles E. Bannister (R)
312 Emily Drive
Lilburn 30247
404-921-0084

District 63
Portion of Gwinnett
Bill Goodwin (R)
3823 Club Forest Drive
Norcross 30092
404-446-2889

District 64
Barrow; Portion of Gwinnett

John Russell (D)
P.O. Box 588
Winder 30680
404-867-5011

District 65
Walton
Neal Jackson (D)
316 N. Broad Street
Monroe 30655
404-267-7557

District 66
*Morgan, Oconee; Portion of
Newton*
Frank E. Stancil (D)
P.O. Box 694
Watkinsville 30677
404-548-6228

District 67
Portion of Clarke
Hugh Logan (D)
1328 Prince Avenue
Athens 30601
404-548-2501

District 68
Portion of Clarke
Bob Argo (D)
P.O. Box 509
Athens 30603
404-353-2345

District 69
Portion of Carroll
Charles Thomas (D)
P.O. Box 686
Temple 30179
404-562-3028

District 70
Portion of Carroll, Douglas
Carol W. Lee (D)
546 Burwell Road
Carrollton 30117
404-832-7414

District 71
Portion of Carroll, Coweta
Neal Shepard (R)
P.O. Box 836
Newnan 30264
404-253-0231

District 72—Post 1
Clayton

William J. (Bill) Lee (D)
5325 Hillside Drive
Forest Park 30050
404-761-6522

District 72—Post 2
Clayton
Jimmy Benefield (D)
6656 Morning Dove Place
Jonesboro 30236
404-471-8825

District 72—Post 3
Clayton
Charles E. Holcomb (D)
P.O. Box 122
Jonesboro 30237
404-478-4383

District 72—Post 4
Clayton
Rudolph Johnson (D)
5604 Reynolds Road
Morrow 30260
404-961-1718

District 72—Post 5
Clayton
Frank I. Bailey, Jr. (D)
P.O. Box 777
Riverdale 30274
404-572-0609

District 73
Portion of Henry
Wesley Dunn (D)
P.O. Box 353
McDonough 30253
404-957-6093

District 74
Portion of Newton
Denny M. Dobbs (D)
125 Hardwick Drive
Covington 30209
404-786-6691

District 75
*Portion of Coweta, Pike,
Spalding*
John L. Mostiler (D)
150 Meadovista Drive
Griffin 30223
404-228-1172

District 76
Portion of Spalding
Suzi Johnson (D)

P.O. Box 277
Orchard Hill 30266
404-228-2017

District 77
Heard; Portion of Coweta,
Troup
J. Crawford Ware (D)
P.O. Box 305
Hogansville 30230
404-637-8655

District 78
Butts, Lamar; Portion of
Henry
Larry Smith (D)
P.O. Box 4155
Jackson 30233
404-775-5377

District 79
Upson; Portion of Pike
Marvin Adams (D)
709 Greenwood Road
Thomaston 30286
404-647-6131

District 80
Jasper, Monroe; Portion of
Crawford, Jones
Kenneth Waldrep (D)
87 N. Lee Street
Forsyth 31029
912-994-5171

District 81
Portion of Troup
Wade Milam (D)
P.O. Box 1361
LaGrange 30241
404-882-1182

District 82
Glascock, Lincoln,
Taliaferro, Warren,
Wilkes; Portion of
Jefferson
Ben Barron Ross (D)
P.O. Box 245
Lincolnton 30817
404-359-3164

District 83
Portion of Columbia
James P. (Jim) Hill (R)
471 Stevens Creek Road
Martinez 30907

404-860-0388

District 84
McDuffie; Portion of
Columbia
Warren D. Evans (D)
P.O. Box 539
Thomson 30824
404-595-1841

District 85
Portion of Richmond
Charles W. Walker (D)
1402 Twelfth Street
Augusta 30901
404-722-4222

District 86
Portion of Richmond
Mike Padgett (D)
Route 1, Box 5
Augusta 30906
404-793-9180

District 87
Portion of Richmond
Jack Connell (D)
P.O. Box 308
Augusta 30903
404-736-5932

District 88
Portion of Richmond
George Brown (D)
P.O. Box 1114
Augusta 30903
404-724-0953

District 89
Portion of Richmond
Don E. Cheeks (D)
3047 Walton Way
Augusta 30909
404-863-2305

District 90
Portion of Richmond
Dick Ransom (R)
2748 Mayo Road
Augusta 30907
404-860-0893

District 91
Meriwether, Talbot; Portion
of Coweta
Claude A. Bray, Jr. (D)
P.O. Box 549
Manchester 31816

404-846-8495

District 92
Portion of Muscogee
Calvin Smyre (D)
P.O. Box 181
Columbus 31902
404-571-2243

District 93
Harris; Portion of Muscogee
Roy D. Moultrie (D)
P.O. Box 119
Hamilton 31811
404-628-5361

District 94
Portion of Muscogee
Sanford D. Bishop, Jr. (D)
P.O. Box 709
Columbus 31902
404-324-3531

District 95
Portion of Muscogee
Thomas B. Buck, III (D)
P.O. Box 196
Columbus 31902
404-323-5646

District 96
Portion of Muscogee
Pete Robinson (D)
P.O. Box 2648
Columbus 31994
404-324-3711

District 97
Portion of Muscogee
Mary Jane Galer (D)
7236 Lullwater Road
Columbus 31904
404-324-2931

District 98
Peach; Portion of Crawford,
Macon
Robert Ray (D)
Route One, Box 189
Fort Valley 31030
912-825-7202

District 99
Portion of Bibb
Denmark Groover, Jr. (D)
P.O. Box 755
Macon 31202
912-745-4712

District 100
Portion of Bibb
Frank C. Pinkston (D)
P.O. Box 4872
Macon 31208
912-741-1000

District 101
Portion of Bibb
William C. (Billy)
Randall (D)
2770 Hillcrest Avenue
Macon 31204
912-742-2885

District 102
Portion of Bibb
David E. Lucas (D)
448 Woolfolk Street
Macon 31201
912-742-8486

District 103
Portion of Bibb
Frank Horne (D)
850 Walnut Street
Macon 31201
912-741-6000

District 104
Twiggs, Wilkinson; Portion of Jones
Kenneth (Ken) W.
Birdsong (D)
Route One
Gordon 31031
912-746-3934

District 105
Portion of Baldwin
Bobby Eugene Parham (D)
P.O. Box 606
Milledgeville 31061
912-452-5152

District 106
Greene, Hancock, Putnam
Jesse Copelan, Jr. (D)
P.O. Box 109
Eatonton 31024
404-485-9410

District 107
Washington; Portion of Baldwin, Johnson
Jimmy Lord (D)
P.O. Box 254
Sandersville 31082

912-552-2515

District 108
Portion of Burke, Jefferson
Emory E. Bargeron (D)
P.O. Box 447
Louisville 30434
912-625-7285

District 109
Candler, Emanuel; Portion of Johnson
Larry (Butch) Parrish (D)
224 W. Main Street
Swainsboro 30401
912-237-7032

District 110
Jenkins; Portion of Bulloch, Burke, Screven
John Godbee (D)
401 Lane Street
Brooklet 30415
912-764-5208

District 111
Portion of Bulloch, Screven
Robert Lane (D)
205 Aldred Avenue
Statesboro 30458
912-764-6813

District 112
Marion, Schley, Taylor; Portion of Chattahoochee
Ward Edwards (D)
P.O. Box 146
Butler 31006
912-862-5535

District 113
Portion of Houston
Ted W. Waddle (R)
113 Tanglewood Drive
Warner Robins 31093
912-923-7424

District 114
Portion of Houston
Roy H. (Sonny) Watson,
Jr. (D)
P.O. Box 1905
Warner Robins 31099
912-923-0044

District 115
Portion of Houston, Macon
Larry Walker (D)

P.O. Box 1234
Perry 31069
912-987-1415

District 116
Sumter
George Hooks (D)
P.O. Box 928
Americus 31709
912-924-2924

District 117
Bleckley, Pulaski, Wilcox; Portion of Turner
W. N. (Newt) Hudson (D)
Route One, Box 29A
Rochelle 31079
912-365-2387

District 118
Dodge; Portion of Laurens, Telfair
Terry L. Coleman (D)
P.O. Box 157
Eastman 31023
912-374-5594

District 119
Portion of Laurens
DuBose Porter (D)
125 N. Franklin Street
Dublin 31021
912-272-3545

District 120
Montgomery, Treutlen, Wheeler; Portion of Toombs
L. L. (Pete) Phillips (D)
Box 166
Soperton 30457
912-529-4447

District 121
Evans, Long, Tattnall
Clinton Oliver (D)
P.O. Box 237
Glennville 30427
912-654-2660

District 122
Portion of Chatham
Jim Pannell (D)
P.O. Box 10186
Savannah 31412
912-236-3311

228

District 123
Portion of Chatham
Diane Harvey Johnson (D)
P.O. Box 5544
Savannah 31414
912-232-3695

District 124
Portion of Chatham
DeWayne Hamilton (D)
P.O. Box 14562
Savannah 31406
912-234-6199

District 125
Portion of Chatham
Jack Kingston (R)
30 Wylly Avenue
Savannah 31406
912-234-1671

District 126
Portion of Bryan, Chatham
Anne Mueller (R)
13013 Hermitage Road
Savannah 31406
912-925-2291

District 127
Portion of Chatham
Ray Allen (D)
1406 Law Drive
Savannah 31401
912-233-4914

District 128
Portion of Chatham
Tom Triplett (D)
P.O. Box 9586
Savannah 31402
912-944-3200

District 129
*Effingham; Portion of
Bryan, Liberty*
George Chance (D)
P.O. Box 373
Springfield 31329
912-754-9262

District 130
*Quitman, Randolph,
Stewart, Webster; Portion
of Chattahoochee*
Gerald E. Greene (D)
Route Three, Box 119
Cuthbert 31740
912-732-2750

District 131
*Calhoun, Clay, Terrell,
Portion of Lee*
Bob Hanner (D)
Route One, Box 26
Parrott 31777
912-623-4582

District 132
Portion of Dougherty
John White (D)
P.O. Box 3506
Albany 31706
912-888-0452

District 133
Portion of Dougherty
Tommy Chambless (D)
P.O. Box 2008
Albany 31702
912-436-1545

District 134
Portion of Dougherty
Mary Young (D)
423 Holloway Avenue
Albany 31705
912-883-4489

District 135
Crisp, Dooly
Howard H. Rainey (D)
913 Third Avenue, E
Cordele 31015
912-273-3062

District 136
Worth; Portion of Lee, Turner
Earleen Sizemore (D)
Route 3
Sylvester 31791
912-776-6943

District 137
*Ben Hill, Irwin; Portion of
Telfair*
Paul S. Branch, Jr. (D)
Route 4, Box 499-A
Fitzgerald 31750
912-423-4410

District 138
Portion of Tift
Henry Bostick (D)
P.O. Box 94
Tifton 31793
912-382-4828

District 139
Coffee; Portion of Atkinson
James C. Moore (D)
Route Two
West Green 31567
912-384-3637

District 140
*Baker, Early, Miller; Portion
of Dougherty*
Ralph J. Balkcom (D)
Route One
Blakely 31723
912-723-5074

District 141
Seminole; Portion of Decatur
Walter E. Cox (D)
202 West Street
Bainbridge 31717
912-246-4411

District 142
*Grady; Portion of Decatur,
Thomas*
Bobby Long (D)
1466 Sixth Street, NW
Cairo 31728
912-377-1723

District 143
Portion of Thomas
R. Allen Sherrod (D)
Route 1
Coolidge 31738
912-226-5272

District 144
*Mitchell: Portion of Colquitt,
Thomas*
A. Richard Royal (D)
20 N. Scott Street
Camilla 31730
912-336-7974

District 145
Portion of Colquitt
Hugh D. Matthews (D)
Route 1, Box 913
Moultrie 31768
912-985-2132

District 146
*Berrien, Cook; Portion of
Tift*
Hanson Carter (D)
808 River Road
Nashville 31639

912-686-2515

District 147
Brooks, Echols; Portion of
Lowndes
Henry L. Reaves (D)
Route 2, Box 83
Quitman 31643
912-263-4051

District 148
Portion of Lowndes
James M. Beck (D)
2427 Westwood Drive
Valdosta 31602
912-244-1106

District 149
Lanier; Portion of Lowndes
Robert Patten (D)
Route 1, Box 180
Lakeland 31635
912-482-3565

District 150
Clinch; Portion of Atkinson,
Charlton, Ware
Tom Crosby, Jr. (D)
705 Wacona Drive

Waycross 31501
912-283-1744

District 151
Portion of Camden,
Charlton, Ware
Harry Dixon (D)
1303 Coral Road
Waycross 31501
912-283-6527

District 152
Bacon, Pierce; Portion of
Brantley, Camden
Tommy Smith (D)
Route One
Alma 31510
912-632-4815

District 153—Post 1
Appling, Jeff Davis, Wayne;
Portion of Brantley,
Toombs
Lundsford Moody (D)
Rt. 1, Box 205
Baxley 31513
912-367-4169

District 153—Post 2
Appling, Jeff Davis, Wayne;
Portion of Brantley,
Toombs
Roger C. Byrd (D)
P.O. Box 756
Hazlehurst 31539
912-375-7938

District 154
Portion of Liberty
Joe E. Brown (D)
217 Cherokee Trail
Hinesville 31313
912-876-5166

District 155
Portion of Glynn
Virginia Ramsey (R)
393 Lake Circle Drive
Brunswick 31520
912-265-6103

District 156
McIntosh; Portion of Glynn
Dean G. Auten (R)
628 King Cotton Row
Brunswick 31520
912-265-7052

MEMBERS OF HOUSE ALPHABETICALLY LISTED

Aaron, Betty (D)
District 56

Adams, G. D. (D)
District 36

Adams, Marvin (D)
District 79

Aiken, Fred (R)
District 21—Post 1

Alford, Dean (D)
District 57—Post 3

Allen, Ray (D)
District 127

Anderson, Wendell T.,
Sr. (D)
District 8—Post 1

Argo, Bob (D)
District 68

Athon, Troy (D)
District 57—Post 1

Atkins, Bill (R)
District 21—Post 3

Auten, Dean G. (R)
District 156

Bailey, Frank I., Jr. (D)
District 72—Post 5

Balkcom, Ralph J. (D)
District 140

Bannister, Charles E. (R)
District 62

Bargeron, Emory E. (D)
District 108

Barnett, Bill H. (D)
District 10

Barnett, Mike (R)
District 59

Beck, James M. (D)
District 148

Benefield, Jimmy (D)
District 72—Post 2

Benn, Lorenzo (D)
District 38

Birdsong, Kenneth (Ken)
W. (D)
District 104

Bishop, Sanford D., Jr. (D)
District 94

Bolster, Paul (D)
District 30

Bostick, Henry (D)
District 138

Branch, Paul S., Jr. (D)
District 137

Bray, Claude A., Jr. (D)
District 91

Brooks, Tyrone (D)
District 34

Brown, George (D)
District 88

Brown, Joe E. (D)
District 154

Buck, Thomas B., III (D)
District 95

Burruss, A. L. (Al) (D)
District 20—Post 2

Byrd, Roger C. (D)
District 153—Post 2

Carter, Hanson (D)
District 146

Chambless, Tommy (D)
District 133

Chance, George (D)
District 129

Cheeks, Don E. (D)
District 89

Childers, E. M.
(Buddy) (D)
District 15—Post 1

Childs, Mrs. Mobley
(Peggy) (D)
District 53

Clark, Betty J. (D)
District 55

Clark, Louie (D)
District 13—Post 1

Colbert, Luther S. (R)
District 23

Coleman, Terry L. (D)
District 118

Colwell, Carlton H. (D)
District 4—Post 1

Connell, Jack (D)
District 87

Cooper, Bill (D)
District 20—Post 3

Copelan, Jesse, Jr. (D)
District 106

Couch, Barbara H. (D)
District 40

Cox, Walter E. (D)
District 141

Crawford, John G. (D)
District 5

Crosby, Tom, Jr. (D)
District 150

Cummings, Bill (D)
District 17

Daugherty, J. C. (Julius
C.) (D)
District 33

Davis, Max (R)
District 45

Dean, Douglas C. (D)
District 29

Dixon, Harry (D)
District 151

Dobbs, Denny M. (D)
District 74

Dover, Bill (D)
District 11—Post 1

Dunn, Wesley (D)
District 73

Edwards, Ward (D)
District 112

Evans, Warren D. (D)
District 84

Felton, Mrs. Dorothy (R)
District 22

Foster, Phil (D)
District 6—Post 2

Galer, Mary Jane (D)
District 97

Godbee, John (D)
District 110

Goodwin, Bill (R)
District 63

Greene, Gerald E. (D)
District 130

Greer, John W. (D)
District 39

Groover, Denmark, Jr. (D)
District 99

Hamilton, DeWayne (D)
District 124

Hanner, Bob (D)
District 131

Hasty, W. G. (Bill), Sr. (D)
District 8—Post 2

Hays, Forest, Jr. (D)
District 1—Post 2

Heard, Paul W., Jr. (R)
District 43

Hill, James P. (Jim) (R)
District 83

Holcomb, Charles E. (D)
District 72—Post 3

Holmes, Bob (D)
District 28

Hooks, George (D)
District 116

Horne, Frank (D)
District 103

Hudson, W. N. (Newt) (D)
District 117

Isakson, Johnny (R)
District 21—Post 2

Jackson, Jerry, D. (D)
District 9—Post 3

Jackson, Neal (D)
District 65

Jamieson, Jeanette
District 11—Post 2

Johnson, Diane Harvey (D)
District 123

Johnson, Frank (R)
District 21—Post 4

Johnson, Rudolph (D)
District 72—Post 4

Johnson, Suzi (D)
District 76

Kilgore, Thomas (Mac) (D)
District 42

Kingston, Jack (R)
District 125

Lane, Dick (R)
District 27

Lane, Robert (D)
District 111

Lawler, Terry (D)
District 20—Post 5

Lawrence, Tom (R)
District 49

Lawson, Bobby (D)
District 9—Post 2

Lee, Carol W. (D)
District 70

Lee, William J. (Bill) (D)
District 72—Post 1

Linder, John (R)
District 44

Logan, Hugh (D)
District 67

Long, Bobby (D)
District 142

Lord, Jimmy (D)
District 107

Lucas, David E. (D)
District 107

Lupton, John M. (R)
District 25

Maddox, J. C. (D)
District 7

Mangum, Wm. C.
(Bill) (D)
District 57—Post 2

Martin, Charles (D)
District 60

Martin, Jim (D)
District 26

Matthews, Hugh D. (D)
District 145

McDonald, Lauren
(Bubba), Jr. (D)
District 12

McKelvey, Forrest L. (D)
District 15—Post 2

McKinney, J. E. (Billy) (D)
District 35

Milam, Wade (D)
District 81

Milford, Billy (D)
District 13—Post 2

Moody, Lundsford (D)
District 153—Post 1

Moore, James C. (D)
District 139

Morton, Chesley (R)
District 47

Mostiler, John L. (D)
District 75

Moultrie, Roy D. (D)
District 93

Mueller, Anne (R)
District 126

Murphy, Thomas B. (D)
District 18

Oliver, Clinton (D)
District 121

Oliver, Donald F. (D)
District 1—Post 1

Padgett, Mike (D)
District 86

Pannell, Jim (D)
District 122

Parham, Bobby Eugene (D)
District 105

Parrish, Larry (Butch) (D)
District 109

Patten, Robert (D)
District 149

Peters, Robert G. (D)
District 2

Pettit, Boyd
District 19

Phillips, L. L. (Pete) (D)
District 120

Pinkston, Frank C. (D)
District 100

Porter, DuBose (D)
District 119

Rainey, Howard H. (D)
District 135

Ramsey, Tom (D)
District 3

Ramsey, Virginia (R)
District 155

Randall, William C.
(Billy) (D)
District 101

Ransom, Dick (R)
District 90

Ray, Robert (D)
District 98

Reaves, Henry L. (D)
District 147

Redding, Frank (D)
District 50

Richardson, Eleanor L. (D)
District 52

Robinson, Cas (D)
District 58

Robinson, Pete (D)
District 96

Ross, Ben Barron (D)
District 82

Royal, A. Richard (D)
District 144

Russell, John (D)
District 64

Selman, Mrs. Helen (D)
District 32

Shepard, Neal (R)
District 71

Sherrod, R. Allen (D)
District 143

Sinkfield, Georganna (D)
District 37

Sizemore, Earleen (D)
District 136

Smith, Larry (D)
District 78

Smith, Paul E. (D)
District 16

Smith, Tommy (D)
District 152

Smyre, Calvin (D)
District 92

Stancil, Frank E. (D)
District 66

Steinberg, Cathey W. (D)

District 46

Thomas, Charles (D)
District 69

Thomas, Mable (D)
District 31

Thompson, Steve (D)
District 20—Post 4

Townsend, Kil (R)
District 24

Triplett, Tom (D)
District 128

Twiggs, Ralph (D)
District 4—Post 2

Waddle, Ted W. (R)
District 113

Waldrep, Kenneth (D)
District 80

Walker, Charles W. (D)
District 85

Walker, Larry (D)
District 115

Wall, Vinson (D)
District 61

Ware, J. Crawford (D)
District 77

Watson, Roy H. (Sonny),
Jr. (D)
District 114

Watts, Charlie (D)
District 41

White, John (D)
District 132

Wilder, Tom (R)
District 21—Post 5

Williams, Betty Jo (R)
District 48

Williams, Juanita T. (D)
District 54

Williams, Roger (D)
District 6—Post 1

Wilson, Joe Mack (D)
District 20—Post 1

Wood, Joe T. (D)
District 9—Post 1

Workman, Ken (D)
District 51

Yeargin, Charles W. (D)
District 14

Young, Mary (D)
District 134

LIBRARIES

Georgia has an extensive public and county library system, supplemented by excellent university libraries. The state's first library was established at Savannah in 1736.

The largest public libraries are in Atlanta, Columbus, Macon, and Savannah. The University of Georgia has special collections on Southern and Georgian history. The Asa Griggs Candler Library of Emory University houses collections relating to the Confederacy and to Methodist Church history. The Georgia Historical Society has extensive materials relating to Georgia's earliest days.

The following chart includes the name of the public library system in each county, the total number of books and media, and the total funds.

The accompanying map shows the county and regional library systems.

County	Library System	Region	Total Books & Media	Total Funds (Dollars)
Appling	Okefenokee	49	185,217	380,139
Atkinson	Satilla	39	92,123	206,698
Bacon	Okefenokee	49	185,217	380,139
Baker	DeSoto Trail	43	135,756	240,031
Baldwin	Middle Georgia	25	417,794	1,999,816
Banks	Piedmont	12	162,521	287,339
Barrow	Piedmont	12	162,521	287,339
Bartow	Bartow	8	35,152	138,776
Ben Hill	Fitzgerald-Ben Hill	38	44,190	112,030
Berrien	Coastal Plain	40	337,372	443,051

County	Library System	Region	Total Books & Media	Total Funds (Dollars)
Bibb	Middle Georgia	25	417,794	1,999,816
Bleckley	Ocmulgee	30	172,967	288,183
Brantley	Brunswick-Glynn	50	275,165	648,777
Brooks	Brooks County	47	28,293	50,746
Bryan	Statesboro	36	127,281	400,185
Bulloch	Statesboro	36	127,281	400,185
Burke	Augusta	28	429,393	1,721,645
Butts	Flint River	21	264,751	745,127
Calhoun	Kinchafoonee	42	147,372	307,927
Camden	Brunswick-Glynn	50	275,165	648,777
Candler	Statesboro	36	127,281	400,185
Carroll	West Georgia	14	314,551	686,092
Catoosa	Dalton	2	203,920	482,103
Charlton	Brunswick-Glynn	50	275,165	648,777
Chatham	Chatham-Effingham-Liberty	37	460,640	2,083,446
Chattahoochee	Chattahoochee	34	478,711	1,295,647
Chattooga	Chattooga	6	52,091	101,262
Cherokee	Sequoyah	5	115,202	346,773
Clarke	Athens	13	256,764	720,344
Clay	Kinchafoonee	42	147,372	307,927
Clayton	Clayton	22	181,572	657,332
Clinch	Okefenokee	49	185,217	380,139
Cobb	Cobb County	15	359,235	2,197,914
Coffee	Satilla	39	92,123	206,698
Colquitt	Colquitt-Thomas	44	208,673	378,216
Columbia	Augusta	28	429,393	1,721,645
Cook	Coastal Plain	40	337,372	443,051
Coweta	Troup-Harris-Coweta	23	171,742	483,363
Crawford	Middle Georgia	25	417,794	1,999,816
Crisp	Lake Blackshear	33	253,044	365,975
Dade	Cherokee	1	182,037	308,215
Dawson	Lake Lanier	9	175,410	1,215,085
Decatur	Southwest Georgia	45	112,948	262,332
DeKalb	DeKalb	18	551,202	3,410,470
Dodge	Ocmulgee	30	172,967	288,183
Dooly	Lake Blackshear	33	253,044	365,975
Dougherty	Dougherty	41	168,887	1,015,158
Douglas	West Georgia	14	314,551	686,092
Early	DeSoto Trail	43	135,756	240,031
Echols	South Georgia	48	161,629	366,928
Effingham	Chatham-Effingham-Liberty	37	460,640	2,083,446
Elbert	Elbert County	16	42,560	76,871
Emanuel	Statesboro	36	127,281	400,185
Evans	Statesboro	36	127,281	400,185
Fannin	Mountain	3	63,720	152,026
Fayette	Flint River	21	264,751	745,127
Floyd	Sara Hightower	7	356,853	952,776
Forsyth	Lake Lanier	9	175,410	1,215,085
Franklin	Athens	13	256,764	720,344

County	Library System	Region	Total Books & Media	Total Funds (Dollars)
Fulton	Atlanta-Fulton	17	1,642,402	9,836,329
Gilmer	Sequoyah	5	115,202	346,773
Glascock	Augusta	28	429,393	1,721,645
Glynn	Brunswick-Glynn	50	275,165	648,777
Gordon	Dalton	2	203,920	482,103
Grady	Roddenberry	46	150,261	262,169
Greene	Bartram Trail	20	89,520	235,641
Gwinnett	Lake Lanier	9	175,410	1,215,085
Habersham	Northeast Georgia	4	171,068	380,077
Hall	Chestatee	10	90,929	467,285
Hancock	Uncle Remus	19	131,001	213,096
Haralson	West Georgia	14	314,551	686,092
Harris	Troup-Harris-Coweta	23	171,742	483,363
Hart	Hart County	11	33,905	81,204
Heard	West Georgia	14	314,551	686,092
Henry	Flint River	21	264,751	745,127
Houston	Houston County	31	119,360	368,167
Irwin	Coastal Plain	40	337,372	443,051
Jackson	Piedmont	12	162,521	287,339
Jasper	Uncle Remus	19	131,001	213,096
Jeff Davis	Satilla	39	92,123	206,698
Jefferson	Jefferson County	27	67,674	108,624
Jenkins	Screven-Jenkins	29	107,185	110,350
Johnson	Oconee	26	200,533	520,783
Jones	Middle Georgia	25	417,794	1,999,816
Lamar	Flint River	21	264,751	745,127
Lanier	South Georgia	48	161,629	366,928
Laurens	Oconee	26	200,533	520,783
Lee	Kinchafoonee	42	147,372	307,927
Liberty	Chatham-Effingham-Liberty	37	460,640	2,083,446
Lincoln	Augusta	28	429,393	1,721,645
Long	Brunswick-Glynn	50	275,165	648,777
Lowndes	South Georgia	48	161,629	366,928
Lumpkin	Chestatee	10	90,929	467,285
Macon	Middle Georgia	25	417,794	1,999,816
Madison	Athens	13	256,764	720,344
Marion	Chattahoochee	34	478,711	1,295,647
McDuffie	Bartram Trail	20	89,520	235,641
McIntosh	Brunswick-Glynn	50	275,165	648,777
Meriwether	Pine Mountain	24	119,681	253,921
Miller	Southwest Georgia	45	112,948	262,332
Mitchell	DeSoto Trail	43	135,756	240,031
Monroe	Flint River	21	264,751	745,127
Montgomery	Ohoopee	35	113,642	243,857
Morgan	Uncle Remus	19	131,001	213,096
Murray	Dalton	2	203,920	482,103
Muscogee	Chattahoochee	34	478,711	1,295,647
Newton	DeKalb	18	551,202	3,410,470

235

County	Library System	Region	Total Books & Media	Total Funds (Dollars)
Oconee	Athens	13	256,764	720,344
Oglethorpe	Athens	13	256,764	720,344
Paulding	West Georgia	14	314,551	686,092
Peach	Thomas	32	38,236	98,162
Pickens	Sequoyah	5	115,202	346,773
Pierce	Okefenokee	49	185,217	380,139
Pike	Flint River	21	264,751	745,127
Polk	Sara Hightower	7	356,853	952,776
Pulaski	Ocmulgee	30	172,967	288,183
Putnam	Uncle Remus	19	131,001	213,096
Quitman	Chattahoochee	34	478,711	1,295,647
Rabun	Northeast Georgia	4	171,068	380,077
Randolph	Kinchafoonee	42	147,372	307,927
Richmond	Augusta	28	429,393	1,721,645
Rockdale	DeKalb	18	551,202	3,410,470
Schley	Lake Blackshear	33	253,044	365,975
Screven	Screven-Jenkins	29	107,185	110,350
Seminole	Southwest Georgia	45	112,948	262,332
Spalding	Flint River	21	264,751	745,127
Stephens	Northeast Georgia	4	171,068	380,077
Stewart	Chattahoochee	34	478,711	1,295,647
Sumter	Lake Blackshear	33	253,044	365,975
Talbot	Pine Mountain	24	119,681	253,921
Taliaferro	Bartram Trail	20	89,520	235,641
Tattnall	Ohoopee	35	113,642	243,857
Taylor	Pine Mountain	24	119,681	253,921
Telfair	Ocmulgee	30	172,967	288,183
Terrell	Kinchafoonee	42	147,372	307,927
Thomas	Colquitt-Thomas	44	208,673	378,216
Tift	Coastal Plain	40	337,372	443,051
Toombs	Ohoopee	35	113,642	243,857
Towns	Mountain	3	63,720	152,026
Treutlen	Oconee	26	200,533	520,783
Troup	Troup-Harris-Coweta	23	171,742	483,363
Turner	Coastal Plain	40	337,372	443,051
Twiggs	Middle Georgia	25	417,794	1,999,816
Union	Mountain	3	63,720	152,026
Upson	Pine Mountain	24	119,681	253,921
Walker	Cherokee	1	182,037	308,215
Walton	Piedmont	12	162,521	287,339
Ware	Okefenokee	49	185,217	380,139
Warren	Augusta	28	429,393	1,721,645
Washington	Oconee	26	200,533	520,783
Wayne	Brunswick-Glynn	50	275,165	648,777
Webster	Kinchafoonee	42	147,372	307,927
Wheeler	Oconee	26	200,533	520,783
White	Northeast Georgia	4	171,068	380,077
Whitfield	Dalton	2	203,920	482,103

COUNTY AND REGIONAL LIBRARY SYSTEMS

County	Library System	Region	Total Books & Media	Total Funds (Dollars)
Wilcox	Ocmulgee	30	172,967	288,183
Wilkes	Bartram Trail	20	89,520	235,641
Wilkinson	Middle Georgia	25	417,794	1,999,816
Worth	DeSoto Trail	43	135,756	240,031
Georgia			10,802,135	38,708,463

LICENSE PLATE IDENTIFICATION

Georgia presently issues passenger vehicle license plates which carry three alphabetic (AAA through SZZ) and three numeric characters. The character structure is non-meaningful, but the county of origin is displayed at the bottom of the plate. Only one plate per vehicle is issued.

LITTLE WHITE HOUSE

Franklin D. Roosevelt, four time President of the United States, lived in many sumptuous residences, including the ancestral home at Hyde Park and the White House in Washington, but in building for himself the kind of home he wanted, he built a very modest place. The Little White House, located on a beautiful site on the slopes of Pine Mountain, tells much of the nature of the man who played such an important role in the history of this country and of the world. It is an impressive home, but is small, with comfort and utility stressed. The Little White House, with three bedrooms, has only an entry, a combination living and dining room, a kitchen, and a spacious sun deck.

During his entire time in office, Mr. Roosevelt used the Little White House frequently. He came to Warm Springs first in 1924 hoping to recover from infantile paralysis which struck him in 1921. Believing exercise in the warm buoyant water beneficial, he became interested in developing the resort for others similarly afflicted. The Georgia Warm Springs Foundation and subsequent development of health facilities resulted from his efforts. The site on which the Little White House stands was personally selected by Mr. Roosevelt during his early stays at Warm Springs, and even before he built his house there, he used it for picnics. It is in a natural setting and Mr. Roosevelt permitted only essential landscaping.

The Little White House is retained substantially as it was when President Roosevelt died there on April 12, 1945. Keys to his personality are many: his collection of ship models denotes his great love of the sea; Fala, his dog, is remembered by a chain still hanging in the closet; a riding quirt denotes Mr. Roosevelt's enthusiasm for horseback riding. Mementos which he cherished more because of the giver than for the workmanship are on the walls. Visitors can see the famous unfinished portrait which was being painted when he suffered a stroke; the President's 1938 Ford convertible, fitted with hand controls which enabled him to drive it alone; the unusual Bump Gate; his 1940 Willys Roadster, the guest house where many notables were entertained; the servant's quarters; the Memorial Fountain; and the Walk of States with flags and stones leading to the Franklin D. Roosevelt Museum which depicts the President's life and displays rare items of memorabilia. A 12-minute movie, "FDR in Georgia" is shown here.

Visitors can see the springs and pools where Roosevelt and other polio victims exercised and played in the naturally warm spring water.

Warm Springs, 31830. 404-655-3511. Open daily 9–5, except Thanksgiving and Christmas.

MANUFACTURING

Manufacturing is one of the largest and most profitable industries in Georgia. Georgia is the nation's leader in the production of processed chicken, tufted textile products, paper and board. Transportation equipment, metal goods, chemicals, food products, and apparel are important components to the state economy.

Following are two charts. The first lists 51 of the state's largest manufacturing plants by employment. The second chart shows the major manufactured products by county, the number of manufacturing plants, and the number of employees.

GEORGIA'S 51 LARGEST MANUFACTURING PLANTS BY EMPLOYMENT

Plant & Location	Total Employment
Lockheed Georgia Co. (Marietta)	13,875
General Motors Corp. (Doraville)	5,216
Union Camp Corp. (Savannah)	3,793
Ford Motor Co. Atlanta Assembly Plt. (Atlanta)	3,669
Scientific Atlanta, Inc. (Atlanta)	3,116
Southwire Co. (Carrollton)	3,066
Western Electric Co., Inc. (Norcross)	2,884
Shaw Industries, Inc. (Dalton)	2,561
Dundee Mills (Griffin)	2,524
Riegel Textile Corp. (Trion)	2,177
Gulfstream American Corp. (Savannah)	2,119
Atlanta Newspapers (Atlanta)	2,000
Galaxy Carpet Mills, Inc. (Chatsworth)	1,806
Fieldcrest Mills, Inc. (Columbus)	1,791
Firestone Tire & Rubber Co. (Albany)	1,782
Integrated Products, Inc. (Rome)	1,721
B. F. Goodrich Textile Products (Thomaston)	1,708
The Bibb Co. (Columbus)	1,700
Galaxy Carpet Mills, Inc. (Dalton)	1,685
Salem Carpet Mills (Ringgold)	1,659
General Motors Assembly Div. (Atlanta)	1,650
Patchogue Plymouth (Bainbridge)	1,620
Mead Packaging Div. Mead Corp. (Atlanta)	1,536
Coronet Carpets Div. Coronet Industries (Dalton)	1,508
West Point Pepperell (Dalton)	1,463

Plant & Location	Total Employment
Hazlehurst Mills (Hazlehurst)	1,450
J. P. Stevens & Co., Inc. (Dublin)	1,441
Sunnyland Foods, Inc. (Thomasville)	1,385
Arrow Co. Div. Cluett Peabody & Co. (Atlanta)	1,332
Swift Textiles, Inc. (Columbus)	1,325
Owens-Illinois, Inc. (Atlanta)	1,300
Sewell Manufacturing Co. (Breman)	1,300
Blue Bird Body Co. (Fort Valley)	1,297
Procter & Gamble Paper Products (Albany)	1,275
The William L. Bonnell Co., Inc. (Newnan)	1,225
Burlington Industries, Inc. (Shannon)	1,215
Bremen-Bowden Investment Co. (Bowdon)	1,207
Coats & Clark, Inc. (Albany)	1,205
Roper Appliance (LaFayette)	1,200
ITT Rayonier, Inc. (Jesup)	1,200
Coats & Clark, Inc. (Toccoa)	1,200
World Carpets, Inc. (Dalton)	1,200
Miller Brewing Co. (Albany)	1,200
West Point Pepperell (Lindale)	1,151
Stratton Industries, Inc. (Cartersville)	1,150
Fieldale Corp. (Cornelia)	1,124
Brunswick Pulp & Paper Co. (Brunswick)	1,122
The William Carter Co. Mfg. Div. (Barnesville)	1,121
Scripto, Inc. (Doraville)	1,100
Lithonia Lighting (Conyers)	1,100
Toms Food, Inc. (Columbus)	1,100

MAJOR MANUFACTURING PLANTS AND PRODUCTS

	Number of Mfg. Plants	Number of Employees	Major Manufactured Products
Appling	25	836	apparel, lumber, chemicals, fabricated metal
Atkinson	12	657	lumber, apparel
Bacon	13	940	apparel, food, textiles
Baker	1	165	apparel
Baldwin	19	4,012	textiles, apparel, chemicals, machinery, trans. equipment
Banks	10	1,227	textiles, apparel
Barrow	26	3,723	textiles, apparel, lumber, fiberglass, chemicals, trans. equipment
Bartow	58	7,988	textiles, apparel, paper, chemicals, primary metals, clay, rubber/plastics, trans. equipment
Ben Hill	33	2,844	food, textiles, apparel, lumber, machinery
Berrien	13	1,857	textiles, apparel, lumber

	Number of Mfg. Plants	Number of Employees	Major Manufactured Products
Bibb	153	12,990	food, tobacco, textiles, apparel, lumber, furniture, paper, printing, chemicals, petroleum refining, rubber/plastics, stone/clay/glass/concrete, fabricated metals, machinery, trans. equipment, instruments
Bleckley	10	1,145	textiles, apparel, machinery
Brantley	7	142	apparel
Brooks	8	1,093	food, apparel
Bryan	6	503	apparel, lumber, machinery
Bulloch	42	2,596	food, apparel, lumber, primary metals, instruments, fabricated metals
Burke	21	1,329	apparel, lumber, furniture, fabricated metals, machinery
Butts	12	960	textiles, apparel
Calhoun	9	313	apparel, food, furniture
Camden	12	2,265	paper, chemicals
Candler	11	458	apparel, printing
Carroll	65	11,565	food, textiles, apparel, lumber, furniture, rubber/plastics, primary & fabricated metal, printing
Catoosa	20	2,429	textiles, furniture, machinery
Charlton	7	481	lumber, apparel
Chatham	159	16,898	food, apparel, lumber, paper, printing, chemicals, petroleum refining, rubber/plastics, primary & fabricated metals, trans. equipment, stone/clay/glass/concrete, machinery
Chattahoochee	0	0	—
Chattooga	16	5,442	food, textiles, apparel
Cherokee	29	1,659	food, apparel, rubber/plastics, lumber
Clarke	83	12,586	food, textiles, apparel, lumber, furniture, paper, printing, chemicals, fiberglass, fabricated metals, machinery, instruments
Clay	3	191	food, apparel, stone/clay/glass/concrete
Clayton	87	5,099	food, furniture, paper, chemicals, rubber/plastics, stone/clay/glass/concrete, fabricated metals, machinery, printing, trans. equipment
Clinch	6	218	apparel, lumber
Cobb	182	21,521	food, textiles, apparel, lumber, furniture, paper, printing, chemicals, petroleum refining, leather, primary & fabricated metals, machinery, trans. equipment, instruments, concrete, rubber/plastics
Coffee	50	2,497	food, textiles, apparel, lumber, fabricated metals, trans. equipment
Colquitt	53	4,104	food, textiles, apparel, lumber, primary & fabricated metals, machinery
Columbia	26	2,283	food, apparel, machinery, printing, stone/clay/glass/concrete, trans. euipment
Cook	18	1,799	apparel, lumber, fabricated metals
Coweta	47	5,707	textiles, apparel, lumber, paper, rubber/plastics, primary & fabricated metals, machinery, instruments
Crawford	2	73	lumber, chemicals
Crisp	33	1,864	apparel, machinery, trans. equipment, food, lumber, chemicals

	Number of Mfg. Plants	Number of Employees	Major Manufactured Products
Dade	9	831	primary metals, texiles, trans. equipment
Dawson	4	175	apparel
Decatur	34	3,880	food, textiles, apparel, lumber, rubber/plastics, chemicals, fabricated metals, machinery
DeKalb	351	28,334	food, apparel, paper, printing, chemicals, rubber/plastics, stone/clay/glass/concrete, fabricated metals, machinery, trans. equipment, lumber, furniture, petroleum
Dodge	11	1,444	food, textiles, apparel, rubber/plastics
Dooly	6	648	apparel, lumber
Dougherty	81	10,609	food, textiles, paper, printing, chemicals, rubber/plastics, fabricated metals, machinery, lumber, stone/clay/glass/concrete
Douglas	31	855	textiles, machinery, stone/clay/glass/concrete
Early	26	1,967	food, apparel, lumber, paper
Echols	0	0	—
Effingham	6	197	apparel
Elbert	63	2,366	food, apparel, stone, machinery
Emanuel	35	2,774	apparel, lumber, furniture, rubber/plastics, fabricated metals, machinery, food
Evans	16	1,298	food, apparel, lumber
Fannin	5	584	apparel
Fayette	31	1,635	food, textiles, paper, petroleum refining, rubber/plastics, stone/clay/glass/concrete, fabricated metals, machinery
Floyd	95	11,847	food, textiles, apparel, lumber, paper, furniture, printing, rubber/plastics, stone/clay/glass/concrete, primary & fabricated metals, machinery, instruments
Forsyth	23	1,814	food, apparel, printing, machinery
Franklin	21	1,621	textiles, apparel, concrete, instruments, fabricated metals
Fulton	638	50,295	food, textiles, apparel, lumber, furniture, paper, printing, chemicals, petroleum refining, rubber/plastics, stone/clay/glass/concrete, primary & fabricated metals, machinery, trans. equipment, instruments
Gilmer	14	1,417	food, textiles, lumber, stone/concrete, instruments
Glascock	4	235	apparel
Glynn	52	5,094	food, paper, chemicals, clay/concrete, machinery, lumber, fabricated metals
Gordon	68	5,987	textiles, apparel, clay, food, rubber/plastics, machinery
Grady	23	2,099	food, apparel, machinery
Greene	15	1,529	textiles, apparel, rubber & plastics, lumber
Gwinnett	212	15,611	food, apparel, furniture, paper, printing, rubber/plastics, glass, primary & fabricated metals, machinery, instruments, lumber, chemicals, leather
Habersham	38	4,316	textiles, apparel, lumber, machinery, instruments, food
Hall	105	11,139	food, textiles, apparel, lumber, furniture, paper, printing, chemicals, rubber/plastics, fabricated metals, machinery, trans. equipment, stone/clay/glass/concrete
Hancock	8	344	apparel, lumber

242

	Number of Mfg. Plants	Number of Employees	Major Manufactured Products
Haralson	25	4,591	textiles, apparel, printing, rubber/plastics, fabricated metals
Harris	10	625	food, textiles
Hart	22	2,210	textiles, apparel, machinery, trans. equipment, chemicals
Heard	7	558	apparel, primary metals
Henry	30	2,058	apparel, paper, glass, machinery, fabricated metals
Houston	27	2,364	food, apparel, lumber, glass, concrete, fabricated metals
Irwin	7	452	apparel, lumber
Jackson	17	2,815	food, textiles, apparel, machinery
Jasper	8	881	apparel, lumber
Jeff Davis	22	2,940	apparel, lumber, rubber/plastics, instruments
Jefferson	30	2,457	textiles, apparel, clay, fabricatd metals, machinery, lumber
Jenkins	6	897	apparel, fabricated metals
Johnson	9	1,122	apparel
Jones	6	103	stone/clay/glass/concrete, machinery
Lamar	8	1,664	textiles, apparel, lumber
Lanier	2	102	apparel
Laurens	48	5,309	textiles, apparel, lumber, furniture, paper, chemicals, machinery, food
Lee	3	959	apparel, machinery
Liberty	7	576	apparel, paper
Lincoln	6	360	textiles, apparel
Long	0	0	—
Lowndes	57	5,613	food, lumber, paper, chemicals, fabricated metals, machinery, trans. equipment, apparel, printing, chemicals
Lumpkin	7	842	textiles, machinery
Macon	11	1,043	food, apparel
Madison	14	800	apparel
Marion	3	435	food, furniture
McDuffie	25	1,897	textiles, apparel, petroleum refining, rubber/plastics, lumber
McIntosh	7	472	food, rubber/plastics
Meriwether	24	2,104	food, textiles, apparel, lumber, printing
Miller	7	119	food, apparel, chemicals
Mitchell	35	2,347	food, textiles, apparel, lumber, trans. equipment
Monroe	10	1,498	textiles, apparel, rubber/plastics
Montgomery	6	624	apparel, lumber
Morgan	15	1,777	food, textiles, apparel, lumber, furniture, rubber/plastics
Murray	47	4,208	textiles
Muscogee	147	19,056	food, textiles, printing, chemicals, rubber/plastics, primary & fabricated metals, machinery, trans. equipment, apparel, lumber, stone/clay/glass/concrete
Newton	21	3,247	textiles, apparel, lumber, paper, printing, chemicals, rubber/plastics, primary & fabricated metals, hospital goods

MANUFACTURING

	Number of Mfg. Plants	Number of Employees	Major Manufactured Products
Oconee	15	493	primary metals, textiles
Oglethorpe	7	216	textiles, apparel
Paulding	14	623	textiles, apparel
Peach	16	2,208	apparel, chemicals, trans. equipment
Pickens	14	1,578	apparel, rubber/plastics, stone
Pierce	10	443	apparel, lumber
Pike	3	465	apparel, textiles
Polk	32	3,436	food, textiles, apparel, furniture, paper, chemicals, rubber/plastics, fabricated metals, machinery
Pulaski	7	908	textiles, apparel, paper
Putnam	10	1,406	textiles, apparel, lumber, fabricated metals
Quitman	0	0	—
Rabun	10	1,719	textiles, apparel, instruments
Randolph	10	704	lumber, machinery, apparel
Richmond	143	14,367	food, textiles, apparel, lumber, paper, chemicals, clay, printing, concrete, fabricated metals, machinery, trans. euipment, instruments
Rockdale	47	4,271	food, apparel, lumber, furniture, rubber/plastics, fabricated metals, machinery
Schley	6	435	lumber
Screven	21	1,903	textiles, apparel, machinery
Seminole	11	411	apparel
Spalding	49	7,298	food, textiles, apparel, rubber/plastics, machinery
Stephens	35	4,939	textiles, apparel, furniture, printing, chemicals, fabricated metals, machinery
Stewart	9	303	lumber
Sumter	47	3,372	food, apparel, furniture, chemicals, rubber/plastics, lumber, machinery, stone/clay/glass/concrete, trans. equipment
Talbot	2	81	furniture
Taliaferro	1	2	lumber
Tattnall	20	1,016	apparel, machinery
Taylor	9	469	apparel
Telfair	16	1,650	food, textiles, apparel, lumber, machinery
Terrell	11	1,428	food, apparel, rubber/plastics
Thomas	68	5,480	food, textiles, apparel, lumber, furniture, chemicals, clay, rubber/plastics, concrete, fabricated metals, machinery
Tift	48	3,748	food, textiles, apparel, paper, primary metals, machinery, trans. equipment
Toombs	40	2,637	apparel, chemicals, machinery, food, lumber, fabricated metals
Towns	6	193	apparel
Treutlen	4	495	textiles, apparel
Troup	65	8,701	textiles, apparel, lumber, paper, printing, rubber/plastics, fabricated metals, machinery, stone, glass, concrete, food
Turner	11	937	textiles, apparel, lumber
Twiggs	5	1,061	clay

	Number of Mfg. Plants	Number of Employees	Major Manufactured Products
Union	8	1,240	apparel, leather, food
Upson	17	5,059	textiles, apparel, lumber, paper, machinery
Walker	35	5,761	food, textiles, paper, rubber/plastics, fabricated metals, apparel, machinery
Walton	35	4,309	food, textiles, apparel, rubber/plastics, clay, fabricated metals, lumber
Ware	45	2,522	food, tobacco, textiles, apparel, lumber, rubber/plastics, concrete, trans. equipment
Warren	7	1,057	apparel, lumber, furniture, rubber/plastics
Washington	25	2,513	textiles, apparel, clay, glass, lumber
Wayne	30	2,085	textiles, apparel, furniture, chemicals
Webster	2	146	lumber
Wheeler	1	215	apparel
White	11	926	textiles, apparel
Whitfield	222	24,495	food, textiles, apparel, paper, printing, chemicals, rubber/plastics, leather, stone, concrete, lumber, machinery
Wilcox	4	270	apparel
Wilkes	28	1,700	textiles, apparel, lumber, rubber/plastics
Wilkinson	11	1,863	apparel, clay
Worth	17	1,246	food, textiles, apparel, lumber
Georgia	5,468	529,332	

MEDICAL RESOURCES

LICENSED HEALTH PROFESSIONALS

	1984			1983		
County	Chiropractors	Dentists	Osteopaths	Physicians	Public Health Nurses	Veterinarians
Appling	1	3	0	8	3	3
Atkinson	0	0	0	0	2	1
Bacon	0	2	0	4	1	0
Baker	0	0	0	0	1	0
Baldwin	3	27	0	85	7	2
Banks	0	2	0	0	1	1
Barrow	3	10	0	9	2	3
Bartow	5	11	0	15	3	4
Ben Hill	3	5	1	10	2	4
Berrien	1	4	0	8	2	0
Bibb	11	93	0	315	39	14
Bleckley	0	5	0	4	2	0
Brantley	0	0	1	1	2	0
Brooks	1	4	0	6	4	4
Bryan	0	11	0	2	2	1
Bulloch	4	13	1	36	4	7
Burke	1	4	0	11	4	3
Butts	2	2	0	6	2	1
Calhoun	0	2	1	2	1	2
Camden	1	6	0	10	2	0

MEDICAL RESOURCES

County	1984			1983		
	Chiropractors	Dentists	Osteopaths	Physicians	Public Health Nurses	Veterinarians
Candler	1	2	0	4	3	1
Carroll	5	23	0	53	4	7
Catoosa	4	6	1	19	4	2
Charlton	0	0	0	4	1	0
Chatham	18	132	3	401	55	17
Chattahoochee	0	0	0	0	1	0
Chatooga	2	7	0	8	3	2
Cherokee	14	17	1	23	4	7
Clarke	10	48	0	157	26	120
Clay	0	1	0	3	1	0
Clayton	24	62	1	133	19	7
Clinch	0	2	0	3	1	0
Cobb	168	214	9	409	32	44
Coffee	6	6	0	24	3	6
Colquitt	3	9	2	35	7	2
Columbia	3	12	1	97	6	2
Cook	1	4	0	6	2	2
Coweta	5	12	0	31	4	7
Crawford	0	1	0	1	1	0
Crisp	2	6	0	15	6	2
Dade	2	4	2	13	1	1
Dawson	1	0	0	2	1	0
Decatur	2	6	0	19	3	5
DeKalb	77	455	42	1,170	75	74
Dodge	3	5	0	10	3	3
Dooly	0	3	0	4	2	1
Dougherty	12	61	0	141	30	17
Douglas	8	18	4	45	9	2
Early	2	2	0	3	1	2
Echols	0	0	0	0	1	0
Effingham	1	1	0	5	3	1
Elbert	2	10	0	12	3	2
Emanuel	2	4	3	12	3	2
Evans	1	3	0	5	2	1
Fannin	1	5	1	7	1	1
Fayette	8	20	0	16	3	4
Floyd	9	35	2	146	27	13
Forsyth	4	14	0	15	3	2
Franklin	2	5	0	9	1	7
Fulton	172	655	5	2,062	130	90
Gilmer	1	4	0	7	1	3
Glascock	0	0	0	0	1	0
Glynn	9	31	4	116	20	9
Gordon	3	9	0	15	3	3
Grady	2	6	0	11	3	3
Greene	0	2	0	5	2	4
Gwinnett	39	97	17	114	17	27
Habersham	5	8	3	14	3	4
Hall	12	50	1	112	16	18
Hancock	0	0	0	3	5	0
Haralson	2	5	0	11	3	1
Harris	0	2	0	8	2	2
Hart	0	6	0	7	2	2
Heard	1	1	0	1	2	1

246

| County | 1984 | | | 1983 | | |
	Chiropractors	Dentists	Osteopaths	Physicians	Public Health Nurses	Veterinarians
Henry	6	9	1	18	5	3
Houston	5	36	0	56	8	13
Irwin	0	2	0	1	2	2
Jackson	2	7	0	10	4	5
Jasper	0	2	1	2	2	2
Jeff Davis	1	3	0	4	2	0
Jefferson	1	2	1	12	3	2
Jenkins	0	3	0	1	2	2
Johnson	0	2	0	1	2	0
Jones	0	1	0	4	2	4
Lamar	2	2	0	5	2	1
Lanier	0	1	1	3	1	0
Laurens	4	13	0	62	10	5
Lee	0	1	0	4	2	0
Liberty	1	8	2	27	4	1
Lincoln	0	2	0	1	2	0
Long	0	0	0	0	1	0
Lowndes	8	39	0	89	19	11
Lumpkin	0	4	0	7	2	2
Macon	0	5	2	3	2	2
Madison	0	2	0	5	2	2
Marion	0	0	0	3	1	2
McDuffie	1	9	0	9	3	3
McIntosh	1	0	1	0	1	0
Meriwether	2	2	0	11	3	2
Miller	0	2	0	4	1	0
Mitchell	1	5	0	8	3	5
Monroe	0	5	0	8	3	1
Montgomery	0	0	0	2	1	1
Morgan	1	5	0	7	2	5
Murray	1	4	1	5	5	2
Muscogee	14	83	1	312	39	24
Newton	2	15	2	18	3	3
Oconee	1	4	0	10	2	5
Oglethorpe	0	1	0	3	1	0
Paulding	6	5	2	9	3	2
Peach	1	8	0	11	3	4
Pickens	2	4	0	6	12	1
Pierce	1	4	0	6	2	2
Pike	0	1	0	3	1	0
Polk	2	12	0	13	5	2
Pulaski	0	4	0	9	1	1
Putnam	1	2	0	5	2	2
Quitman	0	0	0	0	1	0
Rabun	1	5	0	16	1	1
Randolph	0	1	0	3	2	1
Richmond	14	247	2	772	43	19
Rockdale	5	18	0	25	4	5
Schley	0	0	0	0	2	0
Screven	1	4	0	6	3	1
Seminole	0	2	0	6	1	3
Spalding	4	18	0	53	7	7
Stephens	5	7	0	39	2	2
Stewart	0	0	0	2	2	1

| County | 1984 | | | 1983 | | |
	Chiropractors	Dentists	Osteopaths	Physicians	Public Health Nurses	Veterinarians
Sumter	1	10	0	32	6	6
Talbot	0	0	0	0	3	1
Taliaferro	0	0	0	0	1	0
Tattnall	0	6	0	8	3	2
Taylor	0	1	0	3	4	1
Telfair	1	5	0	6	4	3
Terrell	1	5	0	3	1	2
Thomas	5	23	1	73	8	10
Tift	3	10	0	38	4	15
Toombs	4	10	0	19	4	8
Towns	1	6	0	6	1	1
Treutlen	0	1	0	3	2	0
Troup	4	27	0	71	12	1
Turner	1	1	0	4	2	3
Twiggs	0	1	0	1	1	1
Union	1	1	0	6	1	1
Upson	0	10	0	24	3	3
Walker	8	13	0	21	11	3
Walton	4	10	1	18	3	4
Ware	5	14	1	56	19	5
Warren	0	1	0	1	2	0
Washington	1	4	0	10	5	2
Wayne	1	6	2	20	31	2
Webster	0	0	0	0	2	0
Wheeler	0	0	0	2	1	0
White	1	3	0	5	1	4
Whitfield	6	28	0	82	15	6
Wilcox	0	0	0	0	2	0
Wilkes	2	4	0	7	2	4
Wilkinson	0	1	0	4	2	1
Worth	1	3	0	7	3	3
Georgia	833	3,173	128	8,307	1,054	839

HOSPITALS AND NURSING HOMES

| | Hospitals | | Nursing Homes | |
	Number of Facilities	Bed Cap.	Number of Facilities	Bed Cap.
Appling	1	41	2	101
Atkinson	0	0	0	0
Bacon	1	47	1	88
Baker	0	0	0	0
Baldwin	1	160	4	449
Banks	0	0	0	0
Barrow	1	44	1	156
Bartow	1	62	1	118
Ben Hill	1	75	2	245
Berrien	1	71	1	54

	Hospitals		Nursing Homes	
	Number of Facilities	Bed Cap.	Number of Facilities	Bed Cap.
Bibb	4	1,030	10	1,275
Bleckley	1	64	1	75
Brantley	0	0	0	0
Brooks	1	45	1	186
Bryan	0	0	0	0
Bulloch	1	164	4	309
Burke	1	57	2	156
Butts	1	28	1	197
Calhoun	1	40	1	60
Camden	1	39	1	69
Candler	1	60	3	298
Carroll	3	287	4	350
Catoosa	1	237	2	145
Charlton	1	50	1	92
Chatham	3	1,100	11	1,224
Chattahoochee	0	0	0	0
Chattooga	1	31	1	90
Cherokee	2	85	3	234
Clarke	2	524	4	446
Clay	1	35	1	49
Clayton	1	367	3	386
Clinch	1	49	1	92
Cobb	4	1,146	8	886
Coffee	1	157	2	148
Colquitt	1	155	4	277
Columbia	0	0	1	120
Cook	1	40	1	80
Coweta	2	244	2	116
Crawford	0	0	1	100
Crisp	1	70	2	243
Dade	1	39	1	65
Dawson	0	0	0	0
Decatur	1	82	2	207
DeKalb	6	1,844	16	2,012
Dodge	1	113	2	200
Dooly	1	47	1	102
Dougherty	2	673	2	418
Douglas	2	456	1	246
Early	1	49	1	127
Echols	0	0	0	0
Effingham	1	45	1	56
Elbert	1	64	3	187
Emanuel	1	73	3	260

	Hospitals		Nursing Homes	
	Number of Facilities	Bed Cap.	Number of Facilities	Bed Cap.
Evans	1	73	1	87
Fannin	1	51	1	101
Fayette	0	0	0	0
Floyd	2	515	6	561
Forsyth	1	36	2	203
Franklin	1	95	1	144
Fulton	17	4,744	23	3,036
Gilmer	1	51	1	60
Glascock	0	0	1	104
Glynn	1	340	4	370
Gordon	1	65	2	218
Grady	1	60	1	108
Greene	1	68	1	71
Gwinnett	4	364	4	510
Habersham	1	59	2	196
Hall	2	462	5	402
Hancock	0	0	2	152
Haralson	1	85	3	242
Harris	0	0	1	100
Hart	1	98	2	209
Heard	1	29	1	60
Henry	1	104	1	180
Houston	2	295	5	402
Irwin	1	34	2	113
Jackson	1	90	2	122
Jasper	1	28	1	44
Jeff Davis	1	60	1	74
Jefferson	1	101	2	244
Jenkins	1	40	1	99
Johnson	0	0	2	153
Jones	0	0	2	162
Lamar	0	0	1	117
Lanier	1	40	1	62
Laurens	1	190	3	387
Lee	0	0	0	0
Liberty	1	50	1	169
Lincoln	0	0	0	0
Long	0	0	0	0
Lowndes	2	359	4	367
Lumpkin	1	52	1	102
Macon	1	50	3	248
Madison	0	0	1	100
Marion	1	30	1	50

	Hospitals		Nursing Homes	
	Number of Facilities	Bed Cap.	Number of Facilities	Bed Cap.
McDuffie	1	47	1	150
McIntosh	0	0	0	0
Meriwether	1	38	2	171
Miller	1	38	1	83
Mitchell	1	54	2	143
Monroe	1	40	3	275
Montgomery	0	0	0	0
Morgan	1	26	1	67
Murray	1	42	1	120
Muscogee	3	961	6	1,006
Newton	1	87	2	199
Oconee	0	0	1	100
Oglethorpe	0	0	0	0
Paulding	1	83	1	136
Peach	1	76	1	75
Pickens	1	40	3	149
Pierce	1	62	1	29
Pike	0	0	1	50
Polk	2	108	3	289
Pulaski	1	56	1	102
Putnam	1	50	1	92
Quitman	0	0	0	0
Rabun	2	88	1	117
Randolph	1	40	1	80
Richmond	4	2,081	10	1,180
Rockdale	1	100	1	164
Schley	0	0	0	0
Screven	1	76	1	128
Seminole	1	66	1	62
Spalding	1	222	3	350
Stephens	1	99	1	181
Stewart	1	32	0	0
Sumter	1	188	3	423
Talbot	0	0	0	0
Taliaferro	0	0	0	0
Tattnall	1	40	2	252
Taylor	0	0	0	0
Telfair	1	52	2	219
Terrell	1	34	1	74
Thomas	1	246	4	267
Tift	1	168	2	278
Toombs	1	92	2	317
Towns	1	42	1	30

251

	Hospitals		Nursing Homes	
	Number of Facilities	Bed Cap.	Number of Facilities	Bed Cap.
Treutlen	0	0	1	50
Troup	1	280	4	416
Turner	1	40	1	76
Twiggs	0	0	1	132
Union	1	45	1	92
Upson	1	119	3	302
Walker	0	0	3	306
Walton	1	101	3	235
Ware	1	257	3	442
Warren	0	0	1	110
Washington	1	56	4	214
Wayne	1	138	3	224
Webster	0	0	0	0
Wheeler	1	22	1	62
White	0	0	2	149
Whitfield	1	297	3	330
Wilcox	0	0	2	203
Wilkes	1	66	1	47
Wilkinson	0	0	0	0
Worth	1	50	1	59
Georgia	170	25,752	326	33,730

MILITARY POSTS

There are ten military bases in Georgia. These installations, the branch of service which is domiciled on each, and the nearest large town follow.

Base	Branch of Service	Town
Dobbins Air Force Base	Air Force	Marietta
Fort Benning	Army	Columbus
Fort Gillem	Army	Atlanta
Fort Gordon	Army	Augusta
Fort McPherson	Army	Atlanta
Fort Stewart	Army	Savannah
Hunter Army Air Field	Army	Savannah
Kings Bay Submarine Support Base	Navy	Savannah
Moody Air Force Base	Air Force	Valdosta
Robins Air Force Base	Air Force	Macon

MILEAGE CHART

Mileages are approximated	ALBANY	ATHENS	ATLANTA	AUGUSTA	BAINBRIDGE	BRUNSWICK	COLUMBUS	CORDELE	DALTON	DUBLIN	GAINESVILLE	LaGRANGE	MACON	MILLEDGEVILLE	ROME	SAVANNAH	TIFTON	VALDOSTA	WAYCROSS
ALBANY	0	200	174	210	57	172	86	40	260	112	227	129	107	138	223	216	42	80	113
AMERICUS	38	164	134	194	95	203	61	32	222	95	187	104	72	103	188	206	73	118	143
ATHENS	200	0	66	101	257	256	167	159	132	119	39	131	92	72	129	214	202	247	230
ATLANTA	174	66	0	157	231	274	109	144	88	139	53	68	84	93	68	256	183	234	240
AUGUSTA	210	101	157	0	267	189	217	170	245	98	140	222	124	93	225	133	197	216	177
BAINBRIDGE	57	257	231	267	0	198	124	97	305	168	282	167	164	195	261	245	84	80	141
BRUNSWICK	172	256	274	189	198	0	255	170	362	147	298	268	189	194	340	78	129	118	57
CARROLLTON	170	115	49	206	209	303	85	163	96	170	102	41	115	131	53	288	204	251	265
CARTERSVILLE	212	101	41	197	259	313	134	185	48	179	71	91	125	134	28	296	224	275	281
COLUMBUS	86	167	109	217	124	255	0	93	181	141	162	44	93	124	138	252	128	166	198
CORDELE	40	159	144	170	97	170	93	0	232	72	187	136	67	98	208	174	41	88	113
DAHLONEGA	245	60	71	161	303	319	180	208	73	175	21	139	141	128	91	313	254	301	325
DALTON	260	132	88	245	305	362	181	232	0	227	93	137	172	181	43	344	271	322	328
DUBLIN	112	119	139	98	168	147	141	72	227	0	158	149	55	47	208	124	101	137	111
ELBERTON	233	36	102	79	285	249	206	188	162	134	69	167	121	96	165	196	227	263	224
FITZGERALD	68	187	174	173	110	126	139	43	262	75	208	169	93	115	239	157	26	62	68
GAINESVILLE	227	39	53	140	282	298	162	187	93	158	0	121	120	107	99	252	228	275	265
GRIFFIN	133	89	40	153	189	244	78	110	128	110	93	60	55	70	108	227	151	198	208
JESUP	149	223	243	151	184	40	213	128	331	112	262	253	159	159	311	65	107	99	38
LaGRANGE	129	131	68	213	167	268	44	136	137	149	121	0	93	124	94	266	170	209	239
MACON	107	92	84	124	164	189	93	67	172	55	120	93	0	31	152	172	108	148	155
MILLEDGEVILLE	138	72	93	93	195	194	124	98	181	47	107	124	31	0	160	171	139	177	160
MOULTRIE	38	215	202	224	57	148	124	56	290	128	243	168	123	154	261	197	27	42	91
NEWNAN	152	103	37	194	200	274	76	141	119	149	90	33	94	109	74	266	176	223	247
ROME	223	129	68	225	261	340	138	208	43	208	99	94	152	160	0	324	250	297	308
SAVANNAH	216	214	256	133	249	78	252	174	344	124	252	266	172	171	324	0	176	167	104
STATESBORO	180	160	211	81	233	110	213	140	299	72	199	221	127	108	279	53	149	163	102
THOMASTON	106	113	68	169	163	225	57	86	156	100	121	49	45	75	129	217	127	174	191
THOMASVILLE	62	244	230	248	39	163	148	85	318	155	270	188	150	181	281	212	56	43	106
TIFTON	42	202	183	197	84	129	128	41	271	101	228	170	108	139	250	176	0	49	71
TOCCOA	253	50	98	125	307	295	207	211	128	169	45	166	144	122	138	242	252	295	275
VALDOSTA	80	247	234	216	84	118	166	88	322	137	275	209	148	177	297	167	47	0	61
WAYCROSS	113	230	240	177	145	57	198	113	328	111	265	239	155	160	308	104	71	61	0

MISS GEORGIA

Each year a "Miss Georgia" is selected in competition at Columbus. The winner represents the state in the annual "Miss America" contest. Since the contest's inception in 1945, the following "Miss Georgias" have been selected.

1945 Doris Coker
1946 Mary Lou Henderson
1947 Robbie Sauls
1948 Gwen West
1949 Dorothy Johnson
1950 Louise Thomas

1951 Carol Taylor
1952 Neva Jane Langley
1953 Lucia Hutchinson
1954 Mary Jane Doar
1955 Jeanine Parris
1956 Jane Morris

1957 Jody Shattuck	1971 Cynthia Cook
1958 Jeanette Ardell	1972 Lisa Lawalin
1959 Kayanne Shoeffner	1973 Gail Bullock
1960 Sandra Talley	1974 Gail Nelson
1961 Glenda Brunson	1975 Seva Day
1962 Eugenia "Jeanie" Cross	1976 Sandy Adamson
1963 Nancy Middleton	1977 Pam Souders
1964 Vivian Davis (deceased)	1978 Deborah Mosely
1965 Mary Jane Yates	1979 Sandra Eakes
1966 Maudie Walker	1980 Kristl Anne Evans
1967 Sandra McRee	1982 Bobbie Eakes
1968 Burma Davis	1983 Tammy Fulwider
1969 Marilyn Olley	1984 Camille Bentley
1970 Nancy Carr	1985 Samantha Mohr

MUSEUMS

ALBANY

Albany Museum of Art, 311 Meadowlark Dr., Albany 31707. 912-435-0977. Small permanent collection of purchase awards from our annual arts festivals; African art collection. *Hours & Admission Prices:* Tues.-Fri. 11–5; Sat.-Sun. 2–5. No charge. Closed New Year's; Memorial Day; July 4; Labor Day; Thanksgiving Day; Christmas.

Thronateeska Heritage Foundation, Inc., 100 Roosevelt Ave., Albany 31701. 912-432-6955. History Museum featuring costumes; pioneer tools; rocks; minerals; shells; historic artifacts; Indian artifacts; Nelson Tift furnishings; antique carriages; 1880's Hearse; Confederate War Items; local artifacts of the history of Southwest Georgia area; railroad cars with model train exhibit; 1911 steam locomotive. Historic Buildings: 1913, Union Station; 1857, depot; 1854, Kendall-Jarrard House; 1919, Railway Express Bldg.; manuscripts. *Hours & Admission Prices:* Tues.-Sun. 2–5; Train: Wed., Sat.-Sun. 2–5; Planetarium: Wed. 4:00; Fri. 7:30; Sat. 2:30 & 4:00; Sun. 3:00. Museum: no charge; Planetarium: adults $1; children & senior citizens 50¢. Closed New Year's; Thanksgiving; Christmas.

ANDERSONVILLE

Andersonville National Historic Site, Andersonville 31711. 912-924-0343. Civil War P.O.W. camp featuring items related to the Andersonville Prison located in War Museum; limited number of items related to P.O.W. camps; Civil War & later conflicts. Historic House Museum: 1872, Cemetery Sexton's residence; 1908, Cemetery Chapel. *Hours & Admission Prices:* Daily 8:30–5. No charge. Visitor Center closed Christmas.

ATHENS

Athens-Clarke Heritage Foundation, Fire Hall #2, Prince Ave., Athens 30601. 404-353-1801. Museum housed in 1901 Victorian Fire Hall featuring photographs; period furnishings; period herb garden; c. 1820 Brumby House. *Hours & Admission Prices:* Mon.-Fri. 10–4; other times by appointment. No charge. Closed Legal Holidays.

The Garden Club of Georgia, Inc., 325 S. Lumpkin St., Athens 30602. 404-542-3631. Historic House Museum in 1857 brick house, state headquarters for The Garden Club of Georgia Inc., located on the campus of the University of Georgia featuring 18th & 19th century furniture and rugs; Founders Memorial Garden; old smoke house contains memorabilia, pictures relating to the first garden club in America, c. 1891. *Hours & Admission Prices:* Mon.-Fri. 9–4; $1 per person.

Georgia Museum of Art, the University of Georgia, Jackson St., North Campus, Athens 30602. 404-542-3253. American paintings and sculpture; American and Japanese graphics; Kress Study Collection. *Hours & Admission Prices:* Mon.-Sat. 9–5; Sun. 1–5. No charge. Closed Legal Holidays.

Lyndon House Art Center, 293 Hoyt St., Athens 30601. 404-549-3838. Activities include guided tours; lectures; gallery talks; arts festivals; meeting & workshops for local art organizations; formally organized education/awareness programs for children, adults, specialized groups & general public; art courses in painting, printmaking, weaving & youth art; stained glass; internships for student at the University of Georgia. *Hours & Admission Prices:* scheduled exhibitions Mon.-Fri. 1:30–5. No charge; donations accepted. Closed City of Athens Legal Holidays.

Navy Supply Corps Museum, Navy Supply Corps School, Athens 30606. 404-354-7348. Nautical history museum; artifacts relating to logistics; Supply Corps functions; housed in 1907 Carnegie Library. *Hours & Admission Prices:* Mon.-Fri. 9–4:30. No charge.

The State Botanical Garden of Georgia, 2450 S. Milledge Ave., Athens 30605. 404-542-1244. Collections: Woody plant collections; native flora; native & adapted trees & shrubs including shade & ornamental trees. *Hours & Admission Prices:* Grounds: Oct.-April Daily 8–5; May-Sept. Daily 8–8; Callaway Building: Mon.-Fri. 8–5; Sat. & Sun. 2–4:30. No charge.

Taylor-Grady House, 634 Prince Ave., Athens 30601. 404-549-8688. 1838 antebellum home belonging to Henry W. Grady, called the spokesman of the New South. *Hours & Admission Prices:* Mon., Wed., Fri. 10–12; adults $1; children under 12 50¢. Closed Thanksgiving; Christmas; last week in December.

University of Georgia Museum of Natural History, Biological Science Bldg., University of Georgia, Athens 30602. 404-542-1663. Anthropology, botany, entomology, geology, mycology, zoology of Georgia & the Southeast. *Hours & Admission Prices:* Mon.-Fri. 8–5; tours by appointment. No charge. Closed Holidays.

ATLANTA

Atlanta Botanical Garden, P.O. Box 77246, Atlanta 30357. 404-876-5858. 300-vol. library of botany, horticulture, taxonomy books available for research for members & visitors on premises; botanical gardens; visitors center; auditorium; classroom. Gifts relating to horticulture, books & containers for sale. *Hours & Admission Prices:* April-Oct. Daily 9-dusk; Nov.-March Mon.-Sat. 9–4; Sun. 12–4; no charge; scheduled tours adults $1; students 25¢. Closed New Year's; July 4; Thanksgiving; Christmas.

The Atlanta College of Art, 1280 Peachtree St., N.E., Atlanta 30309. 404-898-1164. Art Gallery, 13,000-vol. library of bin arts books available for inter-library loan during regular library hours; classrooms. Art supplies for sale. *Hours & Admission Prices:* Tues.-Fri. 10–5; Sat. 11–3. No charge. Closed Holidays.

The Atlanta Cyclorama, 800 Cherokee Ave., S.E., Atlanta 30315. 404-658-7625. Historic Structure: c. 1885, cyclorama 42-ft. high x 356 ft. in circumference depicting 1864, Battle of Atlanta. *Hours & Admission Prices:* Daily 9:30–4:30; adults $3; senior citizen $2.50; children 6–12 $1.50; group rates available.

Atlanta Historical Society, 3101 Andrews Drive, N.W., Atlanta 30305. 404-261-1837. Manuscripts; 50,000 photographs; maps, books; architectual drawings; Atlanta newspapers; Margaret Mitchell memorabilia; early 19th century furniture and tools; extensive costume collection; folklife collection; Civil War artifacts; decorative arts. Historic Houses: 1840, Tullie Smith House; 1890, Victorian Playhouse; 1928, Swan House; Palladian style mansion. *Hours*

& Admission Prices: Mon.-Sat. 9-5:30; Sun. 12-5; Library: Mon.-Sat. 9-5; adults $5; children 6-12 $2; family & senior citizens, rates avaliable. Closed New Year's; Christmas.

Atlanta Museum, 537-39 Peachtree St., N.E., Atlanta 30308. 404-872-8233. Housed in 1900, R. M. Rose Mansion, last Victorian mansion standing on Peachtree St. in downtown area & home of distiller of Four Roses Liquor; confederate money; collections of George Washington, Thomas Jefferson, Robert E. Lee, Jefferson Davis, John Tyler, John C. Calhoun, Napoleon, Gen. Robert Toombs, F. D. Roosevelt, Hitler; Georgian and Confederate history; Margaret Mitchell personal items; Coca Cola items; early captured Japanese Zero plane; early Chinese items; early glass, porcelains, bronzes, furniture; original Eli Whitney cotton gin; Eli Whitney gun collection; paintings; sculpture; decorative arts; Indian artifacts. *Hours & Admission Prices:* Mon.-Fri. 10-5; adults $2; children $1; special group rates. Closed New Year's; July 4; Labor Day; Thanksgiving; Christmas.

Atlanta Zoological Park, 800 Cherokee Ave., Atlanta 30315. 404-658-7060. *Hours & Admission Prices:* Daily 10-5:30; adults $2.50; children $1.25; group rates available; tours no charge.

Callanwolde Fine Arts Center, 980 Briarcliff Rd., N.E., Atlanta 30306. 404-872-5338. Performing Arts Center; housed in 1917-1920, Callanwolde, home of Charles Howard Candler, son of Asa Candler of Coca Cola fame, exhibit space; classrooms; gallery; rental gallery. Paintings, prints, sculpture, woven items, pottery, jewelry for sale. *Hours & Admission Prices:* Mon.-Thurs. 9-9; Fri. 9-4; Sat. 10-4. No charge. Closed Legal Holidays.

Emory University Museum of Art and Archaeology, Carlos Hall, 571 Kilgo Circle, Atlanta 30322. 404-727-4282. Archaeology; ethnology; prints; drawings; photography; painting; sculpture. *Hours & Admission Prices:* Tues.-Sat. 11-4:30, no charge.

Fernbank Science Center, 156 Heaton Park Dr., N.E., Atlanta 30307. 404-378-4311. Skins; hides; entomology; ornithology; herbarium; geology; skeletal; gems; minerals; birds; mammals; insects. Classes in nature art, molding, casting, taxidermy; guided tours; lectures; films. *Hours & Admission Prices:* Mon. 8:30-5; Tues.-Fri. 8:30 a.m.-10 p.m.; Sat. 10-10; Sun. 1-8. No charge for museum. Planetarium: adults $1.50; students 75¢. Closed National Holidays.

Georgia State Museum of Science and Industry, Room 431, Georgia State Capitol, Atlanta 30334. 404-656-2846. Rocks; minerals; dioramas of industry; reptiles; Indian artifacts; mounted birds, animals and fish. *Hours & Admission Prices:* Mon.-Fri. 8-5:30; Sat. 10-2; Sun. 1-3. No charge. Closed Legal Holidays.

Georgia State University Art Gallery, Georgia State University, University Plaza, Atlanta 30303. 404-658-2257. American contemporary paintings, prints, photographs & crafts. *Hours & Admission Prices:* Mon.-Fri. 8-8. No charge. Closed New Year's; July 4; Labor Day; Thanksgiving; Friday after Thanksgiving; Last Week in December.

The High Museum of Art, 1280 Peachtree St., N.E., Atlanta 30309. 404-892-3600. Western art from early Renaissance to present; decorative arts with emphasis on 18th, 19th & early 20th century American objects; 18th century European ceramics; graphics; sculpture; objects representing most sub-Saharan & African styles; 19th and 20th century photography. *Hours & Admission Prices:* Tues., Thurs.-Sat. 10-5; Wed. 10-9; Sun. 12-5. adults $3; students and senior citizens $1; children under 18 and members no charge; no charge Thurs. 1-5. Closed New Year's; July 4; Labor Day; Thanksgiving; Christmas.

Martin Luther King, Jr. Center for Nonviolent Social Change, 449 Auburn Ave., N.E. Atlanta 30312. 404-524-1956. History Museum, Educational Center & Archive located on the grounds of the Martin Luther King, Jr. National Historic Site. Furnishings of the King family; personal effects of Dr. King; artwork; memorabilia donated by the public; works of art executed by artists in memory of Dr. King. Historic House: 1895, birth home of Dr. Martin Luther King, Jr. Historic Site: Tomb of Dr. King. *Hours & Admission Prices:* Center: Mon.-Sat. 9-5; Sun. 2-5, No charge. Various fees & tours; call for verification & reservations. Closed Legal Holidays.

Martin Luther King, Jr., National Historic Site and Preservation District, 522 Auburn Ave., N.W., Atlanta 30312. 404-221-5190. Neighborhood Dr. Martin Luther King, Jr. grew up, includes birthplace, boyhood home, church & gravesite. Historic photos; local history; oral history.

Photographic Investments Gallery, 468 Armour Dr., Atlanta 30324. 404-876-7260. 19th century photography representing all processes & images worldwide. *Hours & Admission Prices:* Mon.-Fri. 10-4; Sat.-Sun. by appointment. No charge. Closed Legal Holidays.

Wren's Nest, 1050 Gordon St., S.W., Atlanta 30310. 404-753-8535. Historic House, 1881, home of Joel Chandler Harris, author of the Uncle Remus Stories. Original furnishings belonging to the Harris family; personal artifacts of Mr. Harris including his typewriter, hat & umbrella and rolltop desk which he used while employed at the Atlanta Constitution and where the Uncle Remus stories were introduced; photographs and other memorabilia related to Harris, his family and the Uncle Remus stories. *Hours & Admission Prices:* Mon.-Sat. 9:30-5; Sun. 2-5; adults $2.50; Senior Citizen $2; teens $1.25; children under 12 75¢; group rates available. Closed New Year's Eve; New Year's; Easter; July 4; Labor Day; Thanksgiving; Christmas Eve; Christmas Day.

AUGUSTA

Augusta Richmond County Museum, 540 Telfair St., Augusta 30901. 404-722-8454. Local and military history; regional archaeology; natural science; geology; costumes; early American artifacts. Historic House: 1850, Brahe House at 456 Telfair St. *Hours & Admission Prices:* Tues.-Sat. 10-5; Sun. 2-5. No charge. Closed National Holidays.

Ezekiel Harris House, 1840 Broad St., Augusta 30904. 404-733-6768. Furnishings, late 18th century artifacts. *Hours & Admission Prices:* conducted tours: by appointment; call Historic Augusta 404-733-6768; adults $2; children 50¢.

Gertrude Herbert Memorial Institute of Art, 506 Telfair St., Augusta 30901. 404-722-5495. Paintings; graphics; monthly changing exhibitions. Historic House: 1818, Ware's Folly. *Hours & Admission Prices:* Tues.-Fri. 10-5; Sat.-Sun. 2-5. No charge. Closed New Year's; Easter; May 30; July 4; August; Thanksgiving; Christmas.

Laney-Walker Museum, Inc., 821 Laney-Walker Blvd., Augusta 30901. 404-724-5614. African art; Afro-American arts; local artists. *Hours & Admission Prices:* Call for hours. No charge.

Meadow Garden, 1320 Nelson St., Augusta 30904. 404-724-4174. Historic House: Meadow Garden, 1791-1804 residence of George Walton, signer of the Declaration of Independence. *Hours & Admission Prices:* Tues.-Sat. 10-4; adults $2; children 50¢.

BLAIRSVILLE

Brasstown Bald Visitor Center, Hwy. 19 & 129 S. Blairsville 30512. 404-745-6928. Park Museum, located within the Chattahoochee National Forest. Natural history; exhibits pertaining to "Man and the Mountain." *Hours & Admission Prices:* Memorial Day-Oct. Daily 10-6; mid April-Memorial Day Sat.-Sun. 10-5:30. No charge.

BLAKELY

Kolomoki Mounds Museum, Rt. 1, Blakely 31723. 912-723-5296. 13th Century Indian Burial Mound and village site. Archaeology; Indian artifacts; excavated mound. *Hours & Admission Prices:* Tues.-Sat., Holiday Mondays 9-5; Sun. 2-5:30; 17 & over $1; 6-17 50¢; children under 6 no charge. Closed Thanksgiving; Christmas.

BRUNSWICK

Hofwyl-Broadfield Plantation, Rt. 2, Box 83, Brunswick 31520. 912-264-9263. Dairy equipment; rice tools; furnishings from the period 1830-1972. *Hours & Admission Prices:* Tues.-Sat. 9-5; Sun. 2-5:30; adults $1; youth 50¢; groups of 15 or more 25¢; children, no charge. Closed Mondays except Holiday Mondays; Thanksgiving; Christmas.

BUFORD

Bowman-Pirkle House, 2601 Buford Dam Rd., Buford 30518. 404-945-3543. 1818 plantation homestead belonging to one of the first white settlers in the area. Pioneer furniture & furnishings; utensils; barn & corn crib; blacksmith shop; smokehouse; covered wagon; tannery; syrup mill. *Hours & Admission Prices:* Tues.-Fri. 8:30-4; Sun. 2-5:30; No charge.

Lanier Museum of Natural History, 2601 Buford Dam Rd., Buford 30518. 404-945-3543. Located in Lanier Water Park. Birds; mammals; fish; butterflies & insects; rocks; minerals; fossils; shells; Indian artifacts; snakes; old & rare books; photographs; paintings; large collection of "touch" items. *Hours & Admission Prices:* Tues.-Fri. 10-4:30; Sun. 2-5:30. No charge.

CALHOUN

New Echota, Rt. 3, Calhoun 30701. 404-629-8151. 1825 Capital town of Cherokee Nation. Historic Buildings, 1828 Rev. Samuel Worcester's Mission, Vann Tavern, replica of Cherokee Phoenix Print Shop, Courthouse. *Hours & Admission Prices:* Tours: Tues.-Sat. 9:30, 11, 1:30, 3, adults $1; children 6-11 50¢; children 5 & under, no charge; organized groups of 15 or more 25¢. Closed Thanksgiving; Christmas.

CARTERSVILLE

Etowah Indian Mounds Historical Site, Rt. 2, Cartersville 30120. 404-382-2704. Archaeological excavations of prehistoric Indian center. *Hours & Admission Prices:* Tues.-Sat., Holiday Mondays 9-5; Sun. 2-5:30; adults $1; children 12-17 50¢; 12 & under no charge; groups of 15 or more 25¢. Closed New Year's, Thanksgiving, Christmas.

Roselawn Museum, 224 West Cherokee Ave., Cartersville 30120. 404-386-0300. 1880, Victorian mansion, former home of evangelist Samuel Porter Jones. Furniture; documents; clothing & costumes; silver; memorabilia belonging to Samuel Porter Jones; documents & memorabilia belonging to Rebecca Latimer Felton, first woman U.S. Senator. *Hours & Admission Prices:* Mon.-Fri. 9-5; other times by appointment; adults $1; children 50¢. Closed All Holidays.

CEDARTOWN

The Polk County Historical Society, College St., Cedartown 30125. 404-748-5906. Museum housed in 1921, former Hawke's Childrens' Library. *Hours & Admission Prices:* 4th Sun. of each month 12-6. No charge; donations accepted.

CHATSWORTH

Fort Mountain State Park, Rt. 7, Box 1K, Chatsworth 30705. 404-695-2621. Pre-historic stone wall. Woodland period; ceremonial sites; fault zone geology. *Hours & Admission Prices:* Daily 7-10. No charge.

Vann House, Rt. 7, Box 235, Chatsworth 30705. 404-695-2598. 1804, Vann House with furniture; personal items. *Hours & Admission Prices:* Winter: Tues.-Sat., Holiday Mondays 9-5; Sun. 2-5; Summer: Tues.-Sat., Holiday Mondays 9-5:30; Sun. 2-5:30; adults 18 & over $1; children 12-17 50¢; children under 12 no charge; groups of 15 or more, 25¢. Closed Thanksgiving; Christmas.

CLEVELAND

White County Historical Society, Rt. 3, Box 4, Cleveland 30528. 404-865-3225. Historic Building: 1859-60, Courthouse, old newspapers; Civil War documents; diaries and letters. *Hours & Admission Prices:* call for hours. No charge.

COCHRAN

Middle Georgia College Museum, Cochran 31014. 912-934-6221. Housed in 1860s Pace House, home of Paleman J. King, 1st president of college, & 1890 Ebenezer Hall, home of presidents of original college. Period furniture; historical documents. *Hours & Admission Prices:* Mon.-Fri. 10-4; other times by appointment; adults $1. Closed School Holidays.

COLUMBUS

Columbus Museum of Arts and Sciences, Inc., 1251 Wynnton Rd., Columbus 31906. 404-323-3617. Paintings; sculpture; graphics; archaeology; general natural history; decorative arts; paleontology; southern history; ethnology; costumes. *Hours & Admission Prices:* Mon.-Sat. 10–5; Sun. 2–5. No charge. Closed New Year's; July 4; Thanksgiving; Christmas.

Confederate Naval Museum, 202 4th St., Columbus 31902. 404-327-9798. Confederate naval gunboats; CSS Muscogee and CSS Chattahoochee, on display; other exhibits pertaining to Confederate Navy and Marine Corps. *Hours & Admission Prices:* Tues.-Sat. 10–5; Sun. 2–5. No charge. Closed Thanksgiving; Christmas.

Historic Columbus Foundation, Inc., 700 Broadway, Columbus 31901. 404-322-0756. Historic Houses: 1850, The Rankin House, houses an authenticated Victorian furniture collection; 1828, The Walker-Peters-Langdon House, houses 1828–1835 furnishings; 1870, 700 Broadway House, houses late Victorian furnishings; 1840, Pemberton House, houses mid-Victorian furnishings & authenticated Coca-Cola collectibles & memorabilia. *Hours & Admission Prices:* Museum: Mon.-Fri. 9–5. No charge; donations accepted. Heritage Tour: Wed. & Sat. 10–12; adults $5; children $2.50.

CORDELE

Georgia Veterans Memorial Museum, Rt. 3, Box 385, Cordele 31015. 912-273-2190. Historic aircraft; fighting vehicles; uniforms; weapons; accoutrements. *Hours & Admission Prices:* Tues.-Sat., Holiday Mondays 9–5; Sun. 2–5:30. No charge. Closed New Year's; Thanksgiving; Christmas.

CRAWFORDVILLE

Confederate Museum, Alexander St., Crawfordville 30631. 404-456-2221. Arms & memorabilia of Civil War. Historic House: 1875, Liberty Hall, home of Alexander H. Stephens; furnishings; slave quarters & outbuildings. *Hours & Admission Prices:* Tues.-Sat., Holiday Mondays 9–5; Sun. 2–5:30; adults $1; youth 12–17 50¢; children 11 and under no charge; special group rate 15 or more 25¢ per person. Closed Thanksgiving; Christmas.

DAHLONEGA

Dahlonega Courthouse Gold Museum, 1-A Public Square, Dahlonega 30533. 404-864-2257. Native Georgian gold & Dahlonega Mint coins; mining equipment; photographs. *Hours & Admission Prices:* Tues.-Sat., Holiday Mondays 9–5; Sun. 2–5:30; adults $1; children 12–17 50¢; children under 12, no charge; organized groups of 15 or more 25¢ per person. Closed Thanksgiving; Christmas.

DALTON

Creative Arts Guild, 520 West Waugh St., Dalton 30720. 404-278-0168. Various types of art media; guided tours; lectures; concerts; dance recitals; arts festivals; drama; rental Gallery; docent programs; permanent, temporary, and traveling exhibitions. *Hours & Admission Prices:* Mon.-Fri. 9–5; Sat. 11–2. Closed New Year's; Memorial Day; July 4; Thanksgiving; Christmas.

Crown Gardens and Archives, 715 Chattanooga Ave., Dalton 30720. 404-278-0217. Hand-made tufted bedspreads; machines for making spreads, material; textiles; artifacts pertaining to the Black community; Sims Collection of hand-carved wooden objects; c. 1890, furniture from the Loveman home; records of Mills; 1860, Whitfield Co. Census Index; 1860, Murray Co. Census Index. *Hours & Admission Prices:* Tues.-Sat. 9–5. No charge. Closed New Year's; July 4; Thanksgiving; Christmas.

DARIEN

Fort King George Historic Site, P.O. Box 711, Darien 31305. 912-437-4770. Aboriginal & Spanish artifacts; reproductions of uniforms, weapons and accoutrements of British garrison.

Hours & Admission Prices: Tues.-Sat., Monday Holidays 9–5; Sun. 2–5:30; adults $1; youth 50¢; groups of 15 or more 25¢; children 5 and under no charge. Closed Thanksgiving; Christmas.

DECATUR

Dalton Galleries, Agnes Scott College, College & Candler, Decatur 30030. 404-373-2571. Art gallery featuring Harry L. Dalton collection; Steffen Thomas collection; Ferdinand Warren collection; Clifford Clarke collection. *Hours & Admission Prices:* Mon.-Fri. 9 a.m.-10:30 p.m.; Sat. 9–5; Sun. 2–5. No charge.

DeKalb Historical Society Museum, Old Courthouse on the Square, Decatur 30030. 404-373-1088 & 3076. Museum housed in the Old Courthouse on Decatur Square; three exhibit rooms containing memorabilia of the first hundred years, 1822–1922, of DeKalb; Civil War memorabilia; manuscripts. Historic Buildings: 1830–40, Benjamin Swanton House; 1825, Thomas-Barber Cabin; 1822, John Biffle Cabin. *Hours & Admission Prices:* Museum: Mon.-Fri. 8:30–4:30. No charge. Swanton House & Biffle Cabin: open by appointment; adults $2; children 50¢. Closed National Holidays.

DUBLIN

Dublin-Laurens Museum, Academy & Bellevue Aves., Dublin 31021. 912-272-9242. Housed in 1904, restored Carnegie Library; textiles; photographs; farm tools & implements; art memorabilia. *Hours & Admission Prices:* Tues., Thurs., Sat. 1–4:30; other times by appointment. No charge.

DULUTH

Southeastern Railway and Museum, 3966 Buford Hwy., Duluth 30136. 404-476-2013. Railroad & transportation equip.; locomotives; rolling stock; business records; blueprints; maps; books; magazines; trade journals & house organs; newspaper articles. *Hours & Admission Prices:* Sat. 9–5. No charge; donations accepted. Closed July 4, Christmas, New Year's.

DUNWOODY

Chattahoochee River National Recreation Area, 1900 Northridge Rd., Dunwoody 30338. 404-394-8324. Herbarium; biological specimens of the area. Historic Structures: 1840, Allenbrook; 1850, ruins of Akers Mill-Marietta Paper Mill; 1840 Ivy (Laurel) Mill Ruins; prehistoric village sites, rock shelters and fish weirs; historic Indian village sites and Civil War remains. Recreational and educational opportunities; guided walks; lectures; canoe/kayak/raft rentals; shuttle service; skill instructional clinics. *Hours & Admission Prices:* Daily call for hours. 404-394-8335. No charge.

EATONTON

Uncle Remus Museum, 360 Oak St., Eatonton 31024. 404-485-6856. Slave cabin, c. 1820, furniture; artifacts; books of Joel Chandler Harris, author of the Uncle Remus stories. *Hours & Admission Prices:* June-Aug. Mon.-Sat. 10–12 & 1–5; Sun. 2–5; Sept.-May Mon., Wed.-Sat. 10–12 & 1–5; adults 50¢; students 25¢. Closed New Year's; Christmas.

ELBERTON

Elberton Granite Museum & Exhibit, 1 Granite Plaza, Elberton 30635. 404-283-2551. Historical exhibits; artifacts; educational displays; granite monuments. *Hours & Admission Prices:* mid Jan.-mid Nov. Daily 2–5; other times on limited schedule. No charge. Closed Holidays.

FARGO

Stephen C. Foster State Park, Fargo 31631. 912-637-5274. Natural history of Okefenokee Swamp; lumbering; turpentining. *Hours & Admission Prices:* Daily 7–7. No charge. Boat tours: $3 adults; children $1.50; children under 8, no charge.

FORT BENNING
National Infantry Muesum, U.S. Army Infantry Center, Fort Benning 31905. 404-544-4762. Militaria; weapons; military art; local Indian and early military archeological materials; archives of photographs; collection of firearms including experimental U.S. items; presidential collection; 1896, Sutler's store. *Hours & Admission Prices:* Tues.-Fri. 10-4:30; Sat.-Sun. 12:30-4:30. No charge. Closed New Year's; Thanksgiving; Christmas.

FORT OGLETHORPE
Chickamauga-Chattanooga National Military Park, Fort Oglethorpe 30742. 404-866-9241. Civil War relics; Fuller gun collection of American military shoulder arms. Historic Houses: 1866, Cravens House; 1850, Brotherton, Snodgrass and Kelley Cabins. *Hours & Admission Prices:* May-Oct. Daily 8-5:45; Nov.-April Daily 8-4:45. No charge. Closed Christmas.

FORT STEWART
24th Infantry Division and Fort Stewart Museum, Wilson Ave. & Utility St., Fort Stewart 31314. 912-767-7885. Artifacts, uniforms, arms, equipment & photographs from the Civil War through the Vietnam War; towed & self propelled artillery pieces; tanks; anti-aircraft equip. *Hours & Admission Prices:* Tues.-Fri. 12-4; Sat.-Sun. 1-5; other times by appointment. No charge. Closed Federal Holidays.

FORT VALLEY
American Camellia Society, Rural Rt. 3 Box 155, Fort Valley 31030. 912-967-2358. Rare books; original paintings & prints; gallery of Boehm Porcelains; 10 acre garden; greenhouse of plants. *Hours & Admission Prices:* Mon.-Fri. 8:30-4. No charge; donations accepted. Closed National Holidays.

INDIAN SPRINGS
Indian Museum, Indian Springs State Park, Indian Springs 30231. 404-775-7241. Pottery; items that reflect stages of Indian civilization. *Hours & Admission Prices:* Memorial Day-Labor Day Tues.-Sat. 9-5; Sun. 2-5.

JEFFERSON
Crawford W. Long Medical Museum, U.S. Highway 129, Jefferson 30549. 404-367-5307. Located on site of the first operation using ether, performed by Dr. Crawford W. Long. History of the discovery of anaesthetic. *Hours & Admission Prices:* Tues.-Sat. 10-5; Sun. 2-5. No charge; donations accepted. Closed New Year's; July 4; Labor Day; Memorial Day; Thanksgiving; Christmas.

JEKYLL ISLAND
Jekyll Island Museum, Old Village Rd., Jekyll Island 31520. 912-635-2236. Furnishings; documents; photographs; clothing & memorabilia; Tiffany stained-glass window. Historic Houses: 1896, Moss Cottage, former home of Struther-Macy; 1903, Goodyear cottage, former F. H. Goodyear home; 1892, Indian Mound, former McKay-W. Rockefeller home; 1898, Sans Souci Apartments, former J. P. Morgan apartments; 1887, Jekyll Island Club House; 1917, Crane Cottage, former R. T. Crane, Jr. home; 1893, Hollybourne Cottage, former C. S. Maurice home; 1927, Villa Ospo, former W. Jennings home; 1928, Villa Marianna, former F. M. Gould home; 1905, Cherokee Cottage, former Shrady-James home; 1904, Faith chapel; 1914, service facilities including Club Dock; 1927, J. P. Morgan, Jr. indoor tennis court; 1891, infirmary; Baker-Crane Stable; Boat engineer's house and servants quarters; 1742, tabby ruins of Major Horton House; 1880, DuBignon Cottage; 1901, Misletoe Cottage, former Portor-Claflin home. *Hours & Admission Prices:* Memorial Day-Labor Day Daily 9-6; Labor Day-Memorial Day Daily 10-5; tours at 10 & 2; adults $6; students 6-18 $4; 12 group rates available, children $1.

JULIETTE

Jarrell Plantation Georgia State Historic Site, Jarrell Plantation Rd., Juliette 31046. 912-986-5172. Tools; furnishings; clothing; implements; grist mill; cotton gin; planing mill; boiler and steam engines; syrup evaporators; cane mill; saw mill; blacksmith forge. *Hours & Admission Prices:* Tues.-Sat. 9–5; Sun. 2–5:30; adults $1; children 12–17 50¢; groups of 15 or more 25¢; children 12 & under no charge. Closed Thanksgiving; Christmas.

KENNESAW

Big Shanty Museum, 2829 Cherokee St., Kennesaw 30144. 404-427-2117. Industrial Museum located on the site where the Great Locomotive chase began. Civil war locomotive; general and related memorabilia. Historic Structure: c. 1875, railroad depot. *Hours & Admission Prices:* March-Nov. Mon.-Sat. 9:30-5:30; Sun. 12–5:30; Dec.-Feb. Fri.-Sun. 12–5:30; adults $2; children 9–15, 50¢; 8 and under with adult no charge.

LAGRANGE

Chattahoochee Valley Art Association, 112 Hines St., LaGrange 30240. 404-882-3267. Contemporary American works of art housed in 1892 Victorian structure, originally a county jail. Guided tours; lectures; gallery talks; workshops; formally organized education programs for children & adults; temporary exhibitions. Museum Sponsors: annual Affair on the Square, art festival; LaGrange National. *Hours & Admission Prices:* Tues.-Fri. 9–5; Sat. 9–4; Sun. 1–5. No charge. Closed New Year's; July 4; Thanksgiving; Christmas.

LAWRENCEVILLE

Gwinnett Historical Society, 221 N. Clayton St., Lawrenceville 30245. 404-962-1450. Museum with post cards; scrapbooks; county newspapers 1872–1907; 1853 ca-sword U.S. Navy & scabbard; family history files; Cemetery card file; 120-vol. official Records of the War of the Rebellion; 1880 Soundex cards for state of Georgia; manuscript collections; photo ablums. *Hours & Admission Prices:* Mon.-Fri. 9:30–12:30. No charge; donations accepted.

LINCOLNTON

Elijah Clark State Park Museum, Rt. 4, Lincolnton 30817. 404-359-3458. Archives; uniforms; history artifacts of 1770's; reconstructed log house and outbuildings. *Hours & Admission Prices:* Memorial Day-Labor Day Tues.-Sat. by appointment. No charge.

LITHIA SPRINGS

Sweetwater Creek State Park, Rt. 1, Mount Vernon Rd., Lithia Springs 30057. 404-944-1700. Located at the site of the ruins of an 1842 textile mill burned in Gen. Sherman's Atlanta Campaign. Boating; canoeing; hiking; picnicking. *Hours & Admission Prices:* April 15-Sept. 14; Sept. 15-April 14. No charge.

LUMPKIN

Bedingfield Inn, Cotton St., Lumpkin 31815. 912-838-4201. Historic Building Museum, 1836 Stagecoach Inn; decorative arts. *Hours & Admission Prices:* Tues.-Sun. 1–5; adults $1; students 50¢. Closed New Year's; Thanksgiving; Christmas.

Providence Canyon State Park, Rt. 2, Box 54A, Lumpkin 31815. 912-838-6202. Natural history museum; self-guided tours; wildflower audio-visual program. *Hours & Admission Prices:* Tues.-Sat. 9–5; Sun. 2–5:30. No charge. Closed Mondays except Holiday Mondays; Thanksgiving; Christmas.

Westville Village Museum, Troutman Rd., Lumpkin 31815. 912-838-6310. Early 19th century decorative arts; 1825–1860 appropriate Georgia landscaping & gardens. 34 Historic Houses & Structures dating from 1800–1864: 1850, Randle-Morton Store; 1832, Stewart County Academy; 1842, Grimes-Feagin House; 1843, McDonald House; 1836, Cabinet Shop; 1838, Shoemakers Shop; 1838, Singer House; 1845, Doctor's Office; 1854, Chattahoochee

County Courthouse; 1851, Climax Presbyterian Church; 1831, Bryan-Worthington House; 1840, Bagley Gin House; Log Cabins; Patterson-Marrett Farmhouse; Mule Barn; 1827, Wells House; 1850, Blacksmith Shop; c. 1850, Carriage Shelter; Adam's Store; 1836, Lawson House; 1840, Yellow Creek Camp Meeting Tabernacle; 1840, Moye Whitehouse; Pottery Pug Mill; Damascus Methodist Church. *Hours & Admission Prices:* Mon.-Sat. 10-5; Sun. 1-5; adults $3.50; senior citizens & college students $2.50; children $1.50; group rates available. Closed New Year's; Thanksgiving; Christmas.

MACON

Hay House Museum, 934 Georgia Ave., Macon 31201. 912-742-8155. 1855-60 Italianate Mansion; period furnishings; ceramics; pictures; decorative arts relative to house & region. *Hours & Admission Prices:* Tues.-Sat. 10:30-4:30; Sun. 2-4; adults $3; students $1.50; children $1; group rates available; members no charge. Closed All Legal Holidays.

Middle Georgia Historic Society, Inc., 935 High St., Macon 31201. 912-743-3851. Housed in 1840 birthplace of poet Sidney Lanier, documents and photographs; archives of Middle Georgia; memorabilia of Sidney Lanier. *Hours & Admission Prices:* Lanier Cottage: Mon.-Fri. 9-1 & 2-4; Sat. 9:30-12:30; adults $2; senior citizens $1.50; students $1; children 5-12 50¢. Closed New Year's; July 4; Labor Day; Thanksgiving; Christmas.

Museum of Arts and Science, 4182 Forsyth Rd., Macon 31210. 912-477-3232. Archaeological artifacts; exotic moths and butterflies; zyghoriza fossil; rocks & minerals; local wildlife specimens; toys; paintings; drawings; prints and sculpture by Georgian, American and European artists. Historic House: c. 1928, The Kingfisher Cabin. *Hours & Admission Prices:* Mon.-Thurs. 9-5; Fri. 9-9; Sat. 9-5; Sun. 1-5. Museum: adults & children 50¢; members no charge; no charge on Mon., Thurs., Sat. Planetarium programs: Fri. 7:30 p.m.; Sat. 2 p.m.; Sun. 3 p.m.; adults $1.50; children $1; members no charge. Closed New Years; July 4; Labor Day; Thanksgiving; Christmas.

Ocmulgee National Monument, 1207 Emery Hwy., Macon 31201. 912-742-0447. Museum: Indian artifacts; archaeology representing six culture levels covering 10,000 years; anthropology; history; ethnology; British Colonial Trading Post; Lamar Type Site. Historic Building: A. D. 1016, Earthlodge. *Hours & Admission Prices:* Mon.-Sat. 9-7. No charge. Closed New Years; Christmas.

MADISON

Madison-Morgan Cultural Center, 434 S. Main St., Madison 30650. 404-342-4743. Artifacts, photographs, papers pertaining to the history of Madison, Morgan County & the Piedmont region of Georgia; decorative arts; costumes; architectural fragments; tools; household utensils; Civil War materials; school related artifacts & furnishings, housed in the 1895 Madison Graded School, in Madison Historic District. *Hours & Admission Prices:* Mon.-Fri. 10-4:30; Sat.-Sun. 2-5; adults $2; tour groups $1.50; students $1; members & children under 6 no charge; Wednesday no charge except to tour groups. Closed Holidays.

MARIETTA

Cobb County Youth Museum, 649 Cheatham Hill Dr., Marietta 30064. 404-427-2563. Jet trainer; a caboose; street car stop; changing exhibits of living history. *Hours & Admission Prices:* scheduled school and group tours Mon.-Fri. 9:30-1:30; children $3; puppet show 1st Sunday of Oct., Nov., March & June 2-4. No charge on Sundays.

Kennesaw Mountain National Battlefield Park, Jct. Stilesboro Rd. and Old Hwy. 41, Marietta 30060. 404-427-4686. Museum: located on the site of a Civil War battlefield. Dress and weapons of Civil War soldiers. Historic House: 1836 Kolb Farm. *Hours & Admission Prices:* Oct.-Apr. Daily 8:30-5; May-Sept. Mon.-Fri. 8:30-5; Sat.-Sun. 8:30-6. No charge. Closed New Year's; Christmas.

MIDWAY
Midway Museum, Inc., U.S. Hwy. 17, Midway 31320. 912-884-5837. Permanent exhibitions; 1700's-1800's furnishings; museum related items for sale. *Hours & Admission Prices:* Tues.-Sat. 10-4; Sun. 2-4; adults $1; children 6-18 50¢; children under 6 no charge. Closed Holidays.

Sunbury Historic Site, Rt. 1, Midway 31320. 912-884-5999. Military Museum; 1814 earthwork. *Hours & Admission Prices:* Tues.-Sat., Holidays 9-5; Sun. 2-5:30; adults $1; children 12-17 50¢; groups over 15 25¢. Closed Thanksgiving; Christmas.

MILLEDGEVILLE
Museum & Archives of Georgia Education, 131 Clark St., Milledgeville 31061. 912-453-4391. Memorabilia & artifacts relating to education; books; school furniture; housed in c. 1900, Victorian building; 3,000-vol. library of textbooks prior to 1950; records of school systems; biographical information on computers of state's retired teachers available for research by special request; reading room; exhibit space. *Hours & Admission Prices:* Mon.-Fri. 12-5; Sat. 10-12; Sun. 4-5:30. No charge.

MITCHELL
Hamburg State Park Museum, Mitchell 30820. 912-552-2393. Industrial Museum: housed in 1920, water turbine powered gin and milling complex; farm tools; ginning equipment; milling machinery. Corn meal for sale. *Hours & Admission Prices:* Tues.-Sat. 9-5; Sun. 2-5:30. No charge. Closed Thanksgiving; Christmas.

PINE MOUNTAIN
Callaway Gardens, Pine Mountain 31822. 404-663-2281. Southeastern U.S. native plants. Historic House: 1799, Log Cabin; guided tours; lectures; films; concerts; art festivals; formally organized educational programs for children, adults, undergraduate & graduate college students; summer intern program for students in horticulture & natural history; slide lending library. *Hours & Admission Prices:* Nov., Feb. Daily 7-5; March-May, Oct. Daily 7-6; June-Aug. Daily 7-7; Dec.-Jan. Daily 8-5; adults $3.50; children 6-11 $1; annual pass $20.00.

RICHMOND HILL
Fort McAllister, P.O. Box 198, Richmond Hill 31324. 912-727-2339. 1861 Confederate Fort; restored earthworks; military; summer living history demonstrations. *Hours & Admission Prices:* Tues.-Sat., Holiday Mondays 9-5:30; Sun. 2-5:30; adults $1.; children 50¢ children under 11 no charge; 25¢ per person for prearranged group. Closed Thanksgiving; Christmas.

RINCON
Georgia Salzburger Society Museum, Rt. 1, Box 478, Rincon 31326. 912-754-6333. Tools; furniture; letters; books; Bibles; deeds; maps; records of early settlers or their descendants before or just after the Civil War; Historic Church: 1769, Jerusalem Lutheran Church. *Hours & Admission Prices:* Wed., Sat.-Sun. 3-5. No charge; donations accepted.

ROME
Chieftains Museum, 80 Chatillon Rd., Rome 30161. 404-291-9494. Local history artifacts; items from Archaic Indian occupation to present time; trading post artifacts from archaeological dig; antique furniture; costumes; relics of Sherman's March through Rome; photographs; housed in 1794 log cabin, expanded into a plantation house, 1820, & belonging to Cherokee leader Major Ridge. *Hours & Admission Prices:* Tues.-Fri. 11-3; Sun. 1-5. No charge. Closed Christmas thru second week in January; National Holidays.

ROSSVILLE
The Chief John Ross House, P.O. Box 32, Rossville 30741. 404-861-0342. Cherokee alphabet; arrowheads; pictures; letters; furniture; rugs & linens; guided tours; arts festivals; perma-

nent exhibitions. *Hours & Admission Prices:* May-Sept. Mon.-Tues., Thurs.-Sun. 1-5. No charge.

ROSWELL
Bulloch Hall, 180 Bulloch Ave., Roswell 30075. 404-992-1731 & 587-1840. Historic House: c. 1839, Antebellum Greek Revival House and Cottage, childhood home of Mittie Bulloch, mother of Theodore Roosevelt. Period furnishings; family photos; costumes; manuscripts. *Hours & Admission Prices:* Wed. 10-3; $2 per person. Closed Christmas; New Year's.

ST. MARYS
Cumberland Island National Seashore, P.O. Box 806, St. Marys 31558. 912-882-4335. National Park & Historic District: human occupation on island since 200 B.C. Historic site: c. 1800-1900, Indian Village Site & Dungeness Ruins. Historic Houses: c. 1880-1910, Plum Orchard Mansion; 1800, Tabby House; Ice House Museum; outbuildings. *Hours & Admission Prices:* Office: Daily 8:30-4:30. Ferry: May-Oct. Daily; Oct.-May Thurs.-Mon.; leaves from St. Marys at 9:15 & 1:45; adults $7.80; children $4; call office for reservations.

ST. SIMONS ISLAND
Coastal Center for the Arts, 2012 Demere Rd., St. Simons Island 31522. 912-638-8770. Gallery. Yesterday's Gold Isles series, early primitive paintings of the area; guided tours; lectures; films; gallery talks; concerts; dance recitals; arts festivals; drama; study clubs; TV programs; formally organized education programs for children & adults; docent program; traveling exhibitions. *Hours & Admission Prices:* Mon.-Sat. 11-5. No charge; fees charged for special events. Closed New Year's; July 4; Labor Day; Thanksgiving; Christmas.

Fort Frederica National Monument, Frederica Rd., St. Simons Island 31522. 912-638-3639. Park Museum. Historic sites: 1736-1746, ruins of 18th century English barracks, fort and house foundations; study collection of artifacts found at Fort Frederica and town of Frederica. *Hours & Admission Prices:* Daily 8-5. No charge. Closed Christmas.

The Methodist Museum, Box 407, St. Simons Island 31522. 912-638-4050. On site of Oglethorpe & John & Charles Wesley's activities in 1736. John & Charles Wesley memorabilia, letters, land grants. *Hours & Admission Prices:* Mon. 1-4; Tues.-Fri. 9-12 & 1-4; Sat. 9-12. No charge. Closed New Year's; July 4; Thanksgiving; Christmas.

Museum of Coastal History, 610 Beachview Dr., St. Simons Island 31522. 912-638-4666. Located on the site of Colonial Fort St. Simons. Artifacts, books, journals, manuscripts, photographs, slides, graphic arts, audio-visual material of the coastal Georgia area from 1788–present. Historical Structures: c. 1872, Lighthouse; 1890, Oil House. *Hours & Admission Prices:* Winter, Spring & Fall: Tues.-Sat. 1-4; Sun. 1:30-4; June-Labor Day. Tues.-Sat. 10-5, Sun. 1:30-5; adults $1.50; children under 12 $1; children under 6 no charge; tour group rates available. Closed New Year's; Thanksgiving; Christmas Eve; Christmas; Easter.

SAVANNAH
Archives Museum, Temple Mickve Israel, 20 E. Gordon St., Savannah 31401. 912-233-1547. Housed in c. 1876, Gothic style, Congregation Mickve Israel Synagogue, oldest congregation in the South & third oldest in the Nation. 18th–20th century artifacts of Jewish life. 20,000-vol. library pertaining to Jewish studies available for research by special permission. Ceremonial objects, books & jewelry for sale. *Hours & Admission Prices:* Mon., Tues. & Thurs. 10-12. When tour guide available. No charge. Closed Holidays.

Bethesda Museum-Cunningham Historic Center, 9520 Ferguson Ave., Savannah 31406. 912-355-0905. Lady Huntington memorabilia; George Whitefield memorabilia; historic figure dolls; model of first Bethesda buildings; The Union Society through the years; photographs; copy of American papers collection in Cambridge; ship models and artifacts; documents & portraits; exhibits relating to the 13th colony and the Bethesda Home for Boys. *Hours & Admission Prices:* Mon.-Fri. 8:30-5. No charge.

Davenport House Museum, 119 Habersham St., Savannah 31401. 912-236-8097. Chippendale, Hepplewhite and Sheraton furniture; Davenport china. *Hours & Admission Prices:* Mon.-Sat. 10–4:30; Sun. 1:30–4:30; adults $2.50; students 10–17 $1.25; children under 10 no charge. Closed Holidays.

Georgia Historical Society, 501 Whitaker St., Savannah 31499. 912-944-2128. Housed in 1874–1875, building designed by Detlef Lienau. Books, manuscripts, maps, photographs, prints, newspapers, paintings, portraits, artifacts, relating to the history of Georgia and Savannah; manuscripts. *Hours & Admission Prices:* Mon.-Fri. 10–6; Sat. 9:30–1. No charge. Closed National Holidays.

Historic Savannah Foundation, Inc., William Scarbrough House, 41 W. Broad St., Savannah 31401. 912-233-7787. Furniture & furnishings of the period. Historic House: 1820, Davenport House. *Hours & Admission Prices:* Scarbrough House: Mon.-Fri. 10–4; adults $1.50; students 75¢. Davenport House: Mon.-Sat. 10–4:30; Sun. 1:30–4:30; adults $2; students 75¢. Closed Major Holidays.

Juliette Gordon Low Girl Scout National Center, 142 Bull St., Savannah 31401. 912-233-4501. Historic House Museum: 1818–1821, Wayne-Gordon House; memorabilia, art and furniture of Juliette Gordon Low and the Gordon family; Girl Scouts of the USA. *Hours & Admission Prices:* Mon.-Tues., Thurs.-Sat. 10–4; Sun. 11–4:30; Girl Scout adults $2; Girl Scouts under 18 $1.25; non-Girl Scout adults $2.25; under 18 $1.50; under 6 no charge. Closed New Year's; Thanksgiving; Christmas Eve; Christmas; Sundays in Dec. & Jan.

Kiah Museum—A Museum for the Masses, 505 W. 36 St., Savannah 31401. 912-236-8544. Howard J. Morrison, Jr. Zoology Exhibit; Harmon Foundation Collection of African Art; personal items of Marie Dressler, movie actress; 18th & 19th century furniture, china, silver, glass; art works from the 15th century; contemporary art; photography of William Anderson; Indian artifacts and crafts from Hilton Head Island; pre-Civil War and Civil War artifacts; items of Ulysses Davis, a Savannah folk artist; 15,000,000 year old fossil from Chesapeake Bay-Maryland area; Windsor chair, c. 1790. *Hours & Admission Prices:* Sept.-June first & third weeks of the month Tues.-Thurs. 11–5; other days by appointment. No charge.

Museum of Antique Dolls, 505 President St., East, Savannah 31401. 912-233-5296. Antique dolls; doll houses; doll furniture; paper dolls; china, glass, silver, linens for dolls; toys; banks; Victorian clothing; fashion prints; children's books; other artifacts relating to childhood. *Hours & Admission Prices:* Tues.-Sat. 10–5; $1.50 per person. Closed September; Major Holidays.

Oatland Island Education Center, 711 Sandtown Rd., Savannah 31410. 912-897-3773. Wild animals indigenous to state of Georgia; Phillips barn; Martin Cane mill. Historic Houses: 1835, Delk-Dawson House; 1835, Wayne County Cabin. *Hours & Admission Prices:* Mon.-Fri. 8:30–5 by calling in advance or writing to the director; other times by appointment. Call for admission fees. Closed Easter; July 4; Labor Day; Thanksgiving; Christmas.

Old Fort Jackson, 1 Ft. Jackson Rd., Savannah 31404. 912-232-3945. Military Museum; objects relating to Fort Jackson and Savannah's history. *Hours & Admission Prices:* Summer: Daily 9–5; Winter: Tues.-Sun. 9–5; adults $1.75; students, retired persons & military personnel $1.25. Closed New Year's; Thanksgiving; Christmas.

Owens-Thomas House, 124 Abercorn, Savannah 31401. 912-233-9743. Historic Building: 1816–1819, originally designed as home of Richard Richardson and later owned by Owens-Thomas families. Period rooms housing 18th and 19th century decorative arts; European and Chinese export porcelains; American Silver; English and American furniture before 1830; Oriental and European carpets. *Hours & Admission Prices:* Oct.-Aug. Sun.-Mon. 2–5; Tues.-Sat. 10–5; adults $2.50; students $1; special groups of 10 or more $1; children under 6 no charge. Closed Major Holidays.

Savannah Science Museum, Inc., 4405 Paulsen St., Savannah 31405. 912-355-6705. Reptile and amphibian programs and exhibits; planetarium presentations; laser shows; educational puppet shows; classes in the natural, physical, health, and technological sciences. *Hours & Admission Prices:* Tues.-Sat. 10-5; Sun. 2-5; non-member adults $1; children & senior citizens 50¢; second Sundays no charge; members no charge. Closed New Year's; July 4; Labor Day; Thanksgiving; Christmas.

Ships of the Sea Maritime Museum, 503 E. River St., Savannah 31401. 912-232-1511. Ship models; ships in bottles; figureheads; scrimshaw; marine oil paintings; ships chandlery; 19th century English tavern signs; macrame; historical artifacts; housed in an old restored cotton warehouse located on Savannah's historic riverfront. *Hours & Admission Prices:* Daily 10-5; adults $2; senior citizens & active military $1; children 75¢; special group rates available.

Telfair Academy of Arts and Science, Inc., 121 Barnard St., Savannah 31401. 912-232-1177. Art Museum & Historic House: housed in 1818, Regency mansion, designed by architect William Jay; 1883, wing added by architect Detlef Lienau. Many Telfair family objects from late 18th and early 19th century, including pieces commissioned from Duncan Phyfe; Savannah-made silver; portraits. Art museum wing contains 18th, 19th & 20th century American & European paintings; prints; drawings; porcelain; costumes; collection of works by Kahil Gibran. *Hours & Admission Prices:* Tues.-Sat. 1-5; Sun. 2-5; adults $2; students & children 12 & over $1; senior citizens & children under 12 50¢; children under 6 no charge. Closed Holidays.

William Scarbrough House, 41 West Broad St., Savannah 31402. 912-233-7787. Museum: housed in restored 1819 Regency style mansion; various exhibits; local history; decorative arts; architecture; five exhibition rooms. *Hours & Admission Prices:* Mon.-Fri. 10-4; adults $1.50; students 10-17 75¢; children under 10 no charge. Closed National Holidays.

Wormsloe Historic Site, P.O. Box 13852, Savannah 31406. 912-352-2548. Ruins of 1739, fortified house; archaeological artifacts from period c. 1733-1850. *Hours & Admission Prices:* Tues.-Sat. 9-5; Sun. 2-5:30; adults $1; children 12-17 50¢; group rate of 15 or more 25¢ each; children under 11 no charge. Closed Mondays except Holiday Mondays; Thanksgiving; Christmas.

STATESBORO

Georgia Southern Museum, Box 8061, Rosenwald Bldg., Statesboro 30460. 912-681-5444. Exhibits emphasizing natural, cultural, & geological history; fossil skeletons; 29-foot Mosasaur; 20-foot Middle-eocene whale; Southeastern Indians; timber raftsmen; fossil oysters; fish; invertabrates. *Hours & Admission Prices:* Tues.-Fri. 9-4; Sat. & Sun. 2-5. No charge. Closed New Year's; July 4; Labor Day; Thanksgiving; Christmas.

STOCKBRIDGE

Panola Mountain State Park, 2600 Hwy. 155, Stockbridge 30281. 404-474-2914. Granite monadnock; ecology; butterflies; moths; skippers. Visitor center; trails; scenic vistas; picnic area. *Hours & Admission Prices:* mid April-mid Sept. 7-9; mid Sept.-mid April 7-6. No charge.

STONE MOUNTAIN

Georgia's Stone Mountain Park, Box 778, Stone Mountain 30086. 404-469-9831. General Museum. Indian artifacts; Civil War; preservation projects; Revolutionary War, Colonial; early automobiles; musical instruments; 19th century band organs; c. 1830, Georgia-made furniture; 18th and 19th century English and American furniture. Historic Houses: 1790, Thornton House; 1845, Kingston House; 1845, Dickey House; 1845, Clayton House; 1869, Grist Mill; 1892, Covered Bridge. *Hours & Admission Prices:* Park: Daily 6 a.m.-12 midnight; Museums: Summer Daily 10-9; Winter Daily 10-5:30; Plantation: adults $2.50; children $1.50; Auto Museum: adults $2.50; children $1.50; Heritage Museum: adults 50¢; children no charge. Closed Christmas.

THOMASVILLE
Lapham-Patterson House, 626 N. Dawson St., Thomasville 31792. 912-266-0405. Historic House: c. 1884, Lapham-Patterson House, Victorian home; furnishings; period rooms. *Hours & Admission Prices:* Tues.-Sat., Holiday Mondays 9–5; Sun. 2–5:30; adults $1; children 50¢; group rates 25¢ each; tour 75¢ each. Closed Thanksgiving; Christmas.

TIFTON
Georgia Agrirama—The State Museum of Agriculture, Interstate 75 Exit 20 at 8th St., Tifton 31793. 912-386-3344. Agriculture equipment; printing and typesetting equipment; furniture and furnishings of the period; naval stores implements. Historic Buildings: 1896, farmhouse; 1882, log cabin; 1879, grist mill; 1888, printing office; 1899, railroad depot; 1887, doctor's office; 1882, church; 1879, commissary. *Hours & Admission Prices:* Winter: Mon.-Sat. 9–5; Sun. 12:30–5. Summer: Daily 9–6; Family $8.50; adults $3; children 6–16 $1.50; children under 5 no charge; groups of 20 or more, discount rates available. Closed New Year's; Thanksgiving; December 22, 23 & 24; Christmas.

TOCCOA
Historic Traveler's Rest, Rt. 3, Toccoa 30577. 404-886-2256. Museum: 1825 former stagecoach inn; furnishings; guided tours; permanent exhibitions. *Hours & Admission Prices:* Tues.-Sat. 9–5; Sun. 2–5:30; adults $1; children 12–17 50¢. Closed Thanksgiving; Christmas.

TYBEE ISLAND
Fort Pulaski National Monument, Box 98, Tybee Island 31328. 912-786-5787. History Museum and Park located on land purchased for Ft. Pulaski. Civil War cannon and projectiles; uniform accessories; personal effects of soldiers; bottle collection; c. 1862 antique and replica room furnishings; c. 1890 battery Horace Hambright. *Hours & Admission Prices:* Memorial Day-Labor Day Daily 8:30–6:45; Labor Day-Memorial Day Daily 8:30–5:15; $1 per car. Closed New Year's; Christmas.

Tybee Museum, Tybee Island 31328. 912-786-4077. Housed in old Spanish-American War Coastal Defense Battery. Guns and pistols; antique dolls. *Hours & Admission Prices:* April-Sept. Daily 10–6; Oct.-March Daily 1–5; adults $1; children under 13 accompanied by adult no charge; special rates for school and scout groups.

VALDOSTA
The Crescent, Valdosta Garden Center, 900 N. Patterson St., Valdosta 31601. 912-244-4632. Nature Center & Historic House: 1898, antebellum mansion, home of former U.S. Sen. William S. West; completely furnished with antique pieces; Day Lily & Azalea gardens. *Hours & Admission Prices:* Fri. 2–5; other times by appointment. No charge; donations accepted.

Valdosta State College Art Gallery, Valdosta 31698. 912-333-5832. Library; planetarium; reading room; exhibit space; auditorium; theater; classrooms. *Hours & Admission Prices:* Mon.-Fri. 10–4. No charge. Closed School Holidays.

WARM SPRINGS
Little White House Historic Site, Little White House Historic Site, Warm Springs 31830. 404-655-3511. 1932 Georgia home of Pres. Roosevelt, where he died April 12, 1945; c. 1900 Georgia M. Wilkins Home which houses the museum. Personal items; gifts to Pres. Roosevelt from individuals, states and foreign countries; personal & official correspondence. *Hours & Admission Prices:* Daily 9–5; adults $3; children 6–12 $2; group rate $2. Closed Thanksgiving; Christmas.

WASHINGTON
Robert Toombs House, 216 E. Robert Toombs Ave., Washington 30673. 404-678-2226. Historic house; outbuildings; orchard; furniture and furnishings from the period c. 1840–1900.

Hours & Admission Prices: Summer: Tues.-Sat. 9–5; Sun. 2–5; adults $1; children 2–17 50¢. Closed Thanksgiving; Christmas.

Washington—Wilkes Historical Museum, 308 E. Robert Toombs Ave., Washington 30673. 404-678-2105. 1836, Barnett-Slaton House, built by Albert Gallatin Semmes. Confederate history. Guided tours; permanent exhibitions. *Hours & Admission Prices:* Tues.-Sat. 10–5; Sun. 2–5; adults $1; children 6–12 50¢; group rates available. Closed New Year's; Thanksgiving; Christmas Eve; Christmas.

WATKINSVILLE
Eagle Tavern Welcome Center, U.S. Highway 441, Watkinsville 30677. 404-769-5197. Historic Building: stage coach stop, c. 1700's, furnishings. *Hours & Admission Prices:* Mon.-Fri. 9–5; other times by appointment. No charge.

WAYCROSS
Okefenokee Heritage Center, North Augusta Ave., Waycross 31501. 912-285-4260. Museum. History of Okefenokee Swamp and areas surrounding the swamp; renovated 1912 train, including steam engine and tender, 1 baggage car, 1 baggage/postal car, passenger car and caboose. Historic Buildings: 1900's Depot; c. 1832, General Thomas Hilliard House; late 1800's, print shop; Power House exhibit of antique vehicles; Nature Trails. *Hours & Admission Prices:* Tues.-Sat. 10–5; Sun. 2–4; adults $2; children 5–18 $1; 25% group rate discount. Closed National Holidays.

Southern Forest World, North Augusta Ave., Waycross 31501. 912-285-4056. Artifacts & specimens relating to the history & development of forestry in the South, including a 38′ tall model of a Loblolly Pine; a cross-section of the nation's largest Slash Pine; 1905, steam powered logging locomotive; naval stores tools & cups; giant Cypress; working scale model of a turpentine still; 22′ fire tower. *Hours & Admission Prices:* Tues.-Sat. 10–5; Sun. 2–4; adults $2; youth 5–18 $1; children under 5 no charge; tour groups 25% discount when prearranged. Closed Major Holidays.

WINDER
Fort Yargo State Park, Georgia Hwy. 81, Winder 30680. 404-867-3489. Historic Building: restored 1790 Timber Blockhouse used during the Creek Indian Wars. *Hours & Admission Prices:* by reservation only for conducted tours.

WINTERVILLE
Carter-Coile Country Doctors Museum, Bolton Drive, Winterville 30683. 404-742-8600. Housed in 1874 frame building used as an office by Dr. Warren Carter and Dr. Frank Coile. Medical equipment, furnishings, instruments, books, & special anatomy exhibits received from medical and other health personnel chiefly used in Clarke, Ga. and adjacent counties in the late 1800's and early 1900's and from Loree Florence, first woman graduate, 1926, of University of Georgia Medical School. *Hours & Admission Prices:* Call 404-742-5891 or 742-8284 for appointment. No charge; donations accepted.

NATIONAL FORESTS

Two National Forests, administered by the Department of Agriculture, U.S. Forest Service, lie within Georgia's borders. Both forests are located in the northern section of the state.

Oconee National Forest, containing 260,855 acres, is divided into two sections. The largest and southern-most division lies immediately north of

Macon between Interstate Highways 75 and 20. The other, smaller segment is situated in Greene County, north of Interstate Highway 20.

Chattahoochee National Forest, a huge expanse of land stretching along the Tennessee border, consists of 1,571,790 acres. It is divided into three sections, the largest of which lies east of U.S. Highway 411 and running to the South Carolina border. The other two areas are situated immediately east and west of Interstate Highway 75.

NATIONAL HISTORIC LANDMARKS

National Historic Landmarks are buildings, structures, sites, and objects of *National* significance that commemorate and illustrate the history and culture of the United States. Listed are the National Historic Landmarks in Georgia.

ATHENS

Henry W. Grady House. 634 Prince Avenue. Built circa 1845. Home (1863–72) of a major proponent of national reconciliation in the era following the War Between the States, who delivered his famous "New South" speech in 1886 in New York City.

ATLANTA

Dixie Coca-Cola Bottling Company Plant. 125 Edgewood Avenue. Built in 1891. This small brick building served in 1900–01 as the headquarters of what has become the Coca-Cola Bottling Company.

Fox Theatre. 660 Peachtree Street. Built in 1929. Known as "The Fabulous Fox," designed in a Neo-Mideastern Eclectic style, and one of the largest movie palaces at the time of its opening in 1929.

Joel Chandler Harris House. 1050 Gordon Street, SW. Built pre-1881. Harris, author of the "Uncle Remus" tales, lived here from 1881 until his death in 1908. The house contains many original furnishings.

Martin Luther King, Jr. Historic District. Includes the environs in which Martin Luther King, Jr. grew up. His birth home, grave, and the church which he served as assistant pastor are within the district.

State Capitol. Capitol Square. Built in 1889. This monumental domed and columned structure prefigures the American Renaissance style. Its neoclassicism reflects Georgians' hopes for national unity after the War Between the States, and the spirit of the New South.

Stone Hall (Fairchild Hall), Atlanta University. Morris-Brown College. Built in 1882. Stone Hall is closely associated with the history of the university, founded in 1866 by the American Missionary Association to provide education for freed blacks.

Sweet Auburn Historic District. Built in the early 20th century. The center of Black economic, social, and cultural activities in Atlanta from the 1890s to the 1930s. The Sweet Auburn District reflects an important element in the life of the Afro-American community in a segregated South.

AUGUSTA

College Hill (Walton-Harper House). 2216 Wrightsboro Road. Built in 1795. Property once owned by George Walton, a signer of the Declaration of Independence. He served as Georgia's Governor, Chief Justice of the State Supreme Court, and U.S. Senator.

Stephen Vincent Benét House (Commandant's House). 2500 Walton Way. Built in the 19th–20th centuries. Stephen Vincent Benét, known for his poetry and short stories, began his writing career in this Z-story Federal-style house after moving here in 1911.

Historic Augusta Canal and Industrial District. West bank of the Savannah River. Built in 1845–80s. Intact canal system and mills representative of industrial aspects of the New South. The best surviving example of an engineering system singularly important to the southeastern United States.

Stallings Island. 8 miles northwest of Augusta in the Savannah River. Built before 2000 B.C. One of the most important shell mound sites in the Southeast, giving information on Archaic Indians who lived in the Savannah River drainage area.

George Walton House (Meadow Garden). 1230 Nelson Street. The home of George Walton from 1791 to 1804. Appointed to the Continental Congress in 1776, at 26 he became the youngest signer of the Declaration of Independence. After the war he served as Georgia's Governor and as a United States Senator. Now owned by the Daughters of the American Revolution.

BLAKELY

Kolomoki Mounds. Built circa 1400–1600. Excavations have revealed details of burial practices at this type site for the Kolomoki culture. Contains one of the largest mound groups on the Southeastern coastal plain. Now a state park.

CARTERSVILLE

Etowah Mounds. 3 miles south of Cartersville. Built circa 1350. Important as an expression of the eastern expansion of Mississippian culture.

COLUMBUS

Columbus Historic Riverfront Industrial District. East bank of the Chattahoochee River, 8th–38th Streets North. Built in the 19th century. The area exemplifies use of hydrotechnology and its contributions to the growth of an important Southern textile center.

Octagon House. 527 1st Avenue. Built in 1829–30. Among the few fully realized double octagon houses in the United States. Exemplifies a fad that climaxed following publication of Squire Fowler's *A Home for All* on octagon design.

Springer Opera House. 105 10th Street. Built in 1871. This opera house hosted celebrated entertainers in the late 19th and early 20th centuries. It was coverted to a movie house after the Depression of the 1930s sapped the traditions of the circuit of live theatrical "road show."

CRAWFORDVILLE
Liberty Hall. Built in 1858–59, ell; circa 1875 main house. Alexander Stephens, the Vice-President of the Confederate States of America, who also enjoyed a remarkable political career before and after the War Between the States, lived at his Liberty Hall estate from 1834 until his death in 1883.

DAHLONEGA
Calhoun Mine. Associated with the discovery of gold in Georgia and the subsequent gold rush, which drove the Cherokees from their land.

GORDON
New Echota. Built in 1825. First national capital of the Cherokees, established in 1825. Contains first Cherokee newspaper shop.

JEKYLL ISLAND
Jekyll Island. Riverview Drive and Old Village Boulevard. Built in 1880s–1930. A millionaires' village established in the 1880s provided a setting for fashionable architecture. The complex is administered by the Georgia State Parks Authority.

LAGRANGE
Belleview (Benjamin Harvey Hill House). 204 Ben Hill Street. Built in 1853–55. Georgia statesman's home. A significant example of the "domesticated temple" form of the Greek Revival style, with noteworthy plaster cornices.

MACON
Carmichael House. 1183 Georgia Avenue. Built in the late 1840s. Exemplifies the variety and individuality possible within the Greek Revival style, in its use of classical detail in combination with a modified Greek cross plan and spiral staircase in a central tower.

Hay House. 934 Georgia Avenue. Built in 1855–60. An Italian Renaissance villa that offers a striking contrast to Georgia's Neoclassical antebellum mansions. Among interior features are curved marble stairs and a 50-foot ballroom.

MILLEDGEVILLE

Governor's Mansion. 120 S. Clark Street. Built in the 1840s. A Palladian facade with prostyle portico and a plan with round and octagonal rooms distinguish this, the home of Georgia governors when Milledgeville was State capital from 1804 to 1868.

ROME

Chieftains (Major Ridge House). 80 Chatillon Road. Built circa 1792. The hand-hewn log cabin built by Major Ridge, a Cherokee leader, is incorporated into the present larger house. Ridge operated a ferry and trading post and was the speaker of the Cherokee National Council.

ROSSVILLE

John Ross House. Lake Avenue and Spring Streets. Two-story square-timbered log house, home of the Cherokees' most prominent leader, a hero of the 1812 Creek War and senior Cherokee leader during the War Between the States.

SAVANNAH

Central of Georgia Railroad Shops and Terminal (Depot and Trainshed). W. Broad Street at Liberty. Built in 1860–66. Early attempt to build a comprehensive railroad terminal and shop complex. The trainshed is the oldest remaining example of early iron roof construction, the first step in the evolution of modern steel building methods.

Green—Meldrim House. Bull and Harvis Streets. Built in 1850–54. This Gothic Revival house, built for the Green family, was General William T. Sherman's headquarters in 1864–65.

Juliette Gordon Low Birthplace. 10 Oglethorpe Avenue. Built in 1818–21. Low established the Girl Scout movement in the United States, holding the first meeting in her carriage house. She became the first president of the Girl Scouts after their incorporation in 1915.

Owens-Thomas House. 125 Abercorn Street. Built in 1816–19. English Regency style residence with such unique features as indirect lighting, curved walls and doors, and an elegant central stairway.

Savannah Historic District. Built in 1732. The district retains much of James Oglethorpe's original city plan and includes many buildings of architectural merit.

William Scarbrough House. 41 W. Broad Street. Built in 1818–19. Marks the height of neo-classical townhouse design in the United States. Reception hall and mezzanine have been called one of the grandest spatial compositions in United States architecture.

Telfair Academy of Arts and Sciences. 121 Barnard Street. Built in 1818–20. Among the oldest museums in the southeast, opened as a free art museum in 1886. Includes an 1818 townhouse with later additions and renovations in the 1880s, retaining masterful classical elements. Houses an important collection of paintings, including colonial and Federal portraits.

ST. CATHERINE'S ISLAND
St. Catherine's Island. 10 miles off the Georgia coast, S. Newport vicinity. Built in 16th–20th centuries. Important Spanish mission center (1566–1684). Button Gwinnett, delegate to the Continental Congress and signer of the Declaration of Independence, purchased the island in 1765 and lived here.

THOMASVILLE
Lapham-Patterson House. 626 N. Dawson Street. Built in the 1880s. Built as a resort home for a Chicago businessman, this 3-story Victorian mansion represents the eclectic, picturesque, and romantic resort cottage of the High Victorian 1880s. Its design and detailing are both exuberant and individualistic.

THOMPSON
Thomas E. Watson House. 310 Lumpkin Street. Built circa 1875. Watson was a principal founder of the Populist Party and first to urge a united front between white and black farmers. Embitterment, after defeat at the polls in 1892 and 1896, led to an extreme reversal of his attitudes and gave him a considerable following among Southern rural whites.

TOCCOA
Traveler's Rest. 6 miles east of Toccoa. Built in 1764. Erected by Major Jesse Walton, soldier in the Revolution and in conflicts with Native Americans. Example of an early tavern and inn in a rural frontier environment.

WARM SPRINGS
Warm Springs Historic District. Built in 1924–45. The district includes two vacation homes (1928–32 and 1932–45) of Franklin D. Roosevelt, who found relief from his polio in the "warm springs" that gave this town its name, and the Warm Springs Hospital, founded by Roosevelt to aid fellow victims of the ravaging disease. Roosevelt's efforts led to the "March of Dimes." He died at his "Little White House" in Warm Springs (April 12, 1945).

WASHINGTON

Robert Toombs House. E. Robert Toombs Avenue. Built in 1797, enlarged circa 1835, 1840, 1870. Toombs served in the United States Congress and became Secretary of State of the Confederacy and a general in the Confederate Army. House enlarged by original owners and by Toombs.

Tupper-Barnett House. 101 W. Robert Toombs Avenue. Built circa 1832–60. Among the finest examples of 19th century conversions of Federal period homes into Neoclassical mansions by addition of colonnades. Symbolic of the wealth brought to the South by the cotton trade, this house has a finely detailed Doric peristyle colonnade skillfully joined to an existing structure.

NATIONAL PARKS

Georgia contains eight units of the National Park Service. These units, along with their acreages and the nearest large town follow.

Andersonville National Historic Site commemorates the largest Confederate military prison. This was built in 1864 after Confederate leaders decided to move a large number of Federal prisoners from Richmond to a place of greater security and more abundant food. The information program at the site tells how they miscalculated and of the tragedy that ensued. Located near Albany; 476 acres.

Chickamauga and Chattanooga National Military Park is located on one of the most important battlefields of the War Between the States. Exhibits and an audio-visual program at the Visitor Center explain the battle and its place in Civil War history. Situated in Chattanooga, TN; 8,095 acres.

Cumberland Island National Seashore is one of the finest remaining natural preserves on the east coast. There are over 28,000 acres of forest, marsh, dunes, and spacious, unspoiled beach. Reached only by boat from St. Marys. Near Savannah; 36,978 acres.

Fort Frederica National Monument on St. Simons Island was established by Georgia's founder, General James Edward Oglethorpe, in 1736. It played a vital role in the English-Spanish struggle (1739–1748) for control of what is now the southeastern United States. Ruins of the fort and town may be seen by taking a self-guided walk through the historic area. Near Savannah; 214 acres.

Fort Pulaski National Monument in Savannah is an early 19th century fort whose bombardment by Federal rifled canon in 1862 first demonstrated the ineffectiveness of old-style masonry fortification. Most of the fort is in the original condition. It contains 5,623 acres.

Kennesaw Mountain National Battlefield Park in Marietta marks the locale of the skirmish that led to the fall of Atlanta in 1864. Living history demonstrations are staged here during summer months. Contains 2,884 acres.

Ocmulgee National Monument preserves remnants of important Indian mounds and villages of the Macon area. These represent 10,000 years of cultural evolution in the Indian mound-building civilizations of the South. Contains 683 acres.

Martin Luther King, Jr. National Historic Site in Atlanta is a district of 23 acres surrounding the birthplace, boyhood home, church and memorial gravesite of the famed Civil Rights leader. Tours and other interpretive programs are slated to focus on the continuing memorial to Dr. King through the Center for Social Change which is located here.

For more information write Tour Georgia, Georgia Department of Industry and Trade, P.O. Box 1776, Atlanta 30301.

NATIONAL WILDLIFE REFUGES

The U.S. Department of Interior, Fish and Wildlife Service, maintains eight National Wildlife Refuges in Georgia. These units, their mailing addresses, and the facilities available are described below. Always check with the refuge manager (regarding activities, fees, schedules, etc.) before making a trip to a refuge.

Blackbeard Island, Georgia Coastal Complex, Box 8487, Savannah 31402. Facilities: foot trails, environmental study area, hunting, fishing, and a refuge leaflet.

Harris Neck, Georgia Coastal Complex, Box 8487, Savannah 31402. Facilities: foot trails, auto tour, environmental study area, hunting, fishing, a refuge leaflet, and food and lodging nearby.

Okefenokee, Box 117, Waycross 31501. Facilities: visitor center, contact station, foot trails, auto tour, bicycling, non-motorized boating, environmental study area, hunting, fishing, camping, picnicking, refuge leaflet, species list, and food and lodging nearby.

Located in southeastern Georgia and extending slightly into northern Florida, this is the largest national wildlife refuge in the eastern U.S. The refuge contains approximately 396,000 acres of the 438,000-acre Okefenokee Swamp. The threatened American alligator, red cockaded woodpecker, Florida sandhill crane, round-tailed water rats, and osprey may be observed in the refuge.

Piedmont, Round Oak 31038. Facilities: visitor center, contact station, foot trails, auto tour, environmental study area, hunting, fishing, refuge leaflet, species list, and food and lodging nearby.

Savannah, Georgia Coastal Complex, Box 8487, Savannah 31402. Facilities: foot trails, auto tour, environmental study area, hunting, fishing, refuge leaflet, species list, and food and lodging nearby.

Tybee, Georgia Coastal Complex, Box 8487, Savannah 31402. Facilities: environmental study area, and refuge leaflet.

Wassaw, Georgia Coastal Complex, Box 8487, Savannah 31402. Facilities: foot trails, environmental study area, hunting, and refuge leaflet.

Wolf Island, Georgia Coastal Complex, Box 8487, Savannah 31402. Facilities: environmental study area, and refuge leaflet.

NATURAL RESOURCES

A wide variety of productive mineral deposits are found in the state of Georgia. These include asbestos, cement rock, coal, raw clay, granite, limestone, graphite, manganese, mica, talc, silver, and gold. Georgia is a leader in the production of barite, bauxite, and marble and about 75% of the kaolin produced in the United States, as well as being one of the leading states in the production of fuller's earth. In various parts of northern and central Georgia, minor deposits of such precious stones amethysts, diamonds, and rubies may be found. Some of the most common minerals are listed in the chart that follows.

MINERAL PRODUCTION

County	Number of Active Surface Mines	Number of Acres Permitted	Minerals Produced
Baldwin	4	228	Sand, Gravel, Kaolin
Banks	1	11	Crushed Stone
Barrow	2	34	Crushed Stone, Sand
Bartow	8	495	Limestone, Barite, Ochre, Umber, Sand, Gravel, Shale
Bibb	7	608	Clay, Fill Material, Sand
Brantley	2	54	Sand
Burke	1	5	Fill Material
Carroll	4	76	Crushed Stone, Sand, Gravel, Granite
Charlton	1	8	Sand
Chatham	17	335	Fill Material, Sand
Chattooga	1	5	Fill Material
Cherokee	2	45	Sand, Limestone
Clarke	1	78	Granite
Clayton	1	147	Granite
Cobb	3	171	Sand, Gravel, Granite
Columbia	2	49	Clay, Shale, Crushed Stone

County	Number of Active Surface Mines	Number of Acres Permitted	Minerals Produced
Cook	2	247	Sand, Peat
Coweta	1	77	Granite
Crawford	4	84	Sand, Fill Material
Dawson	1	11	Sand, Gravel
Decatur	10	1,099	Fill Material, Sand, Fuller's Earth
DeKalb	5	597	Sand, Gravel, Granite
Dougherty	2	89	Sand, Gravel
Douglas	7	314	Sand, Gravel, Clay, Granite
Effingham	4	110	Sand, Gravel, Fill Material
Elbert	4	35	Granite, Sand
Evans	1	20	Sand
Fannin	—	—	Stone
Fayette	2	317	Granite
Floyd	7	437	Shale, Limestone, Clay, Crushed Stone
Forsyth	4	579	Sand, Granite, Quartzite
Fulton	13	497	Sand, Schist, Fill Material, Granite
Gilmer	2	70	Granite, Crushed Stone
Glascock	1	80	Kaolin
Glynn	5	33	Fill Material, Sand
Gordon	2	286	Limestone, Shale
Grady	2	105	Fuller's Earth, Sand
Greene	3	138	Sand, Gravel, Feldspar, Amethyst
Gwinnett	4	489	Sand, Granite
Habersham	2	63	Granite
Hall	1	264	Granite, Limestone
Hancock	1	27	Kaolin
Hart	2	153	Mica
Heard	1	15	Gravel
Henry	1	178	Granite
Houston	5	605	Limestone, Fill Material, Kaolin
Jackson	2	12	Sand, Gravel
Jasper	1	10	Feldspar
Jefferson	3	198	Kaolin, Fuller's Earth
Jones	2	350	Granite
Laurens	2	6	Fill Material, Sand
Lee	2	232	Sand, Limestone
Lincoln	1	188	Kyanite
Long	2	16	Sand
Lowndes	3	148	Fill Material, Sand
Lumpkin	3	21	Roadbase, Sand, Gravel
Macon	2	96	Bauxite

County	Number of Active Surface Mines	Number of Acres Permitted	Minerals Produced
Marion	1	65	Sand
McDuffie	2	53	Sand, Kaolin
Miller	1	4	Peat
Monroe	1	190	Granite
Montgomery	1	50	Sand
Murray	2	50	Limestone, Slate
Muscogee	6	348	Clay, Sand, Gravel, Granite
Newton	2	28	Granite, Sand
Paulding	2	24	Granite, Crushed Stone
Peach	1	47	Sand
Pierce	3	40	Fill Material, Sand
Pike	1	51	Sand
Polk	2	112	Slate, Sericite
Rabun	1	93	Granite
Richmond	22	1,364	Kaolin, Fill Material, Sand, Clay, Shale, Granite
Spalding	1	97	Granite
Stephens	2	42	Granite
Sumter	3	134	Bauxite, Kaolin, Fill Material
Talbot	2	63	Sand
Tattnall	1	5	Sand
Taylor	2	66	Sand
Thomas	6	460	Fuller's Earth, Sand, Fill Material
Toombs	1	10	Sand
Towns	1	6	Crushed Stone
Troup	1	87	Granite
Turner	1	20	Sand
Twiggs	32	3,797	Kaolin, Clay, Sand
Union	1	68	Roadbase
Walker	3	125	Limestone, Shale
Walton	1	46	Granite
Ware	3	25	Sand, Fill Material
Warren	8	867	Kaolin, Granite
Washington	32	5,136	Kaolin, Gravel
Wayne	1	23	Sand
Wheeler	3	28	Sand
White	1	7	Fill Material
Whitfield	1	284	Limestone
Wilkinson	29	5,630	Kaolin
Georgia	363	30,217	

NEWSPAPERS

DAILY AND SUNDAY NEWSPAPERS

ALBANY (Dougherty County)
The Albany Herald
P.O. Box 48, 31703
912-888-9300
Circulation:
  Daily 37,913
  Sunday 42,869
Pub. Days: Daily

AMERICUS (Sumter County)
Americus Times-Recorder
Vienna Road, 31709
912-924-2751
Circulation: 7,217
Pub. Days: Daily
  ex. Sunday

ATHENS (Clarke County)
Athens Banner-Herald
P.O. Box 912, 30613
404-549-0123
Circulation:
  Daily 12,965
  Sunday 19,695
Pub. Days: Daily

Athens Daily News
P.O. Box 912, 30613
404-549-0123
Circulation:
  Daily 10,039
  Sunday 26,915
Pub. Days: Daily

ATLANTA (Fulton County)
The Atlanta Constitution
P.O. Box 4689, 30302
404-526-5151
Circulation:
  Daily 236,270
  Sunday 519,755
Pub. Days: Daily

The Atlanta Journal
P.O. Box 4689, 30302
404-526-5151
Circulation:
  Daily 184,046
  Sunday 519,755
Pub. Days: Daily

Fulton County Daily Report
190 Pryor St., SW, 30303
404-521-1227
Circulation: 1,521
Pub. Days: Mon.-Fri.

AUGUSTA (Richmond County)
The Augusta Chronicle
P.O. Box 1988, 30913
404-724-0851
Circulation:
  Daily 59,763
  Sunday 84,586
Pub. Days: Daily

The Augusta Herald
P.O. Box 1988, 30913
404-724-0851
Circulation:
  Daily 18,312
  Sunday 84,586
Pub. Days: Daily

BRUNSWICK (Glynn County)
The Brunswick News
P.O. Box 1557, 31521
912-265-8320
Circulation: 14,711
Pub. Days: Daily
  ex. Sunday

CARROLLTON (Carroll County)
The Daily Times-Georgian
P.O. Box 460, 30117
404-834-6631
Circulation: 13,334
Pub. Days: Tues.-Sun.

CARTERSVILLE (Bartow County)
The Daily Tribune News
P.O. Box 70, 30120
404-382-4545
Circulation: 7,446
Pub. Days: Mon.-Fri.

COLUMBUS (Muscogee County)

The Columbus Enquirer
P.O. Box 711, 31994
404-324-5526
Circulation:
  Daily 33,947
  Sunday 68,304
Pub. Days: Daily

The Columbus Ledger
P.O. Box 711, 31994
404-324-5526
Circulation:
  Daily 26,200
  Sunday 68,304
Pub. Days: Daily

CONYERS (Rockdale County)
The Rockdale Citizen
P.O. Box 136, 30207
404-483-7108
Circulation: 7,763
Pub. Days: Mon.-Fri.

CORDELE (Crisp County)
The Cordele Dispatch
P.O. Box 1058, 31015
912-273-2277
Circulation: 5,420
Pub. Days: Mon.-Fri.

DALTON (Whitfield County)
The Daily Citizen-News
P.O. Box 1167, 30720
404-278-1011
Circulation: 14,061
Pub. Days: Daily
  ex. Sunday

DUBLIN (Laurens County)
The Courier Herald
Drawer B, Court Square Station 31040-2249
912-272-5522
Circulation: 10,457
Pub. Days: Daily
  ex. Sunday

GAINESVILLE (Hall County)
The Times

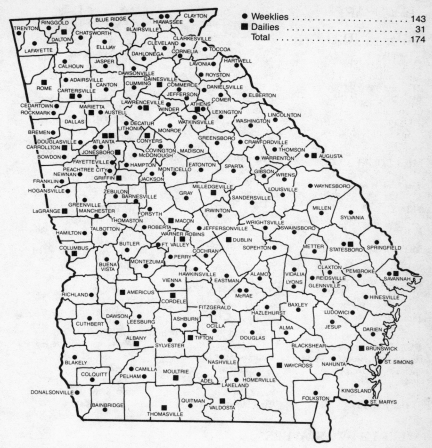

● Weeklies 143
■ Dailies 31
   Total 174

P.O. Box 838, 30503
404-532-1234
Circulation:
   Daily 21,948
   Sunday 23,000
Pub. Days: Daily
   ex. Saturday

GRIFFIN (Spalding
   County)
Griffin Daily News
P.O. Drawer M, 30224
404-227-3276
Circulation: 13,753
Pub. Days: Daily
   ex. Sunday

JONESBORO (Clayton
   County)
Clayton News/Daily
P.O. Box 368, 30237
404-478-5753
Circulation: 8,894
Pub. Days: Mon.-Fri.

LAGRANGE (Troup
   County)
LaGrange Daily News
P.O. Box 929, 30241
404-884-7311
Circulation: 15,023
Pub. Days: Daily
   ex. Sunday

LAWRENCEVILLE
   (Gwinnett County)
Gwinnett Daily News
P.O. Box 1,000, 30246
Circulation:
   Daily 31,176
   Wed. & Sat. 26,824
Pub. Days: Daily

MACON (Bibb County)
**The Macon Telegraph
   and News**
120 Broadway, 31213
912-744-4200
Circulation:
   Daily 71,954

Sunday 86,263
Pub. Days: Daily

MARIETTA (Cobb
County)
**The Marietta Daily
Journal**
P.O. Box 449, 30060
404-428-9411
Circulation:
Daily 25,879
Sunday 27,275
Pub. Days: Daily

MILLEDGEVILLE
(Baldwin County)
The Union Recorder
P.O. Box 520, 31061
912-452-0567
Circulation: 6,797
Pub. Days: Tues.-Sat.

MOULTRIE (Colquitt
County)
The Moultrie Observer
P.O. Box 889, 31768
912-985-4545
Circulation: 8,088
Pub. Days: Daily
ex. Sunday

ROME (Floyd County)
The Rome News-Tribune
305 E. 6th Ave., 30161
404-291-6397
Circulation:
Daily 23,309

Sunday 25,163
Pub. Days: Daily
ex. Saturday

SAVANNAH (Chatham
County)
Savannah Morning News
P.O. Box 1088, 31411
912-236-9511
Circulation:
Daily 56,700
Sunday 73,000
Pub. Days: Daily

Savannah Evening Press
P.O. Box 1088, 31411
912-236-9511
Circulation:
Daily 56,700
Sunday 73,000
Pub. Days: Daily

STATESBORO (Bulloch
County)
The Statesboro Herald
P.O. Box 888, 30458
912-764-9031
Circulation: 6,484
Pub. Days: Daily

THOMASVILLE (Thomas
County)
**Thomasville Times-
Enterprise**
P.O. Box 650, 31792
912-226-2400
Circulation: 11,154

Pub. Days: Daily
ex. Sunday

TIFTON (Tift County)
The Tifton Gazette
211 N. Tift, 31793
912-382-4321
Circulation: 9,501
Pub. Days: Mon.-Sat.

VALDOSTA (Lowndes
County)
The Valdosta Daily Times
P.O. Box 968, 31601
912-244-1880
Circulation: 17,602
Pub. Days: Daily

WARNER ROBINS
(Houston County)
The Daily/Sunday Sun
P.O. Box 2768, 31093
912-923-6432
Circulation:
Daily 10,203
Sunday 11,076
Pub. Day: Daily
ex. Saturday

WAYCROSS (Ware County)
Waycross Journal-Herald
P.O. Box 219, 31502
912-283-2244
Circulation: 12,785
Pub. Day: Daily
ex. Sunday

WEEKLY NEWSPAPERS

ADAIRSVILLE (Bartow
County)
The North Bartow News
P.O. Box 374, 30103
404-773-3754
Circulation: 1,339
Pub. Day: Thurs.

ADEL (Cook County)
The Adel News-Tribune
131 S. Hutchinson Ave.,
31620
912-896-2233
Circulation: 3,257
Pub. Day: Wed.

ALAMO (Wheeler County)

**The Wheeler County
Eagle**
P.O. Box 409, 30411
912-537-2076
Circulation: 1,357
Pub. Day: Wed.

ALMA (Bacon County)
**The Alma Times-
Statesman**
P.O. Box 428, 31510
912-632-7201
Circulation: 3,310
Pub. Day: Thurs.

ASHBURN (Turner
County)

The Wiregrass Farmer
109 N. Gordon St., 31714
912-567-3655
Circulation: 2,621
Pub. Day: Thurs.

ATHENS (Clarke County)
The Athens Observer
P.O. Box 112, 30613
404-548-6346
Circulation: 11,000
Pub. Day: Thurs.

ATLANTA (Fulton
County)
Atlanta Business Chronicle
1800 Water Pl., NW

St. 100, 30339
404-952-6397
Circulation: 17,620
Pub. Day: Mon.

The Southern Israelite
P.O. Box 77388, 30357
404-876-8248
Circulation: 6,185
Pub. Day: Fri.

AUGUSTA (Richmond County)
Richmond County Times
P.O. Box 632, 30903
404-798-5653
Circulation: 3,528
Pub. Day: Thurs.

AUSTELL (Cobb County)
Sweetwater News Enterprise
P.O. Box 99, 30001
404-948-2563
Circulation: 16,000
Pub. Day: Thurs.

BAINBRIDGE (Decatur County)
The Post-Searchlight
301 N. Crawford St., 31717
912-246-2827
Circulation: 5,775
Pub. Days: Wed. & Sat.

BARNESVILLE (Lamar County)
The Herald-Gazette
P.O. Box 220, 30204
404-358-0754
Circulation: 3,995
Pub. Day: Wed.

BAXLEY (Appling County)
The Baxley News-Banner
P.O. Box 409, 31513
912-367-2468
Circulation: 4,687
Pub. Day: Thurs.

BLACKSHEAR (Pierce County)
The Blackshear Times
P.O. Box 410, 31516
912-449-0693
Circulation: 3,600
Pub. Day: Thurs.

BLAIRSVILLE (Union County)
North Georgia News
P.O. Box 748, 30512
404-745-6343
Circulation: 5,165
Pub. Day: Thurs.

BLAKELY (Early County)
Early County News
209 S. Main St., 31723
912-723-4376
Circulation: 3,475
Pub. Day: Wed.

BLUE RIDGE (Fannin County)
The Blue Ridge Summit-Post
P.O. Box 989, 30513
404-632-2019
Circulation: 1,657
Pub. Day: Fri.

BOWDON (Carroll County)
The Bowdon Bulletin
109 Shirley St., 30108
404-258-2146
Circulation: 2,433
Pub. Day: Thurs.

BREMEN (Haralson County)
The Haralson Gateway-Beacon
222 Tallapoosa St., 30110
404-537-2434
Circulation: 5,958
Pub. Day: Thurs.

BUENA VISTA (Marion County)
Patriot-Citizen
P.O. Box 108, 31803
404-846-3188
Circulation: 1,125
Pub. Day: Thurs.

BUTLER (Taylor County)
Taylor County News
P.O. Box 1979, 31006
912-862-5101
Circulation: 2,170
Pub. Day: Thurs.

CALHOUN (Gordon County)

The Calhoun Times
P.O. Box 8, 30701
404-629-2231
Circulation: 7,850
Pub. Days: Wed. & Sat.

CAMILLA (Mitchell County)
The Camilla Enterprise
13 S. Scott St., 31730
912-336-5265
Circulation: 3,733
Pub. Days: Wed. & Fri.

CANTON (Cherokee County)
The Cherokee Tribune
64 Academy St., 30114
404-479-1441
Circulation: 7,800
Pub. Days: Sun. & Wed.

CARTERSVILLE (Bartow County)
The Herald Tribune
P.O. Box 70, 30120
404-382-4545
Circulation: 1,157
Pub. Day: Thurs.

CEDARTOWN (Polk County)
The Cedartown Standard
P.O. Box 308, 30125
404-748-1520
Circulation: 3,618
Pub. Days: Tues. & Thurs.

CHATSWORTH (Murray County)
The Chatsworth Times
P.O. Box 130, 30705
404-695-4646
Circulation: 4,807
Pub. Day: Wed.

CLARKESVILLE (Habersham County)
Tri-County Advertiser
P.O. Box 256, 30523
404-754-4139
Circulation: 5,475
Pub. Day: Wed.

CLAXTON (Evans County)
The Claxton Enterprise
24 S. Newton St., 30417

912-739-2132
Circulation: 3,240
Pub. Day: Wed.

CLAYTON (Rabun
County)
The Clayton Tribune
P.O. Box 435, 30525
404-782-3312
Circulation: 4,450
Pub. Day: Thurs.

CLEVELAND (White
County)
White County News
Box 456, 30528
404-865-4718
Circulation: 2,716
Pub. Day: Thurs.

COCHRAN (Bleckley
County)
The Cochran Journal
106 Cherry St., 31014
912-934-6303
Circulation: 2,779
Pub. Day: Wed.

COLQUITT (Miller
County)
Miller County Liberal
P.O. Box 37, 31737
912-758-5549
Circulation: 2,597
Pub. Day: Thurs.

COMER (Madison County)
The Comer News
422 Main St., 30629
404-783-2553
Circulation: 1,430
Pub. Day: Thurs.

COMMERCE (Jackson
County)
The Commerce News
35 S. Broad St., 30529
404-335-5121
Circulation: 3,621
Pub. Day: Wed.

CORNELIA (Habersham
County)
The Northeast Georgian
P.O. Box 190, 30531
404-778-4215
Circulation: 6,295
Pub. Day: Tues.

COVINGTON (Newton
County)
The Covington News, Inc.
P.O. Box 1278, 30209
404-786-3401
Circulation: 5,453
Pub. Day: Thurs.

CRAWFORDVILLE
(Taliaferro County)
The Advocate-Democrat
P.O. Box 149, Greensboro
30642
404-453-7988
Circulation: 671
Pub. Day: Fri.

CUMMING (Forsyth
County)
The Forsyth County News
P.O. Box 210, 30130
404-887-3126
Circulation: 4,915
Pub. Days: Wed. & Sun.

CUTHBERT (Randolph
County)
**Cuthbert Times & News
Record**
208 W. Dawson St.
31740
912-732-2731
Circulation: 1,891
Pub. Day: Thurs.

DAHLONEGA (Lumpkin
County)
The Dahlonega Nugget
P.O. Box 476, 30533
404-864-3613
Circulation: 3,515
Pub. Day: Thurs.

DALLAS (Paulding
County)
Dallas New Era
P.O. Box 246, 30132
404-445-3379
Circulation: 6,100
Pub. Day: Wed.

DANIELSVILLE
(Madison County)
The Danielsville Monitor
P.O. Box 9, 30633
404-795-3102
Circulation: 1,560
Pub. Day: Fri.

DARIEN (McIntosh
County)
The Darien News
106 Broad St., 31305
912-437-4251
Circulation: 2,600
Pub. Day: Thurs.

DAWSON (Terrell County)
The Dawson News
139 W. Lee St., 31742
912-995-2175
Circulation: 2,697
Pub. Day: Thurs.

DAWSONVILLE (Dawson
County)
Dawson County Advertiser
P.O. Box 225, 30534
404-265-2345
Circulation: 1,430
Pub. Day: Thurs.

DECATUR (DeKalb
County)
Decatur-DeKalb News Era
739 DeKalb Ind. Way,
30033
404-292-3536
Circulation: 7,989
Pub. Day: Thurs.

DONALSONVILLE
(Seminole County)
Donalsonville News
P.O. Box 338, 31745
912-524-2343
Circulation: 3,000
Pub. Day: Thurs.

DOUGLAS (Coffee
County)
The Douglas Enterprise
P.O. Box 551, 31533
912-384-2323
Circulation: 5,165
Pub. Day: Wed.

DOUGLASVILLE
(Douglas County)
Douglas County Sentinel
P.O. Box 1586, 30133
404-942-6571
Circulation: 6,886
Pub. Days: Tues. & Thurs.

EASTMAN (Dodge
County)

Times Journal-Spotlight
277 College Ave., 31023
912-374-5562
Circulation: 4,451
Pub. Day: Thurs.

EATONTON (Putnam
County)
The Eatonton Messenger
P.O. Box 402, 31024
404-485-3501
Circulation: 2,976
Pub. Day: Thurs.

ELBERTON (Elbert
County)
**The Elberton Star-
The Elbert Beacon**
P.O. Box 280, 30635
404-283-3100
Circulation: 4,635
Pub. Days: Tues. & Thurs.

ELLIJAY (Gilmer County)
Times-Courier
13 River St., 30540
404-635-4313
Circulation: 4,690
Pub. Day: Thurs.

FAYETTEVILLE (Fayette
County)
Fayette County News
P.O. Box 96, 30214
404-461-6317
Circulation: 2,500
Pub. Day: Wed.

FITZGERALD (Ben Hill
County)
The Herald-Leader
P.O. Box 40, 31750
912-423-9331
Circulation: 5,035
Pub. Day: Wed.

FOLKSTON (Charlton
County)
Charlton County Herald
P.O. Box 68, 31537
912-496-7304
Circulation: 2,174
Pub. Day: Wed.

FORSYTH (Monroe
County)
**The Monroe County
Reporter**

P.O. Box 795, 31029
912-994-2358
Circulation: 3,726
Pub. Day: Wed.

FORT VALLEY (Peach
County)
Leader-Tribune
205 Main St., 31030
912-825-2432
Circulation: 4,300
Pub. Day: Wed.

FRANKLIN (Heard
County)
The News and Banner
P.O. Box 97, 30217
404-675-3374
Circulation: 1,050
Pub. Day: Wed.

GIBSON (Glascock
County)
Gibson Record and Guide
P.O. Box 306, Warrenton
30828
404-465-3395
Circulation: 744
Pub. Day: Fri.

GLENNVILLE (Tattnall
County)
The Glennville Sentinel
P.O. Box 218, 30427
912-654-2515
Circulation: 2,848
Pub. Day: Thurs.

GRAY (Jones County)
The Jones County News
P.O. Box 637, 31023
912-986-3929
Circulation: 1,923
Pub. Day: Thurs.

GREENSBORO (Greene
County)
The Herald-Journal
P.O. Box 149, 30642
404-453-7988
Circulation: 3,644
Pub. Day: Fri.

GREENVILLE
(Meriwether County)
**The Meriwether
Vindicator**
P.O. Box A, 30222

404-846-3188
Circulation: 2,400
Pub. Day: Fri.

HAMILTON (Harris
County)
Harris County Journal
P.O. Box 75, 31811
404-846-3188
Circulation: 1,742
Pub. Day: Thurs.

HAMPTON (Henry
County)
Hampton News
P.O. Box 708, 30228
404-946-3026
Circulation: 1,293
Pub. Day: Tues.

HARTWELL (Hart
County)
The Hartwell Sun
P.O. Box 700, 30643
404-376-8025
Circulation: 5,286
Pub. Day: Thurs.

HAWKINSVILLE
(Pulaski County)
**Hawkinsville Dispatch &
News**
329 Commerce St., 30136
912-783-1291
Circulation: 2,747
Pub. Day: Wed.

HAZELHURST (Jeff
Davis County)
**The Jeff Davis County
Ledger**
102 Railroad St., 31539
912-375-4225
Circulation: 3,206
Pub. Day: Wed.

HIAWASSEE (Towns
County)
Towns County Herald
P.O. Box 375, 30546
404-745-6343
Circulation: 2,155
Pub. Day: Thurs.

The Mountain News
P.O. Box 417, 30546
404-896-4244
Circulation: 2,400
Pub. Day: Thurs.

HINESVILLE (Liberty County)
Coastal Courier
P.O. Box 498, 31313
912-876-0156
Circulation: 5,063
Pub. Days: Wed. & Fri.

HOGANSVILLE (Troup County)
Hogansville Herald
P.O. Box 426, 30240
404-846-3188
Circulation: 1,200
Pub. Day: Thurs.

HOMERVILLE (Clinch County)
The Clinch County News
210 E. Dame Ave., 31634
912-487-5337
Circulation: 1,710
Pub. Day: Thurs.

IRWINTON (Wilkinson County)
Wilkinson County News
P.O. Box 205, 31042
912-946-2218
Circulation: 2,082
Pub. Day: Thurs

JACKSON (Butts County)
Jackson Progress-Argus
P.O. Box 249, 30233
404-775-3107
Circulation: 4,095
Pub. Day: Wed.

JASPER (Pickens County)
Pickens County Progress
P.O. Box 67, 30143
404-692-2457
Circulation: 4,850
Pub. Day: Thurs.

JEFFERSON (Jackson County)
The Jackson Herald
P.O. Box 908, 30549
404-367-5233
Circulation: 6,804
Pub. Day: Wed.

JEFFERSONVILLE (Twiggs County)
Twiggs Co. New Era
P.O. Box 292, 31044

912-945-3566
Circulation: 1,540
Pub. Day: Wed.

JESUP (Wayne County)
The Press-Sentinel
P.O. Box 666, 31545
912-427-3757
Circulation: 6,835
Pub. Days: Tues. & Thurs.

KINGSLAND (Camden County)
The Southeast Georgian
P.O. Box 1059, 31548
912-729-5231
Circulation: 3,188
Pub. Day: Thurs.

LAFAYETTE (Walker County)
Walker County Messenger
P.O. Box 766, 30728
404-638-1859
Circulation: 3,775
Pub. Days: Wed. & Fri.

LAKELAND (Lanier County)
Lanier County News
P.O. Box 278, 31635
912-482-3367
Circulation: 1,438
Pub. Day: Thurs.

LAVONIA (Franklin County)
Franklin County Citizen
P.O. Box 148, 30553
404-356-8557
Circulation: 3,607
Pub. Day: Thurs.

LAWRENCEVILLE (Gwinnett County)
The Home Weekly
P.O. Box 603, 30246
404-963-9205
Circulation: 4,946
Pub. Day: Wed.

LEESBURG (Lee County)
The Lee County Ledger
P.O. Box 715, 31763
912-759-2413
Circulation: 1,475
Pub. Day: Thurs.

LEXINGTON (Oglethorpe County)
The Oglethorpe Echo
P.O. Box 266, 30648
404-743-5510
Circulation: 2,545
Pub. Day: Thurs.

LINCOLNTON (Lincoln County)
The Lincoln Journal
P.O. Box 399, 30817
404-359-3623
Circulation: 1,625
Pub. Day: Thurs.

LITHONIA (DeKalb County)
Lithonia Observer
P.O. Box 129, 30058
404-482-7339
Circulation: 1,311
Pub. Day: Thurs.

LOUISVILLE (Jefferson County)
The News and Farmer & Wadley Herald
P.O. Box 487, 30434
912-625-7722
Circulation: 2,790
Pub. Day: Thurs.

LUDOWICI (Long County)
The Ludowici News
P.O. Box 218, 31316
912-545-2103
Circulation: 1,180
Pub. Day: Thurs.

LYONS (Toombs County)
The Lyons Progress
P.O. Box 312, 30436
912-526-3516
Circulation: 2,860
Pub. Day: Wed.

MADISON (Morgan County)
The Madisonian
Drawer 191, 30650
404-342-2424
Circulation: 3,996
Pub. Day: Wed.

MANCHESTER (Meriwether County)

Manchester Star-Mercury
P.O. Box 426, 31816
404-846-3188
Circulation: 4,074
Pub. Day: Wed.

McDONOUGH (Henry
County)
The Henry Herald
P.O. Box 233, 30253
404-957-9161
Circulation: 7,138
Pub. Day: Wed.

McRAE (Telfair County)
The Telfair Enterprise
P.O. Box 269, 31055
912-868-6015
Circulation: 3,134
Pub. Day: Wed.

Telfair Times
P.O. Box 429, 31055
912-868-5776
Circulation: 2,770
Pub. Day: Wed.

METTER (Candler
County)
**Metter News and
Advertiser**
15 S. Rountree, 30439
912-685-6566
Circulation: 2,776
Pub. Day: Wed.

MILLEN (Jenkins County)
The Millen News
409 Cotton Ave., 30442
912-982-5460
Circulation: 2,125
Pub. Day: Thurs.

MONROE (Walton County)
The Walton Tribune
P.O. Box 808, 30655
404-267-8371
Circulation: 5,049
Pub. Days: Tues. & Thurs.

MONTEZUMA (Macon
County)
Citizen & Georgian
P.O. Box 387, 31063
912-472-7755
Circulation: 2,500
Pub. Day: Tues.

MONTICELLO (Jasper
County)
The Monticello News
P.O. Box 30, 31064
404-468-6511
Circulation: 2,119
Pub. Day: Thurs.

NAHUNTA (Brantley
County)
The Brantley Enterprise
P.O. Box 454, 31553
912-462-5610
Circulation: 700
Pub. Day: Thurs.

NASHVILLE (Berrien
County)
The Berrien Press
P.O. Box 666, 31639
912-686-3523
Circulation: 3,800
Pub. Day: Wed.

NEWNAN (Coweta
County)
**The Newnan
Times-Herald**
16 Jefferson St., 30263
404-253-1576
Circulation: 12,005
Pub. Days: Tues. & Thurs.

OCILLA (Irwin County)
The Ocilla Star
P.O. Box 25, 31774
912-468-5433
Circulation: 2,312
Pub. Day: Wed.

PEACHTREE CITY
(Fayette County)
**This Week in Peachtree
City**
P.O. Box 2468, 30269
404-487-7729
Circulation: 2,500
Pub. Day: Wed.

PELHAM (Mitchell
County)
The Pelham Journal
P.O. Box 409, 31779
912-294-3661
Circulation: 3,381
Pub. Day: Wed.

PEMBROKE (Bryan

County)
Bryan County Times
109-A N. Main St., 31321
912-653-4570
Circulation: 1,650
Pub. Day: Wed.

PERRY (Houston County)
**The Houston Home
Journal**
1010 Carroll Lane, 31069
912-987-1823
Circulation: 4,197
Pub. Day: Thurs.

PHENIX CITY, AL
(Stewart County)
**The Stewart-Webster
Journal**
P.O. Box 1267, 36867
205-298-0679
Circulation: 1,765
Pub. Day: Thurs.

QUITMAN (Brooks
County)
The Quitman Free Press
P.O. Box 72, 31643
912-263-4615
Circulation: 3,147
Pub. Day: Wed.

REIDSVILLE (Tattnall
County)
The Tattnall Journal
P.O. Box 278, 30453
912-557-6761
Circulation: 3,255
Pub. Day: Thurs.

RINGGOLD (Catoosa
County)
The Catoosa County News
P.O. Box 40, 30736
404-935-2621
Circulation: 3,851
Pub. Day: Wed.

ROBERTA (Crawford
County)
The Georgia Post
P.O. Box 860, 31078-0860
912-836-3195
Circulation: 1,404
Pub. Day: Thurs.

ROCKMART (Polk
County)

The Rockmart Journal
P.O. Box 609, 30153
404-684-7811
Circulation: 3,010
Pub. Day: Wed.

ROYSTON (Franklin
County)
The News Leader
P.O. Box 6, 30662
404-245-7351
Circulation: 1,827
Pub. Day: Thurs.

ST. MARYS (Camden
County)
Camden County Tribune
P.O. Box 470, 31558
912-882-4927
Circulation: 3,167
Pub. Day: Thurs.

ST. SIMONS ISLAND
(Glynn County)
The Islander
P.O. Box 539, 31522
912-264-6751
Circulation: 2,516
Pub. Day: Mon.

SANDERSVILLE
(Washington County)
The Sandersville Progress
P.O. Box 431, 31082
912-552-3161
Circulation: 4,517
Pub. Day: Thurs.

SOPERTON (Treutlen
County)
The Soperton News
P.O. Box 537, 30457
912-529-6624
Circulation: 2,818
Pub. Day: Wed.

SPARTA (Hancock County)
The Sparta Ishmaelite
P.O. Box 306, Warrenton,
30828
404-444-5330
Circulation: 1,511
Pub. Day: Thurs.

SPRINGFIELD
(Effingham County)
The Herald
P.O. Box 247, 31329

912-754-6123
Circulation: 4,260
Pub. Day: Wed.

STATESBORO (Bulloch
County)
Southern Beacon
P.O. Box 888, 30458
912-764-9031
Circulation: 2,000
Pub. Day: Wed.

SWAINSBORO (Emanuel
County)
The Blade
P.O. Box 938, 30401
912-237-9971
Circulation: 5,633
Pub. Day: Wed.

SYLVANIA (Screven
County)
The Sylvania Telephone
P.O. Box 10, 30467
912-564-2045
Circulation: 3,813
Pub. Day: Thurs.

SYLVESTER (Worth
County)
The Sylvester Local News
P.O. Box 387, 31791
912-776-7713
Circulation: 3,689
Pub. Day: Wed.

TALBOTTON (Talbot
County)
Talbotton New Era
P.O. Box 248, 31827
404-846-3188
Circulation: 921
Pub. Day: Thurs.

THOMASTON (Upson
County)
The Thomaston Times
P.O. Box 430, 30286
404-647-5414
Circulation: 6,315
Pub. Days: Mon. & Wed.

THOMSON (Dade
County)
The McDuffie Progress
P.O. Box 1090, 30824
404-595-1601

Circulation: 3,725
Pub. Day: Wed.

TRENTON (Dade County)
Dade County Sentinel
P.O. Box 277, 30752
404-657-6182
Circulation: 5,082
Pub. Day: Wed.

VIDALIA (Toombs
County)
The Vidalia Advance
P.O. Box 669, 30474
912-537-3131
Circulation: 4,331
Pub. Day: Thurs.

VIENNA (Dooly County)
Vienna News-Observer
P.O. Box 186, 31092
912-268-2096
Circulation: 2,115
Pub. Day: Thurs.

WARRENTON (Warren
County)
The Warrenton Clipper
P.O. Box 306, 30828
404-465-3395
Circulation: 1,599
Pub. Day: Fri.

WASHINGTON (Wilkes
County)
The News-Reporter
P.O. Box 340, 30673
404-678-2636
Circulation: 4,660
Pub. Day: Thurs.

WATKINSVILLE (Oconee
County)
The Oconee Enterprise
P.O. Box 535, 30677
404-769-5175
Circulation: 2,490
Pub. Day: Thurs.

WAYNESBORO (Burke
County)
The True Citizen
620 Academy Ave., 30830
404-554-2111
Circulation: 4,495
Pub. Days: Mon. & Thurs.

WINDER (Barrow County)

The Winder News
P.O. Drawer C, 30680
404-867-7557
Circulation: 5,436
Pub. Day: Wed.

WRENS (Jefferson County)
The Jefferson Reporter
P.O. Box 277, 30833
404-547-6629

Circulation: 1,885
Pub. Days: Wed. & Mon.

WRIGHTSVILLE
(Johnson County)
The Wrightsville Headlight
P.O. Box 290, 31096
912-864-3528
Circulation: 1,800
Pub. Day: Thurs.

ZEBULON (Pike County)
Pike County Journal &
Reporter
P.O. Box 789, 30295
404-567-3446
Circulation: 2,185
Pub. Day: Wed.

OCCUPATIONS (See chart beginning on the next page.)

PEANUTS

Peanuts represent Georgia's number one agricultural product. The 1984 crop was a bin-buster, with a record setting production of 2.16 billion pounds, with a record value of $521 million. Peanuts alone accounted for one-third of the total value of all crops in 1984. Georgia remains unchallenged as the nation's leading peanut producing state.

Below are a few tantalizing recipes using peanuts or peanut butter in them. Try them today and get set for a pleasant, tasty surprise.

Cream of Peanut Butter Soup

1/2 cup butter or margarine
1 tablespoon onion, minced
1 tablespoon all-purpose flour

1 cup peanut butter
1 quart chicken stock
Salt and pepper to taste
1 cup cream

Melt butter or margarine, add onion and simmer until tender, but not brown. Add flour and peanut butter and stir to a smooth paste. Add stock gradually, season and cook 20 minutes in a double boiler, stirring constantly until thickened. Strain and add cream.

Makes 8 to 10 servings.

Waldorf Salad

2 cups diced apple
1/2 cup raisins
1/2 cup diced celery
1/2 cup chopped salted peanuts

Toss ingredients together. Serve on a bed of lettuce with dressing.

Makes 4 servings.

DRESSING:
1/4 cup creamy peanut butter
1/4 cup honey
1/2 cup mayonnaise

Blend ingredients. Serve over Waldorf Salad.

(Recipes continued on page 294.)

289

	Executive, Admin'tive, Managerial	Professional Specialties	Technicians & Related Support	Sales	Clerical	Farming, Fishing, Forestry	Precision Production, Craft/Repair	Machine Operators, Assemblers, Inspectors	Trans. and Mat'l Moving	Handlers, Equipment, Cleaners Helpers Laborers	Household Occupations	Protective Services	Other Service Occupations
Appling	288	438	113	406	494	737	1,009	1,092	382	402	55	63	441
Atkinson	72	136	8	105	207	407	249	379	184	191	11	18	115
Bacon	238	250	64	253	436	451	591	569	214	174	35	36	340
Baker	52	89	44	54	154	429	125	240	39	66	19	4	142
Baldwin	1,036	2,095	801	1,226	1,651	161	1,687	1,144	506	408	130	471	2,287
Banks	244	261	61	245	410	390	506	970	270	280	8	60	212
Barrow	579	541	175	755	1,055	226	1,450	2,359	615	610	64	94	731
Bartow	1,158	1,098	303	1,299	2,420	462	2,797	4,385	1,278	1,108	113	172	1,456
Ben Hill	311	507	122	663	669	354	736	1,184	457	318	89	70	465
Berrien	345	412	87	532	648	652	704	1,206	353	307	55	43	377
Bibb	6,591	7,237	1,834	7,369	10,668	478	7,920	4,552	2,688	3,714	932	1,226	6,441
Bleckley	296	349	155	314	719	379	551	702	220	112	84	37	389
Brantley	158	217	29	307	362	247	650	532	263	260	3	25	222
Brooks	306	436	78	476	534	850	625	719	267	319	54	64	690
Bryan	299	232	44	320	500	135	692	401	329	286	20	49	388
Bulloch	1,382	1,927	314	1,481	2,008	1,134	1,854	1,319	621	714	177	169	1,719
Burke	331	699	126	509	801	744	829	1,274	305	580	116	144	651
Butts	260	379	103	361	671	144	814	1,221	213	291	122	120	458
Calhoun	128	169	41	84	180	353	194	375	149	173	63	43	141
Camden	444	382	83	472	651	110	716	732	375	353	20	102	621
Candler	224	283	88	364	231	365	365	371	118	142	34	28	276
Carroll	1,816	2,509	591	2,130	3,530	449	3,637	4,162	1,192	1,314	210	234	2,155
Catoosa	1,404	1,282	454	1,834	2,933	131	2,580	2,572	1,264	762	22	159	1,128
Charlton	155	195	66	151	303	130	325	334	256	179	38	66	352
Chatham	8,061	10,034	2,315	8,969	12,790	704	11,008	4,716	4,847	4,605	1,259	1,557	8,985
Chattahoochee	101	157	27	202	288	18	100	112	90	96	9	19	216
Chattooga	345	606	168	579	797	164	1,263	3,035	518	676	52	49	750
Cherokee	2,016	1,889	654	2,246	3,738	729	4,455	3,022	1,208	1,197	47	397	1,737
Clarke	3,036	6,831	1,914	3,238	5,082	568	2,735	2,792	1,054	1,215	396	446	3,639
Clay	54	126	39	54	119	175	85	150	62	108	19	6	141
Clayton	7,132	5,148	2,104	7,675	17,130	281	11,728	4,335	4,681	4,379	173	1,523	6,101
Clinch	160	267	21	155	275	161	217	635	308	232	51	49	178
Cobb	23,950	17,965	5,306	20,912	31,596	982	19,807	8,085	4,781	5,312	458	1,895	12,195
Coffee	865	859	146	969	1,351	1,399	1,166	1,132	644	682	76	155	780
Colquitt	1,023	1,206	286	1,635	1,853	1,500	1,827	2,325	621	913	151	227	1,125
Columbia	1,834	2,169	576	1,779	2,642	209	2,545	1,463	682	703	134	245	1,496
Cook	377	381	110	308	640	545	679	919	347	390	49	66	578

County													
Coweta	1,217	1,611	508	1,187	2,210	269	2,655	2,897	954	1,156	324	317	1,270
Crawford	189	236	83	230	409	161	527	611	174	147	42	30	199
Crisp	619	623	267	627	978	570	834	1,055	404	460	185	81	912
Dade	216	432	82	260	590	130	787	1,050	400	276	29	8	588
Dawson	137	134	3	133	197	191	381	486	99	129	0	38	182
Decatur	832	927	326	702	1,155	836	1,229	1,718	654	538	96	134	960
DeKalb	37,521	36,793	9,028	31,336	53,990	1,446	21,846	12,664	7,765	8,793	1,612	2,817	22,593
Dodge	398	630	142	487	840	411	791	1,163	250	357	52	72	479
Dooly	213	374	67	217	373	624	363	678	184	294	115	54	478
Dougherty	4,141	4,629	1,268	4,567	6,634	677	5,223	4,001	1,939	2,175	510	664	4,212
Douglas	2,492	1,781	670	2,217	4,604	213	4,390	2,303	1,551	1,368	76	468	2,023
Early	369	433	71	411	523	727	559	576	295	305	135	47	461
Echols	47	54	4	33	87	107	124	156	65	76	4	9	56
Effingham	248	476	162	516	817	316	1,581	888	717	462	43	96	479
Elbert	566	643	153	618	1,020	220	1,301	1,691	491	582	94	86	610
Emanuel	449	601	154	698	818	666	997	1,726	469	419	50	57	596
Evans	279	228	66	320	358	345	402	509	230	207	64	44	371
Fannin	355	441	99	370	479	184	883	944	400	384	8	48	409
Fayette	1,712	1,483	701	1,501	2,854	155	2,059	711	633	621	65	145	919
Floyd	2,783	3,510	982	3,555	5,217	407	4,759	5,710	1,662	1,810	318	547	3,808
Forsyth	1,062	936	278	1,220	1,984	524	2,290	1,602	1,005	708	55	123	919
Franklin	390	515	92	425	575	395	1,007	1,603	365	376	31	59	431
Fulton	33,022	35,455	7,871	29,778	50,745	1,885	21,028	15,852	10,197	12,982	3,793	3,907	32,396
Gilmer	254	359	70	366	409	275	687	978	325	280	8	45	307
Glascock	59	42	22	42	101	101	116	220	56	91	10	9	73
Glynn	2,430	2,648	658	2,875	3,463	581	3,388	1,891	1,100	1,094	310	541	3,640
Gordon	876	855	254	1,086	1,755	433	1,562	3,637	836	734	52	248	904
Grady	466	553	237	636	791	1,253	1,111	1,227	397	742	85	93	581
Greene	225	256	17	167	406	387	568	1,075	286	426	90	35	396
Gwinnett	12,861	8,900	2,812	10,713	17,942	609	11,353	6,727	2,765	2,678	305	1,028	5,281
Habersham	691	907	169	749	1,167	491	1,614	2,340	487	854	28	122	839
Hall	3,213	3,182	776	3,449	4,554	1,268	5,148	5,834	1,749	2,487	148	495	2,857
Hancock	86	331	108	146	278	176	356	640	189	229	59	72	558
Haralson	469	494	225	625	941	125	1,222	1,953	455	449	63	111	637
Harris	659	513	107	624	804	345	951	871	380	425	78	141	666
Hart	462	585	128	573	672	258	1,182	2,385	262	419	104	63	589
Heard	97	234	60	179	245	127	440	599	199	144	7	44	206
Henry	1,474	1,113	457	1,594	3,238	115	2,958	1,673	983	977	203	244	1,244
Houston	3,187	3,418	1,229	3,044	5,317	590	4,920	2,226	952	1,607	225	511	3,107
Irwin	198	220	67	255	327	687	408	505	201	186	44	24	310
Jackson	778	828	135	741	1,449	710	1,664	2,273	533	705	61	166	1,128
Jasper	263	276	80	184	278	170	369	553	151	259	47	36	266
Jeff Davis	381	357	112	323	537	422	654	1,033	204	267	42	35	431

	Executive, Admin'tive, Managerial	Professional Specialties	Technicians & Related Support	Sales	Clerical	Farming, Fishing, Forestry	Precision Production, Craft/Repair	Machine Operators, Assemblers, Inspectors	Trans. and Mat'l Moving	Handlers, Equipment, Cleaners Helpers Laborers	Household Occupations	Protective Services	Other Service Occupations
Jefferson	339	510	85	425	712	619	768	1,605	389	419	161	42	660
Jenkins	166	179	54	281	263	422	430	696	239	189	60	34	190
Johnson	121	177	88	195	295	196	585	966	205	196	53	38	261
Jones	593	677	171	708	1,133	164	1,019	790	416	437	42	166	562
Lamar	372	363	176	231	590	145	699	1,110	262	301	99	81	440
Lanier	119	145	75	125	240	203	304	308	82	147	21	21	143
Laurens	1,188	1,406	311	1,350	1,884	667	2,003	2,719	703	695	178	129	1,469
Lee	494	430	101	544	856	383	790	609	152	287	40	78	391
Liberty	612	766	144	935	1,087	205	1,001	592	404	384	99	135	1,115
Lincoln	141	253	46	156	257	171	420	734	212	186	33	12	190
Long	90	157	44	90	205	130	260	152	109	112	5	35	214
Lowndes	2,575	2,890	614	3,308	3,846	885	3,144	3,035	1,231	1,490	279	491	3,402
Lumpkin	247	350	69	169	435	409	677	696	256	272	6	41	575
Macon	317	411	80	232	603	518	564	780	299	389	113	88	530
Madison	506	458	164	548	1,072	329	1,356	1,486	519	416	43	95	651
Marion	115	105	17	98	183	243	213	310	108	188	28	15	252
McDuffie	540	634	136	739	940	251	1,191	1,252	463	450	89	105	688
McIntosh	235	210	39	205	242	260	360	410	230	217	21	55	301
Meriwether	468	622	160	464	901	275	1,065	1,996	608	716	108	60	802
Miller	150	206	75	230	318	595	325	466	108	89	48	36	255
Mitchell	498	488	195	510	921	1,059	1,059	1,648	342	599	125	54	709
Monroe	472	544	82	510	809	299	823	1,201	347	385	160	136	629
Montgomery	155	208	44	188	291	279	269	471	198	148	36	41	219
Morgan	272	374	73	399	536	443	445	878	365	259	120	43	534
Murray	573	482	85	502	1,184	243	1,284	2,868	668	369	0	69	403
Muscogee	6,832	7,170	1,803	7,565	10,235	386	7,105	6,218	2,609	2,900	926	1,349	7,205
Newton	843	1,038	273	1,339	2,125	207	2,251	3,004	1,000	1,010	143	184	1,248
Oconee	538	760	267	661	1,044	305	652	744	259	226	37	70	405
Oglethorpe	263	273	100	166	411	236	688	924	218	193	67	30	246
Paulding	677	688	281	849	1,651	185	2,185	1,825	608	553	20	232	944
Peach	492	992	211	462	999	482	974	1,002	308	466	87	86	710
Pickens	285	335	100	364	426	118	844	1,113	329	373	16	58	449
Pierce	274	288	85	406	501	533	839	602	282	227	52	48	425
Pike	251	273	184	196	491	288	476	848	165	300	30	62	252
Polk	804	876	280	988	1,435	176	1,826	3,264	929	894	141	278	1,065
Pulaski	228	335	117	232	421	333	490	589	118	184	32	42	337
Putnam	253	387	109	321	478	316	545	1,033	206	265	67	146	301

County													
Quitman	43	52	13	58	65	103	85	131	42	81	9	11	75
Rabun	326	363	108	373	469	133	652	1,047	219	236	28	46	465
Randolph	187	273	15	249	330	521	316	494	170	220	149	56	351
Richmond	5,805	9,510	2,899	6,715	10,794	595	8,013	6,030	2,834	3,963	845	1,284	9,831
Rockdale	1,893	1,453	453	1,857	3,073	106	2,955	1,584	968	794	41	304	1,137
Schley	55	76	37	105	163	106	188	193	84	67	27	22	147
Screven	266	432	145	403	634	557	717	1,210	281	231	100	25	438
Seminole	262	265	96	358	392	435	370	447	156	266	45	83	348
Spalding	1,445	1,635	527	1,981	2,941	335	2,761	3,935	951	1,353	299	347	1,666
Stephens	597	808	249	667	1,156	134	1,441	2,196	410	515	46	117	788
Stewart	135	154	29	115	184	237	170	310	80	183	89	32	182
Sumter	1,093	1,498	299	855	1,807	821	1,541	1,569	559	598	247	133	1,187
Talbot	103	232	44	125	232	195	308	622	239	224	54	14	193
Taliaferro	42	57	8	44	63	46	72	205	49	52	7	1	61
Tattnall	324	530	133	415	754	801	630	805	294	307	45	318	534
Taylor	190	215	50	165	308	336	428	458	199	296	84	24	222
Telfair	276	418	91	320	422	458	534	789	284	239	35	73	357
Terrell	238	389	24	377	476	445	501	685	351	327	130	55	374
Thomas	1,457	1,652	452	1,233	1,963	1,127	1,893	1,859	781	1,028	275	199	1,611
Tift	1,086	1,355	505	1,235	1,900	1,043	1,704	1,681	683	788	209	100	1,372
Toombs	623	824	203	839	1,190	535	1,139	1,284	689	420	77	200	718
Towns	160	233	41	124	162	65	401	287	149	108	0	27	235
Treutlen	115	122	25	118	261	182	306	452	123	115	23	16	189
Troup	1,868	1,774	506	1,765	2,253	388	2,861	4,661	921	1,284	413	325	1,866
Turner	317	261	65	306	437	317	514	673	264	115	73	50	375
Twiggs	140	171	121	179	457	89	653	418	349	365	47	35	240
Union	173	310	56	211	306	368	536	546	202	245	19	42	341
Upson	797	853	255	717	1,198	231	1,560	3,123	387	705	155	180	1,115
Walker	1,574	1,385	462	2,238	2,914	331	3,702	4,808	1,556	1,485	85	387	1,756
Walton	823	709	243	1,004	1,613	374	2,519	2,849	757	910	122	159	963
Ware	1,293	1,432	299	1,559	1,824	506	2,227	1,232	965	765	160	217	1,285
Warren	104	162	28	118	196	192	302	479	143	167	52	12	196
Washington	455	695	262	440	638	450	1,033	1,323	468	433	162	50	671
Wayne	492	628	237	584	855	406	1,244	1,062	531	540	79	153	831
Webster	54	35	9	34	88	150	98	142	84	54	28	8	63
Wheeler	103	174	49	96	188	296	186	414	139	84	16	22	164
White	245	389	112	404	517	317	704	675	251	261	20	76	361
Whitfield	3,081	2,104	556	2,656	4,868	444	3,909	7,600	2,058	1,461	133	447	2,517
Wilcox	105	283	52	243	262	432	404	424	160	144	52	17	210
Wilkes	323	371	101	432	436	310	492	904	279	296	73	70	422
Wilkinson	251	348	267	227	355	104	726	588	367	265	61	17	459
Worth	471	562	103	532	907	836	972	1,033	433	448	114	75	501
Georgia	237,945	250,429	67,417	239,377	382,738	66,750	297,604	274,920	112,669	122,618	23,331	34,559	225,478

293

Strawberry Dips

½ cup creamy peanut butter
2 ounces milk chocolate, melted

2 tablespoons prepared, whipped topping
14 large, fresh strawberries
3 ounces semi-sweet chocolate, melted

In a medium bowl, combine peanut butter, milk chocolate and whipped topping; mix well. Slice strawberries in half lengthwise. Spread peanut butter mixture on half of sliced strawberries. Top with remaining strawberry halves. Refrigerate until filling is set. Dip each filled strawberry into melted semi-sweet chocolate coating only half the berry. Refrigerate until ready to serve.

Makes 14 filled strawberries.

Peanut-Banana Shake

1 medium banana
½ cup creamy peanut butter
1 cup skim milk

2 tablespoons honey
½ teaspoon cinnamon
1 cup club soda

Cut the banana into thin slices and freeze. When banana slices are frozen, place bananas in blender container and add peanut butter, milk, honey and cinnamon. Blend on medium speed until well mixed. Before serving, blend in club soda.

Makes 3 (8-ounce each) servings.

Orange Peanutwich

½ orange
1 English muffin, split
⅓ cup crunchy peanut butter

1 teaspoon honey
¼ teaspoon grated orange rind

Cut peel and all white membrane from orange half. Cut into two slices. Toast English muffin. Spread peanut butter on each English muffin half. Top with an orange slice. In a small saucepan, heat honey and orange rind. Drizzle over orange slices on muffins.

Makes 2 servings.

Oriental Chicken

2 chicken breasts, boned and skinned
½ cup orange juice
1 tablespoon soy sauce
1 tablespoon sherry
1 tablespoon corn starch

¼ teaspoon red pepper flakes
2 tablespoons peanut oil
1 cup scallions, cut into 2-inch pieces
½ cup salted peanuts
Hot cooked rice

Cut chicken into 1-inch pieces. In a medium bowl, combine orange juice, soy sauce, sherry, corn starch, pepper flakes and ginger; mix well. Add chicken; let stand 30 minutes. Heat oil in skillet. Add chicken with marinade and stir-fry over high heat 2–3 minutes. Remove chicken. Add scallions and peanuts; stir-fry 1 minute. Return chicken to skillet; cook 1 minute. Serve over hot cooked rice.

Makes 4 servings.

Peanut Pie

3 eggs
1/2 cup sugar
1 1/2 cup dark corn syrup
1/4 cup butter, melted

1/4 teaspoon salt
1/2 teaspoon vanilla
1 1/2 cup chopped, roasted peanuts
9" unbaked pie shell

Beat eggs until foamy. Add sugar, syrup, butter, salt and vanilla. Continue to beat until thoroughly blended. Stir in peanuts. Pour into unbaked pie shell. Bake in preheated 375 °F. oven for 45 minutes. Delicious served warm or cold, may be garnished with whipped cream or ice cream.

Makes a 9" pie.

Chili Nuts

1 tablespoon peanut oil
1 egg white
2 teaspoons chili powder
1 teaspoon ground cumin

1 teaspoon garlic salt
1/8 teaspoon Tabasco sauce
1 pound unsalted dry roasted peanuts

Grease bottom of a 15 1/2x10 1/2-inch jelly roll pan or baking sheet with peanut oil. In medium bowl, beat egg white until foamy. Fold in chili powder, cumin, garlic salt and Tabasco sauce. Add peanuts; stir to coat evenly. Spread peanuts in pan. Bake in a 325 °F. oven for 20 minutes. Remove from oven; break up pieces if necessary. Store in airtight container.

Makes 1 pound.

Nuts and Bolts Mix

2 packages (6 ounces each) dried apricots,
    chopped
1/2 cup vacuum packed wheat germ

2 cups salted peanuts
1 cup raisins
1 cup toasted flaked coconut

In a medium bowl, combine apricots and wheat germ; toss well. Stir in peanuts, raisins and coconut. Store in airtight container. Eat as a snack, pack in small plastic bags for toting, spoon into plain yogurt, or add to cereal and milk for breakfast.

Makes 6 cups.

POPULATION

The following charts provide information on farm, rural, and urban population in Georgia; population by age groups; comparison of Georgia cities with others in the Southeast, and Georgia population figures every ten years since 1790.

FARM, RURAL, URBAN POPULATION: 1980

County	Urban[1]	Rural Nonfarm	Rural[2] Farm	Total Population
Appling	3,586	10,001	1,978	15,565
Atkinson	0	5,208	933	6,141
Bacon	3,819	3,821	1,739	9,379
Baker	0	3,109	699	3,808
Baldwin	21,153	13,171	362	34,686
Banks	0	7,929	773	8,702
Barrow	6,705	13,927	722	21,354
Bartow	9,508	30,386	866	40,760
Ben Hill	10,187	5,313	500	16,000
Berrien	4,808	7,045	1,672	13,525
Bibb	127,792	22,129	335	150,256
Bleckley	5,121	4,926	720	10,767
Brantley	0	7,818	883	8,701
Brooks	5,188	8,590	1,477	15,255
Bryan	0	10,034	141	10,175
Bulloch	14,866	18,707	2,212	35,785
Burke	5,760	12,234	1,355	19,349
Butts	4,133	9,129	403	13,665
Calhoun	0	5,343	374	5,717
Camden	3,596	9,651	124	13,371
Candler	3,520	3,194	804	7,518
Carroll	17,492	37,724	1,130	56,346
Catoosa	18,433	18,027	531	36,991
Charlton	0	7,043	300	7,343
Chatham	189,373	12,792	61	202,226
Chattahoochee	15,074	6,645	13	21,732
Chattooga	4,843	16,395	618	21,856
Cherokee	15,166	35,204	1,329	51,699
Clarke	62,397	12,012	89	74,498
Clay	0	3,333	220	3,553
Clayton	141,291	8,934	132	150,357
Clinch	3,104	3,378	178	6,660
Cobb	271,109	26,478	131	297,718
Coffee	10,980	12,795	3,119	26,894
Colquitt	15,703	16,776	2,897	35,376
Columbia	23,712	16,045	361	40,118
Cook	5,592	6,723	1,175	13,490
Coweta	11,499	27,088	681	39,268

County	Urban[1]	Rural Nonfarm	Rural[2] Farm	Total Population
Crawford	0	7,190	494	7,684
Crisp	10,914	7,534	1,041	19,489
Dade	0	11,966	352	12,318
Dawson	0	4,623	151	4,774
Decatur	10,532	13,087	1,876	25,495
DeKalb	470,862	12,076	86	483,024
Dodge	5,330	10,200	1,425	16,955
Dooly	2,785	7,114	927	10,826
Dougherty	87,181	13,143	394	100,718
Douglas	37,420	16,996	157	54,573
Early	5,855	5,956	1,347	13,158
Echols	0	2,027	270	2,297
Effingham	0	17,810	517	18,327
Elbert	5,686	12,449	623	18,758
Emanuel	7,552	11,482	1,761	20,795
Evans	2,702	5,163	563	8,428
Fannin	0	14,463	285	14,748
Fayette	10,297	18,458	288	29,043
Floyd	51,216	27,879	705	79,800
Forsyth	0	26,556	1,402	27,958
Franklin	0	13,797	1,388	15,185
Fulton	565,341	24,325	238	589,904
Gilmer	0	10,421	689	11,110
Glascock	0	2,133	249	2,382
Glynn	30,360	24,564	57	54,981
Gordon	5,563	23,411	1,096	30,070
Grady	8,752	8,713	2,380	19,845
Greene	2,878	8,037	476	11,391
Gwinnett	116,611	49,464	828	166,903
Habersham	3,203	21,148	669	25,020
Hall	18,058	55,761	1,830	75,649
Hancock	0	9,279	187	9,466
Haralson	6,589	11,406	427	18,422
Harris	924	14,200	340	15,464
Hart	4,855	12,815	915	18,585
Heard	0	6,242	278	6,520
Henry	6,034	29,745	530	36,309
Houston	64,118	12,810	677	77,605
Irwin	3,436	3,932	1,620	8,988
Jackson	4,092	19,832	1,419	25,343
Jasper	0	6,962	591	7,553
Jeff Davis	4,249	6,142	1,082	11,473
Jefferson	2,823	14,497	1,083	18,403
Jenkins	3,988	3,868	985	8,841
Johnson	2,526	5,288	846	8,660

POPULATION

County	Urban[1]	Rural Nonfarm	Rural[2] Farm	Total Population
Jones	3,018	13,125	436	16,579
Lamar	4,887	6,904	424	12,215
Lanier	2,647	2,492	515	5,654
Laurens	19,000	15,838	2,152	36,990
Lee	1,554	9,524	606	11,684
Liberty	26,326	11,179	78	37,583
Lincoln	0	6,337	379	6,716
Long	0	4,277	247	4,524
Lowndes	37,533	29,276	1,163	67,972
Lumpkin	2,844	7,362	556	10,762
Macon	4,830	8,424	749	14,003
Madison	0	16,402	1,345	17,747
Marion	0	4,778	519	5,297
McDuffie	7,001	11,174	371	18,546
McIntosh	0	8,016	30	8,046
Meriwether	4,626	16,010	593	21,229
Miller	0	5,760	1,278	7,038
Mitchell	9,739	9,759	1,616	21,114
Monroe	4,624	9,591	395	14,610
Montgomery	0	6,244	767	7,011
Morgan	2,907	7,437	1,228	11,572
Murray	0	19,040	645	19,685
Muscogee	167,507	2,538	63	170,108
Newton	10,586	23,433	470	34,489
Oconee	418	11,382	627	12,427
Oglethorpe	0	8,079	850	8,929
Paulding	2,508	23,171	431	26,110
Peach	9,000	9,759	392	19,151
Pickens	0	11,335	317	11,652
Pierce	3,222	7,308	1,367	11,897
Pike	0	8,233	704	8,937
Polk	12,244	19,620	522	32,386
Pulaski	4,357	3,836	757	8,950
Putnam	4,833	4,988	474	10,295
Quitman	0	2,242	115	2,357
Rabun	0	10,324	142	10,466
Randolph	4,340	4,518	741	9,599
Richmond	165,974	15,451	204	181,629
Rockdale	11,284	25,303	160	36,747
Schley	0	3,086	347	3,433
Screven	3,352	9,293	1,398	14,043
Seminole	3,320	4,797	940	9,057
Spalding	24,459	23,045	395	47,899
Stephens	9,104	12,372	287	21,763
Stewart	0	5,720	176	5,896

County	Urban[1]	Rural Nonfarm	Rural[2] Farm	Total Population
Sumter	16,120	11,945	1,295	29,360
Talbot	165	6,074	297	6,536
Taliaferro	0	1,870	162	2,032
Tattnall	4,144	11,890	2,100	18,134
Taylor	0	7,454	448	7,902
Telfair	3,388	6,804	1,253	11,445
Terrell	5,647	5,374	996	12,017
Thomas	18,463	17,955	1,680	38,098
Tift	13,749	17,451	1,662	32,862
Toombs	14,591	6,513	1,488	22,592
Towns	0	5,526	112	5,638
Treutlen	2,981	2,710	396	6,087
Troup	30,837	18,816	350	50,003
Turner	4,766	3,728	1,016	9,510
Twiggs	0	9,084	270	9,354
Union	0	8,857	533	9,390
Upson	12,298	13,350	350	25,998
Walker	30,815	25,015	640	56,470
Walton	11,445	18,703	1,063	31,211
Ware	22,910	13,369	901	37,180
Warren	0	6,111	472	6,583
Washington	6,068	11,962	812	18,842
Wayne	9,365	10,402	983	20,750
Webster	0	1,862	479	2,341
Wheeler	0	4,555	600	5,155
White	0	9,586	534	10,120
Whitfield	20,939	44,122	728	65,789
Wilcox	0	6,876	806	7,682
Wilkes	4,662	5,680	609	10,951
Wilkinson	2,768	7,446	154	10,368
Worth	5,860	9,856	2,348	18,064
Georgia	3,408,267	1,933,749	121,089	5,463,105

[1]Urban areas are places with 2500 or more inhabitants.

[2]A farm is a place with $1000 or more in sales of crops, livestock, or other farm products during the preceding calendar year.

POPULATION BY AGE: 1980

County	0–5 Years	6–18 Years	19–34 Years	35–64 Years	65+ Years
Appling	1,635	3,977	3,875	4,471	1,607
Atkinson	636	1,598	1,432	1,802	673
Bacon	1,036	2,282	2,229	2,814	1,018
Baker	416	940	905	1,063	484
Baldwin	2,776	7,791	10,307	10,133	3,679
Banks	801	1,921	2,229	2,735	1,016
Barrow	2,001	4,967	5,375	6,523	2,488

POPULATION

County	0–5 Years	6–18 Years	19–34 Years	35–64 Years	65+ Years
Bartow	3,661	9,971	10,234	12,885	4,009
Ben Hill	1,655	3,484	3,902	4,730	2,229
Berrien	1,243	3,197	3,295	4,242	1,548
Bibb	13,383	33,577	41,044	46,104	16,148
Bleckley	880	2,548	2,797	3,300	1,242
Brantley	892	2,288	2,207	2,519	795
Brooks	1,518	3,906	3,298	4,278	2,255
Bryan	1,190	2,575	2,698	2,960	752
Bulloch	2,949	8,270	11,942	9,108	3,516
Burke	2,212	4,968	4,715	5,167	2,287
Butts	1,223	3,126	3,918	3,928	1,470
Calhoun	553	1,441	1,282	1,597	844
Camden	1,376	3,361	3,584	3,938	1,112
Candler	654	1,715	1,671	2,255	1,223
Carroll	4,947	13,415	15,761	16,313	5,910
Catoosa	3,378	8,698	9,765	12,073	3,077
Charlton	776	2,028	1,704	2,094	741
Chatham	19,545	44,338	57,346	59,934	21,063
Chattahoochee	1,908	5,427	12,022	2,198	177
Chattooga	1,889	4,843	5,123	7,258	2,713
Cherokee	5,223	12,384	15,120	14,839	4,133
Clarke	5,430	13,306	33,161	16,711	5,890
Clay	328	851	764	1,031	579
Clayton	14,853	37,097	47,380	44,506	6,521
Clinch	679	1,767	1,644	1,915	655
Cobb	25,340	66,098	94,606	95,369	16,305
Coffee	2,846	6,522	7,085	7,670	2,771
Colquitt	3,446	8,484	8,282	10,795	4,369
Columbia	4,228	9,999	11,745	12,124	2,022
Cook	1,327	3,430	3,099	4,014	1,620
Coweta	3,737	9,246	9,678	12,310	4,297
Crawford	728	2,001	1,933	2,263	759
Crisp	2,065	4,700	4,764	5,533	2,427
Dade	1,165	2,912	3,418	3,759	1,064
Dawson	420	1,104	1,233	1,513	504
Decatur	2,689	6,260	6,231	7,241	3,074
DeKalb	37,296	106,273	152,369	153,103	33,983
Dodge	1,504	4,168	3,836	5,201	2,246
Dooly	1,183	2,718	2,425	3,009	1,491
Dougherty	10,959	25,358	29,475	27,626	7,300
Douglas	5,656	14,053	15,334	16,082	3,448
Early	1,353	3,461	2,851	3,756	1,737
Echols	258	577	573	628	261
Effingham	1,896	4,692	4,619	5,551	1,569
Elbert	1,710	4,162	4,517	5,835	2,534
Emanuel	2,256	4,897	4,872	6,138	2,632
Evans	845	2,095	1,993	2,406	1,089
Fannin	1,096	3,008	3,244	5,168	2,232
Fayette	2,564	7,606	7,041	10,110	1,722
Floyd	6,307	17,473	20,490	26,020	9,510
Forsyth	2,617	6,655	7,513	8,820	2,353
Franklin	1,198	3,366	3,594	5,009	2,018
Fulton	48,259	121,738	183,852	174,599	61,456
Gilmer	929	2,393	2,669	3,669	1,450
Glascock	187	499	517	774	405
Glynn	4,836	12,400	14,266	17,351	6,128

300

County	0–5 Years	6–18 Years	19–34 Years	35–64 Years	65+ Years
Gordon	2,718	7,257	7,567	9,580	2,948
Grady	1,937	4,897	4,590	5,772	2,649
Greene	1,241	2,640	2,623	3,226	1,661
Gwinnett	16,841	39,503	51,928	50,068	8,563
Habersham	2,055	5,413	7,081	7,733	2,738
Hall	6,713	16,993	20,005	24,405	7,533
Hancock	945	2,605	2,201	2,514	1,201
Haralson	1,524	4,298	4,261	6,040	2,299
Harris	1,289	3,443	3,608	5,237	1,887
Hart	1,618	4,355	4,360	5,853	2,399
Heard	576	1,548	1,523	2,047	826
Henry	3,447	8,479	9,527	11,656	3,200
Houston	7,595	19,094	22,226	24,548	4,142
Irwin	826	2,191	1,933	2,773	1,265
Jackson	2,239	5,820	6,452	7,925	2,907
Jasper	756	1,683	1,873	2,223	1,018
Jeff Davis	1,145	2,846	2,922	3,411	1,149
Jefferson	1,850	4,649	4,358	5,028	2,518
Jenkins	846	2,169	2,160	2,606	1,060
Johnson	896	1,959	1,980	2,607	1,218
Jones	1,586	4,010	4,426	5,156	1,401
Lamar	1,069	2,918	2,967	3,726	1,535
Lanier	603	1,443	1,344	1,592	672
Laurens	3,557	8,596	8,844	11,376	4,617
Lee	1,191	3,035	3,435	3,266	757
Liberty	4,683	7,892	17,264	6,444	1,300
Lincoln	629	1,569	1,582	2,129	807
Long	548	1,060	1,345	1,185	386
Lowndes	6,761	15,992	20,891	18,405	5,923
Lumpkin	879	2,437	3,292	3,085	1,069
Macon	1,501	3,451	3,476	3,809	1,766
Madison	1,622	4,215	4,645	5,506	1,759
Marion	466	1,418	1,220	1,541	652
McDuffie	1,820	4,470	4,684	5,713	1,859
McIntosh	741	2,156	1,966	2,285	898
Meriwether	2,149	5,133	5,125	6,218	2,604
Miller	684	1,711	1,564	2,114	965
Mitchell	2,297	5,640	4,985	5,849	2,343
Monroe	1,191	3,391	3,809	4,447	1,772
Montgomery	659	1,569	2,052	1,886	845
Morgan	1,108	2,925	2,812	3,270	1,457
Murray	1,961	5,011	5,330	5,865	1,518
Muscogee	15,998	38,126	50,387	50,453	15,144
Newton	3,244	8,687	8,605	10,376	3,577
Oconee	1,154	2,871	3,699	3,646	1,057
Oglethorpe	771	2,220	2,127	2,749	1,062
Paulding	2,543	6,382	7,088	7,825	2,272
Peach	1,840	4,751	5,359	5,511	1,690
Pickens	983	2,555	2,829	3,762	1,523
Pierce	1,213	2,939	2,903	3,554	1,288
Pike	826	2,118	2,062	2,871	1,060
Polk	2,715	7,391	7,523	10,461	4,296
Pulaski	809	2,120	2,013	2,782	1,226
Putnam	898	2,398	2,558	3,265	1,176
Quitman	204	599	497	718	339
Rabun	745	2,163	2,444	3,557	1,557

POPULATION

County	0–5 Years	6–18 Years	19–34 Years	35–64 Years	65+ Years
Randolph	955	2,272	2,205	2,608	1,559
Richmond	16,559	40,586	58,524	50,717	15,243
Rockdale	3,420	9,395	9,325	12,023	2,584
Schley	323	948	778	958	426
Screven	1,421	3,211	3,481	4,079	1,851
Seminole	856	2,188	2,052	2,758	1,203
Spalding	4,578	11,308	11,906	14,908	5,199
Stephens	1,859	4,676	5,531	6,894	2,803
Stewart	550	1,531	1,268	1,714	833
Sumter	2,792	7,100	8,058	7,746	3,664
Talbot	605	1,599	1,602	1,867	863
Taliaferro	169	432	409	596	426
Tattnall	1,622	3,786	5,128	5,463	2,135
Taylor	666	1,969	1,817	2,422	1,028
Telfair	1,122	2,580	2,618	3,403	1,722
Terrell	1,273	3,014	2,857	3,305	1,568
Thomas	3,540	9,244	9,201	11,502	4,611
Tift	3,316	7,973	9,094	9,187	3,292
Toombs	2,327	5,491	5,396	6,856	2,522
Towns	329	1,161	1,319	1,878	951
Treutlen	604	1,487	1,403	1,749	844
Troup	4,629	10,978	12,921	14,910	6,565
Turner	1,086	2,343	2,202	2,707	1,172
Twiggs	996	2,374	2,295	2,710	979
Union	707	2,060	2,164	3,030	1,429
Upson	2,136	5,667	5,981	8,459	3,755
Walker	5,191	12,492	13,920	18,642	6,225
Walton	2,975	7,882	7,492	9,486	3,376
Ware	3,618	8,661	9,112	11,363	4,426
Warren	608	1,630	1,482	1,890	973
Washington	1,857	4,643	4,648	5,279	2,415
Wayne	2,035	4,918	5,250	6,361	2,186
Webster	219	591	555	691	285
Wheeler	524	1,276	1,112	1,483	760
White	797	2,206	2,512	3,298	1,307
Whitfield	6,254	15,450	17,867	20,566	5,652
Wilcox	713	1,721	1,722	2,350	1,176
Wilkes	960	2,402	2,528	3,474	1,587
Wilkinson	1,032	2,621	2,591	2,998	1,126
Worth	1,685	4,684	4,435	5,263	1,997
Georgia	498,159	1,254,159	1,555,944	1,638,112	516,731

POPULATION COMPARISON—LARGE CITIES IN THE SOUTHEAST

City	July 1, 1982			April 1, 1980		
	Population	Rank in United States	Rank in Southeast	Population	Rank in United States	Rank in Southeast
Memphis, TN	645,760	16	1	646,170	15	1
New Orleans, LA	564,561	20	2	557,927	22	2
Jacksonville, FL	556,370	23	3	540,920	23	3
Nashville-Davidson, TN	455,252	26	4	455,651	26	4
ATLANTA, GA	428,153	30	5	425,022	30	5
Miami, FL	382,726	34	6	346,865	41	6
Baton Rouge, LA	361,572	41	7	346,029	42	7
Charlotte, NC	323,972	48	8	315,474	49	8
Louisville, KY	293,531	50	9	298,694	50	9
Birmingham, AL	283,239	53	10	286,799	51	10
Virginia Beach, VA	282,588	54	11	262,199	57	13
Tampa, FL	276,413	55	12	271,599	54	11
Norfolk, VA	266,874	57	13	266,979	56	12
St. Petersburg, FL	241,214	61	14	238,647	59	14
Richmond, VA	218,237	66	15	219,214	65	15
Shreveport, LA	210,881	68	16	205,820	67	16
Lexington-Fayette, KY	207,668	69	17	204,165	68	17
Mobile, AL	204,586	70	18	200,452	71	19
Jackson, MS	204,195	71	19	202,895	70	18
Montgomery, AL	182,406	79	20	177,857	76	20
Knoxville, TN	175,298	84	21	175,045	77	21
COLUMBUS, GA	174,348	85	22	169,441	88	23
Chattanooga, TN	168,016	90	23	169,728	87	22
Little Rock, AR	167,974	91	24	167,602	89	24
Greensboro, NC	157,337	99	25	155,642	100	25
Hialeah, FL	154,713	103	26	145,254	108	28
Raleigh, NC	154,211	104	27	150,255	105	27
Fort Lauderdale, FL	153,755	106	28	153,279	101	26
Newport News, VA	151,240	108	29	144,903	109	29
SAVANNAH, GA	145,699	111	30	141,655	112	31
Huntsville, AL	145,421	112	31	142,513	111	30
Winston-Salem, NC	140,846	115	32	138,584	116	32
Orlando, FL	134,255	121	33	128,291	124	33
Hampton, VA	124,966	127	34	122,617	128	34
Hollywood, FL	122,051	131	35	121,323	129	35
Chesapeake, VA	119,749	135	36	114,486	137	37
MACON, GA	118,730	136	37	116,896	135	36
Portsmouth, VA	105,807	153	38	104,577	154	38
Alexandria, VA	104,276	159	39	103,217	160	39
Tallahassee, FL	102,579	166	40	101,482	166	40
Columbia, SC	101,457	169	41	101,202	168	41
Durham, NC	101,242	171	42	100,538	170	42
Roanoke, VA	100,187	175	43	100,220	171	43

POPULATION, PAST

The following figures give the population of Georgia at each decade since 1790. Also given are figures showing the percentage increase in population for each decade and the population of Georgia as a percentage of the entire nation's population.

Year	Population	% Increase	% of U.S.
1790	82,548		2.1
1800	162,686	97.1	3.1
1810	252,433	55.2	3.5
1820	340,989	35.1	3.5
1830	516,823	51.6	4.0
1840	691,392	33.8	4.1
1850	906,185	31.1	3.9
1860	1,057,286	16.7	3.4
1870	1,184,109	12.0	3.1
1880	1,542,180	30.2	3.1
1890	1,837,353	19.1	2.9
1900	2,216,331	20.6	2.9
1910	2,609,121	17.7	2.8
1920	2,895,832	11.0	2.7
1930	2,908,506	0.4	2.4
1940	3,123,723	7.4	2.4
1950	3,444,578	10.3	2.3
1960	3,943,116	14.5	2.2
1970	4,589,575	16.4	2.3
1980	5,463,087	19.0	2.3

PRESIDENTIAL ELECTION RESULTS

The popular vote in the 1972, 1976, 1980 and 1984 elections of the Democratic and Republican candidates:

County	1972 George S. McGovern	1972 Richard M. Nixon	1976 Jimmy Carter	1976 Gerald Ford	1980 Jimmy Carter	1980 Ronald Reagan	1984 Walter Mondale	1984 Ronald Reagan
Appling	512	2,755	3,585	961	2,985	1,961	1,958	2,929
Atkinson	309	924	1,560	347	1,449	747	901	944
Bacon	192	1,771	2,395	594	1,622	1,427	1,010	1,778
Baker	345	965	1,162	305	1,035	510	691	675
Baldwin	1,435	4,826	4,674	3,612	4,368	3,639	3,853	5,717
Banks	356	1,336	2,387	330	2,091	746	1,063	1,549
Barrow	867	3,423	4,756	1,364	3,876	2,284	2,367	4,123
Bartow	1,590	4,836	8,166	1,876	7,490	3,135	4,780	7,104
Ben Hill	703	2,104	2,449	814	2,544	1,459	1,859	2,313
Berrien	371	2,285	3,394	555	2,869	1,487	1,670	2,395
Bibb	10,201	27,402	31,902	12,819	31,770	15,175	26,427	24,170
Bleckley	377	2,308	2,605	972	2,014	1,261	1,465	1,912
Brantley	338	1,587	2,294	358	2,066	882	1,517	1,679
Brooks	643	2,430	2,653	1,102	2,230	1,546	1,661	2,229
Bryan	263	1,409	2,045	761	1,966	1,212	1,398	2,265
Bulloch	1,524	5,683	5,199	3,156	4,921	3,750	3,644	6,117
Burke	1,058	2,846	3,014	1,565	3,047	1,871	3,127	3,137
Butts	727	1,968	2,898	819	2,574	1,210	1,820	2,141
Calhoun	495	892	1,394	436	1,414	652	1,077	776
Camden	753	2,380	2,962	995	2,924	1,439	2,164	2841
Candler	238	1,427	1,388	646	1,358	1,030	1,014	1,497
Carroll	2,158	8,296	10,050	3,640	8,202	5,815	5,590	11,436
Catoosa	894	6,008	6,020	3,799	4,921	5,962	3,089	7,908
Charlton	310	1,244	1,750	452	1,469	779	1,111	1,368
Chatham	15,566	38,079	32,075	24,160	28,413	26,499	28,271	38,482
Chattahoochee	121	345	506	178	476	256	428	459
Chattooga	923	3,188	4,686	1,087	4,279	1,946	2,576	2,953
Cherokee	1,159	5,509	6,539	2,609	6,020	5,250	3,499	11,146
Clarke	6,090	11,465	11,342	6,610	10,519	8,094	10,132	11,503
Clay	283	632	947	295	909	316	750	419

305

	1972		1976		1980		1984	
County	George S. McGovern	Richard M. Nixon	Jimmy Carter	Gerald Ford	Jimmy Carter	Ronald Reagan	Walter Mondale	Ronald Reagan
Clayton	3,740	23,681	21,432	12,905	17,540	19,160	11,763	31,553
Clinch	239	1,127	1,414	383	1,325	513	625	862
Cobb	7,688	43,977	45,002	34,324	39,157	51,977	28,414	97,429
Coffee	607	3,934	4,601	1,417	4,038	2,499	2,633	4,200
Colquitt	930	6,900	6,928	2,181	5,353	3,593	3,208	5,815
Columbia	946	4,839	4,674	3,423	5,335	6,293	3,727	12,294
Cook	525	2,135	2,882	670	2,461	1,188	1,510	1,860
Coweta	1,560	5,751	6,195	3,044	5,697	4,480	3,650	7,981
Crawford	512	1,167	1,842	378	1,673	642	1,423	1,298
Crisp	682	3,623	3,747	1,328	3,403	1,861	2,128	2,895
Dade	148	2,110	2,263	1,388	1,735	2,114	1,150	2,750
Dawson	230	828	1,384	370	1,072	729	643	1,322
Decatur	1,196	4,292	3,736	2,500	3,242	2,919	2,656	4,134
DeKalb	30,671	104,750	86,872	67,160	82,743	74,904	77,329	104,697
Dodge	884	4,346	5,267	848	4,635	1,719	2,513	2,765
Dooly	590	1,904	2,441	655	2,364	1,083	1,726	1,435
Dougherty	3,625	12,878	11,461	9,337	13,430	12,726	12,904	16,920
Douglas	982	6,610	7,805	3,959	6,807	6,945	4,371	12,428
Early	513	2,396	2,405	1,157	2,110	1,538	1,494	2,239
Echols	68	404	585	111	515	259	227	453
Effingham	497	3,175	2,906	1,654	2,783	2,528	2,055	4,266
Elbert	884	2,875	4,730	961	4,014	1,967	2,670	3,366
Emanuel	916	3,684	4,603	1,493	3,971	2,199	2,458	3,920
Evans	375	1,666	1,631	746	1,456	1,090	1,193	1,601
Fannin	949	3,783	3,402	2,646	2,526	3,196	1,965	4,159
Fayette	450	3,401	3,718	2,837	3,798	6,351	2,861	12,575
Floyd	3,372	15,485	15,151	7,713	13,710	9,220	8,873	15,437
Forsyth	549	2,968	4,693	1,443	4,325	3,157	2,275	6,841
Franklin	435	2,022	4,192	687	3,528	1,387	1,838	2,549
Fulton	74,329	96,256	129,849	61,552	18,748	64,909	125,567	95,149
Gilmer	768	2,729	2,499	1,261	2,246	2,170	1,234	2,972
Glascock	41	578	704	371	614	510	317	827
Glynn	3,002	9,443	9,459	5,403	7,540	7,214	6,574	11,724
Gordon	870	4,344	6,052	1,698	5,199	3,107	2,607	5,566

County							
Grady	874	3,732	3,758	1,209	3,023	2,018	2,261	3,886
Greene	919	1,679	2,534	652	2,571	961	1,992	1,599
Gwinnett	2,896	18,181	20,838	13,912	21,958	27,185	14,139	54,749
Habersham	172	971	5,120	1,315	4,394	2,224	2,125	4,647
Hall	2,440	10,686	12,804	5,093	12,124	7,760	7,421	15,076
Hancock	1,502	1,595	2,117	651	2,205	573	2,109	644
Haralson	767	3,460	4,550	1,301	3,606	2,229	1,938	3,945
Harris	701	2,617	2,861	1,544	2,807	2,001	2,096	3,138
Hart	784	2,308	4,605	860	4,539	1,577	2,496	2,842
Heard	276	1,239	1,593	433	1,348	875	810	1,492
Henry	1,460	5,155	5,717	2,622	5,635	5,326	4,096	9,142
Houston	2,556	13,576	13,164	5,404	10,915	9,005	9,226	14,255
Irwin	335	1,851	2,012	561	1,555	1,056	905	1,330
Jackson	1,055	4,124	5,931	1,239	4,591	2,209	2,717	4,202
Jasper	463	1,289	1,852	689	1,546	879	1,122	1,431
Jeff Davis	302	1,857	2,405	622	2,059	1,191	1,380	2,233
Jefferson	1,184	2,777	3,115	1,309	3,305	1,605	2,816	2,999
Jenkins	484	1,769	1,820	563	1,632	824	1,108	1,399
Johnson	417	2,201	2,210	698	1,854	1,123	1,199	1,733
Jones	861	2,483	3,471	1,317	3,239	1,828	2,781	3,401
Lamar	666	1,844	2,785	847	2,453	1,298	1,605	2,198
Lanier	193	850	1,269	207	1,116	470	741	852
Laurens	2,130	7,350	8,617	3,281	7,860	4,392	5,471	7,181
Lee	390	1,441	1,727	1,110	1,670	1,942	1,284	2,972
Liberty	1,217	2,337	3,328	979	3,099	1,507	2,803	3,229
Lincoln	340	1,246	1,583	576	1,617	806	1,115	1,357
Long	236	764	1,243	222	1,202	514	816	1,099
Lowndes	2,015	7,812	8,830	4,512	5,989	6,622	6,167	10,437
Lumpkin	385	1,477	2,301	547	1,951	1,024	1,110	1,991
Macon	837	2,005	3,013	638	3,025	894	2,521	1,515
Madison	572	2,606	3,367	1,115	2,980	2,330	1,690	3,768
Marion	164	850	1,314	291	1,174	567	951	846
McDuffie	996	2,990	3,024	1,694	2,667	1,928	2,006	3,284
McIntosh	833	1,367	1,978	535	2,104	876	1,796	1,512
Meriwether	1,213	3,420	4,830	1,450	3,876	1,838	2,864	3,195
Miller	118	1,269	1,536	476	1,127	900	526	1,348
Mitchell	1,120	2,400	4,495	1,572	3,566	2,231	2,791	2,737

County	1972		1976		1980		1984	
	George S. McGovern	Richard M. Nixon	Jimmy Carter	Gerald Ford	Jimmy Carter	Ronald Reagan	Walter Mondale	Ronald Reagan
Monroe	789	2,181	2,962	1,078	2,542	1,242	2,189	2,420
Montgomery	337	1,370	1,610	626	1,663	948	950	1,365
Morgan	668	2,007	2,274	904	2,276	1,323	1,714	2,301
Murray	644	2,643	3,511	889	3,094	1,538	1,649	3,521
Muscogee	8,234	28,449	24,092	13,496	23,272	15,203	20,835	23,816
Newton	1,380	4,647	6,294	2,137	5,611	3,206	3,389	5,810
Oconee	464	2,029	2,228	1,184	2,141	2,065	1,467	3,471
Oglethorpe	326	1,712	1,854	811	1,611	1,187	1,238	2,122
Paulding	1,004	2,814	5,420	1,432	4,686	2,845	2,621	6,048
Peach	2,413	3,747	3,989	1,163	3,415	1,642	3,369	2,652
Pickens	520	2,101	2,571	973	2,358	1,612	1,329	2,801
Pierce	269	1,982	2,628	544	1,918	1,027	1,501	1,978
Pike	423	1,432	1,903	776	1,755	1,271	1,203	1,855
Polk	1,317	4,929	6,115	1,944	5,421	2,949	3,262	5,435
Pulaski	444	1,966	2,318	485	1,997	1,153	1,440	1,509
Putnam	604	1,963	2,040	835	1,951	1,166	1,336	1,830
Quitman	140	502	677	313	589	240	490	361
Rabun	366	1,477	2,398	591	2,327	1,070	1,267	2,191
Randolph	798	1,603	2,186	747	1,861	879	1,454	1,578
Richmond	9,219	24,362	24,042	17,893	24,104	19,619	21,208	29,869
Rockdale	791	3,560	4,640	2,974	4,395	5,300	3,291	10,121
Schley	162	694	783	268	613	453	403	614
Screven	575	2,402	2,168	1,176	2,117	1,490	1,747	2,583
Seminole	376	1,851	2,074	681	1,794	1,117	1,350	1,636
Spalding	1,702	7,183	7,593	3,739	7,176	4,809	4,878	8,571
Stephens	871	3,773	5,560	1,340	4,529	2,045	2,272	4,057
Stewart	353	1,020	1,632	433	1,440	611	1,308	805
Sumter	1,268	4,533	5,328	2,053	4,956	2,957	3,725	4,607
Talbot	508	990	1,634	459	1,635	572	1,494	778
Taliaferro	372	585	748	236	670	270	550	318
Tattnall	492	2,892	3,556	1,326	2,864	2,082	1,954	3,641
Taylor	514	1,580	1,962	504	1,845	815	1,340	1,292
Telfair	687	2,245	3,534	637	2,700	1,173	2,049	1,980
Terrell	686	2,057	2,348	1,168	2,010	1,378	1,598	1,744

County								
Thomas	2,171	6,668	6,147	3,263	5,695	4,294	4,039	6,427
Tift	816	4,591	5,185	2,162	4,572	3,280	2,736	4,429
Toombs	675	4,080	4,047	2,126	3,255	2,835	2,385	4,470
Towns	404	1,573	1,786	1,175	1,510	1,475	1,007	1,960
Treutlen	210	1,346	1,567	465	1,307	668	843	1,086
Troup	2,056	8,350	7,699	4,422	7,716	5,398	5,272	9,340
Turner	437	2,120	2,265	416	1,990	898	1,270	1,329
Twiggs	1,113	2,363	2,515	513	2,213	747	1,755	1,143
Union	742	2,317	2,795	1,154	1,700	1,546	1,112	1,914
Upson	896	4,892	4,219	2,897	4,713	2,788	2,943	4,803
Walker	1,574	8,728	8,007	4,807	6,809	7,088	5,000	10,734
Walton	1,140	3,994	5,402	1,687	4,525	2,618	2,481	4,995
Ware	1,724	6,578	7,719	2,661	6,307	3,715	4,435	5,547
Warren	475	1,175	1,335	720	1,517	779	1,258	1,087
Washington	1,246	3,901	3,865	1,657	3,452	1,822	3,034	2,887
Wayne	733	3,677	4,489	1,499	3,843	2,213	2,434	3,698
Webster	108	483	622	165	608	312	534	402
Wheeler	294	1,093	1,378	344	1,599	550	774	833
White	343	1,537	2,125	625	2,017	1,175	1,090	2,369
Whitfield	1,955	8,591	10,475	4,498	9,691	6,404	5,284	11,957
Wilcox	315	1,863	2,153	346	1,780	827	1,212	1,218
Wilkes	646	2,195	2,461	1,067	2,350	1,212	1,586	1,837
Wilkinson	751	2,196	2,652	837	2,365	1,116	2,102	1,756
Worth	542	2,942	2,790	1,156	2,567	2,076	1,685	2,910
Georgia	289,529	881,496	979,409	483,743	890,733	654,168	706,628	1,068,722

PUBLIC ASSISTANCE

Medicaid Recipients, Households Participating in the Food Stamp Program, 1982.

County	Medicaid Recipients	Households Participating in the Food Stamp Program	Aid to Families With Dependent Children	Persons Under Age 18 Receiving Aid to Families With Dependent Children
Appling	1,764	792	267	522
Atkinson	952	425	134	239
Bacon	1,342	659	218	423
Baker	551	242	86	152
Baldwin	2,967	1,209	620	1,200
Banks	465	282	27	42
Barrow	1,762	784	245	507
Bartow	2,602	1,710	459	772
Ben Hill	2,016	983	296	569
Berrien	1,423	647	185	359
Bibb	15,894	8,042	3,603	6,610
Bleckley	1,164	583	214	389
Brantley	631	369	68	118
Brooks	2,261	985	371	768
Bryan	1,089	525	199	386
Bulloch	3,192	1,438	627	1,168
Burke	3,510	1,545	694	1,376
Butts	1,580	609	294	520
Calhoun	1,039	357	142	275
Camden	1,038	548	205	355
Candler	1,223	470	118	237
Carroll	4,204	2,071	686	1,252
Catoosa	1,716	1,171	314	540
Charlton	944	430	179	327
Chatham	20,173	9,566	4,425	8,486
Chattahoochee	314	251	58	107
Chattooga	2,121	1,118	366	658
Cherokee	1,997	970	262	445
Clarke	4,885	2,215	977	1,824
Clay	759	266	139	245
Clayton	5,162	2,728	1,003	1,743
Clinch	1,062	440	175	312
Cobb	6,952	2,747	1,061	1,757
Coffee	3,026	1,371	517	952
Colquitt	4,075	2,209	828	1,692
Columbia	1,864	900	379	680
Cook	1,437	645	196	419
Coweta	3,310	2,192	805	1,528
Crawford	865	396	156	274
Crisp	3,410	1,385	606	1,256
Dade	776	541	120	212
Dawson	410	200	30	56
Decatur	3,541	1,606	638	1,348
DeKalb	17,421	7,580	4,168	7,385
Dodge	2,228	1,105	340	668
Dooly	1,803	698	327	653
Dougherty	12,435	5,134	2,846	5,778
Douglas	2,357	953	338	601
Early	2,561	1,133	480	1,036
Echols	198	128	45	80

County	Medicaid Recipients	Households Participating in the Food Stamp Program	Aid to Families With Dependent Children	Persons Under Age 18 Receiving Aid to Families With Dependent Children
Effingham	1,437	635	293	532
Elbert	2,259	1,170	387	727
Emanuel	3,322	1,556	524	1,132
Evans	1,270	527	198	357
Fannin	1,385	710	144	259
Fayette	450	270	76	108
Floyd	5,806	3,141	1,252	2,303
Forsyth	1,239	661	123	209
Franklin	1,486	697	171	287
Fulton	85,213	35,978	17,179	31,983
Gilmer	1,006	629	114	222
Glascock	344	119	27	40
Glynn	4,052	2,365	784	1,437
Gordon	1,810	909	272	500
Grady	2,121	1,018	353	669
Greene	1,106	583	179	367
Gwinnett	3,169	1,262	330	588
Habersham	1,427	650	118	200
Hall	4,408	2,431	677	1,162
Hancock	2,048	801	381	701
Haralson	1,688	978	208	372
Harris	1,237	540	198	322
Hart	1,691	828	188	329
Heard	667	261	107	210
Henry	2,252	864	424	736
Houston	4,289	1,817	929	1,670
Irwin	1,137	538	194	397
Jackson	1,822	800	189	327
Jasper	661	492	101	164
Jeff Davis	1,055	545	114	198
Jefferson	3,228	1,297	642	1,194
Jenkins	1,465	672	229	414
Johnson	1,199	539	181	375
Jones	1,221	500	238	428
Lamar	1,097	530	185	349
Lanier	834	381	144	274
Laurens	4,165	2,234	654	1,242
Lee	964	454	188	366
Liberty	2,444	1,308	552	1,000
Lincoln	699	362	125	228
Long	556	230	95	157
Lowndes	5,996	2,607	1,149	2,257
Lumpkin	909	417	82	153
Macon	2,500	1,256	528	984
Madison	1,249	708	144	258
Marion	908	411	130	234
McDuffie	2,091	724	430	686
McIntosh	1,161	624	239	394
Meriwether	2,447	1,071	432	855
Miller	1,005	435	147	293
Mitchell	3,425	1,454	657	1,422
Monroe	1,331	522	240	408
Montgomery	1,037	505	132	238
Morgan	1,245	567	199	409

311

PUBLIC ASSISTANCE

County	Medicaid Recipients	Households Participating in the Food Stamp Program	Aid to Families With Dependent Children	Persons Under Age 18 Receiving Aid to Families With Dependent Children
Murray	882	397	105	178
Muscogee	15,138	7,292	3,392	6,267
Newton	2,739	1,529	577	1,116
Oconee	518	185	54	85
Oglethorpe	872	535	166	311
Paulding	1,655	854	217	369
Peach	2,433	1,317	580	1,071
Pickens	994	420	114	203
Pierce	1,148	611	167	286
Pike	681	204	103	177
Polk	3,062	1,392	491	901
Pulaski	1,230	623	214	385
Putnam	1,087	611	185	348
Quitman	428	245	89	153
Rabun	917	504	87	137
Randolph	1,250	611	209	412
Richmond	16,789	7,993	3,969	7,381
Rockdale	1,389	836	238	419
Schley	446	237	82	160
Screven	2,158	1,000	411	715
Seminole	1,254	592	227	450
Spalding	3,974	1,741	823	1,451
Stephens	1,784	759	244	435
Stewart	1,096	483	247	464
Sumter	3,775	1,669	762	1,425
Talbot	782	426	172	292
Taliaferro	359	204	62	99
Tattnall	2,594	1,022	395	775
Taylor	1,458	61	279	512
Telfair	1,703	774	244	452
Terrell	1,779	659	271	526
Thomas	3,912	1,860	749	1,440
Tift	3,227	1,375	545	1,087
Toombs	3,185	1,356	498	991
Towns	489	247	30	53
Treutlen	1,036	470	144	311
Troup	4,456	1,979	704	1,365
Turner	1,362	546	283	576
Twiggs	1,317	553	300	525
Union	853	409	75	127
Upson	2,537	909	469	825
Walker	3,062	1,971	539	929
Walton	2,286	995	348	653
Ware	4,128	2,070	666	1,289
Warren	1,045	433	186	312
Washington	2,716	1,072	531	908
Wayne	2,522	1,048	425	776
Webster	315	168	71	121
Wheeler	939	388	120	240
White	682	247	27	42
Whitfield	3,048	1,608	425	679
Wilcox	1,227	466	148	311
Wilkes	1,411	699	263	477
Wilkinson	1,063	528	244	402

County	Medicaid Recipients	Households Participating in the Food Stamp Program	Aid to Families With Dependent Children	Persons Under Age 18 Receiving Aid to Families With Dependent Children
Worth	2,113	908	405	829
Georgia	435,866	217,027	88,883	165,650

PUBLIC GOLF COURSES

There are over 110 public golf courses in Georgia. These courses and their locations, along with the number of holes and par of each, are given in the table below:

Albany
Metro Golf Course; Ga. 91 N.; 9 holes; par 35.
Turner Field Golf Course; Turner Field Rd.; 9 holes; par 36.

Americus
Brickyard Plantation Golf Course; 7 mi. East on U.S. 280; 9 holes; par 35.

Ashburn
Wanne Lake Country Club; Ga. 112; 9 holes; par 36.

Athens
Creekwood Country Club; Kathwood Dr.; 9 holes; par 34.
University Golf Course; Milledge Extension; 18 holes; par 73.

Atlanta
Adams Park Golf Course (City Course); 2300 Wilson Dr., SW; 18 holes; par 72.
Bobby Jones Golf Course; 384 Woodward Way, NW; 18 holes; par 71.
Brown's Mill Golf Course; 430 Cleveland Ave., SE; 18 holes; par 72.
Candler Park Golf Course (City); 585 Candler Park Dr., NE; 9 holes; par 32.
North Fulton Golf Course; 216 W. Wieuca Rd., NE; 18 holes; par 71.
Piedmont Park Golf Course; Piedmont Park/10th St., NE; 9 holes; par 33.
Sugar Creek Golf Course; 2706 Bouldercrest Rd., SE; 18 holes; par 72.

Augusta
Augusta Golf Club; Highland Ave.; 18 holes; par 71.
Forest Hill Golf Club; Comfort Rd.; 18 holes; par 72.

Austell
Dogwood Golf and Country Club; 4207 Flint Hills Rd.; 18 holes; par 72.
Lithia Springs Golf Course; West Bankhead Hwy.; 9 holes; par 34.

Avondale
Avondale Golf Club; 30 Covington Rd.; 9 holes; par 35.

Avondale Estates
Forest Hills Golf Club; 205 Clarendon Ave.; 9 holes; par 34.

Bainbridge
Industrial Park Golf; U.S. 27 N./Ind. Air Park; 9 holes; par 35.

Barnesville
Barnesville Golf Course; College Dr.; 9 holes; par 36.

Baxley
Appling County Country Club; U.S. 1 South; 9 holes; par 36.

Blairsville
Butternut Creek Golf Course; U.S. 19; 9 holes; par 32.

Bremen
East Maple Lakes Golf Course; Cashtown Rd.; 9 holes; par 36.

Brunswick
Glynco Golf Course; Ga. 303, off U.S. 17 N.; 9 holes; par 36.

Buena Vista
Cedar Creek Golf and Country Club; Just off Ga. 137 N.; 9 holes; par 36.

Buford
PineIsle Golf Course; Lake Lanier Islands; 18 holes; par 72.

Carrolton
Goldmine Golf Club; R. 3 off Bonner Goldmine Rd.; 9 holes; par 36.

Cartersville
Green Valley Greens; Exit 125 off I-75, Rudy York Rd.; 9 holes; par 36.
Royal Oaks; Exit 124 off I-75, Dallas Hwy.; 9 holes; par 36.

Cedartown
Cedar Valley Country Club; U.S. 27 South; 9 holes; par 36.

Clarkesville
Heritage Golf Course; Stonepile Rd. off Ga. 197; 9 holes; par 36.

313

Clayton
Rabun County Country Club; Old U.S. 441; 9 holes; par 36.

Cleveland
Skitt Mountain Golf Course; Ga. 254; 18 holes; par 72.

College Park
Gordon Morris Memorial Golf Course; 3711 Fairway Dr.; 9 holes; par 36.

Columbus
Bull Creek Municipal Golf Course; 7333 Lynch Rd.; 18 holes; par 72.
Victory Drive Golf Course; 603 Lumpkin Rd.; 9 holes; par 27.

Commerce
Commerce Golf and Country Club; Hwy. 15, 9 holes; par 36.

Conyers
Fieldstone Golf and Country Club; 2720 Salem Rd.; 18 holes; par 72.
Highland Golf Club; 2271 Flat Shoals Rd.; 18 holes; par 72.
Honey Creek Golf and Country Club; 635 Clubhouse Dr.; 18 holes; par 72.

Covington
Newton County Golf Course; Brown Bridge Rd.; 18 holes; par 72.

Dallas
Dallas Country Club Estates; Hwy. 92 South to Nebo Rd.; 9 holes; par 36.

Dalton
Tunnel Hill; Exit 137 off I-75, Hwy. 41 North; 9 holes; par 36.

Decatur
Clifton Springs Par 3 Golf Course; 2340 Clifton Springs Rd.; 9 holes; par 27.

Demorest
Piedmont College Golf Course; Demorest/Mt. Airy Rd.; 9 holes; par 36.

Douglas
South Georgia College Golf Course; South Georgia College Campus; 9 holes; par 35.

Dublin
Riverview Park; Off Ga. 19 S.; inside Dublin city limits; 18 holes; par 72.

Folkston
Folkston Golf and Country Club; Okefenokee Dr., North; 9 holes; par 35.

Forsyth
Forsyth Golf Club; Country Club Dr.; 9 holes; par 36.

Gainesville
Chattahoochee Golf Club; Tommy Aaron Dr.; 18 holes; par 72.

Griffin
Griffin Municipal Golf Course; Country Club Dr.; 18 holes; par 72.

Gay
Beaver Lake Golf and Country Club; Old Ga. 85 (5 mi. N. of Gay); 18 holes; par 72.

Haddock
Jonesco Golf Course; Hwy. 22. 4 mi. E. of Gray; 9 holes; par 36.

Hartwell
Hartwell Golf Course; U.S. 29 South; 18 holes; par 72.

Jackson
Deer Trail Golf Course, Biles Rd.; 9 holes; par 36.

Jakin
Green Valley Golf and Recreation Center, U.S. 84 (6 mi. W. of Donalsonville); 9 holes; par 36.

Jasper
Bent Creek; East of Jasper; 18 holes; par 72.
Arrowhead; Ga. 5; 9 holes; par 36.

Jekyll
Jekyll Island Golf Courses:
Indian Mound; 322 Capt. Wylly Rd.; 18 holes; par 72.
Oceanside; Beachview Dr.; 9 holes; par 36.
Oleander; 322 Capt. Wylly Rd.; 18 holes; par 72.
Pine Lakes; 322 Capt. Wylly Rd.; 18 holes; par 72.

Jonesboro
Country Greens Golf Course; 9350 Thomas Rd.; 18 holes; par 71.
Flint Acres Golf Course; 360 Hewell Rd.; 27 holes; pars 35/35/36.

La Grange
American Legion; 9 holes; par 35.
Highland Country Club; 18 holes; par 72.

La Fayette
Municipal Golf Course; 638 S. Main Street; 9 holes; par 36.

Lake Park
Francis Lake Golf Course; Exit 2, I-75 N.; 18 holes; par 72.

Lawrenceville
Windy Hills Country Club; Camp Perrin Rd.; 9 holes; par 36.

Lindale
Lin Valley Country Club; Eden Valley Rd.; 9 holes; par 36.

Lithonia
Idlewood Golf Course; 6465 Browns Mill Rd.; 9 holes; par 72.
Mystery Valley Golf Course; 694 Shadow Rock Dr.; 18 holes; par 72.

Lula/Homer
Pine Hills Golf Course; Lula/Homer Rd.-Ga. 51; 9 holes; par 72.

Loganville
Overlook Golf Club; Sharon Rd.; 18 holes; par 72.

Macon
Bowden; Hwy. 49 at Miller Field Rd., N. of Macon; 18 holes; par 70.

Manchester
Pebblebrook Golf Club; State Rd. 85; 9 holes; par 36.

Marietta
Par 56 Golf Course; 1471 Cobb Pkwy.; 18 holes; par 56.
Westwood Golf Club; 2250 Callaway Rd., SW; 18 holes; par 71.

McRae
Little Ocmulgee State Park; 441, 2 mi. N. of McRae; 18 holes; par 72.

Milledgeville
Little Fishing Creek; Hwy. 22 West; 18 holes; par 72.

Millen
Magnolia Country Club; Waynesboro Rd.; 9 holes; par 36.

Monroe
Monroe Golf and Country Club; Jersey Rd.; 18 holes; par 72.

Pine Mountain
Garden View (Callaway Gardens); U.S. 27; 18 holes; par 70.
Lake View (Callaway Gardens); U.S. 27; 18 holes; par 72.
Mountain View (Callaway Gardens); U.S. 27; 18 holes; par 72.
Skyview (Callaway Gardens); U.S. 27; 9 holes; par 31.

Rockmart
Goodyear Golf Course; Goodyear Ave.; 9 holes; par 36.
Prospect Valley Golf Course; Prospect Rd.; 9 holes; par 36.

Royston
Victoria Bryant State Park; 9 holes; par 36.

Rutledge
Hard Labor Creek State Park; Hwy. 24; 18 holes; par 72.

St. Marys
St. Marys Country Club; St. Marys Rd. off I-95; 9 holes; par 36.

Savannah
Bacon Park Golf Course; Skidaway; 18 holes; par 71.
Mary Calder Golf Course; St. Marys Rd. off I-95; 9 holes; par 35.

Senoia
Brown Bell Golf Course; Hwy. 16 between Newnan and Senoia; 9 holes; par 36.

Stone Mountain
Stone Mountain Park Golf Course; Stone Mountain Park; 18 holes; par 72.

Swainsboro
Swainsboro Golf and Country Club; Gum Log St.; 9 holes; par 36.

Sylvania
Brier Creek Country Club; Hwy. 301 N.; 9 holes; par 36.

Tallapoosa
Talley Mountain Golf Course; Hwy. 78; 9 holes; par 36.

Thomasville
Glen Arven Country Club; Old U.S. 19; 18 holes; par 72.
Country Oaks Golf Course; Ga. 122 E.; 9 holes; par 35.

Thunderbolt
Bonaventure Golf Club; 295 Bonaventure Rd.; 9 holes; par three course.

Toccoa
Toccoa Golf Club Inc.; Black Mountain Rd.; 9 holes; par 72.

Trenton
Big Sandy Golf Course; Hwy. 136 West to 301 South; 9 holes; par 36.

Union Point
Greene County Country Club; U.S. 278; 9 holes; par 36.

Valdosta
Valdosta Country Club; Country Club Dr.; 36 holes.

Varnell
Nob North; Exit 135 off I-75; or Ga. 71; 18 holes; par 72.

Washington
Washington-Wilkes Country Club; U.S. 78; 9 holes; par 36.

Winder
Crossed Arrows; Hwy. 29; 18 holes; par 72.

Wrens
Four Seasons Country Club; Hwy. 80; 9 holes; par 36.

RADIO STATIONS

COMMERCIAL RADIO STATIONS

Adel
WBIT-TV
Box 508, 31620

WDDQ-FM
P.O. Box 508, 31620
912-896-4571

Albany
WALG-AM
P.O. Box W, 31702
912-436-7233

WGPC-AM/Stereo FM
2011 Gillionville Rd.,
31707
912-883-6500

WJAZ-AM
P.O. Box 505, 31702
912-432-9181

WJIZ-FM
P.O. Box 545, 31702
912-432-7447

WKAK-FM
P.O. Box W, 31702
912-436-9929

WQDE-AM
P.O. Box 1624, 31702
912-436-0544

Alma
WULF-AM
P.O. Box 1987, 31510
912-632-4411

Americus
WADZ-FM
605 McGarrah St.,
31709
912-924-1290

WDEC-AM
P.O. Box 1307, 31709
912-924-1290

WISK-AM
P.O. Box 727, 31709
912-924-6500

WPUR-FM
P.O. Box 727, 31709
912-924-6500

Ashburn
WMES-AM
Box 848, 31714
912-567-3355

Athens
WAGQ-Stereo FM
2500 W. Broad St.,
Executive Office Park,
Suite 205, 30606
404-546-7350

WGAU-AM
850 Bobbin Mill Rd.,
30606
404-549-1340

WNGC-FM
850 Bobbin Mill Rd.,
30606
404-549-1340

WRFC-AM
255 S. Milledge Ave.,
30605
404-549-6222

Atlanta
WAEC-AM
1665 Peachtree St., NW,
30309
404-875-777

WAOK-AM
401 W. Peachtree St.,
NE, Suite 1947,
30365
404-659-1380

WCNN-AM
3954 Peachtree Rd.,
NE, 30319
404-261-6800

WFOX-FM
2000 Riveredge Pkwy.,
Suite 797, 30328
404-953-9369

WGKA-AM
P.O. Box 52128, 30305
404-231-1190

WGST-AM
550 Pharr Rd., 30363
404-231-0920

WIGO-AM
1422 W. Peachtree St.,
NW, 30309
404-892-8000

WKHX-FM
360 Interstate N, Suite
101, 30339
404-955-0101

WKLS-AM/Stereo FM
1800 Century Blvd.,
NE, Suite 1200,
30345
404-325-0960

WPCH-Stereo FM
550 Pharr Rd., NE,
30363
404-261-9500

WPLO-AM
120 Ralph McGill Blvd.,
Suite 1000, 30365
404-898-8900

WQXI-AM/Stereo FM
3340 Peachtree Rd.,
Suite 240, 30026
404-261-2970

WRMM-FM
1459 Peachtree St.,
30309
404-892-7766

WSB-AM/Stereo FM
1601 W. Peachtree St.,
NE, 30309
404-897-7000

WTJH-AM
P.O. Box 967, 30364
404-344-2233

WVEE-Stereo FM
120 Ralph McGill Blvd.,
Suite 1000, 30365
404-898-8900

WXLL-AM
P.O. Box 49485, 30359
404-321-1830

WYZE-AM
1111 Broadway, SE,
30312
404-622-4444

WZGC-FM
P.O. Box 54577, 30308
404-881-0093

Augusta
WBBQ-AM
P.O. Box 2066-13, 30913
803-279-6610

WBIA-AM
P.O. Box 1230, 30903
404-724-2421

WGAC-AM
P.O. Box 1131, 30903
404-863-5800

WGUS-AM
P.O. Box 1475, 30903
803-279-1380

WHGI-AM
P.O. Box 669, 30903
404-722-6077

WKZK-AM
2 Milledge Rd., 30904
404-738-9191

WRDW-AM
P.O. Box 1405, 30903
404-724-1480

WTHB-AM
P.O. Box 1584, 30903
803-279-2330

WYMX-FM
P.O. Box 669, 30903
404-722-1302

WZZW-FM
P.O. Box 1584, 30903
404-279-2300

Austell
WCKZ-AM
P.O. Box 746, 30001
404-941-0016

Bainbridge
WJAD-FM
P.O. Box 706, 31717
912-246-1650

WMGR-AM
P.O. Box 706, 31717
912-246-1650

WYSE-AM
1317 E. Carter St.,
31717
912-246-9973

Barnesville
WBAF-AM
Rte. 2, Box A, 30204
404-358-1090

Baxley
WUFE-AM
Highway 341 West,
31513
912-367-3000

Blackshear
WBSG-AM
Box 400, 31516

WKUB-FM
P.O. Box 112, 31516
912-449-3391

Blakely
WBBK-AM/FM
P.O. Box 568, 31723
912-723-4311

Blue Ridge
WPPL-FM
Box 938, Highland St.,
30513
404-632-2803

Bremen
WSLE-AM
P.O. Box 397, 30110
404-537-3275

Brunswick
WBGA-AM
801 Mansfield St., 31520
912-265-3870

WGIG-FM
801 Mansfield St., 31520
912-265-3870

WMOG-AM
F. J. Torras Causeway,
31520
912-265-5980

WPIQ-FM
Hwy. 303, Rte. 6, 31520
912-264-3820

WYNR-AM
Hwy. 303, Rte. 6, 31520
912-264-3820

Buford
WDYX-AM
Box 609, 30518
404-945-9953

WGCO-FM
Box 609, 30518
404-945-9953

317

Cairo
WGRA-AM
U.S. 84 W, 31728
912-377-4392

Calhoun
WEBS-AM
427 S. Wall St., 30701
404-629-2238

WJTH-AM
102 Memorial Rd.,
30701
404-629-6397

Camilla
WCLB-AM
Drawer 113, 31730
912-336-5614

WOFF-FM
P.O. Box 434, 31730
912-336-8767

Canton
WCHK-AM
P.O. Box 231, 30114
404-479-2101

WCHK-FM
P.O. Box 1290, 30114
404-479-2101

Carrollton
WBTR-FM
Bremen Rd., 30117
404-836-0092

WLBB-AM
Bremen Rd., 30117
404-832-7041

WPPI-AM
808 Newman Rd., 30117
404-834-1058

Cartersville
WBHF-AM
West Avenue, 30120
404-382-3000

WYXC-AM
Route 6, N. Tennessee
Rd., 30120
404-382-1270

Cedartown
WGAA-AM
413 Lake View Dr.,
30125
404-748-1340

Chatsworth
WQMT-FM
P.O. Box 738, 30705
404-695-6777

Clarkesville
WIAF-AM
109 Washington St.,
30523
404-754-6272

Claxton
WCLA-AM/FM
316 N. River St., 30417
912-739-3055

Clayton
WGHC-AM
P.O. Box 1149, 30525
404-782-4251

Cleveland
WRWH-AM
Box 181, 30528
404-865-3181

Cochran
WVMG-AM
Industrial Park, 31014
912-934-4548

WVMG-Stereo FM
P.O. Box 570, Industrial
Park, 31014
912-934-4548

Columbus
WCGQ-FM
Box 1537, 31994
404-324-0338

WCLS-AM
P.O. Box 229, 31902
205-298-1580

WDAK-AM
1846 Buena Vista Rd.,
31902
404-322-5447

WEIZ-Stereo FM
P.O. Box 2744, 31902
205-298-1001

WFXE-FM
Box 1998, 31902
404-324-0261

WHYD-AM
1825 Buena Vista Rd.,
31906
404-323-3603

WOKS-AM
P.O. Box 1998, 31902
404-324-0261

WPNX-AM
P.O. Box 687, 31902
404-322-2270

WRCG-AM
P.O. Box 1537, 31902
404-324-0338

WVOC-Stereo FM
P.O. Box 5387, 31906
404-324-2441

Commerce
WJJC-AM
220 Little St., 30529
404-335-3155

Conyers
WCGA-AM
954 S. Main St., 30207
404-483-1000

Cordele
WFAV-FM
P.O. Box 340, 31015

WMJM-AM
20th Ave., E, 31015
912-273-1404

Cornelia
WCON-AM/FM
1 Burrell St., 30531
404-778-2241

Covington
WGFS-AM
P.O. Box 869, 30209
404-786-1430

Cumming
WHNE-AM
Box 609, 30130
404-887-3136

Cuthbert
WCUG-AM
P.O. Box 348, 31740
912-732-3725

Dahlonega
WDGR-AM
P.O. Box 292, 30533
404-864-4477

Dallas
WKRP-AM
362 W. Memorial Dr.,
30132
404-445-1500

Dalton
WBLJ-AM
P.O. Box 809, 30720
404-278-3300

WRCD-AM
P.O. Box 1284, 30720
404-278-5511

WTTI-AM
118 N. Hamilton
St.-Dalton Federal
Bldg., 30720
404-226-2700

Dawson
WAZE-FM
Box 390, 31742
912-995-5846

WHIA-AM
110 N. Main St., 31742
912-995-5846

Decatur
WAVO-AM
P.O. Box 111, 30031
404-292-3800

WGUN-AM
215 Church St., 30031
404-373-2521

Donalsonville
WGMK-FM
P.O. Box 236, 31745
912-524-5124

WSEM-AM
Box 87, 31745
912-524-5123

Douglas
WDMG-AM/FM
620 E. Ward St., 31533
912-384-3250

WOKA-AM/FM
Rocky Pond Rd., 31533
912-384-8153

Douglasville
WDGL-AM
8470 Hospital Dr.,
30134
404-942-5186

Dublin
WKKZ-FM
Glenwood Ave., 31021
912-272-9270

WMLT-AM
807 Belleview, 31021
912-272-4422

WQZY-FM
P.O. Box 130, 31021
912-272-4422

WXLI-AM
Glenwood Ave., 31021
912-272-9270

Eastman
WUFF-AM
731 College, Box 626,
31023

WUFF-FM
721 College St., 31023
912-374-3437

Eatonton
WXPQ-AM
202A Jefferson St.,
31024
404-485-8055

Elberton
WSGC-AM
Jones St., 30635
404-283-1400

WWRK-FM
Jones St., 30635
404-283-1400

Ellijay
WLEJ-AM
P.O. Box 635, 30540
404-276-2016

Fitzgerald
WBHB-AM
601 W. Roanoke Dr.,
31750
912-423-2077

Forsyth
WFNE-FM
P.O. Box 693, 31029
912-994-9494

Fort Valley
WXKO-AM
P.O. Box 1150, 31030
912-825-5547

Gainesville
WDUN-AM
1102 Thompson Bridge
Rd., NW, 30501
404-532-9921

319

WGGA-AM
P.O. Box 1318, 30501
404-532-6211

WLBA-AM
303 Washington St.,
30501
404-532-6331

WWID-Stereo FM
1102 Thompson Bridge
Rd., NW, 30501
404-532-9921

Glennville
WKIG-AM/FM
226 E. Bolton St., 30427
912-654-3580

Greensboro
WGRG-FM
P.O. Box 376, 30642
404-453-4140

Greenville
WGRI-AM
P.O. Box 156, 30224

Griffin
WHIE-AM
P.O. Drawer G, 30223

WKEU-AM/FM
1000 Memorial Dr.,
30223
404-227-5507

Hartwell
WKLY-AM
Box 666, 30643
404-376-2233

Hawkinsville
WCEH-AM/FM
P.O. Box 489, 31036
912-892-9061

Hazlehurst
WVOH-AM/FM
P.O. Box 757, 31539
912-375-4511

320

Hinesville
WGML-AM
P.O. Box 15, 31313
912-876-3599

Homerville
WBTY-FM
303 Court St., 31634
912-487-5350

Jackson
WJGA-Stereo FM
P.O. Box 3878, 30233
404-775-3151

Jasper
WYYZ-AM
Hood Rd., 30143
404-692-6446

Jesup
WIFO-Stereo FM
P.O. Box 647, 31545
912-427-3711

WLOP-AM
P.O. Box 647, 31545
912-427-3711

WSOJ-Stereo FM
P.O. Box 251-B, 31545
912-427-2003

LaGrange
WJYA-FM
304 Broome St., 30240
404-883-6420

WLAG-AM
304 Broome St., 30241
404-882-3505

WTRP-AM
806 Franklin Rd., 30241
404-884-8611

WWCG-Stereo FM
P.O. Box 1429, 30241
404-882-3505

LaFayette
WLFA-AM
P.O. Box 746, 30728
404-638-3276

Lawrenceville
WLAW-AM
P.O. Box 33, 30246
404-963-2222

Louisville
WPEH-AM/FM
Box 425, 30434

Lyons
WBBT-AM
389 N. Victory Dr.,
30436
912-526-8122

Macon
WAYS-FM
P.O. Box 5008, 31208
912-741-9494

WBML-AM
P.O. Box 6298, 31208
912-743-5453

WDDO-AM
544 Mulberry St., 31202
912-745-3375

WDEN-Stereo FM
173 First St., 31202
912-745-3383

WIBB-AM
P.O. Box 6517, 31213
912-742-2505

WMAZ-AM
P.O. Box 5008, 31213
912-741-9494

WNEX-AM
P.O. Box 6318, 31208
912-745-3301

WPEZ-FM
Box 900, 31202
912-746-6286

WPTC-AM
173 First St., 31202
912-745-3383

WQXM-AM/FM
P.O. Box 356, 31208
912-628-2000

Madison
WYTH-AM
U.S. 441 South, 30650
404-342-1250

Manchester
WUFJ-AM
Main St., 31816

WVFJ-FM
Main St., 31816
404-846-3115

Marietta
WFOM-AM
835 S. Cobb Drive,
30060
404-428-3396

WJYA-AM
P.O. Box 1080, 30061
404-424-1080

McDonough
WZAL-AM
12 N. Cedar St., 30253
407-957-1549

McRae
WDAX-AM/FM
P.O. Box 247, 31055
912-868-5611

Metter
WHCG-FM
S. Broad St., 30439
912-685-2136

WMAC-AM
P.O. Box 238, 30439
912-685-2136

Milledgeville
WKGQ-AM
P.O. Box 832, 31061
912-452-7291

WKZR-FM
1250 W. Charlton St.,
31061
912-452-0586

WMVG-AM
1250 W. Charlton St.,
31061
912-452-0586

Millen
WGSR-AM
P.O. Box 869, 30442
912-982-4142

Monroe
WKUN-AM
702 East Spring St.,
30655
404-267-6558

Montezuma
WMNZ-AM
Box 511, 31063

Morrow
WSSA-AM
P.O. Box 831, 30260
404-361-8843

Moultrie
WMGA-AM
Box 1380, 31768
912-985-1130

WMTM-AM/Stereo
FM
Hwy. 33 SE, 31768
912-985-1300

Nashville
WNGA-AM
Box 645, 31639

Newnan
WNEA-AM
8 Madison St., 30264
404-253-4711

WCOH-AM
154 Boone Dr., 30263
404-253-4636

Ocilla
WSIZ-AM
Hwy. 129 N, 31774
912-468-7429

Perry
WPGA-AM/FM
P.O. Drawer 980, 31069
912-987-2980

Quitman
WSFB-AM
P.O. Box 632, 31643
912-263-4373

Reidsville
WTNL-AM
P.O. Drawer 820, 30453
912-557-6731

Rockmart
WPLK-AM
W. Elm St., 30153
404-684-7848

WZOT-FM
W. Elm St., Box 192,
30153
404-684-7848

Rome
WIYN-AM
P.O. Box 5226, 30161
404-291-9496

WKCX-FM
710 Turner-McCall
Blvd., 30161
404-291-9705

WLAQ-AM
Box 228, 30161
404-232-7767

WQTU-FM
E. 6th Ave., 30161
404-295-1023

321

WRGA-AM
E. 6th Ave., 30161
404-291-9742

WROM-AM
710 Turner-McCall
Blvd., 30161
404-291-9766

Rossville
WRIP-AM
203 Alice Rd., 30741
615-867-9898

Royston
WBLW-AM
431 Radio Ranch, 30662
404-245-6101

Sandersville
WSNT-AM/FM
312 Morningside Dr.,
31082
912-552-5182

Savannah
WAEV-FM
P.O. Box 9705, 31412
912-232-0097

WCHY-FM
P.O. Box 1247, 31402
912-964-7794

WEAS-Stereo FM
Box 737, 31404
912-234-7264

WJCL-FM
P.O. Box 13646, 31406
912-925-0022

WKBX-AM
P.O. Box 876, 31402
912-897-1529

WNMT-AM
P.O. Box 7042, 31408
912-964-8124

WSGA-AM
P.O. Box 8247, 31401
912-233-8807

WSGF-FM
Box 876, 31402
912-897-1529

WSOK-AM
24 W. Henry St., 31402
912-232-3322

WWAM Radio
P.O. Box 2026, 31402
912-236-4444

WWJD-AM
P.O. Box 5860, 31414
912-238-0059

WWSA-AM
P.O. Box 1247, 31402
912-964-7794

WZAT-Stereo FM
P.O. Box 8247, 31412
912-233-8807

Smyrna
WYNX-AM
2460-A Atlanta St., SE,
30080
404-436-6171

Soperton
WMPZ-AM/FM
1003 Main St., 30457
912-529-3311

Springfield
WGEC-FM
P.O. Box C, 31329
912-754-6486

Statesboro
WMCD-FM
P.O. Box 958, 30458
912-764-5446

WPTB-AM
Williams Rd., 30458
912-764-6621

WWNS-AM
561 E. Oliff St., 30458
912-764-5446

Summerville
WGTA-AM
State Highway 100,
30747
404-857-2466

Swainsboro
WJAT-AM/Stereo FM
P.O. Box 289, 30401
912-237-2011

WXRS-AM/FM
P.O. Box 1590, 30401
912-237-1590

Sylvania
WSYL-AM
P.O. Box 519, 30467
912-564-7461

Sylvester
WRSG-AM
102 N. Isabella St.,
31791
912-776-3421

Tallapoosa
WKNG-AM
P.O. Box 606, 30176
404-574-7655

Thomaston
WSFT-AM
Box 689, 30286
404-647-5421

WTGA-AM/FM
P.O. Box 550, 30286
404-647-7121

Thomasville
WLOR-AM
Tallahassee Hwy., 31792
912-226-7911

WPAX-AM
P.O. Box 129, 31792
912-226-1240

WTUF-FM
Tallahassee Hwy., 31792
912-226-7911

Thomson
WTHO-FM
1530 Hickory Hill Dr.,
  30824
404-595-5122

WTWA-AM
1530 Hickory Hill Dr.,
  30824
404-595-1561

Tifton
WCUP-FM
P.O. Box 1466, 31794
912-382-1100

WTIF-AM
P.O. Box 968, 31794
912-382-1340

WWGS-AM
1434 N. Tift Ave.,
  31794
912-382-1234

Toccoa
WLET-AM/FM
423 Prather Bridge Rd.,
  30577
404-886-2191

WNEG-AM
100 Boulevard, 30577
404-886-3131

Valdosta
WAFT-FM
94 W. Morven Rd.,
  31603
912-244-5180

WGAF-AM
P.O. Box 100, 31601
912-242-5520

WGOV-AM
P.O. Box 1207, 31601
912-242-4513

WJEM-AM
P.O. Box 368, 31603
912-242-1565

WLGA-FM
P.O. Box 1327, 31603
912-244-8642

WVLD-AM
P.O. Box 1529, 31601
912-242-4821

Vidalia
WTCQ-Stereo FM
Hwy. 280 W, 30474
912-537-9202

WVOP-AM
Hwy. 280 W, 30474
912-537-9202

Vienna
WWWN-AM
Hwy. 41 N, 31092
912-273-1550

Warner Robins
WCOP-AM
P.O. Box 916, 31093
912-929-0523

WRBN-AM/FM
707 Elberta Dr., 31093
912-922-2222

Washington
WLOV-AM/FM
P.O. Box 400, 30673
404-678-2125

Waycross
WACL-AM/FM
Memorial Dr., 31502
912-283-4660

WAYX-AM
P.O. Box 1989, 31501

WQCW-FM
1600 Carswell Ave.,
  31501
912-283-1230

Waynesboro
WBRO-AM
McBean Rd., 30830
404-554-2139

WWGA-FM
P.O. Box 815, 30830
404-554-3942

West Point
WCJM-FM
705 W. 4th Ave., 31833
404-645-1310

WZZZ-AM
705 W. 4th Ave., 31833
404-645-1310

Winder
WIMO-AM
Old Monroe Hwy.,
  30680
404-867-9158

Wrens
WRNZ-FM
Drawer 869, 30833
404-547-2596

PUBLIC/EDUCATIONAL RADIO STATIONS

Athens
WUOG-Stereo FM
P.O. Box 2065, 30602
404-542-7100

Atlanta
WABE-FM
740 Bismark Rd., NE,
  30324
404-873-4477

WCLK-FM
111 James P. Brawley
  Dr., SW, 30314
404-522-8776

323

WRAS-FM
Georgia State University
Plaza, 30303
404-658-2240

WREK-Stereo FM
P.O. Box 32743, 30332
404-894-2468

WRFG-FM
P.O. Box 5332, 30307
404-523-3471

Augusta
WACG-FM
Augusta College, 30910
404-737-1661

WLPE-FM
3213 Huxley Dr., 30909
404-736-9568

Carrollton
WWGC-FM
P.O. Box 10014, 30118
404-834-1355

Cartersville
WCCV-FM
P.O. Box 921, 30120
404-382-8333

Cochran
WDCO-FM
1540 Stewart Ave., SW,
30310
404-656-5961

Columbus
WFRC-FM
1010 7th Place, Phenix
City, Ala., 36867
205-291-0399

WTJB-FM
University Lane, Troy,

Ala., 36082
205-566-5814

Cumming
WWEV-FM
P.O. Box 1511, 30130
404-889-0095

Fort Valley
WHGW-FM
2711 Chelsea Terrace,
Baltimore, 21217

Gainesville
WBCX-FM
Brenau College, 30501
404-534-6187

La Grange
WOAK-FM
1291 Hamilton Rd.,
30241
404-884-2950

Marietta
WGHR-FM
1112 Clay St., 30060
404-424-7354

McDonough
WMVV-FM
19 Griffin St., 30253
404-957-2211

Milledgeville
WXGC-FM
P.O. Box 3146, 31061
912-453-4101

Savannah
WHCJ-FM
P.O. Box 20484, 31404
912-356-2399

WSVH-FM
409 E. Liberty St.,
31401
912-238-0911

WYFS-FM
1300 Battlefield Blvd.,
Chesapeake, VA,
23320

Statesboro
WVGS-FM
P.O. Box 11619, 30460
912-681-5507

Tifton
WABR-FM
Abraham Baldwin
Agriculture College,
31794
912-386-2005

Toccoa Falls
WRAF-FM
P.O. Box 800128, Toccoa
Falls College, 30598
404-886-1912

Valdosta
WVVS-FM
P.O. Box 142, 31698
912-333-5661

Warm Springs
WJSP-FM
1540 Stewart Ave., SW,
30310
404-656-5961

Waycross
WXGA-FM
1540 Stewart Ave., SW,
Atlanta, 30310
404-656-7483

RAILROADS

Listed below are the railroads which operate within the State of Georgia.
The three-letter abbreviation after some lines indicates the name of the
larger system of which that line is a part.

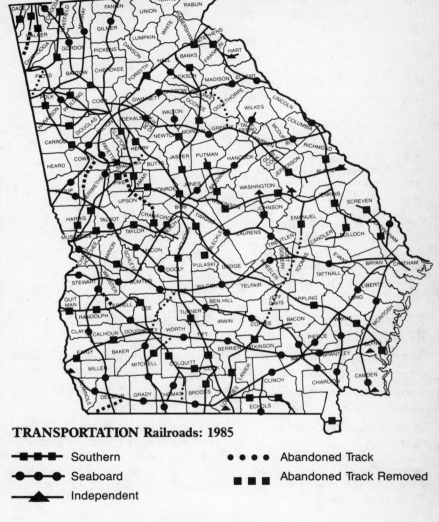

TRANSPORTATION Railroads: 1985

▪■▪■▪■ Southern

●●●●●● Seaboard

▲ Independent

●●●● Abandoned Track

■■■ Abandoned Track Removed

Alabama Great Southern Railroad Company
(SOU)
AMTRAK service
Atlanta and West Point Rail Road Company
(SBD)
Central of Georgia Railroad Company (SOU)
Chattahoochee Valley Railway Company

Chattahoochee Industrial Railroad
Colonel's Island Railroad Company
Gainesville Midland Railroad Company (SBD)
Georgia Northern Railway Company (SOU)
Georgia Southern and Florida Railway Company
   (SOU)
Hartwell Railway Company
Live Oak, Perry and South Georgia Railway
   Company (SOU)
Louisville and Wadley Railway Company
Sandersville Railroad Company
Seaboard System Railroad, Inc.
St. Marys Railroad Company
Southern Railway Company
Tennessee, Alabama & Georgia Railway
   Company (SOU)
Valdosta Southern Railroad
Western Railway of Alabama (SBD)

SOU = Southern Railway Company
SBD = Seaboard System Railroad, Inc.

RELIGIOUS BODIES WITH HEADQUARTERS IN GEORGIA

The following religious denominations maintain their headquarters in Georgia. Number of churches and membership figures are as follows:

Presbyterian: Presbyterian Church of America. Organized 1973; *address* P.O. Box 1428, Decatur 30031; churches, 888; membership, 180,392.

Presbyterian: Presbyterian Church (USA). Organized in 1706 as Presbyterian Church, US; merged in 1983 with the former United Presbyterian Church, currently maintains its original headquarters until a joint headquarters location site is chosen. *Address* 341 Ponce de Leon Avenue, NE, Atlanta 30365; churches, 13,042; membership, 3,202,392 (figures as of 1982, prior to merger).

REVOLUTIONARY WAR

The first battle of the Revolutionary War took place April 19, 1775, in Concord, Massachusetts, but the difficulties which led up to the war began ten years earlier. The French and Indian Wars had created such massive debts that Parliament imposed the Stamp Act as a means of recovering some of the funds, but the colonists objected.

Georgia was the last to join the other colonies in protest for several reasons. A substantial sum of money had been invested by Parliament and private citizens to get the colony of Georgia started. The fact that the governor Parliament had appointed, Sir James Wright, was well-liked, capable and very loyal to the King was another factor. The strong family ties of Georgians with the mother country were of great influence also.

The Stamp Act, which was passed by Parliament March 22, 1765, met with much opposition. William Pitt, Earl of Chatham and Edmund Burke (for whom Chatham and Burke counties were named), spoke out in Parliament on behalf of the colonists. Benjamin Franklin, hired by Georgia in 1768 to act as its agent in England, also spoke out against the British taxes.

The Liberty Boys, as the local organization of the Sons of Liberty were called, were determined that no stamps would be sold in Georgia. Their behavior made Governor Wright very nervous.

The Liberty Boys made their feelings known in October of 1765 when the celebration of the King's birthday usually took place by hanging in effigy dummies of the governor and the stampseller, who had not yet arrived. They paraded about Savannah shouting, "Liberty, Property, and NO STAMPS!"

Only seventy stamps were sold in all of Georgia, and they were for clearance papers for a ship with perishable cargo. Some South Carolina citizens became so angry that the stamps were bought that they threatened to burn the ship.

Georgia's first, and for a long time only, newspaper, the *Georgia Gazette*, was forced to suspend its publication in May, 1765, after publishing for just two years. The editor, James Johnston, cited the Stamp Act as the reason because it had made publication too expensive.

The paper was again published in May, 1766, when it was reported that the Stamp Act would be repealed. This event took place July 16, 1766, when Parliament voted to repeal it by a vote of 275 to 176.

In 1767 taxes were again imposed by Parliament for paint, lead, glass, paper and tea. The colonists rebelled by boycotting British exports, until finally all taxes were repealed except tea (three cents per pound).

The Boston Tea Party, which took place as a result of the tea tax, brought the war nearer. The British closed the port at Boston, and said it would remain closed until the tea was paid for; but the tax was never paid. As a result, food supplies from England were not permitted shipment to the colonies.

When the First Continental Congress was held in September, 1774, the Tories, loyal to the King, were influential enough to prevent Georgia from sending any delegates to it. But when the call for a Second Continental Congress was sounded, Georgia held its first Provincial Congress in January, 1775, and elected three delegates to go to Philadelphia. These delegates refused to attend because they were convinced that all of Georgia was not fairly represented.

The Puritans in Georgia were concerned because their kinsmen in Boston were hungry; so they sent their own delegate, Dr. Lyman Hall. He carried food and money on the journey, and sat in on the deliberations of the Second Continental Congress, but did not attempt to vote.

George Washington was named commander-in-chief of America's raw troops by Congress. In the colonies there were about 282,000 men capable of serving in the troops, but at any one time he never had more than 25,000 of them on active duty.

Fourteen months after the Boston Tea Party, April 19, 1775, the first shooting war took place at Lexington, about sixteen miles outside Boston. Georgia organized a Council of Safety, June 22, 1775, two months after the war started in Lexington. The Council called for a meeting of the Second Provincial Congress.

The Second Provincial Congress met in July, 1775, and at this meeting Georgia seceded from England. Also, five delegates were chosen to attend the Second Continental Congress: Archibald Bulloch, Lyman Hall, John Houstoun, Noble Wymberly Jones, and Reverend Joachim Zubly. In February, 1776, the delegates to the Continental Congress were Bulloch, Hall, and Houstoun, and George Walton and Button Gwinnett, who replaced Jones and Zubly. Hall, Walton, and Gwinnett were the representatives from Georgia who signed the Declaration of Independence.

The war took place in the north for the first three and a half years. In November, 1778, the British failed in their first effort to move the war south. Savannah was captured, however, in December, 1778, and held by the British for three and one half years.

In January, 1779, Sunbury and Fort Morris were captured and in February Augusta fell under siege. The Americans were successful in defeating the British near Kettle Creek, about eight miles from Washington, Georgia, in February, 1779; but the British overcame the Americans at Brier Creek a month later.

The British held the colony of Georgia during the year of 1780. Ogeechee Ferry was the site of the last Revolutionary battle fought on Georgian soil.

Parliament negotiated for peace in February, 1782; and in July, 1782, the British surrendered Savannah. The Treaty of Paris, signed in November, 1782, ended the war. England, France, and America ratified a more detailed treaty, and it was signed September, 1783.

In 1786, a group representing several states met in Annapolis, which suggested that the Continental Congress should meet to work out problems and strengthen the Articles of the Confederation. When the men did meet, they drew up what is probably the most powerful political document in the world, the Constitution of the United States of America.

RIVERS

The major rivers of Georgia are shown on the accompanying map. For the sake of space, only the more important streams can be shown.

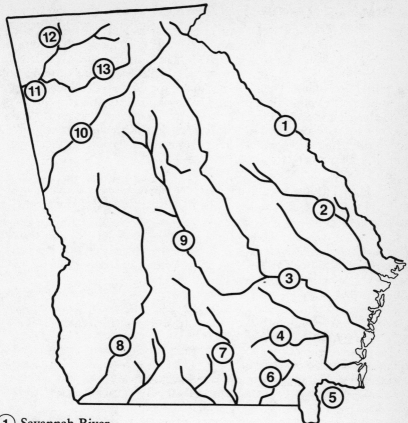

1 Savannah River
2 Ogeechee River
3 Altamara River
4 Satilla River
5 St. Mary's River
6 Suwannee River
7 Alapaha River

8 Flint River
9 Ocmulgee River
10 Chattahoochee River
11 Coosa River
12 Oostanaulie River
13 Etowah River

SENATORS, UNITED STATES

Mack Mattingly
Washington, D.C. 20510
Telephone: 202-224-3643

Sam Nunn
Washington, D.C. 20510
Telephone: 202-224-3521

SHERMAN'S MARCH

General William Tecumseh Sherman's march, which ravaged the countryside, is shown on this map. Sherman's troops—63,000 men—left Atlanta on
November 16, 1864, after setting fire to it, and headed to the sea, following
the rail line. They traveled over a swath of 30 miles on either side of the rail
line, pilfering the land. Their aim was to destroy General Lee's food supply
and to break the will of the people. They took food, livestock, vehicles of
various kinds, and other objects from plantations and small farms along the
way. Among the cities and towns they passed through were Milledgeville,
Sandersville, Louisville, and Millen. They reached Savannah, their desti-
nation, on December 21.

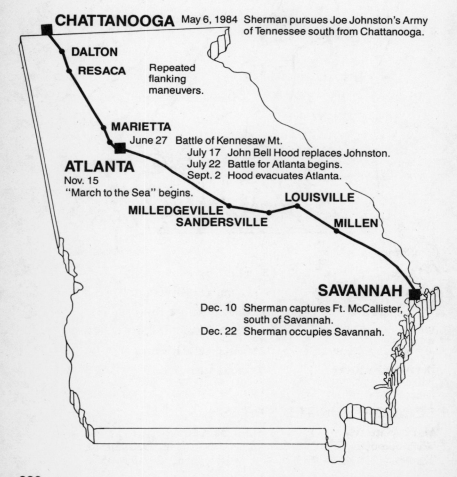

CHATTANOOGA May 6, 1984 Sherman pursues Joe Johnston's Army
of Tennessee south from Chattanooga.

DALTON

RESACA Repeated
flanking
maneuvers.

MARIETTA
June 27 Battle of Kennesaw Mt.
ATLANTA   July 17 John Bell Hood replaces Johnston.
Nov. 15   July 22 Battle for Atlanta begins.
"March to the Sea" begins.   Sept. 2 Hood evacuates Atlanta.

LOUISVILLE
MILLEDGEVILLE
SANDERSVILLE   **MILLEN**

SAVANNAH
Dec. 10 Sherman captures Ft. McCallister,
south of Savannah.
Dec. 22 Sherman occupies Savannah.

SPORTS

GEORGIA SPORTS HALL OF FAME

1956
Selby H. Buck
Clint Castleberry
Joe H. Jenkins
Vernon "Catfish" Smith
Claude T. "Gabe"
 Tolbert
John Varnedoe

1957
John R. Carson
R. L. "Shorty" Doyal
Harold E. McNabb
Charles N. Roberts
Eric P. Staples
John G. "Stumpy"
 Thomason

1958
Joseph W. Bean
W. O. Cheney
Quinton Lumpkin
George M. Phillips
Jack Roberts
Sidney Scarborough

1959
Ray Beck
Sam Burke
H. D. Butler
George Mathews
Mark Smith
A. Drane Watson

1960
Wright Bazemore
Dwight Keith, Sr.
Henry I. Langston
Julian H. "Joe" Pittard
James Skipworth, Jr.
Thomas J. Slate

1961
George Gardner
Thomas E. Greene

Oliver Hunnicutt
Thomas H. Paris
Alfred W. Scott
Kimsey R. Stewart

1962
D. B. Carroll
Vassa "Gus" Cate
Sam Glassman, Sr.
William Henderson
Jim Nolan
George H. O'Kelly

1964
William A. Alexander
Lucius "Luke" Appling
Tyrus Raymond Cobb
Robert G. Hooks
Robert T. Jones, Jr.
Robert McWhorter
Albert H. Staton
Bobby Walthour, Sr.

1965
Robert L. "Bobby"
 Dodd
Bryan M. "Bitsy" Grant
William L. "Young"
 Stribling
Charley Trippi

1966
Frank B. Anderson, Sr.
Wallace "Wally" Butts
Ivy M. "Chick" Shiver
Louise Suggs

1967
John Heisman
Charles Morgan
Nap Rucker
Frank Sinkwich
Forrest "Spec" Towns

1969
Jim Cavan
Spurgeon Chandler
Allen Ralph "Buck"
 Flowers
Joseph T. "Phoney"
 Smith

1971
Frank Broyles
Earl Mann
Harry Mehre
Herman J. Stegeman

1972
Joel H. Eaves
Joe Guyon
Carlton Lewis
Tom Nash, Jr.
Alline Banks Sprouse

1973
Weems O. Baskin
Wayman O. Creel
Howell T. Hollis
John R. Mize

1974
Paul Anderson
James "Doc" Harper
Dorothy Kirby
Martin W. "Marty"
 Marion
Jim Parker
Everett Strupper

1975
Henry L. "Hank"
 Aaron
William F. "Bill"
 Fincher
Fred Missildine
Larry Morris
Doug Sanders
Cecil H. Travis

331

1976
James P. "Buck" Cheves
Theo "Tiger" Flowers
Dan Magill
Virlyn Moore, Jr.
Wyomia Tyus
Perrin Walker
Whitlow Wyatt
Charles Yates

1977
David "Red" Barron
Sterling A. Dupree
Sam J. "Sambo" Elliott
Elmer B. Morrow
Henry R. "Peter" Pund
Francis A. Tarkenton
Rudolph P. "Rudy"
    York

1978
Vince Dooley
J. Timothy "Tim"
    Flock
Alexa Stirling Fraser
James E. "Jimmy" Orr
Nolen Richardson
Harold Sargent
Doug Wycott

1979
Arnold Blum
Alice Coachman Davis
Charles Grisham
Frank "Hop" Owens
William A. "Billy"
    Paschal
Johnny Rauch

B. L. "Crook" Smith
George "Tweedy"
    Stallings
Sidney "Beau Jack"
    Walker

1980
Tommy Aaron
Maxie Baughan
Edmund R. "Zeke"
    Bratkowski
Edith McGuire Duvall
John "Whack" Hyder
H. Boyd McWhorter
Ralph Metcalfe
Garland Pinholster
Sherrod Smith

1981
Thomas William Barnes
Marion Campbell
William C. Hartman, Jr.
Leonard Moore Hauss
Herbert Maffett
George A. Morris, Jr.

1982
James C. Bagby, Sr.
Lew Cordell
Edward B. Hamm
Milton Leathers
George Poschner

1983
Robert T. "Bobby"
    Davis
Mary Louise Fowler
James T. "Jim" Hearn

Tommy Nobis
Reid Patterson
James B. "J. B." Scearce
Mildred McDaniel
    Singleton

1984
Joseph J. Bennett
Jimmy Carnes
George C. Griffin
Roger Kaiser
Oscar Bane Keeler
Melvyn Pender, Jr.
Williams Thomas
    Stanfill

1985
John Donaldson
Leonidas Epps
William L. Goodloe, Jr.
Watts Gunn
J. C. "Jakes" Hines
Fred W. Hooper
Phil Niekro
William L. Shaw

1986
Morris M. Bryan, Jr.
Bobby Lee Bryant
Walter Frazier, Jr.
Joe Gerson
Billy Lothridge
Anthony "Zippy"
    Morocco
Martha Hudson
    Pennyman
Jacob E. "Jake" Scott,
    III

GEORGIA PARTICIPANTS IN THE XXII OLYMPICS

John Crist (Decathlon)
Teresa Edwards
    (Basketball)
Vern Fleming
    (Basketball)
Sam Graddy (Track)
Lea Henry (Basketball)

Evander Holyfield
    (Boxing)
Bob Jaugstetter
    (Rowing)
Roger Kingdom (Track)
David Larson
    (Swimming)

Ed Liddie (Judo)
Steve Lundquist
    (Swimming)
Antonio McKay (Track)
Mark Smith (Fencing)

STATE DEPARTMENTS

Administrative Services, Department of
Suite 1520, West Tower
200 Piedmont Avenue, Atlanta 30334
404-656-5514
Commissioner of Administrative
Services, Larry L. Clark

Agriculture, State Department of
Agriculture Building
404-656-3600
Commissioner, Thomas T. Irvin,
Room 204

Audits, State Department of
270 Washington Street, Room 214
404-656-2174
State Auditor, William M. Nixon

Banking and Finance, Department of
2990 Brandywine Road, Suite 200
Atlanta, 30341
404-393-7330
Commissioner, Edward D. Dunn

Building Authority, Georgia
1 Martin Luther King Dr., SW
404-656-3253
Director of Administration, Steve Polk

Campaign and Financial Disclosure Commission, State
2082 East Exchange Place, Suite 235
Tucker, 30084
404-493-5795
Chairman, Oliver C. Bateman

Community Affairs, State Department of
40 Marietta Street, NW, Suite 800
404-656-3836
Commissioner, Jim Higdon

Comptroller General, Office of
Seventh Floor, West Tower,
Floyd Bldg.
200 Piedmont Avenue, SE
404-656-2056
Comptroller General, Johnnie L.
Caldwell

Courts, Administrative Office of the
Suite 550, 244 Washington Street
Atlanta, 30334
404-656-5171
Director, Robert L. Doss, Jr.

Court of Appeals of Georgia, Office of
Judicial Building, 4th Floor
Telephone: 404-656-3450

Chief Judge Harold R. Banke
Legal Assistant James H. Morawetz
(For list of other judges see
COURTS.)

Defense, Department of
P.O. Box 17965, Atlanta, 30316
404-656-1700
The Adjutant General & Director,
Georgia Emergency Management
Agency, Maj.-Gen. Joseph W.
Griffin

Education, State Department of
Twin Towers East, Suite 2066
404-656-2800
State Superintendent of Schools,
Dr. Charles McDaniel

Employees' Retirement System of Georgia
Two Northside 75, Atlanta, 30318
404-656-2960
Board of Trustees, William B. Stark

Forestry Commission, State
Central Office: P.O. Box 819
Macon, 31298-4599
912-744-3211
Director and Executive Secretary,
John W. Mixon

Human Resources, Department of
47 Trinity Ave., SW
404-656-5680
Commissioner, James G. Ledbetter,
Ph.D.

333

General Assembly, Offices of
State Capitol, 3rd Floor
Senate:
404-656-5030
President, Zell Miller

House of Representatives:
Speaker, Thomas B. Murphy
404-656-5020

Governor, Office of
State Capitol, Rooms 201–203
404-656-1776
Governor, Joe Frank Harris

Industry and Trade, Department of
230 Peachtree Street, NW
Atlanta, 30303
404-656-3545
Commissioner, George Berry

Investigation, Georgia Bureau of
3121 Panthersville Road,
Decatur, 30334
404-244-2535
Director, E. P. Peters

Judicial Administration

District 1: 912-944-2040
Administrative Judge
A. Blenn Taylor, Jr., Brunswick
District Court Administrator
Daniel E. DeLoach, Jr., Savannah

District 2: 912-333-5266
Administrative Judge
George A. Horkan, Jr., Moultrie
District Court Administrator
Roger E. Douglas, Valdosta

District 3: 912-744-6207
Administrative Judge
Hal Bell, Macon
District Court Administrator
David L. Ratley, Macon

District 4: 404-371-4901
Administrative Judge
Curtis V. Tillman, Decatur
District Court Administrator
Richard F. Jugar, Decatur

District 5: 404-656-5358
Administrative Judge

John S. Langford, Atlanta
District Court Administrator
John T. Shope, Atlanta

District 6: 404-228-7430
Administrative Judge
Andrew J. Whalen, Jr., Griffin
District Court Administrator
Fred Roney, Griffin

District 7: 404-382-5374
Administrative Judge
Jere F. White, Cartersville
District Court Administrator
William Martin, Cartersville

District 8: 912-526-6116
Administrative Judge
Walter C. McMillan, Jr.,
  Sandersville
District Court Administrator
Jack L. Bean, Lyons

District 9: 404-535-5307
Administrative Judge
Charles A. Pannell, Jr., Dalton
District Court Adminstrator
Reggie Forrester, Gainesville

District 10: 404-828-3256
Administrative Judge
William M. Fleming, Jr., Augusta
District Court Administrator
Tom Gunnels, Augusta

Juvenile Court Judges, Council of
244 Washington St., Suite 550,
Atlanta, 30334
404-656-6411
Executive Director, J. Chris Perrin

Labor, State Department of
Labor Building, Room 288
404-656-3011
Commissioner, Joe D. Tanner

Law, Department of
Judicial Building, Room 132
404-656-3300
Attorney General, Michael J. Bowers

Legislative Counsel:
404-656-5000
Frank H. Edwards

Legislative Fiscal Officer (Acting):
404-656-5054
Paul Lynch

Legislative Budget Analyst:
404-656-5050
John N. (Pete) Hackney

Library, State
Judicial Building, Room 301
404-656-3468
State Librarian, Carroll T. Parker

Lieutenant Governor, Office of
State Capitol, Room 240
404-656-5030
Lieutenant Governor, Zell Miller

Medical Assistance, Department of
Floyd Veterans Memorial Building
West Tower, 2 Martin Luther King,
Jr., Drive, SE Atlanta, 30334
404-656-4479
Commissioner, Aaron J. Johnson

**Merit System of Personnel
Administration, State**
200 Piedmont Avenue, West Tower
404-656-2705
Commissioner, Charles E. Storm

Natural Resources, Department of
270 Washington St., SW
404-656-3500
Commissioner of Natural Resources,
J. Leonard Ledbetter

**Offender Rehabilitation,
Department of**
Floyd Veterans Memorial Building
East Tower, Room 756
2 Martin Luther King, Jr., Drive, SE
Atlanta, 30334
404-656-4593
Commissioner, David C. Evans

Pardons & Paroles, State Board of
Floyd Veterans Memorial Building
Fifth Floor, East
2 Martin Luther King, Jr., Drive, SE
Atlanta, 30334
404-656-5651
Chairman, Michael H. Wing

Planning and Budget, Office of
Trinity-Washington Building,
6th Floor
270 Washington St., SW
404-656-3820
Director, Clark T. Stevens

**Prosecuting Attorneys' Council of
Georgia**
3951 Snapfinger Pkwy.,
Decatur, 30035
404-289-6278
Director, Joseph L. Chambers

Public Safety, Department of
959 E. Confederate Ave., SE
(P.O. Box 1456), Atlanta, 30371
404-656-6063
Commissioner, State Patrol,
Col. Hugh Hardison

Public Service Commission, Office of
244 Washington St., Room 162
404-656-4501
Chairman, Robert C. (Bobby) Pafford

Regents, Board of
244 Washington St., SW, Room 468
404-656-2200
Chairman Sidney D. Smith, Jr.

Revenue, State Department of
270 Washington St., SW, Room 410
404-656-4015
Commissioner, Marcus E. Collins, Sr.

Secretary of State, Office of
State Capitol, Room 214
404-656-2881
Secretary of State, Max Cleland

**Soil and Water Conservation
Committee, Georgia**
624 South Milledge Avenue
Athens, 30603
404-542-3065
Executive Director, F. Graham
Liles, Jr.

Student Finance Committee
2082 East Exchange Place, Suite 200
Tucker 30084
404-493-5402

Executive Director, Donald E. Payton

Supreme Court of Georgia, Office of
244 Washington Street, SW
404-656-3470
Chief Justice Harold N. Hill, Jr.
(For a complete list of justices, see
COURTS.)

Teacher's Retirement System of Georgia
Two Northside 75, Suite 400
Atlanta, 30381
404-656-2954
Executive Secretary-Treasurer, Gerald S. Gilbert

Transportation, Department of
2 Capitol Square
404-656-5206
Commissioner, Thomas D. Moreland

Veterans Service, State Department of
Floyd Veterans Memorial Building,
Suite E-970, Atlanta, 30334
404-656-2300
Commissioner, Pete Wheeler

Workers' Compensation, State Board of
1000 South Omni International
Atlanta, 30335
404-656-3875
Chairman, Herbert T. Greenholtz, Jr.

STATE FORESTS

There are only two state forests which are owned and managed by the Georgia Forestry Commission.

- **Dixon Memorial State Forest**—35,789 acres located in Ware and Brantley Counties.
- **Baldwin State Forest**—2,702 acres located in Baldwin and Wilkinson Counties.

Two other forests, the **Paulding Forest** and the **Dawson Forest** are owned by the city of Atlanta, but managed by the GFC. There is also the **B. F. Grant Memorial Forest, Hardeman Forest,** and **Whitehall Forest** that are owned and managed by the University of Georgia. The **Rock Eagle Forest** is operated by the Extension Service.

STATE OFFICERS

Governor
Joe Frank Harris

Lieutenant Governor
Zell Miller

Secretary of State
Max Cleland

Attorney General
Michael J. Bowers

Commissioner of Agriculture
Tommy Irvin

Comptroller General
Johnnie L. Caldwell

State School Superintendent
Dr. Charles McDaniel

Commissioner of Labor
Joe D. Tanner

Addresses and telephone numbers listed under **STATE DEPARTMENTS.**

STATE PARKS AND HISTORIC SITES

Map Key	County	Park or Site	Address, Zip	Telephone	Activities, Facilities and Rentals[1]
1	Barrow	Fort Yargo, Will-A-Way, (reserved for handicapped	Winder 30680 Winder 30680	404-867-3489 404-867-5313	TT,DS,S,B,F, C,S,B,F
2	Bartow	Red Top Mountain	Cartersville 30120	404-974-5182	TT,DS,C,S,B, F,CS
3	Bartow	Etowah Mounds	Route 1, Cartersville 30120	404-382-2704	M
4	Bryan	Ft. McAllister Historic Site	P.O. Box 198, Richmond Hill 31324	912-727-2339	M
5	Butts	Indian Springs	Indian Springs 30231	404-775-7241	TT,DS,C,S,B, F,M
6	Camden	Crooked River	St. Mary's 31558	912-882-5256	TT,DS,C,S, B,F
8	Carroll	John Tanner	Route 7, Carrollton 30117	404-832-7545	TT,DS,C,B, F,CS
9	Charlton	Stephen C. Foster	Fargo 31631	912-637-5274	TT,DS,C,B,F, CS
10	Chatham	Skidaway Island	Savannah 31406	912-598-0393	TT,DS,S,F,
11	Chatham	Wormsloe	P.O. Box 13852, 7501 Skidaway Road, Savannah 31406	912-352-2548	M
12	Chattooga	James H. Floyd	Route 1, Summerville 30747	404-857-5211	TT,DS,B,F
13	Clay	George T. Bagby	Route 2, Georgetown 31754	912-768-2660	TT,DS,C,B,F
14	Coffee	General Coffee	Route 2, Nicholls 31554	912-384-7082	TT,DS,S,F
15	Columbia	Mistletoe	Route 1, Appling 30802	404-541-0321	TT,DS,C,S, B,F
16	Colquitt	Reed Bingham	P.O. Box 459, Adel 31620	912-896-3551	TT,DS,S,B, F,CS
16	Cook	Reed Bingham	P.O. Box 459, Adel 31620	912-896-3551	TT,DS,S,B, F,CS
17	Crisp	Georgia Veterans	Route 3, Cordele 31015	912-273-2190	TT,DS,C,S,B, F,M
18	Dade	Cloudland Canyon	Rising Fawn 30738	404-657-4050	TT,DS,C, F,CS
19	Dawson	Amicalola Falls	Star Route, Dawsonville 30534	404-265-2885	TT,DS,C,F
20	Douglas	Sweetwater Creek Conservation Park	Route 1, Mt. Vernon Road, Lithia Springs 30057	404-944-1700	B,F
21	Early	Kolomoki Mounds	Route 1, Blakely 31723	912-723-5296	TT,DS,S,B, F,M
22	Elbert	Bobby Brown	Route 4, Box 232, Elberton 30635	404-283-3313	TT,DS,S,B,F
7	Emanuel	George L. Smith, II	P.O. Box 57, Twin City 30471	912-763-2759	F,TT,DS
23	Franklin	Victoria Bryant	Route 1, Box 267, Royston 30662	404-245-6270	TT,DS,S,F
24	Franklin	Tugaloo	Route 1, Lavonia 30553	404-356-4362	TT,DS,C,S,B, F,CS

Map Key	County	Park or Site	Address, Zip	Telephone	Activities, Facilities and Rentals[1]
25	Glynn	Hofwyl Plantation Historic Site	Route 2, Box 83, Brunswick 31520	912-264-9263	M
26	Gordon	New Echota	Route 3, Calhoun 30701	404-629-8151	M
27	Harris	F. D. Roosevelt	Pine Mountain 31822	404-663-4858	TT,DS,C,S,B, F,CS
28	Hart	Hart	1515 Hart Park Road, Hartwell 30643	404-376-8756	TT,DS,C,S,B, F,CS
29	Henry	Panola Mountain Conservation Park	2600 Highway 155 Southwest, Stockbridge 30281	404-474-2914	M
30	Jenkins	Magnolia Springs	Route 5, Box 488, Millen 30442	912-982-1660	TT,DS,C,S,F
31	Jones	Jarrell Plantation	Route 1, Juliette 31046	912-986-5172	M

Map Key	County	Park or Site	Address, Zip	Telephone	Activities, Facilities and Rentals[1]
32	Liberty	Sunbury	Route 1, Box 236, Midway 31320	912-884-5999	M
33	Lincoln	Elijah Clark	Route 4, Box 107-B, Lincolnton 30817	404-359-3458	TT,DS,C,S,B, M,F
34	Lumpkin	Dahlonega Gold Museum	Public Square Box 2042, Dahlonega 30533	404-864-2257	M
35	Madison	Watson Mill Bridge	Box 118-A, Noel Road, Comer 30629	404-783-5349	TT,DS,F
36	McIntosh	Ft. King George	P.O. Box 711, Darien 31305	912-437-4770	M
37	Meriwether	FDR Little White House Historic Site	Warm Springs 31830	404-655-3511	M
38	Monroe	High Falls	Route 5, Box 108, Jackson 30233	912-994-5080	TT,DS,S,B,F
39	Morgan	Hard Labor Creek	Rutledge 30663	404-557-2863	TT,DS,C,S,F, CS,B
40	Murray	Fort Mountain	Route 7, Box 1-K, Chatsworth 30705	404-695-2621	TT,DS,C,S,F
41	Murray	Vann House	Route 7, Box 235, Chatsworth 30705	404-695-2598	M
35	Oglethorpe	Watson Mill Bridge	Route 1, Box 118-A, Comer 30629	404-783-5349	TT,DS,F
42	Paulding	Pickett's Mill Historic Site	Route 6, Box 474, Dallas 30132	404-424-6177	M
43	Rabun	Black Rock Mountain	Mountain City 30562	404-746-2141	TT,DS,C, CS,F
44	Rabun	Moccasin Creek	Route 1, Clarkesville 30523	404-947-3194	TT,DS,B,F,B
45	Seminole	Seminole	Route 2, Donalsonville 31745	912-861-3137	TT,DS,C,S, B,F
46	Stephens	Traveler's Rest	Route 3, Toccoa 30577	404-886-2256	M
47	Stewart	Providence Canyon	Route 2A, Box 54A, Lumpkin 31815	912-838-6202	M
48	Taliaferro	A. H. Stephens Memorial	Box 235, Crawfordville 30631	404-456-2221 404-456-2602	M
		A. H. Stephens State Park	Box 235, Crawfordville 30631		TT,S,F,CS,M
49	Tattnall	Gordonia-Altamaha	P.O. Box 1047, Reidsville 30453	912-557-6444	TT,S,B,F
50	Telfair	Little Ocmulgee	McRae 31055	912-868-2832	TT,DS,C,S,B, F
51	Thomas	Lapham-Patterson House	626 N. Dawson Street, Thomasville 31792	912-226-0405	M
52	Union	Vogel	Route 1, Box 97, Blairsville 30512	404-745-2628	TT,DS,C,S, F,CS
39	Walton	Hard Labor Creek	Rutledge 30663	404-557-2863	TT,DS,C,S,B, F,CS
53	Ware	Laura S. Walker	Route 6, Box 205, Waycross 31501	912-283-4424	TT,DS,S,B,F
54	Washington	Hamburg	Route 1, Box 223, Mitchell 30820	912-552-2393	TT,DS,B,F, CS,M

339

Map Key	County	Park or Site	Address, Zip	Telephone	Activities, Facilities and Rentals[1]
50	Wheeler	Little Ocmulgee	McRae 31055	912-868-2832	TT,DS,C,S, B,F
55	White	Unicoi Unicoi Lodge/Conference Center	P.O. Box 256, Helen 30545	404-878-2201	TT,DS,C,S, F,CS
56	Wilkes	Robert Toombs House	P.O. Box 605, Washington 30673	404-678-2226	M

STATE PATROL PHONE NUMBERS

City	County	Phone Number	City	County	Phone Number
Albany	Dougherty	404-439-4248	La Fayette	Walker	404-638-1400
Americus	Sumter	912-928-1200	La Grange	Troup	404-882-8104
Athens	Clarke	404-542-8660	Lawrenceville	Gwinnett	404-963-9246
Atlanta	Fulton/DeKalb	404-656-6077	Madison	Morgan	404-342-1515
Blue Ridge	Fannin	404-632-2215	Manchester	Meriwether	404-846-3106
Brunswick	Glynn	912-265-6050	Marietta	Cobb	
Calhoun	Gordon	404-629-8694	Milledgeville	Baldwin	912-453-4717
Canton	Cherokee	404-479-2155	Newnan	Coweta	404-253-3212
Cartersville	Bartow	404-382-3232	Perry	Houston	912-987-1100
Cedartown	Polk	404-748-3334	Reidsville	Tattnall	912-557-4378
Conyers	Rockdale	404-922-4634	Rome	Floyd	404-295-6002
Cordele	Crisp	912-273-3131	Savannah	Chatham	912-232-6414
Cuthbert	Randolph	912-732-2167	Statesboro	Bulloch	912-764-5654
Dalton	Whitfield	404-278-1448	Swainsboro	Emanuel	912-237-7818
Donalsonville	Seminole	912-524-2177	Sylvania	Screven	912-564-2018
Douglas	Coffee	912-384-1600	Thomaston	Upson	404-647-7153
Dublin	Laurens	912-272-2300	Thomasville	Thomas	912-228-2300
Forest Park	Clayton	404-656-4610	Thomson	McDuffie	404-595-2622
Forsyth	Monroe	912-994-5159	Tifton	Tift	912-386-3333
Gainesville	Hall	404-532-5305	Toccoa	Stephens	404-886-4949
Griffin	Spalding	404-227-2121	Valdosta	Lowndes	912-247-3442
Helena	Telfair	912-868-6441	Villa Rica	Carroll	404-459-3661
Hinesville	Liberty	912-876-2141	Washington	Wilkes	404-678-3232
Jekyll Island	Glynn	912-635-2303	Waycross	Ware	912-283-6622

To inquire about Georgia road conditions, call:
Weekdays 8:15 to 4:45   404-656-5882
Nights and Weekends   404-656-5267

STATE SYMBOLS

The following list and illustrations present the state symbols, nickname, seal and flag.

State Flower
Cherokee Rose

State Bird
Brown Thrasher

State Tree
Live Oak

State Fish
Largemouth Bass

State Song
"Georgia on My Mind"

State Motto
"Wisdom, Justice, and Moderation"

State Nickname
"The Empire State of the South"

State Seal

State Flag

TAXES

SALES TAX

Georgia has a three percent state sales tax. The maximum combined state and local rate is five percent.

There is a 1% local transit tax (M) in two counties that started April 1, 1972. The local option 1% sales tax (L) is in effect in 140 counties that originated on April 1, 1976. A Special 1% tax (S) was started on July 1, 1985 and now has 26 counties participating.

The first two local taxes are permanent and would take a public majority vote to remove. The new Special 1% sales tax is voted in to finance specified

341

COUNTIES IMPOSING LOCAL OPTION SALES TAX

⊠ Counties without tax

☐ Counties with tax

capital projects and has automatic "sun-set" provisions that remove this tax in a period of five years or less.

County	% Rate on 4-1-86	County	% Rate on 4-1-86	County	% Rate on 4-1-86
Appling	3	Bibb (L)	4	Candler (L)	4
Atkinson (L)	4	Bleckley (L)	4	Carroll (L)	4
Bacon (L)	4	Brantley (L)	4	Catoosa (L)	4
Baker	3	Brooks (L)	4	Charlton (L)	4
Baldwin (L)	4	Bryan (L)	4	Chatham (LS)	5
Banks (L)	4	Bulloch (L)	4	Chattahoochee (L)	4
Barrow (L)	4	Burke (L)	4	Chattooga (LS)	5
Bartow (L)	4	Butts (L)	4	Cherokee (S)	4
Ben Hill (L)	4	Calhoun (L)	4	Clarke (LS)	5
Berrien (LS)	5	Camden (L)	4	Clay (L)	4

County	% Rate on 4-1-86	County	% Rate on 4-1-86	County	% Rate on 4-1-86
Clayton	3	Heard (L)	4	Putnam (L)	4
Clinch (L)	4	Henry (L)	4	Quitman (L)	4
Cobb (S)	4	Houston (L)	4	Rabun (L)	4
Coffee (L)	4	Irwin (L)	4	Randolph (L)	4
Colquitt (L)	4	Jackson (L)	4	Richmond (L)	4
Columbia (L)	4	Jasper (L)	4	Rockdale	3
Cook (L)	4	Jeff Davis (L)	4	Schley (L)	4
Coweta (LS)	5	Jefferson (L)	4	Screven (L)	4
Crawford (L)	4	Jenkins (L)	4	Seminole (L)	4
Crisp (L)	4	Johnson (L)	4	Spalding (L)	4
Dade (LS)	5	Jones (L)	4	Stephens (L)	4
Dawson (L)	4	Lamar (L)	4	Stewart (L)	4
Decatur (L)	4	Lanier (LS)	5	Sumter (L)	4
DeKalb (M)	4	Laurens (L)	4	Talbot (L)	4
Dodge (L)	4	Lee (L)	4	Taliaferro	3
Dooly (LS)	5	Liberty (L)	4	Tattnall (LS)	5
Dougherty (LS)	5	Lincoln (L)	4	Taylor (L)	4
Douglas (LS)	5	Long	3	Telfair (L)	4
Early (L)	4	Lowndes (L)	4	Terrell (L)	4
Echols	3	Lumpkin (L)	4	Thomas (S)	4
Effingham (L)	4	Macon (L)	4	Tift (L)	4
Elbert (L)	4	Madison (LS)	5	Toombs (L)	4
Emanuel (L)	4	Marion (L)	4	Towns (L)	4
Evans (L)	4	McDuffie (LS)	5	Treutlen (L)	4
Fannin (L)	4	McIntosh (L)	4	Troup (L)	4
Fayette (L)	4	Meriwether (L)	4	Turner (LS)	5
Floyd (L)	4	Miller (L)	4	Twiggs (L)	4
Forsyth (L)	4	Mitchell (L)	4	Union (L)	4
Franklin	3	Monroe (L)	4	Upson (L)	4
Fulton (LM)	5	Montgomery (L)	4	Walker (L)	4
Gilmer (L)	4	Morgan (L)	4	Walton (LS)	5
Glascock	3	Murray (L)	4	Ware (LS)	5
Glynn (LS)	5	Muscogee (L)	4	Warren (L)	4
Gordon (L)	4	Newton (L)	4	Washington (L)	4
Grady (L)	4	Oconee (LS)	5	Wayne	3
Greene (L)	4	Oglethorpe (S)	4	Webster	3
Gwinnett (S)	4	Paulding (L)	4	Wheeler (L)	4
Habersham (L)	4	Peach (LS)	5	White (L)	4
Hall (LS)	5	Pickens (L)	4	Whitfield (L)	4
Hancock (L)	4	Pierce (L)	4	Wilcox (L)	4
Haralson (L)	4	Pike (L)	4	Wilkes	3
Harris (L)	4	Polk (L)	4	Wilkinson (L)	4
Hart (S)	4	Pulaski (L)	4	Worth (L)	4

STATE INCOME TAX

Georgia Personal Income Tax: 1982

County	Adjusted Gross Income Less Deficit		Net Taxable Income	Amount of Tax Liability	
	Total	Average Per Return		Total	Average Per Return
Appling	$ 69,196,634	$14,635	$ 44,902,749	$ 1,946,204	$412

| County | Adjusted Gross Income Less Deficit | | Net Taxable Income | Amount of Tax Liability | |
	Total	Average Per Return		Total	Average Per Return
Atkinson	21,952,781	12,502	13,569,310	558,783	318
Bacon	36,240,436	13,417	22,182,636	928,357	344
Baker	12,032,572	12,560	7,584,357	308,331	322
Baldwin	198,857,030	17,662	136,704,528	6,178,312	549
Banks	30,748,677	13,564	19,217,573	789,805	348
Barrow	127,213,973	15,379	83,244,514	3,775,021	456
Bartow	250,340,098	16,341	167,523,405	7,434,359	485
Ben Hill	76,014,283	15,378	49,390,692	2,175,201	440
Berrien	58,727,337	14,671	38,642,569	1,656,027	414
Bibb	1,017,082,610	19,085	700,815,275	33,830,162	635
Bleckley	53,868,189	15,618	35,478,332	1,564,381	454
Brantley	34,543,809	14,681	22,057,797	927,965	394
Brooks	44,821,686	12,437	27,423,530	1,134,038	315
Bryan	52,984,750	16,348	36,297,373	1,562,718	482
Bulloch	170,992,544	16,205	112,690,201	5,053,513	479
Burke	86,451,613	15,098	56,496,500	2,492,578	435
Butts	65,586,876	15,239	42,361,599	1,856,109	431
Calhoun	24,187,815	14,203	15,194,447	653,509	384
Camden	78,139,479	17,655	53,157,490	2,438,118	551
Candler	29,462,631	13,904	18,514,427	786,620	371
Carroll	337,907,188	16,485	224,086,484	9,967,888	486
Catoosa	171,724,272	17,625	114,114,969	5,001,451	513
Charlton	26,411,452	15,825	17,033,692	747,892	448
Chatham	1,302,389,209	19,111	904,853,137	43,100,018	632
Chattahoochee	10,319,439	11,999	6,537,641	254,167	296
Chattooga	100,542,635	14,084	64,789,689	2,683,152	376
Cherokee	370,504,119	19,625	252,728,709	12,105,362	641
Clarke	438,479,630	17,355	298,337,142	13,802,809	546
Clay	10,744,480	14,231	7,244,052	318,628	422
Clayton	1,168,685,669	19,899	811,773,839	38,733,395	659
Clinch	25,227,322	14,866	16,267,922	700,752	413
Cobb	3,021,865,033	22,926	2,172,188,174	107,116,501	813
Coffee	112,276,151	14,508	72,141,499	3,144,912	406
Colquitt	164,352,142	15,439	107,142,737	4,711,347	443
Columbia	277,231,450	19,530	189,143,803	8,748,538	616
Cook	52,680,887	13,666	32,661,374	1,364,910	354
Coweta	267,932,503	18,691	180,499,692	8,303,628	579
Crawford	30,241,875	15,509	19,754,762	867,258	445
Crisp	88,102,264	14,307	56,109,245	2,466,279	401
Dade	43,079,389	16,730	28,580,846	1,261,268	490
Dawson	30,796,257	15,585	20,245,534	869,102	440
Decatur	98,982,106	14,941	62,875,903	2,741,581	414
DeKalb	4,018,819,706	21,592	2,831,487,289	138,207,567	743
Dodge	74,762,737	14,238	47,886,954	2,065,701	393
Dooly	42,038,865	14,627	26,942,073	1,205,686	420
Dougherty	618,461,885	19,060	421,715,314	19,706,872	607
Douglas	402,665,720	19,996	272,533,749	12,589,016	625
Early	51,454,183	15,750	34,329,353	1,560,953	478
Echols	6,124,258	14,901	4,056,120	176,300	429
Effingham	103,747,089	18,464	71,399,493	3,284,594	585
Elbert	90,187,870	13,729	56,995,170	2,439,797	371
Emanuel	84,085,656	13,760	52,273,813	2,230,751	365

| County | Adjusted Gross Income Less Deficit | | Net Taxable Income | Amount of Tax Liability | |
	Total	Average Per Return		Total	Average Per Return
Evans	39,913,670	14,994	25,863,122	1,154,265	434
Fannin	59,165,033	14,017	38,752,512	1,650,949	391
Fayette	318,789,025	25,601	223,066,461	10,943,475	879
Floyd	491,180,157	17,592	330,098,653	15,045,965	539
Forsyth	192,528,769	19,465	131.654,471	6,143,837	621
Franklin	73,969,424	13,696	46,179,815	1,934,777	358
Fulton	5,246,214,352	21,518	3,686,739,080	184,259,468	756
Gilmer	50,605,974	13,748	31,872,649	1,339,006	364
Glascock	10,726,958	13,931	7,100,190	303,209	394
Glynn	377,172,828	18,758	257,851,163	12,147,544	604
Gordon	171,127,188	15,445	112,850,021	4,894,652	442
Grady	76,592,867	13,923	47,775,090	2,009,372	365
Greene	49,401,422	13,359	30,469,127	1,387,480	375
Gwinnett	1,765,926,172	23,695	1,243,955,352	61,018,902	819
Habersham	133,923,179	15,163	87,320,214	3,733,402	423
Hall	519,865,364	17,414	345,693,943	15,692,359	526
Hancock	29,224,081	12,172	17,620,521	736,451	307
Haralson	102,106,529	15,556	66,787,156	2,901,813	442
Harris	81,171,707	16,657	53,352,390	2,387,232	490
Hart	80,861,225	15,052	53,260,827	2,438,852	454
Heard	27,340,813	14,458	17,914,329	757,622	401
Henry	274,976,347	19,634	185,044,372	8,657,165	618
Houston	534,841,216	19,818	375,941,698	17,550,064	650
Irwin	33,112,204	14,434	21,651,634	960,976	419
Jackson	128,511,357	14,309	82,067,047	3,457,696	385
Jasper	36,687,876	15,841	25,084,259	1,120,160	484
Jeff Davis	54,854,245	14,263	35,494,732	1,522,994	396
Jefferson	76,566,303	13,975	48,843,641	2,090,381	382
Jenkins	32,104,073	13,632	20,021,038	849,715	361
Johnson	33,643,009	13,193	21,363,693	909,582	357
Jones	87,604,688	17,871	60,398,002	2,761,315	563
Lamar	57,218,455	14,724	36,231,636	1,558,162	401
Lanier	18,544,096	13,996	11,735,713	477,962	361
Laurens	194,387,677	15,905	127,393,345	5,637,020	461
Lee	66,311,377	17,995	44,121,602	1,988,326	540
Liberty	91,195,547	14,695	60,884,799	2,635,781	425
Lincoln	28,186,557	12,983	17,434,981	721,401	332
Long	15,524,183	14,841	9,995,414	431,704	413
Lowndes	339,611,515	16,792	225,075,452	10,316,403	510
Lumpkin	48,453,644	14,374	31,606,096	1,324,344	393
Macon	53,015,170	14,641	34,015,691	1,489,639	411
Madison	91,511,555	14,958	58,965,728	2,502,426	409
Marion	19,435,078	13,639	12,468,940	530,280	372
McDuffie	91,502,803	14,557	58,589,135	2,537,827	404
McIntosh	28,774,379	12,938	17,793,203	739,479	332
Meriwether	95,170,832	14,660	61,565,058	2,655,641	409
Miller	25,490,075	14,044	16,040,124	680,563	375
Mitchell	83,814,927	13,443	52,511,975	2,302,530	369
Monroe	74,914,873	16,361	49,784,761	2,239,137	489
Montgomery	24,883,974	13,393	15,978,127	705,445	380
Morgan	58,580,317	14,982	37,129,804	1,617,989	414
Murray	105,967,102	14,948	69,658,551	3,006,419	424

County	Adjusted Gross Income Less Deficit		Net Taxable Income	Amount of Tax Liability	
	Total	Average Per Return		Total	Average Per Return
Muscogee	910,615,612	17,495	605,838,563	28,223,499	542
Newton	216,153,728	17,159	142,533,495	6,359,424	505
Oconee	81,013,819	18,645	54,270,593	2,517,033	579
Oglethorpe	38,191,970	14,093	24,306,748	1,018,995	376
Paulding	157,562,817	17,907	105,500,916	4,756,632	541
Peach	108,992,050	18,552	73,718,744	3,566,414	607
Pickens	60,632,977	14,949	40,042,503	1,717,609	423
Pierce	51,319,906	14,452	32,541,858	1,395,768	393
Pike	43,949,633	15,770	28,295,653	1,229,730	441
Polk	170,000,968	15,399	112,215,620	4,867,126	441
Pulaski	44,035,081	16,118	29,156,149	1,302,539	477
Putnam	58,847,780	16,628	39,497,710	1,769,071	500
Quitman	6,005,202	13,648	3,847,665	171,121	389
Rabun	49,469,267	13,594	30,721,536	1,305,012	359
Randolph	30,124,940	12,825	18,624,413	802,170	341
Richmond	1,019,009,854	17,620	695,982,755	31,765,661	549
Rockdale	299,082,957	21,282	204,849,556	9,729,117	692
Schley	13,406,057	14,896	8,792,508	389,274	433
Screven	59,023,874	14,570	37,893,656	1,599,124	395
Seminole	35,487,590	14,252	22,604,616	984,543	395
Spalding	284,109,942	16,714	186,396,469	9,208,871	542
Stephens	118,495,417	14,864	76,001,656	3,825,011	480
Stewart	19,948,934	13,416	12,654,932	551,004	371
Sumter	143,867,156	16,563	96,289,438	4,419,978	509
Talbot	23,554,604	13,006	14,447,504	595,835	329
Taliaferro	6,688,718	11,414	4,097,960	166,887	285
Tattnall	68,387,496	13,852	43,928,083	1,883,532	382
Taylor	33,270,944	14,637	22,161,266	942,059	414
Telfair	48,467,547	13,018	29,872,397	1,222,755	328
Terrell	48,274,502	14,169	31,100,272	1,353,145	397
Thomas	202,441,608	16,321	132,133,048	5,904,315	476
Tift	167,285,823	16,362	110,977,199	4,933,971	483
Toombs	111,633,786	15,593	74,579,948	3,346,927	468
Towns	21,391,055	12,237	13,082,603	527,311	302
Treutlen	22,171,464	13,158	13,997,864	591,690	351
Troup	293,772,617	16,654	194,691,710	8,841,110	501
Turner	36,748,153	13,171	22,948,389	985,294	353
Twiggs	36,199,303	15,417	24,061,476	1,087,680	463
Union	35,931,570	12,634	21,958,146	896,647	315
Upson	130,219,081	14,283	83,921,335	3,512,595	385
Walker	284,453,332	16,813	189,736,406	8,310,979	491
Walton	173,674,123	16,236	113,380,589	5,070,942	474
Ware	190,653,166	16,309	126,809,114	5,616,663	480
Warren	23,244,302	13,059	14,647,837	610,503	343
Washington	90,213,487	15,947	60,789,658	2,788,590	493
Wayne	104,325,190	16,253	68,874,152	3,074,909	479
Webster	9,335,719	15,638	6,380,822	292,632	490
Wheeler	16,739,947	12,363	10,221,832	413,205	305
White	49,865,602	13,463	31,067,772	1,300,475	351
Whitfield	441,396,663	17,255	300,048,269	13,746,330	537
Wilcox	27,540,845	13,266	17,506,653	748,542	361
Wilkes	53,353,718	14,186	34,071,294	1,452,166	386

County	Adjusted Gross Income Less Deficit			Net Taxable Income	Amount of Tax Liability	
	Total	Average Per Return			Total	Average Per Return
Wilkinson	55,778,388	17,502		38,664,202	1,740,181	546
Worth	81,232,589	15,508		52,764,866	2,330,722	445
Other	837,503,889			1,011,009,774	42,183,169	354
Georgia	$36,730,568,217	$18,027		$25,559,712,006	$1,198,733,931	$588

TELEVISION STATIONS

COMMERCIAL TV STATIONS

Albany
WALB-TV (Channel 10)
NBC
Gray Communications
Systems, Inc.
P.O. Box 3130, 31708
912-883-0154

WTSG (Channel 13)
Gordon
Communications, Inc.
Box 450, 31706
912-453-3100

Atlanta
WAGA-TV (Channel 5)
CBS
Storer Communications,
Inc.
P.O. Box 4207, 30302
404-875-5551

WATL-TV (Channel 36)
WATL-TV
575 Ponce de Leon
Ave., 30308
404-892-3636

WGNX-TV
(Channel 46)
Tribune Broadcasting
Co.
P.O. Box 98097, 30359
404-325-4646

WSB-TV (Channel 2)
NBC
Cox Broadcasting Corp.
1601 W. Peachtree St.,
NE, 30309
404-897-7000

WTBS (Channel 17)
Superstation, Inc.
1050 Techwood Dr.,
NW, 30318
404-892-1717

WVEU (Channel 69)
Broadcasting Corp. of
Georgia
2700 NE Expressway,
Bldg. A
Phoenix Business Park,
30345
404-325-6929

WXIA-TV (Channel 11)
ABC
Pacific & Southern
Broadcasting Co., Inc.
1611 W. Peachtree St.,
NE, 30309
404-892-1611

Augusta
WAGT-TV (Channel 26)
NBC

P.O. Box 1526, 30903
404-722-0026

WJBF (Channel 6)
ABC, NBC
Fuqua Television, Inc.
Box 1404, 30903
803-722-6664

WRDW-TV
(Channel 12)
Television Station
Partners
Drawer 1212, 30903
803-278-1212

Columbus
WLTZ (Channel 38)
NBC
Columbus TV, Inc.
Box 12289, 31995
404-561-3838

WRBL-TV (Channel 3)
CBS
Columbus Broadcasting
Co., Inc.
1350 13th Ave., 31902
404-322-0601

WTVM (Channel 9)
ABC
SFN Communications of
Columbus, Inc.

347

1909 Wynnton Rd.,
  31906
404-324-6471

WXTX (Channel 54)
Columbus Family TV,
  Inc.
Box 12188, 31907
404-561-5400

Macon
WGXA (Channel 24)
  ABC
Russell Rowe
  Communications
Box 340, 31297
912-745-2424

WMAZ-TV (Channel
  13) CBS
Multimedia Broadcasting
  Co.
Box 5008, 31213
912-746-1313

WMGT (Channel 41)
  NBC
Morris Network, Inc.
Box 4328, 31208
912-745-4141

Savannah
WJCL (Channel 22)
  ABC
Lewis Broadcasting
  Corp.
10001 Abercorn St.,
  Extension, 31406
912-925-0022

WSAV (Channel 3) NBC
P.O. Box 2429, 31402
912-236-0303

WTOC (Channel 11)
  CBS
American Savannah
  Broadcasting Co.
516 Abercorn St., 31401
912-234-1111

Thomasville-Tallahassee
  (Fla.)
WCTV (Channel 6)
  CBS
John H. Phipps
P.O. Box 3048,
  Tallahassee, FL 32315
904-893-6666

Toccoa
WNEG-TV
  (Channel 32)
Stephens County
  Broadcasting Co.
Box 970, 30577
404-886-0032

Valdosta
WVGA (Channel 44)
  ABC
Hi-Ho Broadcasting,
  Inc.
Box 1588, 31601
912-242-4444

PUBLIC/EDUCATIONAL TV STATIONS

Athens
WGTV (Channel 8)
GA Public TV Network
1540 Stewart Ave., SW,
  Atlanta, 30310
404-656-5979

Atlanta
WPBA-TV (Channel 30)
Atlanta Board of
  Education
740 Bismark Rd., NE,
  30324
404-873-4471

Chatsworth
WCLP-TV (Channel 18)
GA Public
  Telecommunications
  Commission
Rt. 7, Box 1H, 30705
404-695-2422

Cochran
WDCO-TV (Channel
  15)
GA Public
  Telecommunications
  Commission
P.O. Box 269,
  31014–0269
912-934-2220

Columbus
WJSP-TV (Channel 28)
GA Public
  Telecommunications
  Commission
Rt. 1, Box 17, Warm
  Springs, 31830
404-655-2145

Dawson
WACS-TV (Channel 25)

GA Public
  Telecommunications
  Commission
Rt. 1, Box 75A, Parrott,
  31777
912-623-4883

Pelham
WABW-TV
  (Channel 14)
GA Public
  Telecommunications
  Commission
P.O. Box 249, 31779
912-294-8313

Pembroke
WVAN-TV (Channel 9)
GA Public
  Telecommunications
  Commission

P.O. Box 367,
31321–0367
912-653-4996

Valdosta
WTKV (Channel 33)
Coastal Plains Area Arts
Inc.

601 N. Lee St., 31601
912-247-3333

Waycross
WXGA-TV (Channel 8)
GA Public
Telecommunications
Commission

P.O. Box 842, 31501
912-283-4838

Wrens
WCES-TV (Channel 20)
GA Public
Telecommunications
Commission
P.O. Box 525, 30833
404-547-2107

TIME ZONE
The State of Georgia lies entirely within the Eastern Time Zone.

TOURIST ATTRACTIONS

ALBANY
Chehaw Wild Animal Park, Ga. 99, off US 19 bypass. 100 acre wildlife preserve. Animals roam free in natural habitat. Visitors protected by trails and elevated walkways.

Heritage Plaza, 100 Roosevelt. Thronateeska Heritage Museum (see "Museums"), and 1857 train depot, Jarrad House—oldest frame in the city c. mid 1800s and the Hilsman Kitchen c. late 1800s.

Little Theatre, 514 Pine Ave. Restored antebellum home. Annually, a major season of five comedies, musicals, and dramas, summer musical, children's theatre productions, and theatre classes for young people. 912-439-7141.

Sand Hill, Radium Springs Rd., US 82. Fossil sand dunes.

ALVATON
White Oak Creek Bridge, 3 mi. SE of city, c. 1880. Long truss design. 80 feet long.

ATLANTA
Atlanta International Raceway, I-75 S. at Hampton. 1½ mi. paved oval track. 2 Grand National race events annually. NASCAR, FIA sanctioned, plus Indy car races, motorcross and other motor sports.

Atlanta Stadium, 521 Capitol Ave. Home of the Braves Baseball team 404-577-9100, Falcons Football team 404-588-5425.

Archives, 330 Capitol Ave., SE. Houses the history of the State of Georgia. Research, displays, exhibits. M–F 8:00–4:30, Sa 9:30–3:30.

Capitol, downtown, Capitol Sq. Dome sheeted in gold brought from Dahlonega. Houses State Museum of Science and Industry, Hall of Flags, Georgia Hall of Fame. M–F 8-5.

City Hall, 68 Mitchell St., SE. Built 1929. M–F 8-5.

Fort Peachtree, 2630 Ridgewood Rd., NW. Site of first settlement in city, later a trading post. Log cabin, Indian pottery, arrowheads, artifacts. M–F 10-6.

Fox Theatre, 660 Peachtree St. MARTA'S North-South rail line to North Avenue Station. Opulently detailed 1929 movie palace. 4,000 seat theatre and three grand ballrooms for parties, conventions, performances. National Historic Landmark. Guided tour, Fox Theatre District, M at 1:00 p.m. and Sa at 11:00. It begins in front of the Fox Theatre on Peachtree St.

Governor's Mansion, 391 W. Paces Ferry Rd., NW. Greek Revival. Federal period furnishings. T–Th 10–11:45.

Herndon Mansion, 587 University Place, NW., c. 1910. Home of Alonzo F. Herndon, founder of black-owned and managed Atlanta Mutual Aid Society, now Atlanta Life Insurance Co. Tu–F 1-4.

Historical Society Complex, 3099 Andrews

349

Dr., NW. 3 major structures—McElreath Hall houses an extensive collection of Atlanta historical data, Swan House is a 1928 Palladian style mansion and the Tullie Smith House is an 1840s farmhouse museum. Tu-Sa 10:30–4:30. MARTA Routes 4 Ridgewood or 23 Oglethorpe.

Martin Luther King Jr. National Historic Site. Begin at Information Center, 413 Auburn Ave., NE. MARTA's East-West rail line to King Memorial Station then take Route 99 Georgia Tech or take Route 3 Auburn Avenue. Includes tomb, birthplace, Ebenezer Church where he pastored. Tour hours: 404-221-3919.

Oakland Cemetery, 248 Oakland Ave. Est. 1850. Author Margaret Mitchell and golfer Bobby Jones are among the famous buried here.

Omni Sports Arena, Techwood Viaduct. Home of the Hawks Basketball Team 404-681-3600.

Peachtree Center and Omni Complex, downtown. MARTA'S East-West rail line to Omni Station; North-South rail line to Peachtree Center. Ultra modern hotels, restaurants, shopping. Omni also has cinemas, sports arena. Open DA, shop hours vary.

Rhodes Hall, 1516 Peachtree St. Built 1903. Victorian Romanesque Revival. M–F 8–4:30.

Six Flags Over Georgia, I-20 W., 12 mi. W. of downtown. MARTA'S East-West rail line to Hightower Station then take Route 201 Six Flags. 331 acre family entertainment center. Over 100 rides, shows, attractions. Spring: Weekends March 17–May 28, extended hours April 16–20. Summer: Su–F 10–10, Sa 10–12. 404-948-9290.

State Farmer's Market, 10 mi. S. of city off I-75, Forest Parkway Exit. Fresh fruits, vegetables, henhouse eggs, smokehouse meats, plants, shrubs, cafeteria. DA 24 hours.

Stone Mountain. From Atlanta, take I-20 E. to I-285 N. From I-75 or I-85 N. or S., take I-285 E., exit I-285, Stone Mountain/Athens Exit. MARTA'S East-West rail line to Avondale Station then take Route 120 Stone Mountain. 3,200 acre family recreation park surrounding world's largest granite mono-

lith, world's largest work of sculptural art salutes the Confederacy, antebellum plantation, scenic railroad, riverboats, skylift, camping, motel, historic trails, fishing, boating. Summer: 10–9, DA otherwise 10–5:30 except Dec. 24, 25.

Sweet Auburn Historic District, Auburn Ave. Called "richest Negro street in the world" at one time, hub of Black enterprise 1890–1930.

Wren's Nest, 1050 Gordon St., SW. Home of Joel Chandler Harris who created Uncle Remus. M–Sa 9:30–4, Su 2–5 National Historic Landmark

Zero Mile Post. Underground. Erected 1850. Marks the birthplace of Atlanta.

AMERICUS
Carter Library, Ga. Southwestern College. Memorabilia associated with US President Jimmy Carter who grew up in the area. Photos, slide and video tape presentation. M–F 8–5, Sa 11–4, Su 2–10.

Historic District. Victorian, antebellum. Greek Revival structures c. 1800 to present. Driving tour information at chamber office.

Lindbergh Memorial, Souther Airfield. Commemorates Charles A. Lindbergh's visit, purchase and solo flight of the single engine "Jenny" in 1923, four years prior to his historic solo flight over the Atlantic Ocean.

ANDERSONVILLE
Andersonville National Historic Site, Ga. 49. Confederate prison constructed in 1864 and in operation for 14 months. Over 12,900 Union prisoners died here. National Cemetery, Confederate prison, museum, State monuments and special programs throughout the year. Prisoner of War Museum chronicles all American Wars from the Revolution to Viet Nam. Daily 8:30–5, Memorial Day 8:30–7.

Confederate Village, across from prison. Restored Village includes Museum, log church, prison officials' quarters, living farm, craft and antique stores, picnic areas, open air theatre and camping. Special programs periodically feature encampments with skirmishes between Confederate and Union troops.

Trail. 75 mi. driving tour. Includes Camellia Gardens, river ferry. Americus Historic District, Veterans Memorial State Park, Lake Blackshear, Plains, in addition to Andersonville sites.

APPLING
Old Kiokee Baptist Church, Augusta/ Washington Hwy., 3 mi. N. of city. Oldest Baptist Church in Georgia. Est. 1771.

ASHBURN
Peanut Monument. Visible along I-75. Largest in the world. Commemorates peanut processing industry. Tours of the world's largest peanut shelling plant. By appointment: 912-567-2541.

ATHENS
Athens of Old Tours. Begin at 280 E. Dougherty St., a Federal style house built in 1820 which serves as the Athens Welcome Center. Known as the Church-Waddel-Brumby House, the city's oldest surviving residence. Information on easy-to-follow-do-it-yourself tours of over 50 local historic sites, including the University of Georgia Campus, first state chartered university in the country. M–Sa 9–5, Su 2–5.

Double Barreled Cannon, Cannon Park, downtown. Only one of its kind in the world. Invented 1863. Failed to fulfill its mission of simultaneously firing two balls connected by a chain.

Fire Station Number Two, 489 Prince Ave. Built 1901. Victorian, two-story brick firehouse in the shape of a truncated triangle. Gallery and headquarters of the Athens-Clarke Heritage Foundation.

Founders Memorial Garden, 325 S. Lumpkin St. Built 1857. Filled with 18th and 19th century antiques. State headquarters of the Garden Club of Georgia. M–F 9–12, 1–4.

Joseph Henry Lumpkin House, 248 Prince Ave. Home of Georgia's first Chief Justice. Built 1843. Restoration underway.

Taylor Grady House, 634 Prince Ave. Built 1840. Former Atlanta Constitution Editor and nationally known orator Henry W. Grady lived there while attending the University

and it was later bought by his father and kept in the family until 1872. Greek Revival architecture. M & F, 10–12, W 10–12, 2–5.

Tree That Owns Itself, Finley and Dearing St. Deeded the land that extends from the tree 8 feet on all sides by an early University professor who enjoyed its shade.

University Botanical Gardens, US 441 S. from city to S. Milledge Ave. Follow signs. Rose garden, annual/perennial garden, plant collections and five miles of nature/hiking trails. DA 8–5 October through April; 8–8 May through September.

University President's Home, 507 Prince Ave. Built 1856. Greek Revival. Corinthian columns on three sides. Doric columns at rear face a formal five acre garden. Open special occasions.

AUGUSTA
Appleby House, 2260 Walton Way. Built 1830. Branch library. Summer garden concerts.

Augusta College Administration Building, 2500 Walton Way. Served as Augusta Arsenal. Est. 1793 by order of General George Washington, the Arsenal has been on this site since the 1820s.

Confederate Monument, 7th and 8th at Broad. 76 foot marble shaft containing life-size figures of Confederate heroes.

Confederate Powder Works, 1717 Goodrich St. An obelisk chimney 176 feet high is all that remains of the facility which once manufactured more than two million pounds of gun powder. The chimney stands in front of the Sibley Mill built in 1880 and beside the Augusta Canal, built 1845.

Cotton Exchange, 775 Reynolds St. Built 1887. At one time, Augusta was the largest inland cotton market in the world.

First Christian Church/Parsonage, 629 Greene St. Built 1876 with an endowment from Augusta philanthropist Emily Tubman who also built the adjoining church. Parsonage houses Augusta Heritage Trust and Historic Augusta, Inc. M–F 9–4:30.

First Presbyterian, 7th and Telfair St. Built 1808. Woodrow Wilson's father pastored here during the former president's childhood.

Garden Center, 598 Telfair St. Built 1835. Chartered 1828, the first medical college in Georgia.

Harris Home, 1822 Broad St. Built 1797. 18th century furnishings. By appointment: 404-724-2324.

Meadow Garden, 1320 Nelson St. The parttime residence of George Walton, one of the Georgia signers of the Declaration of Independence. DA except Su & M 10–4.

Old Slave Market Column, 5th at Broad. Legend says a traveling minister, once refused permission to preach in the Lower Market, went into a rage and declared that the Market Place be destroyed. In 1878 a cyclone destroyed the building, except for this one pillar. Some say the curse persists.

St. Paul's Episcopal, 605 Reynolds St. Site of founding of Augusta 1735. Celtic cross marks the location of Fort Augusta, known during the Revolution as Fort Cornwallis.

Signer's Monument, Green St. at Monument St. 50 foot obelisk of Stone Mountain granite honoring Georgia's signers of the Declaration of Independence. Two of the three, Lyman Hall and George Walton are buried here.

Springfield Baptist, 114 Twelfth St. Built 1801 by the Methodists. Sold to the Springfield Congregation in 1884. One of the oldest Black Baptist churches in the country.

Ware's Folly, 506 Telfair St. Built 1818. Federal style. Called "Ware's Folly" because the construction price of $40,000 seemed exorbitant at the time. Now houses Gertrude Herbert Memorial Institute of Art. Tu-F 11-5, Sa & Su 2-5. Closed M, July 4, Thanksgiving and Christmas.

Woodrow Wilson Boyhood Home, 419 7th St. Tu-Sa 9-5.

Yerby Home, 1112 8th St. Black author Frank Yerby grew up and lived here until his graduation from Paine College.

BAINBRIDGE
Willis Park, downtown. Restored Victorian gazebo. Focal point for driving tour of re-

stored antebellum and Victorian homes in city.

BLAIRSVILLE
Blood Mountain Archeological Area, 15 mi. S. of city off US 19 & 129 via Appalachian Trail. Site of Cherokee and Creek Indian battle before the arrival of the white man.

Brasstown Bald Mountain, S. of city via US 19 & 129, via Ga. 180, then Ga. 66. Highest point in Georgia: 4,784 feet. 360° panoramic view of three states. Visitors center: May 23–Sept. 30: W–Su. Oct. 1–Oct. 31: DA.

Richard Russell Scenic Hwy., S. of city via 19 & 129. E. on Ga. 180. Designated Ga. 348. 14.1 mi. mountain drive. Elevations range from 1,600–3,000 feet.

Track Rock Archeological Area, 3 mi. S. of city, E. on county road 95 (town Creek Rd. for 5 mi.). A 52 acre preserved petroglyph of ancient Indian origin. Carvings resemble animal and bird tracks, crosses, circles and human footprints.

BLAKELY
Confederate Flag Pole, Courthouse Sq. Erected 1861. Last remaining.

Kolomoki Indian Mounds, 9 mi. N. of city. Historic settlement dating to A.D. 800, includes seven burial, temple and game mounds as well as ceremonial plaza. Museum depicts Indian cultures of the area. Historic Site.

Peanut Monument, Courthouse Sq. Salutes local peanut production.

BRUNSWICK
Coastal Exhibit Room, US 17 S. Marine exhibits, aquariums representing marine communities and a "petting" aquarium of spidercrabs, fiddler crabs, etc., for children. M-F 8-5. Operated by the Georgia Department of Natural Resources.

Coffin Park, US 17 & US 25. Tennis, baseball, football, auditorium.

Courthouse, downtown. Built 1907. Surrounded by moss-draped live oaks, tung and Chinese pistachio trees.

Lanier's Oak, US 17. The poet, Sidney Lanier, sat here to write many of his works, including "Marshes of Glynn."

Lover's Oak, Albany St. near Prince St. Over 900 years old.

Marshes of Glynn Overlook, US 17. Landscaped garden, picnicking. Unobstructed view of the largest salt marshes on the US east coast.

Oglethorpe Monument, Queen's Square. Honors James Edward Oglethorpe, founder of the Colony of Georgia.

Old Towne, downtown. Victorian architecture abounds. English street names such as Gloucester and Norwich have remained since before the American Revolution (many other American cities changed such names following the war). Driving tour map can be purchased at Old City Hall on Newcastle. National Register of Historic Places.

CAIRO

Hartsfield Farms. The Old Store. Ga. 112, 3 mi. N. of city. Early 1900s. Pot bellied stove, phonograph, other antiques. Locally made crafts, Tu-Sa 11-7.

Roddenbery Memorial Library, 320 N. Broad St., History exhibits, wildlife, Art exhibits. M, Tu, W, F, 9-6; Th 9-8 Sa 9-12.

CALHOUN

Calhoun Musicland. Country/Western music, entertainment. Red Bud Rd., off I-75.

Confederate Cemetery, Hwy. 41, exit off I-75 at Resaca.

New Echota, exit 131, I-75. Capital of the Cherokee Indian Nation, 1825—1838. Inventor of the Cherokee alphabet, Sequoyah, lived here. See where and how the alphabet was used to print the only Indian newspaper in North America. Historic Site.

Etowah Indian Mounds, 3 mi. SW of city. Occupied between A.D. 1000 and A.D. 1500. Largest Indian settlement in the Etowah Valley. Climb mounds, visit museum. Historic Site.

Lowery Covered Bridge, also known as Euharlee Creek Bridge, 6 mi. W. of city, via Ga. 113, 2 mi. No. on county road to Euharlee. Built 1886. 1 span wide, 116' long. Town

lattice design. Numbers still legible on timbers indicate the bridge was assembled elsewhere to assure perfect fit, then rebuilt over the stream.

Weinman Mineral Center, I-75 S., Exit 126, Culver Rd. Simulated limestone cave to explore, adjoining 20 linear foot waterfall. "Touch and Feel" exhibits. Precious gems, including rare amethyst collection. Tu-Sa 10-5, Su 2-5.

CARNESVILLE
Cromer's Mill Covered Bridge (or Nail's Creek Bridge), 8 mi. S. of city via Ga. 106, E. on county road. Built 1906. One span wide, 132 feet long. Town lattice design.

CLARKESVILLE
Mark of the Potter, Soque River, Ga. 197. Watch a potter at work and see the pet mountain trout from a porch built over the river. M-Sa 10-6, Su 1-6.

CHATSWORTH
Vann House, US 76, 3 mi. W. of city. Built 1804. Example of Cherokee Indian wealth and culture. Historic Site.

Fort Mountain Crafts Village, top of Fort Mountain. Shops featuring handcrafted items unique to Georgia. Miniature golf. 404-695-9371.

CHICKAMAUGA
Chickamauga and Chattanooga Battlefield, US 27. Nation's oldest and largest military park. 5,000 acres. Visitor center houses slide program, bookstore and a 355 weapon collection of military shoulder arms. 50 miles of hiking trails slope Lookout Mountain. Open year round. Center closed Christmas. Operated by the National Parks Service.

Historic Chickamauga, downtown. Frontier and Victorian buildings. Many have National Register of Historic Places nominations. Visitor center, 30 min. slide show. Free 12 passenger limousine tour by appointment: 404-375-2650. Center M-Sa 8:30-6.

Gordon Lee Home, Chickamauga Battlefield. Built 1847. Served as Union Army headquarters and then as a hospital during the two bloodiest days of the War Between the States. Open May 29-Labor Day: Tu-Sa 12-5, Su 2-5.

CLAYTON

Bartram Trail. First blazed by Quaker naturalist William Bartram over 200 years ago. Mid-point of the trail is 3 mi. E. of city in Warwoman Dell on Warwoman Rd. Continues appx. 40 mi., marked with yellow and black signs.

CLEVELAND

Babyland General Hospital, Hwy. 129. Birthplace of "Lil People" and Cabbage Patch Kids. Visiting hours: M–Sa 9–6, Su 1–6.

Old White County Courthouse, downtown. Built 1857—1859. Used until 1965. Houses county historic society.

CLINTON

Historic District. Only Clinton, of Georgia's early 19th century county seats, has survived sufficiently free of modern development to give an idea of the layout and appearance of an early town. Twelve houses built between 1808—1830 and the Methodist Church, built 1921, still stand. Self-guided driving tours.

COCHRAN

Pace House, 406 Beech St. Built 1870s. Said to be the oldest house in the city. Two-story, white frame, plantation plain style.

COLUMBUS

Bartletts Ferry, N. of city on the Chattahoochee River. Also known as Lake Harding. 5,850 acres.

Columbus College Fine Arts Auditorium, Algonquin Dr. Quarterly productions by Dept. of Speech and Theatre. Musical presentations on a continuing schedule.

Fountain City. A designation inspired by the numerous fountains throughout the city.

Golden Park, Lumpkin Blvd. Home of the Columbus Astro's baseball team. Season begins in April.

Heritage. Originates Ga. Visitor Center, Hwy. 27. Two hours. Guided bus. Interiors include 4 house museums and Springer Opera House. W & Sa 10.

Historic Columbus Foundation, 700 Broadway. Two-story Italian villa style townhouse c. 1870. M–F 9:30–4, Sa & W Heritage Tour 10.

Historic District, part of the original city. Includes Chattahoochee Promenade, a riverwalk outdoor museum, amphitheatre. Historic Columbus Foundation headquarters, Columbus Ironworks, Steamboat Wharf, house museums, restaurants, antique stores and working artisan studios as well as a growing number of residential renovations.

Illges, 1428 2nd Ave. Built 1850. Embellished 1870. Greek Revival. Corinthian columns, flying balcony, wrought iron trim.

Ironworks Convention and Trade Center, 801 Front Ave. 19th century structure that produced farm implements and munitions and weapons during the War Between the States. Renovation preserved massive timbers, exposed beams, old brick walls. Serves as a convention and meeting facility boasting 70,000 sq. ft. of exhibit space, 16 meeting rooms, outdoor amphitheatre and in-house catering services. National Register of Historic Places.

Jubilee Riverboat. Steamboat Wharf. Authentic split sternwheel riverboat. Excursions available.

Patterson Planetarium, 2900 Woodruff Farm Rd. Daily shows 9:30, 10:45 and 12:45 by appointment.

Pemberton, 11 7th St. Home of Dr. John Styth Pemberton from 1855 to 1860, when he originated the Coca-Cola formula. Adjoining kitchen-apothecary.

Rankin, 1440 2nd Ave. Restored French Empire. Double walnut staircase. By appointment: 404-322-0756.

Springer Opera House, 103 Tenth St. State Theatre of Georgia. Restored Victorian theatre where Edwin Booth and FDR appeared. Museum sections house memorabilia of artists who have performed at the Springer and papers of Abe Feder. Tours Tu 11:00, Heritage or by appointment. National Register of Historic Places.

Three Arts Theatre, 1020 Talbotton Rd. Home of the Columbus Symphony.

Walkers-Peters-Langdon, 716 Broadway. Built 1828. Federal cottage style. Restored furnishings. M–F 9:30–4:30, Sa & W Heritage Tour 10.

CONYERS

Monastery of the Holy Ghost, 8 mi. SW of city via Ga. 138 & 212. Founded 1944 by a group of monks who practice self-sufficiency, cultivating their food. Men may visit inside 10–noon, year round. After-noons-winter:2:30–4:30, summer: 3:30–5:30. Women may attend services in church and visit grounds, which include a green-house and gift shop. Greenhouse: Th, F, Sa 2:30–4:30.

CORNELIA

Big Red Apple Monument, downtown. Honors the area's apple growing industry.

COVINGTON

Historic Homes. Predate War. Between the States and can be viewed on driving tour.

CRAWFORDVILLE

Alexander H. Stephens Home and Confederate Museum, Ga. 22. Antebellum home of the Vice President of the Confederacy. Historic Site.

CULLODEN

Historic Buildings. Pre-Civil War village. Built 1802, the Methodist Church has the oldest brick of any Methodist Church in the State. The Courthouse, c. 1894, features old furnishings and pressed metal ceiling.

DAHLONEGA

Crisson's Gold Mine, 3 mi. N. of city on Wimpy Rd. Gold panning, picnicking. April 12–Nov. 7.

DALLAS

New Hope Church Monument. Marks the spot of a crucial battle in the War Between the States where General John B. Hood's Confederate Corps met General Joseph Hooker's Army Corps of the Union Army.

DALTON

Creative Arts Guild, old firehouse, 520 W. Waugh St. Community Center for visual and performing arts M–F 9–5, Sa–Su 2–4.

Crown Gardens and Archives, 715 Chattanooga Ave. Built 1884. Former office of Crown Cotton Mills. A center for local history, meetings, exhibits, genealogy material, bedspread material. Tu–Sa 9–5, Su & M: Closed.

Praters Mill Country Fair, Ga. 2, right on Ga. 2, 10 mi. NE of city. Exit I-75 at Hwy. 201 (Tunnel Hill). Travel N. 4.5 mi. to Ga. 2, right on Ga. 2, continue 2.6 mi. Built 1859. Site of country fairs twice a year: Mother's Day and Columbus Day weekends.

DARIEN

Butler Island, Altamaha River Delta. US 17 S. Owned by Pierce Butler. Was one the richest rice plantations in the world. His wife, actress Fannie Kemble, wrote a book about her life on the island.

Fort King George. The southernmost outpost of the British Colonies in 1721. Former Indian village and Spanish mission site. Historic Site.

Hofwyl-Broadfield Plantation, 7 mi. S. of city, US 17. Antebellum rice plantation. Visitors center explains rice culture. House open to visitors. Historic Site.

DILLARD

Hambidge Center. Est. 1934. See hand-weaving, pottery at this community center for the arts. Programs also feature dance, music, nature, creative writing, photography, painting and art history.

DUBLIN

Chappell's Mill, 13 mi. N. of city. US 441. Built 1811. Still in operation. Uses original dam which brings 75 acres under water. M–F 8–5, Sa 8–12.

Fish Trap Cut, Oconee River, Ga. 19. Believed built 1000 B.C. to A.D. 1500 a large rectangular mound, a smaller round mound and a canal that may have been used as an aboriginal fish trap. National Register of Historic Places.

Historic Buildings. Greek Revival and Victorian homes can be seen driving along Bellevue Ave. Carnegie Library, built 1904, restored 1972 at Bellevue, Church St. and Academy Ave. intersection, houses Laurens County Historical Society and historic exhibits. Tu–Th Sa 1–5.

EATONTON

Rock Eagle Center, US 129 & 441. Named

for a huge rock mound on the site believed to be made by the Indians nearly 4,000 years ago. Measures 101 feet head to tail, 120 feet across wing span. Can be seen year round.

Thompkins Inn, US 441, 6 mi. N. of city. Built 1811. One of 19 early 19th century buildings in the area featured on a driving tour map available at the chamber of commerce.

Uncle Remus Museum and Statue, downtown. Statue, courthouse lawn. Museum recalls slave cabin setting of Joel Chandler Harris' stories about Uncle Remus and his famous "critters" which Harris began writing about while living in the area. Summer: DA 10–12 & 1–5, Su 2–5, Sept.—May: Closed–Tu.

ELLIJAY
Apple Capitol of Georgia and home of Carter's Lake.

FAYETTEVILLE
Fayette County Courthouse, downtown. Built 1825. Oldest continually used courthouse in Georgia. M, Tu, Th, F 8–4:30, W & Sa 8–12.

Fife House, 140 Lanier St. Only unaltered antebellum home in county. Housed faculty, students of the Fayetteville Academy (1855–57), which was attended by the fictional Scarlett O'Hara in Margaret Mitchell's *Gone With the Wind.* Fayetteville Methodist Church steeple bell is from the original academy.

Margaret Mitchell Library, between Ga. 85 and Lee St. Begun by Margaret Mitchell. One of the most complete War Between the States reference libraries.

FORSYTH
Commercial Historic District. Courthouse Square and surrounding eight blocks has 40 structures of mostly mid-1800s construction.

FORT GAINES
Driving Tour. Frontier homes, hotels, apothecary of the 1890s. Globe Tavern, cemetery, The Dill House dates to 1800s.

Frontier Village. Authentic log cabins brought from outlying areas.

Outpost Replica, S. Ga. 39, right on Commerce St., then 3 blocks on left. Reconstructed fort, one-third of original (c. 1816–1830) used to protect settlers from Creek, Seminole Indian attacks.

FORT VALLEY
Peaches. This is the heart of Georgia's peach production area. Blossoms peak mid-March. Fruit available June–August. Travel US 341 for best views.

GAINESVILLE
Green Street Station, downtown. Mark Trail of comic strip fame is alive here in a collection left by Ed Dodd. Also featured is a historical exhibit of Northeast Georgia, a collection of North Georgia Arts and Crafts, the Elachee Creative Museum and Nature Science Center and crafts. M–Sa 10–4, Su 2–5.

Poultry Park, Broad St. at Grove. Gardens and statuary salute the local poultry industry and the city's status as "Broiler Capital of the World."

Road Atlanta, 40 mi. N. of city, US 29. Premier road racing circuit with a 2.52 mi. asphalt track for cars, motorcycles, go karts. Home of Sports Car Club of America National Championship Race. Racing and sports car museum. M–F 9–5.

Quinlan Arts Center, US 129 and Ga. 60. Traveling exhibits of regional, state and national artists. M–F 10–12 & 1–4, Su 2–4.

GREENSBORO
Courthouse, downtown. Antebellum, Greek Revival.

Old Greene County "Gaol," downtown. Built 1807. Rock jail patterned after bastilles of the 19th century.

HARTWELL
Train Rides. All aboard the Red Carpet Line for a 2–hour excursion aboard an authentic steam engine pulled train. March 15–Memorial Day weekend: Weekends, June–Oct: DA except W., Nov.—Dec. 15: Weekends. For hourly departures: 404-376-4901.

HAWKINSVILLE
Harness Training Tracks. Hwy. 129.

Horses arrive in Nov. and train until early March for the series of races held every year in late March or early April.

Opera House, Broad and Lumpkin St. Built 1907. Restoration underway. Houses chamber of commerce. One of the oldest steam pumpers for fire fighting in the world, built 1883, is restored and on display on the side lawn. National Register of Historic Places.

Taylor Hall, Kibbee St. Built 1824. Restored. National Register of Historic Places.

HELEN
Bavarian Alpine Architecture is throughout Helen. Stone streets, unique shops, specialty foods. Oktoberfest in the Fall, Fasching Karnival in the winter and a variety of Spring events, such as a Balloon Race, make this a year round resort. Shop and restaurant hours vary.

Old Sautee Store, Ga. 17 & 255. Unusual collection of old store merchandise from the early days when the General Store serviced every need of the pioneer. M–Sa 9:30–5:30, Su 1–6.

Stovall Covered Bridge, 3 mi. N. of city on Ga. 255. Georgia's smallest covered bridge. Built 1895. Kingpost design. One span wide, 33 feet long. Featured in the movie, *I'd Climb the Highest Mountain.*

HINESVILLE
Liberty County Jail, 301 Main St. At the completion of this jail, 1882, it was described by the press as "a handsome structure with all the modern conveniences"—running water, inside plumbing, fireplaces, 12″ brick walls and 36″ concrete floors. In use until 1972. Houses chamber of commerce office/ visitor center.

JEKYLL ISLAND
Faith Chapel. Built 1904. English Gothic stained glass window designed, installed and signed by Louis Comfort Tiffany. Tours DA 10, 12, 2. Extend to 4 p.m. from Easter to Labor Day weekend.

Goodyear Cottage. Center for the Cultural Arts. Tu–Su 12–4 p.m.

Horton House. Remains of a two story tabby house dating to 1742 when Major William Horton, one of General Edward Oglethorpe's (founder of Georgia) officers established an outpost here. Nearby, Georgia's first brewery ruins and the cemetery of the DuBignon family, first owners of Jekyll.

Millionaires' Village. From the beginning of the Jekyll Island Club in 1886 until the beginning of World War II, Jekyll was the remote winter retreat of Rockefellers, Morgans, Vanderbilts, Goodyears, Goulds and Pulitzers. Tour restored cottages DA. Details, group tour information: 912-635-2727.

JULIETTE
Jarrell Plantation, 8 mi. SE of city. 7.5 acre working farm complex spanning 1840s–1940s, complete with animals, crops, steam powered mill, blacksmith shop, can syrup evaporators. Self-guided tour and scheduled special activities. Historic Site.

Juliette Grist Mill. Built 1927. World's largest waterpowered grist mill at one time. Great picnic spot.

KENNESAW
Big Shanty Museum, 293 N. Houses The General, one of two vintage locomotives used in the Great Locomotive Chase. Artifacts, War Between the States. DA 9:30–6.

The Doll Gallery, Rt. 4, 2000 Old US 41 Hwy. KOA Atlanta-North Campgrounds. Antique and Modern Doll Museum. A fantasy land of over 1500 dolls; old, bisque, new, character, wax. Unique displays of the world. M–Sa 7 p.m.–10 p.m., Su 1–5 p.m.

LAGRANGE
Bellevue, 204 Ben Hill St. Built 1853. Greek Revival. Recently restored. Open Tu–Su. National Register of Historic Places.

Callaway Memorial Tower, Truitt & 4th Ave. Built 1929. Salutes Fuller E. Callaway, Sr., textile magnate of the area. Patterned after Campanile of St. Mark's Square in Venice, Italy.

Chattahoochee Valley Art Association, downtown. Built as a jail in the early 1800s. Recently restored.

LaFayette Fountain, LaFayette Square. Salutes Marquis de LaFayette for whose French estate La Grange was named. Replica of the LaFayette statue in LePuy, France.

LEESBURG
Chehaw Indian Monument, 3 mi. N. of city, Ga. 195. Marks site of Indian town home of the Chehaws, a friendly agricultural people of the Creek tribe.

LOUISVILLE
Old Time Capital of Georgia, 1796–1805.
Old Market, downtown Louisville. Built 1758. Bell cast in France in 1772.

Pre-Revolutionary Cemetery, Ga. Hwy. 4, S. Thirty gravesites.

LUMPKIN
Bedingfield Inn and Drug Store Museum, town square. Restored 1836 stagecoach inn and family residence, with period furnishings. Museum fully equipped in turn of the century fashion. Tu–Su 1–5.

Stagecoach Trail. Driving tour of 30 pre-1850 houses marked with stagecoach signs. Brochure available at Bedingfield Inn.

Westville, 1/2 mi. S. of city square. Re-created village of 1850. Authentic buildings were moved here, restored and furnished. Craftsmen demonstrate skills, such as basket-weaving, blacksmithing. M–Sa 10–5, Su 1–5.

MACON
Cannonball House, 856 Mulberry St. Built 1853. Struck by cannonball during federal attack, 1864. Restored. Houses Confederate museum. Tu–F 10:30–1 & 2:30–5, Sa & Su 1:30–4:30.

City Auditorium, Cherry & First St. Built 1925. Restored 1978. South's largest pipe organ, world's largest copper dome. Painting depicted the leading characters in the area's history across the proscenium which measures 10 feet wide, 60 feet long.

Fort Benjamin Hawkins, US 80 E. Reconstructed blockhouse of the style built when the federal government established the first modern settlement here in 1806. By appointment: 912-742-2627.

Grand Opera House, 651 Mulberry St. Built 1853. Restored 1970. One of the largest stages in the US. By appointment: 912-745-7925.

Hay House, 934 Georgia Ave. Built 1855–1861. Italian Renaissance, 24 rooms, priceless furnishings, secret room and 18 handcarved marble mantels and exquisite plaster cornices. Tu–Sa 10:30–4:30, Su 2–4. Closed holidays.

Kingfisher Cabin, 4182 Forsyth Rd. (grounds Museum of Arts and Sciences). Dwelling and workshop of author Harry Stillwell Edwards.

Ocmulgee Indian Mounds, US largest archaeological restoration of ancient Indian civilization in the East. Visitor center, earthlodge, mounds and lodges detail the lifestyle of six groups of Indians that occupied the area 8,000 B.C. to A.D. 1717. Ceremonial earthlodge believed to be one of the oldest public buildings in the US. DA 9–5. Closed Christmas and New Year's Day.

Rose Hill Cemetery, Riverside Dr. DA 8–4, National Register of Historic Places.

Sidney Lanier Cottage, 935 High St. Birthplace of Sidney Lanier, Georgia poet for whom Lake Lanier Islands are named. By appointment: 912-743-3851. National Register of Historic Places.

US Federal Building/Post Office, College St. Murals by George Beattie depict the history of the area.

MADISON
Historic Homes. Referred to as "town Sherman refused to burn," Madison has a large collection of privately owned antebellum homes, over half of which are shown during home tours in May and December.

Presbyterian Church, S. Main St. Built 1800s. Old English style. Tiffany windows and a silver communion service which was stolen during the War Between the States and later returned by federal orders. Still used today.

MARIETTA
Kennesaw Battlefield, Old US 41 & Stilesboro Rd. Commemorates one of the most decisive battles of the War Between the States. Museum, slide presentation, exhibits. 18 mi. hiking trail. Picnicking. DA 8:30–5. Ex-

tended hours in summer. Closed Christmas
Day and New Year's Day.

MARSHALLVILLE
Camellia Gardens, at Massee Lane Farms.
From I-75 S., exit Byron onto Ga. 49. Headquarters American Camellia Society. Camellia gardens, library, Boehm porcelains.
Blossoms peak Jan. 15–Mar. 15. Gardens
open daylight hours, year round.

MERIDIAN
Sapelo Island. Home of the Sapelo Island
National Estuarine Sanctuary. Formerly the
home of millionaire R. J. Reynolds, currently
operated by the Georgia Department of Natural Resources and the University of Georgia
Marine Institute. Tours are available year
round on W & Sa & F during summer
months. All day tours are available to the
first 28 who make reservations: 912-264-
7330.

METTER
Commissary, I-16, Exit Metter 23. Fully restored 1930 lumber mill commissary. Houses
visitor center. M–F 8–12, 1–5.

Guido Gardens, Hwy. 121 S. Fountain, gazebo.

"The Sower" Studios, adjacent Guido Gardens. Radio, film center for religious broad-
caster Michael A. Guido. Tours M–F 8–12,
1–5.

MIDWAY
Church, US 17. Built 1729. Congregation
produced two signers of the Declaration of
Independence, two Revolutionary generals
and a US senator. Old slave gallery and high
pulpit remain unchanged. Cemetery across
US 17 dates to early days of Colonial Georgia.

Sunbury, 8 mi. E. of I-95. Marks the spot of
Georgia's second largest Colonial seaport, an
important site of the Revolutionary War and
War of 1812. Visitor center displays history
of the earthen Fort Morris and the "last"
town of Sunbury. Historic Site.

MILLEDGEVILLE
Capital of Georgia, 1806–1867.
Marlor Home, 200 N. Wayne St. Built 1830.
Headquarters Allied Arts. For exhibit infor-
mation: 912-452-3950.

**Museum and Archives of Georgia Educa-
tion,** 131 S. Clark St. across from Old Governor's Mansion. Built 1900. Photographs and
memorabilia of the Georgia education systems. M–F 12–5.

Old Governor's Mansion, 120 S. Clark St.
Home of ten Georgia governors. Built 1838.
Greek Revival. Restored 1967. Tu–Sa 9–5,
Su 2–5. Closed M. Thanksgiving, Christ-
mas, New Year's.

Old State Capitol, 201 E. Green St.
Milledgeville was laid out in 1803 as the state
capital and today retains its original plan of
parallel streets. This structure, used as the
State Capitol from 1807–1867, has been rebuilt and is a part of the Georgia Military
College.

Stetson-Sanford House. W. Hancock. Built
1812. Received nationwide acclaim for architectural design and beauty of worksmanship.

Trolley Tours, Historic District. Originate
Milledgeville Chamber of Commerce, 130 S.
Jefferson. Tu & F 10 a.m. By appointment:
912-452-4687.

MONTICELLO
Town Square. Incorporated 1808. All buildings 1889—1906.

MONTROSE
Sanders Hill. Plantation House. National
Register of Historic Places.

MILLEN
National Fish Hatchery, Hwy. 25, 5 mi.
from city. 26-tank aquarium displays fish
raised by the hatchery. DA 8–4 April–
September, M–F 8–4 October–March.

MONROE
Davis Edwards House. Built 1845. Restored
1981. Mystery room featured in the children's book, *Uncle Robert's Secret,* by Wylly
Folk St. John.

Kilgore's Mill Covered Bridge, N. of city
on Walton-Barrow County lines. Built 1892.
100 foot spans of Apalachee River. No sup-
ports in the river. Lattice type truss design.

McDaniel/Walker Homes, McDaniel St.
Homes of two former Georgia governors face
each other. Confederate Major Henry Dick-

359

erson McDaniel, Governor 1883–86 and Clifford M. Walker, 1923–27, occupied these brick residences built in 1887 and 1916.

Selman-Pollack-Williams Home, McDaniel St. Built 1832.

Social Circle, National Historic District. Est. 1980. More than 50 homes built before 1900.

MONTEZUMA
Flint River Ferry, 8 mi. N. of city, Ga. 127 at Flint River. 50 foot flat steel barge. Drawn by cable. Daily. Honk horn for ferryman.

Tours. Historic driving tour of Oglethorpe. Montezuma and Marshallville. Guide brochure available at the Macon County Chamber office and Andersonville National Historic Site.

NEWNAN
Historic Homes of the antebellum style are privately owned, but can be seen on a driving tour.

OXFORD
Historic District includes antebellum homes, Oxford College, Confederate cemetery and Methodist Church c. 1841, recently restored. National Register of Historic Places.

PERRY
Cranshaw's One Horse Farm & Day Lily Gardens, Sandefur Rd. 6 mi. N. of city. 400 varieties of lily on 25 acres. Pet peacocks. Picnic facilities. Lilies in bloom May and June.

Heileman Brewery, US 341 S. to Ga. 247 S., 5 mi. from city. Tour hours: 9, 10, 11 and 1, 2, 3, 4 M–F.

Peach Blossom Trail, US 341 N. Pink and white blossoms line the road between Perry and points north from mid- to late-March.

Peach Picking, US 41 N. of city. Orchards along this highway allow visitors to pick their own peaches and/or buy fresh from roadside stands from mid-May to mid-August.

PLAINS
Carter Hometown, US President Jimmy Carter grew up and reared his children here. See his home, birthplace, campaign headquarters, peanut warehouses.

RICHMOND
Fort McAllister, 10 mi. E. of I-95, Ga. 144. Earthwork. Key to Savannah's fortifications during War Between the States. Held under Naval assaults. Fell to Sherman, December, 1864. State Park Campground adjacent, picnic facilities, boat ramp, etc. Historic Site.

ROME
Capitoline Statue, Municipal Building. "Romulus & Remus" presented to the city by the Governor of Rome, Italy, 1929.

ROSSVILLE
John Ross House. A 1797 two story log cabin. Home of John Ross, Cherokee Indian Nation Chief. Open Spring and Fall: Sa & Su 2–6. Summer: DA 2–6.

Lake Winnepesaukah Amusement Park, 1 mi. off US 27. Carousel, paddleboats, roller coaster, other rides. Picnicking. Entertainment weekends. May–Labor Day: Th–Su 12 noon—11 p.m. April & early Sept: Sa & Su 12 noon—11 p.m.

ROSWELL
Chattahoochee Nature Center, 9135 Willeo Rd. Natural Science Education Center offering animal rehabilitation program; nature trails and scenic boardwalk; on the banks of the Chattahoochee River. M–Sa 9–5; Su 1–5.

Crabapple Community, N. US 19, left 5 mi. Ga. 372. Originated as a cotton producing community. Cotton mill, mercantile stores (one c. 1849) have been restored and house antiques. M–Sa 10:30–5:00, Su 1–6. Antique Fair held third Saturday in May and October.

Historic Homes. Founded 1838 by a group of affluent families from the Georgia coast led by Roswell King, the city today features 15 structures which survived the War Between the States. The Roswell Historical Society, 98 Bulloch Ave., recommends a walking or driving tour. Stop by M–F 10–4. Write: Box 274, Roswell 30077 or call 404-992-1665.

ST. MARYS
Oak Grove Cemetery. Dates 1788. Graves from each American war. Tombstones with

French inscriptions indicate a move by Arcadian settlers from Nova Scotia, Canada in 1755.

Orange Hall, Osborne St. Antebellum style. Houses chamber of commerce office. Tour information Th–M 1–4:30.

Toonerville Trolley, Osborne St. Featured in 1930s Wash Tubbs cartoon.

ST. SIMONS
Bloody Marsh Battle Site, Frederica Rd. 1742 battle was a turning point in the Spanish invasion of Georgia.

Christ Church, Frederica Rd. Founded by John and Charles Wesley, 1736. Present structure built 1884 by Anson Green Phelps Dodge, Jr., as a memorial to his wife. M–F: winter—1–4, summer—2–5, Su services 8, 9, & 11.

Epworth-By-The-Sea. Methodist center on the site of the former Hamilton Plantation. Museum and former slave cabins open to the public.

Fort Frederica, Frederica Rd. Built by Oglethorpe 1736. Most expensive British fortification in country. Visitor center: DA 9–5. Film every hour, 10–4. DA park hours vary with season.

Retreat Plantation. Famous long staple, sea island cotton first raised here. Tabby ruins of slave hospital and plantation home still stand. Now part of the Sea Island Golf Club.

St. Simons Sojourns Tours. The islands' landmarks, lore and legends woven into an absorbing narrative. Available daily from the Pier Village, 223½ Mallory St. 912-638-1585.

SANDERSVILLE
Old Wooden Jail, N. of city. Built 1783. Site of Aaron Burr's incarceration in 1807 while en route to Virginia to stand trial for treason.

SAVANNAH
Site of founding of Georgia, 1733. Georgia Colonial Capital until 1782.
Barbra Negra, River St. Former whaling vessel. When in port, tours DA.

Bethesda Home for Boys, Ferguson Ave. 500 acre campus. 239 years old. Oldest continuously operating home for boys in country. Cunningham Historical Center houses items associated with home since 1700. M–F, 9–4.

Bonaventure Cemetery, Bonaventure Rd., edging Wilmington River. Once a lavish plantation. Moss-hung oaks, camellias, azaleas, dogwoods.

Cathedral of St. John the Baptist, 222 E. Harris St. Oldest Roman Catholic Church in Georgia, home of the Diocese of Savannah.

Christ Episcopal, 28 Bull St. First church in Georgia. Present structure replaced two others and was erected in 1840. John Wesley founded what is believed to be the world's first Sunday school here.

Colonial Park Cemetery, Abercorn and Oglethorpe St. Second burial ground for the early Colonists. 1750–1853.

Davenport, 324 E. State St. Built 19th century. Federal style. M–Sa 10–4:30, Su 1:30–4:30.

Factor's Walk, Bay St. Center of Commerce during the years when cotton was king. World cotton prices were set here. Ornate iron bridgeways connect buildings which once were cotton factors' (merchants') offices. Other landmarks nearby include the City Exchange Bell, Old Cotton Exchange, Washington Guns, Old Harbor Light, fountain commemorating three famous ships named for Savannah and Oglethorpe Bench which marks the site of the landing of General Oglethorpe February 12, 1733 and founding of the colony that was to become the State of Georgia.

First African Baptist, 403 W. Bryan. Organized 1788. First Black church in USA. Present structure built 1859.

Fort Jackson, 3 mi. from city on the Savannah River. Oldest remaining brickwork fort in city. Built 1809–49. Displays, artifacts depicting the history of city and the coast. Tu–Sa 9–5.

Fort Pulaski, US 80 E. of city. Built 1829–42. Robert E. Lee's first engineering assignment. DA: winter—8:30–5:15, summer—8:30–6:45.

Fort Wayne, Bay at E. Broad St. Built mid-

1800s. Named after General "Mad Anthony" Wayne.

Girl Scout Center, Bull & Oglethorpe, birthplace Juliette Gordon Low, founder of the Girl Scouts in Savannah in 1912. Restored to the period of her childhood. M, Tu, Th, Sa 10-4, Su 2-4:30, except Dec. & Jan.

Independent Presbyterian, 25 W. Oglethorpe Ave. Founded 1755. Woodrow Wilson married Ellen Axson, granddaughter of the pastor, here in 1885.

Isle of Hope. Community of privately owned antebellum homes overlooking Skidaway River.

Low Home, 329 Abercorn St. Built 1848 by Andrew Low, a cotton merchant whose son married Juliette Gordon. M–S 10:30-4:30.

Lutheran Church of the Ascension, Bull & State St. Organized 1741 by Salzburgers. Present church constructed 1878-79. Stained glass Ascension window.

Mickve Israel Temple, 20 W. Gordon. Oldest congregation in US practicing Reform Judaism. Founded 1733.

National Historic Landmark. Largest registered urban landmark district in the nation (2½ square mi.). More than 1100 restored buildings.

Olde Pink House, 23 Abercorn St. Built 1771. Georgia's first bank (1812). Headquarters Union General York 1864-65.

Owens Thomas, 124 Abercorn St. General LaFayette was a guest here in 1825. Tu–Sa 10-5, Su & M 2-5. Closed Sept.

Riverfront Plaza, River St. 9 block concourse dotted with fountains, benches, plantings, museums, pubs, restaurants, artist galleries, studios and boutiques housed in restored cotton warehouses. Waving girl statue, along the concourse, salutes Florence Martus, said to have greeted every ship that entered the Port of Savannah 1887-1931.

St. Johns Church and Parish House, 14 W. Macon St. Built 1852. Chimes, stained glass windows show Gothic influence. Parish House is former Green-Meldrim House, headquarters of Sherman after his 1864 march.

Scarborough, 41 W. Broad St. Built 1818. Houses Historic Savannah Foundation offices. M-Sa 10-4, Su 2-4, closed Th.

Squares, 21 half acre parks in historic district. Laid out by State's founder, James Edward Oglethorpe. Each has a story behind its name and a central monument, fountain, etc. Some not to be missed are: *Columbia, Habersham, York & State St.*, eastern limit when Savannah was walled city, 1757-1790. *Emmett Park,* Bay and E. Broad St., named for Irish Patriot Robert Emmett. Contains the old Harbor Light, erected 1852 and fountain. *Forsyth Park,* Gaston & Park Ave., fountain dates 1858, fragrance garden for the blind. *Johnson Square,* Bull, Bryan & Congress, monument and grave of Nathanael Greene, surrounded by sites of first inn, public oven, mill and general store in Georgia. *Madison Square,* Bull, Harris & Charlton St., honors President James Madison and Sgt. William Jasper who fell in the Seige of Savannah 1779.

Thunderbolt, off US 80. Shrimping village along intercoastal waterway.

Tours, *Black Heritage.* Three walking and/or driving routes highlight sites significant in Black History from early slave times. By appointment, 24 hours in advance: 912-233-2027. *Carriage.* Historic district by day, evening service to restaurants in restored horsedrawn carriages. By appointment: 912-236-6756. *Capt. Sam's Riverboat Tours:* 912-234-7248. *Harbor.* Paddlewheel sightseeing, area excursions and charters. River St. at the foot of Bull St. *Trolley Tours* by appointment: 912-233-0083. *Victory Drive,* US 80. Do-it-yourself driving along route of early 1900 mansions. *Visitor Center,* 301 W. Broad St. Restored 1860 railroad station in historic district. Information, orientation, complimentary slide show, trained tour advisors, parking. M-F 8:30-5. Weekends, holidays 9-5. Closed Christmas.

Trustees Garden, E. Broad near Bay St. America's first public experimental garden. Herb Shop and Pirate's House where it is believed Blackbeard died.

Victorian Historic District. One square mi. adjacent to landmark district. Restorations underway.

Wesley Monumental Methodist, 429 Abercorn St. Commemorates the memory of John Wesley, founder of Methodism.

Wormsloe. Country estate established 1736 by Noble Jones one of the first Colonists, 500 acres. After over two centuries of single family ownership, estate (minus house, library and 65.5 acres) was bought by the State. Visitors center, exhibits, audio visual program, ruins of a tabby fortification and Fort Wimberly earthworks. Tu–Sa 9–5, Su 2–5:30.

SOPERTON

Troup's Tomb, 5 mi. SW of city via Ga. 46. Tomb of Georgia Governor George M. Troup located on his plantation. Ornate iron gate leads to elaborate granite tomb.

Visitor Center, Ga. 29 at I-16. Renovated log cabin built 1845. DA 9–5.

SPARTA

Historic Landmarks. Beautiful old homes, courthouse on square. Hotel Lafayette, across from Courthouse. Known as Edwards House and Drummers Home. Haven for refugees of the War Between the States.

STARR'S MILL

Scenic Stop, I-85 & Ga. 74. Mill believed to be over 200 years old.

SYLVANIA

Brier Creek Battle Site, 10 mi. E. of city, Brannen Bridge Rd. Revolutionary Battle Site. Breastworks visible.

TALLULAH FALLS

Gorge, US 441. Believed to be the oldest natural gorge in North America. 1½ mi. long, 2,000 feet deep. Stop by Terrora Park Center for specifics.

Traveler's Rest, 6 mi. W. of Toccoa US 123. Built 1815–1830. Served as a plantation house, tavern, trading post and post office. Authentic furnishings. Historic Site.

THOMASTON

Auchumpkee Covered Bridge, 12 mi. S. of city, Allen Rd. Built 1898.

Pettigrew-White-Stamps House, S. Church & Andrews Dr. Built early 1800s. By appointment: 404-647-7838. Holds annual Christmas Open House.

THOMASVILLE

Confederate Prison, Wolf St. 5 acres bounded by a 6 feet to 8 feet deep ditch, 10 feet to 12 feet wide. Temporary when Andersonville officials feared a raid by Sherman. Now a park. Part of the original ditches visible.

Lapham-Patterson House, 626 N. Dawson St. Built 1884. Victorian. Historic Site.

Paradise Park, S. Broad St. 26 acre forest. Heart of the city. A natural wonder.

Pebble Hill Plantation, US 319 S. Site of an antebellum plantation, a winter resort home representative of the shooting plantations in the Thomasville area frequented by wealthy northern industrialists. Great number of out buildings house exhibits and artifacts including a carriage and automobile collection. Grounds open to the public Tu–Su 10–5. Guided house tours available for adults (over 12 yrs.) Tu–Su 10–5.

Thomasville Oak, E. Monroe & E. Crawford St. Nearly 300 years old. Limb spread of 155 feet, 65 feet high, 22 feet wide.

Tours: *Historic District*. Information, brochure at chamber office 401 S. Broad St. *Plantation*. M–Sa. Original chamber office.

Test Gardens, 1 mi. E. of city, US 84 (1840 Smith Ave.). Over 2000 plants on 2 acres. Varieties labeled for easy identification. Devoted to testing new and unnamed varieties for All American Rose Selections (one of 25 locations in the USA). Mid–April to mid–Nov.: Daylight hours.

THOMSON

Old Rock House, c. 1885. 4 mi. NW of city. Ga. 150 to 223 W. Stone residence, post Revolutionary, considered one of oldest dwellings in the State. By appointment: 404-595-5584.

Wrightsboro. Begun in 1768 by Quakers. Church built 1810. By appointment: 404-595-5584.

TIFTON

Agrirama, I-75 & 8th St. Exit 20. Living history village of rural Georgia prior to 1900. Over 35 authentic restorations. Gristmill, cotton gin, turpentine still, logging train, rural village. Summer: DA 9–6, Labor Day–May 31: M–Sa 9–5, Su 12:30–5.

Wiregrass Opry. Saturday nights, April–Oct. Outdoor performances include bluegrass, gospel, country music and clogging.

Fulwood Park, Tift Ave. & 12th St. 35 acres Virgin pines, azaleas, cookout, picnic facilities.

TOOMBSBORO
Swampland Opera House, intersection Ga. 57 & 112. Country, gospel, bluegrass music every Sa 4–12 except Christmas week.

TYBEE ISLAND
Fort Screven, near museum. Built 1875. Manned during Spanish-American War and WWI & II. Winter: DA except Tu 1–5, summer: DA 10–6.

Lighthouse, N. end of beach. One of the first public structures in Georgia. Marks the mouth of the Savannah River. Sa–Su 2–5.

UNADILLA
Southeastern Arena, S. Railroad St. One of the largest indoor horse arenas in the Southeast. Activities include horse and cattle shows, rodeo performances, circus and musical concerts. Open year round.

VALDOSTA
Barber House and Valdosta-Lowndes Co. Chamber of Commerce. Built 1915 for E. R. Barber, world's second bottler of Coca-Cola. Known for its outstanding examples of architectural design and craftsmanship. Walking or guided tours available M–F 9–5.

Crescent House, 904 N. Patterson St., US 221, 41 & 75. Built 1898. Third floor ballroom seats 300. F 2–5.

Lowndes County Historical Society, 305 W. Central Ave. Records, old photographs, exhibits of the naval and sea island cotton industries and local historical displays representative of Valdosta, once known as the smallest American city with a street car system. Su 3–6.

Converse-Dalton House, 305 N. Patterson St. 1902 Colonial home is the Jr. Service League's speech and hearing clinic. Tours available to the public M–F 9–5.

VIENNA
Tours: Historic driving, brochures available at City Hall.

VININGS VILLAGE
Antique shopping, West Paces Ferry Rd. Antique, gift shops, ski slope, teahouse.

WARM SPRINGS/PINE MOUNTAIN
Roosevelt's Little White House & Museum, Ga. 85 W. & US 27 A. Built 1932 by President Franklin Delano Roosevelt so that he could be close to Warm Springs for therapy for polio. House is exactly the way it was the day he died there in 1945. Every day of the year: 9:30–4:30.

WASHINGTON
Callaway Plantation, 5 mi. W. of city, US 78. Early American buildings furnished to illustrate life in the various periods of the history of the area. April 15–Dec. 10: DA 10–5:30, Su 1–5:30.

Kettle Creek Battlefield, 8 mi. SW of city off Ga. 44. Site of a decisive battle during Revolutionary War.

Toombs House, Augusta Rd. Core of home of Confederate General Robert Toombs, built 1797. Historic Site.

Mary Willis Library, Liberty and Jefferson St. Built 1888. High Victorian style. Tiffany windows.

Washington-Wilkes Historical Museum, 308 E. Robert Toombs St. Built 1835. Confederate gun collection. Indian artifacts. Tu-Sa 9–1, 2–5, Su 2–5:30.

WATKINSVILLE
Eagle Tavern, downtown. Early Georgia stage stop and store. Late 1700s furnishings. M–F 9–5, Weekends by appointment: 404-769-5197.

WAYCROSS
Okefenokee Entrance, 8 mi. S. of city, US 1. Guided boat trips, serpentarium show, observation tower, wildlife exhibits, ecology and swamp life exhibits, interpretive dis-

plays, 2 hour guided trip and all day excursions by appointment: 912-283-0583. DA hours seasonal.

Okefenokee Heritage Center/Southern Forest World, N. Augusta Ave. between US 1 & 82. 1912 steam locomotive, train, and depot; late 1800s print shop; the exhibit building houses antique arts, vehicles, nature trails info, an 1840s farm house and other exhibits of arts, sciences, and local history. Experience the fascinating story of the development of forestry in the South. Climb a fire tower and walk up inside a 38 foot tall model of a Loblolly pine. Tu–Sa 10–5, Su 2–4, Closed M. 912-285-4260 or 4056.

WAYNESBORO
Dell-Goodall House, 6 mi. N. of US 301. 18th century dwelling said to have been spared when an evangelist asked God to destroy the town of Jacksonborough.

Shell Bluff, off Ga. 80, 13 mi. NE of city. A 150′ x 140′ bluff composed of giant fossilized oyster shells deposited over 60 million years ago.

WILLACOOCHEE
McCranie's Turpentine Still, just west of city limits on US 82, is a preserved wood burning turpentine still; operated from 1936–42, 19th century design.

WINDER
Old Railroad Station. Built 1912. Late American Queen Anne style. A polychromed, serpentine clay tile roof, smooth-cut limestone lintels and window sills. Restored. Houses chamber of commerce.

WOODBURY
Big Red Oak Creek Bridge, 4 mi. N. of city. c. 1840s. Town lattice design. 116 feet long.

TOURIST INFORMATION

VISITOR CENTERS

The State of Georgia maintains the following Visitor Centers where tourist, driving, and accommodations information can be obtained.

I-75 South/Ringgold (Tennessee Line) 404-937-4211
I-75 North/Valdosta (Florida Line) 912-559-5828
I-85 South/Lavonia (South Carolina Line) 404-356-4019
I-85 South/West Point (Alabama Line) 912-645-3353
I-20 West/Augusta (South Carolina Line) 404-828-4610
I-20 East/Tallapoosa (Alabama Line) 404-574-2621
I-95 South/Savannah (South Carolina Line) 912-964-5094
I-95 North/Kingsland (Florida Line) 912-729-3253
US 301/Sylvania (South Carolina Line) 912-829-3331
US 280/Columbus (Alabama Line) 404-571-7455
US 280/Plains 912-824-7477
Atlanta Airport (Baggage Claim Escalator) 404-767-3231

WELCOME CENTERS

There are twenty-two Local Welcome Centers in the state. Some are located in historic sites and some have local arts and crafts. They work with the Georgia Department of Industry and Trade, area Chambers of Commerce and Convention and Visitors Bureaus. For more information, call Georgia

Tourist Division, 404-656-3595 or write Georgia Local Welcome Centers, P.O. Box 1776, Atlanta 30301.

Albany Local Welcome Center
501 North Slappey Drive
Albany 31702 (Dougherty County)
912-883-6900

Andersonville Visitors Center
Old Railroad Depot
Andersonville 31711 (Sumter County)
912-924-2558

Athens Local Welcome Center
280 East Dougherty Street
Athens 30603 (Clarke County)
404-549-6800

Atlanta Local Welcome Center
3393 Peachtree Road NE
  Lenox Square Mall
Atlanta 30326 (Fulton County)
404-233-6767

Atlanta Local Welcome Center
233 Peachtree Street, NE
  Peachtree Center
Atlanta 30303 (Fulton County)
404-523-6517

Brunswick-Golden Isles Welcome Center
I-95 between exits 8 and 9
Brunswick 31520 (Glynn County)
912-264-0202

Brunswick-Golden Isles Local Welcome Center
Glynn Avenue on U.S. 17
Brunswick 31520 (Glynn County)
912-264-5337

Claxton Welcome Center
4 North Duval Street
Claxton 30417 (Evans County)
912-739-2281

Clayton County Local Welcome Center
8712 Tara Blvd.
Jonesboro 30236 (Clayton County)
404-478-6549

Dalton Local Welcome Center
524 Holiday Avenue
Dalton 30720 (Whitfield County)
404-278-7373

Eagle Tavern Welcome Center
U.S. Hwy. 441—Main Street
Watkinsville 30677 (Oconee County)
404-769-5197

Gainesville Local Welcome Center
230 Sycamore Street
Gainesville 30501 (Hall County)
404-532-6206

Helen Welcome Center
Main Street
Helen 30545 (White County)
404-878-2521

Metter Welcome Center
I-16
Metter 30439 (Candler County)
912-685-6151

Million Pines Visitors Center
I-16 at Soperton Exit
Soperton 30457 (Treutlen County)
912-529-6263

Rabun County Local Welcome Center
Hwy. 441
Clayton 30525 (Rabun County)
404-782-5113

Rome Local Welcome Center
Civic Center Hill
Rome 30161 (Floyd County)
404-295-5576

Savannah Visitors Center (Downtown)
301 West Broad Street
Savannah 31401 (Chatham County)
912-233-6651

Thomasville-Thomas County Local
    Welcome Center
401 Broad Street
Thomasville 31792 (Thomas County)
912-226-1131

Toccoa-Stephens County Local
    Welcome Center
907 East Currahee Street
Toccoa 30571 (Stephens County)
404-886-2132

VEHICLE REGISTRATION

TYPE VEHICLE CLASSIFICATION BY COUNTIES
(Estimated): 1984

County	Passengers	Trucks	Trailers	Motorcycles	Buses	Total
Appling	7,602	4,693	1,384	231	56	13,966
Atkinson	2,586	1,705	309	70	19	4,689
Bacon	4,390	2,563	690	96	38	7,777
Baker	2,006	1,047	190	70	13	3,326
Baldwin	16,240	5,636	1,698	553	88	24,215
Banks	5,940	3,206	939	236	41	10,362
Barrow	14,384	5,947	2,959	568	75	23,933
Bartow	25,656	11,236	3,170	1,502	145	41,709
Ben Hill	7,628	3,435	1,029	236	38	12,366
Berrien	6,784	4,106	960	244	34	12,128
Bibb	81,041	20,316	7,754	2,266	327	111,704
Bleckley	5,047	2,389	833	189	45	8,503
Brantley	4,184	2,807	956	108	32	8,087
Brooks	6,756	3,770	837	171	48	11,582
Bryan	5,514	2,752	1,016	245	36	9,563
Bulloch	17,704	7,645	1,922	670	134	28,075
Burke	9,262	4,232	1,077	297	68	14,936
Butts	6,954	2,733	899	233	38	10,857
Calhoun	2,340	1,171	311	61	20	3,903
Camden	8,050	3,467	1,262	342	66	13,187
Candler	3,651	1,960	506	123	23	6,263
Carroll	31,418	12,814	3,635	1,329	180	49,376
Catoosa	24,277	9,277	1,816	983	79	36,454
Charlton	3,472	1,935	610	83	25	6,125
Chatham	114,458	25,245	12,620	3,447	532	156,302
Chattahoochee	1,756	567	147	106	10	2,566
Chattooga	11,256	4,807	1,033	367	48	17,511
Cherokee	36,224	16,464	5,221	1,786	154	59,849
Clarke	37,073	8,577	2,790	1,189	183	49,812
Clay	1,602	785	243	38	14	2,682
Clayton	109,143	30,602	12,499	4,432	467	157,143
Clinch	2,599	1,931	595	65	23	5,213
Cobb	256,077	56,581	24,235	9,090	686	346,669
Coffee	12,221	6,631	1,950	501	77	21,380
Colquitt	17,414	8,138	2,460	468	98	28,578
Columbia	27,433	8,580	4,008	974	177	41,172
Cook	5,825	2,907	932	149	29	9,842
Coweta	26,202	9,753	3,215	987	144	40,301
Crawford	4,026	2,173	626	145	35	7,005
Crisp	8,861	4,136	1,381	466	37	14,881
Dade	6,320	3,186	461	207	34	10,208
Dawson	6,701	3,224	569	288	25	10,807
Decatur	11,615	5,166	1,973	339	79	19,172

VEHICLE REGISTRATION

County	Passengers	Trucks	Trailers	Motorcycles	Buses	Total
DeKalb	321,297	48,662	18,617	8,433	1,135	398,144
Dodge	7,924	3,813	933	229	57	12,956
Dooly	4,629	2,656	763	140	39	8,227
Dougherty	49,133	13,783	6,087	1,793	251	71,047
Douglas	36,469	13,575	4,439	1,494	175	56,152
Early	5,372	2,720	774	158	45	9,069
Echols	1,010	727	199	30	11	1,977
Effingham	10,315	5,352	2,343	436	65	18,511
Elbert	10,590	4,826	1,362	288	70	17,136
Emanuel	9,304	4,359	937	275	70	14,945
Evans	4,449	2,159	558	114	29	7,309
Fannin	8,286	4,498	853	344	59	14,040
Fayette	28,826	10,141	3,825	1,286	121	44,199
Floyd	45,125	15,525	4,584	1,889	244	67,367
Forsyth	20,796	10,002	3,771	940	108	35,617
Franklin	10,278	4,918	1,624	332	66	17,218
Fulton	318,081	57,402	20,766	6,775	1,444	404,468
Gilmer	7,100	4,036	792	298	53	12,279
Glascock	1,190	680	136	41	9	2,056
Glynn	32,614	9,475	4,251	1,170	137	47,647
Gordon	17,469	8,059	2,414	700	57	28,699
Grady	9,122	4,558	1,454	322	51	15,507
Greene	4,972	2,317	651	104	27	8,071
Gwinnett	155,958	42,659	17,702	6,067	523	222,909
Habersham	13,605	6,424	1,850	406	66	22,351
Hall	47,632	17,787	6,045	1,764	284	73,512
Hancock	3,743	1,321	210	52	28	5,354
Haralson	11,439	5,175	1,401	457	56	18,528
Harris	9,563	4,338	909	300	57	15,167
Hart	10,729	4,516	1,253	281	61	16,840
Heard	3,583	2,005	502	121	23	6,234
Henry	25,261	10,954	3,757	1,153	123	41,248
Houston	46,945	13,147	5,555	2,549	234	68,430
Irwin	3,842	2,209	542	121	16	6,730
Jackson	14,321	6,316	1,690	527	84	22,938
Jasper	4,307	2,110	705	166	23	7,311
Jeff Davis	5,674	3,009	1,225	120	54	10,082
Jefferson	8,001	3,613	1,014	179	53	12,860
Jenkins	3,856	1,830	412	92	21	6,211
Johnson	3,607	1,803	437	75	10	5,932
Jones	10,805	4,605	1,606	483	58	17,557
Lamar	6,644	2,543	760	276	74	10,297
Lanier	2,292	1,453	361	69	8	4,183
Laurens	19,270	8,186	2,207	525	94	30,282
Lee	6,577	3,024	1,410	325	57	11,393
Liberty	17,092	4,575	1,274	984	66	23,991
Lincoln	3,381	1,659	609	78	38	5,765
Long	2,337	1,432	715	74	23	4,581
Lowndes	36,261	12,381	4,433	1,562	209	54,846
Lumpkin	6,217	3,337	852	330	43	10,779
Macon	6,198	2,665	815	160	52	9,890
Madison	10,391	5,168	1,598	377	80	17,614
Marion	2,554	1,371	264	61	22	4,272
McDuffie	9,638	4,006	1,482	277	54	15,457
McIntosh	3,765	1,605	551	95	18	6,034
Meriwether	9,978	4,138	995	348	79	15,538
Miller	3,098	1,787	396	63	13	5,357

County	Passengers	Trucks	Trailers	Motorcycles	Buses	Total
Mitchell	8,996	4,297	1,362	194	64	14,913
Monroe	8,162	3,408	924	303	48	12,845
Montgomery	3,247	1,866	732	95	25	5,965
Morgan	6,323	3,025	889	223	56	10,516
Murray	10,977	6,041	1,563	579	62	19,222
Muscogee	96,466	21,286	7,002	3,532	392	128,678
Newton	21,124	7,814	2,527	710	113	32,288
Oconee	8,481	3,604	1,232	367	48	13,732
Oglethorpe	5,079	2,674	829	198	42	8,822
Paulding	17,577	8,875	2,367	736	105	29,660
Peach	8,999	3,254	1,300	349	67	13,969
Pickens	7,512	4,229	869	320	36	12,966
Pierce	5,779	3,405	1,077	175	44	10,480
Pike	5,266	2,751	800	267	41	9,125
Polk	18,004	7,599	1,707	591	98	27,999
Pulaski	4,352	1,900	648	172	27	7,099
Putnam	5,593	2,748	1,048	176	40	9,605
Quitman	849	374	138	10	14	1,385
Rabun	6,532	3,706	840	207	53	11,338
Randolph	3,468	1,750	374	81	38	5,711
Richmond	101,116	22,037	7,876	2,887	452	134,368
Rockdale	26,968	9,053	3,274	1,088	99	40,482
Schley	1,617	901	212	65	18	2,813
Screven	6,579	3,503	720	197	44	11,043
Seminole	4,373	2,188	828	112	28	7,529
Spalding	27,115	8,842	2,743	958	137	39,795
Stephens	13,331	4,919	1,807	509	94	20,660
Stewart	2,470	1,262	261	54	31	4,078
Sumter	13,764	5,521	2,088	563	74	22,010
Talbot	3,408	1,506	282	101	25	5,322
Taliaferro	1,046	442	89	34	5	1,616
Tattnall	7,668	4,140	1,089	207	65	13,169
Taylor	3,485	1,961	516	121	31	6,114
Telfair	5,386	2,756	777	104	42	9,065
Terrell	4,888	2,074	668	117	29	7,776
Thomas	19,115	7,598	2,743	537	126	30,119
Tift	15,978	7,151	2,576	704	122	26,531
Toombs	11,306	5,351	1,872	355	74	18,958
Towns	4,090	2,178	720	175	15	7,178
Treutlen	3,155	1,590	313	86	17	5,161
Troup	27,356	9,186	2,773	827	131	40,273
Turner	3,792	2,312	450	131	23	6,708
Twiggs	4,590	2,173	592	170	43	7,568
Union	5,556	3,482	823	336	36	10,233
Upson	13,812	5,318	1,415	415	47	21,007
Walker	28,034	11,128	2,306	1,067	118	42,653
Walton	17,615	7,778	2,210	578	107	28,288
Ware	17,344	7,282	2,738	636	104	28,104
Warren	2,885	1,238	325	80	17	4,545
Washington	8,067	4,181	1,063	172	68	13,551
Wayne	10,461	5,395	1,900	297	79	18,132
Webster	1,048	631	115	9	10	1,813
Wheeler	2,312	1,317	393	59	18	4,099
White	6,674	3,657	830	270	43	11,474
Whitfield	39,078	15,594	7,081	1,597	199	63,549
Wilcox	3,047	1,880	388	110	23	5,448
Wilkes	5,846	2,839	922	173	55	9,835

County	Passengers	Trucks	Trailers	Motorcycles	Buses	Total
Wilkinson	4,871	2,685	685	136	32	8,409
Worth	9,507	5,281	1,211	411	61	16,471

VOTERS, REGISTERED

In order to become a registered voter in the state of Georgia, you must be 18 years old or older; a resident of the state for 1 year; and in the county 6 months.

REGISTERED VOTERS: 1968–1984

	Total Number					
	1968	1972	1976	1980	1982	1984
Appling	7,959	8,942	8,465	8,404	7,797	8,114
Atkinson	3,494	3,897	3,443	3,544	3,273	3,549
Bacon	5,578	6,171	5,862	5,600	5,026	5,331
Baker	2,528	2,686	2,402	2,336	2,554	2,422
Baldwin	10,908	11,706	12,593	12,083	13,434	14,334
Banks	4,343	3,492	4,043	4,030	4,012	4,459
Barrow	8,076	9,592	9,476	8,898	8,245	9,558
Bartow	12,625	14,732	15,697	15,105	14,923	18,157
Ben Hill	6,428	6,398	6,000	6,761	6,749	8,222
Berrien	8,172	6,750	6,596	7,091	6,213	7,014
Bibb	64,944	67,142	62,812	61,190	62,385	72,581
Bleckley	4,941	5,239	5,044	5,243	5,127	5,647
Brantley	4,389	4,295	3,746	4,314	4,666	5,391
Brooks	5,590	6,583	6,151	5,057	5,951	6,016
Bryan	4,042	4,252	4,888	4,976	4,832	6,046
Bulloch	14,664	15,340	13,700	13,564	14,497	17,339
Burke	7,748	7,100	6,943	7,105	7,557	9,462
Butts	5,051	5,793	5,953	5,302	5,541	6,344
Calhoun	2,993	3,090	3,710	3,600	3,395	3,372
Camden	5,893	5,977	6,038	6,812	6,188	7,369
Candler	3,658	3,413	3,398	3,756	3,307	4,107
Carroll	19,648	22,285	21,216	20,500	20,909	24,865
Catoosa	13,481	15,200	16,252	14,450	15,432	18,379
Charlton	3,078	3,236	3,524	3,286	3,575	4,051
Chatham	77,035	79,508	81,154	74,912	78,909	94,606
Chattahoochee	817	937	1,033	1,081	1,175	1,488
Chattooga	9,397	9,237	9,375	9,626	8,851	10,054
Cherokee	14,805	13,412	16,301	16,986	19,624	23,877
Clarke	20,800	28,419	30,346	26,722	27,083	33,428
Clay	1,787	2,040	1,939	2,102	1,502	1,925
Clayton	30,496	41,859	51,093	47,778	49,763	61,518
Clinch	3,123	3,275	3,213	3,699	3,194	3,209
Cobb	68,011	86,659	113,765	119,936	130,574	178,191
Coffee	12,941	10,467	10,857	9,866	10,304	11,817
Colquitt	13,293	13,625	13,257	11,642	11,859	13,833
Columbia	7,690	9,245	13,494	16,045	16,514	22,608
Cook	7,028	6,294	5,225	4,590	5,280	5,662
Coweta	15,584	18,162	13,714	12,743	13,925	17,445
Crawford	2,452	3,136	3,479	3,404	3,318	4,207
Crisp	8,384	8,559	7,732	7,317	7,961	8,057

	Total Number					
	1968	1972	1976	1980	1982	1984
Dade	5,923	7,000	7,859	8,000	5,770	6,700
Dawson	2,863	2,597	2,676	2,469	2,656	3,143
Decatur	9,988	10,332	9,762	9,094	9,776	10,386
DeKalb	158,124	206,461	231,358	213,356	217,671	263,675
Dodge	10,694	11,589	12,352	11,380	9,539	11,203
Dooly	5,374	4,453	4,512	5,125	5,352	5,132
Dougherty	27,022	29,824	30,808	33,136	36,888	44,156
Douglas	10,767	13,138	18,072	19,600	20,140	23,706
Early	6,096	5,526	4,991	5,190	4,954	5,832
Echols	976	1,074	1,170	1,395	1,208	1,365
Effingham	4,883	6,581	6,911	7,984	8,784	9,997
Elbert	9,379	9,809	8,988	8,783	8,698	9,179
Emanuel	9,928	9,747	9,997	9,641	9,122	10,277
Evans	3,372	3,792	3,766	3,969	3,702	4,110
Fannin	8,663	9,837	11,122	11,495	11,273	11,517
Fayette	4,843	6,299	10,092	12,861	15,280	20,461
Floyd	30,743	33,970	33,523	32,951	31,198	34,522
Forsyth	6,645	7,526	9,011	11,376	12,367	13,679
Franklin	11,677	11,721	9,749	7,681	7,346	8,227
Fulton	273,339	303,937	305,296	291,635	290,740	350,942
Gilmer	5,490	5,925	6,478	6,838	7,147	6,818
Glascock	1,492	1,330	1,536	1,690	1,388	1,575
Glynn	20,367	23,143	21,773	23,066	22,675	27,838
Gordon	12,508	14,131	16,666	15,894	15,403	17,500
Grady	8,144	7,984	7,929	7,641	7,254	8,461
Greene	6,528	5,625	5,211	5,080	5,930	6,110
Gwinnett	30,050	39,382	55,212	61,983	74,265	106,856
Habersham	10,851	9,148	9,434	9,070	9,179	10,166
Hall	21,286	22,541	26,131	27,600	29,007	33,159
Hancock	4,972	5,697	6,519	6,273	6,663	7,059
Haralson	9,674	9,819	10,146	10,155	9,120	10,555
Harris	5,954	6,533	6,646	6,643	6,767	8,297
Hart	7,890	7,983	8,802	9,242	8,666	9,305
Heard	3,403	3,768	3,357	3,213	3,274	3,763
Henry	11,677	12,066	14,029	14,437	16,510	19,674
Houston	19,663	25,337	29,060	26,596	28,686	35,130
Irwin	5,825	5,000	4,236	3,786	3,631	3,752
Jackson	9,284	9,836	10,389	10,067	9,417	10,757
Jasper	3,334	3,445	4,300	3,980	4,449	4,533
Jeff Davis	6,485	5,951	6,880	6,482	5,560	6,286
Jefferson	8,347	8,011	6,260	7,366	7,407	9,248
Jenkins	3,885	4,197	4,211	3,958	3,913	4,200
Johnson	4,279	4,161	4,931	5,016	4,474	5,038
Jones	5,764	6,294	7,142	6,985	8,316	9,659
Lamar	5,313	5,239	5,142	5,142	5,121	5,475
Lanier	2,589	2,538	2,591	2,880	2,528	2,864
Laurens	19,144	17,627	17,632	17,930	17,951	20,757
Lee	2,998	3,597	4,260	4,508	5,001	6,102
Liberty	5,844	6,435	6,623	7,021	7,267	8,830
Lincoln	3,383	3,667	4,277	3,403	3,489	4,095
Long	3,031	2,992	3,537	2,572	2,643	3,030
Lowndes	17,060	20,254	21,968	18,680	20,260	24,935
Lumpkin	3,817	3,795	4,200	4,347	4,231	4,975
Macon	5,419	5,083	5,574	5,624	5,579	6,233
Madison	5,314	5,883	6,711	7,313	7,446	8,197

371

VOTERS, REGISTERED

	Total Number					
	1968	1972	1976	1980	1982	1984
Marion	1,901	1,851	2,492	2,600	2,627	3,088
McDuffie	6,198	7,650	8,898	8,275	6,621	8,383
McIntosh	3,521	4,651	5,187	4,733	4,717	5,080
Meriwether	7,899	8,422	9,448	8,971	8,579	9,559
Miller	3,209	3,816	4,354	2,768	3,277	3,511
Mitchell	7,551	8,041	9,638	8,703	7,915	9,345
Monroe	5,441	5,909	6,689	5,772	5,628	6,432
Montgomery	4,002	4,341	3,935	4,347	3,814	4,342
Morgan	4,968	5,348	5,664	5,917	6,016	6,110
Murray	6,207	6,257	7,389	6,548	6,573	9,158
Muscogee	53,709	55,887	57,991	52,950	55,097	65,613
Newton	11,271	14,600	13,993	13,090	12,250	13,506
Oconee	3,500	3,853	4,622	5,162	5,664	6,971
Oglethorpe	4,190	3,761	4,142	3,877	3,751	4,401
Paulding	9,042	11,469	12,569	10,963	11,100	13,074
Peach	6,442	9,610	9,499	7,614	7,804	9,435
Pickens	5,603	6,013	7,042	7,403	6,353	7,257
Pierce	5,325	5,082	5,398	5,147	5,718	6,000
Pike	4,329	3,929	4,022	4,130	4,164	4,707
Polk	14,756	13,481	13,205	13,205	11,706	13,530
Pulaski	4,544	4,234	4,366	4,403	4,747	5,216
Putnam	4,136	4,757	4,208	4,075	4,537	5,421
Quitman	921	1,142	1,494	1,390	1,223	1,467
Rabun	4,833	5,016	5,059	5,314	5,523	6,512
Randolph	4,090	4,563	4,397	4,364	3,835	4,585
Richmond	55,717	57,832	61,704	59,243	63,384	78,346
Rockdale	6,832	8,690	12,774	14,329	15,543	19,314
Schley	1,397	1,615	1,708	1,555	1,672	1,661
Screven	6,408	5,629	5,766	5,010	6,046	7,330
Seminole	3,762	4,467	4,391	4,527	4,471	4,980
Spalding	15,773	15,985	17,486	16,541	17,164	19,994
Stephens	8,828	9,832	11,838	10,714	9,799	11,060
Stewart	2,788	3,365	3,890	3,729	4,052	4,314
Sumter	11,628	12,853	12,025	12,048	11,767	13,205
Talbot	2,315	3,205	3,291	3,337	3,974	4,426
Taliaferro	1,820	2,024	1,890	1,746	1,717	1,626
Tattnall	9,799	8,951	9,705	7,821	8,139	9,238
Taylor	4,028	4,029	4,524	4,400	4,290	4,446
Telfair	6,912	6,928	6,812	6,689	6,477	6,742
Terrell	5,751	6,216	6,873	5,041	4,932	5,729
Thomas	14,816	14,879	16,320	14,264	14,757	17,055
Tift	10,038	9,861	11,196	11,185	11,893	13,307
Toombs	8,646	9,804	10,662	9,755	9,678	11,634
Towns	4,329	4,184	4,217	4,724	4,206	4,647
Treutlen	4,058	3,596	3,813	3,630	3,538	3,553
Troup	18,269	18,835	19,111	18,370	18,881	22,164
Turner	4,149	4,789	4,509	3,838	3,838	4,283
Twiggs	3,403	4,354	4,528	4,752	4,391	4,913
Union	4,991	6,295	6,925	7,543	5,876	6,783
Upson	9,185	9,781	10,695	9,784	10,440	12,472
Walker	23,523	23,629	21,328	17,907	18,587	22,431
Walton	9,725	10,963	10,561	9,913	9,461	11,701
Ware	15,918	16,618	16,172	14,404	14,027	15,947
Warren	3,475	3,494	3,578	4,830	3,535	3,707
Washington	8,507	11,073	9,456	8,142	8,259	9,475

	Total Number					
	1968	1972	1976	1980	1982	1984
Wayne	9,189	10,178	10,128	8,350	9,358	10,589
Webster	1,177	1,246	1,329	1,550	1,532	1,501
Wheeler	3,001	2,824	3,013	3,166	3,404	3,186
White	5,090	5,286	4,480	4,675	4,926	5,565
Whitfield	20,182	21,086	22,282	21,385	21,796	25,500
Wilcox	4,476	4,545	4,439	4,055	4,159	4,605
Wilkes	5,354	5,082	5,154	4,971	5,053	5,222
Wilkinson	4,918	5,698	5,126	4,921	4,852	5,421
Worth	6,424	6,709	6,438	6,602	6,566	8,062
Georgia	1,960,426	2,167,888	2,301,575	2,231,223	2,284,184	2,732,332

WAR BETWEEN THE STATES

On January 3, 1861, Georgia state troops seized the mighty United States fortress, Fort Pulaski, near the mouth of the Savannah River. Then, on January 19, the State Legislature voted, 164 to 133, to take Georgia out of the Union. The next week, the State Militia occupied Fort Jackson, near Savannah, and the U.S. Federal Arsenal at Augusta.

Before the war was over, there had been 108 major engagements on Georgia soil, the least of any Confederate state with the exception of Alabama, Florida, and Texas. By far, Georgia's most active year in the war was 1864, when 92 of those 108 conflicts occurred. In addition to these, there were scores of lesser skirmishes.

The results of the various Georgia campaigns were mixed. At Chickamauga, in September of 1863, Confederate General Braxton Bragg scored a technical victory, but failed to follow up on his success. Consequently, the entire area around Chattanooga was lost. By May, 1864, Union General William T. Sherman and 112,000 soldiers were positioned near Chattanooga and began the long march to Atlanta. In front of them was Confederate General Joseph E. Johnston and 60,000 Southern troops. In mid-May, the two armies clashed at Resaca, and after holding the Federals for several days, Johnston was finally forced to retreat south. Sherman assaulted Johnston again in late June at Kennesaw Mountain. Johnston's valiant victory there did not deter his superiors from replacing him as commander of the Army of Tennessee, however.

By now, Sherman was at Atlanta's doorstep, and the impetuous John Bell Hood, Johnston's replacement, was eager for a contest. Within two days, in July, 1864, Hood lost over 11,000 troops in two ill-planned attacks against Sherman. The Union Army was then free to encircle Atlanta and the Confederate Army. Over a month of waiting ensued. Finally, with Confederate supply lines cut and overwhelmingly outnumbered, the Confederates evacuated Atlanta on September 1.

General Hood started to return to Tennessee and was subsequently overpowered at Franklin and Nashville. In the meantime, General Sherman headed for Savannah with 60,000 troops. In a path of destruction over 50 miles wide, Sherman destroyed everything in sight. By his own estimate, the General suggested that $100,000,000 worth of damage was done to property along the way. When he reached Savannah in December, he made President Lincoln a "Christmas-gift" of the city. The fall of Atlanta and Sherman's "march to the sea" all but obliterated further resistance in the Deep South.

In June, 1868, Georgia was readmitted to the Union, along with several other Southern states. The proud residents began the long, hard road to recovery amidst a shattered economy and a ruined land. As the title of perhaps the most famous book ever written by a Georgian indicates, the good years prior to the war were, indeed, "Gone With the Wind."

Today, there are several military parks which commemorate the War Between the States in Georgia, among them Chickamauga and Chattanooga National Military Park, Andersonville National Historic Site, Kennesaw Mountain National Battlefield Park, and Fort Pulaski National Monument. See the section on "National Parks" for more details of these and other interesting sites from the War Between the States.

WOMEN'S RIGHTS

Georgia has been an outstanding leader in matters having to do with women and women's rights. Among the more important of these issues and their associated dates are:

1802—Sarah Porter Hillhouse becomes the first woman in the U.S. to own and edit a newspaper *(The Washington Gazette)*.

1819—The first women's foreign missionary society is formed.

1836—Wesleyan College at Macon becomes the first college in the world chartered to confer degrees to women.

1866—Georgia becomes the first state to pass legislation allowing women to have full property rights.

1912—Juliette Gordon Low of Savannah organizes the Girl Scouts of America.

1922—Georgia elects Rebecca Felton as the first woman U.S. senator.

ZIP CODES

Post Office and County	ZIP Code	Post Office and County	ZIP Code	Post Office and County	ZIP Code
Abac, Tifton	31794	**Adairsville**, Bartow	30103	S Decatur	30030
Abbeville, Wilcox	31001	**Adel**, Cook	31620	**Ailey**, Montgomery	30410
Acworth, Cobb	30101	**Adrian**, Emanuel	31002	**Airport Mall Facility,**	
Oak Grove	30101	**Agnes Scott College,**		Atlanta	30320

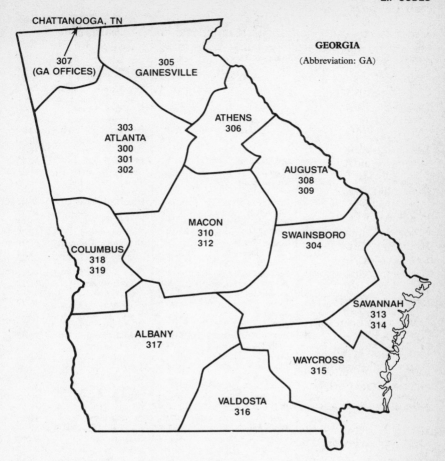

CHATTANOOGA, TN

307
(GA OFFICES)

305
GAINESVILLE

GEORGIA
(Abbreviation: GA)

ATHENS
306

303
ATLANTA
300
301
302

AUGUSTA
308
309

MACON
310
312

SWAINSBORO
304

COLUMBUS
318
319

SAVANNAH
313
314

ALBANY
317

WAYCROSS
315

VALDOSTA
316

Post Office and County	ZIP Code	Post Office and County	ZIP Code	Post Office and County	ZIP Code
Alamo, Wheeler	30411	**Alpharetta,** Fulton	30201	**Argyle,** Clinch	31623
Alapaha, Berrien	31622	**Alps Road,** Athens	30604	**Arlington,** Calhoun	31713
Albany, Dougherty	31706	**Alston,** Montgomery	30412	**Armuchee,** Floyd	30105
Bridgeboro (Worth		**Alto,** Habersham	30510	**Arnoldsville,**	
Co.)	31705	**Alvaton,** Gay	30202	Olgethorpe	30619
Federal Station	31702	**Ambrose,** Coffee	31512	**Ashburn,** Turner	31714
Four Points	31705	**Americus,** Sumter	31709	**Athens,** Clarke	30603
Marine Corps		Georgia		Alps Road	30604
Logistics Base	31740	Southwestern		Campus	30605
Alexander,		College	31709	Gaines Community	30605
Waynesboro	30801	**Andersonville,** Sumter	31711	Georgia University	30612
Allenhurst, Liberty	31301	**Appling,** Columbia	30802	Navy Supply Corps	
Allentown, Wilkinson	31003	**Arabi,** Crisp	31712	School	30606
Alma, Bacon	31510	**Aragon,** Polk	30104		

Post Office and County	ZIP Code	Post Office and County	ZIP Code	Post Office and County	ZIP Code
Atlanta, Fulton	30301	**Attapulgus,** Decatur	31715	**Bowdon Junction,**	
Airport Mail Facility	30320	**Auburn,** Barrow,	30203	Carroll	30109
Ben Hill	30331	Carl	30203	**Bowersville,** Hart	30516
Bolton	30318	**Augusta,** Richmond	30903	**Bowman,** Elbert	30624
Briarcliff (DeKalb		Fort Gordon	30905	**Box Springs,** Talbot	31801
Co.)	30359	Martinez (Columbia		Juniper (Marion Co.)	31801
Briarwood	30344	Co.)	30907	**Braselton,** Jackson	30517
Capitol Hill	30334	Medical Ctr.		**Bremen,** Haralson	30110
Cascade Heights	30311	Eisenhower Hosp	30905	**Briarcliff,** Atlanta	30359
Central City	30302	Peach Orchard	30906	**Briarwood,** Atlanta	30344
Chamblee (DeKalb		The Hill	30904	**Bridgeboro,** Albany	31705
Co.)	30366	**Austell,** Cobb	30001	**Brinson,** Decatur	31725
Civic Center	30308	**Avera,** Jefferson	30803	**Bristol,** Pierce	31518
College Park	30337	**Avondale Estates,**		**Bronwood,** Terrell	31726
Cumberland (Cobb		DeKalb	30002	**Brookfield,** Tift	31727
Co.)	30339	**Axson,** Atkinson	31624	**Brooklet,** Bulloch	30415
Doraville (DeKalb		**Baconton,** Mitchell	31716	Stilson	30415
Co.)	30362	**Bainbridge,** Decatur	31717	**Brooks,** Fayette	30205
Downtown	30301	West Bainbridge	31717	**Broxton,** Coffee	31519
Druid Hills (DeKalb		**Baker Village,**		**Brunswick,** Glynn	31520
Co.)	30333	Columbus	31903	Main Office Boxes	31521
Dunwoody (DeKalb		**Baldwin,** Banks	30511	Glynco	31520
Co.)	30338	**Ball Ground,** Cherokee	30107	Jekyll Island	31520
East Atlanta		**Barnesville,** Lamar	30204	Saint Simons Island	31522
(DeKalb Co.)	30316	**Barney,** Brooks	31625	Sea Island	31561
East Point	30364	**Bartow,** Jefferson	30413	**Buchanan,** Haralson	30113
Eastwood (DeKalb		**Barwick,** Brooks	31720	**Buckhead,** Morgan	30625
Co.)	30317	**Baxley,** Appling	31513	**Buena Vista,** Marion	31803
Embry Hills B		**Beallwood,** Columbus	319	**Buford,** Gwinnett	30518
(DeKalb Co.)	30341	**Bellville,** Claxton	30414	**Butler,** Taylor	31006
Emory University		**Belvedere,** Decatur	30032	**Byromville,** Dooly	31007
(DeKalb Co.)	30322	**Bemiss,** Valdosta	31601	**Byron,** Peach	31008
Executive Park		**Benevolence,**		**Cadwell,** Laurens	31009
(DeKalb Co.)	30347	Randolph	31721	**Cairo,** Grady	31728
Federal Reserve	30308	**Ben Hill,** Atlanta	30331	**Calhoun,** Gordon	30701
Fort McPherson	30330	**Berlin,** Colquitt	31722	**Calvary,** Grady	31729
Gate City	30312	**Berryton,** Summerville	30748	**Camak,** Warren	30807
Greenbriar	30331	**Bethlehem,** Barrow	30620	**Camilla,** Mitchell	31730
Hapeville	30354	**Bibb City,** Columbus	31904	**Campus,** Athens	30602
Industrial	30336	**Big Canoe,** Jasper	30143	**Canon,** Franklin	30520
Lakewood	30315	**Bingville,** Savannah	31403	**Canoochee,** Emanuel	30416
Lenox Square	30326	**Bishop,** Oconee	30621	**Canton,** Cherokee	30114
Martech	30377	**Blackshear,** Pierce	31516	**Canton Plaza,**	
Morris Brown	30314	**Blairsville,** Union	30512	Marietta	30066
North Atlanta		**Blakely,** Early	31723	**Capitol Hill,** Atlanta	30334
(DeKalb Co.)	30319	**Bloomingdale,**		**Carl,** Auburn	30203
Northlake		Chatham	31302	**Carlton,** Madison	30627
(DeKalb Co.)	30345	**Blue Ridge,** Fannin	30513	**Carnesville,** Franklin	30521
North Side	30355	**Bluffton,** Clay	31724	**Carrollton,** Carroll	30117
Old National	30349	**Blythe,** Richmond	30805	West Georgia	
Peachtree Center	30343	**Bogart,** Oconee	30622	College	30118
Sandy Springs	30358	**Bolingbroke,** Monroe	31004	West Georgia	
Six Flags Over		**Bolton,** Atlanta	30318	College	30117
Georgia (Cobb Co.)	30336	**Bonaire,** Houston	31005	**Carters,** Chatsworth	30705
Toco Hills		**Boneville,** McDuffie	30806	**Cartersville,** Bartow	30120
(DeKalb Co.)	30329	**Boston,** Thomas	31626	**Cascade Heights,**	
Tuxedo	30342	**Bostwick,** Morgan	30623	Atlanta	30311
West End	30310	**Bowdon,** Carroll	30108	**Cassville,** Bartow	30123

Post Office and County	ZIP Code	Post Office and County	ZIP Code	Post Office and County	ZIP Code
Castle Park, Valdosta	31601	Fort Benning		Snapfinger	30035
Castle Park Sta Boxes,		(Chattahoochee		South Decatur	30032
Valdosta	31604	Co.)	31905	Vista Grove	30033
Cataula, Harris	31804	Lindsay Creek	31907	**Deepstep,** Sandersville	31082
Cave Spring, Floyd	30124	Upatoi	31829	**Demorest,** Habersham	30535
Cecil, Cook	31627	Windsor Park	31904	Habersham	30544
Cedar Springs, Early	31732	Wynnton	31906	**Denton,** Jeff Davis	31532
Cedartown, Polk	30125	**Comer,** Madison	30629	**DeSoto,** Sumter	31743
Centerville, Warner		**Commerce,** Jackson	30529	**Devereux,** Sparta	31087
Robins	31028	**Concord,** Pike	30206	**Dewy Rose,** Elbert	30634
Central City, Atlanta	30302	**Conley,** Clayton	30027	**Dexter,** Laurens	31019
Chamblee, Atlanta	30366	**Conyers,** Rockdale	30207	**Dillard,** Rabun	30537
Chatsworth, Murray	30705	**Coolidge,** Thomas	31738	**Dixie,** Brooks	31629
Carters	30705	**Coosa,** Floyd	30129	**Dobbins A F B,**	
Chauncey, Dodge	31011	**Cordele,** Crisp	31015	Marietta	30060
Cherrylog, Gilmer	30522	**Cornelia,** Habersham	30531	**Doerun,** Colquitt	31744
Chester, Dodge	31012	**Cotton,** Mitchell	31739	**Donalsonville,**	
Chestnut Mountain,		**Court Square, Dublin**	31021	Seminole	31745
Gainesville	30502	**Covena,** Emanuel	30422	**Doraville,** Atlanta	30362
Chickamauga, Walker	30707	**Covington,** Newton	30209	**Douglas,** Coffee	31533
Chula, Tift	31733	Starrsville	30209	**Douglasville,** Douglas	30133
Cisco, Murray	30708	**Crandall,** Murray	30711	**Dover,** Screven	30424
Civic Center, Atlanta	30308	**Crawford,** Olgethorpe	30630	**Downtown,** Atlanta	30301
Clarkdale, Cobb	30020	**Crawfordville,**		**Downtown,** Columbus	31902
Clarkesville,		Taliaferro	30631	**Druid Hills,** Atlanta	30333
Habersham	30523	**Crescent,** McIntosh	31304	**Dry Branch,** Twiggs	31020
Hollywood	30523	Valona	31332	**Dublin,** Laurens	31021
Clarkston, DeKalb	30021	**Culloden,** Monroe	31016	Lollie	31021
Claxton, Evans	30417	**Cumberland,** Atlanta	33339	Court Square	31021
Bellville	30414	**Cumming,** Forsyth	30130	East Dublin	31021
Clayton, Rabun	30525	**Cusseta,**		Scott (Johnson Co.)	31095
Clermont, Hall	30527	Chattahoochee	31805	**Dudley,** Laurens	31022
Cleveland, White	30528	**Custer Terrace,**		**Duluth,** Gwinnett	30136
Climax, Decatur	31734	Columbus	31905	**Dunaire,** Decatur	30032
Clinchfield, Houston	31013	**Cuthbert,** Randolph	31740	**Dunwoody,** Atlanta	30338
Cloudland, Chattooga	30709	**Dacula,** Gwinnett	30211	**Du Pont,** Clinch	31630
Clyattville, Valdosta	31604	**Dahlonega,** Lumpkin	30533	**Eastanollee,** Stephens	30538
Clyo, Effingham	31303	North Ga College	30597	**East Atlanta,** Atlanta	30316
Cobb, Sumter	31735	**Daisy,** Evans	30423	**East Dublin,** Dublin	31021
Cobb County Center,		**Dallas,** Paulding	30132	**East Ellijay,** Gilmer	30539
Smyrna	30080	**Dalton,** Whitfield	30720	**Eastman,** Dodge	31023
Cobbtown, Tattnall	30420	East Side	30721	**East Point,** Atlanta	30364
Cochran, Bleckley	31014	**Damascus,** Early	31741	**East Side,** Dalton	30721
Empire (Dodge Co.)	31026	**Danburg,** Tignall	30668	**Eastwood,** Atlanta	30317
Cogdell, Clinch	31628	**Danielsville,** Madison	30633	**Eatonton,** Putnam	31024
Cohutta, Whitfield	30710	**Danville,** Twiggs	31017	**Eden,** Effingham	31307
Colbert, Madison	30628	**Darien,** McIntosh	31305	**Edison,** Calhoun	31746
Coleman, Randolph	31736	**Davisboro,**		**Elberton,** Elbert	30635
College, Fort Valley	31030	Washington	31018	**Eldorado,** Tifton	31794
College Park, Atlanta	30337	**Dawson,** Terrell	31742	**Elke,** Houston	31025
Collins, Tattnall	30421	**Dawsonville,** Dawson	30534	**Ellabell,** Bryan	31308
Colquitt, Miller	31737	Juno	30534	**Ellaville,** Schley	31806
Columbus, Muscogee	31902	**Dearing,** McDuffie	30808	**Ellenton,** Colquitt	31747
Baker Village	31903	**Decatur,** DeKalb	30031	**Ellenwood,** Clayton	30049
Beallwood	31904	Agnes Scott College	30030	**Ellerslie,** Harris	31807
Bibb City	31904	Belvedere	30032	**Ellijay,** Gilmer	30540
Custer Terrace	31905	Dunaire	30032	**Elmodel,** Newton	31748
Downtown	31902	North Decatur	30033	**Embry Hills,** Atlanta	30341

Post Office and County	ZIP Code	Post Office and County	ZIP Code	Post Office and County	ZIP Code
Emerson, Bartow	30137	Gaines Community,		Hardwick, Baldwin	31034
Emory University		Athens	30605	Harlem, Columbia	30814
Atlanta	30322	Gainesville, Hall	30503	Harrison, Washington	31035
Empire, Cochran	31026	Chestnut Mountain	30502	Hartsfield, Colquitt	31756
Enigma, Berrien	31749	Westside	30501	Hartwell, Hart	30643
Epworth, Fannin	30541	Garden City,		Hawkinsville, Pulaski	31036
Esom Hill, Polk	30138	Savannah	31408	Hazlehurst, Jeff Davis	31539
Eton, Murray	30724	Garfield, Emanuel	30425	Helen, White	30545
Evans, Columbia	30809	Gate City, Atlanta	30312	Helena, Telfair	31037
Everett, Glynn	31536	Gay, Meriwether	30218	Hephzibah, Richmond	30815
Executive Park,		Alvaton	30202	Hiawassee, Towns	30546
Atlanta	30347	Geneva, Talbot	31810	High Shoals, Oconee	30645
Experiment, Spalding	30212	Georgetown, Quitman	31754	Hill City, Resaca	30735
Fairburn, Fulton	30213	Georgia Southern,		Hillsboro, Jasper	31038
Fairmount, Gordon	30139	Statesboro	30460	Hilltonia,	
Fair Oaks, Marietta	30060	Georgia Southern,		Sylvania	30467
Fargo, Clinch	31631	Statesboro	30458	Hinesville, Liberty	31313
Farmington, Oconee	30638	Georgia Southwestern		Fort Stewart	31314
Fayetteville, Fayette	30214	College, Americus	31709	Hiram, Paulding	30141
Woolsey	30214	Georgia University,		Hoboken, Brantley	31542
Inman	30232	Athens	30612	Hogansville, Troup	30230
Peachtree City	30269	Gibson, Glascock	30810	Holcomb Bridge,	
Federal Reserve,		Gillsville, Hall	30543	Roswell	30077
Atlanta	30308	Girard, Burke	30426	Holly Springs,	
Federal Station,		Glenn, Heard	30219	Cherokee	30142
Albany	31702	Glennville, Tattnall	30427	Hollywood,	
Felton, Haralson	30140	Glenwood, Wheeler	30428	Clarkesville	30523
Fitzgerald, Ben Hill	31750	Glynco, Brunswick	31520	Homer, Banks	30547
Fleming, Liberty	31309	Godfrey, Madison	30650	Homerville, Clinch	31634
Flintstone, Walker	30725	Good Hope, Walton	30641	Hortense, Brantley	31543
Flippen, McDonough	30215	Gordon, Wilkinson	31031	Hoschton, Jackson	30548
Flovilla, Butts	30216	Stevens Pottery		Howard, Taylor	31039
Indian Springs	30231	(Baldwin Co.)	31031	Huber, Macon	31201
Flowery Branch, Hall	30542	Gough, Keysville	30811	Hull, Madison	30646
Folkston, Charlton	31537	Gracewood,		Hunter Army Airfield,	
Forest Park, Clayton	30050	Richmond	30812	Savannah	31409
Main Office Boxes	30051	Grantwood, Coweta	30220	Ideal, Macon	31041
Forsyth, Monroe	31029	Graves, Terrell	31755	Ila, Madison	30647
Fort Benning,		Gray, Jones	31032	Indian Springs,	
Columbus	31905	Wayside	31032	Flovilla	30231
Fort Gaines, Clay	31751	Grayson, Gwinnett	30221	Industrial, Atlanta	30336
Fort Gordon, Augusta	30905	Graysville, Catoosa	30726	Inman, Fayetteville	30232
Fort McPherson,		Greenbriar, Atlanta	30331	Iron City, Seminole	31759
Atlanta	30330	Greensboro, Greene	30642	Irwinton, Wilkinson	31042
Fort Oglethorpe,		Greenville,		Irwinville, Irwin	31760
Rossville	30742	Meriwether	30222	Jackson, Butts	30233
Fortson, Muscogee	31808	Griffin, Spalding	30223	Jacksonville, Telfair	31544
Fort Stewart,		Main Office Boxes	30224	Jakin, Early	31761
Hinesville	31314	Grovetown, Columbia	30813	Jasper, Pickens	30143
Fort Valley, Peach	31030	Guyton, Effingham	31312	Big Canoe	30143
College	31030	Habersham, Demorest	30544	Jefferson, Jackson	30549
Four Points, Albany	31705	Haddock, Jones	31033	Jeffersonville, Twiggs	31044
Fowlstown, Decatur	31752	Hagan, Evans	30429	Jekyll Island,	
Franklin, Heard	30217	Haldra, Lowndes	31632	Brunswick	31520
Franklin Springs,		Hamilton, Harris	31811	Jenkinsburg, Butts	30234
Franklin	30639	Hampton, Henry	30228	Jersey, Walton	30235
Fry, McCaysville	30555	Hapeville, Atlanta	30354	Jesup, Wayne	31545
Funston, Colquitt	31763	Haralson, Coweta	30229	Jewell, Warren	31045

Post Office and County	ZIP Code	Post Office and County	ZIP Code	Post Office and County	ZIP Code
Jonesboro, Clayton	30236	**Lyons,** Toombs	30436	**Maxeys,** Union Point	30671
Main Office Boxes	30237	**Mableton,** Cobb	30059	**Mayfield,** Sparta	31087
Juliette, Monroe	31046	**Macon,** Bibb	31208	**Maysville,** Banks	30558
Junction City, Talbot	31812	Huber P		**McCaysville,** Fannin	30555
Juniper, Box Springs	31801	(Twiggs Co.)	31201	Fry	30555
June, Dawsonville	30534	Macon Mall	31212	**McDonough,** Henry	30253
Kathleen, Houston	31047	Mercer University	31207	Flippen	30215
Kennesaw, Cobb	30144	Mulberry Street	31202	**McIntyre,** Wilkinson	31054
Keysville, Burke	30816	Pio Nono	31203	**McRae,** Telfair	31055
Gough	30811	Riverside	31209	**Meansville,** Pike	30256
Kibbee, Vidalia	30474	Shurlington	31211	**Medical Ctr.**	
Kings Bay, Kingsland	31547	South Macon	31205	**Eisenhower**	
Kingsland, Camden	31548	Wesleyan College	31297	**Hosp,** Augusta	30905
Kings Bay	31547	Wilson Airport	31297	**Meigs,** Thomas	31765
Kingston, Bartow	30145	**Macon Mall,** Macon	31212	**Meldrim,** Effingham	31318
Kite, Johnson	31049	**Madison,** Morgan	30650	**Menlo,** Chattooga	30731
Knoxville, Crawford	31050	Godfrey	30650	**Mercer University,**	
LaFayette, Walker	30728	**Madras,** Coweta	30254	Macon	31207
LaGrange, Troup	30240	**Main Office Boxes,**		**Meridian,** McIntosh	31319
Main Office Boxes	30241	Brunswick	31521	**Mershon,** Pierce	31551
Lakeland, Lanier	31635	**Main Office Boxes,**		**Mesena,** Warren	30819
Lakemont, Rabun	30552	Forest Park	30051	**Metter,** Candler	30439
Lake Park, Lowndes	31636	**Main Office Boxes,**		**Midland,** Muscogee	31820
Lakewood, Atlanta	30315	Griffin	30224	**Midville,** Burke	30441
Lavonia, Franklin	30553	**Main Office Boxes,**		**Midway,** Liberty	31320
Lawrenceville,		Jonesboro	30237	**Milan,** Telfair	31060
Gwinnett	30245	**Main Office Boxes,**		**Milledgeville,** Baldwin	31061
Main Office Boxes	30246	LaGrange	30241	**Millen,** Jenkins	30442
Leary, Calhoun	31762	**Main Office Boxes,**		**Millwood,** Ware	31552
Lebanon, Cherokee	30146	Lawrenceville	30246	**Milner,** Lamar	30257
Leesburg, Lee	31763	**Main Office Boxes,**		**Mineral Bluff,** Fannin	30559
Lenox, Cook	31637	Rome	30162	**Mitchell,** Glascock	30820
Lenox Square, Atlanta	30326	**Main Office Boxes,**		**Molena,** Pike	30258
Leslie, Sumter	31764	Smyrna	30081	**Monroe,** Walton	30655
Lexington, Oglethorpe	30648	**Main Office Boxes,**		**Montezuma,** Macon	31063
Lilburn, Gwinnett	30247	Valdosta	31603	**Monticello,** Jasper	31064
Lilly, Dooly	31051	**Main Office Boxes,**		**Montrose,** Laurens	31065
Lincolnton, Lincoln	30817	Warner Robins	31099	**Moody A F B,**	
Lindale, Floyd	30147	**Manassas,** Tattnall	30438	**Valdosta**	31601
Lindsay Creek,		**Manchester,**		**Moody Afb (official),**	
Columbus	31907	Meriwether	31816	Valdosta	31699
Lithia Springs,		**Manor,** Ware	31550	**Moreland,** Coweta	30259
Douglas	30057	**Mansfield,** Newton	30255	**Morgan,** Calhoun	31766
Lithonia, DeKalb	30058	**Marble Hill,** Pickens	30148	**Morganton,** Fannin	30560
Lizella, Bibb	31052	**Marietta,** Cobb	30061	**Morris,** Quitman	31767
Locust Grove, Henry	30248	Canton Plaza	30066	**Morris Brown,** Atlanta	30314
Loganville, Walton	30249	Dobbins A F B	30060	**Morrow,** Clayton	30260
Lollie, Dublin	31021	Fair Oaks	30060	**Morven,** Brooks	31638
Louisville, Jefferson	30434	Southern Tech	30060	**Moultrie,** Colquitt	31768
Louvale, Stewart	31814	**Marine Corps**		**Mountain City,** Rabun	30562
Lovejoy, Clayton	30250	**Logistics Base 3,**		**Mountain View,**	
Ludowici, Long	31316	Albany	31704	Clayton	30070
Lula, Hall	30554	**Marshallville,** Macon	31057	**Mount Airy,**	
Lumber City, Telfair	31549	**Martech,** Atlanta	30377	Habersham	30563
Lumpkin, Stewart	31815	**Martin,** Stephens	30557	**Mount Berry,** Rome	30149
Luthersville,		**Martinez,** Augusta	30907	**Mount Vernon,**	
Meriwether	30251	**Matthews,** Jefferson	30818	Montgomery	30445
Lyerly, Chattooga	30730	**Mauk,** Taylor	31058	**Mountville,** Troup	30261

379

Post Office and County	ZIP Code	Post Office and County	ZIP Code	Post Office and County	ZIP Code
Mount Zion, Carroll	30150	Peachtree Center,		Riverside, Macon	31209
Mulberry Street,		Atlanta	30343	Roberta, Crawford	31078
Macon	31202	Peachtree City,		Robins A F B, Warner	
Murrayville, Hall	30564	Fayetteville	30269	Robins	31098
Musella, Crawford	31066	Pearson, Atkinson	31642	Rochelle, Wilcox	31079
Mystic, Irwin	31769	Pelham, Mitchell	31779	Rockledge, Laurens	30454
Nahunta, Brantley	31553	Pembroke, Bryan	31321	Rockmart, Polk	30153
Nashville, Berrien	31639	Pendergrass, Jackson	30567	Rock Spring, Walker	30739
Navy Supply Corps		Penfield, Union Point	30658	Rocky Face, Whitfield	30740
School, Athens	30606	Perkins, Jenkins	30822	Rocky Ford, Screven	30455
Naylor, Lowndes	31641	Perry, Houston	31069	Rome, Floyd	30161
Nelson, Cherokee	30151	Philomath, Oglethorpe	30659	Main Office Boxes	30162
Newborn, Newton	30262	Pinehurst, Dooly	31070	West End Sta	
Newington, Screven	30446	Pine Lake, DeKalb	30072	Boxes	30164
Newnan, Coweta	30264	Pine Log, Rydal	30171	Mount Berry	30149
Raymond	32063	Pine Mountain, Harris	31822	West End	30161
Newton, Baker	31770	Pine Mountain Valley,		Roopville, Carroll	30170
Elmodel	31748	Harris	31823	Rossville, Walker	30741
Nicholls, Coffee	31554	Pineview, Wilcox	31071	Fort Oglethorpe	
Nicholson, Jackson	30565	Pio Nono, Macon	31203	(Catoosa Co.)	30742
Norcross, Gwinnett	30098	Pitts, Wilcox	31072	Roswell, Fulton	30077
Norman Park, Colquitt	31771	Plainfield, Dodge	31073	Holcomb Bridge	30076
Norristown, Emanuel	30447	Plains, Sumter	31780	Royston, Franklin	30662
North Atlanta, Atlanta	30319	Plainville, Gordon	30733	Rupert, Taylor	31081
North Decatur,		Pooler, Chatham	31322	Rutledge, Morgan	30663
Decatur	30033	Portal, Bulloch	30450	Rydal, Barlow	30171
North Ga College,		Porterdale, Newton	30270	Pine Log	30171
Dahlonega	30597	Port Wentworth,		Saint George,	
Northlake, Atlanta	30345	Savannah	31407	Charlton	31646
North Side, Atlanta	30355	Poulan, Worth	31781	Saint Marys, Camden	31558
Norwood, Warren	30821	Powder Springs, Cobb	30073	Saint Simons Island,	
Nunez, Emanuel	30448	Powersville, Peach	31074	Brunswick	31522
Oakfield, Worth	31772	Preston, Webster	31824	Sale City, Mitchell	31784
Oak Grove, Acworth	30101	Pulaski, Candler	30451	Sandersville,	
Oakman, Gordon	30732	Putney, Dougherty	31782	Washington	31082
Oak Park, Swainsboro	30401	Quitman, Brooks	31643	Deepstep	31082
Oakwood, Hall	30566	Rabun Gap, Rabun	30568	Sandy Springs,	
Ochlocknee, Thomas	31773	Ranger, Gordon	30734	Atlanta	30358
Ocilla, Irwin	31774	Ray City, Berrien	31645	Sapelo Island,	
Oconee, Washington	31067	Rayle, Wilkes	30660	McIntosh	31327
Odum, Wayne	31555	Raymond, Newnan	30263	Sardis, Burke	30456
Offerman, Pierce	31556	Rebecca, Turner	31783	Sargent, Coweta	30275
Ogeechee Road,		Redan, DeKalb	30074	Sasser, Terrell	31785
Savannah	31405	Red Oak, Fulton	30272	Sautee-Nacoochee,	
Oglethorpe, Macon	31068	Register, Bulloch	30452	White	30571
Oglethorpe, Savannah	31416	Reidsville, Tattnall	30453	Savannah,	
Okefenokee, Waycross	31501	Rentz, Laurens	31075	Chatham	31402
Old National, Atlanta	30349	Resaca, Gordon	30735	Bingville	31403
Oliver, Screven	30449	Hill City	30735	Garden City	31418
Omaha, Stewart	31821	Rex, Clayton	30273	Hunter Army	
Omega, Tift	31775	Reynolds, Taylor	31076	Airfield	31409
Orchard Hill, Spalding	30266	Rhine, Dodge	31077	Ogeechee Road	31405
Oxford, Newton	30267	Riceboro, Liberty	31323	Oglethorpe	31416
Palmetto, Fulton	30268	Richland, Stewart	31825	Port Wentworth	31407
Parrott, Terrell	31777	Richmond Hill, Bryan	31324	State College	31404
Patterson, Pierce	31557	Rincon, Effingham	31326	Wilmington Island	31410
Pavo, Thomas	31778	Ringgold, Catoosa	30736	Windsor Forest	31406
Peach Orchard,		Rising Fawn, Dade	30738	Wright Square	31412
Augusta	30906	Riverdale, Clayton	30274	Scotland, Telfair	31083

380

Post Office and County	ZIP Code	Post Office and County	ZIP Code	Post Office and County	ZIP Code
Scott, Dublin	31095	Stovall, Meriwether	30283	Twin City, Emanuel	30471
Scottdale, DeKalb	30079	Suches, Union	30572	Tybee Island,	
Screven, Wayne	31560	Sugar Valley, Gordon	30746	Chatham	31328
Sea Island, Brunswick	31561	Summertown,		Tyrone, Fayette	30290
Senoia, Coweta	30276	Swainsboro	30466	Ty Ty, Tift	31795
Seville, Wilcox	31084	Summerville,		Unadilla, Dooly	31091
Shady Dale, Jasper	31085	Chattooga	30747	Union City, Fulton	30291
Shannon, Floyd	30172	Berryton	30748	Union Point, Greene	30669
Sharon, Taliaferro	30664	Sumner, Worth	31789	Maxeys	30671
Sharpsburg, Coweta	30277	Sunny Side, Spalding	30284	Penfield	30658
Shellman, Randolph	31786	Surrency, Appling	31563	Upatoi, Columbus	31829
Shiloh, Harris	31826	Suwanee, Gwinnett	30174	Uvalda, Montgomery	30473
Shurlington, Macon	31211	Swainsboro, Emanuel	30401	Valdosta, Lowndes	31601
Siloam, Greene	30665	Oak Park	30401	Castle Park Sta	
Silver Creek, Floyd	30173	Summertown	30466	Boxes	31604
Six Flags Over		Sycamore, Turner	31790	Main Office Boxes	31603
Georgia, Atlanta	30336	Sylvania, Screven	30467	Moody A F B	
Smarr, Monroe	31086	Hilltonia	30467	(official)	31699
Smithville, Lee	31787	Sylvester, Worth	31791	Valdosta State	
Smyrna, Cobb	30080	Talbotton, Talbot	31827	College	31698
Main Office Boxes	30081	Talking Rock, Pickens	30175	Bemiss	31601
Cobb County Center	30080	Tallapoosa,		Castle Park	31604
Snapfinger, B Decatur	30035	Haralson	30176	Clyattville	31604
Snellville, Gwinnett	30278	Tallulah Falls, Rabun	30573	Moody A F B	31699
Social Circle, Walton,	30279	Talmo, Jackson	30575	Valdosta State	
Soperton, Treutlen	30457	Tarrytown,		College, Valdosta	31698
South Base, Warner		Montgomery	30470	Valona, Crescent	31332
Robins	31098	Tate, Pickens	30177	Vanna, Hart	30672
South Decatur,		Taylorsville, Bartow	30178	Varnell, Whitfield	30756
Decatur	30032	Tazewell, Marion	31828	Vidalia, Toombs	30474
Southern Tech,		Temple, Carroll	30179	Kibbee	
Marietta	30060	Tennga, Murray	30751	(Montgomery Co.)	30474
South Macon, Macon	31205	Tennille, Washington	31089	Vienna, Dooly	31092
Sparks, Cook	31647	The Hill, Augusta	30904	Villa Rica, Carroll	30180
Sparta, Hancock	31087	The Rock, Upson	30285	Vista Grove, Decatur	30033
Mayfield	31087	Thomaston, Upson	30286	Waco, Haralson	30182
Devereux	31087	Thomasville, Thomas	31792	Wadley, Jefferson	30477
Springfield, Effingham	31329	Thomson, McDuffie	30824	Waleska, Cherokee	30183
Springvale, Randolph	31788	Tifton, Tift	31794	Walthourville, Liberty	31333
Stapleton, Jefferson	30823	Abac	31794	Waresboro, Ware	31564
Starrsville,		Eldorado	31794	Warm Springs,	
Covington	30209	Tiger, Rabun	30576	Meriwether	31830
State College,		Tignall, Wilkes	30668	Warner Robins,	
Savannah	31404	Danburg	30668	Houston	31093
Statenville, Echols	31648	Toccoa, Stephens	30577	Main Office Boxes	31099
Statesboro, Bulloch	30458	Toccoa Falls	30598	Centerville	31028
Georgia Southern	30460	Toccoa Falls, Toccoa	30598	Robins A F B	31098
Georgia Southern	30458	Toco Hills, Atlanta	30329	South Base	31098
Statham, Barrow	30666	Toomsboro,		Warrenton, Warren	30828
Stephens, Oglethorpe	30667	Wilkinson	31090	Warthen, Washington	31094
Stevens Pottery,		Townsend, McIntosh	31331	Warwick, Worth	31796
Gordon	31031	Trenton, Dade	30752	Washington, Wilkes	30673
Stillmore, Emanuel	30464	Trion, Chattooga	30753	Watkinsville, Oconee	30677
Stillwell, Effingham	31330	Tucker, DeKalb	30084	Waverly, Camden	31565
Stilson, Brooklet	30415	Tunnel Hill, Whitfield	30755	Waverly Hall, Harris	31831
Stockbridge, Henry	30281	Turin, Coweta	30289	Waycross, Ware	31501
Stockton, Lanier	31649	Turnerville,		Okefenokee	31501
Stone Mountain,		Habersham	30580	Waynesboro, Burke	30830
DeKalb	30086	Tuxedo, Atlanta	30342	Alexander	30801

Post Office and County	ZIP Code	Post Office and County	ZIP Code	Post Office and County	ZIP Code
Waynesville, Brantley	31566	White, Bartow	30184	Winston, Douglas	30187
Wayside, Gray	31032	White Oak, Camden	31568	Winterville, Clarke	30683
Wesleyan College,		White Plains, Greene	30678	Woodbine, Camden	31569
Macon	31201	Whitesburg, Carroll	30185	Woodbury,	
West Bainbridge,		Whitestone, Gilmer	30186	Meriwether	30293
Bainbridge	31717	Wildwood, Dade	30757	Woodland, Talbot	31836
West End, Atlanta	30310	Wiley, Rabun	30581	Woodstock, Cherokee	30188
West End, Rome	30161	Willacoochee,		Woolsey, Fayetteville	30214
West End Sta Boxes,		Atkinson	31650	Wray, Irwin	31798
Rome	30164	Williamson, Pike	30292	Wrens, Jefferson	30833
West Georgia College,		Wilmington Island,		Wright Square,	
Carrollton	30118	Savannah	31410	Savannah	31412
West Georgia College,		Wilson Airport,		Wrightsville, Johnson	31096
Carrollton	30117	Macon	31201	Wynnton, Columbus	31906
West Green, Coffee	31567	Winder, Barrow	30680	Yatesville, Upson	31097
Weston, Webster	31832	Windsor Forest,		Young Harris, Towns	30582
West Point, Troup	31833	Savannah	31406	Zebulon, Pike	30295
Westside, Gainesville	30501	Windsor Park, S			
Whigham, Grady	31797	Columbus	31904		